RIDEOUT'S PRINC
OF
LABOUR LAW

AUSTRALIA AND NEW ZEALAND
The Law Book Company Ltd.
Sydney : Melbourne : Perth

CANADA AND U.S.A.
The Carswell Company Ltd.
Agincourt, Ontario

INDIA
N.M. Tripathi Private Ltd.
Bombay
and
Eastern Law House Private Ltd.
Calcutta and Delhi
M.P.P. House
Bangalore

ISRAEL
Steimatzky's Agency Ltd.
Jerusalem : Tel Aviv : Haifa

RIDEOUT'S PRINCIPLES
OF
LABOUR LAW

by

ROGER W. RIDEOUT, LL.B., Ph.D.
Of Gray's Inn, Barrister,
Professor of Labour Law,
University College London

FIFTH EDITION

LONDON
SWEET & MAXWELL
1989

First Edition   1972
Second Edition   1976
Third Edition   1979
Fourth Edition   1983
Fifth Edition   1989

Published in 1989 by
Sweet & Maxwell Ltd. of
South Quay Plaza, 183
Marsh Wall, London
Computerset by
Promenade Graphics Limited, Cheltenham

Printed and Bound in Great Britain by
Hartnolls Limited, Bodmin, Cornwall.

British Library Cataloguing in Publication Data
Rideout, Roger W.
Rideout's Principles of Labour Law—5th ed.
1. Great Britain, Employment. Contracts Law
I. Title
344.106'24

ISBN 0–421 397705
ISBN 0–421 397802

PREFACE

It is now traditional for each new edition of a student textbook in law to be longer than its predecessor and this book has, thus far, been no exception to that rule. The result is often that the textbook contains at least twice as much subject matter as could be covered in any undergraduate course. This of course, may be designed to give the teacher a selection of topics but, frequently, many of these topics are well recognised as outside any known teaching programme. Such had certainly become the case with the later chapters of this book. The decision to eliminate them prompted consideration of whether much other material, which added to a student's knowledge of the law but did not significantly develop an ability to discuss and criticise, might not also be eliminated.

Many short books are rejected by teachers because they attempt to cover a large amount of detail briefly. It seemed to me that if it was possible to encompass a course in forty-five hours of seminars it ought to be possible to produce a relatively short book, pruned of somewhat arid exposition, so that most of those matters which were dealt with were presented in such a manner as to prompt some depth of thought. The sacrifice that has been made will mean that many details of labour law simply are not recorded in these pages. The book is an instrument for study, not for reference. The benefit is that the student is not required to purchase considerably more pages than are needed for the course undertaken. The caution that must be given, however, is that the student will have to be prepared to absorb a greater proportion of this book than of many textbooks to which he or she has become accustomed.

This must not be taken to imply that argument excludes exposition. That approach would leave most undergraduates uncertain of the law they were supposed to be discussing. Considerable portions of this book are, in fact, still simply expositions of aspects of the law. It is hoped, however, that they fit into the pattern of a course which, overall, is one of critical assessment of the way the law has developed and may continue.

This attempt to comply with modern teaching demands in law, in which the taking of notes from a lecture gives place to consideration of a particular aspect in a seminar, has meant that a large proportion of this book has been rewritten. In the process I have taken a certain amount of risk. Nowhere will this be more clear, I imagine, than in the approach to unfair dismissal. For years the Court of Appeal has been saying that there is not all that much law in the process of assessing fairness. The chapter is an attempt to accept that proposition and depict what does happen in practice. The risk is that many will still look for a step by step journey through procedural considerations which may form the substance of reported cases on appeal but do not seem to occur as distinct elements of consideration in the decision-making process of the members of industrial tribunals.

In its first edition this book led rather than followed. It is hoped that the present lead towards shorter undergraduate course books which, nevertheless retain their ability to inspire discussion will be welcomed by those who may turn to encyclopedias as works of reference.

University College London   R. W. RIDEOUT
January 1989

CONTENTS

TABLE OF CASES

●

TABLE OF STATUTES

TABLE OF RULES

ABBREVIATIONS

This following principal works on United Kingdom Labour Law are referred to in this text by the names of their authors only.

Davies and Freedland: *Labour Law Text and Materials* (2nd Ed.) (Weidenfeld and Nicolson 1984)
Elias, Napier and Wallington: *Labour Law: Cases and Materials* (Butterworth 1980)
Wedderburn (Lord): *The Worker and The Law* (2nd and 3rd Eds.) (Penguin Books 1971 and 1986)

CHAPTER I

THE SUPPLY OF LABOUR

Introduction

The now common use of the term Labour Law to cover the material in this
book is somewhat misleading. The title *Law of Employment*, possibly at one
time regarded as too narrow to comprehend the ancillary topics then commonly included in such a course, would probably be a more precise definition
of that topic which is the direct descendant of the law of master and servant
and which, instinctively in the hands of the legislator, judge, writer or student, is, at the very least, dominated by the relationship between employer
and employee. The justification for not dealing more widely with the supply
and use of labour is that there must be limits to any course of study. Most
general books on labour law do, as this one, consider in an early chapter the
various forms in which labour is supplied, but none would be capable of comprehending all the law relating to the self-employed, to temporary and casual
staff and to the vast range of different relationships for the supply of various
services.

Yet employment, properly so called, though in no danger of being sup-
planted as the principal labour relationship, is increasingly being supplemented by other forms. In so far as a trend can be detected the courts are
increasingly ready to recognise these forms as different from employment
and, therefore, not subject to the rules of law which are confined to those who
work under a contract of service. Already the legislature shows signs of
responding by broadening the scope of such legislation, for instance to all who
personally supply their labour.[1] There have, of course, always been those who
provided their labour outside an employment relationship. The legislature is
responding to the fact that it is increasingly possible to choose this type of
independence in circumstances otherwise indistinguishable from those of the
employee. The more numerous the variations of circumstance the more varied the choice of suitable response.

We may, therefore, find two craftsmen in the construction industry performing the same tasks. One, who is likely to be older, is employed. He finds,
despite the fact that the prophesy proved correct that employers would not
lightly give up the prerogative of management to dismiss, a greater feeling of
security. He also finds, in his regular hourly rate of pay, less pressure to over-
work. Management engaging both types of labour do not necessarily see this
as a disadvantage. The self-employed worker in his desire to complete the job
and be paid for it may well cut corners—or, more likely, leave them to be
completed by employed colleagues. The self-employed relieve the employer

---

[1] *e.g.* Sex Discrimination Act, 1976; Race Relations Act, 1975.

1

of a certain amount of overhead office costs, for they will be left to make their own tax returns and pay their own national insurance contributions. They may have a vague hope of avoiding both but will certainly admit to a belief that, in the end, they pay less. The employed worker knows this but worries more about the risks of unemployment and injury at work—for both of which the national insurance system will provide him, but not the self-employed, with benefits. It follows from these attitudes that the self-employed worker is the more mobile. He will find another job when the quantity of work available begins to diminish or become more complex. By definition he is less careful—more likely to believe it will not happen to him. So he may often be accused of being a safety risk, which is more likely to mean he is a risk to others than to himself. He is probably paid by the job and so it is unlikely that he will be paid for holidays or sickness. But he answers that the employer knows this and that the job rate will have been calculated to include such an element at normal speeds. His profit derives from his speed. He would prefer to be paid in cash, but then his employed counterpart is likely to be paid in cash in this country. The employer is somewhat wary of him. He cannot rely on him turning up for work on any day if a more pressing, or more lucrative, opportunity is presented. So he cannot calculate with any reliability when the job will be done. He may take steps to alleviate the worst of the effect of this by specifying a deadline, but he knows he has few sanctions. He lacks the control, which lies ultimately in a disciplinary sanction, which he has over the employee. So despite the overheads which attach to employment and its apparently inherent lack of incentive, he will not want too high a proportion of people who go on working with no supervision when he has gone home but do not subsequently report for work for two or three days.

This is a simple picture on both sides. The self-employed worker may not differ so much in other industries. He may be virtually identical to the employee, save, for example, that a fee is paid for his services, at the same intervals as the wages of others, to a company he has formed. He may on the other hand, be a member of a group of the self-employed, which group has a leader who receives the fees and shares them out and might resemble a small employer who works with his men but for the fact that, by tacit agreement, he is only the first among equals. To make distinctions even less clear the employer himself—perhaps it would be better to say "itself"—is more often unidentifiable. He turns out to be "they" and is located in the minds of workers as a group of more senior management who are actually in essentially similar positions to other employees. They have a higher position in the hierarchy which even trade unions accept as setting them apart. This, like most of what we have so far considered, is a difference based more on attitudes of mind than any significant reality. That there is no necessary difference is, in this case, demonstrated by the fact that the distinction does not exist at all in socialist economies and may not be recognised in practice to anything like the same extent in other capitalist countries. The gap between British managerial employees—seen as the employers—is more marked than in, say, West Germany or Japan, in both of which many people would blame it for much of the disruption that occurs in British industry.

It can be seen, therefore, that many of our apparently defined categories rest on habit and presumption. They also raise far reaching questions of policy. In 1968 a Committee of Inquiry, under the chairmanship of Professor

Phelps Brown reported on the engagement of Labour in the Construction Industry.[2] It had been set up, probably as a result of trade union concern expressed to the Royal Commission on Trade Unions, primarily to consider the problem of "The Lump" in the Construction Industry. Trade unions were concerned at what was suspected to be the dramatic growth in that industry of the practice of engaging self-employed gangs of workers. One, perhaps the, major concern of the unions was that the members of such gangs resisted organisation into trade unions—partly because they had no wish to join— because they moved from site to site before union organisers could catch up with them or, having done so, ensure that they paid union dues. As a result, some construction unions were in severe financial difficulty. Trade unions also complained that these groups creamed off the most remunerative work at enhanced rates, ignored safety provisions, failed to support, as does an employed labour force as a whole, the older slower worker more prone to sickness and injury, and provided the employer with a bargaining counter against union claims on behalf of employees. The government was not then inclined to support the lump. It is one thing to say that it demonstrates a healthy entrepreneurial attitude or makes use of an urge to work hard in return for high remuneration. Those on the lump, however, significantly failed to pay taxes or national insurance contributions and, by their mobility, made enforcement of such obligations difficult. Even the employers, as we have already seen, regarded with concern any major increase in the practice as producing an imbalance between the relative reliability of the slower, but controllable, employee and a desire to have the work done quickly. Inevitably, the Committee of Inquiry came to the conclusion that there was room for both systems but that some of the main drawbacks of "the lump" could and should be subjected to control. The proposed legislative measures were never enacted because of a change of government, but some control was achieved over the payment of taxation. The lump, as a problem, faded from the headlines rather than being dealt with. The withdrawal of Selective Employment Tax—which was levied per capita on employees of employers but not in respect of the self-employed—may have destroyed one of the main incentives to its uncontrolled growth.

In somewhat similar fashion, the supply of temporary workers through agencies is seen as a problem by most Western European governments, many of which prohibit various forms of the practice. It is undeniable that there is a demand from both employees and employers for such a system; notwithstanding that it can be presented as the selling of human labour for a profit which should belong to the worker and, if uncontrolled, as a means of depriving the employer of available labour save at premium rates. The agency system of securing employment enables the worker who only seeks to be engaged intermittently, or on a part-time basis, to be offered a wide selection of the market. On the other hand, not only is the system open to ideological objections, but it too may deprive employers of important elements of control forcing them to resort to expensive forms of labour for no better reason than that those who would otherwise be available for direct recruitment have been attracted away from that market.

In the face of such a variety of forms of the supply of labour it is surprising

---

[2] Cmnd. 3714 (1968).

that the law should have so neglected provision for those which do not fall within the master-servant category of the contract of service. Only those falling within that category are subject to a wide range of statutory obligations and benefits.

The reader must take care in applying what follows. In 1988 the Inland Revenue issued a popular pamphlet on the tax position of the self-employed which began, "There is no legal definition of employment." No doubt designed to induce its recipients to accept the Revenues' guidelines on such a definition which it proceeded to set out, this bold and incorrect assertion is difficult to counter by those who have difficulty in saying what constitutes the legal definition of so practically important a dividing line in methods of supply of labour.

The significance of employment, as against other working arrangements, was demonstrated in *Young and Woods Ltd* v. *West*.[3] The Court of Appeal decided that the claimant was an employee, and thus entitled to claim a remedy for unfair dismissal, despite an agreement between himself and his employer that he should be treated as self-employed. Ackner L.J. pointed out that this false designation, which had been accepted by the Inland Revenue, had resulted in a tax advantage of some £500 over five years simply as a result of assessment under Schedule D instead of Schedule E. The statement of facts in the All England Report headnote to *Ready Mixed Concrete (South East) Ltd.* v. *Minister of Pensions and National Insurance*[4] indicates some of the considerable anticipated advantages from the deliberate alteration of the relationship in that case:

> "It was considered that not only would the scheme further the policy of keeping and [sic] making and selling of concrete separate from its delivery but also that the scheme would benefit the group by stimulating speedy and efficient cartage, the maintenance of trucks in good condition, and the careful driving thereof, and would benefit the owner driver by giving him an incentive to work for a higher return without abusing the vehicle in a way which often happened if an employee were given a bonus scheme related to the use of his employer's vehicle."[5]

Unfortunately, the apparent immediate economic and psychological advantages may tempt workers to accept the far less protected status of self-employment; persuading themselves that prospective disadvantages will not materialise. In *M.J. Ferguson* v. *John Dawson and Partners (Contractors) Ltd.*[6] the plaintiff had stumbled and fallen off an unguarded flat roof whilst engaged in throwing scaffold boards to the ground below. The question whether he was entitled to the £30,387 awarded by the court of first instance depended solely on whether he was employed or self-employed. Megaw L.J. said:

> "It is conceded by the defendants that if the plaintiff was employed under a contract of service, they were, subject only to the issue as to 'appropriate time', under a duty to the plaintiff; they failed to carry out that duty; and that failure was the cause of the accident. But, say the defendants, the plaintiff was employed under a

---

[3] [1980] I.R.L.R. 201.
[4] [1968] 2 Q.B. 497.
[5] See also *Massey* v. *Crown Life Assurance Co.* [1978] I.C.R. 590.
[6] [1976] I.R.L.R. 346.

contract for services: he was 'self-employed'; he owed a statutory duty to himself to take the statutory precautions. (*Smith* v. *Wimpey Bros.* [1972] 2 Q.B. 329) It was for him, under the regulations, not for the defendants, to ensure that the guard rail was erected. The defendants were under no such duty."

In view of the fact that the learned judge is here able to use "employed" in two different senses it is unfortunate that the distinction between service and services should have loomed so large in case and statute law.

Whilst the courts may be criticised for a recent tendency to let more and more situations fall outside the definition of employment the legislature may be blamed for failing to appreciate the extent of such excluded areas or the irrelevance of characteristics of employment to the incidence of the legislative benefit or obligation under discussion. Rarely, it appears, is such neglect explicable on the ground of the lack of feasibility of extending the legislative effect more widely. Interestingly, anti-discrimination legislation[7] has returned to an application to all under contract personally to execute work or labour which, until 1986, had a continuous application through the Truck Acts from 1831 in a form which could already be seen as a conscious attempt to avoid the bypassing of a restriction by avoidance of the technical master-servant relationship. This wider application is also retained in the Wages Act 1986. It is not entirely surprising that the initial judicial approach to this attempt to limit avoidance techniques should have revealed a failure to understand that purpose and an instinctive adherence to a habit of legalistic thought concerning the definitions used. In *Tanner* v. *Post Office*,[8] for example, the E.A.T. refused to include the small businessman, working in that instance as a sub-post master, on the wholly artificial ground that he could delegate his functions and so was not *obliged* to offer his personal services. The legislation might be thought to have referred to one who, in practice, under his contract did offer personal service rather than intending to enable those with a largely theoretical right to delegate to exclude themselves. It is unfortunate, therefore, that the opposite approach adopted by the E.A.T. in *Mirror Group of Newspapers Ltd.* v. *Gunning*,[9] in which a contract, the purpose of which was to deal with the sale of goods, was held to fall within the category because such sale would necessarily involve personal execution of labour by the retail newsagent, should have cast the net too wide. The Court of Appeal correctly held that the contract was not one the primary purpose of which was personal service. A comparison of these two cases, however, reveals the difficulty of devising, within the small number of words considered proper for such a purpose in United Kingdom legislation, a definition which will be adequate for the peculiar demand for legislative provision of United Kingdom courts without, at the other extreme, indicating to such courts the need to include obviously unintended situations. The cases also, however, prompt the realisation that there may well be situations where, for instance, it is wholly relevant that a restriction should not also extend to those responsible for the provision of services. In a situation of rapid economic change such as has not been seen in almost 200 years of the law of master and servant encouragement of those who would once normally have entered employment to become small

---

[7] Sex Discrimination Act 1976, s.82(1); Race Relations Act 1976, s.78(1).
[8] [1981] I.C.R. 374.
[9] [1986] I.R.L.R. 27.

businessmen may well mean that this distinction, the classic dividing line between the field of labour law and the relatively unregulated area of the provision of labour outside that field, will produce anomaly and strain and, finally, be destroyed.

THE DEFINITION OF EMPLOYMENT

Nevertheless, for the time being, it is the contract of service defining the boundaries of what once would have been described as the master-servant relationship which most commonly decides the application of what we call labour law. The student will be startled to find, so early in his study, a lack of precision in so vital a dividing line so extensive as to suggest that the supposed definition has no fixed meaning at all. As he or she continues to consider the nature of the contract of employment it will be found that the same extensive variability applies to the rights and duties imposed by that contract. Both variables are part of the same attempt to comprehend, or to respond to, the almost infinite variety of forms of the provision of labour. If the contract of employment were not such a flexible concept it would have had to be discarded long ago as the strains it imposed by forcing such variety into stereotypes became intolerable. Exactly the same consideration, viewed from the different angle of the need to apply common rights and duties to as wide a coverage of situations of this variety as could reasonably be said to produce a homogenous group, has led to the formulation of an imprecise and, therefore, flexible definition of that group. In both cases, of course, there arise situations in which the general width and flexibility has to be applied in an individual case so as to produce a precise answer. Let us take an example in each of these two areas of consideration so as to make the point. It should be apparent that it is impossible to dictate that all employees should be treated *politely* unless we are to give that word such a width of meaning that the obligation is to treat an employee with such a degree of courtesy as is reasonable in the circumstances. That is precisely the position at which the courts, after avoiding the issue for almost a century and a half, have arrived. It means, however, that in any individual case a court looking at all the circumstances will have to exercise a good deal of discretion in deciding the relative incidence of courtesy to be applied by the airline operator to the airline pilot in front of his crew. Similarly, it is not possible to define employment as extending to all those who are paid wages unless, by wages we are to mean something as wide as remuneration. At once it is clear that that definition would comprehend all forms of personal execution of work and service, unless provided at no charge. So the courts must search in the first place for a characteristic which applies only to those work situations it is considered appropriate to subject to the regulation of labour law. This thought will prompt the question: why not a different group for each different incident? Why, for example, should the same group be entitled to unemployment benefit under the national insurance scheme as are entitled to receive a written statement of the terms and condition on which they work? The answer is that it is convenient for bundles of rights to attach to the same broad groups, otherwise the law becomes as various as the situations it seeks to regulate. As we have already suggested this desire for uniformity is often pursued for its own sake, to the point of anomaly. In general, however, it is submitted that a reasonable degree of uniformity must be sought. So it is that the courts search for one or more characteristics that will sweep into a group, tolerably suited to a common range of regulation, all that variety of arrangements which can suitably be covered. It is inconceivable that one or more characteristics could be selected which could be defined with precision in any individual case and so, again, it must be accepted that the courts will exercise considerable discretion in any case which the parties have thought worthy of dispute. We must now examine the struggle to define, even in the widest terms, a characteristic which can bring together a range of situations which we wish to call employment.

In the nineteenth and early twentieth centuries there was at least general agreement that the characteristic was subjection to the right of another to control the manner of doing the work. Originally defined as if such control was constantly exercised[10] it was still surviving in the modified form of a supposed right in 1957.[11] The modification is important because it reveals not only realisation that no one particularly wishes to employ someone who often has to be controlled—the effort making it more economic to get the controller to do the job—but also the unreality of asking the courts to look for evidence of the existence of a right which is not exercised. It can be said, for instance, that though the airline pilot is usually allowed to apply his own skill and experience to fly the plane he will find himself subject to control if he chooses to do so in an unusual and unacceptable manner. What we have done, if we say that, is to conclude that the airline pilot is an employee so that this consequence follows. In fact, there is probably no evidence to indicate whether or not he can be controlled in such circumstances. We assume he can because we know other things about the relationship which suggest that this must be so. If we knew more we might discover that the pilot owned the plane and had been paid a fee to fly from A to B and was free to do so, so far as the person who had engaged his resources was concerned, in any manner he saw fit.

In other words, the supposed test of control became nothing more than an *ex post facto* rationalisation of a conclusion reached on the basis of other factors, save in those cases where control was already exercised and which would so obviously be regarded as master-servant situations as not to be the subject of dispute. It follows that, somewhere in those other factors, are concealed the characteristics upon which the decision as to employment is made. So the courts threw away the blue print and began again to search the entrails for the true characteristic of employment. Initially, they produced some startlingly meaningless suggestions. In *Short* v. *J. and W. Henderson Ltd.*[12] Lord Thankerton purported to rely on a list first mentioned in 1928:[13]

> "(a) the master's power of selection of his servant; (b) the payment of wages or other remuneration; (c) the master's right to control the method of doing the work, and (d) the master's right of suspension or dismissal."

This list re-appeared in a surprising number of cases without the courts apparently realising that it was only because of the use of predetermined

---

[10] *Yewens* v. *Noakes* [1880] 6 Q.B. 530.
[11] *Gibb* v. *United Steel Co. Ltd.* [1957] 1 W.L.R. 668.
[12] [1946] 174 L.T. 417 at 421.
[13] *Park* v. *Wilsons and Clyde Coal Co. Ltd.* [1928] S.C. 121.

words like "master," "servant," "wage," "dismissal," that it appeared to be
talking of employment. If for them were substituted "contractor," "worker,"
"payment" and "termination" only the reference to the discarded test of control served as any form of distinction between employment and self-employment. In 1951[14] Kahn-Freund had suggested that the power of the employer
was to organise a system into which the work in question was incorporated. It
seems fair to assume that Denning L.J. had seen this suggestion when, in
Stevenson Jordan and Harrison Ltd. v. MacDonald and Evans,[15] he said:

> "One feature which seems to run through the instances is that, under a contract of
> service, a man is employed as part of a business, and his work done as an integral
> part of the business; whereas under a contract for services, his work, although
> done for the business, is not integrated into it but is only accessory to it."

This "organisation" test was applied in a few cases.[16] Its drawback, as
McKenna J. pointed out in Ready Mixed Concrete (South East) Ltd. v. Minister of Pensions,[17] is that it does not disclose what degree of integration into
the organisation is required. Whether he realised it or not, McKenna J. not
only provided a definition of organisation but also answered his own problem
when he said:

> "Control [to which we might add "of the organisation" since the word cannot
> apply to anything else] includes the power of deciding the thing to be done, the
> way in which it shall be done, the means to be employed in doing it, the time
> when, and the place where it shall be done."

The organisation is surely the running of the business and the worker is
integrated into it when that organisation is applied to his job. McKenna J.'s
list was clearly not exhaustive. He, like the organisation test, is inviting us to
consider a wide range of characteristics of a working situation (the organisation) and to ask whether those characteristics are imposed on the worker as a
method of working by the control exercised by the employer. So all the organisation test has done, and all McKenna J. did in the Ready Mixed Concrete
case, is to broaden the concept of subjection to control by an employer of a
range of characteristics of the working situation going beyond the way in
which the job is done.

It is suggested that McKenna J. also introduced into the discussion an
unnecessary, even a misleading, division of function when he said that the
definition must be applied in two stages; namely, a prima facie decision based
on a few major characteristics followed by a more detailed testing of this conclusion by a search for inconsistencies. Among the major characteristics the
only new element he suggested was the requirement of personal service; that
is to say, absence of the power to delegate. This is of little value. The situation
in the Ready Mixed Concrete case was quite exceptional in that numerous
lengthy draft contracts had been proposed and submitted to the Ministry one
by one in an attempt to secure a decision in favour of self-employment. Each

---

[14] [1951] 14 M.L.R. pp. 505–8.
[15] [1952] 1 T.L.R. 101.
[16] e.g. Cassidy v. Ministry of Health [1951] 2 K.B. 343; Bank voo Handel en Scheepraart N.V. v.
   Slatford [1953] 1 Q.B. 248; Whittaker v. Minister of Pensions [1967] 1 Q.B. 156.
[17] [1968] 2 Q.B. 497.

of those drafts expressly dealt with the power to delegate. The right to delegate was also provided in *Hitchcock* v. *Post Office*[18]; but this situation is unlikely to occur frequently. Mostly, the right to delegate could only be an assumption derived from a decision already made as to the category into which the contract fell. McKenna J. admitted that control, in the sense he used it of control of the organisation of the job, would remain the other major prima facie factor. As has been suggested, assessment of that control will involve a review of all the major organisational factors, unless the prima facie conclusion is to be so much of an untested assumption as to be worthless. The effect of re-listing inconsistencies, or of discovering inconsistencies which should have been taken into account in the first place, is to bias the argument. If the prima facie test concluded that the contract was not one of employment it would be unlikely that "inconsistencies" would prove strong enough to suggest the contrary; but if the conclusion was in favour of employment consideration of inconsistencies without counterbalancing them with consistencies, would lead to a false conclusion. McKenna J. did not balance inconsistency with consistency. The industrial tribunal in *O'Kelly* v. *Trusthouse Forte PLC*[19] did, but used the exercise not as a second stage but as part of a single stage of conclusion. It is suggested, therefore, that it is better to ignore the idea of a two stage approach. The truth is that McKenna J. was trying to explain the mental process which does indeed jump to a conclusion and then test it. The courts function, however, is not to jump to a conclusion but to examine the matter in detail; in other words, to weigh all the relevant factors and decide in which direction they point.

McKenna J. suggested that employment will be indicated if these factors point towards control of the job organisation. His ultimate conclusion, however, is expressed differently as an answer to the question whether they point towards the worker being a small businessman. Here he is asking, as one stage or two is immaterial, whether the factors indicate fundamental inconsistency with employment. The alternative is most likely to be the status of a small businessman. This suggests that the courts considering a working situation alleged to be employment should consider not so much the characteristics of that status but those of the most likely alternative. This approach was adopted by Cooke J. in *Market Investigations Ltd.* v. *Minister of Social Security*[20] although it is almost inevitable so soon after McKenna's decision that he should purport to adopt the two stage approach:

> "I therefore proceed to ask myself two questions: First, whether the extent and degree of the control exercised by the company, if no other factors were taken into account, be consistent with her being employed under a contract of service, bearing in mind the general test I have adumbrated.
>
> As to the first question: The facts found by the Minister show that the control of the company is exercised at two stages. Before the interviewer engages herself for the particular survey, she will probably have seen the company's 'Interviewer's Guide.' This document contains detailed instructions on the technique of interviewing, and much of it is couched in imperative language. . . . On the Minister's

---

[18] [1980] I.C.R. 100.
[19] [1983] I.C.R. 728.
[20] [1969] 2 Q.B. 173 at p. 185.

findings, I have no doubt that the instructions in the 'Interviewer's Guide,' after having been seen by the interviewer, are incorporated into the terms of any contract which the interviewer may thereafter make with the company to participate in a particular survey.

The second stage of control comes after the interviewer has agreed to take part in a particular survey, that is to say, after the contract has been made. The interviewer is then sent instructions which according to the Interviewer's Guide give details of whom to interview, what to say to informants, how to handle the questionnaire and other forms, and also deal with contact with the office. In addition to that, the interviewer might in particular cases be required to attend the office of the company for instructions, or might receive instructions from a supervisor.

The control which the company had the right to exercise was, however, limited in various ways. They had no right to instruct Mrs Irving as to when she should do the work. The only requirement imposed on her was that the work should be completed within a specified period. During that period Mrs Irving was free to do similar work for other organizations, so that the company had no right to prohibit her from doing that. No doubt it would be agreed before Mrs Irving accepted the assignment that her work would be in a given area; if so, the company would have no right to send her to another area. In addition to those limitations on the right of the company to give instructions to her, there was a practical limitation on the possibility of giving instructions to her while actually working in the field, because, as found by the Minister, the supervisor would then have no means of getting into touch with her.

It is apparent that the control which the company had the right to exercise in this case was very extensive indeed. It was in my view so extensive as to be entirely consistent with Mrs Irving's being employed under a contract of service. The fact that Mrs Irving had a limited discretion as to when she should do the work was not in my view inconsistent with the existence of a contract of service . . . Nor is there anything inconsistent with the existence of a contract of service in the fact that Mrs Irving was free to work for others during the relevant period. It is by no means a necessary incident of a contract of service that the servant is prohibited from serving any other employer. Again, there is nothing inconsistent with the existence of a contract of service in the master having no right to alter the place or area within which the servant has agreed to work. So far as concerns practical limitations on a master's power to give instructions to his servant, there must be many cases when such practical limitations exist. For example, a chauffeur in the service of a car hire company may, in the absence of radio communication, be out of reach of instructions for long periods.

I therefore turn to the second question, which is whether, when the contract is looked at as a whole, its nature and provisions are consistent or inconsistent with its being a contract of service.

Mr Pain, for the company, points first to the fact that Mrs Irving was appointed on each occasion to do a specific task at a fixed fee. He points to the fact that the company's officers were of the opinion that they could not have dismissed Mrs Irving in the middle of an assignment. He says that these factors are more consistent with the conception of a contract of services than a contract of service.

As to the first factor, appointment to do a specific task at a fixed fee, I do not think that this is inconsistent with the contract being a contract of service. See, for example, *Sadler* v. *Henlock* [1855] 4 E. & B. 570.

. . . Then Mr Pain says that the fact that the contract makes no provision for time off, sick pay and holidays, suggests that it is not a contract of service. I cannot accept that this is a test which is of great assistance in the present case. The fact that the contract makes no provision for time off is merely a reflection of the fact that there are no specified hours of work. I have already dealt with this. The fact that there is no provision for sick pay and holidays is merely a reflection of the fact that the contract is of very short duration. If a man engages himself as an extra kitchen hand at a hotel for a week in the holiday season, there will be no provision for sick pay and holidays, but the contract will almost certainly be a contract of service.[21]

The company then refer to the fact that Mrs Irving's work was performed under a series of contracts, each for a specific survey. They say that the relationship of master and servant is normally conceived of as a continuous relationship, and that the fact that there is a series of contracts is more consistent with those contracts being contracts for services than contracts of service. For my part, I doubt whether this factor can be usefully considered in isolation. It must I think be considered in connection with the more general question whether Mrs Irving could be said to be in business on her own account as an interviewer."

Subsequent cases have consistently adopted the same approach of reviewing the elements of the employment situation which the court considers most significant and applying them either to the degree of control the employer exercises over the conduct of the job (the organisation test),[22] or, more frequently, to the degree of independence, or lack of obligation, of the worker (the small businessman test).[23] In *Withers* v. *Flackwell Heath Football Supporters Club*[24] Bristow J. refers to both before stating that the ultimate test is the small businessman test.

Both the "organisation" and the "small business" test seek to discover the extent of the workers independence. As Davies and Freedland point out[25] the "organisation" test suggests a social, whilst the "small business" test suggests an economic, bias to the enquiry. But "social" is used in this context in the sense of the purely industrial environment of the worker, and it is more meaningful to pay attention to their second suggestion that the one considers the employer's circumstances whilst the other concentrates on the employee's situation. Though this is true, too much should not be made of it. It is suggested that this distinction is only that of looking for independence from one standpoint or another and that choice of the standpoint rarely depends on a predetermined (biased) point of view but rather on the type of factors presented to the tribunal or court for its consideration. So far as industrial tribunals are concerned the evidence will usually be confined to a very few factors on which basis the tribunal will have to do the best it can.

The "small businessman" test emphasising the economic position of the worker is in theory, as Davies and Freedland indicate,[26] the more "scientific" test. It is submitted, however, that it is not correct to say that it is more likely to avoid impressionistic and intuitive classification. This depends on the facts

---

[21] This conclusion is, a few years later, much less likely to be reached.

[22] In *Midland Sinfonia Concert Society Ltd.* v. *Secretary of State for Social Services* [1981] I.C.R. 454 the court was referred to every known test and several new ones, announced that it was applying the control test but eventually considered the degree of obligation which is characteristic of the small businessman test.

[23] *Young and Woods Ltd.* v. *West* [1980] I.R.L.R. 201; *Hitchcock* v. *The Post Office* [1980] I.C.R. 100; *Nethermere (St. Neots) Ltd.* v. *Taverna and Gardner* [1984] I.R.L.R. 240; *O'Kelly* v. *Trusthouse Forte PLC* [1983] I.C.R. 728.

[24] [1981] I.R.L.R. 307.

[25] At p. 88.

[26] At p. 89.

one has available. To take a typical example, a worker may be engaged full-time for one employer reporting to the office each day and, in practice, working the same number of hours as employees. But he may be paid by way of a fee remitted to a company he controls. The tribunal may well consider this obvious indication of the status of a small businessman scarcely less artificial than a statement in the contract that it provides for self-employment. The tribunal may well prefer to search for indications of whether it reflects the real economic position by looking at the organisational factors as did the court in *Hitchcock* v. *The Post Office.*[27] The lack of a practical distinction between the application of the two tests is more alarmingly demonstrated in the majority of recent reported decisions[28] where the courts can be seen to be primarily influenced by a single factor regardless of the test they are said to be applying. That fact, shorn of the more detailed facts in the particular case, is revealed as commitment to regular performance.[29] It can now readily be seen that this element can be comprehended within either test. Superficially, it appears appropriate to the determination either of the existence of commitment within an organisation or, somewhat more questionably, the economic independence of a small businessman. Upon closer examination it is seen to be appropriate to neither. It would lead to a marked tendency to classify casual, and perhaps even part-time, work as self-employment,[30] and to the absurd situation, actually treated seriously in *Nethermere* v. *Gardner*, of producing a different answer according to whether the work was done under a series of contracts or a single agreement.[31] Such lack of regularity of performance may be a factor to be considered—though it is suggested that the question of the status of the worker is more often better to be determined in a snapshot of the position at any one time—but there is great danger of arriving at the wrong result if any factor is to be given this sort of predominance. It is suggested, therefore, that the test to be applied is as to the organisational and economic dependence of the worker but that this must be determined only when the court is satisfied that it has sufficient factors before it to make a balanced decision. Too often, especially in industrial tribunals, a decision is reached on random and inadequate evidence, apparently because tribunals are reluctant to say that no decision is possible and the issue therefore turns on failure to satisfy the burden of proof. There is no reason why, in any given situation, one or more factors may not be seen to carry much more weight than others but there is no justification for the assignment of such preponderence in advance.

The effect of the obsession with the single factor of obligation to regular performance which has sprung from the distinction between employee and small businessman is clearly apparent in the decision of the Court of Appeal

---

[27] [1980] I.C.R. 100.
[28] *Sinfonia* v. *Secretary of State,* (*supra*); *O'Kelly* v. *Trusthouse Forte PLC* (*supra*); *Mailway (Southern) Ltd.* v. *Wilsher* [1978] I.R.L.R. 322; *Nethermere* v. *Gardner* (*supra*); *Addison* v. *London Philharmonic Ltd.* [1981] I.C.R. 267.
[29] *McLeod* v. *Hellyer Bros. Ltd.* [1987] I.R.L.R. 232.
[30] See: *Hepple* and *Napier* [1978] I.L.J. 84.
[31] The absurdity is made worse by the fact that either contractual situation can be viewed as producing a different effect, as a comparison of *Nethermere* and *Airfix Footwear Ltd.* v. *Cope* [1978] I.R.L.R. 396 reveals.

in *McLeod* v. *Hellyer Bros. Ltd.*[32] Trawlermen served under a series of separate "crew agreements" signed for each sailing. Between sailings they registered as unemployed. They claimed dismissal for redundancy in 1984 when, by a "mutual consent discharge", the practice ended. Initially before the industrial tribunal the issue had seemed to be how to treat the intervals between employment. The Court of Appeal held, however, that a "global" contract of employment (whatever that might be) could only derive from a continuing obligation. The effect of this type of reasoning is that that which would once have been treated as a series of short contracts of employment is now regarded, because of the lack of ongoing obligation, as not involving employment at all. The casual employee is in danger of extinction—though to regard him, simply because of this casual effect, as a small businessman seems unreal. If, however, the casual relationships run together into a continuous connection, as in *Airfix Footwear Ltd.* v. *Cope*,[33] it is open to a tribunal to find employment even though the *de facto* situation contains the purely voluntary element which produced a finding of no employment in *Mailway (Southern) Ltd.* v. *Wilsher*.[34] It is easy to say that those decisions are distinguishable as findings of fact. It is much more difficult to elicit any legal principle which such findings of fact are intended to activate.

This century has produced therefore, a test which it was realised was no test and a long, but disorganised, search for a substitute. It should come as little surprise, therefore, to find that this situation had produced two startling suggestions; the one that the parties may settle the issue by agreeing the classification of their own contract and the other that the definition of employment is not a question of law.

In the *Ready Mixed Concrete* case[35] it was stated that the parties' own assessment would be irrelevant unless there was a doubt as to the rights and duties for which they intended to provide. In *Massey* v. *Crown Life Assurance Co.*[36] the Court of Appeal agreed with Lord Denning M.R. that ambiguity could be removed by the parties own statement as to the status of the contract.[37] It is difficult to decide what significance was given to such a statement in *B.S.M. (1257) Ltd.* v. *Secretary of State for Social Services*[38] though it seems to mean that the statement should settle the matter unless that category is inconsistent with the primary purpose of the contracts. Fortunately, this question cannot be left to random choice of preference since any suggestion that the parties have conclusively chosen the category poses immediately a range of policy considerations as to whether they should be allowed to opt out of the consequences the law imposes on employment. So in *Ferguson* v. *John Dawson Ltd.*[39] it was held not permissible to opt out of an employer's safety obligations by a statement that the worker was engaged on a self-employed

---

[32] [1987] I.R.L.R. 232.
[33] [1978] I.R.L.R. 396.
[34] [1978] I.R.L.R. 322.
[35] *Supra*.
[36] [1978] I.C.R. 590.
[37] The EAT misstated this in *Tyne and Clyde Warehouses Ltd.* v. *Hammerton* [1978] I.C.R. 661 but nevertheless it must be the courts duty to see whether the label correctly represents the true relationship.
[38] [1978] I.C.R. 894.
[39] [1976] W.L.R. 346.

basis.[40] The decision in *Young and Woods Ltd.* v. *West*[41] relieved the courts of the worry that a worker might eat his cake in self-employment and have it returned to him by being reclassified as employed by pointing out the possibilities of recovering the eaten portion. In practice this possibility is more theoretical than real but the suggestion has served its purpose and it seems likely that the courts are now aware of the desire of parties to a working relationship to opt for certain incidents regardless of whether they properly attach and are, therefore, most likely to ignore signs of avoidance of such obligation.[42]

The obvious conclusion from the preceding discussion is that there are no rules of law by which to assess the significance of the various factors in the relationship which point one way or another. Yet, as Ackner L.J. (dissenting in part) pointed out in *O'Kelly* v. *Trusthouse Forte PLC*[43] it is axiomatic that the nature of relationship the parties have entered into is a matter of interpretation of the contract and, therefore, of law. Ackner L.J. was, however, in the minority in drawing from this the conclusion that an appeal on a point of law could call in question the weight assigned to various factors. As the Court of Appeal explained in *Nethermere (St. Neots) Ltd.* v. *Taverna and Gardner*[44] the question is one of law but also one which involves questions of degree and fact. The majority of the Court of Appeal in that case seem not to have envisaged much scope for appeal on a point of law apart from the basic issues, one of which Kerr L.J., dissenting, found in the very existence of any contractual obligation. Lord Templeman, delivering the judgment of the House of Lords in *Davies* v. *The Presbyterian Church of Wales*[45] seems to imply a wider field of enquiry on appeal in saying that even if an industrial tribunal took into account all relevant circumstances and reached a conclusion that was reasonable such a conclusion must be reversed if in error, despite the fact that other tribunals might have reached similar erroneous conclusions.

ILLEGALITY

It would seem from the preceding discussion that, with a few obvious exceptions, the courts, in their search for a workable definition of employment have not often been motivated by consideration of the far-reaching policy issues to which an answer one way or another would give rise. It is, of course, possible that McKenna J. in the *Ready Mixed Concrete* case had come to the conclusion reached by the employers that, quite apart from the saving of office costs and other overheads, the real economic advantage of the changed status was that those who think they are working for themselves work harder. In *Nethermere* the Court of Appeal may have understood that the attraction of a system of casual working is the absence of restrictions such a designation as "employment" increasingly imposes. Only in those cases such as *Ferguson* v. *Dawson*

---

[40] See also *Davies* v. *New England College of Arundel Ltd.* [1977] I.C.R. 6; *Tyne and Clyde Warehouses Ltd.* v. *Hammerton* [1978] I.C.R. 661; *Young and Woods Ltd.* v. *West* [1980] I.R.L.R. 201.

[41] *Supra.*

[42] *e.g.* *Withers* v. *Flackwell Heath Football Supporters Club* [1981] I.R.L.R. 307.

[43] [1983] I.R.C. 728.

[44] [1984] I.C.R. 612.

[45] [1986] 1 All E.R. 705.

where the evidence shows a clear intention by the parties to select one status rather than another for policy reasons do the courts allow the language of their decisions openly to reveal considerations of policy. The question of illegality of the contract of employment, on the other hand, is almost entirely a matter of public policy and the courts readily allow themselves to be influenced by a sort of ethical judgment of the parties' intentions. For this reason the principle is clearly established that the doing of an unlawful act— such as the alleged procurement of prostitutes for customers, or the driving of a vehicle without a licence—does not, of itself, preclude enforcement of the contract.[46] Far less logical is the distinction between a term of the contract known to be illegal which is merely unenforceable itself and such a term which renders void the entire contract. Before their repeal in 1986 the Truck Acts rendered illegal and unenforceable provision in the contract for fines not in accordance with section 2 of the 1896 Act.[47] An attempt to agree to waive a breach of statutory duty would similarly be illegal and void.[48] The rest of the contract survives. It can be seen, of course, that it would be counter-productive to avoid the entire contract of employment because it failed to comply with a provision designed to protect the employee. The courts have, accordingly, been in some difficulty deciding the extent to which contracts which they regard as contrary to public policy[49] should be declared void thus depriving the worker of protection which would have been afforded him had he been working under a valid contract of employment.[50] In practice most of the recent cases have concerned attempts to evade[51] payment of income tax. There is, therefore, no sufficient range of types of illegality to justify giving an answer to the question what, if anything, might be regarded as an illegal term not avoiding the whole contract, and what as contrary to public policy. It may seem surprising that a contract deliberately and wrongly described as for services in order to lessen the incidence of tax should not be subjected to the same enquiry as a contract to pay an employee gross wages in cash, in the same way as it is surprising that the legislature can provide that a contract permitting illegal fines remains valid without causing the courts to consider why a contract not to deduct income tax is void. It can only be admitted that the court's views as to the extent of the illegal provisions producing invalidity is vague.

When an illegality having that effect does exist, and such will be the case with deliberate tax evasion, the courts have taken the view that the contract remains valid unless the employee[52] and the employer[53] subjectively know,[54] and not merely ought to have known,[55] of the fraudulent purpose. The court

---

[46] *Coral Leisure Group Ltd.* v. *Barnett* [1981] I.R.L.R. 204. See also: *Saint John Shipping Corporation* v. *Joseph Rank Ltd.* [1957] 1 Q.B. 267.
[47] *Kearney* v. *Whitehaven Colliery Co.* [1893] 1 Q.B. 700.
[48] *Baddeley* v. *Earl of Granville* [1887] 19 Q.B.D. 423; *Wheeler* v. *New Merton Board Mills Ltd.* [1933] 2 K.B. 669.
[49] Which must be the basis of complete invalidity—*Napier* v. *National Business Agency* [1951] 2 All E.R. 264.
[50] *Tomlison* v. *Dick Evans U. Drive Ltd.* [1978] I.C.R. 639.
[51] In *McConnell* v. *Bolik* [1979] I.R.L.R. 422 referred to as "avoidance."
[52] *Davidson* v. *Pillay* [1979] I.R.L.R. 275.
[53] *McConnell* v. *Bolik* [1979] I.R.L.R. 422.
[54] *Newland* v. *Simons and Waller (Hairdressers) Ltd.* [1981] I.R.L.R. 359.
[55] *Corby* v. *Morrison* [1980] I.R.L.R. 218.

is free to infer that the employee must have known,[56] which conclusion, of course, will owe something to whether any reasonable employee should have known. That there were decisions of policy is also apparent from the clear implication in both *Newland's* case and *Corby's* case that the employee's subsequent knowledge has the same vitiating effect as initial knowledge.[57] This has been criticised as severe[58] and it has been suggested that it should be modified so that the vitiating effect only arises where it is necessary to disclose the illegality to enforce the right in question.[59] A more telling criticism at the present time, however, would seem to spring from the lack of any certainty as to when an act of illegality will be regarded as contrary to public policy.[60]

Contract and its Effect

We have spoken thus far of decisions based on the nature of the contract. The lawyer instinctively seizes upon the explanation that the rights of the parties rest upon individual agreements enforceable as such. He knows that this is a lawyers' explanation of a situation in which terms are often negotiated by trade unions or, more often, left unstated and unconsidered. He knows, too, that the idea of an agreement freely entered into by equals has little reality in labour relations—but he knows that that same unreality applies to plenty of other contractual situations. Despite the doubts, reservations and exceptions, the contract of employment is seen by the lawyer as "an apparatus for the regulation of the industrial employment relationship" capable of combining it with other sources of rules but also with a body of legal theory.[61] Wedderburn,[62] not intending to signify approval, said that the lawyer was forced to return to it again and again despite "a certain unreality." Kahn-Freund, even earlier,[63] whilst acknowledging that it was "almost invisible to the naked eye of the layman" saw it as "the cornerstone of the edifice." Even during the brief period since these statements the significance of contract as providing the controlling mechanism has declined. We shall see, for instance, that though the legislative draftsman instinctively defined "dismissal" in contractual terms[64] the rest of the process of determining the fairness of dismissal need not be affected by the presence or absence of contractual rights. The gradual decline in the significance of contract, even for the labour lawyer, has long been noted.[65] More recently, its restrictive effect upon new (statutory) rights has provoked comment.[66] The discussion will take up more time later

---

[56] *Corby* v. *Morrison* [1980] I.R.L.R. 218.
[57] This does not seem to have been the view of Browne-Wilkinson J. in *Coral Leisure Group Ltd.* v. *Barnett* [1981] I.R.L.R. 204.
[58] Hepple and O'Higgins: *Encyclopedia of Labour Relations Law*.
[59] The Q.B.D. adopted this type of argument in *A.R. Dennis and Co. Ltd.* v. *Campbell* [1976] I.C.R. 465, but the Court of Appeal rejected that line of distinction: [1978] I.C.R. 862.
[60] See: Mogridge (1981) 10 I.L.J. 23.
[61] Freedland: *The Contract of Employment* (O.U.P. 1976) at p. 4.
[62] *The Worker and the Law* (Penguin (2nd Ed. 1971) at p. 51).
[63] "Legal Framework" in A. Flanders and H. A. Clegg (Ed.) *The System of Industrial Relations in Great Britain* (Oxford 1954) pp. 45 and 47.
[64] See now, E.P.(C).A. 1978 s.55.
[65] See, *e.g.* Rideout: *The Contract of Employment* (1966) 19 C.L.P. 111.
[66] See for an excellent survey of these effects Hepple: *Do we need the contract of employment?* (1986) I.L.J. 69.

and is merely mentioned here by way of warning that the position of the contract of employment as the machinery of regulation is not only unestablished but controversial.

It is, however, of great significance to the development of specific rights and duties in the area of employment that the contract should have been seen by the common law as the only source of employee rights. When it was suggested that increasing statutory rights, and particularly the recognition by the Redundancy Payments Act 1965 of the need to compensate the employee whose job no longer existed, had at last recognised a property right in employment, a number of academic writers expressed their opinion that this was not so. Apparently, they objected to a formal recognition of employment as an item of property on the ground that this would lead to acknowledgement of a right in the employer simply to buy out the property right of his employee. There is, of course, no reason why this should be so since private individuals seldom are recognised as having a right compulsorily to purchase the property of others. There is, also, considerable reason to suggest that without the concept of property the common law permitted the compulsory buying out of whatever right it did recognise and that the provision of compensation for neither redundancy nor unfair dismissal had done much in practice to inhibit such a power carefully exercised. Oddly enough, the common law did once recognise that the master had a property right in his servant[67] which gave rise to an action in tort for damages for depriving the master of the services of his servant. But this was never more than a remnant of feudalism. However that may be, the common law never recognised any property right in the ordinary employee. This is not the primary reason for the absence of power specifically to enforce the contract of employment but it is the explanation for the common law rule that compensation for wrongful dismissal should be confined to the loss of contractual rights which, in practice, only conferred entitlement to a period of notice before termination.[68] It was this conclusion which deprived the employee in most situations[69] of a worthwhile remedy and so, until the introduction of a statutory claim for unfair dismissal with a wider ranging basis for comparison, deprived the courts of any significant opportunity to develop a body of case law dealing with the principles of individual employment law.

Occasionally, the common law did recognise a property right in a job which it based on vague impressions of status and rested upon the concept of an office holder, which it never defined. In a pragmatic fashion the courts dealing with employment issues which conferred the status of office holding seem to have done so specifically to make available some right which the purely contractual notion of employment would not confer, without giving any significant thought to the reality of distinction between the two.[70] This impressionistic approach has been apparent in all the cases so that it was possible to suggest a higher status than mere employment for a registered schoolteacher in *Malloch* v. *Aberdeen Corporation*[71] but deny it to the head of a

---

[67] Lord Goddard C.J. in *Jones Bros. (Hunstanton)* v. *Stevens* [1955] 1 Q.B. 275 at 282.
[68] *Addis* v. *The Gramophone Co. Ltd.* [1909] A.C. 488.
[69] Not quite all: see *Yetton* v. *Eastood Froy Ltd.* [1966] 1 W.L.R. 104.
[70] *Fisher* v. *Jackson* [1891] 2 Ch. 84.
[71] [1971] 1 W.L.R. 1578.

department in a University in *University Council of the Vidyodaya University of Ceylon* v. *Silva*.[72] It would have been possible to utilise such a category for some workers who, for technical reasons could not be brought within that of employment as, for instance, ministers of religion who appear to be excluded by the absence of a contractual status.[73] Policemen, in the absence of statutory provision deeming them to have characteristics of employment,[74] are excluded because their authority "is original not delegated" and they are "ministerial officers exercising statutory rights independent of contract."[75] Whilst this may not raise problems of policy in individual cases where the result appears appropriate[76] conferment of property rights, including specific enforcement and the common law right to a fair hearing, on wide categories of such workers whilst other virtually indistinguishable categories were denied such rights induced the courts to treat office holding as a rare phenomenon not to be defined in case this led to a widespread, but illogical, conferment of its advantages.

In other areas of the law, however, policy considerations may differ and recognition of such a category may be convenient. The category is adopted by statute in the law of taxation and for these purposes it has been found both convenient and good policy to define the class.[77]

The advantages of office holding over employment lie primarily with the worker and this may explain why they have not been actively sought, as have those attaching to self-employment. In more recent years these advantages, and particularly specific enforcement and a right to a hearing before dismissal, have been substantially conferred on employment so that it is likely that the category will disappear save, perhaps, as a nominal category for some workers who do not fall within any other.

The idea that employment depends on contract has, as we shall see, a stultifying effect on the *application* of certain new statutory rights. We shall see, however, that it has a far less restrictive effect on the *development* of new rights than might at first seem likely. The implied term is proving an extremely flexible tool to re-tune the contract of employment to provide more effective protection to the employee than it has done before. In theory, given the economic inequality of the parties, the contract could have been used by the employer as a means of manipulating the relationship to suit himself. Yet it was not, and still is not, the parties who manipulate the contract of employment. It is a mistake to assume that because the parties, individually or collectively, negotiate wages, holidays and overtime they thereby fundamentally affect the nature of the relationship. That nature, even in the extreme example of the prerogative of management, is determined by the rights and obligations devised by the law. In the past this law has been created largely by

---

[72] [1965] 1 W.L.R. 77.
[73] In *Barthorpe* v. *Exeter Diocesan Board of Finance* [1979] I.C.R. 900 a lay reader who did have such a contract was regarded as both an employee and an office holder.
[74] *e.g.* The Police Act 1964, s.48.
[75] Att.-Gen. for *New South Wales* v. *Perpetual Trustee Co. Ltd.* [1955] A.C. 457 at 489.
[76] See: *Ridge* v. *Baldwin* [1964] A.C. 40.
[77] As the holders of "a subsisting, permanent, substantive position which had an existence independently from the person who filled it" in *Great Western Railway* v. *Baker* [1923] K.B. 266 at 274. In *Dale* v. *I.R.C.* [1954] A.C. 11 it was too obvious for argument that a trustee was, for revenue purposes, an office holder.

the courts. That they could, had they wished, have introduced a wide range of new rights, with or without the aid of contract, is clearly demonstrated by the suggestion of Woolf J. in *R.* v. *B.B.C., ex parte Lavelle*[78] that, though the relationship was private and so not amenable to the remedies of public law, the requirements of natural justice should attach where it contained an element of public service, statutory support, office or status. In an era before such far-reaching conceptual change was thought of the category of office holder provides an example of the range of devices which would have been available to the courts to develop the common law out of its master/servant attitude. It was the courts which chose not to meet the challenge, as their mean-minded approach to office-holding and their restrictive attitude to the content of the contract of employment both demonstrate. Whether the academic writer imagines changes in such recognition or not, the courts refusal to recognise a property right for the worker in employment and their indication that categories which did recognise such a right were to be regarded as wholly exceptional provides a clear indication of the light in which the courts saw the position of the worker. It is not surprising that this view of the subservience of the employee has not significantly changed even in those areas where contract has either become significantly less dominant or has disappeared altogether. It seems that the characteristic of lack of independence inevitably carries this connotation. It is the characteristics of employment, as the courts see them, and not the instrument in which those characteristics are enchained, which limits the development of labour law. Employment could have been assigned all the advantages of office holding. The courts chose not to do so and chose scarcely to avail themselves of the category of office holder. Significantly, apart from the independence of self-employment, the common law failed to develop any way out of its own property-less view of the position of the worker and so ensured that his subservience dominated labour law.

---

[78] [1982] I.R.L.R. 404.

CHAPTER II

CREATING THE EMPLOYMENT RELATIONSHIP

Parties to a contract often admit terms and conditions not chosen by either of them but dictated by common form, custom, the practice of others or, even, by what the courts are likely to say should be implied in the absence of contrary provision. The element of agreement exists largely in the sense of mutual acceptance of a standard way of achieving a desired result.

The agreement to enter into an employment relationship which lawyers call a contract is one of the most extreme examples of this standardisation of what is nominally an individual agreement. In practice, the employer adapts the standard to his own requirements by manipulation of a very narrow group of terms and conditions. Commonly, he will already be restricted as to his choice of rates of pay, hours, holidays and job description, sickness provision and disciplinary and grievance procedure, by the terms of collective agreements made with trade unions. This will be so even if the employer in question does not directly negotiate with a trade union, since then he is likely to adopt something approaching the standard set by those who do. He may introduce variations to make his offer more attractive. He may fix his own starting times, decide how many shifts he will operate and, so, offer day or night work. He may decide to make available a company pension scheme and slightly enhance the job security of his workforce by offering better than usual rights to notice of dismissal. Occasionally he may venture into areas primarily regulated by judicial decisions, for instance, by introducing covenants in restraint of the future trading activities of his employees. On the whole, however, the principal contribution of the employer to the nature of the relationship derives from managerial power of day-to-day administration and its correlative of discipline and disciplinary procedures. The employer, through management, provides most of the initiative to operate the contract by giving instructions, devising and exercising disciplinary powers, (although disciplinary procedures are often negotiated), offering overtime working and the like but he does not himself significantly mould the contractual situation which permits the exercise of those powers. Since the complaint is well known that the employee's economic dependence affords him little power of negotiation it follows that the employee has even less influence on the content of the contract than the employer chooses to exercise. The employee will decide what job he is looking for, what rate of pay he desires and the hours he wishes to work. His function is then to search for such a package with a variable amount of scope for cushioning the sharper corners of what is offered by individual negotiation of slight variations.

The two main sources of influence on the content of the contract, and, in that sense, the nature of the relationship, of employment are collective agreement and judicial law-making. Early books on the law of master and servant emphasised the latter and ignored the former. In reaction to this, later books have sometimes suggested that the influence of collective agreement on the employment relationship is dominant. This is to look at the relationship primarily in terms of its economic significance. Most wage rates are either fixed by, or follow standards set by, collective agreement. So do associated matters such as numbers of paid holidays, provision of paid sick leave procedures, compensation for loss of employment due to reorganisation, and job description. Disciplinary and grievance procedures are frequently dictated and operated by management, but are quite often negotiated. From the point of view of an employer anxious to operate efficiently and maximise profits and from the point of view of the worker anxious to obtain a good return for his labour these aspects are, no doubt, the most important provisions in the contract. In another sense, however, apart from job description which determines the division of work, the character of employment as a relationship is derived not from these economic incidents but from a much more numerous category of terms and conditions devised, implied, interpreted and regulated by the courts. It is these that used to be presented as the essence of the law of master and servant. The value of the tendency to downgrade them in favour of the negotiated economic terms exemplified above must not be overrated. The nature of the relationship between management and worker is determined much more by the obligation to obey instructions, the right to terminate the relationship, the duty to maintain the trust and confidence of the other party and the more particularised duties such as confidentiality, which may not be felt equally, or at all, by all categories of employee. It is wrong to suppose that because the average employee may think much less often about his duty of care to his employer than about his pay or overtime that the former is less a potential cause of problems for him. The overall influence upon the attitude of the parties to each other of judicially controlled characteristics of the contract is almost certainly greater than the collectively controlled economic aspects which govern the social status and standard of living of the employee.

In this chapter, therefore, we shall examine how the parties come together, put together agreement by interview and letter, knowing that the economic substance of that agreement is quite likely to be predetermined by collective agreement; subsequently realising the significance of what judge-made law says of the nature of that relationship. Apart from the importance of safety standards, legislation has conferred few rights equivalent to these. We shall examine them separately because they clearly have a wholly separate function in forming the employment relationship than do the interrelated activities of the parties, the collective bargainers and the courts.

FORMATION OF THE CONTRACT BY THE EMPLOYER

In *Gill* v. *Cape Contracts Ltd.*[1] the employer required 40 insulation engineers to work at oil terminals in the Shetland Islands. To compensate for inclement working conditions high salaries and guaranteed employment for at least six months were offered. Workers were recruited in Northern Ireland where

---

[1] [1985] I.R.L.R. 499.

their existing employers, annoyed by their leaving, informed them that they
would not be taken on again. Before they left for the new jobs, however, the
recruits were informed that their union had objected to the recruitment of
workers in Northern Ireland rather than Scotland and that, accordingly, they
would not be given the employment offered. The Northern Ireland court held
that the employers had broken a contract, collateral to the contract of
employment, that in consideration for the recruits terminating their existing
contracts they would offer high wages for a minimum of six months. Damages
of about one-third of what would have been earned in that guaranteed period
were awarded to allow for the fact that a considerable portion of the wage was
intended as compensation for the working conditions. Although the court in
this case was able to construct a collateral contract with separate consideration it also cited two cases which had taken the view that a representation
would constitute a warranty in the contract which the representation was
designed to induce.[2] That is, no doubt, true, but if no such contract ever
comes into existence there is no vehicle to contain such a warranty. In other
words, the possibility of a warranty fails to remove most of the difficulty of
granting rights to a worker who is offered employment, and incurs expenditure based on that offer which is withdrawn before the contract of employment comes into existence. It is suggested that the mere fact that the worker
will have to leave his former job to accept the offer is not capable of constituting consideration to support a collateral contract unless, as in *Gill's* case, that
act is incorporated into the deal. The same objection applies to such acts as
selling one house and purchasing another. The difficult question which will
have to be faced is at what point such acts cease to be separate actions of the
worker enabling him to meet his projected obligations and become part of the
bargain he has made with his projected employer. The alternative solution to
the problem appears to lie in the conclusion that the contract of employment
can pre-date the inception of the wage/work aspect of the bargain. We shall
see, in due course, that it can continue after the wage/work bargain has
ended, so it does not seem impossible to arrive at the conclusion that it can
begin earlier. So far, however, lawyers seem unwilling to conclude that there
is a contract of employment—as distinct, in limited circumstances, from a
contract to employ—before work has begun.[2a]

The first steps in the process of making a contract of employment are often
informal. In *Ferguson* v. *John Dawson and Partners (Contractors) Ltd.*[3]
Megaw L.J. gave the following account of a procedure perhaps selected deliberately by the worker for its lack of identifiability:

> " . . . the plaintiff came with four other Irishmen, already working for the
> defendants, and he asked, or perhaps one of his friends asked if he could "come
> along." Mr. Murray's evidence is: 'I said he could start on Monday and that was
> it. But I did inform him there were no cards; we were purely working as a lump
> labour force.' Mr. Ferguson gave a false name, Goff."

---

[2] *Dick Bentley Productions Ltd.* v. *Harold Smyth (Motors) Ltd.* [1965] 2 All E.R. 65; *Esso Petroleum Co. Ltd.* v. *Mardon* [1976] 2 All E.R. 5.
[2a] An employer asked to provide a reference is under a duty of care both to any potential new employer and to the employee seeking the reference to ensure the opinions stated are based on accurate facts—*Lawton* v. *R.O.C. Transhield Ltd.* [1987] I.C.R. 7.
[3] [1974] I.R.L.R. 346.

The Court of Appeal confirmed that this amounted to the creation of a contract of employment. As often, formation of the contract will begin with advertisement by the employer but it does not follow that this will lead to precision, or even clarity, even in the most important of those matters retained within the control of the employer such as assignment to job categories. The headnote in *Deeley* v. *British Rail Engineering*[4] begins:

> "In September 1972, Mr. Deeley answered an advertisement by the employers for a 'Sales Engineer (Export).' His letter of application was headed 'Sales Engineer (Export)' as was the employer's acknowledgment. The actual offer of employment, however, was headed 'Sales Engineer' and enclosed with it were terms and conditions of appointment headed 'Sales Engineer' which stipulated that 'The duties will be as required by the Managing Director of British Rail Engineering Ltd. or as the Railway's Board may from time to time determine.' Mr. Deeley's acceptance of the offer was also headed 'Sales Engineer.'"

The Court of Appeal described the offer and statement of terms and conditions as "the contractual document" and concluded, therefore, that the contract permitted employment outside the "export" field. In *Pedersen* v. *London Borough of Camden*[5] the Court of Appeal held that the letter of appointment should be interpreted in the light of the job advertisement. It is dangerous for courts to try to draw precise lines around "contractual documents" in such an imprecise process as the formulation of the contract of employment. In *Tayside Regional Council* v. *McIntosh*[6] the Scottish EAT described such an approach as very technical and not well-founded in the context of industrial relations. Interviews seem to be the time when the contract maker is at his least guarded.[7] The interview in *Hawker Siddeley Power Engineering Ltd.* v. *Rump*[8] took place after employment had begun but is not untypical of earlier occasions. The employee was asked to sign a contract of employment form indicating that he could be required to travel all over the country. He objected to this because his wife was in bad health. One of the company's managers said "Don't be a fool, there is enough work in southern England to see you out. Sign that contract and I'll get in touch with the office and you'll only work in southern England." Allowing a little time for both parties to assume that what was said was what they later realise should have been said the terms of the contract may be somewhat speculative.[9] In *London Borough of Redbridge* v. *Fishman*[10] a headmaster acting with the authority of the employing authority in interview had indicated that a particular post primarily involved organising a resource centre and not a predominance of actual teaching. The parties may have the intention of dealing with some aspect, or even most aspects as in *Jones* v. *Lee*[11] and never get around to it,

---

[4] [1980] I.R.L.R. 147.
[5] [1981] I.R.L.R. 173.
[6] [1982] I.R.L.R. 272.
[7] See, *e.g. Curtis* v. *Chemical Cleaning and Dyeing Co.* [1951] 1 K.B. 805.
[8] [1979] I.R.L.R. 425.
[9] See, *e.g. Simmonds* v. *Dowty Seals Ltd.* [1978] I.R.L.R. 211—a case concerning subsequent variation of the contract.
[10] [1978] I.R.L.R. 69.
[11] [1980] I.C.R. 310.

or, very commonly, they may simply assume that everyone understands a particular position[12] and make neither provision for, nor mention of, it.

The Statutory Statement of Terms and Conditions of Employment

It is generally true to say that the long-standing statutory attempt to produce more precision in the major terms of employment by requiring the issue of a written statement of such terms[13]; has failed to produce the desired effect. In 1977[14] Leighton and Dunville found that 80 per cent. of a sample of "good employers" issued the statement but there is no doubt that many less well-organised companies do not[15]; to say nothing of those who wish to avoid the implication of employment. More significantly, the terms of the statutory requirement allow avoidance of its purpose.

The statement of terms and conditions of employment requires written notice specifying the following matters to be sent to any employee under a contract normally involving not less than 16 hours' employment per week and who has been continuously employed by the same employer for 13 weeks (excepting civil servants, registered dock workers and the husband or wife of the employer). No statement is required where terms do not differ from those of a previous employment with the same employer which ended not more than six months before. Provision must be included for:

(a) The date when employment began and the date on which the employee's period of continuous employment (including that with any other employer) began;

(b) The scale or rate of remuneration or the method of calculating the remuneration;

(c) The intervals at which remuneration is paid (that is, whether weekly or monthly or by some other period);

(d) Any terms and conditions relating to hours of work (including any terms and conditions relating to normal working hours);

(e) Any terms and conditions relating to:

    (i) entitlement to holidays, including public holidays, and holiday pay (the particulars given being sufficient to enable the employee's entitlement, including any entitlement to accrued holiday pay on the termination of employment, to be precisely calculated);

    (ii) incapacity for work due to sickness or injury, including any provisions for sick pay (This is now extended by the terms of the Social Security and Housing Benefits Act 1982 which introduces a Statutory Sick Pay scheme. Regulations made under this Act require an employer to make it clear to the employee how and when he wants notification of incapacity to be given);

    (iii) pensions and pension schemes, with the exception of statutory pension schemes which require such information to be given to new employees;

---

[12] *O'Brien* v. *Associated Fire Alarms Ltd.* [1968] 1 W.L.R. 1916.

[13] Originally contained in the Contracts of Employment Act 1963 and now, as amended, in E.P.C.A. 1978, s.1.

[14] [1977] 6 I.L.J. 133.

[15] See Leighton (1984) I.L.J. 86.

(f) The length of notice which the employee is obliged to give and entitled to receive to determine his contract of employment; and

(g) The title of the job which the employee is employed to do.

The provision in relation to continuous employment in (a) was inserted by the Employment Protection Act 1975. In view of the complexity of statutory provisions as to continuity, compliance with the requirement is likely to be difficult in some cases. It is worth pointing out that a misstatement to the employee's disadvantage would be ineffective as an attempt to contract out of statutory requirements. An error in the employee's favour, however, was at one time thought to be likely to effect an estoppel.[16] Based on this view there even developed a practice whereby an employer taking on the employees of another might be asked to insert a false statement as to continuity so as to confer potential benefits in respect of any future redundancy. Such a practice was robbed of its validity by a decision that, since continuity conferred juris-diction on industrial tribunals, it could not be created by an estoppel contra-dicting the actual facts.[17]

In addition, the Employment Protection Act 1975 added a requirement that the statement should contain a note specifying any disciplinary rules applicable to the employee, or refer to a reasonably accessible document con-taining such rules.[18] The same Act amended two further requirements, first introduced by the Industrial Relations Act 1971, so as to provide for notifi-cation, by description or otherwise, of a person to whom the employee can apply if he is dissatisfied with any disciplinary decision, or where he seeks redress of any employment grievance, and the manner in which such appli-cation should be made. An explanation of any further steps in such pro-cedures where they exist, or reference to a reasonably accessible document explaining them, must also be included.[19]

The requirement that the statement shall specify the job title was designed to furnish significant assistance in the law of redundancy. It should be noted that what is required is not a job description. The more detailed the "title" the more restrictive of movement within the contract it is likely to prove. The main disadvantages to the employer of a generalised statement would seem to be that employees may fear loss of status if lumped together in broad categor-ies. The legislative requirement to state a title seems, therefore, intended to induce wide general job classifications for the purpose of measuring redun-dancy.

Instead of setting out the details of these matters in the statement, the stat-ment itself may refer to other documents available for inspection by the employee during normal working hours and containing the requisite infor-mation. Amendments must be notified in the same way within four weeks of the date of coming into effect of the amendment but it is possible to avoid this requirement by making reference to future documents.[20]

---

[16] See *Evenden* v. *Guildford City Association Football Club* [1975] Q.B. 917.

[17] *Secretary of State for Employment* v. *Globe Elastic Thread Ltd.* [1979] I.C.R. 706.

[18] The government proposes to remove this obligation from small employers.

[19] E.P.C.A. 1978, s.1(4)(c).

[20] An industrial tribunal, when considering the adequacy of the statement was held to have no power to declare the meaning of the contract nor to rectify a manifest error, *Construction Industry Training Board* v. *Leighton* [1978] 2 All E.R. 723.

It is very common for employees to speak of this statement as a contract of employment and it was, indeed, presented as a "worker's charter" in the run up to the 1964 election. It seems likely that Lord Denning saw it in that light in *Gascol Conversions Ltd.* v. *Mercer*[21] despite the clear statement by Parker C.J. in *Turriff Construction Ltd.* v. *Bryant.*[22] Lord Denning was following his own assessment expressed in *Camden Exhibition and Display Ltd.* v. *Lynott,*[23] although the decision in the later case can be based on the fact that the document described itself as a contract and the employee signed a receipt which itself described the document as a contract. Subsequent decisions[24] make it clear that the courts will not regard the statutory statement as more than evidence of the terms of the contract. More significantly, it is usually only evidence of one party's view.[25] Even as such it will be likely to have a considerable effect, especially when used as an instrument to incorporate documents such as collective agreements and employee manuals[26] when it takes effect at the commencement of the relationship.[27] At that stage, as we shall see, it is much easier for the courts to infer the consent of the employee to such a statement than at a later stage when the statement is re-presented with the intention of amending existing obligations.[28] Although sometimes the courts seem to speculate on technicalities, such as which statement came last,[29] the truth probably is that neither they nor industrial tribunals respond favourably to the fact that the employee might be confused by the change as distinct from failing to notice what existed at the outset of the employment relationship. It would be misleading to say that when choosing between two different terms put forward by the employer the courts are inclined to select that most favourable to the employee because, in practice, they take into account a number of other indicators such as the fact that the employee probably understood the position. Nevertheless, tribunals are unlikely to wish to see the employee prejudiced by an unclear diversity of statements.

The legislative purpose in making provision for a written statement of terms and conditions was not to provide a vehicle for tying the parties to a rigid contract, as the approach in *Gascol Conversions Ltd.* v. *Mercer*[30] would have done, but rather, to inform the employee of what his rights and obligations are. The statement is the servant, not the master, of the contract. It is, therefore, entirely right that the tribunals and courts should not seek to use the statement as an instrument to sort out uncertainties in other sources. It is also entirely in accordance with this that industrial tribunals should have power to determine what particulars ought to have been included in the state-

---

[21] [1974] I.C.R. 420.

[22] [1967] I.T.R. 292.

[23] [1965] 3 All E.R. 28.

[24] *Hawker Siddeley Power Engineering Ltd.* v. *Rump* [1979] I.R.L.R. 425; *System Floor (U.K.) Ltd.* v. *Daniel* [1981] I.R.L.R. 475; *Jones* v. *Associated Tunnelling Co. Ltd.* [1981] I.R.L.R. 477.

[25] *System Floor Ltd.* v. *Daniel, supra.*

[26] *Camden Exhibition Ltd.* v. *Lynott, supra.*

[27] It is in this sense that Leighton and Dunville (1977) 6 I.L.J. 133 are correct in suggesting that it assumes the character of a contract.

[28] *Jones* v. *Associated Tunnelling Co. Ltd. supra.*

[29] *Trusthouse Forte (Catering) Ltd.* v. *Adonis* [1984] I.R.L.R. 382.

[30] *Supra.*

ment.[31] The tribunal "may either confirm the particulars . . . or may amend those particulars, or may substitute other particulars for them, as the tribunal may determine to be appropriate".[32] In exercising this function the tribunal is quite simply asking what the contract is and it may seek the answer in any way in which tribunals or courts would normally decide what was contained in a contract of employment[33] though it may not deal with any terms not required to be contained in the statement.[34]

Finally, it is equally consistent with this informative, non-creative, function of the statement that it should be used to incorporate by reference other existing documents. Not only would it be wasteful to require repetition of those documents but the chance this would give for summaries and alterations in meaning would force the statement into an unintended role as a correcting agent. It may well be that the requirement of making those documents available for inspection by the employee is inadequate to inform him of their content, but the principle is sound. Its application may, however, have some unexpected effects. It may, for instance, serve to confirm, as included in the contract, a document the incorporation of which would otherwise be in doubt. This may have the effect of turning what might be seen as mere information into terms of the contract. It is suggested that in this way the legislative decision to inform the employee of whatever procedure existed for processing grievances by including that requirement in the statutory statement was instrumental in turning that procedure into a contractual right.

This may appear as a welcome development permitting the employee to enforce what he assumed he could rely on. The same provision may work in favour of the employer, permitting him to incorporate a succession of varying documents. So, in *Robertson* v. *British Gas Corporation*[35] the employer had sought to make use of this "rolling" contractual statement by providing:

> "The provisions of the Agreement of the National Joint Council for Gas Staffs and Senior Officers relating to remuneration and increments will apply to you. Any payment which may, from time to time, become due in respect of incentive bonuses will be calculated in accordance with the rules of the scheme in force at the time."

It was made clear in *Burroughs Machines Ltd.* v. *Timmoney*[36] that termination of a collective agreement would not, as such, affect individual contractual rights which had accrued as a result of that agreement. *Robertson's* case, however, supposing that it is theoretically open to contracting parties to provide that some future speculative event may alter their contractual rights and obligations, raises the question of whether this has been achieved by the terms of incorporation in this instance. It must be appreciated that this method of incorporating changing documents is widely adopted by employers because it avoids the need to reissue the contractual statement within four weeks of any change that takes place. In *Robertson's* case the Court of Appeal held that complete withdrawal of incentive bonuses was contrary to the contractual

---

[31] E.P.C.A. 1978, s.11.
[32] E.P.C.A. 1978, s.11(6).
[33] *Mears* v. *Safecar Security Ltd.* [1982] I.R.L.R. 183.
[34] *Construction Industry Training Board* v. *Leighton* [1978] 2 All E.R. 723.
[35] [1983] I.C.R. 351.
[36] [1977] I.R.L.R. 404.

right of the employee to be the subject of such bonuses which had been incor-porated by the employee's letter of appointment. The approach would seem to permit the conclusion that no such "rolling" provision could be effective to change any contractual right, whether or not it had been established at the beginning of the relationship. Even the argument that the employee had pre-viously accepted advantages conferred by the rolling provision would not seem to stop him subsequently objecting to disadvantageous changes. Kerr L.J. alone dealt with this problem. He took the view that the rolling provision would permit changes in the provision but would not permit unilateral revision by withdrawal from the collective agreement. In abstract terms it may be asked why an obligation to adhere to such rules as exist from time to time should not operate if no rules exist. In practice the view of Kerr L.J. is almost certainly what the parties would have understood to be the purport of the reference in the statement of terms. Whatever the answer to this particu-lar point, this type of decision does establish the power of the statutory state-ment to confer contractual effect on documentary evidence which changes from time to time.

Despite this it can be seen that the employer who seeks to use the statement as in *Hawker Siddeley Power Engineering Ltd.* v. *Rump* and *Jones* v. *Associ-ated Tunnelling*[37] as a vehicle of unilateral change, or to incorporate pro-visions forgotten when the relationship began, is perverting its intention. The courts have accepted that the normative provisions are dictated elsewhere and that the statement is primarily designed to carry information as to what they are. This, it is submitted, is precisely the original legisative intent.

RESTRICTIONS UPON THE FORMATIVE STAGE

(a) *Discrimination*

As we saw in Chapter 1, the parties have considerable freedom to devise the type of relationship that suits them. The form in which that relationship is stated may be dictated by third-party intervention but is not regulated by legislation, save to the extent we have noticed of issuing a written statement of selected terms and conditions after the employment has commenced. Con-siderable statutory restriction has been imposed on the right of the employer to terminate employment because the employee is, or is not, a member of a trade union but it has not been thought feasible to restrict the employer's freedom to engage, or refuse to engage, labour on these grounds.

The main source of restriction on the freedom of the employer to choose who he employs and how he conducts the process of engagement is legislation aimed at race and sex discrimination.[38] We shall consider these provisions in more detail in Chapter VII but it will be useful to summarise their effect on the formation of the relationship. Discrimination to which the legislative pro-hibitions apply is defined as[39]:

A person discriminates against another (a woman) in any circumstances rel-evant for the purposes of any provision of this Act if:

---

[37] *Supra.*
[38] S.D.A. 1975; R.R.A. 1976. The E.P.A. 1970 operates to amend the contract after it has been made.
[39] R.R.A. 1976, s.1; S.D.A. 1975, s.1.

(a) on racial grounds (the grounds of her sex) he treats that other (her) less favourably than he treats or would treat other persons (a man); or

(b) he applies to that other (her) a requirement or condition which he applies or would apply equally to persons not of the same racial group as that other (a man) but

    (i) which is such that the proportion of persons of the same racial group as that other (woman) who can comply with it is considerably smaller than the proportion of persons not of that racial group (men) who can comply with it, and

    (ii) which he cannot show to be justifiable irrespective of the colour, race, or nationality or ethnic or national origins (or sex) of the persons to whom it is applied, and

    (iii) which is to the detriment of that other (her) because he (she) cannot comply with it.

Segregating a person on racial grounds is declared to amount to less favourable treatment. In the field of employment discrimination against married persons arises in the same circumstances as are set out above.

The two types of discrimination defined here are normally known as "direct" and "indirect." It will be observed that direct discrimination requires a subjective intention, whilst indirect discrimination requires only the imposition of a condition which has a discriminatory effect. For instance, to require applicants to be Welsh speaking is not direct discrimination since the ground is language. It is, however, likely to be indirect discrimination since a smaller proportion of persons of other national origins than Welsh, are able to speak that language. The employer may, however, seek to show that the condition is justifiable. The extent to which good business practice, as distinct from necessity, can be pleaded as justification is the most hard-fought issue in the field of discrimination in employment and is examined more fully at pages 241–242.

It is unlawful to publish, or to cause to be published, an advertisement which indicates, or might reasonably be understood as indicating an intention by a person to do any act of discrimination even if, in the case of racial discrimination, the doing of that act would be lawful.[40] Clearly, this covers indirect discrimination, and the Race Relations Code of Practice[41] accordingly states that employers should not confine advertisements to areas or publications which would exclude or reduce (one might add, or be reasonably understood as intended to exclude or reduce) the number of applicants of a particular group (the same applies to a particular sex). Enforcement of this prohibition is uneven. It is unlawful to apply for a waitress or a person of above average physical strength unless this can be justified, but a great deal of advertising is conducted through magazines apparently primarily aimed at women, although the Equal Opportunities Code recommends advertisement in publications likely to reach both sexes. The same code recommends that employers should not use recruitment agencies whose sources are confined wholly or mainly to a particular group.

---

[40] S.D.A. 1975 s.38: R.R.A. 1976 s.29.
[41] S.I. 1983/1081.

It will have been noted that prohibition on discriminatory advertising can arise from a reasonable understanding that it will have that effect. All other prohibitions on discrimination require the discrimination to be proved in fact to exist. So far as the formulation of the contract is concerned both Acts[42] forbid unlawful discrimination in the arrangements for selection, rejection or deliberate omission to offer employment and in the terms of the offer. In *Perera* v. *Civil Service Commission (No. 2)*,[43] for instance, an application was made for selection as an administrative trainee and an upper age of 32 was specified. The complainant, who was 39, claimed that because a large number of "coloureds" entered the country as adults a smaller proportion of them, than of whites, could comply with the condition. In this instance the Court of Appeal took the view that the age limit was not mandatory and so did not constitute a "requirement or condition." This is not untypical of a degree of strict construction apparent in Court of Appeal decisions and contrasts with many decisions of the EAT, especially in the formative stage of the legislation under the presidency of Phillips J. The approach of the Court of Appeal, if maintained, is likely to lead to a more narrow view of the need to prove proportionate effect statistically rather than, as often happens in industrial tribunals, by reference to popular impressions.

The problems for the applicant of proving discrimination are considerable. Some assistance in this task is afforded by the decision of the House of Lords in *Science Research Council* v. *Nasse, BL Cars Ltd.* v. *Vyas*[44] that confidentiality of documents was not a bar to disclosure if such disclosure was necessary for the fair disposal of the proceedings. Nevertheless, the need, particularly when direct discrimination is alleged, for information about the other candidates remains a barrier to many complaints. The variety of recruitment practices itself tends to facilitate discrimination. Individual recommendation is a common form of employer access to the labour market and will, of course, tend to the perpetuation of members of the existing group of employees.[45] A tradition of reserving certain job categories for men or women is widespread as are the disadvantages in pay and promotion prospects that accompany it. There is, no doubt, a high level of rejection of applicants on grounds of colour and sex based on generalised statements of the qualities and capacities of the group in question. As the Race Relations Code of Practice[46] indicates, the damaging effect of discrimination may often be found at levels of administration such as reception and personnel staff so that a company selection policy seeking to prevent discrimination never comes into operation. Chiplin and Sloane[47] point out that discrimination within the family in domestic situations is often to blame for a knock-on effect in employment. More women than men work only part-time, not because of employer discrimination but because they "choose" to do so under pressure from their obligations to the home.

---

[42] S.D.A., s.6; R.R.A., s.4.
[43] [1983] I.R.L.R. 166.
[44] [1979] I.C.R. 921.
[45] See *R.* v. *Commission for Racial Equality ex p. Westminster City Council* [1985] I.R.L.R. 426.
[46] S.I. 1983/1081.
[47] *Tackling Discrimination at the Workplace* (1982) p. 131.

(b) *Other statutory restrictions*

Some, more piecemeal, controls apply at the formative stage of the employment. The examples are, however, scattered and indicate clear reluctance to interfere with the freedom of the employer to choose the workforce he desires.

The minimum age at which children may be employed at all is 13.[48] Those under school-leaving age[49] may not be employed in a ship registered in the United Kingdom nor in any factory, mine or transport, nor in any other industrial undertaking unless only members of the same family are employed there.[50] The Secretary of State has power to regulate the employment of children under school-leaving age in entertainment.[51] Local authorities may require information concerning children's employment and may prevent the employment of a child in unsuitable ways, times or periods even though this is not otherwise unlawful.

Many long-standing restrictions on hours of work for women employed in factories were repealed, in the interests of non-discrimination, in 1986.[52] Some restrictions remain for women and young persons. For all workers under 16 the weekly limit is 44 hours.[53] The daily spread of work must not exceed 11 hours (12 in a five-day week), to begin no earlier than 7 a.m. for workers under 16, nor end later than 6 p.m. for them and 8 p.m. for young persons (1 p.m. on Saturday, or such other short day as the Secretary of State shall prescribe if satisfied that the exigencies of the trade require it). Unless the work of a male young person over the age of 16 is vital to the continuous employment of men with whom he is working, in which case he may work a continuous spell of five hours, young persons may not work a spell of more than four-and-a-half hours without at least a half-hour break. If a 10-minute break is permitted during the spell it may be increased to five hours.

It is permissible to increase these maximum hours where the pressure of work in the factory demands it, but in no such case shall more than 100 overtime hours annually be permitted, and they shall not be at the rate of more than six hours in any week, nor for more than 25 weeks in the year. Even then the maximum working day may not exceed 10 hours, spread over 12 hours.[54] The Secretary of State may permit an increase in these maxima in special circumstances.[55]

Young persons may not be employed outside the factory during meal or rest intervals, or outside the period of employment, save, if over the age of

---

[48] Children and Young Persons Act 1933, s.18(1) as amended by the Children Act 1972, s.1.

[49] Currently 16. See Raising of the School Leaving Age Order 1972 (S.I. 1972 No. 444).

[50] Factories Act 1961, s.167; Mines and Quarries Act 1954, ss.124(2) and 160; Employment of Women, Young Persons and Children Act 1920, s.1.

[51] Employment of Children Act 1973, s.1.

[52] S.D.A. 1986, s.7.

[53] Factories Act 1961, s.87(1).

[54] *Ibid.* s.89.

[55] Such special regulations have been made for a number of industrial processes including: Aerated Water (S.R. & O. 1938 No. 727); Biscuit Manufacture (S.R. & O. 1938 No. 1528); Bread and Flour Confectionery and Sausage Manufacture (S.R. & O. 1939 No. 509); Chocolates and Sugar Confectionery (S.R. & O. 1938 No. 1245); Dyeing and Cleaning (S.R. & O. 1929 No. 642); Ice-Cream Manufacture (S.R. & O. 1939 No.857); Laundering (S.R. & O. 1938 No. 728). But see E.P.A. 1970.

16, in a shop, in which case the employment counts as employment in the factory. Except for defined exceptions those under 18 may not be employed at night (A period of 11 consecutive hours including those between 10 p.m. and 5 a.m.—Women, Young Persons and Children Act 1920, Hours of Employment (Conventions) Act 1936). The remaining provisions limiting the hours of work for women are not to be affected by legislation for equal opportunities, although they will be kept under review.

The Mines and Quarries Act 1954 continues the prohibition on young persons working below ground and also limits hours of employment of young persons above ground.[56]

So far as women were concerned the legitimacy of such regulations, in the light of the EEC Equal Treatment Directive, was called into question by the decision of the European Court of Justice in *Johnston* v. *Chief Constable of the Royal Ulster Constabulary*[57] that it must be shown that the protection of women is specifically necessary.

The Shops Act 1950 contains a very detailed set of provisions concerning the hours of shop assistants, their half-holidays, meal times and overtime, which were inspired by the exceptionally long, continuous periods of work expected at one time in the retail trades where shopkeepers tended to wait for each other to close for the day. A proposal to relax these restrictions in 1986 was defeated by a combination of trade unions and the churches.

An alien may not hold public office[58] nor be employed in the civil service without certification.[59] Neither these nor any other restrictions on employment of aliens, applies, however, to the nationals of States members of the European Economic Community.[60] Any non-patrial, as defined by the Immigration Act 1971, may have restrictions placed on his right to accept or change employment when he is given leave to enter the country.

(c) *The disabled*

Apart from statutory domination of the law relating to safety at work and the more recent anti-discrimination legislation, statute law has not, in the United Kingdom, played a significant role in the direct imposition upon either employer or employee of social obligations. The Disabled Persons (Employment) Act 1944 and associated legislation is one of the few examples of such legislation.

A disabled person is one who, on account of injury, disease, or congenital deformity is substantially handicapped in obtaining or keeping employment, or in undertaking work on his own account, of a kind which apart from that injury, disease or deformity, would be suited to his age, experience and qualifications. Such a person may, after his disability has continued for 12 months,[61] apply for registration as disabled.[62] An employer of 20 or more employees (which includes apprentices) is required to employ a percentage of

---

[56] But see the amendment in S.D.A. 1975, s.21(1) and 1986, s. 7(2), and note that proposals have been made for repeat of these restrictions upon women in 1990.
[57] [1986] I.R.L.R. 263. But other EEC countries have more extensive prohibitions.
[58] Act of Settlement 1700.
[59] Aliens Employment Act 1955, s.1.
[60] Immigration (Revocation of Employment Restrictions) Order 1972 (S.I. 1972 No. 1647).
[61] Disabled Persons (Employment) Act 1958, s.2.
[62] Disabled Persons (Employment) Act 1944, s.7.

disabled persons and, where he does not currently meet that quota, to allocate vacancies for that purpose. The employer is required not to take into his employment other than a disabled person if immediately after such engagement the quota would not be met.[63] The general quota is currently 3 per cent.[64] There is power to fix special percentages for specified industries but this power has only been used in relation to crews of British ships where the percentage is 0·1.[65] The Minister may issue a permit in a particular case, which may be subject to conditions, entitling an employer who would otherwise be bound to engage a disabled person to avoid the obligation where it appears to the Minister that it would be expedient to do so having regard to the nature of the work for which the applicant desires to engage and the qualifications and suitability for the work of any available registered disabled person, or if he is satisfied that there are insufficient such persons available.[66]

The 1944 Act contains a very early example of partial protection from dismissal[67] of a registered disabled person if his dismissal would produce a failure to meet the quota. No particular sanctions are provided and the prohibition on dismissal does not operate where the employer has reasonable cause for dismissal. This aspect of the protection of the disabled has, therefore, clearly been overtaken by the provision of general remedies for unfair dismissal but, more significantly, its very existence in this attenuated and easily avoidable form reveals the major weakness of the legislation, which seems to have been founded on pious hopes rather than the provision of effective enforcement procedures. Apart from being largely unpoliced and ineffective, some of the provisions of the legislation appear not only condescending but detrimental. Nowhere is this more apparent than in the Disabled Persons (Designated Employments) Order 1946.[68]

In what appears to have been an effort either to introduce a spark of life into the implementation of the obligation or, at least, to appear to be endeavouring to do so, the annual returns of all companies which are required to attach to their balance sheets a directors' report must, from September 1, 1980, include in that report a statement as to the policy applied during the financial year to which the report relates to the employment of disabled people.[69]

This legislation is significant in principle because it imposes a positive obligation to employ a quota of a minority group. Such an approach suffers from two linked defects in that it does not confer a specific right on any individual and leaves enforcement to administrative systems unsupported by substantial public pressure. In this type of situation the unaffected public obtain the result they deserve. If, as has been suggested (by the Manpower Services Commission in 1981), this protection of the disabled was taken over by anti-discrimination provisions individuals would obtain an enforceable right but

[63] *Ibid.* s.9 subject to certain exceptions.
[64] Disabled Persons (Standard Percentage) Order 1946 (S.R. & O. No. 1258).
[65] Disabled Persons (Special Percentage) (No. 1) Order 1949 (S.R. & O. 1949 No. 236).
[66] Disabled Persons (Employment) Act 1944, s.11.
[67] *Ibid.* s.9(5). See *Seymour* v. *British Airways Board* [1983] I.R.L.R. 55 (EAT).
[68] S.R. and O. 1946 No. 1257 made under the Disabled Persons (Employment) Act 1944, s. 12 which reserves to the disabled alone employment as lift and car park attendants.
[69] Companies (Directors' Report) (Employment of Disabled Persons) Regulations 1980 (S.I. 1980 No. 1160).

would suffer problems of proof and unconscious prejudice similar to those that occur in the case of sex and race discrimination. On the other hand, prohibition of indirect discrimination might well induce a greater degree of reconsideration of the justification for rejection of the disabled.

(d) Rehabilitated offenders

The Rehabilitation of Offenders Act 1974 forbids exclusion from office, profession, occupation or employment on the ground that the applicant has a criminal conviction deemed, under the provisions of the Act, to be spent.[69a] No direct remedy is provided if such refusal occurs. The legislative intention appears to be to persuade employers to stop asking the improper questions and to allow the employee (without fear of recission of the contract for misrepresentation) to decline to answer if asked. The Act has more effect in controlling subsequent termination when such an offence comes to light since it has the effect of preventing the offence being put forward as a reason for dismissal. The application of the Act is subject to a considerable number of exceptions in respect of specified professions and occupations.[70]

INCORPORATION OF COLLECTIVE AGREEMENTS IN THE CONTRACT

(a) The theoretical basis of incorporation:

The initiative of the employer in proposing terms is moderated by the effect of collective bargaining in producing collectively agreed terms.[71] Even where this does not occur the initiative of the employer in proposing such terms will often be influenced by standards set by collective bargaining by other employers in the industry and locality with which he has to compete for labour.

It is the assignment of the power to decide the terms of the contract by collective agreement with a representative organisation which causes most potential conflict between the idea of an individual contract and the reality of industrial organisation which does not, and cannot, operate on an individual basis. Judicial explanations of how the assimilation is to be achieved are ephemeral. Most textbook writers stride into the mist, followed hesitantly by their readers. The writer usually emerges on the other side declaring that he has mapped a path through and little aware that the readers either do not emerge at all or have little idea how they found the way. To provide a map in advance would seem elementary common sense but will provoke the criticism that it is designed to divert attention away from suggestions and decisions that do not accord with the preconceived pattern. Despite this objection it seems valuable to offer one explanation of the judicial approach to incorporation of collective agreements which the reader may thereafter modify for himself.

Paths appear to start at three different points and one of them, express incorporation, if it can be followed, will avoid uncertainty altogether. In N.C.B. v. Galley[72] the statement that the provisions of a collective agreement on certain aspects were to be followed was considered sufficiently clear to

---

[69a] s.4(3)(b).
[70] Rehabilitation of Offenders Act 1974 (Exemptions) Order (S.I. 1975/1023.)
[71] On the practice of collective bargaining see Chap. 8 infra.
[72] [1958] 1 W.L.R. 16.

leave no room for doubting their inclusion. The potential of this explanation has been greatly extended by the statutory provision for the written statement of the most significant terms and conditions of employment expressly to incorporate other documents.[73] The most common of such documents are likely to be written collective agreements. It is submitted that there can be little argument about the effect of a statement that "Your right to paid holidays is in accordance with the national agreement for [the industry]." If there is added "as amended from time to time" the question of which of successive agreements is referred to is placed beyond doubt. The only significant doubt remaining is whether this raises only a rebuttable presumption, since the essential individuality of contract permits individual objection to exclude the collective agreement. It seems probable that this is so wherever the alleged express incorporation is by way of the statutory written statement, since this is only evidence of the contract and so must, of necessity, be rebutted by the stronger contrary evidence of a clearly expressed individual objection.

There may be a query as to whether alleged express incorporation applies, as there was in *Camden Exhibition* v. *Lynott*,[74] where express incorporation of working-rule agreements on hours was thought by two members of the Court of Appeal to apply to an agreement not to impose unreasonable restrictions on voluntary overtime working. Russell L.J., it is submitted, was right when he concluded that the latter agreement applied to resort to industrial action rather than the number of hours worked.

Agency is a deceptively attractive explanation of the incorporation of a collective agreement in the individual contract. In representing its members a trade union can, at least for some legal purposes, be seen as their agent. This was accepted in *Heatons' Transport Ltd.* v. *T.G.W.U.*[75] Arnold J. in *The Burton Group Ltd.* v. *Smith*[76] warned against the conclusion that it was an agent in every case. That might lead to problems if some collective agreements were not being incorporated because it could be said that they were the product of "union policy" rather than the wishes of the affected members. That apart, however, even non-members can be dealt with, not as Kilner Brown J. did in *Land and Wilson* v. *West Yorkshire M.C.C.*,[77] by excluding them until they indicate acceptance of the agreement, but by implying that they too authorise the union to act on their behalf.

Both judicial pronouncements do not, save for rare exceptions, support the application of anything but a popular idea of agency to the collective bargaining process. It is suggested that agency should be treated as no more than a popular expression. Neither trade union members nor other employees in the "bargaining unit" normally authorise the union to achieve a defined objective. By the very nature of the process the union must have discretion to take a decision on what it will accept. It may, and often does, emerge to put a proposition to its members for their decision. In that event they are bound not as principals but because they have actually accepted the negotiated term of

---

[73] E.P.C.A. 1978, s.4.
[74] [1966] 1 Q.B. 555.
[75] [1972] I.C.R. 308.
[76] [1977] I.R.L.R. 351.
[77] [1979] I.C.R. 452.

employment. In other situations most trade union officials would regard themselves as possessing considerable freedom. If the union's authority is open-ended so that it regards itself as entitled to agree in detail without reference to its members then the actual details of the agreement are reached on its own authority and some other explanation than agency has to be found for incorporating *those details* in the contracts of affected individuals. Apologies for this cavalier treatment of the agency theory are due to those many writers who have argued it out. It has never been clearly rejected by the courts, any more than it has been clearly accepted.[78] It derives substantial support only from *Heatons Transport Ltd.* v. *T.G.W.U.*[79] which was concerned with authorisation, in broad general terms, for a course of conduct rather than specific agreement. Occasionally there is bound to be a clear example of agency in specific terms, as in *Edwards* v. *Skyways Ltd.*[80] but the impracticability of the suggestion based on agency made by Kilner Brown J. in *Land and Wilson* v. *West Yorkshire M.C.C.*[81] justifies the doubts about its creation expressed in *The Burton Group Ltd.* v. *Smith.*[82]

The only explanation acceptable to a lawyer must be some form of deemed individual acceptance of the detailed terms in question. What actual evidence is the court likely to find of that save absence of rejection? In *Joel* v. *Cammell Laird Ltd.*[83] the court insisted on actual individual knowledge of the term and, in *Duke* v. *Reliance Systems Ltd.*[84] either on such knowledge or "adherence without objection for a substantial period." Both cases, therefore, support a basis in acceptance without apparently realising that "knowledge" will disclose nothing about acceptance, and "adherence over a period" is an impossible test since the terms of the contract of employment cannot develop gradually over a defined, let alone an unspecified, period of time. If we cannot say when adherence reaches the point of acceptance it cannot furnish the explanation for incorporation. Anyway, no one in practice supposes that a collective agreement is at first unincorporated but later, without more, becomes part of the individual contract. Either there is acceptance at the outset, or some later act of acceptance is necessary. All the court is doing in suggesting incorporation by the time of the judgment is finding, in a certain set of facts, a useful excuse for an implied acceptance which must derive its support from some factor other than the passage of time.

That factor, it is submitted, is judicial acceptance of the common expectation of both parties to the contract of employment that the terms of relevant collective agreements will govern the relationship. The courts have accepted that where collective bargaining occurs it is regarded by all, save a possible dissident group, as the appropriate way to govern the terms of employment. If lawyers are to regard those terms as part of a contract then it follows that it is appropriate to incorporate the agreement into the contract. They mean to

---

[78] Although Brian Napier, in Elias, Napier and Wallington: *Labour Law Cases and Materials*, Chap. 3, p. 407, makes a determined effort to prove such rejection.
[79] [1972] I.C.R. 308.
[80] (1964) 1 W.L.R. 349.
[81] *Supra.*
[82] [1977] I.R.L.R. 351.
[83] [1969] 4 I.T.R. 206.
[84] [1982] I.R.L.R. 347.

imply no subjective value judgment when they say this is the "proper" way to regulate the employment relationship.[85] It is the proper way for the courts to permit its regulation by contract because it is the way that all involved expect it to occur. Varying judicial expressions may be used to indicate the satisfactory nature of this conclusion, as in *Howman and Son Ltd.* v. *Blyth*,[86] support was found in its reasonableness. Of course, it may suit the individual to deny that expectation when it imposes some burden upon him and the concept of "contract" forces a laywer to accept as effective clear proof of objection. But the courts are not anxious to fragment employment obligations by ready permission to opt out of the common pattern that they themselves have always supported.[87] The lawyers' desire to achieve this end may appear to be inhibited by the device of individual contract which he has chosen to support it.[88] In fact, there is no need to feel such inhibition. Why should one not be taken to have agreed to be governed by the rules one knows a specified procedure will produce from time to time? This is precisely why the courts accept the implication of an established custom regardless of actual knowledge.[89] We do not need to turn collective agreements into customs, as *Duke* v. *Reliance Systems*[90] demands, before being able to assume acceptance of the rules that are produced. Regulation by the terms of a collective agreement is as readily assumed at the present time as regulation by trade custom once was. Both, therefore, produce terms incorporated into the individual contract of employment because, as a fact and by no artificial legal explanation, the parties to the contract expect that this will be so.

The justification for incorporation of a collective agreement in an individual contract of employment is that the parties to the contract, regardless of union membership, expect employment to be regulated in this way. It is in this sense that Otto Kahn-Freund spoke of the collective agreement as "crystalised custom."[91] If the legal explanation for incorporation follows that assumption it is unnecessary to look for knowledge or express acceptance. The employee may properly be regarded as a passive acceptor of established practice as was the case with the trade custom in *Sagar* v. *Ridehalgh and Son Ltd.*[92] The judgment in *Joel* v. *Cammell Laird Ship-repairers Ltd.*[93] for instance, confuses the implication of established practice with incorporation by consent. The E.A.T. in *Howman and Son Ltd.* v. *Blyth*[94] need not have supported its conclusion in favour of incorporation by reference to its reasonableness. Any other explanation than expectation will turn the legal explanation

---

[85] *Gray Dunn* v. *Edwards* [1980] I.R.L.R. 23; *Nelson and Woolett* v. *The Post Office* [1978] I.R.L.R. 548.

[86] [1983] I.C.R. 416.

[87] See: *Meek* v. *Port of London Authority* [1918] 1 Ch. 415; *Singh* v. *British Steel Corporation* [1974] I.R.L.R. 131.

[88] As Browne-Wilkinson J. in *Duke* v. *Reliance Systems Ltd*, *supra*, insisted that contract needed consent and that consent required knowledge or custom.

[89] As in *Sagar* v. *Ridehalgh and Son Ltd.* [1931] 1 Ch. 310.

[90] *Supra.*

[91] O. Kahn-Freund: *System of Industrial Relations in Great Britain*, ed. Flanders and Clegg (1954) pp. 58–9.

[92] [1931] 1 Ch. 310.

[93] [1969] 4 I.T.R. 206.

[94] [1983] I.C.R. 416.

away from practice and even, as in *Duke* v. *Reliance Systems Ltd.*[95] from practicability.

This explanation produces a sharp distinction between the effect of change introduced by collective agreement and that initiated unilaterally by the employer.[96] It is submitted that there is no reason why the law should hesitate to produce such a difference by recognising that, in practice, however it comes to achieve that position, the trade union bargaining for an "industrial unit" acts as the representative of each individual in the unit. Collective bargaining is a (perhaps, "the") proper way to regulate the employment relationship.[97] From the point of view of industrial organisation it is nonsense to individualise, and thus fragment, the relationship and this does not happen in practice. If collective agreement does not produce common terms, employer initiative will. The alternative safeguard of express individual objection may, as Kahn-Freund always insisted, be a valuable safeguard of individual liberty, even in the face of the understanding that the collective agreement will be accepted. But in the light of worker acceptance of collective representation there is no need to press contract theories to demand further evidence of acceptance such as is appropriate to change introduced by one party alone.

(b) *Terms appropriate for incorporation*

So long as the trend of present legislative policy does not reverse judicial acceptance of collective organisation the principal issue in dispute in future is likely to be the appropriateness of a term for incorporation. If objection to incorporation is made it is more likely to be on the ground that the particular clause of the collective agreement is inappropriate to an individual contract of employment or, which may sometimes be a deviation from this conclusion, was not intended to be so incorporated. In 1971, when specific examples, like rules, were considered more reliable than is now the case Lord Wedderburn ventured the following comment[98]:

> "For example, it is not easy to incorporate into any individual worker's contract the clauses: 'Each Trade Union party to this agreement may have Shop Stewards' (Vehicle Building 1961) or 'the proportion borne by the aggregate number of men [in certain departments] shall not exceed one boy to every four (or fractional part of four) men' (Boot and Shoe 1962). These are matters between the unions and the employers. Other clauses could be incorporated only with some semantic jugling: *e.g.* 'No female shall be allowed to use nails longer than $1\frac{3}{4}$ inches' (Packing-case Agreement, 1942). Many other clauses (quite apart from wages, hours, and the like) are capable of being incorporated, *e.g.* 'Secretaries of Line Committees shall be allowed free rail travel on the Region concerned when engaged in the execution of their secretarial duties' (Railways 1960). With minimum ingenuity this could be expressed as an implied term of the individual contract of employment of each Secretary if the lawyers so desired. Presumably, too, a '100 per cent. membership' agreement can become an individual obligation to join a union if incorporated into the employment contract."[99]

---

[95] [1982] I.R.L.R. 347.

[96] See, *e.g. Jones* v. *Associated Tunnelling Ltd.* [1981] I.R.L.R. 477.

[97] As was accepted in *Gray Dunn and Co. Ltd.* v. *Edwards* [1980] I.R.L.R. 23; *Nelson and Woolett* v. *The Post Office* [1978] I.R.L.R. 548.

[98] *The Worker and the Law* (Penguin) (2nd ed.) at p. 193.

[99] But can it grant an individual right to compel the employer to operate the "closed shop" until the agreement is rescinded?

The fact, which this paragraph is designed to indicate, that almost everything, including the examples it gives, has some individual application has
deterred subsequent writers from attempting even so much guidance on the
type of collectively agreed clause which would be considered not to have been
intended to have individual effect. The decision in *Gallagher* v. *The Post
Office*[1] belongs to the same formative era but lacks the clarity of principle on
which the above quotation was founded. The policy underlying the decision
not to incorporate a recognition agreement into an individual contract is
clear. The plaintiff, when first employed by the Post Office (which then incorporated telecommunications) as a telephonist, had been advised by his training instructor that he was entitled to join either what was then called the
Union of Post Office Workers or the Guild of Telephonists. The latter, which
had broken away from the former many years before, was composed entirely
of male telephonists and was recognised by the Post Office as entitled to bargain for them. This had been a viable arrangement no doubt because male
telephonists usually worked the night shift and women did not. It would probably have become less viable, even if the Guild had nominally admitted
women, as legislation against sex discrimination operated to make such overt
distinctions difficult to maintain. The principal reason why, on reorganisation
as a public corporation in 1969, the Post Office decided to cease to recognise
the Guild, is likely to have been pressure from the UPW (established trade
unions never really learn to live with breakaways) coupled with the feeling
that the existence of the Guild would, of itself, create disputes and problems.
The plaintiff, who had joined the Guild, sought an injunction to prevent
breach of an alleged implied term in his contract of employment that the Post
Office would recognise both unions. This was presented as dependent on a
term that the employee was entitled to join either union and Brightman J.
rejected that term on the ground that there was no need for it since contractual silence would leave the plaintiff free to join either union. Since he had
apparently destroyed the basis for the implication of recognition the learned
judge did not consider that possibility in isolation. Clearly it strengthens the
argument that if there were an implied right to join a union non-recognition
would effectively destroy the substance of such a right. That is, however, not
the only available ground on which to imply an obligation to recognise a
union and it is a pity that some of the others were not explored since they
might have been more difficult to dispose of. The learned judge was able to
support his decision by other arguments such as inference from the type of
wording of the agreement and the non-managerial function of the training
instructor but it is submitted that he was really concerned to resist an overlap
between collective procedure and individual right. To put it another way, he
saw the relationship between employer and union as distinct from that
between employer and employee and did not want two separate lines to be
joined in a triangular arrangement. To have done so would seriously have
restricted the prerogative of the employer to manage his relations with his
employees whatever sources he may draw on to constitute that relationship.
Typically, United Kingdom courts do not see the situation as involving three-
party co-operation in the running of industry but separate two-party relationships radiating from employer initiative. Contract theory, of course, virtually

---

[1] [1970] 3 All E.R. 712.

compels such a view. So Brightman J. saw the statutory obligation imposed on the Post Office to consult with organisations representing its workforce as intended to acknowledge the distinction he made and, with it, the freedom of an employer to choose not only with whom, but the extent to which, he bargains.

The same policy is apparent in *Associated Newspaper Group Ltd.* v. *Wade*[2] In declining to incorporate into the contract of employment the terms of a rule of the employee's trade union the court openly disclosed its reluctance to acknowledge an employment triangle:

> "If the union rules are incorporated into the contract then the union has more power of direction over the employee than the employer . . . In those circumstances there is no doubt which of the two masters he will obey . . . That being the case it seems to me there would have to be very strong evidence indeed before one could come to the conclusion that the rules . . . had become part of the contract."

In *Partington* v. *NALGO*,[3] however, such a triangular situation was created. Policy pointed to that conclusion because the union had assigned to the employer some of the control it would normally seek to exert over its own members. Geoffrey Lane L.J. revealed an obvious willingness to consider collective agreements, even affecting collective action, to be appropriate for individual incorporation. In that case the collective agreement specifically permitted an employer to require certain employees in particular situations to work during a strike called by the union. Since the employer would have had such a right by implication, unless he had very clearly relinquished it, the readiness to imply the right from the collective agreement is not surprising, especially as the actual decision concerned expulsion from the union of an employee who had obeyed the instruction of an employer which the union itself had agreed the employer was entitled to give.

It is tempting[4] to infer that the distinction is, therefore, between procedural and substantive agreements. Usually that distinction will provide a starting point for incorporation but procedural agreements may have obviously individual characteristics and substantive agreements raise policy issues in respect of long-term effects which complicate so simple a test. This was the cause of disagreement in the Court of Appeal in *Camden Exhibitions and Display Ltd.* v. *Lynott*[5] where the majority of the court saw an agreement not to resort to individual action as part of the definition of individual job obligation, and so correctly to be incorporated in the contract of employment; whilst Russell L.J., rightly, it is suggested, saw it as a procedural agreement relating to the manner in which industrial relations would be conducted. Interestingly, Lord Denning M.R., in the majority, presents no reasons at all for his conclusion which he is content to express thus:

> "Can the men put a collective embargo on overtime. This is a difficult point. On the whole I think this working rule means that the men will not, officially or

---

[2] [1979] 1 W.L.R. 697.
[3] [1981] I.R.L.R. 537.
[4] See, *e.g.* Elias, Napier and Wallington: *Labour Law: Cases and Materials* p. 412 note.
[5] [1966] 1 Q.B. 555.

unofficially, impose a collective embargo on overtime when it is required to ensure the due and proper performance of contracts."

The reluctance of the courts to impose, by incorporation into the contract of employment, long-term procedural fetters on managerial freedom also found expression in *British Leyland (U.K.) Ltd.* v. *McQuilken.*[6] With the same lack of reasoned argument, Lord McDonald in the Scottish EAT decided not to incorporate an agreement as to the options to be offered to individual employees subject to a reorganisation under which their present jobs were to be terminated. All he said, but it is significant, was that this should be seen as a long-term plan dealing with policy rather than the rights of individuals. That, of course, entirely begs the question since what is seen by the employer as a long-term plan is, for the employee to whom it is, or is not, applied, a matter of immediate rights, or lack of rights. "Long-term plans," if enforceable, impinge on the freedom of management to take substantive decisions either unilaterally or in negotiation with trade unions or individuals and the courts have not favoured a fetter on managerial discretion in the organisation of industry.

If it is correct to deduce, from the fact that that is the outcome of judicial decisions, that the courts, consciously or not, are reluctant to render enforceable long-term restrictions on managerial freedom, but that this reluctance does not extend to long-term restrictions on the freedom of trade unions to take industrial action, or otherwise limit their options, justification can be seen for the caution of the legislature in 1974[7] in excluding from incorporation, without express provision to that effect, any restriction on the right to take industrial action. It is plainly not safe to assume that, as a procedural agreement, it will normally be regarded as inappropriate for individualisation.

The courts are unlikely to admit to so brash a policy nor, indeed, would its expression be sufficiently general to cover any situation which they might have to consider. They are more likely to agree that they seek to discover the intention of the parties. They may be wrong to assume that trade unions intended to allow management to enforce negotiated restrictions on their bargaining freedom but did not intend to limit management's business options in the long term. Nevertheless, that is the conclusion they seem to have reached. The important point to note is that the intention with which the courts concern themselves is that of the collective parties. This is another step away from individual contract towards recognition of the collective regulation of employment. If the courts had been applying the law of individual contract they would have been bound to see the issue as one of what the parties to the contract of employment intended to incorporate. In practice they appear much more ready to search for the collective intention. In *Loman and Henderson* v. *Merseyside Transport Services Ltd.*[8] the employer gave evidence that a local agreement which guaranteed pay based on a 68-hour week was not intended to be enforceable but had as its purpose the elimination of local problems. What he appears to have meant was that the local agreement

---

[6] [1978] I.R.L.R. 245.
[7] Trade Union and Labour Relations Act 1974, s.18(4).
[8] [1968] 3 I.T.R. 108.

would be adhered to for as long as it suited both parties but that the only ulti-mately binding provision was contained in a national agreement providing for a basic 41-hour week. No doubt, the trade union would probably have agreed that, at the risk of industrial action, the employer was free to terminate the local agreement. Both would have shied off the suggestion that the individual employee had an enforceable right to demand observance of its terms. The employee, of course, would have taken a different view. His only interest was local and he would see the local agreement as resolving a dispute in his favour and as conferring on him an entitlement to be paid in accordance with its terms. Although the decision to the same effect in *Gascol Conversions Ltd.* v. *Mercer*[9] depended on other reasoning Lord Denning M.R. accepted the pre-ference for the collective intention expressed in *Loman*. In *Gascol* this was actually expressed in the collective agreement by the words: "where the [national] agreement is at variance with other national and local working agreements, it is to take precedence" and, in passing, Lord Denning indicated his acceptance of this expression of intent. The same emphasis was placed on the collective intention, by the EAT, in *Marley* v. *Forward Trust Group Ltd.*[10] It was agreed that the employee's contract of employment included matters set out in the relevant personnel manual. The personnel manual referred to a collective agreement on the handling of redundancies. That col-lective agreement stated that it was binding in honour only. Popplewell J. said that the intention of the parties was to be judged by the agreement they had entered into and, by this, he clearly meant the collective agreement (though at one point he refers to it as "the contract"). At this point, however, he mis-understood the meaning of the words "binding in honour" and held that they indicated an intention to exclude the collective agreement from the individual contract. The Court of Appeal reversed this.[11] Lawton L.J. relied on *Robert-son* v. *British Gas Corporation*[12] In *Robertson's* case the contract of employ-ment expressly provided for a bonus scheme and all that was necessary was to make the implication that the terms of that scheme were to be found in what-ever collective agreement was then operative. The collective agreement indi-cated no contrary intent by the parties to it. The decision, accordingly, does not deal with the intentions of the collective parties. By relying on the judg-ment in *Robertson* the Court of Appeal must be taken to have indicated its disregard, for individual purposes, of a statement which it chose to see as wholly referring to the position of the parties to the collective agreement. The Court of Appeal was actually extending the policy of giving predominance to collective regulation over individual choice by preferring to restrict a collec-tive disclaimer to its collective aspect whilst continuing to give effect to the collective regulating effect on the individual. No doubt the collective parties can exclude this regulating effect if they choose to make that intention clear beyond a peradventure, but the Court of Appeal was clearly desirous of avoiding a situation in which the general regulatory effect of a collective agreement is set aside by the operation of a side issue. One is forced again to

---

[9] [1974] I.C.R. 420.
[10] [1986] I.R.L.R. 43.
[11] [1986] I.R.L.R. 369.
[12] [1983] I.C.R. 353.

the conclusion that courts, so often accused of taking too much notice of individualism in employment, have accepted that employment is collectively regulated to the extent of avoiding the introduction of pockets of non-regulation which would be caused by emphasis on individual differences.

(c) *Implication into a separate contract*

We shall deal in due course with the problem of variation of the contract by collective agreement. At this point where we are considering the initial impact of the collective agreement on the content of the individual contract it is, however, worth noting a proposition about the structure of the contract of employment so far developed largely to solve the problems of change in its collective sources. In *Land and Wilson* v. *West Yorks MCC*[13] the Court of Appeal decided that the single contract of employment was divisible into one part relating to whole-time employment and another part relating to retained duties in the employee's spare time so that termination of the second part did not affect the first.[14] It is important to note that both reasoned decisions in the Court of Appeal approach this proposition with caution. Brightman L.J., for instance, makes a point of referring to the difference in time and place of work involved. In *Bond* v. *CAV Ltd.*,[15] however, *Land's* case was the only authority referred to by Peter Pain J. for a much wider application of the idea of severance so as to permit a bonus maintenance agreement to be regarded as separate from the rest of the contractual provisions for remuneration. The problem arising from such an extension is to know where lines of separation can be drawn without going so far as to permit an employee to demand payment for such work as he chooses to do despite his refusal to do other work. In *Metropolitan Borough of Solihull* v. *National Union of Teachers*[16] Warner J. accepted that there was an arguable case that a school teacher undertaking the oversight of pupils during the lunch break (in consideration of a free lunch!) entered into a supplemental contract with his employer so that lunchtime supervision could not be said to be voluntary, even though it would normally have been regarded as separate from the functions of a school teacher.

It is obvious that the concept of a subsidiary contract, interference with which does not affect the main contract of employment, could prove a useful way of handling a collectively agreed incident. It is equally clear that the courts are not prepared to confine its use to temporally or geographically separated employment. On the other hand, the court in *Gibbons* v. *Associated British Ports*[17] was not prepared to sever a six-day guarantee agreement from the normal provision for remuneration because the purpose of the agreement had been to close a growing gap in earnings between those on container duties and the rest of the port workers. Tudor Price J. specifically said, however, that he would not rule out the possibility of severing other aspects of the Productivity Agreement.

---

[13] [1981] I.C.R. 334.
[14] Though it seems likely that termination of the first would have had the same effect on the second. See Brightman L.J. at p. 341.
[15] [1983] I.R.L.R. 360.
[16] [1985] I.R.L.R. 211.
[17] [1985] I.R.L.R. 376.

However far the concept of severability is to be taken it is clear that it has a considerable part to play, not only confined to handling the collective agreement, in the judicial approach to breach of the contract of employment. From *Bowes and Partners Ltd.* v. *Press*[18] to *Royle* v. *Trafford Borough Council*[19] courts have from time to time had to deal with a case of an employee prepared to perform a part only of his obligation. The invention of constructive dismissal raises the possibility of an employee bringing the same allegation against an employer. The recent acceptance of a power of deduction of wages for part performance also permits openings for arguments as to severability.

(d) *Custom*

The terms which the parties, individually or collectively, devise may be supplemented by judicial willingness to imply trade customs. No court has ever suggested how long a practice needs to have continued to be regarded as customary. It is probably true to say that the extent of observance is more important than time, but this must not be taken to suggest any weakness in a well-established practice because it only operates at one location. Lawrence L.J. made this assumption as to the nature of the established custom to make deductions for bad work which was in issue in *Sagar* v. *Ridehalgh and Son Ltd.*[20] and concluded that anyone who accepted employment at that mill did so on the basis of the same terms as applied to others. He then considered the matter in the light of the fact that a custom to deduct pay for bad work applied throughout the Lancashire weaving trade and concluded that that would suffice to incorporate the custom into the contract of every weaver in Lancashire "without special mention" and, it seems, without personal knowledge. There is no point in arguing whether custom thus produces an express, or an implied, term. The less documentary evidence that exists the more it will look like implication. In the case of payment during sickness, mobility or an obligation to work particular public holidays much will depend on what is happening in the rest of that industry. That circumstance may be regarded as simply a source of implication or, if very clearly marked, be dignified by the term "custom." The result is the same.

Much of the more formal custom that used to exist will now be found incorporated in collective agreement which has adapted it to changing circumstance and the fact that the employee collectively may have challenged its former tendency to produce working rules in favour of the employer. In *Bond and Neads* v. *CAV Ltd.*,[21] for instance, an alleged custom, entitling the employer to lay off without pay where industrial action interfered with production, was held, if it had existed at all, to have been absorbed into the guaranteed pay provisions of the engineering national agreement. It is not impossible for local aspects of a custom to survive such a process, but in the absence of clear evidence of the continuation of deviant local practice the conclusion reached in that case that there was no surviving scope for the custom is more likely.

---

[18] [1894] Q.B.D. 202.
[19] [1984] I.R.L.R. 184.
[20] [1931] 1 Ch. 310.
[21] [1983] I.R.L.R. 360.

JUDICIAL INTERPRETATION AND CONSTRUCTION

The courts are, not infrequently, faced with a difficult problem in interpreting documentary and oral evidence of express provisions in the contract of employment. Even when a written document is produced the employer (who will almost always be its originator) is often imprecise as to his intention. Partly because collective agreements are not usually regarded as contractually enforceable, the parties to them rarely make significant efforts to be precise. Both employer and union often have good reason to avoid such precision. Precision narrows the possible scope of the provision. A general job title such as "general office duties," for instance, is seen by the employer as allowing much greater flexibility than if it were filled out with a more detailed job description. Where a collective agreement is made in settlement of a dispute it is that objective which the parties will regard as primary. The less precise the words used the easier it is to achieve agreement.

Although the Court of Appeal was of the opinion that the rule book in question did not form part of the contract of employment in *Secretary of State for Employment* v. *ASLEF (No. 2)*[22] Lord Denning's account of its content would not be untypical of many examples of this very common written source of terms. He said[23]:

> "Some of them are quite out of date, such as that the coal in the engine must not be stacked too high. Others contain trivial details, such as that the employees must on duty be neat in appearance. A few are important in this case, particularly rule 2(1), which says that employees must see that the safety of the public is their chief care under all circumstances . . . Rule 126(1) . . . says: 'The driver and fireman *must* . . . satisfy themselves that the engine is in proper order.' Rule 176 is a compendious rule which is worth noting: 'Inspectors, shunters, guards, drivers, signalmen and all others concerned, must make every effort to facilitate the working of trains and prevent any avoidable delay."

The normal "employee handbook" is even more varied. Even when the clearly non-contractual sections have been eliminated (such as the managing director's letter of welcome and the statements of the company's employment and safety policies) the court will have to consider whether a statement such as "misconduct or lack of ability may result in warnings, suspension, demotion or a transfer or dismissal" has contractual effect and, if so, what it means. Disciplinary procedures would be a major source of problems of interpretation were it not that whatever their meaning their operation will be judged most often on the basis of fair or unfair dismissal. This is demonstrated by the decision of the Court of Appeal in *Dietman* v. *London Borough of Brent.*[24] Lesser forms of discipline are rarely challenged in the courts.[25] The impetus to produce statements of grounds for disciplinary action following the extension of the content of the statutory statement of terms and conditions to cover this aspect led to more wild generality than has appeared in any other part of the contract of employment.

---

[22] [1972] I.C.R. 19.
[23] At p. 54.
[24] [1988] I.R.L.R. 299. See on tribunal interpretation, *Cawley* v. *South Wales Electricity Board* [1985] I.R.L.R. 89.
[25] But see *Post Office* v. *Strange* [1981] I.R.L.R. 2 515.

Probably the most common single source of demand for judicial interpretation is the job description. These disputes reveal very clearly the difficulty of
ascertaining what the contractual provision originally meant in the light of a
much later dispute leading both parties to a highly developed view of what
they earlier thought. It is impossible to be really sure what the parties
intended to be the meaning of the job title "copy typist/general duties clerk"
in *Glitz* v. *Watford Electric Co. Ltd.*[26] since, by the time the dispute arrived in
court, they were not likely to agree. As we shall see, the fact that for some
three years the clerk did not operate a duplicator would usually only be evidence that she had not been asked to do so. There was not likely to be previous evidence that she had, by refusal of such a request, indicated that she did
not think herself so obligated or that the employer, by making the request,
had indicated his contrary view. Interpretation of such a term as the location
of the work may well be made easier by other indicators, such as the
employee's social circumstances, but job content is unlikely to be controlled
by such factors. It may well be that the general understanding in the company
itself will settle the matter. Alternatively there may be a general understanding in the industry; although, surprisingly, the same job title is likely to conceal considerable differences of detailed content between almost any two
individual employers one chooses to select. In the last resort, if such factors
are non-existent or inconclusive, a form of common sense the courts call
reasonableness will have to be called into play. This reasonableness will owe a
great deal to a mixture of second-hand experience and sense of what will produce a working relationship. In *Glitz* the court felt that, in a relatively small
office, a "general duties clerk" would be expected to operate a duplicator.
The issue in *Peter Carnie & Son Ltd.* v. *Paton*,[27] decided by the Scottish EAT,
was slightly more complicated. It was not disputed that someone whose job
description was "general garage duties/stores" would be expected to carry out
a wide range of jobs as a general handyman. The employee, however,
enjoyed working as a receptionist but was held not to be entitled to a substantial amount of work in that capacity. In *Haden Ltd.* v. *Cowan*[28] the employer
had again sought to secure a range of services. On this occasion the basic job
title was, however, more restricted to "divisional contracts surveyor." To this
had been added a requirement to "undertake, at the direction of the company, any and all duties which reasonably fall within the scope of his capabili-
ties." The Court of Appeal considered the job title to indicate work different
from that of ordinary quantity surveyors but regarded the additional provision as a qualification upon that, rather than as an extension to a broad
range of duties unconnected with the basic job.
    The influence of judicial reasonableness on interpretation of written
sources of contract of employment—thus assimilating the results with those
achieved by implication—is clearly apparent in the decision of Hodgson J.
and of the Court of Appeal in *Dietman* v. *Brent London Borough Council.*[29]
The plaintiff had been the supervisor of a social worker responsible for a child
in the authority's care who had been killed by her stepfather. The authority

---

[26] [1979] I.R.L.R. 89.
[27] [1979] I.R.L.R. 260.
[28] [1982] I.R.L.R. 314.
[29] Q.B. [1987] I.C.R. 737; C.A. [1988] I.R.L.R. 299.

appointed an independent panel of inquiry which concluded that the plaintiff "by her non-intervention in flawed social work was grossly negligent." On receipt of the report of that inquiry the authority forthwith, and without a hearing, dismissed the plaintiff. She took an internal appeal without success. The authority contended that she had been guilty of "gross misconduct" within its written disciplinary procedure incorporated in its contracts of employment. Gross misconduct was defined as "misconduct of such a nature that the [authority] is justified in no longer tolerating the continued presence at the place of work of the employee." Examples were then given which were expressly said to be non-exhaustive but which the Court of Appeal said all involved an element of intention. Hodgson J. said that use of the term "gross negligence" was unfortunate. It is, of course, quite likely that it was the presence of the emotive word "gross" in both the description of the employee's fault and their disciplinary procedure which influenced the authority to ignore the difference between "negligence" and "misconduct." Hodgson J. and the Court of Appeal concluded that "gross negligence" would not amount to gross misconduct in the context in question. Napier[30] pointed out that by giving examples specifically not intended to detract from the generality of the definition the employer had, in fact, narrowed that definition. There can be little doubt that what an employer sees as explanatory examples may be read by the employee as demonstrative of a single particular type of situation. Judicial application of the *ejusdem generis* rule is not the legal abstraction that it might seem, therefore.

We may draw from this decision the conclusion, well known to lawyers, that the more detailed a statement becomes the narrower it is. If employers are tending to add more to the written content of contracts of employment they must bear in mind that though this may reduce the scope for judicial implication it broadens the scope for judicial interpretation. More specifically, it becomes clear that the employer's options will not effectively be kept open by use of such phrases as "examples include."

The courts also considered the meaning of the reference to "instant dismissal" which, in its letter of dismissal, the authority had equated with "summary dismissal" and which it argued meant dismissal without a hearing. The Court of Appeal rejected this contention holding that "instant" referred to dismissal without notice. This is in line with the well-established meaning of "summary dismissal" at common law but the Court of Appeal confused this analogy by continuing to refer to the employee as having been summarily dismissed. In the context of unfair dismissal "summary" has come to mean "dismissal without a warning" and it remains to be seen whether use of this term (which most non-lawyers would equate with "instant") as meaning something like "immediate", will ever be seen by the courts to refer to procedural omission. It is suggested that neither term is capable of referring to dismissal without a hearing and that the courts in applying principles of "reasonable" interpretation would require a clear and specific exclusion of this element.

Interpretation of the expressions used may not resolve the dispute. In *London Borough of Redbridge* v. *Fishman*,[31] for instance, the employee was

---

[30] Brian Napier: "Disciplinary Procedure Unfair Dismissal and the Contract of Employment" 138 N.L.J. 197.

[31] [1978] I.C.R. 569.

appointed "full time permanent teacher in charge of Resources Centre." No doubt her status was that of an assistant teacher. The dispute was as to whether this status took priority over the initial appointment to the Resources Centre. The words used indicate nothing as to a degree of flexibility. "Interpretation" becomes more a question of reasonable implication of the extent of the terms of engagement which, here, were held not to include substantial periods of class-room teaching. There is room in this process for a significant element of changeable policy. It is difficult to deny such an element in the refusal of the EAT in *Rank Xerox Ltd.* v. *Churchill*[31a] to interpret the requirement that the employee might be required "to transfer to another location" as confined to movement within a reasonable distance of their homes. The suggestion that such interpretation would be nonsense since the employer's rights would then vary according to the employee's unilateral decision as to where to live fails to accord with a line of previous such implications and prompts the question why such a conclusion would be more startling than the scope given to the employer by job flexibility clauses.

Interpretation of collective agreements will involve the same technique, but a different understanding of the likely reaction of the parties. It is true one of the parties—the employer—is the same in both situations but his reactions, intentions and expectations may well be different when he is dealing collectively with a trade union. This difference may be seen at its simplest, and probably least significant, in *Stevenson* v. *Teesside Bridge and Engineering Ltd..*[32] A dispute had arisen on the geographical mobility of the employee. No express mobility clause existed in documents representing the individual contract of employment. The national collective agreement, however, though similarly refraining from stating any express obligation contained extensive provisions for travelling and subsistence allowances. The employee, who had been working within travelling distance of his home, declined offers of work on other sites not within travelling distance because he doubted the chance of overtime at those locations. If he had no obligation to move to those other sites his dismissal following the completion of work on his "home" site would have been by reason of redundancy, entitling him to statutory compensation. If he was obliged to travel, his contractual workplace was the wide area where there was work for him so that he could not have been said to have been terminated for redundancy. The industrial tribunal, and Ashworth J. in the Divisional Court (which at that time heard appeals from industrial tribunals) based the decision in favour of an obligation to move on the general expectation of mobility in the industry and the clear evidence that the employee himself had, earlier, accepted that he was obliged to move. Lord Parker C.J. looked more to the meaning of the collective agreement and concluded that the very detailed nature of the provisions indicated that the negotiators had assumed that they were regulating an obligation rather than a voluntary undertaking. Whether this is a justified inference or not, it is submitted that it would have carried a different weight if it had been applied to the similar terms offered by an employer directly to his employees.

The decision of the Inner House of the Court of Session in *Burroughs Machines Ltd.* v. *Timmoney*[33] is generally recognised as one of the triumphs

---

[31a] [1988] I.R.L.R. 280.
[32] [1971] 1 All E.R. 296.
[33] [1977] I.R.L.R. 404.

of judicial understanding of the nature and purpose of collective agreements. Employees claimed statutory redundancy compensation. That is only available following a dismissal and they had only been laid off without pay due to a strike by other employees at their workplace. If the employees could show that this lay-off was in breach of contract they could found their claim on what is known as "constructive dismissal."[34] A Guarantee of Employment Agreement had been entered into between the Engineering Employers' Federation, of which the employer was then a member, and the Confederation of Shipbuilding and Engineering Unions. As we have seen[35] there can be little doubt that the terms of this agreement were incorporated into the individual contracts of employment. As subsequently amended, the agreement provided that hourly-rated manual workers, after a qualifying period of service, should be entitled to a minimum of 40 hours' pay in any week during which less than 40 hours' paid work was provided. A condition was attached to this guarantee, expressed to be available to "federated employers," permitting its withdrawal if the failure to supply the work was brought about by the dislocation of production by industrial action in that or any other federated establishment. The employer in question had resigned from the E.E.F. 16 years after the agreement was first made. It was accepted that this resignation, effectively cancelling the collective agreement, could not unilaterally destroy the right of the individual employee. The employees argued, however, that as the employer was no longer a federated employer he could not rely on a provision only expressed to be available to federated employers. The court held that the clear meaning of the agreement was that the employees' right was to be conditional upon the freedom of the employer to withdraw it when, otherwise, it would have arisen from industrial action. It rejected the suggestion that the collective agreement must be incorporated according to the strict construction of the words used. The intention was to limit the concession and it was that intention which should be effected. Collective agreements frequently take the form of package deals, more frequently of carefully conditioned concessions. If the process of transfer to the individual contract were to lose sight of what is probably the most inherent characteristic of a negotiated compromise the courts would have lost touch with reality and the collective parties would respond in ways which could, at the very least, complicate industrial relations.

It will be apparent that the process of interpretation of existing provisions and of implication so as to qualify or amend them shade into each other. It matters little whether it is said that the words used by the parties are capable of comprehending a certain consequence, or that the same consequence is reasonable and so should be implied. Many decisions which have been arrived at via one path could equally have been reached by the other. In *Cresswell* v. *Board of Inland Revenue*,[36] for example, the job description of the tax inspector could have been interpreted as referring to the same job when computerised or, alternatively, the job description could have been qualified by an implied duty to be reasonably flexible. In many other decisions, such as *Fishman*, it is not entirely clear whether the court is interpreting the conversation at an interview or implying a right from a reasonable expectation. If the

---

[34] *Infra*, pp. 134 *et seq.*
[35] *Supra*, p. 36 *et seq.*
[36] [1984] I.R.L.R. 190.

general assumption of the courts in such cases is that it does not matter this must depend on acceptance of the existence of the preconditions for implication. The process of interpretation has already established that the parties intended to have a provision dealing with the matter at issue. If no such indication exists the courts are compelled to consider whether to imply a term and they have consistently indicated that they will only do so where it is necessary that there should be some provision for the matter.[36a] Students will recognise this requirement of necessity, even when it is not so expressed, as the test of business efficacy.[37] As a matter of fact the courts are not always right in regarding it as satisfied. In *Bristol Garage Ltd.* v. *Lowen*,[38] for instance, the court said that implication of a qualification to the employer's right to deduct from wages a shortage in the till was necessary because no employee would accept employment if such a right arose from theft or dishonesty of a third party. However undesirable the practice may have been felt to be there is little doubt that, in the industry in question, absence of such a qualification to the general right would not render employment impossible, and such an unqualified right exists in other occupations as well. However that may be, the requirement that some term be shown to be necessary is established.[39]

Many examples, such as the location of the job and the job description, are so obviously necessary that the student will not expect to see the court formally establishing the point. What is not required is that the courts should seek to establish that the parties would have included the term had they thought about it. Indeed evidence that they would not is not fatal.[40] The search for "a testy, oh! of course"[41] would in any event, strictly speaking only have served the same end as discussion whether such a term was necessary since the parties would only be assumed to concede this in a case of necessity. Almost never could the detail of the term be constructed save on the assumption that the parties react in the same way as the court.

Uniformly, the courts concentrate their attention on the initiation of the contract—at which time, rebuttably, they presume agreement. Secondarily they consider whether there is evidence of agreement to vary that position. The contract, therefore, appears to move, if at all, by fits and starts (which is frequently the case) rather than by a process of development. In practice, consideration of the latter process is not infrequent since the courts will consider subsequent practice as evidence of the situation at the point of initiation. Where there is clear evidence of an initial position later process will not change the position unless it can be more or less identified as a point at which an agreed variation occurred.[42] Care must be exercised, therefore, before subsequent practice is adopted as evidence in the absence of other indications. It must be remembered that the court is searching for evidence of obli-

---

[36a] The Court of Appeal clearly stated this requirement when rejecting an invitation to imply a term in an agreement to provide articles that the clerk should have passed the solicitor's final examinations—*Stubbs* v. *Trower, Still and Keeting* [1987] I.R.L.R. 321.

[37] See *Luxor (Eastbourne) Ltd.* v. *Cooper* [1941] A.C. 108.

[38] [1979] I.R.L.R. 86.

[39] e.g. *Gallagher* v. *The Post Office* [1970] 3 All E.R. 712; *Jones and Associated Tunnelling Co. Ltd.* [1981] I.R.L.R. 477.

[40] *Mears* v. *Safecar Security Ltd.* (1981) I.C.R. 409 (EAT); (1982) I.R.L.R. 183 (C.A.)

[41] *Southern Foundries Ltd.* v. *Shirlaw* (1940) A.C. 701.

[42] e.g. *Horrigan* v. *Lewisham London Borough Council* [1978] I.C.R. 15.

gation. In *O'Brien* v. *Associated Fire Alarms Ltd.*[43] Salmond L.J. accepted seven years' practice of working in Liverpool alone as indicative of an absence of contractual obligation to work elsewhere. It is, of course, only evidence that the employee never has worked elsewhere and that may be because he has not been asked to do so. Lord Denning M.R., on the other hand, asked only what circumstances suggested it was reasonable to impose upon the parties. He relied on evidence almost entirely outside the employment situation. Social and domestic circumstances may provide clear indication of what work obligations it is reasonable to impose or, even, what the parties would have adopted had the matter been left to them. It is often suggested that surprise should be felt, and a fresh explanation sought, for the opposite conclusion in *Managers (Holborn) Ltd.* v. *Hohne*[44] where it was held that the employee had no contractual right to resist a move, after 11 years of work in London's High Holborn, to New Oxford Street, a few hundred yards away. Davies and Freedland[45] claim that *Hohne* supposed an initial mobility whilst *O'Brien* supposed an initial immobility. With respect there is nothing to support a contention that the presumptive degree of mobility was different in either case. O'Brien was far more mobile than Hohne had ever been. O'Brien could almost certainly have been asked to work anywhere within the boundaries of Liverpool. The only evidence was that both employees had their domestic and social base at a certain location. The conclusion in one case was that the employee could not be required to move an unreasonable distance from that base, in the other that the employee could be required to move within a reasonable area having regard to that base. The test is always the same namely what, in the circumstances, is it reasonable to imply. The courts, however, may not always answer that, being content simply to say that whatever the term it is certainly reasonable or unreasonable to require particular conduct. In *Courtaulds Northern Spinning Ltd.* v. *Sibson*[45a] the Court of Appeal pointed out that the reasonableness of implying a contractual right is in no way dependent on the reasonableness of exercising that right in particular circumstances. If there is no commercially sound reason for moving an employee to another location the right to do so may still exist and be exercised. In that case the court was prepared to imply a right to require an HGV driver to operate from any depot within reasonable travelling distance of his home. Considerable importance was attached to the fact that the employee only started and finished work at that place. It might have been more correct to emphasise the fact that such an employee would normally have transport from his home to the depot.

Although the subsequent practice to which Salmond L.J. referred in *O'Brien* did not produce any evidence to support the imposition of obligation or lack of it, there are plenty of circumstances in which subsequent practice will tend to indicate acceptance of an obligation. If a specific payment is made for particular work, for instance, it is reasonable to infer that the payer assumed an obligation to make it. It is a little less obvious that the receiver assumed a right to receive it until he had done so several times. This may, on

---

[43] [1968] W.L.R. 1916.
[44] [1977] I.R.L.R. 230.
[45] At p. 298.
[45a] [1988] I.R.L.R. 305.

the face of it, look as if we are suggesting a contract developing over a period. All the court is doing, however, is to take a subsequent course of conduct as evidence of an initial understanding. To what extent then do the courts look for guidance to the parties and to what extent do the courts impose the contract they think ought to exist?

As was said in *Jones* v. *Associated Tunnelling Co. Ltd.*[46] there must be a contractual provision as to the place of work. Often neither express provision nor subsequent practice will provide any reliable indication of what that term should be. If we suppose that Mrs. Hohne would have agreed that she could be moved within the central London area it is only because we conclude that such agreement would be reasonable. A contract to work at only one location would be entirely efficacious. In *O'Brien* business efficacy would have permitted either answer and the supposed intention of the parties, though clear enough in relation to a move of 120 miles, would have provided no answer to a disputed move of 20 miles. By the time the parties in fundamental disagreement in *Jones* have been supposed to be told they must agree and then supposed to have reached that agreement it becomes clear that what they might have said has little to do with the reality that the court is imposing its own decision. A glance at any of the judgments which purport to apply business efficacy to the contract of employment reveals that the courts almost always use that supposed principle to lend an appearance of technical authority to a decision that has already been reached.[47] In only one reported case[48] does it seem that the court has ever allowed business efficacy to divert it from a conclusion it considered to be reasonable. If, therefore, the process of implication is one of asking what term would be reasonable, and it is the court which decides what is reasonable, is there any point in pretending that the court is enquiring of the parties?

The Court of Appeal in *Mears* v. *Safecar Securities Ltd.*[49] plainly thought not. Stephenson L.J. stated that implication into the contract of employment had been recognised as often involving a legal incident of the relationship. "We can" he said "treat as an agreed term a term which would not have been at once assented to by both parties at the time they made the contract." This might suggest that in the end, having been told they must agree, the minds of the parties must be searched. In *Howman & Son Ltd.* v. *Blyth*[50] the EAT decided unequivocally that it was free to apply its own view as to what was a reasonable term, rather than purporting to defer to that of the parties. In *Jones* v. *Associated Tunnelling Co. Ltd.*[51] Browne-Wilkinson J. in the EAT distinguished the House of Lords decision in *Trollope and Colls Ltd.* v. *North Western Regional Hospital Board*[52] on the ground that it was not there necessary for such a term to be implied. This is obviously a logical conclusion. If terms were to be implied as a legal incident, regardless of the intention of the parties, that can only be on the assumption that it is necessary to have a term dealing with the matter in question. The courts have, therefore, given them-

[46] [1981] I.R.L.R. 477.
[47] See *e.g. Gallagher* v. *The Post Office* [1970] 3 All E.R. 712.
[48] *Express Lift Co.* v. *Bowles* [1977] I.R.L.R. 99.
[49] [1982] I.C.R. 626.
[50] [1983] I.C.R. 416.
[51] *Supra.*
[52] [1973] 2 All E.R. 260.

selves extensive powers in relation to gaps left by the parties in the contract of employment. Provided only that it is considered necessary that a matter should be provided for it is open to them to insert such term as they consider reasonable in the circumstances without the need to determine the parties' intention to that effect. There can be no denying that this allows for the introduction of judicial policy. The most obvious feature of circumstances is that they change. In *Mears* case itself the Court of Appeal discarded what Stephenson L.J. recognised to have been a legal incident that, in the absence of contrary evidence, an employee off work due to sickness should be paid. As Freedland has pointed out[53] that legal incident has an irregular and unconvincing history but it is suggested that its appearance is most likely to have been an attempt to protect the employee. The major development of sick-pay schemes in the past 20 or so years, so that they now extend to a majority of employees of all types and not merely to white-collar workers, has had a dual effect. On the one hand it has made it more difficult to impose, as a legal incident, an obligation to pay wages during sickness until dismissal when the overwhelming practice is to place specific time limits on such payments. On the other hand, those limitations are not nearly as restrictive as was once the case so that contractual implication of the common practice can more realistically be founded on an assumption of reasonableness rather than the economic advantage of the employer.

The obvious question to which to seek an answer is how far the courts are likely to go in the implication of terms on the basis of policy. In *Secretary of State for Employment* v. *ASLEF (No. 2)*[54] Sir John Donaldson in the N.I.R.C. had propounded a duty upon the employee of active co-operation. The Court of Appeal considered that this went too far but, led by Lord Denning M.R., was prepared to imply a contractual obligation not wilfully to disrupt the undertaking. This would have introduced into the idea of breach of contract a mental element. An employee might, in good faith, refuse to do voluntary overtime, but if his motive was wilful disruption be acting in breach of contract. It is, no doubt, the difficulty of accepting this concept and of instituting an enquiry as to the intent of the individual which has prevented the adoption of the Court of Appeal's suggestion. In practice, it is suggested, it is the more extensive obligation of Sir John Donaldson which is more likely to be accepted, especially if the popular idea of industrial relations as properly involving a community of interest gains ground. The barrier which must be crossed is acceptance of the necessity of such a contractual provision. There is little room to argue that such a requirement would be other than reasonable in the light of decisions that it is reasonable to dismiss employees who stand upon their contractual rights and refuse to co-operate,[55] the conclusion that an employee must accept reasonable changes in the method of performing his job,[56] and, above all, the considerable potential for expansion of the duty to maintain trust and confidence, hitherto primarily imposed on the employer. The question must be of the extent to which a difference of public opinion on

---

[53] Freedland: *The Contract of Employment* (OUP). pp. 108–114.
[54] [1972] I.C.R. 19.
[55] *e.g. Horrigan* v. *Lewisham London Borough Council* [1978] I.C.R. 15; *Woods* v. *W.M. Car Services Ltd.* [1982] I.C.R. 693.
[56] *Cresswell* v. *Board of Inland Revenue* [1984] I.R.L.R. 190.

any issue will deter the courts. In *Secretary of State* v. *ASLEF (No. 2)* the Court of Appeal was well aware of the fact that a signalman who went home at the end of his shift knowing there was no one else to undertake his duties might argue that it was not his job to rectify management's failure to provide for the operation of his section of the railways, but, nevertheless, thought that he would have a contractual duty not deliberately to exploit that situation. Many would currently contend that industry is not a partnership but an arena in which the interests and power of capital confront those of organised labour, yet the courts have consistently favoured the view that management should be free to manage, despite the contrary suggestion that the interest of the employee is at least as important.

Nowhere is the development of a judicial policy more clear than in the collecting of the various strands of the job obligation. In *Langston* v. *AUEW*[57] Lord Denning M.R. put forward the view that employees do not agree to work only for money but, to some extent, for the satisfaction of working. He was prepared to imply an obligation to provide work on that basis. It is a short step to consider the balance of work and this was done by a process of selection of concrete evidence in *Pederson* v. *Camden London Borough Council*[58] In the latter case Phillips J. could, with the backing of authority, have concluded that the employee could be employed anywhere within the range of activities which fell within the scope of a "catering manager." The industrial tribunal had not, as Phillips J. suggested, confused a decision on the scope of the contract with one on the reasonableness of dismissal but clearly felt the employer to have a contractual right to use the whole range of the job to suit his economic needs. It was appreciation of the consequence of this that the employee could be left only with "humdrum" and "residual" duties which forced Phillips J. to consider no less a policy issue than whether an employee has a right to job satisfaction. It is clear from decisions such as *Peter Carnie*[59] that the courts do not at present accept any general right of this nature. Those decisions like *Pederson* which support such a right in individual circumstances depend on evidence that a spread of work is a reasonable expectation.

In *Glitz* v. *Watford Electric Co Ltd.*[60] it had been considered reasonable, in the light of the managerial needs of a small office, to expect from the employee—whether by way of interpretation or implication makes no difference—a degree of flexibility. In *Cresswell* v. *The Board of Inland Revenue*[61] Walton J. could have decided that, at its outset, the work did not involve the operation of a computer and that this limited method had been confirmed by a long-established practice containing no evidence of variation. This would not have been out of line with the reluctance to assume employee obligations to suit managerial convenience revealed in *O'Brien* or *Horrigan*. He disclosed a different attitude in the statement[62]:

> "It is a very fine line from (counsel for the employee's submission) that employees have a vested right to preserve their working obligations completely unchanged as

---

[57] [1974] I.C.R. 180.
[58] [1981] I.R.L.R. 342.
[59] [1979] I.R.L.R. 260.
[60] [1979] I.R.L.R. 89.
[61] [1984] I.C.R. 508.
[62] At p. 517.

from the moment when they first begin to work. This cannot surely, by any stretch of the imagination, be correct."

As expressed, it is clearly well within the bounds of reasonableness to imagine some working obligations to be regarded as fixed unless there is an agreed variation. Applied, in the context of the case, to working methods it may well be reasonable to say:

" . . . the person concerned does not like the new *method* of working and feels that his or her job satisfaction will be less. So be it; a loss of job satisfaction is always regrettable but by itself provides no cause of action."

This statement, however, begs the question since the decision whether to imply a degree of flexibility into the job obligation is likely to be made only on the basis of a conclusion that it is, or is not, reasonable to expect it—not vice versa. However that may be, we are clearly faced with conflicting views as to the balance between the scope for managerial initiative and protection of the employee's established expectations. This issue may be raised in the form of mobility, job flexibility or any other aspect of the rights and obligation of the parties. If its resolution depends on what the courts consider it reasonable to imply in all the circumstances we are likely to encounter different answers. In *Horrigan* v. *Lewisham London Borough Council*[63] the Court of Appeal felt itself bound by the clear contractual statement as to fixed basic hours to deny an obligation to accept some flexibility in hours. In the light of the fact that, despite that absence, it was proposed to concede the reasonableness of dismissal of an employee for insisting on his right to be inflexible, it is fair to ask whether the court would not have implied a contractual obligation to that effect had it been free to do so. Despite the decision in *Cawley* v. *South Wales Electricity Board*[64] there seems no logical reason why the circumstances indicating reasonable implication at the time of making the contract should not exclude an obligation as to flexibility whereas the circumstances at the time of dismissal should indicate that a reasonable employer might dismiss an employee who refused to accept such flexibility.[65] The answer is bound to be significantly affected by how the court sees the reasonable assumptions about the employment relationship. If, at present, they lean in favour of providing managerial flexibility, as against social protection for the employee, there is no reason why that policy should continue to dominate. Interpretation and implication, in short, will continue to reflect judicial assumptions about the proper balance of obligations and other changeable attitudes.

CHANGING CONTRACTUAL TERMS DURING EMPLOYMENT

The experience of most employees and employers will be that the employment relationship is subject to development and change. There is little doubt that the state of the law is that courts will mostly find agreement to initial

---

[63] [1978] I.C.R. 15.
[64] [1985] I.R.L.R. 89.
[65] As in *Woods* v. *W.M. Car Services Ltd.* [1983] I.R.L.R. 413.

terms but will raise barriers, and in particular, will insist on evidence of agreement, to variation. This rigidity is admitted by Browne-Wilkinson J. in *Jones*
v. *Associated Tunnelling Co. Ltd.*[66] when he says that an initial statement is
often compelling evidence but that later statements only furnish evidence of
agreed variation. In *Horrigan* v. *Lewisham London Borough Council*[67] the
employee began work as a driver in 1966 with a clear obligation to work a 40-
hour week. There was no express provision for overtime. The employee frequently had to work up to one-and-a-half hours overtime to complete his
round and, as early as 1968, the employer agreed with trade unions that
drivers who regularly worked overtime would be paid "conditional overtime." In 1976 the employee decided he would no longer work overtime and
he was eventually dismissed for this refusal. The EAT declined, on the available evidence, to imply an initial term, dictated by supposed business efficacy, requiring the working of overtime. It clearly assumed that the only
other source of such an obligation must stem from a variation of the contract
and it severely limited the prospects of implied variation, saying[68]:

> "It is fairly difficult, in the ordinary way, to imply a variation of contract, and it is
> very necessary, if one is so to do, to have very solid facts which demonstrate that it
> was necessary to give business efficacy to the contract, that the contract should
> come to contain a new term implied by way of variation."

This remark and the whole tenor of the judgment reveals reluctance, having ascertained the content of the initial contract, to recognise a change of
obligation. The question of an agreed variation should raise no similar reluctance. The common law was very willing to imply agreement to change from
comparatively short periods of continued working under unilaterally introduced variation. The common law never seems to have been forced, in a
reported case, to deal with a very short period of such apparent acquiescence.
When the practice developed, in line with increasing frequency of such situations, of making an alternative offer to an employee whose existing contract
was only terminated because his job had ceased to exist the NIRC declined to
infer variation of obligation from short periods in the new job.[69] Careful
reference to the shortness of the period of work under the new terms in such
cases indicates, however, that the idea that practice can imply acceptance and
that acceptance is enough to establish a variation of the contract of employment was, then, generally accepted.

This is an interesting approach to the requirements of variation of contract
which, in doctrinal terms, is much more strict. Most significantly, the normal
principle is that variation must be supported by fresh consideration.[70] It
seems that the law of employment never sought to impose such unrealistic
requirements upon a constantly changing situation, but that as soon as any
number of cases was reported on the issue they revealed a judicial realisation
that, if such severe restrictions were inappropriate, care must nonetheless be
taken to protect the party not initiating the proposal for change from over-

---

[66] [1981] I.R.L.R. 477.
[67] [1978] I.C.R. 15.
[68] At p. 19.
[69] *Shields Furniture Ltd.* v. *Goff* [1973] I.C.R. 187; *Ubsdell* v. *Paterson* [1973] I.C.R. 86.
[70] *Stilk* v. *Myrick* (1809) 2 Camp 317.

ready assumptions that the change had been accepted. The question the court must face is the need to strike a balance between the rigidity appropriate to a commercial contract and that to be applied to a contract which, to a considerable extent, is no more than a recasting in lawyer's terms of the practices and expectations of the parties to employment. The courts are also aware that the initiative for change will normally come from the employer, who must accept and implement the change even if it is originally proposed by a trade union in the course of collective bargaining. The employer's unilateral proposal is backed by his economic strength against the desire, if not the need, of the employee to continue in that employment. If the employee clearly objects to the change, as in *Marriott* v. *Oxford and District Co-operative Society Ltd.*[71] and *Hawker Siddeley Power Engineering Ltd.* v. *Rump*[72] there has been seen to be no difficulty in protecting his contractual interests because ordinary contractual principles allow him to stand on his existing rights and obligations. Indeed it may seem to the courts that he is over-protected in such a situation so that, in face of the employee's contractual right to resist change the employer may be regarded as reasonably entitled to terminate employment without liability to pay compensation.[73] But where the employee appears acquiescent the courts have revealed an awareness of the fact that that appearance may be dictated by economic necessity and conceal an underlying lack of realisation of the consequences of the change. In such circumstances the question must be how to produce a contractual approach which does not contradict the practical flexibility of the employment relationship, whilst not permitting the practical reality of employer initiative to deprive the employee of reasonable protection. Whilst, on the one hand, protecting an employee against too ready an assumption of acceptance courts are, on the other, willing to declare reasonable termination of the contracts of those who unduly resist change.[74] Statutory review of the fairness of dismissal allows such a question to be asked. But if the issue must be confined to the contents of the contract (as in a consideration, for instance, of the employee's entitlement to leave the employment and claim a constructive dismissal) the courts have to resort to other means of regulating freedom of action. In these cases they have used implied consent as the regulator, tending to withhold such implication where they consider the employee would be unreasonably stampeded into an unheeding acceptance. The clearest example of this approach is to be found in *Jones* v. *Associated Tunnelling Co Ltd.*[75] The employee commenced work in 1964 for a firm of specialist tunnelling contractors. He worked first at a colliery, called Chatterley Whitfield, which was mentioned in the statement of terms and conditions of employment. Five years later he moved to another colliery about 12 miles from his home. In 1973 he was issued with a fresh statement of terms and conditions stating his place of work as that colliery "or such place or places in the United Kingdom the employers may decide from time to time." A further statement in 1976 confirmed the requirement of mobility without indicating that it covered the whole of the United Kingdom.

---

[71] [1970] I.C.R. 186.
[72] [1982] I.R.L.R. 425.
[73] *Woods* v. *W.M. Car Services Ltd.* [1982] I.R.L.R. 413; *Brandon and Gould* v. *Murphy Bros.* [1983] I.R.L.R. 54.
[74] *e.g. R.S. Components Ltd.* v. *Irwin* [1973] I.C.R. 535.
[75] [1981] I.R.L.R. 477.

In 1980 the employee was required to move to a third colliery very close to the second and equally accessible to his home, but he refused to move, found other employment with the NCB and claimed redundancy compensation. The EAT noted that any contract of employment must contain a provision as to the place of work so that, if none is specified, one must be implied. It followed that, although the court should imply the provision the parties acting reasonably would probably have agreed, it was not essential to the power of the court that evidence should be available of what they would have agreed. The EAT considered it obvious that some mobility was intended but that the evidence suggested that the employee would not have agreed to move anywhere in the United Kingdom and would have insisted on being within daily reach of his home. That was enough to settle the issue in the instant case since the employee had not been required to move beyond that range. Browne-Wilkinson J. added some remarks, *obiter*, about the rationality of the alleged variation. In his view it would be wrong to imply assent to a variation from mere failure to object. The most that could be said of continuation of work in face of unilateral notice of change was that it might imply agreement or lead to an estoppel, but neither alternative should be adopted without caution. He went on, by way of example, to draw a distinction between variations having immediate practical effect and those, like that in the instant case, which had no immediate practical effect. In his view it would be unrealistic to suppose that an employee, even if he read and understood the notice of proposed change, would risk a confrontation in the second type of situation. The imponderable in this decision is the degree of caution which the courts will apply to the implication of consent and, in particular, whether that degree is the same for both parties. Browne-Wilkinson J. quite clearly infers that it is not. It is, of course, much less frequently that the issue of employer consent will arise but, although the employer is normally the initiator of change, it may not always be clear what detail he intended to include. In *Simmonds* v. *Dowty Seals Ltd.*[76] there was no dispute that when the employee was asked to transfer to working nights and agreed his original contract had been changed. The issue was whether it had changed so that he became a permanent night worker or could be switched between the two shifts. The EAT was prepared to assume the agreement of two members of management as to permanency, which was contrary to company policy and would not have been approved by the personnel department. It is true that the need was for a permanent night-shift worker but that situation would have been achieved even if the company had acquired a discretion as to moving the employee back to day-shift work. In other words, when management is looking for someone who will work permanently on a shift it is not necessarily to be implied that it has acquired a right so to do. Perhaps *Simmonds* would have been better regarded as a case of estoppel, but it does suggest that if the employee is able to break through barriers of proof, which are more difficult for him than for management to overcome, management has little ground on which to argue absence of real agreement on its behalf.

The decline in the significance of a purely contractual answer points a way to avoidance of the protective effect of judicial reluctance to permit variation of contract. There is little practical point in informing an employee that he is

---

[76] [1978] I.R.L.R. 211.

entitled to stand upon his contractual right if it is not unfair to dismiss him for doing so.[77] In *Horrigan* v. *Lewisham London Borough Council*[78] the employee's contractual right to refuse overtime was accepted. So also in *Woods* v. *W.M. Car Services Ltd.*[79] her contractual right to adhere strictly to her specified job and pay rate. Both employees were held to have been fairly dismissed as were those who refused to work a Bank Holiday in *Brandon and Gould* v. *Murphy Bros.*[80] To go one stage further, the obligation to accept a reasonable degree of change might easily be implied into the initial contract. It is not clear whether the court in *Cresswell* v. *Board of Inland Revenue*[81] did intend to impose such a general term or saw the obligation mainly as an incident of the absence of contractual limitation on the method by which a job should be done. It is, however, a short step to hold that trust and confidence may be lost (or fidelity fail to be shown) in an employee who uncompromisingly stands on his contractual rights.

It is also apparent that consent to variation may be incorporated in the contract from its inception. In *Jones* v. *Lee and Guilding*[82] the employer had reserved the right to introduce new terms into the contract although he did not do so. In *Cadoux* v. *The Central Regional Council*[83] the right of unilateral change was held to have been agreed from the fact that certain terms of the contract were said to be contained in Local Authority Rules which the employing Authority had the power to change. Lord Denning in *Secretary of State for Employment* v. *ASLEF*[84] had foreseen that some working rules would amount to nothing more than formalised instructions which the employee was under a duty to obey but which the employer was free to vary from time to time. The decision in *Cadoux* indicates no such distinction in principle between the day-to-day conduct of the job and more fundamental aspects usually provided for in matters of contractual obligation.

Variation of previously incorporated collective agreements raises the question of consent in a more complicated form. The contract approach leads the courts to conclude, virtually without argument, that a collective term, incorporated without any real enquiry as to individual consent, and collectively variable cannot unilaterally be altered or rescinded.[85] In *Burroughs Machines Ltd.* v. *Timmoney*[86] this acceptance that one party could continue to rely on the right he had derived from the agreement which had ceased to be applicable was, quite logically, applied to permit the other party to claim his correlative advantage. The objection which might have been raised that, by leaving the bargaining group, the employer had impliedly rescinded all its collective agreements, was avoided by regarding the contractual right retained by the employee as conditional upon acceptance of the corresponding rights con-

---

[77] The Industrial Tribunal confused the two questions in *Cawley* v. *South Wales Electricity Board* [1985] I.R.L.R. 258.
[78] [1978] I.C.R. 15.
[79] [1982] I.C.R. 693.
[80] [1983] I.R.L.R. 54.
[81] [1984] I.R.L.R. 190.
[82] [1980] I.C.R. 310.
[83] [1986] I.R.L.R. 131.
[84] [1972] I.C.R. 19.
[85] See *Gibbons* v. *Associated British Ports* [1985] I.R.L.R. 376 referring to *Morris* v. *C. H. Bailey Ltd.* [1969] 2 Lloyd's Rep. 215.
[86] [1977] I.R.L.R. 404.

ferred on the employer by the package deal collective agreement. This device will not be available unless such a package deal exists, and it will not solve the problem of an amendment of which one party only takes the benefit.

The courts have shown no readiness to adopt the view that an employee may be said to have agreed to the variation of his contract by subsequent, collectively agreed, change when the statutory statement of terms and conditions refers to a particular aspect being covered by "collective agreements as amended from time to time." This type of phrase is often included so as to permit the statement to be deemed to refer to whatever agreement is current, without the separate written notice of amendment which would otherwise be required by statute.[87] The practical objection to allowing it to operate as an agreement to accept collective change is that this would permit the acquired right to be completely abrogated by unilateral cancellation of the collective agreement. This effect would not occur, were it not for the peculiarly British attitude to the contractual enforceability of collective agreements. In *Robertson* v. *British Gas Corporation*[88] the Court of Appeal rejected any such conclusion by using the well-established proposition that the statutory statement was no more than evidence of the contract, asserting that another source of such evidence indicated an irrevocable right to an incentive bonus the details of which might be varied, but only by collective agreement. No such alternative source of evidence existed in *Gibbons* v. *Associated British Ports*.[89] The statutory statement referred to conditions of service as dependent on "national or local agreements for the time being in force." Tudor Price J., in the Queens Bench Division, indicated that, even so, variation would only be effective if the employee's consent could be implied. He refused to imply consent to a variation producing a total absence of provision for bonus payments which had previously been a contractual entitlement but did not indicate how he would view the argument that the mere words of the statutory statement implied consent to change, as distinct from abrogation. It appears from subsequent discussion with counsel, however, that the learned judge did accept what counsel referred to as the "established procedure" of variation by renegotiation of the collective agreement; as the learned judge added, "on behalf of the plaintiff." This is flimsy authority for the suggestion that the courts will feel able to assume the individual's agreement to a collectively agreed variation but not to rescission arising from the recognised freedom of one collective party to withdraw from the agreement. A distinction between variation of the contract of employment by negotiated change and variation by unilateral withdrawal is obvious in contractual terms but not in terms of the understandings common to industrial relations.

Finally, we must consider whether the courts, if they have power to decide the content of a contract by reference to rules of law rather than the intention of the parties,[90] have not also the power to vary the contract without enquiry as to the consent of the parties. It must be pointed out that in many instances of terms introduced as rules of law this enquiry will never be necessary for the term itself has no fixed content. The duty to maintain trust and confidence,

---

[87] E.P.C.A. 1978, s.4(3).
[88] [1983] I.C.R. 351.
[89] [1985] I.R.L.R. 376.
[90] *Mears* v. *Safecar Securities Ltd.* [1982] I.R.L.R. 183.

for example, is broken by any action of one party which is regarded by the courts as intolerable to the other.[91] Our general faith that we are progressing might cause us to reject the idea that what is now regarded as intolerable will become tolerable but the reverse proposition is likely to be agreed. Employers may find, therefore, that what they are free to do today is a breach of contract tomorrow. This has always been so in theory. The content of the duty of fidelity is clearly capable of change and the decision in *Cadoux* v. *Central Regional Council*[92] only relegated local authority rules to the same position as the employer's rule book, envisaged as unilaterally changeable in *Secretary of State for Employment* v. *ASLEF*.[93]

The process of implication in *Mears'* case, however, goes further than this. The sickness provisions which a court would be likely to imply on the basis of such factors as general industrial practice will plainly alter from time to time. In *Mears* the court did not ask what they were 20 years ago in respect of an employee who might have made a contract at that time but seems to have assumed that such an employee would currently be entitled to terms dictated by existing practice. How has the variation occurred? Rules of law do not require consent so change operating on the product of a rule of law is also not dependent on consent. Are we, therefore, in a position where contractually introduced terms are not subject to a process of development but terms introduced by rule of law are?

SUMMARY—THE CONSEQUENCES OF FOUNDING EMPLOYMENT ON CONTRACT

We have now seen how the terms of the contract of employment are assembled by the parties, by collective negotiation and by judicial interpretation and implication. The end result has been presented as a lawyer's device by which those expectations of the parties to the employment relationship which the courts recognise as of legal significance become legal rights and obligations. Whether Lord Wedderburn spoke with approval when he said that the contract of employment is the fundamental institution to which the lawyer is forced to return again and again,[94] he was stating an undoubted fact. Labour law has been built around this concept of an individual contract. Sociologists and economists are apt to suppose that they disclose a fundamental defect in the concept when they point out the inequality of the parties.[95] Inequality of bargaining power not infrequently characterises the relationship of parties to other contracts. Sometimes such inequality prompts protective legislation or judicial caution. Until the past 25 years it did not do so markedly in the field of labour law—the inequality being assumed to have been set off extra-legally by collective forces. This inequality may lead to the conclusion that the terms on which the parties "agree" are unfair but that is not the fault of contract as a concept. Any other legal device for expressing the facts of the employment relationship, short of statutory provision, would incorporate the same accepted inequalities in that relationship. What we have to

---

[91] *e.g. Bliss* v. *South East Thames RHA* [1985] I.R.L.R. 308.
[92] [1986] I.R.L.R. 131.
[93] [1972] I.C.R. 19.
[94] *The Worker and the Law* (Penguin 2nd ed. 1971) at p. 51.
[95] *e.g.* Alan Fox: *Beyond Contract: Work Power and Trust Relations* (1974).

consider is whether contract, as an explanation, has had beneficial or damaging effects which might not have occurred had some other concept for binding together the elements of the relationship been selected.

It is difficult for the law student initially to understand the question. One is surrounded with products of the view of employment as an individual contractual relationship to such an extent that it is not readily apparent that this view produces, as well as explains, consequences. Legislation has unquestioningly accepted the contractual basis and the courts, not surprisingly, have not questioned, but, rather, extended this acceptance. The major statutory rights to claim compensation for redundancy and to complain of unfair dismissal have been attached to this contract. Both depend on an act of "dismissal" which, despite an air of industrial technicality, has no legal meaning beyond termination of the contract, brought about by the employer's initiative. The aspect of the dismissal by which it comprehends a situation in which the employee leaves of his own volition in response to an act of the employer "entitling" him to do so, produced the classic example of judicial acceptance of contract.[96] The statutory definition of redundancy has been tied by the courts to the contractual job definition, whether or not the legislature had actually stated such an intention.[97] Individual statutory rights are often granted by insertion as incorporated terms of the contract,[98] and even where they are expressed as independent rights they tend to be accompanied by provisions enabling them to fit into a pattern of contractual rights.[99] Even in the field of legal regulation of collective industrial action the entire structure depends on the basic illegality of interference with, or breach of, the individual contract of employment. Statute again accepts the concept in this field.[1] Arguments about the value of the definition of employment in the contract of employment[2] are not part of this discussion, as is often supposed. Selection of characteristics which distinguish one type of relationship from another would be equally difficult were the selection made in contract or some other format. Only decisions such as *Davies* v. *Presbyterian Church of Wales*[3] reveal the restrictive effect of the search for a contract.

There are, however, areas where the influence of contract has been avoided. Even the common law, which is prepared to conclude that the employee breaks his contract in going on strike, permits the employer to cease to honour his obligation to pay wages without having accepted the employment breach as a terminating event. Once the door of contract has been opened, a claim for unfair dismissal proceeds to deal with reasonable responses of an employer in a non-contractual manner,[4] and, on more detailed aspects, the absence of contractually required notice to terminate is irrelevant to the question of fairness.[5]

---

[96] *Western Excavating (EEC) Ltd.* v. *Sharp* [1978] I.C.R. 21.
[97] *Nelson* v. *BBC (No. 2)* [1979] I.R.L.R. 346. *Pace* Harvey.
[98] *e.g.* Equal Pay Act 1970.
[99] *e.g.* Maternity pay—E.P.C.A. 1978, s.35(3)(4); Guarantee payments—E.P.C.A. 1978, s.16(1)(2); and paid time off—E.P.C.A. 1978, s.27(5)(6).
[1] *e.g.* E.A. 1980, s.17(2).
[2] pp. 6–14, *supra*.
[3] [1986] 1 All E.R. 785.
[4] *e.g.* *Woods* v. *W.M. Cars Ltd.* [1982] I.R.L.R. 413; *Brandon and Gould* v. *Murphy Bros.* [1983] I.R.L.R. 54.
[5] *Treganowan* v. *Robert Knee Ltd.* [1975] I.C.R. 448.

In other areas the myth of a contract has been maintained by courts which have included in it concepts wholly alien to the English law of contract. The categoric statement of the court in *Mears* v. *Safecar Securities Ltd.*,[6] that it was not necessary to consider what the parties intended but that it was permissible to insert terms as rules of law, may have overwhelming advantages for the process of adaptation of the contract of employment to the reality of industrial organisation. It may owe a great deal to Continental views of contract[7] which appear to be attractive for exactly this reason. But the result is achieved despite, not because of, the English law of contract. It will be necessary, in future, to sustain the aberration if it is not to lead to chaos. The rule of law which springs from the gradual establishment of a practice is capable of changing and it will, for instance, be necessary to explain how, over a period of years, without any noticeable point when variation was accepted by them, workers who commenced employment with one contractual term have acquired a changed term with which new workers are entering employment. Thus, although the contract of employment may be applauded for its flexibility, this flexibility is normally only achieved by departing from contractual rules.

At least two significant effects solely attributable to the application of contract in the law of employment can be isolated. The first is a negative one. We have said that inequality is not the fault of contract but of the facts of the employment situation. But contract is to blame for having no mechanism to correct the effects of such imbalance save where it occurs to such a degree as to be contrary to public policy (*e.g.* as a result of duress or unreasonable restraint of trade). Contractual theory, by assuming equality, actually suppresses any direct enquiry as to the existence of imbalance. The fact is that the employer proposes virtually all the express provisions of the contract which do not derive from collective agreement and does so mostly at a time when the worker's only bargaining strength is his freedom not to take the job. Only because of the gaps left by these proposals have the courts been able to insert balancing factors and this, as we have seen, they do by imposition of rules of law based on what they consider reasonable. The implied duty to maintain trust and confidence[8] is nothing more than a dressing up in contractual language of a requirement of law derived from the essentials of a relationship. It has to do with what the courts consider reasonably necessary to maintain that relationship. If individual freedom inherent in the idea of contract were invoked expressly to displace it the courts could take shelter only in the conclusion that the contract had not produced an employment relationship.

If contractual principles were fully applied, therefore, they would tend to ensure the domination of the employer, checked only by the conclusion that once that dominant position had been initially enshrined in the contract change could be resisted. The courts avoid the first of these concepts by letting in collective agreement on the basis of a pure presumption of acceptance, and by making their own assumptions on the basis of what is reasonable in whatever circumstances, including development of policy, are available for

---

[6] [1982] I.R.L.R. 183.
[7] See: Kahn-Freund (1967) 30 M.L.R. 635.
[8] *e.g. Palmanor* v. *Cedron* [1978] I.C.R. 1008; *Robinson* v. *Crompton Parkinson Ltd.* [1978] I.C.R. 401.

them to consider. It is not contract which has proved flexible but the courts' readiness to depart from contractual theory. It is submitted that the view of the Court of Appeal in *Mears* v. *Safecar Securities Ltd.*[9] is entirely justified. The, so-called, contract of employment has at least as much to do with collective influence and the imposition of rules of law as it has with a search for the individual agreement of the parties. By this means it is possible to introduce factors balancing the economic dominance of the employer, although it is only recently that the courts as producers of rules of law have taken a significant part in this process or admitted it to exist.

The second effect, however, tends to act in opposition to this non-contractual practice. Whilst the contract continues to be asserted as the basis of the employment relationship it is likely to prove impossible for lawyers to overcome its ultimate individuality by overriding the right of either employer or employee to veto the inclusion of any term. Development of a law of expectations apart, even those matters which, according to *Mears*, may be incorporated as rules of law must give way to clear individual provision to the contrary. There is scarcely a need to demonstrate the operation of so obvious an effect of the English law approach to contract. Indeed, in an attempt to provide greater protection for the employee against unilateral change the reality of the power of veto has recently been re-emphasised[10] to reverse the effect of an apparent assumption that consent might be implied from inaction. The decision in *Horrigan* v. *Lewisham Borough Council*[11] demonstrates that the individual veto is as effective against change by developing practice as it is against a specific act and the veto, if maintained, must either stop introduction of the provision or result in the termination of the relationship.[12] The only limitation on the individual veto is that, if sustained at the initiation of the contract, it may operate to exclude some essential characteristic of employment so that if a contract emerges it must be one other than of service.

This produces an important contradiction in judicial approach. Whereas it has been suggested that the courts have so plainly accepted the fact of collective regulation as virtually to presume the incorporation of collective agreements, evidence of individual objection must rebut that presumption. However contrary it would be to accepted standards of bargaining power the individual employee may ordinarily reject a collectively agreed variation of his exsting rights. In practice this is unlikely to occur frequently. Where it does the dispute will be settled by industrial relations machinery or will emerge in the courts by way of a claim for unfair dismissal. In such circumstances the matter can be dealt with, as it was in *Brandon and Gould* v. *Murphy Bros.*[13] solely by reference to the issue of the reasonableness of the employer's response to the situation. Of much greater significance is the power of the employer to go his individual way. The courts equally will not be presented with many examples of the effect of this since the rejected implications and incorporations will only have the effect of inducing the employee not to accept the employment. The employee is not the recipient, but the

---

[9] [1982] I.R.L.R. 183.
[10] *Jones* v. *Associated Tunnelling Co. Ltd.* [1981] I.R.L.R. 477.
[11] [1978] I.C.R. 15.
[12] *Burdett-Coutts* v. *Hertfordshire County Council* [1984] I.R.L.R. 91.
[13] [1983] I.R.L.R. 54; see also *Woods* v. *W.M. Car Services* [1982] I.R.L.R. 413.

initiator, of variation and these disputes will, again, be fought out in the arena of unfair dismissal. But the actual effect is far-reaching, for the employer is thereby entitled to opt out of the collective regulation of the relationship which, otherwise, the courts are so ready to accept. In times of economic decline this step may prove attractive, employers' organisations may be too weak to control their members desirous of taking such a step and the whole structure of collective regulation may be endangered. Yet legislation sustaining this structure by a system of compulsory extension will appear to fly in the face of contractual freedom.

The employment relationship has, therefore, moved near the point envisaged by the present writer in 1966[14] where the essential conflict between a relationship dominated by collective regulation and rule of law and a contract ultimately dictated by agreement of the parties has to be resolved. Sooner or later it will prove absurd readily to presume individual acceptance of collective variation but equally readily to concede the power of individual veto to destroy this presumed collective regulation.

Reference was made earlier in this chapter to the contract of employment as a device by which the expectations of the parties are recognised as giving rise to legal rights and obligations. The important, but imprecise, qualification was added that only those expectations which the courts are prepared to recognise as giving rise to legal obligation are so "contractualised." We have also seen that other expectations which would be capable of contractualisation may be excluded, most often because more formally evidenced provision would conflict with such enforcement. So, for instance, the normal expectation of an employee would be, no doubt, that he could be required to work at the location where he had always worked, in the job he had always done. The employer might, or might not, have a wider vision but the law of contract, looking at the beginning of the relationship, would insist on finding that width evidenced then. As we have seen the courts are prepared to contractualise expectations which would be reasonable if the parties had applied their minds to the matter. The employee who has always worked in one place might not complain if told that his expectations should extend beyond that place, but within reason.[15] But all such expectations are displaced by clear provision to the contrary[16] and the only scope for "expectation" in such a situation is by judicial interpretation.[17] As we have also seen the contractualisation of expectations developed after the commencement of the relationship is even more difficult.[18]

Judicial handling of the contract of employment produces, therefore, considerable inconsistency in relation to "expectation" for a variety of reasons, most of which are the same as those which explain the strains to which the concept of contract is subjected in handling the employment relationship. It may disappoint expectations by its insistence on a formation stage, and

---

[14] Rideout: "The Contract of Employment" (1966) 19 CLP 11.

[15] e.g. Jones v. Associated Tunnelling Ltd. [1981] I.R.L.R. 477; and O'Brien v. Associated Fire Alarms Ltd. [1968] 1 W.L.R. 1916 does not imply narrow confines to the job area.

[16] U.K. Atomic Energy Authority v. Claydon [1973] I.C.R. 128.

[17] Haden v. Cowan [1982] I.R.L.R. 314; Pederson v. London Borough of Camden [1981] I.R.L.R. 173.

[18] Horrigan v. London Borough of Lewisham [1985] I.C.R. 15.

restricted change thereafter,[19] or by declarations of reasonableness founded more on policy than on enquiry into what either party really supposed the position to be.[20] On the other hand, it may be able to detect a common expectation and incorporate it,[21] yet reject the development of one party, now disabused by the other who knows of that expectation simply by the fortuitous appearance of some more formal, contrary, source.[22] It is not surprising that the effect on expectations is unpredictable because it is not the purpose of the law of contract to render such expectations enforceable. It may do so most frequently by implication based on reasonableness, but such processes are subordinate to clear evidence of what existed in practice at the outset.

Much expectation is not necessary to the contract on agreement and, because it develops after the contract has been made, will find no place accorded to it by the courts. It is necessary to know whether an employee can be required to work nights or days[23] but it is not necessary for the courts to render into terms of obligation most of the issues as to how a job should be done. Method, therefore, however much it may have given rise to expectation is simply denied contractual effect.[24]

There has, however, recently appeared, simultaneously in a number of areas of the common law, an apparent desire to confer enforceability on expectations. The principal decision is that in *R.* v. *Foreign Secretary ex p. CSSTU*[25] in which the House of Lords was prepared, in principle, to issue public law remedies against a decision contrary to the expectations of public sector employees; those expectations affecting both substantive and procedural matters. Employees who had previously been free to join a trade union were informed that they would, in future, lose that freedom. We have seen enough to realise that the answer to whether they had an implied right to join a union would be difficult to predict. Certainly, such a right would not be determined on the basis of expectation. It would depend on such questions as whether it was necessary to have more than a freedom[26] and what, in the light of that, it was reasonable to infer as the intentions of the parties. But the House of Lords had no difficulty in accepting that the employees had an expectation and, moreover, an expectation that even if they only possessed freedom that freedom would not be withdrawn without consultation. We shall see in a moment how important this procedural aspect of expectation may be in the development of the law of expectations in employment. It is, of course, possible to argue that this phenomenon is confined to public law because such expectations can only be enforced by public law remedies. If so its development would be confined to only some of those employed by government and its agencies. There is no doubt that such public employees may derive advantages over other employees because of their exceptional access to such

---

[19] *Horrigan* v. *Lewisham LBC, supra.*
[20] *Cresswell* v. *Board of Inland Revenue* [1984] I.R.L.R. 190.
[21] *O'Brien* v. *Associated Fire Alarms Ltd.* [1968] I.W.L.R. 1916; *Mears* v. *Safecar Securities* [1982] I.R.L.R. 183.
[22] *Express Lift Co.* v. *Bowles* [1977] I.R.L.R. 99.
[23] *Simmonds* v. *Dowty Seals Ltd.* [1978] I.R.L.R. 211.
[24] *Cresswell* v. *Board of Inland Revenue* [1984] I.R.L.R. 190; *Secretary of State for Employment* v. *ASLEF* [1972] I.C.R. 19.
[25] [1985] I.R.L.R. 28.
[26] *Gallagher* v. *Post Office* [1970] 2 All E.R. 112.

remedies. Such remedies may have the effect of specifically enforcing the rights of a public employee whereas others, in the private sector, have no such effective method of enforcement.[27] It seems unlikely, however, that the development of a range of enforceable expectations could be confined to public employees and there are already indications that the thinking that has given rise to them does not derive from some source peculiar to public law. It is, in truth, a form of estoppel, but it is estoppel which can be used as a sword as well as a shield. The same development can be detected in the backstreets of labour law. Statute denies to employees past their "normal retirement age" access to industrial tribunals to claim unfair dismissal.[28] In *Department of Health and Social Security* v. *Coy, Jarnell and Hughes*[29] the House of Lords applied the decision in *Waite* v. *Government Communications Headquarters*.[30] Lord Fraser, in the latter case, had said that the words "normal retirement age," in the light of a social policy of securing fair treatment among employees of a particular group, refers to the usual age at which the majority of employees actually retire, rather than the contractual minimum age at which they could be retired. This, in his view, established an expectation among employees in that group. Prima facie this expectation would be fixed by the terms of the contract but if regularly departed from in favour of some other definite, as distinct from variable, age the effect of the contract would be displaced by the established expectation. Obviously, but significantly, the date for establishing a non-contractual expectation must be the time when it is acted upon—that is to say, in this case, the date of retirement. It cannot, like the terms of the contract, be established at the outset of the relationship and no other firm date is available. This introduction of effective expectation in the law of employment is seen to have occurred because of statutory use of a word such as "normal," rather than a word such as "entitled" which has contractual connotations. If these decisions stood alone, therefore, they would not properly be presented as inferring any new level of enforceable expectations. What is here suggested is that, possibly, the same expectations could be enforced by public law remedies under the *CSSTU* case as acquire substantive effect by so simple a statutory device as reference to practice rather than contract. Is it too much to suppose that the two streams of thought have the same source in a policy of protection of expectations? Such expectations must inevitably be capable of overriding contractual positions.

The decision in *DHSS* v. *Coy* illustrates other curious characteristics, the most notable of which is that the expectation can be unilaterally rescinded. The expectation arose from the act of one of the parties and it is open to that party to indicate that he has changed his mind; at which point, assuming that change to be within the knowledge of the other, the expectation must have changed. It is at this point that procedural expectations become important. If the operative date of expectation is that at which action is taken it would be open to the actor to replace an established expectation with a new one and then, almost immediately, properly to act on the new expectation. Procedural

---

[27] R. v. *Home Secretary ex p. Benwell* [1985] I.R.L.R. 6.
[28] E.P.C.A., s.64.
[29] [1985] I.R.L.R. 263.
[30] [1983] I.R.L.R. 341.

expectations, such as that of consultation, will inhibit such unilateral variation, the denial of which has been contract's principal contribution to employee protection in recent years. Bringing all those possibilities together it can be seen that the development of enforceable expectation would enable the employment relationship to be enforced at the point of development which it had reached at the time of the act in question. If the courts were to go along this path, therefore, means would have to be devised of protecting the established expectations more effectively than was envisaged in *DHSS* v. *Coy*.[31] Without such means Horrigan's[32] conduct in consistently working overtime would establish an effective expectation in his employer but Horrigan could replace that expectation at a moment's notice by another, namely; that he will not so work. Expectations may well be set aside by unilateral destruction of their reliability. Probably they cannot immediately be replaced by other expectations. The most likely solution would be to fall back on the basic contractual right until the new expectation has established itself. In practice, the courts would not have to decide when this re-establishment occurred because the only question would be whether it had done so by the date of the action complained of.

Clearly the House of Lords in the *CSSTU* case envisaged a law of enforceable expectations. Equally clearly in *Waite* v. *GCHQ* it only went so far as to give effect to an expectation because it saw statute as intending that it should. But if both conclusions have been reached, and it is feasible to envisage the formulation of rules to govern the definition and enforcement of such expectations, why should the development of them in the employment relationship and their enforcement or effectiveness, so clearly acknowledged in both public and private law, not lead to a general recognition that they can exist to give rise to enforceable rights, not only supplementary to, but overriding contractual positions?

---

[31] *Supra.*
[32] *Horrigan* v. *Lewisham Borough Council* [1987] I.C.R. 15.

Chapter III

THE TERMS OF EMPLOYMENT

Want of certainty

There was a time when textbooks on the law of employment, usually under such a heading as "rights and duties of master and servant," set out a list of standard terms and conditions of employment which, in the absence of express provision to the contrary, would be implied into virtually every contract of employment. The implication was that any other term would have to be established by some special feature of the contract in question. So, for instance, an obligation on the employer to behave with courtesy was not regarded as of general implication[1] but might be implied in particular circumstances.[2] It would still be possible to set out a list of such generally recognised terms as they stood at any given moment, but few would care now to do so.

It is not entirely true that such generalised provisions have become so much less precise as to cease to mean anything now. That was always the case. The duty to obey lawful orders was clear enough in so far as it imposed a reverse duty on the employer not to give unlawful orders. In practice, that aspect which limited the employee's duty of obedience to orders within the scope of his contract was much more significant. That aspect, however, meant nothing until one knew what obligations the contract involved. So the question asked by Roskill L.J. in *Secretary of State for Employment* v. *ASLEF*[3] as to the duties of a signalman whose shift had ended without a relief appearing, found no answer provided by general implied obligations. It all depended what obligations three potentially frustrated commuters were prepared to think he had accepted. In this instance those three inferred that he was there to smooth away the problems caused by a failure in his superiors to provide another employee to continue his duties. Far more directly clear is the lack of meaning in the duty usually stated as one of "fidelity." It was never clear how far it went—whether, for instance, it could extend to prevent competition. Even where it indisputably applied, as to the use of information during employment it would be necessary to discover who "owned" the information.

Nevertheless, the newer generalised duties are noticeably less meaningful. The development of a duty upon both parties to maintain trust and confidence is, as every student at a loss for authority in the midst of an examination answer has discovered, apparently capable of justifying the implication of almost any obligation, whether or not previously recognised, from provision of safety equipment to courteous treatment and support. Such a compendious heading only acquires a meaning from study of the way in which the courts

---

[1] *Veness* v. *Dyson Bell and Co. Ltd.*, *The Times*, May 25, 1965.
[2] *Donovan* v. *Invicta Airways* [1969] 2 Lloyds Rep. 413.
[3] [1972] I.C.R. 19.

have used it. This width, and indeed the very fact that such a vehicle for implication emerged, is what deters the present day labour lawyer from seeking to
set out a list of such terms. The moment one broke down such a generalisation into its established components the question would be asked why the list
of contents should be regarded as so confined. Perhaps the change in attitude
can be expressed more scientifically, at the risk of suggesting greater clarity
than existed then or now. The former terms depended on implication based
on a principle of necessity which was the essential feature of business efficacy.
Recognition of terms as matters of law derived from reasonableness opens up
the prospect of unlimited discretion to suit the facts of the particular case and
even to suit the need to find a repudiatory breach to create a constructive
dismissal.

Is the despairing student, ever searching for "rules," then to be told the
quest is hopeless and that Brightman L.J. was right to say[4] " . . . a reported
case on the construction of one contract of employment is usually of no assistance in construing another contract of employment."? The question whether
the attitudes on implication and interpretation which we have just considered
give rise to any predictable results is easily answered by a negative reference
to policy. Of course these principles leave an enormous scope for policy. Incidentally it is tempting to say that in view of judicial imprecision it is scarcely
suprising that the courts do not require the parties to aspire to certainty in the
terms they formulate.

Inbuilt adaptability

Lord Wedderburn[5] describes the approach in *Woods* v. *W.M. Car Services
Ltd.*[6] as the most important judicial development of the 1980s and states that
it permits the employer "to legislate at the workplace to improve the methods
and profits of 'the business.' " Can we say, therefore, that the policy on implication and interpretation is one of extending management prerogatives?
There is certainly a lot of evidence to support such a conclusion which, if true,
suggests that nothing much has changed since the common law days when,
apart from a right to receive his wages, virtually all implied terms imposed
duties on the employee.

Particularly noteworthy is the attitude of the courts to job flexibility. Whilst
they are plainly moving to a position in which the employee is entitled to a
satisfactory amount of work of a proper quality, they are, equally noticeably,
imposing a steadily increasing obligation upon the employee to accept
changes in technology. From the straightforward interpretation in *Glitz* v.
Watford Electric Co.[7] through the more specialised facts of *Milthorn Toleman
Ltd.* v. *Ford*[8] on expectations of change during a period of notice, to the ultimate view in *Cresswell* v. *Board of Inland Revenue*[9] the attitude to attempts to
adhere to an employee's narrowly stated job description is clear. The result of
Cresswell could have been produced either by implication of a requirement of

---

[4] *J. Sainsbury Ltd.* v. *Savage* [1981] I.C.R. 1, at p. 6.
[5] *The Worker and the Law*, (3rd ed.) at p. 181.
[6] [1982] I.C.R. 693.
[7] [1979] I.R.L.R. 89.
[8] [1978] I.R.L.R. 306.
[9] [1984] I.C.R. 508.

flexibility or of a wide interpretation of the existing job definition. So far as policy is concerned it does not matter which of the two devices was used. The judgment of Walton J., who chose the latter approach, indicates the direction of his thoughts. The union was said to recognise that it could not stand indefinitely in the way of progress but to be worried about a decline in its membership. Fear of compulsory redundancy leading to unemployment was not mentioned although these were the precise terms of the undertaking the union had sought. Computerisation, eliminating the need for human arithmetic, was presented as likely to reduce mistakes—a proposition few of the public believe. The advantage in speed of the automatic despatch of impersonalised communications alone was emphasised. Opposition to computerisation is represented as akin to instinctive opposition to any new machinery. The implication is that, as time proved the Luddites wrong, so it will again. The learned judge appears to have believed the statement "there is extremely little scope for discretion, properly so-called, in the taxing system."[10] So he was, no doubt, in the right frame of mind to conclude that it could not, by any stretch of the imagination, be correct to say that employees had a vested right to preserve their working obligations completely unchanged as from the moment when they first began to work. The question, of course, was not that, but whether they had a choice of acceptance or rejection of change. "There can," he said, "really be no doubt as to the fact that an employee is expected to adapt himself to new methods and one might add techniques introduced in the course of his employment"[11] when and to the extent that management sees fit in the interests of the business. The employee genuinely unable to comply "can be left to be dealt with when the matter arises."[12] There is little doubt in view of this decision how that difficulty is intended to be resolved. Only the ease, after training, of using the new method, not its boredom or any other factor, is considered to impose any duty on the employer. He must offer training but is not subjected to any other obligation to assist adaptation. All this may be, not only justifiable, but a necessary approach to the problems of a businessman, forced to incorporate technological change in order to remain competitive. All that is here demonstrated is that that is the view of the court and the court is prepared to present a one-sided account of the situation to support its view.

SPECIFIC TERMS AND STATUTORY RIGHTS

Payment of wages

From one point of view wages are the most important aspect of the employment relationship, at least if one extends the word to all forms of remuneration constituting, in the lawyer's view, the contractual consideration for the worker's promise to be available for work. Theorists would, no doubt, challenge the assertion that "all labour law, as well as social security, can in simple terms be reduced to one issue: how is work to be remunerated."[13] It

---

[10] At p. 517.
[11] At p. 518.
[12] At p. 518.
[13] G. Lyon-Caen, *Le Solaire* (2nd ed., 1981) p. 1.

would be comforting to those concerned with industrial relations to think that Lord Denning M.R. was correct to say[14]:

> "A skilled man takes a pride in his work. He does not do it merely to earn money. He does it so as to keep himself busy and not idle. Tax his skill, and to improve it. To have the satisfaction which comes of a task well done."

But the law recognises no right to such satisfaction[15] and, outside socialist industrial systems, does little, in the last resort, about its loss, save to compensate for loss of wages. So, it may be argued, the law only comes into the picture when things have gone wrong[16] and its obsession with monetary remedies which refer back to wages is no more than a reflection of its inability, or at least its refusal, to consider remedies which would assist job satisfaction. As everyone knows, however, the reality of industrial relations is of dispute about the nature and quantity of remuneration. The law, therefore, reflects the element on which the parties rely and it is significant that, though Kahn-Freund[17] saw wage fixing legislation as extending to the control of other terms and conditions, that wider concern has, in British industrial relations, been dwarfed by the obsession with wages.

It must be understood, of course, that by "wages" we refer, as does Article 119 of the Treaty of Rome in its use of the word "pay," to the whole return for work including "redundancy payments, unemployment benefits, family allowances and credit facilities, (and, one might add, insurance, medical care, pensions and even, in some circumstances, "expenses") even if parts of the return are immediately subtracted by the employer and paid to third parties on behalf of the employee."[18] A system of law which does not take account of the full range of such remuneration devices, as is the case with the United Kingdom formula for determination of statutory redundancy compensation,[19] is deficient as a means of realistic remedy for wage loss.

This variety of forms of return for work is matched by the range of methods of calculating what, in popular terms, would be regarded as the monetary wage. If payment to the employee of the value of his availability were the only factor one might expect a single system of fixed rates. It has, after all, been said (though the proposition is questionable)[20]:

> "It would not be a breach of contract by the employers to ask the clerical employees to do clerical work of any kind within those terms . . . If the employee is unwilling to do the increased amount of work for the wage which he is being paid, his right . . . is to . . . find another job."

Yet, as the judge who made this remark recognised, the worker is more likely to say " . . . this job is getting a good deal harder. I am producing a good deal more. You ought to agree to pay me an increased wage".[21] Pay-

---

[14] *Langston* v. *AUEW* [1974] I.C.R. 180 at p. 190.
[15] See Professor B. A. Hepple (1981) 10 I.L.J. 65.
[16] See, Kahn-Freund's *Labour and the Law* (3rd ed. by Davies and Freedland) at p. 29.
[17] *Ibid.*, at pp. 39–40.
[18] *Worringham* v. *Lloyds Bank Ltd.* [1981] I.C.R. 558 (European Court of Justice).
[19] *e.g. Lyford* v. *Turquand* [1966] I.T.R. 544.
[20] *Seaboard World Airlines Inc.* v. *TGWU* [1973] I.C.R. 458 at p. 459.
[21] At p. 460.

ment by results is widely recognised, not only by the worker as just, but by the employer as a necessary incentive. A contract based legal system will provide remedies based on whatever remuneration the parties have agreed. The parties consider a variety of alternatives to take account of the fact that some jobs offer satisfaction that cannot be recognised in the contract as remuneration but can be offset against what is. So, "white-collar" workers are much more likely to be found on fixed wages systems in which the remuneration may be stated as an annual sum (albeit, for convenience, actually paid in periodic instalments) invariable by relation to quantity or quality of actual work. It is either a fact of life or a depressing deficiency of the system that direct incentives to higher production are normally considered necessary for jobs involving primarily manual work. Bonus and other production related payments, however, possess a serious disadvantage in that they tend to produce fluctuating net payments. The fluctuations usually depend on the state of the market rather than the enthusiasm of the worker. Inevitably, this has a frustrating and depressing effect on the worker which is, of course, the reverse of the purpose of remuneration. "Measured day work" seeks to eliminate this effect by transferring detriment to a disciplinary provision if the shortfall is the fault of the worker, or to the employer if it is the fault of the market. By way of work study an acceptable standard of productivity is set and a rate of pay calculated in accordance therewith. Any shortfall which is the fault of the worker may lead to invocation of disciplinary sanctions but not to a reduction in wage. In practice, lacking total faith in the philosophy, many employers provide for withholding of a bonus element as one of the disciplinary sanctions and this, as Freedland says,[22] makes the scheme a type of payment by result. Measured day work also tends to lack objectivity because the operation of job evaluation studies is not objective. Different factors in the make-up of the job are rated and the weight given to each rating may well reflect the desired result so that the introduction of such a system may preserve existing differential rates of pay based on history, scarcity value, collective strength or other factors which, though analytical, have no direct relevance to the nature of the job.

If net pay is variable the instinct of the worker is to see himself as receiving an average. The courts, when they have to calculate compensation, are inclined to engage in the same process of simplification.[23]

It is most unlikely in manual employment situations that an employee will be in a position to bargain for an individual rate of pay. Normally he will be offered the "rate for the job." This may still depend on custom, as in *Sagar* v. *H. Ridehalgh and Sons Ltd.*,[24] particularly where pay is determined by piece rates. Much former customary practice has been absorbed into collective agreements. Most commonly these days it is local agreement which will fix hourly or weekly rates. National agreements may often have a direct effect on net pay, however, since not only will they fix holiday pay entitlements but also a basic rate on which overtime premiums may be based. Where neither trade custom nor collective agreement is operative the employer will usually propose the pay rate but, again, it will be based on his standard practice in rela-

---

[22] (1977) 29 C.L.P. 184–6.
[23] *Ogden* v. *Ardphalt Asphalt Ltd.* [1977] I.C.R. 604; *Weevsmay Ltd.* v. *Kings* [1977] I.C.R. 244.
[24] [1931] 1 Ch. 310.

tion to his other employees which, in turn, may be based on rates in the locality and/or industry, themselves derived from collective agreement.

For obvious reasons the "rate for the job" will tend to be applied without exception, although some individual circumstances may serve to produce a peculiar differential. It may, for instance, be desirable to attract a particular employee by some device which maintains his wage in a former employment or to maintain his existing pay rate, or differential, despite movement to a lower paid job or grade. Apart from such pressing individual situations the normal practice is to pay the rate for the job to all those engaged in it. This holds good despite the fact that that rate has been negotiated with a trade union to which not all the workers belong. In the United Kingdom the unofficial attitude of most union officials would be that they were not bargaining for non-members and that it was a matter for the employer whether he offered the same rate to non-unionists. This attitude depends on the assumption that if the employer did offer a different rate it would be lower than that fixed by negotiation. It also operates in the clear knowledge that a differential is unlikely in practice. In *National Coal Board* v. *Ridgway and Fairbrother*[25] it became clear that a differential based on union membership, or non-membership, would be likely to constitute "action short of dismissal".[26] It was certainly not the original purpose of this statutory provision that it should compel collectively agreed rates to be applied to the whole category of workers regardless of union membership but the undoubted effect is that a union would be unable to induce an employer to accept that agreed rates should not be available to non-members.

Despite this collective source the law treats pay, like any other term, as a matter of individual contract. Few problems are likely to arise from this whilst rates, or at least the overall beneficial effect of the package of remuneration, are seen to improve. In *Rigby* v. *Ferodo Ltd.*[27] the House of Lords held that a unilateral reduction of wages by the employer is ineffective to reduce the entitlement of an individual employee who objects.[28] Payment of the lesser amount proposed by the employer confers on the employee an action for debt for the unpaid difference. The employee is not obliged to mitigate his loss—indeed it is difficult to see how he reasonably could—and notice of the reduction will not, without more, be construed as notice to terminate. This decision derives from confirmation by the House of Lords of the "new" rule that repudiatory breach (which a unilateral wage reduction must always be) does not automatically terminate the contract. On the other hand, the courts have not yet resolved the ancilllary problems. The objecting worker may hang on until he is dismissed, or he may himself leave. In either situation, of dismissal or constructive dismissal, he may find that an industrial tribunal finds the employer's breach to be reasonable. It may even be thought intolerable that the employee should refuse to discuss (if that is what has happened) a disad-

---

[25] [1987] I.R.L.R. 80.

[26] Contrary to E.P.C.A. (1978) s.23(1).

[27] [1987] I.R.L.R. 516; see also *Burdett-Coutts* v. *Hertfordshire County Council* [1984] I.R.L.R. 91.

[28] It is likely that clear objection would be necessary. The amount of pay is usually obvious enough for continuation in employment without objection to be treated as implied acceptance; even within the limited confines acknowledged in *Jones* v. *Associated Tunnelling Co. Ltd.* [1981] I.R.L.R. 477.

vantageous re-arrangement of the method of calculating remuneration if such a change was a sensible economic decision on the part of the employer.[29] The scope which tribunals, dealing with claims for unfair dismissal, have been prepared to concede to business interest permits an employer who has reached a rational decision on economies to advance this as a defence to a claim for unfair dismissal as a reasonable ground for his attempt to change the consideration. It is, of course, otherwise, if the cause of the proposal is irrational or arbitrary.[30] Conversely, so far as the law is concerned, an employer is entitled to adhere to existing rates and refuse to negotiate even if there is a long history of annual, or other periodic, review.[31] Established practice is often a source of contractual terms but the courts vision of contract apparently does not extend to comprehension of an implied agreement to regular change notwithstanding that that is the normal assumption of those who are parties to the contract.

It is relatively easy for the legal concept of consideration for the contract of employment to absorb the situation created by the collective agreements in force at the inception of the relationship. As we have seen[32] in relation to variation of any contractual term the implication of consent by the employee (the employer normally being the proposer of change) to subsequent variation is less automatic. Variation by means of collective agreement which, so far as wages are concerned, is frequently a regular event will, once again, pose no problem where the change involves an improvement. The law is free to adopt almost any of the bases for incorporation of collective agreements to explain the effective creation of a new contractual package. The lawyer is bound to experience difficulty, however, when a collective source of wages is unilaterally revoked. In many countries this problem would not arise. If the collective agreement itself has binding effect it can only be varied or rescinded by agreement or effluction of time. In either situation the same arguments that originally incorporated it into the individual contract can be used to remove it. It is possible to argue that since, in the United Kingdom, the common expectation is that collective agreements may be unilaterally rescinded, it is accepted by the parties to the contract of employment that such rescision would destroy the pre-existing right derived from the new situation not governed by agreement. The courts have, however, applied a much simpler contractual argument that unilateral variation can have no effect on the contract. Whereas, therefore, it is commonly understood that collective agreements do not bind the parties, once they have been contractually individualised, no action of the parties to the collective agreement which cannot be assumed to have been accepted by the parties to the contract can remove that right. The effect of this is particularly noticeable in relation to pay. *Rigby* v. *Ferodo Ltd.*[33] prevents unilateral withdrawal from the pay obligation in the contract of employment; the decision in *Gibbons* v. *Associated British Ports*[34] applies

---

[29] *WM Car Services (Peterborough) Ltd.* v. *Woods* [1982] I.R.L.R. 413.
[30] *Pepper and Hope* v. *Daish* [1980] I.R.L.R. 13.
[31] *Leyland Vehicles Ltd.* v. *Ruston* [1981] I.C.R. 403; *Murco Petroleum Ltd.* v. *Forge* [1987] I.R.L.R. 50.
[32] *Supra* p. 57.
[33] [1987] I.R.L.R. 516.
[34] [1985] I.R.L.R. 376.

precisely the same principle despite the non-contractual source of the original obligation.

If the package of remuneration is consideration for the promise to be available for work it is difficult to understand how that consideration is to be apportioned between various aspects of that work.[35] Some authorities took the view that the Apportionment Act 1870 permitted apportionment of wages to the period of time actually worked.[36] Paul Matthews has persuasively argued, however, that the legislative reference to salary would have been understood to refer to remuneration for public office where the emoluments are payable to a successor in title.[37] It is, however, difficult to resist the temptation to argue that the words "other periodical payments in the nature of income" could easily be regarded as referable to pay fixed by reference to periods of time exceeding the day to day basis which the Act deems them to have. If this were so, a small beginning, but not much more, would have been made to break down the "all or nothing" rule hitherto normally applied to remuneration under the contract of employment.[38] On this argument wages were considered due in return for availability to perform every aspect of the service obligation. Failure of that availability as regards any aspect or part of the obligation entitled the employer to reject all performance and withhold all wages as in the case of strike action. Such a rule is, of course, subject to amendment by the express or implied terms of the contract. In *Browning* v. *Crumlin Valley Collieries Ltd.*[39] the employees were available for work but the court was prepared to imply into the contract the supposed understanding of the parties that no wages were due whilst the colliery was closed for necessary safety works. This may now be thought an unlikely implication but there is no doubt of the right to apportion wages to certain tasks and since the repeal of the Truck Acts, to provide for deduction for partial non-performance. The snag about the right described above is that it is actually a right to reject partial performance. If, however, it makes economic sense for the employer to accept such performance as the employees are prepared to offer then he would, until recently, have been required to pay the whole of the contractual wages. It is probably not surprising that the courts have developed two main lines of exception to this "all or nothing" rule.

Part payment

In the first place, the idea has developed that the work obligation can be regulated by separate contracts, each providing its own separate remuneration. This was the solution adopted by the Court of Appeal in *Land and Wilson* v. *West Yorkshire MCC*[40] to save itself falling into the mire of explanations for the incorporation of collective agreements which had caused Kilner Brown J. in the E.A.T., to clutch at some rather theoretical straws. That was rather an obvious case for such apportionment. Regular firemen also worked, if they wished, a stand-by arrangement at times other than when

---

[35] See, *Cutter* v. *Powell* (1795) 6 T.R. 320.
[36] Glanville Williams (1941) 57 L.Q.R. 373 and 382; Freedland at 132–133. The view is based on the decision in *Moriarty* v. *Regents Garage* [1921] 1 K.B. 423.
[37] Salaries in the Apportionment Act 1870 (1982) 2 Legal Studies 302.
[38] *Henthorne* v. *CEGB* [1980] I.R.L.R. 361.
[39] [1926] 1 K.B. 522.
[40] [1981] I.C.R. 334.

they were employed full time. Naturally, separate rules of pay applied to these duties. The attempt by the employing authorities to terminate the stand-by arrangements can readily be seen as the termination of a contract separate from that governing full time employment. It is not really properly described even as ancillary. The same is true of the schoolteachers' agreement to supervise in the lunch hour, which was the subject of dispute in *Metropolitan Borough of Solihull* v. *N.U.T.*[41] although the schoolteachers might have been a little surprised to learn that their "wages" for this obligation consisted of a free school-meal. In *Bond* v. *CAV Ltd.*[42] the idea was extended to a set of agreements dealing with the operation under a new piece-work system of new or renovated machines, incapable of full rates of production. But in *Gibbons* v. *Associated British Ports*[43] the guaranteed wage agreement was held not to be thus severable from the main part of the agreement.

Even if particular duties are not severable, the courts have recently experimented with arguments permitting the withholding of a portion of remuneration for partial non-performance. In *Sim* v. *Rotherham Metropolitan Borough Council*[44] the court had assumed that it would be necessary for the employer to withhold wages and then meet the employee's claim with a counter claim based on equitable set-off. Park J. had not appeared to envisage such complexity in *Royle* v. *Trafford Borough Council*,[45] presumably because the employer had withheld the entire salary of a school teacher who had refused to teach five extra children that it was proposed should be added to a class of 31. The decision was that the employer had accepted partial performance and was obliged to pay for it but was not obliged to pay for non-performance assessed, for want of a better fraction, at 5/36ths. During the period of these decisions *Miles* v. *Wakefield Metropolitan District Council*[46] had been working its way to the House of Lords. In the process, a majority of the Court of Appeal had overruled the judge of first instance (upon whose decision *Royle* had relied) and had held that there was no right to deduct a portion of salary for several hours in the week when the employer had indicated that he was not prepared to accept the employee's offer of partial performance. The House of Lords held that the employee's claim for the unpaid portion of salary failed because he could not show that he was ready to perform his contractual obligation. Two members of the House considered the deduction to depend on a *quantum meruit*, but this can hardly be correct since there is no possibility of implying such an agreement in the contract. The outcome seems to be that the employer is free to reject partial performance entirely but that if he accepts it (on the basis, for instance, that some work is better than none) he may make a proportionate deduction from remuneration. Perhaps he could not claim to recover money once paid but if he takes the initiative the employee cannot support his claim to recover by evidence of availability to do the work. The danger, as usual, lies in the fact that it is the employer who takes the initiative. In practice it is unlikely that an employee will seek in the courts to challenge a partial reduction of wages on the ground that the pro-

---

[41] [1985] I.R.L.R. 211.
[42] [1983] I.R.L.R. 360.
[43] [1985] I.R.L.R. 376.
[44] [1986] I.C.R. 897.
[45] [1984] I.R.L.R. 184.
[46] [1987] I.C.R. 368.

portion is excessive.[47] Yet the proportion when applied to forms of industrial action, such as work to rule, will be much less easy to identify than the five scholars in *Royle* or the three hours on a Saturday morning in *Miles*. Probably, employers will stick to proportionate deduction from basic rates but there would seem no reliable answer if they choose to extend the proportion to other parts of a more complex pattern of remuneration.

Contractual suspension without pay

Contractual theory has lead to the conclusion that an employer is not entitled to suspend without pay unless such a power is included in the contract expressly or by necessary implication.[48] It has never been clear whether necessary implication (which is, after all, the correct basis of the business efficacy and "oh of course" tests) was meant to impose some higher degree of inevitability than commonly justified the inclusion of an implied term. Would standard practice in other parts of the industry suffice? Benedictus and Bercusson[49] present suspension in its disciplinary aspect and note that such suspension rarely continues for more than a few days. *Browning* v. *Crumlin Valley Collieries Ltd.*[50] recognises a wholly different form of suspension (and, incidentally, an example of "necessary" implication). The power to suspend the guarantee pay scheme in *Burroughs Machines Ltd.* v. *Timmoney*[51] is an example of by far the most significant form of indefinite suspension where industrial action, or some other cause, affects trade.

Where there is a power of suspension the courts have taken the view that it is only common sense to suppose that the obligations of both parties are in suspense.[52] In fact, that conclusion depends on the terms of the suspension. A great deal of suspension in recent times has been on full pay; the device being adopted to remove the employee from the workplace pending a disciplinary enquiry. It would be necessary, therefore, to ascertain the purpose of the suspension before one could calculate its effect on the contract of employment and it is certainly not always possible to say that the whole contract is suspended. Sometimes it will be necessary for a court to decide, for instance, whether an employee suspended without pay for a fixed period could withdraw his labour (*i.e.* go on strike) during that period. Would it make any difference if he were suspended on full pay, or indefinitely, so that it could be contended that the employer was at liberty to recall him? Certainly the contract does not appear normally to have been terminated, subject to later renewal, during a suspension. The decision of Goddard L.C.J. in *Marshall* v. *English Electric Co. Ltd.*[53] to the contrary must be regarded as dependent on presumptions about the freedom to terminate virtually at will which would not be implied at the present time.

---

[47] *Sed contra* if the amount is obviously excessive—*Wiluszynski* v. *London Borough of Tower Hamlets* [1988] I.R.L.R. 154.
[48] *Gorse* v. *Durham County Council* [1971] 2 All E.R. 666.
[49] *Labour Law and Materials* (1987) at pp. 251–256.
[50] [1926] 1 K.B. 522.
[51] [1977] I.R.L.R. 404.
[52] *Wallwork* v. *Fielding* [1922] 2 K.B. 66; *Bird* v. *British Celanese* [1945] 1 K.B. 336.
[53] [1945] 1 All E.R. 653.

Guarantee pay

Suspension without pay, not as a disciplinary measure but as a longer term response to the employer's economic difficulties arising from shortage of supplies or lack of a market, has always tended to bear most heavily upon production workers. The reasons for this are fairly obvious. The shortage of supply or demand will reveal itself most quickly in the front line of production. Pay expressed as an hourly or weekly calculation is, perhaps only psychologically, apparently easier to withhold at short notice than "salary" based on a longer notional period. So the white collar worker has, in varying degrees, been cushioned. Trade unions have long responded to this risk by seeking to extend the concept of guarantee payment from piece-workers who, of course, were automatically affected by such shortages, to time-workers, the effect on whom was often only slightly delayed. There is little doubt that the extension of guarantee payments by collective agreement prevented strains which would otherwise have arisen from appearing in the law reports. Nevertheless the risk to the worker of loss of wages resulting from market fluctuations was thought in the mid 1970's to be somewhat haphazardly alleviated. In consequence, provision was made for a "statutory floor" of payment wherever there has been a diminution in the requirements of the employer's business for work of the kind which the individual employee is employed to do, or some other occurrence affecting the normal working of the employer's business in relation to work of that kind, the result of which is that no work is provided throughout a day during any part of which the employee would normally be required to work.[54] It is a floor which has always been very low, emphasising the obvious invitation to enter into collective agreements improving the statutory minimum.

This benefit, which is available to all employees except dock workers, share fisherman,[55] those employed outside Great Britain[56] and those employed by a husband or wife,[57] is not available if the workless day occurs in consequence of a strike, lock-out or other industrial action involving an employee of his employer or of an associated employer.[58] In *Thompson* v. *Priest (Lindley) Ltd.*[59] an industrial tribunal held that a trade dispute need not be the sole factor.[60] No payment may be claimed for holidays or other days which would not normally be working days.[61] The employer has also, as it were, a defence to a claim in two provisions of section 13. The employee is not entitled to a guarantee payment in respect of a workless day if his employer has offered to provide alternative work for that day which is suitable in all the circumstances, whether or not it is work which the employee is under his contract employed to perform, and the employee has unreasonably refused that offer. This is

---

[54] E.P.C.A. 1978, s.12(1).
[55] s.144(2).
[56] s.141(2).
[57] s.146(1).
[58] s.13(3).
[59] [1978] I.R.L.R. 99.
[60] Since that decision "trade dispute" has been replaced by the words "strike, lock-out or other industrial action." Employment Act 1982, Sched. 3, para. 14.
[61] In *North* v. *Pavleigh Ltd.* [1977] I.R.L.R. 461 it was not the fact of non-contractual holidays but the absence of diminution or other "occurrence" which led the tribunal to refuse a payment.

parallel to the defence originally provided by the Redundancy Payments Act 1965. It is suggested that some care should be taken, however, in applying decisions under the earlier Act. It would seem quite likely that industrial tribunals would be inclined to hold that during a period of purely temporary redundancy the employee might be expected to be rather more accommodating in his readiness to take alternative work than would be the case where the performance of that alternative work would continue indefinitely. It has been held[62] that an offer of work upon a different day does not constitute an offer of alternative work within this provision.

The second situation provided for is one where the employee does not comply with reasonable requirements imposed by his employer with a view to ensuring that his services are available. There seems no reason to suppose that this provision was intended only to apply to requirements within the employee's contract of employment, although it is not clear whether such a contractual requirement should be regarded automatically as reasonable. In an industrial tribunal decision[63] the claim arose out of the failure of the heating system at the place of employment because the oil to operate it had run out. The employer had arranged for oil to arrive by 9.30 a.m. He was notified of a slight delay which was likely to mean that the oil would not arrive until 9.45 a.m. Employees were asked to wait in the canteen where they were supplied with tea. They voted to go home when the oil did not arrive at the expected time. In fact, the oil arrived just after 10 a.m. The industrial tribunal held that the employees had failed to comply with a reasonable requirement within what is now section 13(2)(b). It pointed out that they had been supplied with information about the delay and that it had been made clear that there would be no pay if the workforce went home.

In each period of 13 consecutive weeks the employee is entitled to a maximum of five days of guaranteed payment.[64] If the employee normally works less than five days in a week under his contract of employment then he will only be entitled to payment for that lesser number of days.[65] This reduction, however, does not apply in any case where an employee's contract has been varied or a new contract has been entered into in connection with a period of short-time working. In such a case the number of days of payment will be governed by the original contract.[66] At face value, this provision would appear not to refer to a situation where there is a standing contract which provides for a reduction in the working week in certain circumstances. In such a case it would seem possible to hold that the situation before the reduction took effect constituted the normal contractual requirement and the reduced week an abnormal situation. This would, of course, have the effect of entitling the employee to rely upon the pre-reduction situation to govern his entitlement. It is suggested, however, that difficulties might occur in applying this view if the reduction had continued over a considerable period of time. The position was considered by an industrial tribunal in *Trevethan* v. *Stirling Metals Ltd.*[67]

---

[62] *North* v. *Pavleigh Ltd.*, *supra.*
[63] *Meadows* v. *Faithfull Overalls Ltd.* [1977] I.R.L.R. 330.
[64] E.P.C.A. 1978, s.15(3) as amended by Employment Act 1980, s.11.
[65] As to what amounts to normal work, see *Miller* v. *Harry Thornton (Lollies) Ltd.* [1978] I.R.L.R. 430.
[66] s.15(4).
[67] [1977] I.R.L.R. 416.

A regular night-shift worker worked four shifts between 8 p.m. and 6.30 a.m. Day-shift workers worked five eight-hour shifts per week. The night-shift worker was laid off on four isolated days and paid the then statutory maximum guarantee payment of £6.60 per day. On the fifth day of lay-off he was refused a statutory payment on the ground that he had used his statutory entitlement for that quarter. An industrial tribunal held that his entitlement was limited to four days. This decision is obviously correct because the statute provides[68] that where a period of employment straddles midnight then only the day in which the major part of that employment occurs shall be counted as a day of employment.

Some support for the proposition that a permanent alteration does not fall within the provisions of section 15(4) is obtained from the industrial tribunal decision in *Daley* v. *Strathclyde Regional Council.*[69] In that case, night-shift cleaners had been employed on five eight-hour shifts per week. As an alternative to redundancy this was reduced to one week of five eight-hour shifts and one week of four eight-hour shifts, alternating. One trade union did not agree to this and its members claimed guarantee payments for the alternate Fridays. The industrial tribunal held that the agreement meant that those days were days on which they were not normally required to work. The change was a permanent one, and therefore did not, presumably, fall within the meaning of a section which refers to an alteration "in connection with a period of short-time working."[70] In both cases the tribunal's decision that the new arrangement had been accepted appears to be open to question.

There is no need for statute to make it a condition of entitlement that no payment shall be made for the day in question, since it is provided that from the amount of the statutory entitlement there is to be deducted any contractual remuneration paid to the employee in respect of a workless day.[71] The effect, however, is that the day covered by the alternative payment remains one of the statutory days of entitlement.[72] The statute indicates[73] that contractual remuneration is, in fact, only intended to cover remuneration derived from the claimant's contract of employment. It is likely that this would cover such things as sick pay for a day when the employee's colleagues were laid off and he would have been laid off but for the fact that he was already off work, sick. A contractual undertaking by the employer himself to pay some form of guaranteed wage during the period of lay-off will, of course, also justify a set-off against the statutory entitlement. This, in turn, is likely to derive from a collective agreement. It follows from this that the provision in section 18, whereby an exemption order can be obtained in respect of collectively agreed guarantee provisions, is of little value since the collectively agreed amount will be deducted from the statutory amount in any event. There would, however, be some advantage in obtaining an exemption order if, for instance, the collective agreement provided for six weeks of guarantee pay during a year. If it so happened that six weeks of lay-off occurred during a single quarter, then

---

[68] s.12(2).
[69] [1977] I.R.L.R. 414.
[70] See also *Clemens* v. *Peter Richards Ltd.* [1977] I.R.L.R. 332.
[71] s.16(2). This obviously excludes such payments as a trade union might make for unemployment since they would not be remuneration.
[72] *Cartwright* v. *G. Clancy Ltd.* [1983] I.R.L.R. 355.
[73] s.16(1).

only five days of statutory guarantee would be eliminated by that agreement, and the statutory guarantee could be claimed for the remaining three quarters of the year. The effect of an exemption order is to eliminate all statutory payment.

A complaint may be presented to an industrial tribunal, normally within three months of any day on which a guarantee payment is alleged to be due, that the employer has failed to pay the whole, or part, of the payment. If the tribunal finds the claim well founded it must order the employer to pay the amount due.[74] Few cases reach tribunals, partly because of the low rates of payment involved and partly because complaints will normally first be handled by an ACAS conciliation officer.[75]

Sick pay

Wages are the return for the employee's availability for work. Though the obligation is indefinite even a temporary failure to meet it is normally regarded as providing a justification for withholding remuneration, despite the continuation of the contract. No doubt this has a good deal to do with the notion of pay periods since it is the employee on hourly rates who will most quickly experience a loss of pay consequent upon non-availability.

About 90 per cent. of all employees are covered by some form of occupational sick pay scheme, mostly incorporated into the contract of employment. Most schemes, however, provide for part only of full pay or a short period of entitlement to full pay. No presumption or implication can overcome express contractual provision so there is, in practice, only occasional need to consider the common law. Nevertheless, its development seems to shed a different light on judicial response to the question of whether the economic dependence inherent in the nature of employment should be a charge on the employer or on the state than is apparent in relation to lay-off, dismissal for redundancy, and unemployment generally.[76] This suggests that, for some unusual reason, the common law courts had, as late as 1858,[77] sought to impose a paternalistic obligation on the employer.[78] But if this had been the object of the presumption as to sick pay it would surely have disappeared long before 1981. The duty to provide medical care seems to have become confined to specific situations early in the nineteenth century.[79] The attempt at paternalism, if it existed, was frustrated by the freedom of contract which the courts also established and which, in practice, permitted the stronger party to exclude obligations burdensome to him.

Freedland[80] points out that *Cuckson* v. *Stones*,[81] from which is later supposed to have derived the common law rebuttable presumption that wages

---

[74] s.17.

[75] E.P.C.A. 1978, s.133.

[76] See Schwarger, *Wages During Temporary Disability* (1952) 5 Stanford L.R. 30. Freedland remarks that the common law had, by the time of the decision in *Orman* v. *Saville Sportswear Ltd.* [1960] 1 W.L.R. 1055 become remote from practice.

[77] *Cuckson* v. *Stones* (1858), 1 E. and E. 248.

[78] They might have done so earlier by analogy with their own somewhat limited vision of employment within a household which produced for instance, an early duty to provide medical insurance—*Scarman* v. *Castell* (1795) 1 Esp. 270.

[79] *Winnal* v. *Adney* (1802) 3 Bos. and P. 247; *Sellen* v. *Norman* (1829) 4 C. & P. 80.

[80] *The Contract of Employment* (OUP 1976) at p. 110.

[81] *Supra*.

were payable during sickness (so long, of course, as the contract survived), was concerned with a managerial employee engaged for a fixed term of ten years who was, in any event, still able to carry out some of his contractual functions. In other words, the origin of the supposed presumption depended precisely on the distinction between the expectation of white collar workers to a certain continuity of wages and that of manual workers to shoulder the risks of their own incapacity which later characterised express contractual provisions. As Freedland shows, the extension to manual workers in *Marrison* v. *Bell*[82] was immediately countered by a denial of such an entitlement by implied or express qualification.[83] Thus Freedland isolates the decision in *Orman* v. *Saville Sportswear Ltd.*[84] which, he reminds us, was again concerned with employment in a managerial capacity. True, the presumption is stated generally enough by Pilcher J., but one wonders whether courts might readily have implied a contrary understanding in the case of categories of worker used, in 1960 at least, to a normal practice of non-payment.

In *Mears* v. *Safecar Security Ltd.*[85] Slynn J., in the E.A.T., effectively rejected the existence of any presumption; relying, rather, on those authorities which had allowed proof of express or implied terms to formulate the proposition that the question was simply one of what term should be implied as to payment of wages during sickness. As Stephenson L.J. said, in the Court of Appeal, the decision of the E.A.T. "disapproved the conclusion of Pilcher J. . . . and substitutes an approach to the facts and evidence in each case with an open mind unprejudiced by any preconception, presumption or assumption."[86] We know enough now about the implied term to recognise that it is capable of reflecting policy. *Mears'* case itself contains the statement that a term can be implied even though it is one which there is no evidence the parties would have agreed. Nevertheless, this brief account of the judicial experience in controlling remuneration during sickness reveals no sign of any policy save the usual reluctance to concede a right temporarily to cease payment to those envisaging long term, rather than indefinite, employment.

It is more likely that the decision in *Mears* owed something to the development of contractual provision and social security sick pay schemes than that *Cuckson* v. *Stones*[87] owed anything to paternalism. There will now usually be some foundation for expectation as to what is to happen to remuneration during sickness, even if there is no foundation for the story of the employee of the C.E.G.B. who, when asked how much annual holiday he had to come responded, "Two weeks and three weeks sick." Conversely, however, the statutory incorporation into the private employment relationship of a sick pay scheme makes the development of any independent common law policy unlikely.

The Social Security and Housing Benefits Act 1982 transferred, from the national insurance system to employers, the obligation to make sickness payments to their employees for 28 weeks (originally eight weeks) from the com-

---

[82] [1939] 2 K.B. 187.
[83] *Petrie* v. *Mac Fisheries Ltd.* [1940] 1 K.B. 258; *Hancock* v. *BSA Tools Ltd.* [1939] 4 All E.R. 5387; *O'Grady* v. *M. Saper Ltd.* [1940] 2 K.B. 469.
[84] *Supra.*
[85] [1981] I.C.R. 409 affirmed by the Court of Appeal [1982] I.C.R. 626.
[86] At p. 647.
[87] *Supra.*

mencement of the period of incapacity for work, or as long as the employee remains in their employment, whichever is the shorter. Employees with fixed contracts of less than three months or those participating, or having a direct interest in, a trade dispute at their place of employment do not qualify. Nor do pregnant women in the period of 18 weeks beginning with the eleventh week prior to the expected date of confinement. The employer is free to make what sickness payments he is contracted, or agrees otherwise, to make so long as they reach the minimum designated from time to time by statutory instrument. That minimum is nominally wage-related, but for most employees in full time employment, is likely to operate at the maximum rate, currently somewhat less than £50 per week. The employer recovers this minimum rate (together with an 8 per cent. supplement to cover his administrative costs) from his national insurance (and, if necessary) PAYE contributions. To qualify for statutory sick pay the employee must be incapable, by reason of some specific disease or mental or bodily disablement, of doing work of a kind he might reasonably be expected to do for any period of four or more consecutive days; although a day of incapacity counts as part of the same period if it is not separated from an earlier period of incapacity by more than eight weeks. An employee may certify his own incapacity, subject to procedural rules applicable to his employment relationship, for the first seven days of incapacity. Every day of the week counts as part of any requisite consecutive period of days.

So, effectively, the overlap between state sickness pay and private sickness schemes (whereby in some cases both were payable and the state payments were not subject to income tax) has been eliminated.

Suspension from work on medical grounds

Depending on express or implied contractual terms, absence from work because of illness may not affect the employee's right to wages. An employer who suspends an employee for any reason not regarded as affecting that employee's willingness to work may be obliged to continue payment of wages.[88]

In certain cases statute, statutory instrument or recommendation may have the effect of requiring an employer to suspend an employee on medical grounds. It is obviously considered unfair to the employee that in such a circumstance his contract of employment might exclude his right to continuing wages during that period of suspension. It is, accordingly, provided[89] that in such circumstances the suspended employee is entitled to up to 26 weeks' remuneration while so suspended. Any period during which he is actually incapable of work by reason of disease or bodily or mental disablement is, however, excluded from the operation of the right.[90] The entitlement is also inoperative in respect of any period during which his employer has offered to provide him with suitable alternative work (even though not within his contractual obligation) which the employee has unreasonably refused, or during

---

[88] See p. 78, *supra*.
[89] E.P.C.A. 1978, s.19(1). These provisions apply to employees with at least one month's employment ending the day before the first day of claim. (E.A. 1982, Sched. 2).
[90] s.19(2).

which the employee does not comply with reasonable requirements imposed by his employer with a view to ensuring that his services are available.[91]

The amount of remuneration is a week's pay for each week of suspension. Any contractual remuneration actually paid by the employer to the employee goes in discharge of the statutory entitlement and vice versa.[92] Complaint of non-payment may be made, normally within three months of the day of which the claim relates, to an industrial tribunal which may award the amount due.[93]

Methods of wage payment

In the agricultural economy that preceded the industrial revolution payment of wages in kind was a normal, and at times beneficial, system. It is not surprising that it should have appeared in the early factories. It might then have been beneficial since provision for consumer needs was not highly developed in the rapidly expanding industrial areas and an employer, able to buy in bulk, could have passed on the benefit of discount to his employees.

The "truck system"[94] was not widely known for any such advantages. Either the employer paid in overvalued products of his own factory (particularly if the market was depressed and he could not sell them) or he paid wages in token coinage exchangeable only in a few shops. Those who exchanged the goods (often by arrangement with the employer), or the token coinage, employed various devices for undervaluing to add to the commission they would receive on return of the items to the employer. In the result, therefore, truck diminished the value of the wages due. It was particularly popular with small employers. Large employers found it, no doubt, too cumbersome. It enabled small employers to undercut large employers and so inspired one of the those unlikely combinations of capitalist reformers similar to that which, for other reasons, supported early safety legislation—in industries other than their own. The Truck Act 1831 brought together a number of earlier pieces of legislation relating to particular industries into a general requirement that all artisans (with some specific exceptions) should be paid the wages due in current coin of the realm. It did not destroy the truck system but, as Professor Kahn Freund said,[95] it gave workers, when combined in trade unions, the means to insist on the maintenance of statutory standards. Even the introduction of a wages inspectorate in 1887 did not wholly eradicate it and related legislation was required to deal with other methods of reducing the actual wages below those earned. The Checkweighing in Various Industries Act 1919 entitled workers—in practice, their unions—to supervise the weighing of material where wages depended on the amount produced. The Particulars Clause of the Factories Act 1961[96] required occupiers of factories to display notices of piece rates. Shop Clubs which were designed to provide certain long term benefits to members, but were never extensively developed,[97] were

---

[91] s.20.
[92] s.21.
[93] s.22.
[94] "Truck" means "barter" and survives in modern usage in the phrase "to have no truck with . . . "
[95] *Labour and the Law* (2nd ed.) p. 8.
[96] s.315.
[97] In 1966 as Wedderburn notes in the second edition of *The Worker and the Law* at p. 232 membership of certified shop clubs amounted only to 24,000, whilst twelve million workers were members of some 65,000 private pension schemes.

regulated.[98] Statutory steps were also taken to forbid another arrangement for the mutual benefit of employer and publican in the payment of wages in public houses.[99]

The Truck Acts had what was, latterly, their most significant consequence apparently unintended by the legislature in 1831. The words "the whole of the wages due" were construed as requiring payment not only in coin but without deduction. In consequence the legislature was forced, in 1896, to make more detailed provision to permit certain fines and penalties for unsatisfactory performance. These statutory provisions operated alongside certain examples of judicial interpretation of the earlier provisions construing "the wages due," when there was evidence of bad work, as the reduced wages specifically provided for in such circumstances.[1] The operation of the various Truck Acts was haphazard, partly because of the exclusion of particular sections of industry, but largely because of the application of the 1831 Act to "artificers" and the extension, in 1887, effectively to "manual" workers.[2] It is too much to say that among its effects Truck legislation is responsible for the familiarity of the clerical worker with payment by cheque and banks and the unfamiliarity of production workers with anything but cash in hand. Nevertheless, there is no doubt that it did prevent the introduction of modern methods of wage payment, which the Payment of Wages Act 1960 did little, in practice, to facilitate. Other methods of remuneration were also restricted.[3] Despite this, the protective value of the Truck Acts was revealed in a final burst of life shortly before their repeal when they were applied to protect petrol station forecourt attendants from what were often repressive terms of their contract requiring them to make good deficiencies of cash takings.

The Truck Acts employed a wide range of remedies from avoidance of any offending contractual term to inspection and criminal sanction. The suspicion, clearly justified in 1831, that the worker could not be left to protect himself by negotiation of contractual terms was not re-assessed in 1986 when this, by far the longest-standing piece of protective employment legislation, was repealed. The Wages Act 1986 leaves authorisation of deductions from wages (the prohibition on payment in kind disappears) entirely to be regulated by agreement between employer and worker.[4] Deductions (or payment by the worker to the employer) otherwise prohibited may be made if required or authorised by statutory provision or the worker's contract, or otherwise by agreement or consent in writing, and in advance, by the worker.[5] In the case of contractual authorisation the relevant provision must exist prior to the deduction and, either, be in writing of which the worker has a copy, or the

---

[98] Shop Clubs Act 1902.

[99] The Welsh miners who took their wives' shoes to the colliery on pay day seem to have defeated the legislature.

[1] *E.g. Hewlett* v. *Allen* [1894] A.C. 383; although Lord Wright in *Penman* v. *The Fife Coal Co. Ltd.* [1936] A.C. 45 described this decision as going to the limit of what is permissible in a liberal construction of the Act.

[2] See, *e.g. Cameron* v. *Royal London Opthalmic Hospital* [1941] 1 K.B. 350—a stoker in the hospital boiler house was a domestic servant and thus excluded from the Acts.

[3] See *Kenyon* v. *Darwen Cotton Manufacturing Co. Ltd.* [1936] 2 K.B. 193—share purchase scheme.

[4] The Act extends to a worker under a contract personally to perform work or services other than to a client or customer of a profession or business.

[5] Wages Act 1986, s.1(1).

effect of which must have been previously explained to the worker in writing.[6] Deductions may be made, unaffected by these requirements, in the following circumstances:

(a) To recover an overpayment of wages or expenses made by the employer to the worker;

(b) In respect of any penalty imposed by statutory disciplinary provisions;

(c) In respect of deduction to satisfy an employer's statutory obligation, properly made by a public authority, requiring wages to be deducted and paid to a public authority, as, for instance, by attachment of wages[7];

(d) To pay to a third party, in accordance with the relevant notification of that person, amounts due to that person under any provision of the worker's contract to which he has signified his agreement in writing; or otherwise with the prior agreement of the worker signified in writing;

(e) To make payment to the employer, or recover from wages paid by the employer, any amount required by the employer on account of the worker having taken part in any industrial action;

(f) To satisfy an order of a court or tribunal for payment by the worker to the employer, where the worker has signified his prior agreement or consent in writing or has paid the employer for this purpose.

In the case of "retail workers" deductions on account of cash shortages or stock deficiencies may not exceed one tenth of the *gross* wages payable on any pay day save the last in that employment.

Complaints of unauthorised deductions or payments may be made to an industrial tribunal within three months of the deduction or payment. At the time of writing, industrial tribunals are not sure whether they are entitled to consider questions of the interpretation or content of the contract of employment in dealing with these matters. It would seem surprising if, where a question of contract arose, they had to refer the matter to a County Court. On the other hand, to date, tribunals have not dealt with other matters relating to the contract of employment. Some very difficult problems have yet to be solved in this area. It will be necessary, for instance, to decide whether suspension without pay under a non-statutory disciplinary procedure amounts to a deduction of pay if, for instance, it is a response to an alleged repudiatory breach by the employee so that it is not expressly or impliedly covered by the terms of the contract. The definition of industrial action, which in a number of other areas is also calling for clarification, again becomes an issue where, for instance, part of wages is withheld in response to a worker's refusal to perform what is said to be part of his contractual obligation.

Protection against insolvency of an employer

It is provided that certain amounts due to an employee under the provisions of the Employment Protection (Consolidation) Act 1978 shall have priority over other debts in the same way as arrears of wages under section 33 of the Bankruptcy Act 1914.[8] These are amounts in respect of:

---

[6] *Ibid.* s.1(4).
[7] *Infra*, p. 89.
[8] s.121.

(a) a guarantee payment;
(b) remuneration in respect of a period of suspension on medical grounds;
(c) payment for time off work for officials of trade unions engaged in matters concerned with industrial relations or training in aspects thereof under section 27;
(d) payment for time-off to look for work under section 31;
(e) remuneration under a protective award arising out of interim proceedings on a claim for unfair dismissal for trade union activities under section 101 of the Employment Protection Act 1975.

In addition to this priority, an employee may make application in writing to the Secretary of State that his employer is insolvent owing, on the date of the insolvency or of the termination of employment, whichever is later, the whole or any part of any of a number of specified debts. These are[9]:

(a) arrears of pay in respect of one or more (but not more than eight) weeks;
(b) payment due for the statutorily required minimum period of notice;
(c) holiday pay accrued due in the previous 12 months up to a maximum of six weeks' pay;
(d) a basic award of compensation in respect of an unfair dismissal;
(e) any reasonable sum by way of reimbursement of the whole or part of any fee or premium paid by an apprentice or articled clerk;
(f) any amount due in respect of any of the items given priority under section 121 up to the equivalent of eight weeks' pay.[10]

The Secretary of State shall, if satisfied of the basis of the claim pay the amount due up to whatever is the current maximum amount fixed for each weekly payment or a proportionate part thereof.

In addition the Secretary of State may similarly pay any sum in his opinion payable in respect of unpaid payments due from an insolvent employer in respect of an occupational pension scheme. These contributions may be either those due on the employer's own account or on behalf of an employee. This latter situation will only arise where an equal sum has been deducted from the pay of the employee by way of contribution.[11] Certain maxima are specified as to the amount of such payment.[12] The application in writing must come, in this case, from persons competent to act in respect of the scheme.

Where an application is made to the Secretary of State in respect of any of these payments he may require the employer to provide him with such information as he may reasonably require to determine whether the application is well founded. He may also require any person having custody or control of any relevant records or other documents to produce such documents for examination.[13]

Any applicant may, within three months of the decision of the Secretary of State, complain to an industrial tribunal that the Secretary of State has failed

---

[9] s.122. As amended by E.A. 1982, Sched. 2, para. 4.
[10] s.122(4).
[11] s.123(1) and (2).
[12] See s.123(3) and (5).
[13] s.126(1).

to pay the whole or any part of the amount claimed to be due.[14] The industrial tribunal may make a declaration that the Secretary of State ought to make the payment specified in the declaration. Broadly speaking, when the Secretary of State has made any such payment he is subrogated to the rights of the claimant against the employer.

It has been held with reference to a claim for wages due during a period of notice that the claim against the Secretary of State cannot be better than would have been the right against the insolvent employer. The Secretary of State is, accordingly, entitled to the benefit of a contractual set-off.[15]

Payments from company assets

Section 74 of the Companies Act 1980 extends the powers of a company to include provision for the benefit of employees or former employees of the company or any of its subsidiaries in connection with cessation or transfer of the whole or part of the undertaking. The power may be exercised notwithstanding that it is not in the best interests of the company. The power may be exercised only by a resolution of the directors if authorised by the memorandum or articles or, if not so authorised, by an ordinary resolution of the company. The memorandum or articles may, however, require exercise by a special resolution of the company with more than a simple majority. In effect the memorandum or articles can be drafted so as effectively to exclude the exercise since the section goes on to provide that any other requirements of the memorandum or articles must be satisfied before the payment is made.

On a winding up the liquidator may take the payments so authorised out of assets available to shareholders after the discharge of all the company's liabilities. If made before a winding up the payment may only be made out of profits available for the payment of a dividend. So creditors of the company may not be prejudiced.

These provisions replace the rule in *Parke* v. *Daily News Ltd*[15a] that such payments were not in the best interests of the company and so could not be made.

Attachment of earnings

The law relating to the attachment of earnings has been consolidated in the Attachment of Earnings Act 1971. Attachment orders may be made by the High Court to secure payments under a High Court maintenance order; by a county court for county court, or High Court, maintenance orders, a judgment debt over £5 or under an administration order; or by a magistrates' court for a magistrates' court maintenance order, the payment of any sum adjudged to be paid by a conviction and any sum required to be paid by a legal aid contribution order.[16] Generally speaking it is the creditor who is empowered to make the application but the debtor himself may apply to a magistrates' court or, in respect of maintenance payments, to the High Court or a county court. Where a creditor applies it must appear that the debtor has failed to make at least one required payment. In the case of maintenance

---

[14] s.124.
[15] *Secretary of State for Employment* v. *Wilson* [1978] I.C.R. 200. There seems no reason why a similar princple should not apply to all the payments specified.
[15a] [1962] Ch. 927.
[16] s.1.

orders the failure must be by reason of the debtor's wilful refusal or culpable neglect unless, of course, the application is from the debtor.[17]

Where an application is made to a county court to secure the payment of a judgment debt the court may, in the light of the debtor's other debts, make, together with the attachment order or alone, an order for the administration of his estate.[18] The county court, however, will have no such jurisdiction if the total of the debts exceeds the county court limit, presently of £500.

An attachment order, which may incorporate a number of debts, instructs the employer to make periodic deductions from the debtor's earnings at such times as the order requires or the court allows and to pay the amounts deducted to the specified collecting officer. The order must specify a rate of protected earnings below which, in the opinion of the court, the earnings actually paid to the employee should not fall. The collecting officer is normally the county court registrar or a magistrates' clerk or an officer of the High Court.[19] The employer is under a duty to comply with the order seven days after receipt unless, within 10 days, he notifies the court that the person is not in his employment. On every occasion on which he deducts he may also deduct a specified sum for his administrative expenses. He must, on each occasion, give the debtor a written statement of the total deduction.[20] Where, because of the operation of the protected earnings level, it is not possible to deduct the whole amount due then, except in the case of judgment debts or payments under an administration order, the backlog must be made up subsequently.[21] If an employer is faced with more than one attachment order he must deal with them in order of priority dependent on the dates they were made.[22] The employer, the debtor or the creditor may apply to the court to determine what constitutes "earnings."

The order is directed to a particular employer and not to whoever may be employing the debtor from time to time. It, therefore, lapses if the debtor ceases to be in that employment (or, presumably, if he was not in that employment when the order was first served) but it may be redirected by the court to any other person appearing to be the employer. The court will give notice to an employer when an order ceases to have effect or the amount of the debt has been paid. Seven days after this notice the employer will become liable to pay the unreduced wages to the employee again.[23]

Where a court has power to make, or has made, an order it may require the person appearing to it to be the employer to furnish specified particulars of the debtor's actual and anticipated earnings.[24] Failure to comply will render the employer liable to a fine of £25. Of much more significance is the requirement that every person who becomes the debtor's employer and knows of the order, and by which court it was made, must notify the court within seven days of this fact and of the actual or anticipated earnings of the debtor.[25]

---

[17] s.3.
[18] s.4.
[19] s.6.
[20] s.7.
[21] Sched. 3, paras. 5 and 6.
[22] Sched. 3, para. 7.
[23] s.12.
[24] s.14.
[25] s.15.

Trust and confidence

The most significant development in the implied term since 1970 is the recognition of a contractual obligation on both parties to maintain the trust and confidence of the other.[26] It is difficult to decide why this obligation should have emerged, apparently so suddenly, in 1977. It could derive from an attempt to rationalise the duty not wilfully to disrupt the employer's undertaking, favoured by at least two members of the Court of Appeal in *Secretary of State for Employment* v. *ASLEF*[27] but scarcely mentioned by the courts since. All the examples postulated by its supporters in that judgment imply recognition of an element of co-operation, although the Court of Appeal[28] went out of its way to reject that positive aspect of Sir John Donaldson's judgment in the N.I.R.C. It has generally been recognised that it is difficult to see how an employee can be liable for breach of contract solely because of the motive behind his lack of co-operation. Brian Napier points out[29] that implication of a duty of co-operation between employer and employee is one of the most obvious signs of a unitary approach to employment in which partnership as a common interest, rather than conflict of interests, is seen as fundamental. As such the development of such a contractual obligation would have been in line with the resurgence of such a view which began at that time. The judicial innovation may have been nurtured, though it is unlikely to have been initiated, by a realisation that such a term would be likely to confer positive rights on employees. Apart from the right to wages and to an established job location most implied terms favour management's prerogative to manage. Courts rarely consciously develop a device to redress an imbalance they have created, unless some other consideration induces such a development. The early decisions on trust and confidence, however, favour employee rights. Finally, the early decisions on trust and confidence coincide with the resolution of the argument as to the basis of constructive dismissal in favour of a response to a repudiatory breach of contract. Having apparently rejected the argument that an employee might claim compensation for unfair dismissal if he had left employment in response to unreasonable conduct from his employer it was, no doubt, very satisfactory to discover that forms of unacceptable conduct constitute a repudiatory breach. It is most likely, therefore, that a series of factors contributed to this development.[30]

Although it is suggested that such implication first occurred in 1977, decisions in that year around this theme do not clearly define the obligation. This may seem surprising in view of later assertions that such an obligation had always been recognised by the common law. The common law had recognised that maintenance of trust and confidence was essential to continuation

---

[26] Wedderburn *Worker and the Law* (3rd ed.) at p. 181 links this assessment of importance to the decision in *W.M. Car Services Ltd.* v. *Woods* [1982 I.C.R. 693]. That decision applied the obligation so as to require reasonable acceptance by an employee of management initiated reorganisation in the interests of the business.

[27] [1972] I.C.R.7.

[28] [1972] I.C.R. 7.

[29] [1977] I.L.J. 1.

[30] But breach of trust and confident is not to be equated with unreasonableness. *Post Office* v. *Roberts* [1980] I.R.L.R. 347; *White* v. *London Transport Executive* [1981] I.R.L.R. 261.

of the employment relationship.[31] But it was recognised by the common law
not as an implied obligation but as a test to measure the repudiatory character
of some other breach.[32] In *Hill* v. *C.A. Parsons and Co. Ltd.*[33] Sachs L.J.
relied on survival of mutual trust and confidence as a justification for the
unusual step of ordering specific performance. Of course, it is very strongly
arguable that the parties to a contract are under an implied obligation to
maintain a state of affairs known by them to be essential for the performance
of that contract but the common law, even when faced with situations later
said to fall within the scope of destruction of trust and confidence,[34] does not
seem previously to have thought of this line of reasoning.

The earliest cases introducing the obligation as an implied term did so
cautiously, as if it might be confined to especially personal relationships. In
Isle of Wight Tourist Board v. *Combes*,[35] for instance, Bristow J. said:

> "The relationship between somebody in the position of the director of this board
> and his personal secretary must be one of complete confidence. They must trust
> each other; they must respect each other."

But two years later the same situation is clearly recognised as subject to a
general principle.[36]

In fact, an early tribunal decision—*Wood* v. *Freeloader Ltd.*[37]—seems to
regard the duty as a general one and, incidentally, presumes to tell the
employee what she ought to have found intolerable (although there seems
reason to doubt if she did). There was no wild rush in those early cases, however, to invoke "trust and confidence." In *Wigan Borough Council* v.
Davies[38] the E.A.T., like its predecessor two years before,[39] although regarding the resultant situation as intolerable to the employee, preferred to rely on
the more precise implication of a duty to provide an employee with the support necessary to enable her to do the job.[40] It seems probable that the most
obvious early invitation to use breach of trust and confidence as a source of an
obligation to behave fairly lay in the judgment of Lawton L.J. in *Western
Excavating (ECC) Ltd.* v. *Sharp.*[41] Having supported repudiatory breach as
the essential precondition of constructive dismissal, he somewhat inconse-

---

[31] *Boston Deep Sea Fishing and Ice Co.* v. *Ansell* (1888) 39 Ch.D. 339; although it was there rendered as "breach of the confidential relationship" which, it is suggested, would have been
regarded more as "fidelity," and would not have been regarded as mutual.
[32] See, *e.g. Re Rubel Bronze and Metal Co. and Vos* [1918] 1 K.B. 315; *Sinclair* v. *Neighbour*
[1967] 2 Q.B. 279.
[33] [1971] 3 W.L.R. 995. The same point was made in *Powell* v. *London Borough of Brent* [1987]
I.R.L.R. 466.
[34] *E.g. Veness* v. *Dyson, Bell & Co.*, *The Times*, May 25, 1965; *Donovan* v. *Invicta Airways Ltd.*
[1970] 1 Lloyds Rep. 486; and, perhaps, most obviously of all, *Pepper* v. *Webb* [1969] 1
W.L.R. 514.
[35] [1976] I.R.L.R. 413.
[36] *Courtaulds Northern Textiles Ltd.* v. *Andrew* [1979] I.R.L.R. 84.
[37] [1977] I.R.L.R. 455.
[38] [1979] I.C.R. 411.
[39] *Wetherall (Bond St., W.1.) Ltd.* v. *Lynn* [1978] I.C.R. 205.
[40] See too, *Associated Tyre Specialists (Eastern) Ltd.* v. *Waterhouse* [1976] I.R.L.R. 2386. Typical of the continuing misrepresentation of this type of decision as "trust and confidence" see
Southern and Howard: *AIDS and Employment Law* (Financial Training Publications Ltd.
1987) at p. 68.
[41] [1978] I.C.R. 221 at p. 229.

quentially, went on to consider the meaning of employer's "conduct" as if it meant some action more personally intolerable than well established breaches which might equally be said to constitute "conduct." His insistence that there was such a thing as intolerable conduct amounting to a repudiatory breach of contract begs the question what implied term would thereby be broken. Lawton L.J. did not say. Phillips J. in *British Aircraft Corporation Ltd.* v. *Austin*[42] said that it must certainly be an implied term that employers do not behave in a way "which employees cannot be expected to put up with any longer."[43] No one would doubt that, but some lawyers might want to be a little clearer on the necessary basis for such an implication. The court so wished in *The Post Office* v. *Roberts*.[44] The E.A.T. there rejected a proposal to imply a contractual obligation upon an employer to treat an employee in a reasonable manner. It stated that the test of destruction of trust and confidence was whether the act disabled the other party from carrying out his or her obligations. The matter, surprisingly perhaps, was sorted out between Lord McDonald and Sir Ralph Kilner Brown. In *Fyfe and McGrouther Ltd.* v. *Byrne*[45] the former held that a demonstration by the employer of unjustified loss of confidence in the employee could be sufficient to destroy the employee's confidence. One can see, in the way Lord McDonald expressed himself, how the employer was confused in *Courtaulds Northern Textiles Ltd.* v. *Andrew*,[46] into thinking it was his confidence which was in issue and that all he had to do to deny the breach was to show that he had no basis for loss of confidence in the employee. In *Robinson* v. *Crompton Parkinson Ltd.*[47] Kilner Brown J., characteristically, shows himself aware of the discussion he has had with his tribunal members and emphasises, over and over again, the explanation that the confidence is mutual, so that an employee may lose confidence from the very unreasonableness of his employer's apparent loss of confidence in him.

It is a surprising fact that there is no clear statement of principle before this and certainly there is nothing as clear later[48] until the definitive specification of the term by Browne-Wilkinson J. in the E.A.T. in *Woods* v. *W.M. Car Services (Peterborough) Ltd.*[49] Several decisions could, quite sensibly, have been based on the existence of such a term, but ignored it. Two of the most startling are those of Browne-Wilkinson J., himself, in *White* v. *London Transport Executive*[50] and *Wadham Stringer Commercials (London) Ltd.* v. *Brown*.[51] In the first, he thought it unwise to imply anything so detailed as an obligation to "support, assist, offer guidance to and train" during a probationary period. Even more strange, in view of his remarks three months later

---

[42] [1978] I.R.L.R. 332.
[43] See also Slynn J. in *Palmanor Ltd.* v. *Cedron* [1978] I.R.L.R. 303 " . . . so unreasonably that it really went beyond the limits of the contract."
[44] [1980] I.R.L.R. 347.
[45] [1977] I.R.L.R. 29.
[46] [1979] I.R.L.R. 84.
[47] [1978] I.C.R. 401.
[48] In the *Post Office* v. *Roberts, supra*, the Tribunal suggested a list of conduct having the effect of discharging the other party from carrying out its contractual obligations. But this only begs the question of how to assess the effect of conduct on the contract.
[49] [1981] I.C.R. 666, overruled by the C.A., scarcely on a different ground but without damage to the principle, [1982] I.C.R. 693.
[50] [1981] I.R.L.R. 261.
[51] [1983] I.R.L.R. 46.

in *Woods*[52] about cumulative effect is his isolation of each of a series of what he described as minor incidents.[53] In the second, where a "squeezing down" similar to, and at least as serious as that in *Woods* had occurred, which the court described as "demotional degradation," applying the adjective "intolerable" to aspects of it, the E.A.T. preferred to find two specific implied terms at least as detailed as those rejected in *White*. This, it is submitted, is in sharp contrast to *British Aircraft Corporation Ltd.* v. *Austin*,[54] where, despite an indisputable implication of a duty to take reasonable care, the E.A.T. was prepared to regard a single, though lengthy, delay as sufficiently intolerable to amount to a destruction of trust and confidence. In this period only the decision of Talbot J. in *Post Office* v. *Roberts*,[55] adds anything significant to the discussion of "trust and confidence" and that addition is to caution that the conduct must be sufficiently serious to prevent the proper carrying out by the victim of the obligations of employer or employee.[56]

It was thus that Browne-Wilkinson J. was justified in *Woods* v. *W.M. Car Services*[57] in recognising that the existence of an implied obligation to sustain trust and confidence was widely accepted. But it would be very difficult to go any further than that in order to seek to explain when that obligation might be said to be broken:

> "In our view," he said,[58] "it is clearly established that there is implied in a contract of employment a term that the employers will not, without reasonable and proper cause, conduct themselves in a manner calculated or likely to destroy or seriously damage the relationship of confidence and trust between employer and employee. To constitute a breach of this implied term it is not necessary to show that the employer intended any repudiation of the contract; the tribunal's function is to look at the employer's conduct as a whole and determine whether it is such that its effect, judged reasonably and sensibly, is such that the employee cannot be expected to put up with it. The conduct of the parties has to be looked at as a whole and its cumulative impact assessed.[59] We regard this implied term as one of great importance in good industrial relations."

In fact, neither Browne-Wilkinson's definition nor any of the earlier cases suggest that the duty is very extensive. Where the cases had entered on such a duty, and the instances, as we have shown, are few, they had tended to emphasise the negative aspect of intolerable conduct rather than the positive aspect of consideration. This passage, therefore, correctly states that position. On the other hand, the passage, perhaps inadvertently, concentrates on

---

[52] *Supra*.

[53] Later in *Lewis* v. *Motorworld Garages Ltd.* ([1985] I.R.L.R. 465, Ackner L.J. suggested that the accumulation of a series of minor breaches of trust and confidence could add up to a repudiatory breach. But one wonders how there can be *minor* breaches of trust and confidence. Surely it would be better to say that a series of acts lead to an eventual breakdown of trust and confidence. Neil L.J. seems to recognise this point.

[54] [1978] I.R.L.R. 332.

[55] [1980] I.R.L.R. 347.

[56] So too, *Gardner Ltd.* v. *Beresford* [1978] I.R.L.R. 63, decided before the obligation was seen as more than a duty not to teat arbitrarily.

[57] [1981] I.C.R. 666.

[58] At p. 670.

[59] So it must be correct that mere matters of dispute cannot be productive of a breach of trust and confidence: *Frank Wright Holdings Ltd.* v. *Punch* [1980] I.R.L.R. 217; *Financial Techniques Ltd.* v. *Hughes* [1981] I.R.L.R. 32.

the duty of the employer. All the previous consideration had looked at the obligation in the same light although, no doubt, it would have been accepted by all concerned that the duty, as was sometimes specifically said, was mutual. This was too much for the Court of Appeal. Mrs. Woods had had her pay increased by her former employer at the last moment before transfer and after the transferees had agreed to take on staff on their existing terms. She forcefully rejected suggestions that she should work longer for less money. She consulted a solicitor and, on his advice, collected a list of untoward incidents, each one probably trivial in itself but, as Lord Denning M.R. said, magnified by the parties out of all proportion until all trust and confidence was lost *on both sides*. Lord Denning, typically, concentrated on the factual discretion vested in a tribunal to decide whether the conduct in question amounted to a breach of the contractual duty. As to what that duty comprised, all he said, rather generally but categorically, was:

> "It is the duty of the employer to be good and considerate to his servants. Sometimes it is formulated as an implied term not to do anything likely to destroy the relationship of trust and confidence between them . . . the employer must be good and considerate to his servants. Just as a servant must be good and faithful, so an employer must be good and considerate."[60]

This is a very slapdash definition. The history of the development of trust and confidence, as we have seen, reveals all the courts resisting the temptation to adopt anything as wide and uncontrollable as "good and considerate" behaviour. Nor is the mutuality properly expressed by comparison with the employee's duty of faithful service, the content of which is wholly different. Watkins L.J. had the right balance of obligation when he said:

> "The obdurate refusal of the employee to accept conditions very properly and sensibly being sought to be imposed upon her was unreasonable."[61]

Whether he reached the right conclusion is another matter since to him "very properly" meant a prerogative right to introduce "improved business methods in furtherance of seeking success for their enterprise." Quite apart from anything else, it does not fit the facts for, as Fox L.J. said, "while the employer's attempts to vary the conditions of employment were *ill-advised*, they *did not persist in them*."[62] In the result none of the members of the Court of Appeal doubted a mutual duty to maintain trust and confidence, though one of them misstated it in a form neither previously recognised nor workable. Only Watkins L.J. actually applied the duty in reverse to the employer, overstating, as Fox L.J. recognises, the reasonableness of the employer's demands for contractual change.

Interestingly, if the obligation was conceived in the *ASLEF* case in 1972,[63] *Woods* case reveals its most noteworthy characteristic. Trust and confidence overlays the whole contract rather than applying to any particular part of the employment relationship. So it can be destroyed even though the contract is

---

[60] [1982] I.C.R. 693 at p. 698.
[61] At p. 702.
[62] At p. 705. Author's italics.
[63] *Supra.*

observed in all other respects.[64] We have seen that courts may impose terms, as a matter of law, by implication, in the gaps left by the parties "Trust and confidence" enables the courts to impose their view of the conduct essential to a working relationship to override unacceptable contractual provisions. The definition produced by Browne-Wilkinson J. in the overruled E.A.T. decision in *Woods* is most nearly founded on previous cases and is workable. He does not depart from the criteria applied by all, save Lord Denning and Watkins L.J., in regarding the duty as confined to conduct which cannot reasonably be tolerated and therefore necessarily rendering unworkable employment dependent on maintenance of a workable relationship. Even on that view such a duty would be capable of absorbing many other more specific obligations. In other decisions, however, Browne-Wilkinson J. makes no attempt to use it in that extended fashion. This seems to suggest that his reference to the industrial relations value of trust and confidence is intended to emphasise the aspect of relationships. It is, in fact, to the maintenance of personal relationships between employer and employee that all the decisions thus far have been devoted. It is, for instance, significant that no one would consider that the duty of trust and confidence would extend to the method of performance of the employee. If the courts, in extreme cases, are to look at the importation of something like a fiduciary obligation, as in *Sybron Corpn.* v. *Rochem*,[65] they will have to pursue a different line of development.

Confidentiality

The recent development of the employee's long established and usually implied duty to maintain his employer's trade secrets is of a wholly different kind but reveals policy considerations to an equal degree. Instead of a new term the courts have here radically revised an apparently well defined obligation.

The duty of confidentiality in the law of employment has always been derived from the contract of employment. Turner V.C., in *Morison* v. *Moat*,[66] noted that the duty of confidentiality could stem either from contract, equity or the protection of property. In that case he based his decision either on contract or equity. The equitable duty of confidentiality did not, however, develop greatly until the twentieth century.[67] By that time a duty implied into the contract of employment had been established. Despite the development of the equitable duty[68] employment law has continued to rely on contract. Despite more than a century of usage many of the elements of the duty of confidentiality remain unclear. The search for likely development would obviously be greatly assisted if the two strands could be said to produce the same principles. In the fourth edition of this book[69] a high degree of similarity was asserted largely by relying on the contention that the content of an

---

[64] *B.B.C.* v. *Beckett* [1983] I.R.L.R. 43.

[65] [1983] I.R.L.R. 253, see Freedland (1984) 13 I.L.J. 25.

[66] (1851) 9 Hare 241.

[67] *Gartside* v. *Outram* (1856) 26 L.J.Ch. 113 is one of the few nineteenth century decisions clearly founded on equity.

[68] Fully examined in the Report of the Law Commission on Breach of Confidence, (1981) (Cmnd. 8388).

[69] At p. 74.

implied term, like the content of a principle of equity, would depend on what the courts considered reasonable. This has been revealed as a false syllogism; what is reasonable in respect of a former employee allegedly bound by a wide range of confidences is plainly different from what is reasonable for a fiduciary restricted by a duty applicable to a single piece of information acquired from a special relationship. It is, on this occasion, advisable to begin at the point thus reached by the Court of Appeal even though this will prove only a reverse turn in a continuing development.

It is unnecessary to explain the duty of an existing employee, as regards information he has received, in terms of confidentiality. His duty of faithful service will prevent him using, during his employment, a wide range of information concerning his employer's business other than for the purposes of that business. That duty obviously ceases when the relationship of service, from which it derives, ceases. The duty to respect confidentiality, or, as it has always been expressed in the law of employment, not to disclose trade secrets, continues after the employment has ended. For the sake of this discussion it does not matter whether that continuation is explicable as some sort of ancillary continuing contract or, as the present writer prefers it, no more than an obligation for the future springing from a contract which has been executed. Herein lurks the policy issue. An employee moving from one job to another takes with him an accumulation of knowledge and experience. It is his stock in trade. If he is to be prevented from displaying some of it because it is regarded as acquired in confidence during previous employment he is a less attractive proposition to his potential new employer. Everyone acquires this knowledge to some extent. Is everyone to be prevented from using it? If so, how should the courts define the limits of such restriction and, more fundamentally, what justification is there for that restriction? If the obligation is said to extend to information received in confidence, thus equating it to the equitable obligation, some rather awkward answers to the first of these questions are apparent. Equity seems to have settled that confidentiality can attach however trivial the information[70] and, though speaking of trade secrets, the law of employment appeared to have adopted the same view.[71] The "information" was restricted in the hands of an employee even though it could easily be acquired by others and it remained restricted even if others did acquire it, provided only that it had not, at the time of the defendant's acquisition, been sufficiently well known to be regarded as in the public domain.[72]

The courts, therefore, sought to distinguish confidentially acquired information from knowledge not readily severable from the employee's own store of accumulated knowledge, skill and experience.[73] This accumulated store could not be used against his employer's interest during employment if that would be a breach of the duty of fidelity, but it could be used by the employee freely thereafter.[74] The difficulty with this situation lies in defining what is in one category or the other. The decision in *Robb* v. *Green*[75] may be seen as

---

[70] *Underwater Welders and Repairers Ltd.* v. *Street and Longthorne* [1968] R.P.C. 498.
[71] *Cranleigh Precision Engineering Ltd.* v. *Bryant* [1965] 1 W.L.R. 1293.
[72] See, *Saltman Engineering Co. Ltd.* v. *Campbell Engineering Co. Ltd.* [1963] 3 All E.R. 413 n.; *Sun Printers Ltd.* v. *Westminster Press Ltd.* [1982] I.R.L.R. 292.
[73] See, *Printers and Finishers Ltd.* v. *Holloway* [1965] 1 W.L.R. 1.
[74] *Wessex Dairies Ltd.* v. *Smith* [1935] 2 K.B. 80.
[75] [1895] 2 Q.B. 315.

restraining use of a list of customers copied from a round-book before employment ends whilst permitting an approach to the same customers, whose identity is easily remembered, after that termination. The explanation is not in the use of a piece of paper belonging to the employer, yet the distinction between the same information acquired from the employer and subsequently stored in the employee's memory is difficult to comprehend. The existence of such an indefinable line raises a suspicion that it is drawn on the basis of a policy decision.

Even an obviously careful attempt to draw the line does not greatly assist clarity. In *Herbert Morris Ltd.* v. *Saxelby*,[76] for example, the distinction was expressed thus:

> "the general skill and knowledge which an employee of any ability must necessarily obtain as opposed to knowledge of any matter and skill in any process in which [the employer] could be said to have any property at all."

The Court of Appeal was almost certainly trying to avoid the appearance of discretion, so as to establish some certainty upon which a former employee could base his conduct when, in *Faccenda Chicken Ltd.* v. *Fowler*[77] it seized on the practice of referring to respect for trade secrets in employment law, as distinct from confidentiality in aspects of equitable obligation, to propound a difference between the scope of information involved. The court makes the point, incorrectly stated by the judge at first instance,[78] that the duty of fidelity is available to prevent the use even of the employee's own knowledge against his employer's interest during employment. It then goes on to sever the contractual duty from the equitable obligation, stating that in the law of employment the duty is to be governed by an implied term in the contract of employment. Presumably this means that an employer cannot invoke the equitable duty instead, even if it is clear that that duty would apply to the more trivial confidentiality he alleges to have been broken. In *Speed Seal Products Ltd.* v. *Paddington*[79] the plaintiffs' statement of claim had referred to an employee's duty in equity. It appears that employment is, in future, to be regarded as a relationship not giving rise to an equitable duty of confidentiality. This, hitherto unobserved, emphasis on the significant difference between trade secrets and confidential information forced the Court of Appeal for the first time to define that distinction and thus to create the fundamental characteristic of confidentiality in employment law. Unfortunately, the definition leaves as much to unfettered discretion as the former attempt to distinguish personal knowledge from information derived in confidence from an employer. The Court of Appeal made the following points:

(a) The nature of employment may give rise to a higher obligation where confidential information is habitually handled.

This test would be circular unless the Court of Appeal is intending to recognise two categories of confidential information, one of which is not protected by an enforceable obligation to respect that confidentiality. This, it is submitted, is exactly what the Court has in mind since

---

[76] [1916] 1 A.C. 688 at 711.
[77] [1986] I.R.L.R. 69.
[78] [1985] 1 All E.R. 724.
[79] [1986] 1 All E.R. 91.

it had earlier referred to information confidential in the sense only that its disclosure would be a breach of the duty of fidelity. This is to confuse what it had been at pains to distinguish. The duty of fidelity has no connection with confidentiality. What the Court probably means, therefore, is that where the nature of employment requires a high level of fidelity and the habitual handling of information is a characteristic of that employment there will be an indication that the information should be protected but only by the restricted implication of confidentiality as applicable to "trade secrets."

(b) The nature of the material, which will only be protected if it requires protection.

As the Court of Appeal itself points out this is to borrow one aspect of the limitation on enforcement of restrictive covenants. A protection which is not necessary will not be granted. Clearly there is a similarity in effect upon the former employee of a covenant excluding him from seeking employment with competitors in a particular industry and of an obligation not to disclose to competitors information relevant to the working of that industry. In the case of a restrictive covenant, however, the courts, albeit in a somewhat rough and ready fashion, go further than merely to ask whether the protection is necessary. They endeavour to balance protection for the employer with freedom for the employee. They do this primarily by demanding temporal, spacial and industrial limits to the restriction. In other words, a consideration of the nature of the material may well indicate that it requires protection from some user at some time. In the case of trade secrets, does the Court of Appeal intend a positive answer to indicate the need to define the material as totally protected for all time? This would make nonsense of the implicit analogy with public policy as applied to restrictive covenants. The inclusion of this factor in the test does however, plainly indicate that the Court is concerned with the policy of balancing employer and employee interests, even if it has not worked out the detailed problems of doing so.

The remaining two tests are of less significance:

(c) Whether the employer impressed confidentiality on the employee. This shows the defect of test (a) in that it seems hardly relevant to the question whether information falls within a narrow category that the supplier of that information regarded it as falling within a wider category. Information which an employer regards as sensitive may well constitute a trade secret within the narrow category but his insistence on confidence can only indicate that the information falls in a category which may not attract protection. In any event, if an employee is not bound by ordinary confidentiality how can the insistence on that confidentiality indicate the imposition of an enforceable restriction on him?

(d) Whether the information in question can be isolated from the employee's own knowledge.

As has been indicated this is simply the test of the law of ordinary confidentiality for determining whether the information belongs to the employer so that he can impose confidentiality upon it. It is no help in deciding between the wide and narrow concepts of confidentiality envisaged in this judgment.

In the end the only really useful guidance is to be derived from the incontrovertible fact that the Court of Appeal did regard confidential information as a wider category than it wished to protect by an implied term in the contract of employment. It clearly envisaged a narrower subdivision of confidential information which, for convenience, it chose to designate by the old employment law title of trade secret. It gave as examples, manufacturing processes, designs or special methods of construction. Unfortunately, it added "other information of a sufficiently high degree of confidentiality as to amount to a trade secret." The common factors, however, are plainly intended to be significant material directly relevant to production or the conduct of the business. It is this final alternative which remains to be resolved. On it depends protection of such matters as price lists, wage rates, and customer lists. All these have been protected in the past. The indication is that the Court of Appeal did not intend some of them to be protected in the future since it refused protection to sales information relating to the requirements of customers and the prices they paid. There is no doubt, therefore, of one thing. The range of information protected since this decision is considerably narrower than it was before and the former employee is, therefore, much more free to use accumulated knowledge. In virtually every particular case the distinction between an employee's knowledge and experience and his employer's trade secrets should now be obvious.

The price of this attempt to introduce greater definition is the production of an unprotected category of confidential information belonging to a former employer, but which falls short of "trade secrets."

The definition of a trade secret offered by the Court of Appeal in *Faccenda*[80] depends, it is submitted, upon the importance, in its trade context, of the information. It has nothing necessarily to do with whether that information is from some source obviously belonging to the employer or is in the employee's head. It is submitted, therefore, that the Court of Appeal should have felt no difficulty, in *Johnson and Bloy (Holdings) Ltd.* v. *Wolstenholme Rink PLC*[81] in dealing with the argument that though the employee had taken away documents relating to the formulation of certain printing inks, much of the information in question was remembered by him. The comment that he could scarcely complain if an injunction restricted the use of his knowledge, since it was his removal of confidential information which caused the problem may reveal good policy but has little legal basis to support it. The decision in *Roger Bullivant Ltd.* v. *Ellis*[82] is more significant. The respondent, while still in the employment, as Managing Director, of a division of the appellant company acquired a company which became the vehicle of a new business operating in competition with the appellant. The respondent took with him a vast number of documents, including a card index listing the appellant's trade contacts. These were recovered by injunction. Subsequently, the High Court granted an injunction restraining the respondent, and other employees who had left to work for the new company, from entering into, or fulfilling, con-

---

[80] *Supra.*
[81] [1987] I.R.L.R. 499.
[82] [1987] I.R.L.R. 491 (C.A.).

tracts with any person either recorded in the card index or who had been approached while that index was in their possession. The Court of Appeal considered that the material was not a trade secret. The fact that Ellis was in a fiduciary position might have caused it to restrict to that extent the *Faccenda* exclusion of equitable confidentiality from the law of employment had it not been for the need to restrain non-fiduciaries as well. The Court pointed out, however, that the limiting effect of the exclusion of other confidential information in *Faccenda* may not be as extensive as it appears. Unless confidential information other than trade secrets is memorised by the employees the act of carrying it away in documentary form, which will usually occur whilst the employee is still employed, will offend the duty of fidelity applied in *Robb* v. *Green*[83] This obscures the fact that that duty is not dependent even on the existence of confidential information. It seems that we cannot, after all, escape the task of making the distinction between information belonging to the employer, which may not be carried away by the employee during his employment, and information belonging to the employee, unless we accept the somewhat absurd proposition that the employee who can memorise confidential information short of trade secrets is free to use if after his employment ends provided he does not inextricably mix it with documentary information he amasses during his employment in case his memory fails.

Fidelity

During employment the need to protect the employee's freedom to trade is not relevant. Nevertheless the extent of faithfulness required of him is unsettled and the explanation is that, more than almost any other implied term, the actual content of this one will depend on the nature of the employment. The contract of employment is not a contract *uberrimae fidei*[84] nor is an employee (as distinct from a company director) in a fiduciary position. This leaves many specific obligations falling under the general head of fidelity capable of being implied into the contract of employment. The interest lies in what is not so included.

It is well known that in *Bell* v. *Lever Bros. Ltd.* a majority of the House of Lords refused to imply a duty to disclose the employee's own breaches of contractual duty. Familiarity with this proposition, usually from a very early stage in his legal studies, seems to have prevented as much expression of surprise by the student as the situation merits. Business efficacy could easily have been invoked in respect of a post such as that held by *Bell*, who could have commanded little sympathy. The amount of money he received of which disclosure would undoubtedly have deprived him was large. The only reason for not implying such a duty seems to have been an inbred feeling that a person should not be required to incriminate himself. This, however, is an overstatement of the position since the issue in this case was whether the defrauded payer could recover a sum of money. This compares strangely with the well established rule that an employee must account for the smallest secret profit.[85] The rule is not likely to yield to the movement we have already

---

[83] [1895] 2 Q.B. 315.
[84] *Bell* v. *Lever Bros. Ltd.* [1932] A.C. 161.
[85] *Boston Deep Sea Fishing and Ice Co. Ltd.* v. *Ansell* ((1888) 39 Ch.D. 339).

noticed[86] to withhold, rather than recover, wages paid for non-performance but the difference in the end result appears somewhat anomalous. Perhaps most surprising of all is the failure of the House of Lords to imply a term in the particular contract whilst leaving employees generally free from the obligation of disclosure. A later court[87] also hesitated to do this, preferring to interpret an express term to include the obligation. It is strange how courts which are very ready to individualise the detail of established implied terms are almost always reluctant to decide that new obligations should be implied at all on an individual basis. Perhaps, in 1932, the line between a director who has a fiduciary duty of disclosure[88] and a senior member of management, who has not, was more sharply defined. These days, the active members of most Boards of Directors are senior employees. So far as the duties of employees are concerned it is somewhat unreal to draw the line between Board membership and non-membership. It is suggested, therefore, that the decision in *Sybron Corporation* v. *Rochem Ltd.*[89] is indicative of an awareness of the key position in which senior management is placed in respect of the well being of the employer, whether or not the individual is a director. As Freedland points out[90] the relationship between the "high discretion—high reward" category of employee and the employer is one in which commitment and the sacrifice of personal interest are taken for granted. It is ludicrous to suppose that the implication of obligations for high trust employees should be based on decisions relating to low trust employees as if there had to be some common basic term. The argument in *Sybron* supports no such general distinction. It only goes so far as to extend the concept of an individual obligation developed in *Swaine* v. *West*[91] beyond interpretation to implication. It did not impose a duty, even on a high trust employee, to disclose his own misdeeds. Stephenson L.J. points out, however, that the House of Lords in *Bell* v. *Lever Bros.* lays down no rule as to the obligation to disclose the shortcomings of other employees. Whilst refusing to disturb *Swaine*'s conclusion that there was no general implication of such a duty, he finds no need to go further than to accept the finding in that case that the circumstances of a particular contract may give rise to a duty of disclosure. It is suggested that this decision will, in practice, alter the understanding of the law far·more radically. It must be standard practice for senior management not only to disclose what they know of other employees but actively to seek to acquire such information. If that is what is expected of them a decision suggesting that they might be obliged to do so is likely to receive ready acceptance. It is, however, too early to give any confident prediction. In *Horcal Ltd.* v. *Gatland*[92] an employee was held to have no obligation to disclose what, at the time of the contract which the employer sought to set aside, was no more than an anticipation of fraudulent

---

[86] Pp. 76 *et seq. supra* and see *Miles* v. *Wakefield Metropolitan Borough Council* [1987] I.C.R. 368; *Sim* v. *Rotherham Metropolitan Borough Council* [1986] I.C.R. 897.

[87] *Swain* v. *West (Butchers) Ltd.* [1936] 3 All E.R. 261.

[88] *Regal (Hastings) Ltd.* v. *Gulliver* (1941) [1967] 2 A.C. 134 n.

[89] [1983] I.C.R. 801.

[90] *High Trust, Pensions and the Contract of Employment*, (1984) 13 I.L.J. 25 at 33 relying on Alan Fox: *Beyond Contract: Work Power and Trust Relations* (Faber 1974).

[91] *Supra*.

[92] [1983] I.R.L.R. 459.

behaviour. Since the employee in question was the managing director and so in a recognised fiduciary position, Glidewell J.'s statement that he would have imposed a duty of disclosure had the fraud produced a secret profit at the time is unsurprising. It may well be that the Courts will come to refer to fiduciary duties in this field as if they first had to equate the particular employee with a fiduciary before attaching a duty of disclosure.

If disclosure is presently the salient where the break-through is most likely to occur there are a number of other aspects of fidelity which may be extended on the basis of individualised implication. The duty of active co-operation, rejected by the Court of Appeal in *Secretary of State for Employment* v. *ASLEF (No.)*[93] appears a great deal more viable if it is the unrelieved senior manager, rather than the signalman, who is required to stay beyond the end of his normal working hours. The decision of the Court of Appeal in *Hivac Ltd.* v. *Park Royal Scientific Instruments Ltd.*[94] might produce less sleeplessness among students if it were "individualised." It is accepted that it cannot have intended to suggest a general obligation not to work for another in the employee's spare time. Earlier editions of this book have pointed out that the judgment of Lord Greene M.R. relies largely on the need to restrain the risk of passing trade secrets. But in *Nova Plastics Ltd.* v. *Froggatt*[95] the E.A.T. suggested that spare time work causing great harm to the employer could amount to a breach of the implied obligation of loyal service. Of course, the amount of harm actually done can have no bearing on the evidence of an implied term. What is relevant is the potential harm that an individual can do. The threat of disclosure of trade secrets may have proved a useful basis for an injunction in *Hivac* but it is possible that the Court of Appeal was really thinking of the plaintiff's monopoly of the skilled labour force in question. In *Nova Plastics* the industrial tribunal may have come nearer to a general principal than the E.A.T. was prepared to acknowledge when they said that, as an odd job man, the employee's spare time activities would not constitute a breach of trust.

If any one of these developments of the implied term is singled out for examination it can be described variously as indicative of a pluralist or unitary approach or, alternatively, as a recognition of the predominance of management prerogative over employee interest or, conversely, of a need to recognise employee expectations. A few judges such as Browne-Wilkinson J. may have been pursuing some such consistent policy but most are likely to have behaved more pragmatically. The trend is to incorporate into contractual obligations what the courts see as the expectations of the parties. The law, to that extent, follows rather than leads the development of the employment relationship. This process gives rise to noticeable swings in opinion over quite short periods. "Trust and confidence" was undoubtedly developed with a view to protecting an employee's expectation of fair treatment. It's inherent mutuality made it always prone to a swing in the other direction and this duly occurred when it appeared to support resistance to change. Exactly the same swing occurred in respect of job expectation as between decisions which pro-

---

[93] [1972] I.C.R. 19.
[94] [1946] Ch. 169.
[95] [1983] I.R.L.R. 146.

tected an employee's expectation of particular types of work[96] and those which emphasised obligation to accept changes of method.[97]

Employee inventions

The common law

In *Cranleigh Precision Engineering Co. Ltd.* v. *Bryant*[98] the plaintiff's managing director had acquired a patent directly relevant to the plaintiff's products and had used it for his own purposes. Undoubtedly he was under a duty to disclose the information thus acquired but it seems clear that that duty only arose because of the fiduciary relationship which he had as a director. An employee ordinarily is not in a fiduciary relationship. Nevertheless, there is no doubt that at common law an employee is under a duty to disclose to his employer information relevant to what the employee is employed to do. This is certainly true of information which the employee has discovered; *a fortiori* it would seem to apply to similar information which he derives from other sources unless, of course, a duty of confidentiality exists between the employee and that other source.

In *British Reinforced Concrete Co. Ltd.* v. *Lind*[99] the defendant employee was employed in the plaintiffs' drawing office to work out designs and calculations for tenders for supporting roofs of mines. While doing this he worked out a method more satisfactory than that used by his employer. Eve J. held that as the plaintiff was employed to work out solutions to this problem he was bound to offer the best solution he could devise. His employer was, therefore, entitled to secure the details of the new method.

This line of reasoning was developed further in *British Syphon Co. Ltd.* v. *Homewood*[1] where the defendant, while in charge of the plaintiffs' design and development department, designed and patented an improved form of sodawater syphon. Roxburgh J. held that he was employed to give his employer his best service in the broad field of design related to his employer's undertaking. It is clear that, conversely, at common law an invention in the employee's time which does not impinge on what he is employed to do and does not use confidential information would remain the property of the inventor.[2] It is only fair to point out that the judgment of Roxburgh J. in the *British Syphon* case raises some problems. The learned judge said:

"It is common ground that the defendant had not been expressly asked to design any new methods of dispensing soda water by a low-pressure system or any other system, and that he had not been asked to give any advice in relation to any such problem. This is the circumstance which, as far as I can see, differentiates this case from all that have gone before. . . . He was employed to give the plaintiffs technical advice in relation to the design or development of anything connected

---

[96] *Breach* v. *Epsylon Industries Ltd.* [1976] I.C.R. 316; *D. A. Coleman* v. *S. & W. Baldwin* [1977] I.R.L.R. 342.
[97] *e.g. Cresswell* v. *Board of Inland Revenue* [1984] I.R.L.R. 190
[98] (1965) 1 W.L.R. 1293.
[99] (1917) 116 L.T. 243. See also *Triplex Safety Glass Co. Ltd.* v. *Scorah* [1938] 1 Ch. 211; *Sterling Engineering Co. Ltd.* v. *Patchett* [1955] A.C. 534.
[1] [1956] 1 W.L.R. 1190.
[2] *Re Selz Ltd.'s Application* (1953) 71 R.P.C. 158.

with any part of the plaintiffs' business. No particular problem had been put before him, but if, and as often as, any problem of that kind was put before him, it was his duty to be ready to tender his advice and to assist in any matter of design or development. He was paid to stand by in that respect. He had other functions, but those are not material to the present case.

Would it be consistent with good faith, as between master and servant, that he should in that position be entitled to make some invention in relation to a matter concerning a part of the plaintiffs' business and either keep it from his employer, if and when asked about the problem, or even sell it to a rival and say: 'Well, yes, I know the answer to your problem, but I have already sold it to your rival'? In my judgment, that cannot be consistent with a relationship of good faith between a master and a technical adviser. It seems to me that he has a duty not to put himself in a position in which he may have personal reasons for not giving his employer the best advice which it is his duty to give if and when asked to give it.

He has a duty to be free from any personal reason for not giving his employer the best possible advice. *A fortiori*, it seems to me that he is not entitled to put himself into the position of being able to say: 'You retained me to advise you, and I will tell you what I advise you. Do it this way, but you will have to buy the method from your rival, because I have just sold it to him, having invented it yesterday.' That seems to me to be reasoning which, in the absence of authority, makes it right and proper for me to decide that this invention (which, in my judgment, plainly relates to and concerns the business of the plaintiffs, namely, the distribution of soda water to the public in containers of a satisfactory character), if made during a time during which the chief technician is standing by under the terms of his employment, must be held to be in equity the property of the employer. Accordingly, my decision is for the plaintiffs."

It is apparent, therefore, that the common law bears particularly severely on more senior employees, research workers and those with a wider remit, since it is they to whom the implied obligation will most significantly extend. Nevertheless, it is less clear than may once have been the case that an employer can say that he purchases the whole potential of an employee who has no special position within a given area. This is what Sir John Donaldson thought in *Seaboard World Airlines Inc.* v. *Transort and General Workers Union*[3] and it is depressingly reminiscent of the reasoning in *Turner* v. *Mason*[4] Logically the approach of Roxburgh J. would mean that an employer would acquire inventions and patents belonging to any employee at the time of his engagement if they were within the field of his employment. As early as 1903[5] it had been said that it did not follow that the obligation was so extensive in all cases. The employee in no special position and not expected to make discoveries may not be subject to any obligation to disclose them if made. Nevertheless the cases cited are considered to represent the current state of the common law as to information in the hands of an employee who can be expected to be in a position to acquire such information. The only reservation that seems to have been made concerns information which would affect the interests of a fellow employee.[6]

---

[3] [1973] I.C.R. 458.
[4] (1845) 14 M. & W. 112.
[5] *Worthington Pumping Engine Co.* v. *Moore* (1903) 20 R.P.C. 41 at 48.
[6] *Swain* v. *West (Butchers) Ltd.* [1936] 3 All E.R. 261.

The Patents Act 1977

The common law in this respect has been largely replaced by the provisions of the Patents Act 1977. In part this Act was a response to the effect of the normal common law term upon employees with widely defined obligations. In part also it was intended to deal with a problem arising from the employer's use of freedom of contract to impose upon employees who were likely to make discoveries express obligations of even greater scope. The most senior employees might reasonably be said to accept such an obligation in return for their remuneration but the obligation at common law extended to all types of information and so might easily include unspectacular but useful ideas which could be said to be within the scope of virtually any employment. It is, moreover, true to say that no employee could claim possession of an idea derived from, or as a development upon, his employer's property. This would include any improvement upon any piece of information which the employee had received in confidence.

Statute defines the property rights in an invention as between the employer and employee as follows:

> **39.**—(1) Notwithstanding anything in any rule of law, an invention made by an employee shall, as between him and his employer, be taken to belong to his employer for the purposes of this Act and all other purposes if—
>
> (*a*) it was made in the course of the normal duties of the employee or in the course of duties falling outside his normal duties, but specifically assigned to him, and the circumstances in either case were such that an invention might reasonably be expected to result from the carrying out of his duties; or
>
> (*b*) the invention was made in the course of the duties of the employee and, at the time of making the invention, because of the nature of his duties and the particular responsibilities arising from the nature of his duties he had a special obligation to further the interests of the employer's undertaking.
>
> (2) Any other invention made by an employee shall, as between him and his employer, be taken for those purposes to belong to the employee.

This extends to joint inventions but not to inventions of others to which the employee has merely contributed advice or assistance.[7]

This leaves a lot of questions unanswered. The first ground of obligation requires that the employment should be such than an invention, but not *the* invention, might reasonably be expected to result from carrying out his duties. The duties of more senior employees, as we have said, may be very wide. The invention, it is said, must be made in the course of normal duties. This presumably refers not to the contractual duties but to those that it is normal for the employee to perform within the contract. Again, however, it may be difficult in the case of more senior employees to say which duties which they sometimes perform are "normal." The second limb imposes the obligation in respect of inventions made in the course of duty, and not "normal" duty. It is arguable, therefore, that this refers to contractual duties and such an interpretation is the more likely since it will be to the contract that the courts are likely to look to see whether a special obligation arises. It is clear that the courts are left free to decide when to imply such a special obligation

---

[7] s.43(3).

from the nature of the duties. It should be noted, however, that it must be possible to imply such an obligation. An express statement of such an obligation in circumstances which would not otherwise support its implication will not satisfy the test.

An employer would be free by contract to define the employee's duty of confidentiality widely so as to catch as large an area as possible in which the employee's inventions were developments upon such confidential information.[8] Otherwise it is not only impossible for there to be a valid term in the contract of employment diminishing the employee's rights as defined in section 39; but also the employee may not validly dispose of his invention by any advance contract to his employer or to anyone else at the request of the employer. Section 42 provides that no such contract may diminish the rights of an employee in inventions made by him after the date of the contract. An employee is, therefore, free to dispose of inventions he has already made even to his employer.

Even there, however, the employee is protected from disposing of his invention for an inadequate return. When the employee assigns, or grants an exclusive licence over, his *patented* invention to his employer, he may apply to the court or the Comptroller who may decide that the benefit derived by the employee from the assignment or grant is inadequate in relation to the benefit derived by the employer and that it is just to increase that benefit.

Where the employee's *patented* invention vests in the employer under section 39 a similar application may be made. In that case, however, the court or Comptroller must be satisfied that the patent is of oustanding benefit to the employer having regard to the size and nature of the employer's undertaking and that by reason of those facts it is just that the employee should be compensated. In either case compensation shall be such as will secure for the employee a fair share of the benefit the employer has derived, or may reasonably be expected to derive, from the patent or from any further dealing with it. In both cases, however, the jurisdiction may be excluded where a relevant collective agreement (within the meaning of the Trade Union and Labour Relations Act 1974) provides for compensation in respect of inventions of the same description to employees of the same description. The collective agreement in question must be one by or on behalf of a trade union to which the employee belongs and which is in force at the time of making the invention.

Protection of rights on a transfer of undertakings

The collective agreement and consultative aspects of transfer under the Transfer of Undertakings (Protection of Employment) Regulations 1981[9] are discussed elsewhere.[10] We shall here deal with the effect of the Regulations on transfer of individual contractual and statutory rights.

The Regulations are the United Kingdom government's, somewhat tardy, response to its obligation to implement EEC Council Directive 187 of February 14, 1977, called the "Acquired Rights" Directive. They were originally drafted and laid before Parliament in 1978, when they were withdrawn for redrafting. Three years after the two year implementation period for the

---

[8] s.42(3).
[9] S.I. 1981/1794.
[10] See pp. 287–289, *infra*.

Directive had expired, they were again laid before the House of Commons in December 1981, "with a remarkable lack of enthusiasm,"[11] only because the Commission had decided to take action against the United Kingdom for failure to implement the Directive. There is good reason to believe that the Regulations still do not satisfy the Directive. Unfortunately the method of enactment by way of Regulation under the European Communities Act, 1972,[12] though quick, has meant that the provisions have not been merged with existing statutory provisions. The continuity provisions of E.P.C.A. 1978, Sched. 13 relating to continuity of employment, therefore, operate in parallel to Regulation 5 which provides for the automatic transfer of both contractual and statutory rights relating to the contract of employment. If an employee is dismissed a day or two before the transfer and re-engaged immediately afterwards, he may rely on the Schedule but not on the Regulations, but the latter may refer to a wider range of working relationships than employment and to transferred contractual rights as well as merely continuity for statutory purposes.

The most surprising feature of the Regulations is their limitations. They are confined to the transfer of commercial organisations said, rather unconvincingly,[13] to require an interest in financial return, by which one assumes is meant profit. The effect of such a provision on tribunals used to somewhat impressionistic judgment is shown in *Haddow* v. *University of Dundee Students' Association*[14] where the E.A.T. held that the catering activities of a university students' union, the object of which was, at least, to break even, were not trading in the full sense of the word. As with the provisions for continuity of employment there must be an identifiable business to transfer.[15]

Most significantly, however, the Regulations transfer only the rights of those employees in the employment of the transferor immediately before the transfer. In *Teesside Times Ltd.* v. *Drury*,[16] when dealing with E.P.C.A. 1978, Sched. 13, the Court of Appeal, *obiter*, had clearly treated transfer as a process. A number of decisions under these Regulations did so with the result that it seemed that a transferee wishing to avoid the effect of the Regulations would have to dismiss employees at least a week before completion of the transfer. The Court of Appeal overruled these decisions in *Secretary of State* v. *Spence*.[17] The transferor had dismissed his workforce at 11 a.m. on November 28, 1983. They were re-employed by the transferee the next morning, three hours after the completion of the transfer. The Court of Appeal held that they were not employed immediately before the transfer. In *Brook Lane Finance Co. Ltd.* v. *Bradley*[18] at the date of the completion of the transfer the employee in question was already employed by the transferee. He had moved into the service of the latter once the transfer had been settled and largely to help prepare the way for it. The E.A.T. held that the com-

---

[11] H.C.Deb. Vol. 14 cols. 677, 680, 695 and 696.
[12] s.2(2).
[13] *Woodcock* v. *Committee of the Friends School* ([1987] I.R.L.R. 98).
[14] [1985] I.R.L.R. 449.
[15] *BIFTU* v. *Barclays Pank PLC, The Times*, March 21, 1987.
[16] [1980] I.C.R. 338.
[17] [1986] I.R.L.R. 248.
[18] [1988] I.C.R. 423 (E.A.T.); See also *Wheeler* v. *Patel* [1987] I.R.L.R. 211, *Forth Estuary Engineering Ltd.* v. *Lister* [1988] I.R.L.R. 289.

pletion date is the date on which, in law, ownership changes, exactly as at the sale of a house. It discussed the contrary view in *Teesside* v. *Drury* but discarded that authority as *obiter* and upon a different legislative provision.

The regulations make provision for transfer by a series of transactions but only when these occur between the same parties. In *Forth Estuary Engineering Ltd.* v. *Lister*[19] it was pointed out that there was nothing to prevent a series of transactions between different parties, relating to a transfer of business by one of those transactions, resulting in a transfer of the business taking place between two of these parties. If this is right it seems that the provision relating to a series of transactions is largely useless. There will usually be a series of transactions in the transfer of the business but, equally usually, one of them will operate to pass the title. That will be the transfer and that will fix the moment at which employees will be transferred. In more complicated interactions where "the business is inextricably mixed" in the hands of several parties, the provision for a series of transactions will not apply anyway.

There exists in the United Kingdom a practice, largely adopted by the receivers of insolvent companies known as "hiving down." Typically, the receiver transfers the assets of a company to another company—usually a wholly owned subsidiary of the first. Because the two are separate legal entities this gives the receiver a wholly advantageous package of assets to sell, shorn of its liabilities. One of the most significant of such liabilities is the accumulated rights of existing employees. The employees, therefore, are retained by the original, insolvent, company. Their services are loaned to the wholly owned subsidiary which continues to operate the business. In due course when a purchaser is found he will decide which of these employees he wishes to engage and they will be transferred from the original insolvent company to the purchaser, bypassing the operating company whose business the purchaser has, in law, acquired. Those employees who are not wanted become redundant. Their accumulated compensation rights will be met by the original company, or if it is unable to do so, by the Secretary of State for employment.[20] If the automatic transfer provisions were to operate normally they would transfer all the employees to the subsidiary operating company and thence to the purchaser and the economic value of the device would be lost. Other EEC countries might not object to this loss since hiving down provides the opportunity of a hidden subsidy for the costs of business transfer. The United Kingdom government seems, however, to have been able to agree with the Commission a concession in this respect similar to the creation of a timeless zone in the process advocated by Davies and Freedland,[21] but without any protection for the employees adversely affected. Under Regulation 4 the transfer to which the Regulations apply does not occur in this situation until either the intermediate transferee ceases to be a wholly owned subsidiary of the transferor, or the business is transferred to a third party. The effect is that there passes only then the rights and obligations of the employees then in the employment of the original transferor. This allows the ultimate purchaser time to decide which of them he wishes to take on along with the package of assets which he acquires by transfer of the subsidiary intermediary. The

---

[19] [1986] I.R.L.R. 59.
[20] See, *Pambakian* v. *Brentford Nylons Ltd.* [1978] I.C.R. 665 (E.A.T.).
[21] [1980] 9 I.L.J. 95 at 110.

rest of the employees will be dismissed as redundant by the insolvent company before the transfer of the going concern operated by the intermediary. Since that company no longer has a requirement for employees to loan to another, such dismissal is likely to be held to be fair. Professor Hepple[22] questions whether this device is compatible with Article 3(1) of the Directive which does not provide for such a loophole in the requirement for contractual rights to be transferred. As it has turned out, however, the loophole seems considerably less widespread and rather more complex to operate than that obtained by the simple process of dismissing the employees a few hours before the relevant transfer.

If a case arises in which a transferor or transferee is affected by the Regulations it seems likely that it will be by accident or neglect. In *Premier Motors Ltd.* v. *Total Oil*[23] for instance, the possibility arose that an overall owner of premises to whom a franchise reverted for a few moments before it was passed to another might be caught in the web. No doubt, large companies likely to be in such a position have long since decided on a course of evasive action.

Should the Regulations apply they will transfer all contractual and statutory rights and obligations of an employee from the transferor to the transferee. This extends beyond employment, strictly defined, to cover any individual who works for another "under a contract of service or apprenticeship or otherwise, but does not include anyone who provides services under a contract for services."[23a] It may well be, therefore, that casual workers, who have tended recently to be excluded from the category of employees, would be within the operation of these Regulations. In *Angus Jowett Ltd.* v. *NUTGW*[24] it was held that the statutory obligation of an employer to consult before a redundancy with recognised trade unions, imposed by section 99 of the E.P.A. 1975, was not transferred. The regulations speak of "all the transferor's rights, powers, duties and liabilities under or in connection with any such contract." The words "or otherwise arising in connection with the employment of a person" which had appeared in the 1978 draft did not recur in 1981.

It seems likely that statutory rights conferred upon the individual employee will be transferred. It was certainly the intention of the Directive that they should be.[25] On the other hand, Regulation 5 actually destroys some statutory rights. If the contract of employment is automatically transferred there is no dismissal. The affected employee cannot, as he could before the passing of the Regulations, opt to claim compensation for dismissal for redundancy from the transferor,[26] though he might have been met in this by the defence of suitable alternative offer. It is not clear whether the employee retains rights under his former contract with the transferor for such matters as arrears of pay and holiday entitlement or whether the transfer of his contract, including these rights, to the transferee operates, without his consent, as a novation of his contract. The transferred employee may be able to claim to have been

---

[22] [1982] 11 I.L.J. at p. 34.
[23] [1983] I.R.L.R. 471.
[23a] Reg. 2.
[24] [1985] I.R.L.R. 326.
[25] See also Lord Lyell in H.L.Deb., Vol. 425, cols. 1499–1500 (December 10, 1981.)
[26] But see *Lapman* v. *CPS Computer Group PLC*, *The Times*, June 30, 1987. "Redundancy" for other purposes is unaffected.

constructively dismissed by the transference if the latter imposes upon him a substantial change in contractual terms.[27] This is obvious since such a right exists against any employer who unilaterally imposes a change of contract.[28] The Regulations provide, however, that the mere change of employer is not such a change "unless the employee shows that in all the circumstances the change is a significant change and is to his detriment." If the transferor had committed such a breach of contract before the transfer and the employee had preserved that breach, for instance, by objection, he might exercise his right to accept the repudiation when he had moved into the employment of the transferee since Regulation 5 provides that anything done before the transfer is completed, by or in relation to the transferor, shall be deemed to have been done by or in relation to the transferee.

Regulation 8 adds a new ground of automatically unfair dismissal[29] wherever an employee is dismissed by the transferor or the transferee before or after the dismissal and the transfer, or a reason connected with it, is the reason, or principal reason, for the dismissal. This is, however, subject to a sweeping qualification where there is an "economic, technical or organisational reason entailing changes in the workforce of either the transferor or the transferee." If the employer is able to prove such a reason the transfer is to be regarded as being for some other substantial reason within E.P.C.A., s.57(3). A tribunal can then be asked to consider whether the dismissal for that reason was unfair.[30] In 1982[31] Professor Hepple argued that the word "entailing" should be construed to mean "giving rise, as a fact, to" so as to prevent the employer citing his own economic or organisational decision. As Professor Hepple then pointed out such a subjective business decision produces that subjective conclusion as a reason for dismissal in other cases of alleged unfairness. Other EEC countries are more likely to seek objective justification. This issue does not seem to have arisen in reported cases but, strangely, what might have seemed one of the most easily opened loopholes in the protection allegedly afforded by these Regulations has been construed narrowly by the courts. In *Wheeler* v. *Patel*[32] it was held that "economic" should be construed *ejusdem generis* (presumably with "organisational") so as to imply a limitation to the economics of running the business. The aim of the transferor to make a profit by ridding the business of unwanted employees was held not an economic reason. This appears to be in line with the concept of employee protection and reference to that context is probably a better basis for construction since, otherwise, the meaning of "social" would be severely limited. Of greater significance is the decision of the Court of Appeal

---

[27] Regulation 5(5).

[28] See, *Delabole Slate Ltd.* v. *Berriman* [1985] I.R.L.R. 305. The transferee may, however, alter the terms of the contract with the transferred employee by any means permitted by national law—*e.g.* by agreement—*Foreningen at Arbejdscedere I Danmart* v. *Daddy's Dance Hall* [1988] I.R.L.R. 315 (Eur. Ct. J.)

[29] See Chap. V, *infra*.

[30] *McGrath* v. *Rank Leisure Ltd.* [1985] I.R.L.R. 323. The fascinating argument that classification of such a reason as "some other substantial reason" prevented it being put forward, for other purposes, as "redundancy" was destroyed in *Gorictree Ltd.* v. *Jenkinson* [1984] I.R.L.R. 391.

[31] (1982) 11 I.L.J. at p. 37.

[32] [1987] I.R.L.R. 211 (E.A.T.). See also, *Gateway Hotels Ltd.* v. *Stewart* [1988] I.R.L.R. 287 (E.A.T. Sc.).

in *Delabole State Ltd.* v. *Berriman*[33] that the words "involving a change in the workforce" meant a change in the body of workers (*i.e.* usually a reduction). A change in terms of employment as, for instance, by reducing the wages of transferred employees to bring them into line with those already employed by the transferee, may lead to a constructive dismissal which will not be excused by the economic reason and so will be automatically unfair under Regulation 8(1).

---

[33] [1985] I.R.L.R. 305.

CHAPTER IV

TERMINATION OF EMPLOYMENT

At common law

We have seen that employment is a mixture of contract and law. It is certainly not recognised (or recognisable) as status.[1] On the other hand, the task of controlling and defining the relationship has been facilitated by the characteristic failure of the parties to the "contract" to specify large areas of terms and conditions necessary to provide the courts with answers to disputes of rights.

Termination is usually regarded as essentially a contractual concept and the relatively new statute law governing unfair dismissal is widely criticised on the ground that "dismissal" turns out not to be a specialised technical term but merely another name for termination of contract. The lack of specificity in that contract, however, permits a good deal of discretion. No one reading judgments in *Pepper* v. *Webb*[2] in search of clear definition of the repudiatory breach committed by the employee can fail to entertain the suspicion that the Court of Appeal was primarily concerned to endorse the conclusion that continuation of the relationship had become impossible. The development of the modern concept of maintenance of trust and confidence[3] has produced a comprehensible example of termination by breakdown translated into breach of contract. Clearly a great deal of practical reality can be accommodated within the boundaries of contract, no less in handling termination than in the solution of disputes during the continuation of the relationship. On the other hand, some of the most far-reaching solutions derive purely from the application of contractual principle. It must not be assumed that, because even fewer reported cases of wrongful dismissal will now appear than the sparse supply of the past century, these principles are unimportant. The effect of a repudiatory breach on the continuity of the contract and, even more, the availability of specific enforcement will continue to be of considerable importance not only to the common law but also to the operation of statutory remedies. A study of them will also help to reveal the artificiality of much contractual doctrine.

At the outset the fact has to be faced that the common law has never entirely cleared up the question of what it is that is terminated by dismissal or a voluntary leaving. But if termination of the contract were replaced by some idea of the ending of an employment relationship an explanation would be no clearer. It is probable that termination is generally evidenced by the purely visible ending of the wage/work bargain. Even here, however, care must be

---

[1] See Kahn-Freud: *A Note on Status and Contract in British Labour Law* (1967) 30 M.L.R. 635.
[2] [1969] 1 W.L.R. 514.
[3] See pp. 91–96, *supra*.

exercised since the bargain is not for work but for availability to work. A lock-out, for example, breaks the contract not because work ceases but because the obligation to pay for its availability is broken. In that situation it would generally not be said that the relationship has been terminated. Until recently, however, it would have been difficult to explain why this was so, save by resort to intention of one party and reaction of the other. Even where intention to terminate exists contractual doctrine may artificially perpetuate a dead relationship. It has already been seen that the duty to respect trade secrets outlives the employment situation. We shall shortly see that the law now recognises that all rights and duties survive the intention of one party to terminate them, save so far as the contract allows, until the other party accepts the repudiation.

Termination in response to repudiation

A repudiatory breach of contract confers upon the innocent party the option of waiving the breach and asserting continuation of the contract, whether or not in an altered form, or accepting the breach as putting an end to contractual obligations, subject to any remedies that may be available for breach. It has long been acknowledged that the existence of a repudiatory breach does not depend on moral considerations but purely upon determination of whether the guilty party can be said to be no longer prepared to carry out the contract.[4] Nothing in *Laws* v. *London Chronicle (Indicator Newspapers) Ltd.*[5] alters this principle. The Court of Appeal, after more than a century, was simply prepared to be more lenient in its view of what amounted to rejection of one or more of the fundamental obligations of the contract. The guilty party may, therefore, commit a repudiatory breach expecting the contract to survive. Nor are the actual consequences of the breach relevant.[6] Repudiation does not require rejection of every substantial contractual obligation. Refusal to obey a single order, if of sufficient moment, will indicate an intention not to be bound by a contract containing an obligation to obey orders.[7] Repudiation may be brought about, therefore, by a single act the effect of which is temporary.[8] Just as the question in such circumstances is solely whether the breach is sufficiently substantial to indicate rejection of the contractual obligation, so a breach not in itself sufficiently substantial may, if repeated, or accompanied by other breaches, indicate such an intention.[9] In practice, it is not uncommon for the employer to respond to a string of relatively minor shortcomings by a dismissal. There should be no difficulty in understanding why an accumulation of minor faults should be regarded as sufficiently substantial to indicate an intention to reject the contract.

What is more difficult to explain is why the fact that no action has been taken on each successive default should not be construed as a waiver. It could

---

[4] *Turner* v. *Mason* [1845] 14 M. and W. 112.
[5] [1959] 1 W.L.R. 698.
[6] *Savage* v. *British India Steam Navigation Co.* (1930) 46 T.L.R. 294.
[7] Lord Evershed in *Laws* v. *London Chronicle*, *supra*; *Blyth* v. *Scottish Liberal Club* [1983] I.R.L.R. 245.
[8] *McNeill* v. *Charles Crimin (Electrical Contractors) Ltd.* [1984] I.R.L.R. 179.
[9] *Lewis* v. *Motorworld Garages Ltd.* [1985] I.R.L.R. 465.

be argued that it is impossible to waive a breach which could not have been accepted as repudiatory, (although it is not clear that the Court of Appeal in *Lewis* v. *Motorworld Garages Ltd.*[10] either considered, or thought it necessary to consider, whether any of the series of breaches was in itself repudiatory), so that failure to act on it might have been construed as waiver of objection to it. Plainly it would be practical nonsense to expect a party to the contract of employment on each occasion of breach to engage in such enquiry. Nevertheless, failure to object to a repudiatory breach is clearly capable of being construed as waiver.[11] It looks very much as if an innocent party who does not object to what may be a repudiatory breach takes something of a gamble. If further breaches occur he may fortify their effect by the earlier breach; whilst, if they do not, he is likely to be prevented from asserting the repudiatory nature of the breach at a later stage.

The assertion of a mistaken view of a right supposed to derive from contract is not a repudiatory breach if it does not reveal an intention not to be bound by the contract as correctly construed.[12] Actual refusal to perform a present obligation in the mistaken belief that no such obligation exists, however, was held in *Blyth* v. *Scottish Liberal Club*[13] to amount to a repudiatory breach. It is submitted that this must be so since, however mistaken, there is a clear refusal to carry out an essential part of the contract. As Donaldson M.R. pointed out in *Bridgen* v. *Lancashire County Council*[14] it has to be shown that the party did not intend to be bound by the contract as properly construed. There will come a time when he will have to make up his mind to act on one view, thereby indicating an intention not to be bound by any other. It is probably not so much a question of distinction between the assertion of a view and a present refusal to perform, as suggested in *Blyth*[15] since this would tend to prevent any anticipatory breach constituting repudiation. The issue is whether the party concerned has committed himself to a position which, as it turns out, is or will produce a repudiatory breach or is continuing to argue the issue of one view as against another.

The reader will have noticed that nothing has yet been said to indicate any precise definition of a repudiatory breach. We know only that the repudiator must indicate an intention not to be bound by the contractual obligations, properly construed, even though this intention arises because he misunderstands those obligations. It is clear that breach of a single obligation, as also the attitude of mind demonstrated by the accumulation of a series of minor breaches will both suffice to demonstrate such an intention. But the student will be hard pressed to explain convincingly what it is that distinguishes a non-repudiatory breach (giving rise only to a claim for damages) from a repudiatory breach (allowing the innocent party to rescind the contract—and claim damages). It is not much help to say that the question is whether the breach precludes "further satisfactory continuance of the relationship."[16] The very

---

[10] [1985] I.R.L.R. 465.

[11] See *Burdett-Coutts* v. *Hertfordshire County Council* [1984] I.R.L.R. 91.

[12] *Financial Techniques Ltd.* v. *Hughes* [1981] I.R.L.R. 32.

[13] [1983] I.R.L.R. 245.

[14] [1987] I.R.L.R. 58.

[15] *Supra.*

[16] *Re. Rubel Bronze and Metal Co. and Vos* [1918] 1 K.B. 315; *Sinclair* v. *Neighbour* [1967] 2 Q.B. 279.

possibility of waiver indicates that in many situations it is the recipient, not the perpetrator of the act itself, who decides that. Perhaps the statement would have been more useful if the word "contract" had replaced "relationship" but then, of course, any departure by one party would prevent continuation of that particular contract. In *Hill* v. *C.A. Parsons and Co. Ltd.*[17] Sachs L.J. expressed the test as that of an act destroying the confidential relationship. In a particular situation such as that in *Boston Deep Sea Fishing and Ice Co. Ltd.* v. *Ansell*,[18] where it was first used, this is obviously an accurate description. It suited common law practice quite well since most dismissal claims were made by senior employees to whose position the description "confidential" might meaningfully be applied. As a matter of history it seems to have been this use of the expression as a test which led to the adoption as an obligation of the duty to maintain trust and confidence. Our discussion of that term, however, has revealed that it possesses only that meaning which examples of its application assign to it. Although one would not expect the judiciary to wish to be seen resorting to such apparent lack of technicality it is at least as meaningful to say that what is required is a "serious" or "significant" breach. It goes without saying that this assessment will depend on the relation of the act (and its consequences) to the nature of the employment.

It is sometimes necessary to distinguish between termination and repudiation (implying the possibility of continuation) in the field of employment because this is one of the few areas of contract where there is normally a right unilaterally to terminate the contract. In *Burdett-Coutts* v. *Hertfordshire County Council*[19] a letter giving notice of changes in conditions of employment, particularly involving a pay reduction, was held to indicate a repudiatory breach despite the fact that the employer could have given notice to terminate followed by an offer of the new terms. As the facts of this case indicate it is most likely that it will be apparent whether a termination was intended. If there is no such indication the courts will lean in favour of attempted unilateral variation. It is probably for this reason that courts prefer to regard notice of a change of job content rejected by the employee as constructive dismissal (that is, as we shall see, a deemed dismissal arising from employee objection to a repudiatory breach) rather than an actual dismissal arising from the fact that, with or without notice, termination of the contractual job has occurred. In practice, there is not likely to be much difficulty in the distinction. Absence of clear evidence of an intention to terminate the employment relationship will be construed as indicating an intention, whilst maintaining that relationship, to depart from the existing contract.

In *Burdett-Coutts* v. *Hertfordshire County Council*[20] the Court of Appeal held that continuation in employment under protest at an attempted unilateral change amounting to a repudiatory breach would not lead to an assumption that the repudiation had been waived. It is difficult to see how any other conclusion could be reached. The effect of a waiver in the case of a continuing breach such as occurred in that case must be to produce a consensual variation of the contract. This could scarcely be assumed in face of clear rejec-

---

[17] [1972] 1 Ch. 305.
[18] (1888) 39 Ch.D. 339.
[19] [1984] I.R.L.R. 91.
[20] *Supra.*

tion. In *Harrison* v. *Norwest Holst Group Administration Ltd.*[21] the Court of Appeal held that acceptance of repudiation must, similarly, be unequivocal. It must follow that there can be a state of limbo in which, as the Court held in *Harrison*, the guilty party is free to revoke the repudiatory act. Presumably, the innocent party is free, during this time, to accept or waive the breach. The problem which the courts have not satisfactorily resolved is whether this situation in which repudiation has not led to termination, but has not been waived, can continue indefinitely.

The problem is a relatively new one stemming from the change of opinion which has recently occurred[22] in which the contract of employment is seen as no different from other contracts in this respect. Before that change the proposition that a repudiatory breach would automatically terminate the contract of employment was bound to suggest the conclusion that if employment continued the repudiation had been waived. The difficulty experienced by the Courts in *Marriott* v. *Oxford and District Co-Operative Society Ltd. (No. 2)*[23] in explaining the legal position of continuing employment in face of clear evidence of absence of waiver is now largely eliminated. It can now be said that in such a situation the former contract continues. In *Marriott* it only continued for three weeks but in *Harrison* v. *Norwest Holst* it lasted some seven months, as it did in *Burdett-Coutts*. Some idea of the potential consequence of this period of legal limbo, during which the parties to the contract are not agreed as to its terms, is apparent from the facts of *Rigby* v. *Ferodo Ltd.*[24] in which the House of Lords upheld the Court of Appeal's conclusion that a wage reduction of £30 per week unilaterally imposed more than five years before constituted an unwaived repudiatory breach. Even over shorter periods the effect can be startling. In *Evening Standard and Co. Ltd.* v. *Henderson*[25] employers who refused to accept the breach occasioned by an employee leaving without notice were held entitled to prevent the employee working for another during the period of notice that should have been given, thus disposing of the long held view that nothing much can be done, in practice, about such a situation.

Less in practice than in legal theory, problems similarly arise where the repudiation, though unaccepted, does lead to a cessation of the employment relationship because the repudiator refuses to continue it. Again, the common law had, until recently, avoided this problem by adhering to the proposition that a repudiatory breach automatically terminated the contract of employment leaving the innocent party no option but to accept it. The argument was that, since neither party can be specifically compelled to carry out the contract, an indication by one that he rejects it must be effective to terminate it. Presumably, the common law would not in the past have regarded waiver as casting doubt on that argument since it would, earlier, have seen the change resulting from waiver of a continuing breach as constituting a new contract. With the development of the concept of consensual variation it could say that waiver resulted in an amended contract. Deadlock, as we have

---

[21] [1985] I.R.L.R. 240.
[22] See pp. 118–119, *infra*.
[23] [1970] 1 Q.B. 186.
[24] [1987] I.R.L.R. 516 (H.L.).
[25] [1987] I.R.L.R. 64.

just seen, caused problems but these were easily resolved where work actually ceased by concluding that the contract had also ceased.

Fortunately, there can now be no doubt that the common law has changed its stance. The contract of employment is not now regarded as different from any other contract in this respect. The contract continues, despite a repudiatory breach, until that breach is accepted as such by the innocent party.[26] Megarry V.-C., first pointed out the fallacy in the reasoning of the former rule in *Thomas Marshall (Exports) Ltd.* v. *Guinle.*[27] Put simply, he said that there was no reason why a contract, not capable of specific performance, should not survive a unilateral rejection. Actual execution of the contract would cease irretrievably. The rights of the innocent party would, however, continue and he could sue for damages for the continuing failure to acknowledge them. As the facts of *Guinle's* case showed, it would otherwise be possible for one party to shed all his continuing obligations by unilateral rejection of them. Damages would then have to be based on acknowledgment of the effectiveness of that action. Given that contract is not another name for the working relationship, but is a legal concept of a compendium of rights, it must be correct that one can envisage a contract bestowing rights which no longer produce that relationship. Some immediately subsequent decisions revealed difficulty with the application of this new idea where it was clear that that was the case. In *Brown* v. *Southall and Knight*,[28] for instance, Slynn J. in the E.A.T. envisaged a difference between those repudiatory breaches which related only to a significant aspect of the contract, but did not call in question the possibility of a working relationship on some terms, and those "fundamental" repudiations which rejected the relationship in its entirety. Use of the word "fundamental"[29] inevitably prompted the criticism that the concept of fundamental breach had been decisively rejected by the House of Lords in *Photo Production Ltd.* v. *Securicor Transport Ltd.*[30] The expression was not used in *L.T.E.* v. *Clarke*[31] however, in the sense of a breach of obligation not involving any specific contractual term, which is the concept of which the House of Lords disapproved. The distinction attempted in *Brown* v. *Southall and Knight* is, however, theoretically impossible. If the definition of a repudiatory breach is one revealing an intention not to be bound by the contract, degrees of such intention, though they exist in practice, cannot be permitted to produce different legal consequences. In practice, the solution envisaged by Slynn J. would produce the unresolved deadlock to which we have already referred. The explanation for the judicial hesitation to accept the full consequences of the proposition that no repudiatory breach terminates the contract of employment until it is accepted was fear of this very consequence. An employer who, for example, wrongly thinks he has cause to dismiss without notice an employee because of the latter's repudiatory breach will by acting on the assumption, himself commit a repudiatory breach. The employee has no option but to cease work and will frequently do so without registering any

---

[26] *Rigby* v. *Ferodo Ltd.* [1987] I.R.L.R. 516.

[27] [1979] Ch. 227.

[28] [1980] I.C.R. 617.

[29] Particularly by Lord Denning M.R. in *London Transport Executive* v. *Clarke* [1981] I.C.R. 355. See also Shaw L.J. in *Gunton* v. *Richmond Upon Thames L.B.C.* [1980] I.C.R. 755.

[30] [1980] A.C. 827.

[31] *Supra.*

objection sufficiently precise to be treated as non-acceptance so as to put the employer on notice that he must end the contract. The possibility exists that an employee in this position might return years later claiming back wages as a debt on the ground that he had never accepted the repudiation. The employee should not, as Buckley L.J. supposed in *Gunton* v. *Richmond-Upon-Thames London Borough Council*,[32] be prevented from recovering his loss after a reasonable period by the application of the duty of mitigation since he is not claiming damages, but a debt to which the duty of mitigation does not apply. There is considerably more strength in the contention that, in practice, the former employee will in most circumstances commence to act in ways inconsistent with the continuation of his contractual obligation to be available for work—as by finding[33] other employment, or by presenting a claim for unfair (constructive) dismissal.[34] In *W.E. Cox Toner (International) Ltd.* v. *Crook*[34a] Browne-Wilkinson J. said that unreasonable delay in terminating the relationship would be evidence of affirmation, as would any act of calling upon the guilty party for performance. Presumably, the delay principle could also work in reverse if the working relationship had ended and the innocent party took no step to affirm continuation of the contract within a reasonable time.

None of the solutions by way of implied acceptance resolve two general problems. The House of Lords, by holding in *Rigby* v. *Ferodo Ltd.*[35] that the mere fact of working under protest does not amount to waiver of a repudiatory breach, emphasises the point that waiver will not be implied as readily as when it was the only available explanation for a continuing relationship. There is nothing that distinguishes the situation of waiver during continuing employment from that of acceptance of repudiatory termination of employment which justifies treating the latter with less caution. The second problem is likely to prove more important in practice. The former rule that a repudiatory breach, unless waived, terminated the contract at once provided a more or less precise date of termination. The wait for acceptance, especially if that acceptance has to be implied, destroys that precision. In such circumstances the courts are likely to resort to pragmatism. Slynn J., in *Robert Cort and Son Ltd.* v. *Charman*[36] held that the effect of a "dismissive" repudiation was to terminate the right to employment and turn the contractual rights into claims for damages. Therefore, it could be said that the effective date of termination of *employment* was the date of effective repudiation. Very little in this statement is technically correct. The statutory definition of the effective date of termination speaks of termination of the contract rather than termination of employment. Moreover, the employee's right to wages in return for availability for work continues, so that his claim is not merely for damages. However that may be, this dubious logic undoubtedly represents the way in the courts will continue to solve these problems.[36a]

---

[32] [1980] I.C.R. 755.
[33] But not, it is submitted by seeking; although, in *Dietman* v. *London Borough of Brent* [1987] I.R.L.R. 259, Holdgson J. took "determined efforts" to indicate acceptance.
[34] See *F.C. Shepherd and Co. Ltd.* v. *Jerrom* [1985] 275 (E.A.T.); [1986] I.R.L.R. 358 (C.A.)
[34a] [1981] I.C.R. 823.
[35] [1987] I.R.L.R. 516.
[36] [1981] I.C.R. 816.
[36a] See Bingham LJ. in *Batchelor* v. *British Railways Board* [1987] I.R.L.R. 136.

Dismissal with due notice

The existence of a repudiatory breach justifies dismissal without notice which common law courts refer to as summary dismissal. In many cases where dismissal is regarded as morally (and statutorily) "justified," however, no such breach has occurred. This is, for instance, true of dismissal for redundancy or dismissal following a long period of absence through illness or injury. It is probable that the same applies to many situations of dismissal for incompetence. If the employee has warranted his competence, as when he applies for, and is appointed to, a job requiring a particular skill, failure to show that level of competence will amount to a breach of contract or even to misrepresentation justifying rescission. But if the employer has, in a sense, taken a risk; as where he promotes an employee to a different post in which it can only be said that the employee agrees to do his best, it is submitted that there will be no such breach.[37] In other cases the employer may deem it in the interests of his undertaking that he should sever relationships with a particular employee. In *Newell* v. *Gillingham Corporation*,[38] for instance, the plaintiff apprentice was a registered conscientious objector although the court obviously had doubts as to whether such a description was the correct one. His support for the German cause in the second world war, which at the relevant time was at a somewhat critical stage for this country, produced considerable irritation among those who worked with him and he was dismissed. His actions were held not to justify dismissal of an apprentice since the purpose of that contract was instruction and he had not rendered that impossible. Although the irritation had been inspired deliberately it is by no means clear that there would have been a repudiatory breach had he been an ordinary employee.

In cases where it is necessary to terminate the relationship despite the absence of a breach of contract, the common law solution is to regard a term permitting unilateral termination upon a period of notice as so necessary as to justify its implication unless expressly excluded.[39]

The idea that a contract of service might, by implication, be terminated on the giving of reasonable notice was first accepted in *Beeston* v. *Collyer*.[40] The concept seems to have sprung from discussion as to whether a yearly hiring terminated automatically at the end of the year or whether notice in advance of the termination was required.[41] The law of employment had taken over the yearly hiring from the agricultural economy which flourished before the industrial revolution. In that economy it had been customary to regard the hiring of labour as operative from Michaelmas to Michaelmas. Even in 1882 Grose J. was prepared to refer to the normal presumption of a yearly hiring

---

[37] See *Harmer* v. *Cornelius* (1858) 5 C.B.(N.S.) 236; *K.* v. *Raschen* (1878) 38 L.J. 38.
[38] [1941] 1 All E.R. 552.
[39] The Court of Appeal in *Land and Wilson* v. *West Yorkshire M.C.C.* [1981] I.C.R. 334 was prepared to concede a right to terminate one of two separate jobs under a single contract by adequate notice.
[40] (1827) 2 C. & P. 607.
[41] See Cronin and Grime, *Labour Law* (Butterworth 1970). This book is now out of print and, obviously, out of date but it did contain some very useful leads to further thought.

capable of displacement by a term implied by custom,[42] and in 1950 Parker J. said:

" . . . it is old law that an employment, an engagement, for an indefinite period is what is called a general hiring for a year unless something is shown to the contrary."[43]

It was easy to rebut the presumption and in this century it has never been a practicable alternative to termination by notice. In 1910, for instance, Lord Alverstone C.J. said:

"The general principle applicable to contracts of service is that, in the absence of misconduct or of grounds specified in the contract, the engagement can only be terminated after reasonable notice."[44]

In that case the contract stated that save for certain specified grounds of summary dismissal it should be terminable in the absolute discretion of the employer. It was held that this discretion could only be exercised after proper notice. In *De Stempel* v. *Dunkels*[45] the Court of Appeal used the ordinary rules of contractual implication to conclude that the parties to the contract could not have intended otherwise than that the contract should be terminable by notice. It was left to Lord Denning M.R. in *Richardson* v. *Koefod*[46] finally to assert the presumption of terminability by notice and to discard that of the yearly hiring. "The time has now come," he said, "to state explicitly that there is no presumption of a yearly hiring. In the absence of express stipulation, the rule is that every contract of service is determinable by reasonable notice."

It appears that it will only be possible to displace the presumption of a right to terminate upon reasonable notice by very strong words. In *McClelland* v. *Northern Ireland General Health Services Board*[47] both Lords Oaksey and Goddard, in the majority, stated that a contract of service said to be permanent and pensionable could be terminated by notice. They did not look with favour on the decision in *Salt* v. *Power Plant Co. Ltd.*[48] that use of the word "permanent" indicated that the contract was not capable of termination by notice.

Statutory minimum notice

The question of the length of notice that will be considered reasonable is now best approached from the statutory provision of minimum notice rights first introduced in 1963 and contained as amended in the Employment Protec-

---

[42] *Buckingham* v. *Surrey and Hants Canal Co.* (1882) 46 L.T. 885.
[43] *Mulholland* v. *Bexwell Estates Co. Ltd.* (1950) 66 T.L.R. (Pt. 2) 764.
[44] *Re African Association Ltd. and Allen* [1910] 1 K.B. 396. See also *Payzu* v. *Hannaford* [1918] 2 K.B. 348.
[45] [1938] 1 All E.R. 238. see also *Fisher* v. *W.B. Dick and Co. Ltd.* [1938] 4 All E.R. 467; *Adams* v. *Union Cinemas Ltd.* [1939] 3 All E.R. 136 at 143.
[46] [1969] 1 W.L.R. 1812.
[47] [1957] 1 W.L.R. 594. See also *Southern Foundries (1926) Ltd.* v. *Shirlaw* [1940] A.C. 701.
[48] [1936] 3 All E.R. 322; *cf. Ward* v. *Barclay Perkins and Co. Ltd.* [1939] 1 All E.R. 287.

tion (Consolidation) Act 1978.[49] The minimum notice required to be given by an employer to terminate the employment of an employee with one month or more of continuous employment is one week if the period of continuous employment is less than two years. If the period of continuous employment is two years or more the minimum period of notice is one week for each completed year up to a maximum of 12 weeks. The Contracts of Employment Act 1963 broke the principle of reciprocity and since then the minimum period of notice required to be given by an employee with more than one month continuous employment is one week, whatever his length of service. These periods replace any contractual provision for shorter periods but a party may waive his right or accept payment in lieu. It is quite clear that these statutory minimums can be extended both in favour of the employee and of the employer's right to receive notice. There seems no reason to suppose that they cannot be extended by normal common law implication. Custom has often been used as the basis for such implication and it is largely this that has given the common law on notice its peculiarly status-conscious aspect. In *Todd* v. *Kerrick*[50] for instance it was held that a governess could not be treated as a mere menial entitled only to the customary one month's notice available to domestic servants because she enjoyed a different position and status in the family and society.[51] In *Nicoll* v. *Falcon Airways*[52] an airline pilot was held entitled to six months' notice and in *Savage* v. *British India Steam Navigation Co. Ltd.*[53] it was suggested that the master of an ocean-going steamship could be entitled to six months' notice. Lord Denning M.R. in *Hill* v. *C.A. Parsons and Co. Ltd.*[54] concluded that the position of a draughtsman justified him granting the right to six months' notice—a deliberately exaggerated period but no less dependent on concepts of status. The common law did not so extensively examine the notice entitlement of manual workers because they rarely considered it worthwhile to bring claims for wrongful dismissal, least of all in a court from which a published report might emerge. It was generally assumed, however, that the practice of dismissing with wages for the next pay period established the implication of a right to notice corresponding to such pay periods. It was this assumption which, in *Marshall* v. *English Electric Co. Ltd.*[55] enabled the Court of Appeal to hold that suspension of an hourly paid worker could be treated as dismissal on an hour's notice. There is no doubt that implication of such periods of notice would not be countenanced today if the statutory minimum periods did not exist. On the other hand there is nothing to suggest that common law courts if left to themselves would extend these minima by implication in the case of most manual employees.

Statute now confers on the employee entitled to notice not exceeding one

---

[49] s.49. A contract for a fixed term of one month or less under which a employee has served continuously for three months is converted into an indefinite contract. E.P.C.A. 1978, s.49(4) as amended by the E.A. 1982, Sched. 2.

[50] (1852) 8 Exch. 151.

[51] In *Mulholland* v. *Bexwell Estates Co.* (1950) 66 T.L.R. (Pt. 2) 764 the "general manager" of three companies was considered in reality to hold a comparatively lowly position and to be entitled only to three months' notice.

[52] [1962] 1 Lloyd's Rep. 245.

[53] [1930] 46 T.L.R. 294.

[54] [1972] 1 Ch. 305.

[55] [1945] 1 All E.R. 633.

week more than the statutory minimum,[56] certain rights during the minimum statutory period.[57] If the employee is ready and willing to work or is incapable of work through sickness or is absent from work in accordance with his contractual holiday rights he is entitled to be paid the average hourly rate if he has normal working hours or not less than a week's pay for each week of notice if there are no normal working hours. The same rights apply where it is the employee who gives notice, but in that case only for the period of notice required by statute of an employee and from the time when the employee leaves the service of the employer in accordance with the notice. Any amount paid to such an employee under a sick pay scheme will go towards meeting this liability. The right to payment during notice ceases if the employer rightfully treats a breach of contract by the employee during the notice period as terminating the contract. If the employer breaks the contract during the notice period then any payment made by him in respect of a period after that breach will go to mitigate damages for the breach.

Frustration of contract

Because employment is regarded as regulated by contract, the doctrine of frustration of contract is available to excuse performance which has become impossible through no fault of the parties. The doctrine does not require proof of absolute impossibility of performance. Lord Radcliffe said, in *Davis Contractors Ltd.* v. *Fareham U.D.C.*[58]:

" . . . frustration occurs whenever the law recognises that without the default of either party a contractual obligation has become incapable of being performed because the circumstances in which performance is called for would render it a thing radically different from that which was undertaken by the contract."

Frustration is only brought about by inability to perform. Increased risk does not suffice.[59] On the other hand, unforseen inconvenience may mean that the venture as it would now be carried through would be different from that envisaged. In employment one of the most common frustrating events is relatively long non-availability of the service contracted for. It is obvious that the situations in which it will be said that absence makes the projected employment a thing different from what can now be offered, especially where the project was of indefinite length, will be determined by the courts with the exercise of considerable discretionary latitude. Mere absence due to sickness does not put an end to the contract,[60] and five months of such absence during a five year term has been held not to constitute frustration.[61] Ten months, followed by a medical board certificate of suspension, was considered by the Divisional Court to make frustration abundantly clear,[62] but an industrial tribunal has held a year's absence as the result of industrial injury insufficient.[63]

---

[56] E.P.C.A. 1978, s.50.
[57] *Ibid.* Sched. 3.
[58] [1956] A.C. 696.
[59] *Converfarm (Darwen) Ltd.* v. *Bell* [1981] I.R.L.R. 195.
[60] *Warburton* v. *CWS Ltd.* [1917] 1 K.B. 663.
[61] *Storey* v. *Fulham Steel Works Co.* (1907) 24 T.L.R. 89 (C.A.).
[62] *Pritchard* v. *Dinorwic Slate Quarries Ltd.* [1971] I.T.R. 102.
[63] *Watts* v. *Mapus Smith* (1974) COIT 300/116.

That a great deal depends on how the courts see the expectation of the parties is apparent from the old, but leading, case of *Poussard* v. *Spiers & Pond*.[64] The fact that the absence of the lead opera singer for four days at the commencement of the engagement constituted a frustrating event obviously depended on the difficulty of securing a short term replacement at that level of professionalism.

Whether a situation can produce frustration is a question of law. Whether it does so, one of fact. But if a court decides that frustration has occurred the contractual obligations are extinguished as a matter of law and regardless of the fact that the parties have treated them as still subsisting. The promisor is, therefore, entitled to treat himself as discharged from his obligation providing the frustrating event is not of his making. In determining the factual existence of a frustrating event, however, the courts will be heavily influenced by the fact that the parties have treated the obligations as surviving.[65]

Application of the doctrine of frustration is also influenced by consideration of the injustice of forcing the promisor to perform an obligation which circumstances have made fundamentally different from that which the contract envisaged. This, no doubt, is the reason why it was said in *Harman* v. *Flexible Lamps Ltd*.[66] that there was no room for the doctrine where, as is common in employment, the contract is terminable by short notice. Whilst the Court of Appeal in *Notcutt* v. *Universal Equipment Co. (London) Ltd*.[67] said that this circumstance might indicate that courts should approach frustration of the contract of employment with care it rightly discarded the proposition that the availability of other ways of mitigating the consequence of difficulty of performance should affect the principle.

In *Paal Wilson and Co.* v. *Partenreederie*[68] Lord Brandon expounded the doctrine of frustration in somewhat more detail than its definition normally contains. He said:

> "The first essential factor is that there must be some outside or extraneous change of situation, not foreseen or provided for by the parties at the time of contracting, which either makes it impossible for the contract to be performed at all, or at least renders its performance something radically different from what the parties contemplated when they entered into it. The second essential factor is that the outside event or extraneous change of situation concerned, and the consequences of either in relation to the performance of the contract, must have occurred without either the fault or the default of either party to the contract."

Logically, if the parties to the contract have provided for an eventuality, that circumstance cannot frustrate the original venture. The mere provision of machinery for termination (as, for instance, disciplinary procedures capable of handling the events which occurred so as to release the promisor) will not amount to such provision. In *Notcutt* v. *Universal Equipment Co. (London)*

---

[64] [1876] 1 Q.B.D. 410. Compare, *Loats* v. *Maple* (1903) 88 L.T. 288.
[65] *Hebden* v. *Forsey and Son Ltd.* [1973] I.C.R. 607; *The Egg Stores (Stamford Hill) Ltd.* v. *Leibovici* [1977] I.C.R. 260.
[66] [1980] I.R.L.R. 418.
[67] [1986] 3 All E.R. 582; and see Mustill L.J. in *F.C. Shepherd and Co. Ltd.* v. *Jerrom* [1986] I.R.L.R. 358.
[68] [1983] 1 A.C. 854 at p. 909.

Ltd.[69] provision for cessation of payment of wages during sickness was held not to envisage total disablement. It is suggested that though this formulation was sufficient to dispose of the issue in the case it is too narrow. Most contracts of employment now provide for what is to happen to wage entitlement during sickness but it would be surprising if the mere provision for cessation of such entitlement in the case of long term sickness prevented that circumstance frustrating the contract. As *Poussard* v. *Spiers*[70] shows, there is a good deal more to be considered than payment of wages. The obligation to resume active employment when a temporarily disabled employee is again available for work is unlikely to be held to survive long absence just because provision was made for non-payment of wages. One must not be too ready to conclude that a contractual provision for one consequence necessarily indicates that others have been envisaged.

The greatest uncertainty is produced in modern employment law by the last of the more detailed propositions contained in Lord Brandon's formulation. In *Bank Line Ltd.* v. *Arthur Capel and Co.*[71] Lord Sumner said that the doctrine of frustration assumes an absence of fault on either side. A party could not rely on self-induced frustration—which would normally amount to repudiation by the party responsible. Lord Brandon, however, refers to "default" as if it were an alternative to "fault." The question is whether "self-inducement" and "fault," which imply deliberate choice, should encompass "default" which may apply simply to negligence. Text books on labour law have usually said, or assumed, that the courts will not enquire as to whether employee sickness has been brought on by the employee's lack of care. This is probably correct as a reflection of practice, but the theory is not so settled. Viscount Simon L.C. favoured a requirement of deliberate inducement in *Joseph Constantine Steamship Ltd.* v. *Imperial Smelting Corporation Ltd.*[72] but declined to commit himself to a final decision. The problem can be avoided in many instances, as it was by Lawton L.J. in *F.C. Shepherd and Co. Ltd.* v. *Jerrom*,[73] by distinguishing the fault of the promisee from its frustrating consequences. In that case the fault lay in a criminal act but Lawton L.J. pointed out that the imposition of a custodial sentence was the frustrating event. The apprentice could be said to have induced the latter but the sentence itself was incurred neither by his fault or default. It would certainly be surprising if the deliberate act of standing in the rain rather than the onset of pneumonia was said to be part of the frustrating circumstances but it is rather more questionable whether the latter cannot be said to be a direct, if not an inevitable, consequence, of the former default.

The principal argument in *Jerrom's* case concerned the related question of whether a promisee, seeking to sustain the obligations of the promisor, could plead his own default to *avoid* the application of frustration. As Mustill L.J. pointed out, the question would not arise at common law. If the fault is a deliberate act, making performance impossible, it will almost inevitably constitute a repudiatory breach enabling the promisor to treat the contract as dis-

---

[69] *Supra.*
[70] *Supra.*
[71] [1919] A.C. 435, at p. 452.
[72] [1942] A.C. 154 at p. 166.
[73] [1986] I.R.L.R. 358.

charged (though there is a possibility of a significant difference occurring between the automatic effect of frustration and the exercise of the option to rescind which for example may be indefinitely postponed). Even if the act is mere negligent default it is open to the courts to imply an obligation not to create a situation in which performance becomes impossible.[74] In the modern law of employment, however, the exercise by an employer/promisor of the option to rescind would amount to dismissal (which, despite the existence of sufficient cause, might, by reason of procedural defect, be unfair) whereas the operation of frustration would prevent a claim being made by the employee/promisee. This was the advantage which the employee sought to gain in *Jerrom's* case by pleading his own default to avoid frustration. All members of the Court of Appeal declined to permit a party to secure such an advantage in this way. Mustill L.J. explains the point most clearly by stating that frustration concerns the release of the promisor. Each party may, in different ways, be a promisor, but it is in that capacity that self-inducement cannot be pleaded. It is inconceivable that the promisor should be held to his obligation because of the fault of the promisee. The availability of other pleas of discharge may make it sufficient in most cases to state the self-inducement rule as if it applied to either party. In the case of employment contracts it is now necessary to make it clear that it relates to the conduct of the party seeking the advantage of frustration to terminate contractual obligations.

Specific performance

It has, until recently, been regarded as axiomatic that however improper the termination of a working relationship and, now, despite the fact that the contractual relationship may survive, the contract of employment is not capable of specific performance.

Exceptions have been made. It has been held possible to enforce a negative covenant not to work for another employer provided that, in practice,[75] the effect was not to leave the employee no option but to work for the covenantee.[76] In *Vine* v. *National Dock Labour Board*[77] it seems that the unassailable logic of their argument would have freed the House of Lords to conclude that a termination of employment, invalid in the sense of being *ultra vires*, was a nullity. Clearly, Viscount Kilmuir L.C. did not envisage dismissal from employment as likely to be invalid in this sense, and so felt safe distinguishing employment from the special status which registration as a dockworker available for employment had conferred in that case. In *Francis* v. *Municipal Councillors of Kuala Lumpur*[78] the Privy Council rejected the same logical conclusion, though it must be admitted that the *ultra vires* nature of the Council's action was the merest technicality, and preferred the proposition that a declaration would not tend to specific enforcement of the contract of employment—as distinct from a statutory status—even if the purported termination

---

[74] See, *e.g. Condor* v. *The Barron Knights* [1966] 1 W.L.R. 87.
[75] See *Page One Records Ltd.* v. *Britton* [1967] 1 W.L.R. 157.
[76] *Warner Brothers Pictures Incorporated* v. *Nelson* [1937] 1 K.B. 209. See also, *Lumley* v. *Wagner* (1852) 1 De G.M. and G. 604.
[77] [1957] A.C. 488.
[78] [1962] 1 W.L.R. 1411.

was as a nullity. The rule received statutory confirmation[79] so far as enforcement against an employee is concerned. The same rule, or at least the attitude of mind behind it, originally persuaded the legislature not to confer on Industrial Tribunals power to order, as distinct from recommending, re-engagement or reinstatement of an unfairly dismissed employee.

Perhaps it is the change in this last mentioned provision[80] so that industrial tribunals may now order reinstatement or re-engagement, or a belated acknowledgment that modern employment is not normally the distinctly personal relationship which nineteenth century judges, with their domestic staff in mind, thought it to be, which has led to signs that adamant refusal of specific performance is beginning to crack. The reason for the rule may be nothing better than an attitude of mind, or it may be a simple statement of fact. It must be remembered that implied terms of a contract are likely to be reciprocal. The courts cannot order a large impersonal corporation to employ an individual because they will not (or, now, cannot) order that individual to work for the corporation. They will not make an order against the individual because it would require constant supervision, or amount to villeinage.[81] Each of these has been advanced as an objection in principle. In the end, however, the justification for the common law rule lies in the factual impossibility of forcing employment upon an adamantly unwilling party. Although one wonders how it is that the office holder has, by reason of his property right in the office, always been able to seek specific performance.[82] The power of an industrial tribunal is statutory and statute has avoided ultimate confrontation by providing for the award of punitive compensation if the order is not obeyed. In other words, statute seems to accept the ultimate factual impossibility. The position is fraught with a greater insolubility for the common law which could only respond to refusal to obey an injunction by penalties for contempt. The grant of a declaration might seem to be the way out of this trap save that, just because there is no mechanism for its enforcement, courts are not likely to grant a declaration which is likely to be disobeyed.

The majority of the Court of Appeal used the reverse side of the factual impossibility to justify specific enforcement in *Hill* v. *C.A. Parsons and Co. Ltd.*,[83] holding that where mutual trust and confidence remained it was not impossible to enforce the relationship.[84] In *Irani* v. *Southampton and S.W. Hampshire Health Authority*[85] the Chancery Division granted an interim injunction allegedly on the same basis but stating the critical element to be continuing belief in the plaintiff's competence. The reason for dismissal in *Irani's* case, however, was the employer's belief in the incompatibility of the plaintiff and the consultant surgeon with whom he had to work. That, it is submitted, is a matter wholly different from the third party objection in *Hill's*

---

[79] Trade Union and Labour Relations Act 1974, s.16 "No court shall, whether by way of: (a) an order for specific performance or specific implement of a contract of employment, or (b) an injunction or interdict restraining a breach or threatened breach of such a contract, compel an employee to do any work or attend at any place for the doing of work."

[80] E.P.C.A. 1978, s.69.

[81] *Horwood* v. *Millar's Timber and Trading Co. Ltd.* [1917] 1 K.B. 305.

[82] See *Ridge* v. *Baldwin* [1964] A.C. 40.

[83] [1972] 1 Ch. 305.

[84] This was what a later Court of Appeal, in *Chappel & Others* v. *The Times Newspapers Ltd.* [1975] 2 All E.R. 233 regarded as the basis of the decision.

[85] [1985] I.R.L.R. 203.

case. Incompatibility with colleagues is just as likely as incompetence to produce intransigent objection to continuing the relationship.

In *Powell* v. *London Borough of Brent*[86] the Court of Appeal accepted the
proposition that an injunction might be granted specifically to enforce the
contract of employment where sufficient confidence continued on the part of
the employer. It suggested that it would be difficult for the employee to show
the existence of such confidence in face of adamant employer opposition to
such enforcement. The Court of Appeal in that case concluded that there was
no evidence of loss of confidence and that damages would not compensate for
distress and embarrassment and loss of opportunity to do a more demanding
and rewarding job.[87] The availability of an injunction was extended to cover
irrational loss of trust and confidence. This would seem at variance with the
Court of Appeal's assumption based on opposition to enforcement. In *Dietman* v. *London Borough of Brent*[88] Hodgson J. refused an injunction because
of the employees' apparent acceptance of the repudiatory breach, but accepts
its availability to restrain implementation of a decision to dismiss before
proper (contractual) procedures had been adopted, notwithstanding absence
of any remaining vestige of trust and confidence.

Development of a wholly different line of remedies has, recently, presented
another source of specific performance of the contract of employment. A line
of distinction has been developed between purely private employment and
that which derives additional fortification from statute. It is suggested that the
courts had been feeling for an excuse to extend the rights of some employees
beyond the lack of protection afforded by pure contract remedies considerably before the decision in *R.* v. *Home Secretary, ex p. Benwell*[89] which has
apparently settled a line between statutory rights, protected by public law
remedies, and contractual rights, which do not enjoy that benefit. One of the
most obvious advantages is that public law remedies allow the avoidance of an
invalid decision. An early example of this search occurs in the majority
decision of the House of Lords in *Malloch* v. *Aberdeen Corporation*[90] that a
statutory system of registration for school teachers necessarily incorporated
the right to the observance of natural justice in disciplinary procedures. Lord
Wilberforce, having linked the absence of a requirement of natural justice
with inability to order reinstatement, said[91]:

> "One may accept that if there are relationships in which all requirements of the
> observance of rules of natural justice are excluded . . . these must be confined to
> what have been called 'pure master and servant cases,' which I take to mean cases
> in which there is no element of public employment or service, no support by stat-
> ute, nothing in the nature of an office or status which is capable of protection."

In this case the House of Lords, when it referred to public law remedies,
had in mind the grant of a declaration. The question of the availability of
other public law remedies was considered—in the same context of a claim to

---

[86] [1987] I.R.L.R. 466. See also, *Hughes* v. *London Borough of Southwark* [1988] I.R.L.R. 55.
[87] This decision was expressly followed in *Ali* v. *London Borough of Southwark* [1988] I.R.L.R.
100.
[88] [1987] I.R.L.R. 259.
[89] [1985] I.R.L.R. 6, I.C.R. 743.
[90] [1971] 1 W.L.R. 1578.
[91] At p. 1595.

be entitled to a hearing—in *R. v. B.B.C. ex p. Lavell.*[92] Woolf J. pointed out that public law remedies of *mandamus*, prohibition and *certiorari*, or the grant of an injunction on an application for judicial review, are not available to enforce private rights. Since the disciplinary procedure in this instance was purely contractual no such remedy could be granted. His Lordship went on to hold, however, that employment legislation had conferred upon ordinary master and servant relationships many of the attributes of an office. Moreover, the contractual restrictions on dismissal, in his view, made the present case one in which an injunction or a declaration would lie to enforce the contractual right to a hearing were it not for the fact that the plaintiff had opted to pursue a remedy by way of internal appeal. Clearly the grant of an injunction to compel the observance of natural justice would have operated as specific enforcement.

An order for *certiorari* was, incidentally, sought in *R. v. East Berkshire Health Authority ex p. Walsh*[93] to enforce a right to a hearing and set aside a dismissal by an officer having no contractual right so to act. The Court of Appeal, however, refused to go so far as to extend public law remedies to contractual employment simply because the employer was a public authority. It was, the Court said, the existence of statutory support in *Malloch* which led to the conclusion that "public" rights and remedies were available. The line of distinction was applied in *R. v. Home Secretary ex p. Benwell.*[94] The plaintiff was a prison officer. He refused to attend a meeting with the Regional Director unless he was paid a car mileage allowance rather than public transport charges. After an enquiry by the Governor a charge of disobedience was referred to the Home Secretary. An enquiry recommended severe reprimand. The Home Office, however, notified the plaintiff of dismissal after having regard to records of critical remarks concerning the Governor made by the plaintiff to the Press. The plaintiff unsuccessfully invoked the internal appeal procedure (which operated as a rehearing) and then applied for judicial review. The Court granted a declaration that the decision to dismiss was *ultra vires* and *certiorari* to quash it. It was the statutory underpinning of that Code which, in the opinion of Hodgson J. made the difference between *Benwell* and *Walsh*. In *Walsh* the disciplinary procedures derived from collective agreement and were approved by the Minister but they were then incorporated into the contract of employment. The reader may think the distinction somewhat fortuitous. It is not quite true to say that the distinction was that in *Benwell* the Home Office "was performing the duties imposed upon it as part of the statutory terms under which it exercises its power" if this is meant to imply that this was not so in *Walsh*. The truth is that the statutory obligations of public bodies were in the one case being exercised by derivation from legislative authority whereas in the other individual contract was being used. We have already seen how easy it is to imply something so personal as a disciplinary code into a contract. Are we to conclude that a reference to the statutorily authorised Code in some written statement of contract would suffice to deprive the employee of public law remedies?

It is now clear, however, that the Courts will apply such a distinction. The

---

[92] [1982] I.R.L.R. 404.
[93] [1984] I.R.L.R. 278.
[94] [1985] I.R.L.R. 6.

final enquiry must concern what types of fault in a dismissal process will entitle a "public" employee to judicial review. In *Benwell's* case, Hodgson J. first dealt with the well accepted rule that a decision may be set aside if it is so absurd that no reasonable authority could come to it. Public authorities are unlikely to arrive at absurd conclusions. The explanation for decisions so described is usually that something has been taken into account which either does not appear in the account of the evidence or should not have been considered. Since it was clear that this had occurred in *Benwell* the Court preferred to base its orders on that specific fact.

The principal source of guidance on the scope of jurisdiction in this type of case is now the decision of the House of Lords in *Council of Civil Service Unions* v. *Minister for the Civil Service*.[95] The case which concerned the decision to revise the conditions of service of civil servants employed at the Government Communications Headquarters so as to exclude the freedom to join any trade union, involves a number of issues. It will suffice at this point to notice that Lord Diplock held that a decision was susceptible to judicial review under one or more of three main grounds which he described as "illegality," "irrationality" and "procedural impropriety." He allowed for the future development of other grounds such as the EEC concept of "proportionality." "Illegality," he said, relates to the proper application of the law regulating the decision-making power. "Irrationality" describes the principle of unreasonableness discussed in *Benwell's* case and, of course, originally derived from *Associated Provincial Picture Houses Ltd.* v. *Wednesbury Corporation*.[96] "Procedural irregularity," he explained, covers not only natural justice and basic procedural fairness but also legislatively founded procedural rules. This Lord Diplock was prepared to extend to implications derived from "legitimate expectations" which, in this case, were that there would be consultation before a change of terms—including a change in the consultation process itself.

It appears, therefore, that, once the source of authority to act is founded on statutory sources rather than contract, the right of review arises. Public law remedies will be granted for any of the types of defect isolated by Lord Diplock and procedural impropriety is not confined to express breaches of statutory procedure actually granted to that authority. All that is necessary is to show that the action improperly taken has interfered with some interest of the employment. In the GCHQ case that interest did not amount to any enforceable right, let alone one having a statutory foundation. It follows, therefore, that an employee whose *contract* of employment was terminated could seek a public law remedy if the source of the power to take that action was statutory.

"DISMISSAL" STATUTORILY DEFINED

In order to make a claim for unfair dismissal, the employee must show that the dismissal falls within the statutory definition.[97] Despite the obvious intention to separate such claims from contract this definition is nothing more than

---

[95] [1985] A.C. 374.
[96] [1948] 1 K.B. 223.
[97] E.P.C.A. 1978, s.55. The basic elements of the definition are the same for a claim for redundancy compensation—s.83.

a summary of employer initiated termination of the contract of employment. "Dismissal" is a term properly reserved for the employment relation but it has no specialist content of its own. The statutory definition includes three separate types of termination.

(a) Direct termination by the employer

The contract under which the employee is employed by the employer is terminated by the employer, whether it is so terminated by notice or without notice.

This aspect embodies the popular concept of an employer-initiated termination. Nevertheless it does give rise to a few problems. It may occasionally have to be decided whether the words or the action taken amount to a dismissal. There are a number of reported examples of the use of ambiguous words but the best working test was laid down by the E.A.T. in *Tanner* v. *D.T. Kean*.[98] The employee had been instructed by his employer not to use the company's van outside working hours and had been lent £275 to enable him to buy himself a car. His employer discovered the van outside a country club of which he was a member and the employee the part-time doorman. Obviously having lost his temper the employer, among other things, said to the employee "That's it, you're finished with me." Phillips J. said:

> "In our judgment the test which has to be applied in cases of this kind is along these lines. Were the words spoken those of dismissal, that is to say, were they intended to bring the contract of employment to an end? What was the employer's intention? In answering that a relevant, and perhaps the most important question is how would a reasonable employee, in all circumstances, have understood what the employer intended by what he said and did? Then in most of these cases, and in this case, it becomes relevant to look at the later events following the utterance of the words and preceding the actual departure of the employee. . . . A word of caution is necessary because in considering later events it is necessary to remember that a dismissal or resignation, once it has taken effect, cannot be unilaterally withdrawn. Accordingly, as it seems to us, later events need to be scrutinised with some care in order to see whether they are genuinely explanatory of the acts alleged to constitute dismissal, or whether they reflect a change of mind. If they are in the former category they may be valuable as showing what was really intended."

This test was held, however, only to apply where the words are ambiguous. Where there is no ambiguity and the words are understood in a certain sense there is no room for consideration of what a reasonable person might have understood.[99]

Notice of termination has at common law been held to require some precision of date and time. This led to the formulation of a distinction between a mere warning of an impending decision to dismiss and notice of dismissal.[1] A warning of an impending decision on dismissal has, moreover, been held not

---

[98] [1978] I.R.L.R. 110.
[99] *B.G. Gale Ltd.* v. *Gilbert* [1978] I.C.R. 1149. "I am leaving, I want my cards." *Southern* v. *Frank Charlesly and Co.* [1981] I.R.L.R. 278 (C.A.). "I am resigning."
[1] *Morton Sundour Fabrics Ltd.* v. *Shaw* (1967) 2 I.I.R. 1; *Devon County Council* v. *Cook* [1977] I.R.L.R. 188.

to constitute a repudiatory breach such as to justify the employee in leaving and claiming constructive dismissal. It is important, however, to avoid defining a warning as any imprecise notice of impending termination despite the fact that this was the source of the rule in *Morton Sundour*. In *Maher* v. *Fram Gerrard Ltd.*[2] the N.I.R.C. made it clear that notice of dismissal would constitute a dismissal however imprecise. So, in *Jones* v. *Liverpool Corporation*[3] the employee was held to have been dismissed when he did not report for work having been told dismissal would result from such failure on a specific date.

It is clear that the fact that an employee asks to be dismissed[4] or is willing to accept dismissal,[5] does not prevent satisfaction of the statutory definition. On the other hand these situations may be distinguished from that in which the employee effectively asks for and is given permission to leave.[6]

The courts' reluctance to construe notice to dismiss out of an intention to substitute one contract for another[7] is clearly in line with this search for the intention of the parties.

There is no doubt that a freely given mutual consent of both parties to termination will lead to the conclusion that the dismissal was not initiated, in this sense, by the employer.[8] The distinction is vital to the growing practice of employee acceptance of early retirement. Despite this the decision in *Scott* v. *Coalite Fuels and Chemicals Ltd.*[9] seems unacceptably wide. Employees had already received notice of dismissal for redundancy. While working out this notice, they accepted "voluntary early retirement" because this scheme afforded a benefit for a surviving spouse. It was held that the contract was terminated by mutual agreement. If this were correct it could pose a threat to all forms of agreed early leaving.

This situation must be distinguished from that in which the employer seeks in the contract to make provision for automatic termination in certain eventualities. Originally, the E.A.T. held that where it was agreed that the employment would be regarded as terminated if the employee failed to return from leave on a fixed date, the resultant termination was not a dismissal.[10] Even the E.A.T. subsequently showed marked reluctance to follow this decision[11] and there were academic suggestions that it should be confined to a situation in which an agreement had been reached for consideration separate from that supporting the contract of employment. The Court of Appeal

---

[2] [1974] I.C.R. 31.

[3] [1974] I.R.L.R. 55.

[4] *Mercia Rubber Mouldings Ltd.* v. *Lingwood* [1974] I.C.R. 256.

[5] *Burton, Allton and Johnson Ltd.* v. *Peck* [1975] I.C.R. 193; *Morley* v. *C.T. Morley Ltd.* [1985] I.C.R. 499.

[6] *L. Lipton Ltd.* v. *Marlborough* [1979] I.R.L.R. 179. In *Caledonian Mining Co. Ltd.* v. *Basset and Steel* [1987] I.C.R. 425 two employees of a mining contractor were held to have been dismissed after being inveigled into applying for employment with the NCB and resigning in order to relieve their employer of the obligation to make redundancy payments.

[7] *e.g. Burdett-Coutts* v. *Hertfordshire County Council* [1984] I.R.L.R. 91; *Rigby* v. *Ferodo Ltd.* [1987] I.C.R. 457.

[8] *Birch and Humber* v. *The University of Liverpool* [1985] I.C.R. 470. Compare, *Caledonian Mining Co. Ltd.* v. *Bassett and Steel* [1987] I.C.R. 425.

[9] [1988] I.R.L.R. 131 (E.A.T.).

[10] *British Leyland (U.K.) Ltd.* v. *Ashraf* [1978] I.C.R. 979.

[11] *Midland Electric Co. Ltd.* v. *Kanji* [1980] 185; *Tracey* v. *Zest Equipment Co. Ltd.* [1982] I.R.L.R. 268.

in *Igbo* v. *Johnson Matthey Chemicals Ltd.*[12] overruled *Ashraf* on the ground that such an agreement would be void under E.P.C.A., s.140 as an attempt to contract out of the statutory protection. The difficulty in applying this argument is that if there is no dismissal, because the contract is not terminated by the employer alone, there is no statutory protection to contract out of. It must frequently be the case that an employee cannot claim a constructive dismissal because the contract has given the employer the right to take the action of which the employee complains. Such a right could be thoroughly unreasonable as, for instance, a provision subsequently included in the contract of employment that an employee late by five minutes would lose a day's pay, yet it could not be suggested that that agreement destroyed a statutory right to claim unfair constructive dismissal. Nor does there seem to be much value in the apparent distinction taken by the Court of Appeal between a provision originally in the contract and one subsequently inserted. It cannot be argued that an initial agreement not to resort to an industrial tribunal would be valid. The same invalidity must apply to any provision which excludes that right. The issue, therefore, is to what extent it is possible to contract out of the pre-conditions which have to be satisfied before resort can be had to industrial tribunals. In the end, every decision has to answer the question whether a dismissal has occurred. The difficulty in answering the question stems from the inequality of contractual freedom between the parties. When is it to be said that they have agreed a termination and when is the apparent agreement to be regarded as employer initiative to terminate? The decision of Popplewell J. in *Brown* v. *Knowsley Borough Council*[13] demonstrates the uncertainty of the answer to this by holding that contractual provision for termination on the happening or non-happening, of a future event would not amount to a dismissal.

Early leaving

If notice of dismissal has been given by an employer but the employee, of his own initiative, leaves before that notice expires the contract may have been terminated by that leaving and not by the action of the employer. Legislative provisions in relation both to claims for redundancy payment and unfair dismissal provide that there will be deemed to be a dismissal where an employee under notice from his employer, himself gives notice to his employer of his desire to leave on a date earlier than the date on which the employer's notice is due to expire.[14] The development of the two rights from different statutory sources has, however, given rise to significant differences of detail between them. Whereas, in the case of a claim for unfair dismissal, the employee's rights are preserved at whatever point in his period of notice he gives notice or leaves, and regardless of his employer's consent to that leaving, in the case of a claim to redundancy payment the right is only preserved if the employee actually gives notice *in writing*[15] during the minimum statutory period of notice to which he is entitled. Even then the claim is subject to objection by the employer and possible apportionment of the

---

[12] [1986] I.C.R. 505.
[13] [1986] I.R.L.R. 102.
[14] E.P.C.A. 1978, ss.55 and 85. If an employer dismisses an employee during the latter's period of notice that is a dismissal—*Harris and Russell Ltd.* v. *Slingsby* [1973] I.R.L.R. 221.
[15] See, *e.g. Brown* v. *Sugar Manufacturing Co. Ltd.* [1967] I.T.R. 213.

payment.[16] It is, therefore, not improbable that a notice to leave early will be ineffective to satisfy the requirements of the redundancy provisions, but most unlikely that such a notice would fail to satisfy those of the unfair dismissal provisions. If, for any reason, the notice to leave early were invalid the employee's right might still be capable of preservation. In *Hudson* v. *Fuller Shapcott*[17] an industrial tribunal held that the acceptance of the notice to leave early by the employer might be regarded as a consensual variation of the date of dismissal. This view was subsequently accepted by the N.I.R.C.[18] In *Ready Case Ltd.* v. *Jackson*[19] it was held that an industrial tribunal was entitled to attribute to the words "you can piss off" the quality of an agreement to vary the original date of termination. It could also be contended that where the employer's notice amounted to a repudiatory breach an employee's subsequent leaving constituted a constructive dismissal provided that it was clear that the leaving was an acceptance of the repudiation.

(b) Expiry of fixed term

Where under that contract he is employed for a fixed term that term expires without being renewed under the same contract.

A fixed term contract exists where a period of time is specified for its operation. Reference need not be made to actual dates so long as fixed dates are implicit.[20] The effect of the fixed term is not destroyed by provision for earlier termination by notice[21] or by the fact that the work contracted for may end earlier.[22] In the case of fixed term contracts alone the employee can waive his right to claim for unfair dismissal or redundancy if the term is for two years or more and the employee agrees to the waiver in writing.

(c) Constructive dismissal

The employee terminates that contract with or without notice, in circumstances (apart, in the case of a redundancy payment claim, from an employer lockout) such that he is entitled to terminate it without notice by reason of the employer's conduct.

The group of situations comprehended within this heading has come to be commonly called constructive dismissal. This concept has a strange history. It was incorporated in the Redundancy Payments Act 1965 for the obvious reason that, without it, an employer might have appeared able, with impunity, to force an employee to leave his employment without the employer terminating the contract. The Industrial Relations Act 1971, introducing a remedy for unfair dismissal, however, did not include this heading and it was made clear in debate that this was no oversight but that the government did

---

[16] See, *e.g. Jarman* v. *E. Pollard and Co. Ltd.* [1967] I.T.R. 406.

[17] [1970] I.T.R. 266.

[18] *Glacier Metal Co. Ltd.* v. *Dyer* [1974] 3 All E.R. 21. In *C.P.S. Recruitment Ltd.* v. *Bowen* [1982] I.R.L.R. 54, the E.A.T. held that the employee's early leaving was caused by the employer's dismissal.

[19] [1981] I.R.L.R. 312 (E.A.T.).

[20] *Wiltshire County Council* v. *NATFHE* [1980] I.C.R. 455.

[21] *B.B.C.* v. *Dixon* [1979] I.C.R. 281.

[22] *Wiltshire County Council* v. *NATFHE* (*supra*).

not intend to extend the right for unfair dismissal to an employee who left in such circumstances. Nevertheless, in *Sutcliffe* v. *Hawker Siddeley Aviation Ltd.*[23] Sir John Donaldson in the N.I.R.C. described as "academic pedantry" the suggestion that the statutory concept of dismissal for the purpose of claims for unfair dismissal was not intended to include this situation. He pointed out that the then unchallenged effect of a repudiatory breach of the contract would be that the contract was automatically terminated. Accordingly it could be argued that, at common law, where an employee left in response to a repudiatory breach by the employer it was the employer who had terminated the contract. It would not now be so easy to deduce a constructive dismissal from common law doctrines but the view in *Sutcliffe's* case, to which objection could not then be taken, served its turn until statute made express provision for it in 1974. Incidentally, whilst common law was the support for the doctrine of constructive dismissal there could be no question but that the action of the employer had to constitute a repudiatory breach of the contract and that the response of the employee must demonstrably be to that breach. As we shall see these conclusions continue to be applied to the purely statutory concept.

The decision of the Court of Appeal in *Western Excavating (E.C.C.) Ltd.* v. *Sharp*[24] firmly established constructive dismissal as arising only from a repudiatory breach. As a result of a disciplinary suspension without pay Sharp was short of money and sought an advance of accrued holiday pay. His request was refused on the ground that company policy was not to make holiday payments save for holidays. In order to secure his holiday pay and thus solve his immediate financial problems Sharp left his employment. Subsequently he claimed to have been unfairly constructively dismissed. The industrial tribunal and the E.A.T., founding themselves on the test of unreasonable conduct, upheld his complaint, but the Court of Appeal reversed this decision. Lord Denning M.R. said:

> "The new test of 'unreasonable conduct' of the employer is too indefinite by far: it has led to acute difference of opinion between the members of tribunals . . . It is better to have the contract test of the common law. It is more certain: as it can well be understood by intelligent laymen under the direction of a legal chairman. . . . I would adopt the reasoning of the considered judgment of the Employment Appeal Tribunal in *Wetherall (Bond St., W.1) Ltd.* v. *Lynn*[25]:
>> 'Parliament might well have said, in relation to whether the employer's conduct had been reasonable having regard to equity and the substantial merits of the case, but it neither laid down that special statutory criterion or any other. So, in our judgment, the answer can only be, entitled according to law, and it is to the law of contract that you have to look.' "

In the result the certainty that Lord Denning envisaged did not materialise. Our study of the implication of terms[26] will have revealed how relatively easy it is to turn an unreasonable action into a breach of contract by implying an obligation not to commit such an unreasonable act. The more meaningless the alleged term the more discretion is afforded to discover a breach giving rise to

---

[23] [1973] I.C.R. 560.
[24] [1978] I.C.R. 221.
[25] [1978] I.C.R. 205 at p. 211.
[26] See Chap. 2.

unfair dismissal.[27] Nowhere is this more apparent than in the use that has been made of an alleged obligation to sustain mutual trust and confidence.[28]

Correct application of the principle in *Western Excavating Ltd.* v. *Sharp*,[29] however, involves some limitation upon this discretion. Lord Denning made it quite clear that "entitlement" referred to the concept of a repudiatory breach. The breach must be sufficiently serious to justify the employee in treating the contract as at an end. There is little doubt that some earlier reported decisions, not only of industrial tribunals, failed to consider this requirement. It was, however, emphasised in *Walker* v. *Josiah Wedgwood and Sons Ltd.*[30] in which a series of incidents, such as failure to consult the works manager over the appointment of a subordinate and instructing him to pay increases to his subordinates when his own increase was withheld, were considered not indicative of any sufficiently serious breach to amount to repudiation. Although interspersed with examples of acceptance of apparently less serious breaches this insistence seems to have found support from most subsequent judgments.[31] It is nonetheless true to say that by the process of taking particular breaches and applying to them a generalised description such as 'destruction of trust and confidence' it is still possible to make relatively minor breaches look serious, especially when fortified by the fact that continuation of the relationship is, indeed, impossible because the employee has walked out. In *Garner* v. *Grange Furnishing Ltd.*[32] for instance, the E.A.T. allowed a series of incidents to amount to repudiation and added that conduct making it impossible for the employee to stay is plainly repudiatory.

There is no doubt that the need to act upon a repudiatory breach to establish constructive dismissal has led to a considerable increase in judicial attention to the development of implied terms in the contract of employment. As we have seen this raises some very complex considerations haphazard and ill-formulated discussion of which could make the contract of employment a virtually unworkable method of controlling the relationship of employment. Davies and Freedland[33] cite the judgment in *British Leyland (U.K.) Ltd.* v. *McQuilken*[34] and pose the question whether discussion of the implication of a collectively agreed scheme of redundancy into individual contracts of employment was an appropriate way to decide whether a constructive dismissal had occurred. A clause in this agreement provided that employees affected by reorganisation would be interviewed to discover whether they desired retraining or dismissal for redundancy. Subsequently the employer changed his plans, and employees were told they would have the option of transfer to other locations or retraining. Uncertainty continued as to the precise fate of individuals and McQuilken eventually left the employment without ever having been interviewed. The Scottish E.A.T. discussed the doctrine of construc-

---

[27] Early signs of this development were observed by Patrick Elias writing in (1978) 87 I.L.J. 100.
[28] For some extreme examples of the application of implied terms see: *Fyfe and McGrouther Ltd.* v. *Byrne* [1977] I.R.L.R. 29; *Wood* v. *Freeloader Ltd.* [1977] I.R.L.R. 455; *Isle of Wight Tourist Board* v. *Coombes* [1976] I.R.L.R. 413; *Gardner Ltd.* v. *Beresford* [1978] I.R.L.R. 63.
[29] *Supra.*
[30] [1978] I.C.R. 744.
[31] See, *e.g. Adams* v. *Charles Zub Associates Ltd.* [1978] I.R.L.R. 551; *Gillies* v. *Richard Danies and Co. Ltd.* [1979] I.R.L.R. 457; *Graham Oxley Tool Steels Ltd.* v. *Firth* [1980] I.R.L.R. 135.
[32] [1977] I.R.L.R. 206.
[33] At p. 340.
[34] [1978] I.R.L.R. 245.

tive dismissal and concluded that the collective agreement was a long term policy plan not incorporated into individual contracts of employment. It is apparent from the judgment that had it decided otherwise it would have found great difficulty in avoiding a decision that a constructive dismissal had occurred, notwithstanding its ultimate conclusion that the real reason which caused McQuilken to leave was uncertainty about his future.

The difficulty in avoiding complexity of this type is that it is not clear from the statutory definition how closely the reason for the termination must relate to the employer's conduct. All the statute says is that termination must take place in circumstances such that the employee is entitled to terminate. The courts have, however, insisted on a closer relationship than those words would necessarily imply. This is particularly apparent in the judgment in *Walker* v. *Josiah Wedgwood and Sons Ltd.*[35] where Arnold J. in the E.A.T., said:

> "The question has been whether it is sufficient merely to act in such a way as to indicate that the contractual relationship will not be continued, or whether it is necessary to do more than that, namely to indicate that the reason why it will not be continued is the conduct of the employers which is regarded as unjustified by the employee."

The court expressed surprise at the absence of authority on this but relied on some remarks in *Logabax Ltd.* v. *Titherley*[36] to assist it in reaching the conclusion that:

> " . . . it is at least a requisite that the employee should leave because of the breach of the employer's relevant duty to him, and that this should demonstrably be the case. It is not sufficient, we think, if he merely leaves. . . . And secondly, we think it is not sufficient if he leaves in circumstances which indicate some ground for his leaving other than the breach of the employer's obligation to him."

Constructive dismissal has thus become irretrievably tied to contractual principles applying to repudiatory breach. Whether, as formerly, the repudiatory breach itself terminated the contract or, as now, the acceptance terminates the contract, termination must relate to the breach and not to some other fact. In practice, tribunals are likely to imply this relation unless they are precluded by evidence clearly suggesting that the employee left, not because he accepted the breach but for some other reason, such that he had a better job.[37] By similar process of association the employee must leave whilst it is still open to him to accept the breach as repudiation. It is no longer correct to say that he must leave employment promptly. Browne-Wilkinson J. said in *W.E. Cox Toner (International) Ltd.* v. *Crook*[38] that mere continuation at work is not conclusive evidence of affirmation of the contract. Clear objection makes it impossible to imply such affirmation. But whilst the employee leaves the situation in limbo, so that it can neither be said that the repudiation has

---

[35] [1978] I.C.R. 744 at p. 751.
[36] [1977] I.R.L.R. 369.
[37] *Walker* v. *Josiah Wedgwood and Son Ltd.* [1978] I.R.L.R. 105.
[38] [1981] I.C.R. 823.

been accepted or waived, he leaves it open to the other party to withdraw the act of repudiation.[39]

Unilateral variation as constructive dismissal

It is normal for the courts to treat as constructive dismissal the common situation in which an employer, for one reason or another, offers the employee a job different from that which he is by contract obliged to do. As students who have absorbed the principles of the contract of employment frequently point out this situation appears to be one in which the contract has been terminated by the employer. It is fair to reply that this may not always be as obvious as it looks. In *White* v. *London Transport Executive*[40] the employee was employed as a waitress. Subsequently she assisted the manager of the social centre and was paid a supervisor's rate. When the manager left she was appointed to that position on a probationary basis. The probation was not successful and she was offered alternative employment as a waitress. It seems that the E.A.T. thought that her contract was as assistant to the manager since it held that failure to reinstate her in that job was a very small breach. With respect, it is suggested that it was a very large breach, however reasonable it might then have been considered to be. Apart from that, however, it is clear that had she been offered reinstatement at that level the employee could not have complained that removal from a probationary post was a termination of contract by the employer. The proper questions, as the judgment reveals, would have been directed to alleged repudiatory factors such as a possible contractual obligation to conduct periodic appraisal.

In *Land and Wilson* v. *West Yorkshire M.C.C.*[41] the Court of Appeal refused to regard withdrawal of one aspect of the job as a repudiatory breach on the ground that the contract of employment contained two separate elements and that it was necessary to imply a right to terminate one without affecting the other. This is likely to prove an exceptional case. More normally the elimination of a significant part of an employee's duties will be regarded as a repudiatory breach.[42]

To treat all cases of rejection of alternative offers as constructive dismissal might seem to avoid a number of difficult questions which might arise if some were argued as dismissal. In many such circumstances the employer might respond that when making the alternative offer he had taken no decision not to continue the former employment if the offer was rejected. On the other hand, if he could put forward this contention it would also remove the existence of the repudiatory breach necessary to found a constructive dismissal.

The employee must be careful not to presume an anticipatory breach. In *Haseltine Lake and Co.* v. *Dowler*[43] the employee left employment after numerous intimations that if he did not do so he would eventually be dismissed. The E.A.T. held that the employer had not committed himself to a date for dismissal so no question arose that he would inevitably be in breach. In *Financial Techniques (Planning Service) Ltd.* v. *Hughes*[44] the employee

---

[39] *Harrison* v. *Norwest Holst* [1985] I.R.L.R. 240.
[40] [1981] I.R.L.R. 261.
[41] [1981] I.C.R. 334.
[42] See *Coleman* v. *S. and W. Baldwin Ltd.* [1977] I.R.L.R. 342 (E.A.T.).
[43] [1981] I.C.R. 222. See also *International Computers Ltd.* v. *Kennedy* [1981] I.R.L.R. 28.
[44] [1981] I.R.L.R. 32.

resigned without notice before he had otherwise intended to do so, claiming that he was entitled to do so by reason of the employer's refusal to comply with a scheme of bonus payment. The Court of Appeal held that action in support of one point of view during a genuine dispute as to the meaning of the contract did not constitute an anticipatory breach. Templeman L.J., however, was of the opinion that a party who insisted on the correctness of his view might be guilty of such a breach. In the light of these decisions it is apparent that the employee may have difficulty in selecting the right time to leave since he may neither go too early nor leave it too late.

It may be argued that even if it is accepted that there is no real justification for treating such cases as constructive dismissal there is no real harm in doing so. This is almost certainly correct in practice. In theory it is possible to point out that in a case of constructive dismissal the employer does not have to establish a reason to rebut the presumption that it is unfair. In practice such a presumption virtually exists in cases of established constructive dismissal and the employer will have to work hard to prove the reasonableness of the dismissal so that the question becomes one only of the order in which the issues are considered.

Forced resignation as dismissal

One situation has consistently been recognised as giving rise to dismissal, notwithstanding that it does not fit neatly into any of the three statutory categories. An employee who resigns as a result of being given an option either to do so or be dismissed is usually said to have been constructively dismissed.[45] In *Sheffield* v. *Oxford Controls Ltd.*[46] the E.A.T. insisted that for this rule to apply the causal connection between the threat of dismissal and the resignation must be shown. In that case the threat of dismissal if the employee did not resign had been made, but the employee then negotiated terms upon which he left voluntarily.

(d) Extension of "dismissal" for redundancy claims

It is provided, in relation to redundancy claims that[47] where in accordance with any enactment or rule of law:

(a) any act on the part of an employer, or
(b) any event affecting an employer (including, in the case of an individual, his death)

operates so as to terminate a contract under which an employee is employed by him, that act or event shall be treated as a termination of the contract of the employer.

The fact that a contract has been frustrated clearly prevents the application of any of the three general categories of dismissal and so operates, effectively, as a defence to a claim for unfair dismissal.[48] It seems to be generally accepted that the same is true of a claim for redundancy compensation and that (b)

---

[45] See *Penprase* v. *Mander Bros. Ltd.* [1973] I.R.L.R. 167. An industrial tribunal decision.
[46] [1979] I.C.R. 396. See also, *Soctt* v. *Coalite Fuels and Chemicals Ltd.* [1988] I.R.L.R. 131.
[47] E.P.C.A. 1978, s.93(1).
[48] See, *e.g. F.C. Shepherd and Co. Ltd.* v. *Jerrom* [1986] I.C.R. 802.

above is not intended to apply to a frustrating event which, of course, does not *only* affect the employer.

The 1965 Act also made special provision for the employee to produce a notional dismissal from a situation in which he is periodically laid off or kept on short time. The object of this was to prevent employers artificially concealing a redundancy situation by attempting to retain under-employed labour forces (which shows the peculiar effect of enshrining in legislation, which is intended to be more or less permanent, temporary economic purposes.)

Where the employee is laid off or kept on short time,[49] other than where that is wholly or mainly attributable to a strike or lock-out,[50] the employee must give his employer written notice that he intends to claim a redundancy payment in respect of lay-off or short time. The right only arises where the lay-off or short time has occurred in four or more consecutive weeks or in six or more weeks (of which not more than three were consecutive) within a period of 13 weeks. In both cases the notice must be served within four weeks from the last of these weeks of lay-off or short time.[51] It does not matter whether this issue concerns entirely lay-off or short time or whether the two were intermingled.[52]

If the employer serves no counter notice then a redundancy payment may be claimed in the normal way, provided that the employee leaves his employment after giving a week's notice, or such longer period as is required as a minimum period of notice by his contract of employment, within three weeks of serving notice of his intention to claim.[53] If the employer, within seven days of the employee's notice, serves a written counter notice of intention to contest his liability, the issue of liability must be determined by a tribunal.[54] In this case (unless the counter notice is withdrawn), the employee retains his right, provided that he leaves by the proper period of notice within three weeks of being notified by the decision of the tribunal.[55]

The purpose of the counter notice is to enable the employer to invoke the statutory "defence"[56] that, on the date of service of the employee's notice, it was reasonably to be expected that within four weeks from that date the employee (if he remained in the employment) would enter into a period of not less than 13 weeks without lay-off or short time. This expectation is conclusively presumed not to be available if the employee is in fact laid off or put on short time in each of the four weeks following the date of his notice of intention to claim.[57] The work involved in the 13 weeks must be of a kind which the employee was employed to do.[58]

It should be borne in mind that some cases of lay-off or short-time may amount to a breach of contract by the employer entitling the employee to claim the existence of a constructive dismissal which will render satisfaction of

---

[49] E.P.C.A. 1978, s.81.
[50] *Ibid.* s.89(3).
[51] *Ibid.* s.88(1).
[52] *Ibid.* s.89(3).
[53] *Ibid.* ss.88(2) and 89(5)(a).
[54] *Ibid.* s.89(4).
[55] *Ibid.* s.89(5)(c).
[56] *Ibid.* s.88(3) and (4).
[57] *Ibid.* s.89(1).
[58] *Neepsend Steel and Tool Corporation* v. *Vaughan* [1972] I.C.R. 278.

the above conditions unnecessary.[59] It should also be borne in mind that what looks like a series of lay-offs may be better regarded as intermittent employment.[60]

"Effective" and "Relevant" date of dismissal

In practice it is, not infrequently, important to decide the date of dismissal (called the "effective" date for unfair dismissal claims and the "relevant" date for redundancy compensation claims). Where the employment is terminated by notice, statute provides that this date is that on which the notice expires. In the case of fixed term contracts it is said to be the date on which the term expires. The draftsman was a little less sure of his ground when it came to termination without notice, the date of which is said to be that "on which the termination takes effect." These general rules are subject to exception in three situations where the date will be significant, namely:

(a) calculation of the period of employment needed before entitlement to a written statement of terms and conditions of employment;
(b) calculation of the period of employment needed to qualify to make a claim for unfair dismissal or redundancy (*i.e.* to years); and
(c) determination of the quantum of the basic award of compensation for unfair dismissal or of redundancy payment.

It should be noted that for the purpose of deciding whether an application to an industrial tribunal is in time the effective date of dismissal is the actual date and not this extended notional date.

In *London Borough of Newham* v. *Wood*[61] the Court of Appeal affirmed the established rule that in a case of summary dismissal the effective date is that on which the employee ceases work. This is regardless of whether the employee unsuccessfully pursues an internal appeal, even if that appeal has the effect of treating his employment as suspended rather than terminated.[62]

Wedderburn[63] suggests that there is no reason to suppose that the decision of the House of Lords in *West Midlands Co-Operative Society Ltd.* v. *Tipton*[64] alters this. That decision had, in effect, extended the concept of dismissal into a process, ending with the final internal appeal on which any newly emergent facts should be taken into account in favour of the employee. The suggestion is likely to prove justified. The courts have refused to be shaken even by payment of full salary for ten months after notification of dismissal pending appeal.[65]

Although the provision relating to termination by notice seems clear enough it must be borne in mind that, in other circumstances, courts have looked upon a payment of wages in lieu of notice as liquidated damages for

---

[59] See *Davis Transport Ltd.* v. *Chattaway* [1972] I.C.R. 267; *Hanson* v. *Wood* [1968] I.T.R. 14. See also the judgments in *Jones* v. *H. Sherman Ltd.* [1979] I.T.R. 63 and *Johnson* v. *Cross* [1977] I.C.R. 872; although the latter decision arrives at some startlingly improbable conclusions.
[60] *Puttick* v. *John Wright and Sons (Blackwell) Ltd.* [1972] I.C.R. 457.
[61] [1985] I.R.L.R. 509.
[62] *Savage* v. *J. Sainsbury Ltd.* [1980] I.R.L.R. 109. See also *Howgate* v. *Fane Acoustics Ltd.* [1981] I.R.L.R. 161.
[63] 3rd Ed. at p. 223.
[64] [1986] 2 W.L.R. 306.
[65] *Board of Governors of National Heart and Chest Hospitals* v. *Nambiar* [1981] I.R.L.R. 196.

summary dismissal. This point was noted by the E.A.T. in *Leech* v. *Preston Borough Council*[66] which said that it was for the industrial tribunal to decide whether payment in lieu of notice was intended to follow a summary dismissal or whether the employment was intended to continue; the employee being excused from attending her work. Such concession clearly existed in *TBA Industrial Products Ltd.* v. *Morland*[67] where the employee had received notice clearly stating a future date of termination but had asked for, and been given, permission to leave early. In such a case it is open to the courts to find evidence of variation of the original date of termination.[68] On this possibility the Court of Appeal in *Morland*, by a majority, concluded that there was no evidence of variation. It was said by Browne-Wilkinson J. in *Chapman* v. *Letheby and Christopher Ltd.*[69] that the test of intention was the construction to be put upon the situation by a reasonable employee. In that case, he held, a reasonable employee would conclude that he was dismissed on the date specified, despite payment of a "retainer" in lieu of a further nine weeks' notice. This must cast some doubt on the continued validity, in practice, of the presumption of continuing employment during an unworked period of notice, said to exist by the Court of Appeal in *Lee* v. *Arthur Greaves (Lees) Ltd.*[70] It is a rare employee who will think himself not at liberty to work for another during such a period of notice. If that is his conclusion it would be difficult to say that he does not consider his employment at an end. It might then seem somewhat artificial to suggest that though that is his assumption it is not the construction he put on the actual notice of dismissal. It must follow from concentration on the intention of the parties that statutorily presumed extension of notice periods do not affect the date of termination save for those purposes specified by the statute.[71] Pursuit of an internal appeal against termination will not extend the effective date of dismissal[72] unless the employer makes it clear that dismissal is not to take effect until the appeal has been taken.[73] In *Batchelor* v. *British Railways Board*[74] the Court of Appeal held that dismissal occurred when it was stated to take effect even if this statement was a breach of contract contained in a disciplinary procedure intended to provide for continual employment pending the outcome of an appeal. Bingham LJ. raises, however, the interesting possibility that dismissal in breach of contract might amount to a repudiatory breach which the employee could reject, thus perpetuating his employment.

The new approach to repudiatory breach causes a potential problem since, logically, it ought to mean that the contract of employment does not end until the repudiation is accepted. If the repudiatory breach actually denies

---

[66] [1985] I.R.L.R. 337.
[67] [1982] I.R.L.R. 331.
[68] *Stapp* v. *The Staffordshire Society* [1982] I.R.L.R. 326. *In Staffordshire C.C.* v. *Secretary of State for Employment* [1988] I.R.L.R. 3 the E.A.T. endorsed the alternative, adopted by an industrial tribunal, holding that the original dismissal had been withdrawn.
[69] [1981] I.R.L.R. 440.
[70] [1974] I.R.R. 501.
[71] *Slater* v. *Secretary of State for Employment* [1981] I.R.L.R. 303.
[72] *J. Sainsbury Ltd.* v. *Savage* [1981] I.C.R.1.
[73] As would normally have been the case in dismissals such as that which occurred in *Batchelor* v. *British Railways Board* [1987] I.R.L.R. 136.
[74] *Supra.*

the employee the opportunity to work, however, it has been held[75] that, though the contract may continue for some purposes, the inability of the employee to insist on being employed and the transmutation of his employment rights into a right of damages should signal the effective date of termination.

---

[75] *Robert Cort and Son Ltd.* v. *Charman* [1981] I.C.R. 816.

CHAPTER V

UNFAIR DISMISSAL

Introduction

The common law afforded no job security. An employee dismissed for any, or no, reason, had no remedy provided he was given "proper" notice or paid wages in lieu for this period. If this was not done the employer was free to buy out his default by no more than payment of what he would have been obliged to pay during that period of notice. The fact that, in 1963 when the first Contracts of Employment Act was passed, it was considered an advance to fix the statutory minimum period of notice at four weeks for an employee with five years' continuous employment (even now this would only be five weeks) reveals the inadequacy of employment protection.

Breaking away from contract, the legislature, in 1971, based the statutory right to a remedy for dismissal on the unreasonableness of the employer's conduct. Notice to terminate, for example, becomes totally irrelevant to the issue of fairness of dismissal.[1] A dismissal cannot become more reasonable because its effect is deferred. The common law had never conceded even that an employee might demand a fair procedure before dismissal; though, presumably, had it thought about it, it might have afforded him damages for failure to observe a contractually incorporated procedure. A "reasonable" employer, on the other hand, may readily be expected to follow a fair procedure. Jurisdiction in respect of the new right was naturally assigned to the existing industrial tribunals which were already handling claims for compensation arising from dismissal for redundancy. Employees generally had never been all that keen on County (or any other) courts which they might approach for damages for breach of contract or under the Master and Servant Acts. Consequently a tribunal with power to outvote its legally qualified chairman and which contained at least one member who might be assumed to appreciate the problems of the employee was, and is, far more popular. It is easy enough to approach a County Court but few who have not done so think so. The patent simplicity of applying to an industrial tribunal was, in itself, an achievement which should not be underrated. Consequently 29,392 applications in respect of unfair dismissal were made to industrial tribunals in the year ending March 31, 1987.[2] Some ten and a half thousand of these were settled under the auspices of ACAS conciliation, about 9000 were withdrawn and, in the end, 3129 succeeded at a tribunal hearing. But only 103 (1.1 per cent. of cases heard and 0.4 per cent. of all applications) resulted in an order for reinstatement or re-engagement and 70 per cent. of successful applicants

---

[1] *Treganowan* v. *Robert Knee and Co. Ltd.* [1975] I.C.R. 405. Followed in *B.S.C. Sports and Social Club* v. *Morgan* [1987] I.R.L.R. 391.
[2] Employment Gazette Vol. 95 No. 10, pp. 498–501.

received less than £3000 in compensation. Perhaps this matters to the applicant less than it should. He or she often appears primarily to want some public acknowledgment of unfair treatment.

There are, as we shall see[3] considerable barriers to pursuing a claim for unfair dismissal. One may not even be an employee, perhaps, especially in a claim based on constructive dismissal it will appear that the statutory definition of dismissal[4] has not been satisfied; the applicant may have insufficient continuous employment to qualify, or the complaint may be out of time. There will certainly be a great temptation to settle. ACAS maintains a service of employment conciliation officers with a duty to seek a settlement if they consider the effort has a reasonable prospect of success. As in all judicial procedures there is a fair rate of settlement "at the door" of the tribunal.

Assuming the applicant enters the tribunal it is sometimes said that he will be put off by the complexity of the law or of procedure. Upon enquiry those who complain of this are usually not clear what they mean. The law can be complex on preliminary issues such as qualifications to claim but rules have all but disappeared from assessment of the reasonableness of dismissal, and the citation of cases with them. Lawyers either chairing, or appearing before, tribunals, are often worried that the relaxation of procedural requirements has reached the point of affecting the reliability of the decisions and apocryphal stories of the early days, where claimants were asked how they pleaded, would now be viewed as pure fantasy. The legal chairmen whose experiences are almost invariably of an adversarial system, punctuated by examination-in-chief and cross-examination, instinctively apply this and justify the application by saying it is the best way to discover the truth. Low standards of cross-examination, which normally prevail, may suggest that an inquisitorial system in which a story is told and tested by experienced tribunal members may be just as good. However that may be, there is probably enough appearance of legalism in the procedure to worry the lay applicant The worry becomes conviction if he finds no opportunity to say something vital which he feels would have won him the case he lost.

So far, however, we have mentioned nothing fundamental to the system which lessens the value of industrial tribunals. In the first few years of administering unfair dismissal claims, and guided by the National Industrial Relations Court, they applied an identifiable set of rules. Procedure was regarded as involving a requirement of prior warning, unless the case was sufficiently serious to exclude it, and "hearing." The process gave birth to terms such as "gross misconduct" (said to justify dismissal without prior warning) which still appear in dismissal practice (and in the ACAS code of practice). These, in turn led to an invention of sub-rules[5] so that it could even be laid down that a warning was inadequate if it did not say that an employee would be dismissed, rather than might be dismissed, for the next offence. Somehow, forms of dismissal on economic or organisational grounds or for sickness were fitted in to this "misconduct" pattern. The author has argued elsewhere[6] that this "natural justice" model provides no reasonable chance of securing fair-

---

[3] *Infra*, pp. 206 *et seq.*
[4] See pp. 130–139, *supra.*
[5] See, *e.g. Martin* v. *Yorkshire Imperial Metals Ltd.* [1978] I.R.L.R. 440.
[6] R. W. Rideout, *Unfair Dismissal—Tribunal or Arbitration.* (1986) 15 I.L.J. 84.

ness in the hands of an inevitably partial management and that the industrial relations model of consultation and negotiation between two opposed parties, favoured for redundancy cases in *Williams* v. *Compair Maxam Ltd.*,[7] is a better safeguard. However that may be, the rules have given way to a broader, impressionistic, approach, described as that of an industrial jury and expressed by the Court of Appeal as the application of the single pervasive test of reasonableness. Most decisions on the substantive application of this test are decisions of fact which do not give rise to a right of appeal to the Employment Appeal Tribunal. The process should have benefited considerably from the speed with which an unchallengeable conclusion can be reached and the simplicity of the law which frequently makes it pointless to cite precedent.

Fundamental weaknesses, at least from the point of view of its protective potential, are apparent. The most far-reaching of these, it is submitted, lies at the heart in the test of the reasonable employer. He is not to be confused with the reasonable man. A court applying the standard of the reasonable man applies its own standards of reasonableness. The reasonable judge may do a good job in imagining himself on the Clapham omnibus but, in the end, what is reasonable is what he would like to think he would do in that circumstance. An industrial tribunal must ask what, in its experience, reasonable employers do. Employers are scarcely likely to be considered unreasonable if they do what a substantial proportion of employers would do. Industrial tribunals do not consider it part of their function to judge the business merits of management decisions. Once such a decision, as, for instance, to reorganise the workforce, has been made management may adopt a number of courses of implementation, all of which, experience dictates, are reasonable choices. In the same way certain managerial responses are either standard or, at least, widely applied. There is no way in which such action can be described as that of an unreasonable employer. The tribunals, therefore, are unable to produce, or have disentitled themselves from producing, a lead in developing improved practices, such, for instance, as would be taken by the Health and Safety Executive applying the test of reasonable practicability which is not so confined to existing practices. To some extent, therefore, "the employer" sets his own standard of reasonable behaviour and industrial tribunals round up those who fall out of line. This is not to suggest that such a limitation is not desirable, but only to point out the restriction it places on a developing concept of reasonableness.

Industrial tribunals labour under other disadvantages, sometimes of their own making. The idea that the "employer," by which is meant in this context immediately superior management, could not be expected to work harmoniously with an employee, dismissed by management and returned by outside intervention, is entrenched in British industrial psychology, though not that of some other countries. British industrial tribunals accept as the reason for dismissal that which the employer reasonably believes to exist. In other countries the employer may be required to show that the supposed reason exists as a fact.

It is submitted, however, that an overriding defect of the tribunal system is that it stands apart from industrial relations. It is in this respect, more than

---

[7] [1982] I.R.L.R. 83.

any other, that the lawyer has imposed a regime of external adjudication. He either does not know, or does not accept, that many large industrial establishments operate an effective system for dealing with disciplinary disputes, even to the point of reversing dismissals. There is no reason why he should notice that those employers less frequently appear in industrial tribunals. But he should notice that the industrial tribunal takes over where internal dispute settlement leaves off and that it would be better if tribunals operated by industrial relations standards than by legalistic ones.

The reason for dismissal

We turn now to consider the principal issues which have to be determined when dealing with the substantive question of whether a dismissal is fair.

Save in the case of a constructive dismissal, a dismissed employee is entitled, on request, to be supplied, within 14 days, with a written statement giving particulars of the reasons for his dismissal. The statement is admissible in evidence in any proceedings.[8] Failure to supply it entitles the employee to exact a fixed penalty equivalent to two weeks' wages (without any upper limit). Once the reasons are stated, the employer will, in practice, do his case little good by seeking to show that there were other reasons. They, or the written statement, are likely to be disbelieved and, in any event, it is likely to be considered unreasonable to expect the employee to deal with so much uncertainty.

The jurisdiction of an industrial tribunal depends, of course, on its ability to establish reasons. If it is unable to decide what the reasons, or principal reason, actually were[9] it has no means of deciding whether the dismissal is fair or unfair. The statutory presumption that a dismissal is necessarily unfair unless the reason is shown is inevitable.

The process of establishing the reason for dismissal adds nothing to the extensive academic debate about the nature and objectives of legal intervention in the employment relationship and, probably for this reason, has been neglected by recent academic writers. Apart from such legal issues as tend to arise in preliminary tribunal proceedings such, for instance, as employment and qualifications to claim, this is the most technically precise question remaining in the law of unfair dismissal—the question of "dismissal" itself notwithstanding. Perhaps because it tends to be neglected by writers it is also considerably misunderstood.

Paradoxically that aspect which, to the casual observer, would appear to be a tribunal's first consideration is no more than a meaningless charade. Section 57(1)(b) of E.P.C.A. 1978 requires the employer to show that the reason, or principal reason, falls within subsection (2), or is some other substantial reason of a kind such as to justify the dismissal of an employee holding the position which that employee held. Subsection (2) sets out four categories of reasons in language so general as to have almost no meaning, save in the restrictive category of "redundancy." The other three are that the reason:

   (a) related to the capability or qualifications of the employee for perform-

---

[8] E.P.C.A. 1987, s.53(3).
[9] As in *Timex Corporation Ltd.* v. *Thomson* [1981] I.R.L.R. 522.

ing work of the kind he was employed to do (so, presumably, supposing an enquiry into his contractual obligations);

(b) related to the conduct of the employee; or

(c) was that the employee could not continue to work in the position he
held without contravention of a legislative duty or restriction.

Almost inevitably, "redundancy" has assumed the technical position
imposed on it by section 81 although there is no reason why the requirements
of Part VI should affect Part V. If anything turned on the classification, it
would almost certainly have needed to be redrafted for this reason alone since
all those re-organisational reasons falling short of redundancy have to be
classified within the miscellaneous category of "some other substantial
reason." Yet many tribunals solemnly commence proceedings by classifying
the reason and most model forms of decision include a statement of it.[10] If the
word "other" were omitted the requirement to show some substantial reason
of a kind such as to justify dismissal of that employee would suffice to include
all types of reason.

Except, that is, that the word "substantial" seems also to be meaningless.
This must be so otherwise a qualification would be imposed on the miscellaneous category which is not imposed on the "specific" classifications. It
must also be so otherwise determination of the "substantial" nature of the
reason would enter into the area covered by the test of reasonableness set out
in section 57(3). And so it has proved. In *Priddle* v. *Dibble*,[11] Bristow J. in the
E.A.T. said that "justify" did not involve any element of fairness, which was
only to be considered once the employer has shown a reason within the section. The E.A.T. also held, it is submitted, as is obvious, that there was no
common factor among the specified reasons to permit the miscellaneous
category to be construed *ejusdem generis*.

The student will be inclined to ask at this point whether there is any point in
asking more than that the employer should establish the reason for the dismissal. He would be justified. In *Thomson* v. *Alloa Motor Company Ltd.*[12] Lord
McDonald in the Scottish E.A.T. said that the miscellaneous category was
confined to actions of such a nature as to reflect in some way upon the
employer-employee relationship. He held that damage to the employer's
petrol pumps caused accidentally by a petrol pump attendant as she left work
under driving instruction was not of this kind. In *Kent County Council* v. *Gil-
ham (No. 2)*[13] Griffiths L.J. in the Court of Appeal said (*obiter*) that the purpose of the requirement was to prevent the employer dismissing for some
trivial or unworthy reason. A reason which could justify dismissal passes as a
substantial reason. This, it is suggested with respect, is badly put because it
tends to suggest enquiry into the adequacy, rather than the nature, of the
reason and, as Griffiths L.J. said in the next paragraph, that would confuse
subsection 57(1) with subsection 57(3). Lord McDonald is nearer the point.
The matter must have some relevance to the employment relationship. This,

---

[10] See also the discussion of this point in *Monie* v. *Coral Racing Ltd.* [1981] I.C.R. at
pp. 120–121.
[11] [1978] I.C.R. 149.
[12] [1983] I.R.L.R. 403.
[13] [1985] I.R.L.R. 18.

however, is not particularly helpful since "I don't like him" would be a reason relevant to a personal relationship. The colour of the employee's hair may not seem a very reasonable ground on which to base a dismissal but it could be the reason and, if purple with gold streaks, could be relevant. The purpose of this requirement is not to prevent dismissal for a trivial reason. That is the purpose of the test of reasonableness. It is clearly desirable that there should be a separate stage to establish what the reasons were, but beyond that there is no need for a standard of sufficiency. How is it possible to say that what obviously was the reason is not the reason because it cannot be presented as such? If an employee accidentally damages petrol pumps when leaving work and is dismissed accordingly that is the reason for dismissal. The nature of such a ground need not be separated from its adequacy. If it were not so it is difficult to see why the requirement of a third party, not a customer of the employer, as in *Dobie* v. *Burns International Security*[14] should constitute a reason, except that the employer has chosen, by contract with that third party, to make it so.

Another attempt to lay down a rule for excluding existing reasons was made in *Wadley* v. *Eager Electrical Ltd.*[15] where the employee had been dismissed following the arrest of his wife on charges of theft from the employer. The E.A.T. said that the reason must be some act on the part of one side or the other to the contract of employment in breach of the obligation to maintain trust and confidence that would be a substantial reason of a kind to justify dismissal. The only reason for such a demand is the need to give some significant meaning to the words "substantial reason of a kind to justify dismissal." The only way to do that is to attribute to them some content indicating sufficiency. If that were the purpose of the subsection it would mean that the employer was being required to prove an element of reasonableness as to which section 57(3) does not impose on him the burden of proof. *Wadley*, would have been better decided on the ground of the employer's reasonable belief, to consideration of which we will shortly come. There is, it is submitted, only one type of reason which cannot be advanced and that is one expressly precluded from consideration by statute.[16]

Nevertheless, there is some value in the generalised statutory list of sufficient reasons. It would be too severe a requirement that the employer should establish every example constituting part of the motive for dismissal. It will suffice therefore, if the respondent establishes, by sufficient examples, a reason which can be classified within one of these broad headings.

It is required that the employer show the sole or principal reason.[17] This was applied strictly by the House of Lords in *Smith* v. *City of Glasgow District Council.*[18] A charge of unsatisfactory performance in respect of an overspending in the annual Housing Repairs fund was supported by three more specific allegations. An additional charge of failure to implement a proper programme of work in respect of a particular contract was also advanced. Lord Wheatley, in the Inner House of the Court of Session, had taken liter-

---

[14] [1984] I.C.R. 812.
[15] [1986] I.R.L.R. 93.
[16] *e.g. Property Guards Ltd.* v. *Taylor & Kershaw* [1982] I.R.L.R. 175 applying Rehabilitation of Offenders Act 1974, s.4.
[17] E.P.C.A. s.57(1)(a).
[18] [1987] I.R.L.R. 326.

ally the statutory requirement to prove a principal reason but concluded that all four separate charges related to "conduct" which, therefore, constituted the principal reason. In his view, and that of the House of Lords, however, the failure to establish a constituent of the principal reason which must have influenced the decision was fatal to the fairness of dismissal.

It seems likely that tribunals often do identify a principal reason in these broad terms. So, "redundancy" is normally treated as the principal reason for a dismissal whilst the reason for selection of an individual is regarded as subsidiary. The case will proceed to the stage of considering reasonableness once the redundancy is proved and the subsidiary reason for selection will go solely to the issue of reasonableness.[18a] Such a differentiation would be a considerably more artificial exercise in areas outside redundancy or re-organisation, as the decision in *Smith* v. *Glasgow* reveals. In most cases it is likely that a group of reasons can be brought together under one of the very general heads— even if that one is "some other substantial reason." This is certainly what tribunals normally assume and so the question of what is the principal, and what the subsidiary, reason rarely arises for discussion. On the rare occasions when there are obviously reasons which do not fall within the principal head they will be sufficiently considered as going to the reasonableness of the reaction to the principal reason. It seems likely, therefore, that Lord Wheatley was right to conclude that the employer only has to prove a principal reason or principal group of reasons, even if, as he inadvertently demonstrated, it is often easy to classify lack of ability as misconduct, and vice-versa. An employer who fails to establish an alleged subsidiary reason, therefore, will not automatically lose his case. He can still succeed if the tribunal considers it fair to dismiss notwithstanding his taking into account, as a minor element, a matter in which he did not reasonably believe. Does the same apply where, as in *Smith's* case, the employer proves only some of the factors which have led him to conclude that there has been misconduct (or one or more elements of some other general head)? The answer to this would seem to be in the affirmative. The unproved element in the misconduct may be no more than an example. It follows that other examples may be sufficient to establish a reasonable belief in the existence of the principal reason. Whether that misconduct was a reasonable ground for dismissal is for consideration under section 57(3). The same treatment would seem appropriate where the unsubstantiated reason was subsidiary to the principal group. Its non-existence should not stop the case proceeding to the stage of consideration of reasonableness but it will then become a factor for consideration.

The existence of two or more reasons may, however, cause further problems. There is, of course, always the possibility that the way in which the two are presented causes the tribunal to doubt the principal reason. This happened in *Timex Corporation* v. *Thomson*[19] where, if the above analysis is correct, what were presented as subsidiary reasons for applying to the applicant the principal reason of redundancy were suspected of being themselves the

---

[18a] The decision of the House of Lords in *Stockton on Tees B.C.* v. *Brown* [1988] I.C.R. 410 that failure to offer a redundant employee alternative employment because she was pregnant resulted in dismissal for a principal reason connected with pregnancy (E.P.C.A. s. 60) probably rests on the fact that the dismissal could be seen to arise because of the failure of the alternative rather than the original redundancy.

[19] [1981] I.R.L.R. 522.

principal reason. In such a case it must be that the employer has failed to show what is the principal reason.[20]

It is, however, well established that the principal reason will not be invalidated because the facts constituting it are wrongly labelled. An employer who describes an established set of facts as amounting to "misconduct" would not fail to establish these facts as the reason because a tribunal considered them more properly described as showing "incompetence." The exception is long standing,[21] but, it is submitted, must be strictly applied. If the reason accepted by the tribunal depends on any unproven fact, different from that supporting the reason given, then the substitution is not proved. This was clearly the basis of the decision in *Hannan* v. *TNT-IPEC (U.K.) Ltd.*[22] In *Hotson* v. *Wisbech Conservative Club*[23] the person responsible for selling drinks and ordering stock for the club bar failed to provide an explanation of a considerable shortfall of cash receipts as against invoiced purchases. She was dismissed for a reason eventually given in rather obscure language but best summarised as "inefficiency." At the tribunal hearing the respondent's witness agreed with the chairman that the real reason was dishonesty but that the respondent did not want "all the publicity of branding her a thief." The E.A.T. held that this was more than a mere change of label. It is submitted that this is clearly correct. The facts necessary to produce a reasonable belief in dishonesty must include belief in the existence of dishonest intention. It is true that this conclusion may be no more than a deduction from other facts but it is a deduction that in fact such an intention existed. If the respondent is not satisfied of the existence of such a dishonest intention the charge established is a very different thing and is certainly not a mere change of label. The student will be less satisfied with the actual reasoning of Waite J. He seems to have assumed that the facts necessary to support inefficiency and dishonesty were the same but, nevertheless, described the alteration of the charge as too serious and significant to be described as a change of label. Earlier, however, he had given, as an example of a change of label, substitution of "incapability" for "redundancy." It seems that the learned judge defined a change of label as "substitution of a reason no more serious than the original reason." This is the sort of sloppy reasoning by the E.A.T. which causes so many students to despair of finding any substantial ground on which to base the law. In *Hannan's* case "redundancy" was put forward as the reason for dismissal but the tribunal found the reason to be re-organisation (falling within the miscellaneous category of "some other substantial reason"). This is the classic example of mis-labelling resulting from a failure to understand the complexities of the statutory definition of redundancy which, alone among the categories of reasons, cannot be left to broad popular assumptions of the meanings of words. The E.A.T. was more concerned with justice in the tribunal hearing

---

[20] Much the same occurred in *Grootcon (U.K.) Ltd.* v. *Keld* [1984] I.R.L.R. 302 where no less than three possible primary reasons were suggested and the Scottish E.A.T. held that there was insufficient evidence to support the conclusion of an industrial tribunal that the existence of incapability had been proved. So also in *McCrory* v. *Magee* [1983] I.R.L.R. 414 where the tribunal, influenced by the triviality of "failure to take care of the employer's goods" as a type of "gross misconduct," concluded that the real reason was suspicion of dishonesty.

[21] See *Abernethy* v. *Mott, Hay and Anderson* [1974] I.C.R. 323.

[22] [1986] I.R.L.R. 165.

[23] [1984] I.R.L.R. 422.

than with the statutory obligation to show the correct reason but its conclusion that, on one basis or the other, apparently different grounds will only be different labels where the difference does not go to the facts and substance is in line with the authorities. If the aspect with which the E.A.T. was concerned is thought to be material in view of the express statutory prohibition on introducing such a change then it can be pointed out that anything more than a change of label will inevitably suggest that the case would have been conducted differently before the tribunal had the correct reason been given.

Very early in the history of unfair dismissal it was firmly established that the reason must be shown to exist at the time of dismissal, that is to say, when the final decision to dismiss is taken.[24] It is not entirely surprising that the common law allowed an employer to justify summary dismissal for breach of contract of which he did not know at the time[25] but it is probably incorrect in principle to extend the right of dismissal to a situation in which the breach of contract only occurred after the decision to dismiss.[26] When one asks a question "what is fair?" rather than "what is the actual contractual position?" it seems at first sight obvious that the dismissal must stand or fall by the facts known at the time the decision was made. It is, of course, true that this time cannot be fixed with absolute certainty. It is also true that such a rule tends to cut off what may be a developing line of thought. Extraordinary use was made of this effect in *O'Hare* v. *Rotaprint Ltd.*[27] where the E.A.T. held that redundancy had not been established as a reason for dismissal, despite the fact that the result was selection of employees without replacement, because the employer, at the time of dismissal had not progressed beyond the conclusion that he must somehow cut his costs.

This rule should not be presented so as to justify the proposition that nothing matters once the decision has been taken. Whilst a dismissal cannot be supported by a later discovered reason which clearly could not be the reason for the dismissal, it may well be unfair to deny an employee a later right to have that decision reviewed on new facts.[28] If such an opportunity for review exists and permits the revelation that the decision may have been unjustified it may, equally, be unfair for the respondent to decline to reverse it.[29] These concessions to the fact that the process of dismissal must be fair, however, do not effect the conclusion that the reason was, and remains, that in the mind of the respondent at the time of the dismissal.

A little more must, however, be added to make it clear what is the position of discredited reasons. In *St Anne's Board Mill Co. Ltd.* v. *Brien*[30] it was held that a reason in which the employer reasonably believed at the time of dismissal can continue to be relied on despite later doubt, or even certainty that it was not correct. Indeed, it must be relied on. It was the reason and no

---

[24] *Earl* v. *Slater and Wheeler Ltd.* [1972] I.C.R. 508 see also *Abernethy* v. *Mott, Hay and Anderson* [1974] I.C.R. 323 and the House of Lords confirmed this in *W. Devis and Sons Ltd.* v. *Atkins* [1977] I.C.R. 662.

[25] *Boston Deep Sea Fishing and Ice Co. Ltd.* v. *Ansell* (1888) 39 Ch.D. 339.

[26] *Ridgway* v. *Hungerford Market Co.* (1835) 3 Ad. and EP 171. See now on this issue *Cyril Leonard Co. Ltd.* v. *Sim Securities Trust Ltd.* [1972] 1 W.L.R. 80.

[27] [1980] I.R.L.R. 47.

[28] *West Midlands Co-operative Society Ltd.* v. *Tipton* [1985] I.C.R. 444.

[29] *Greenall Whitley P.L.C.* v. *Carr* [1985] I.R.L.R. 289.

[30] [1973] I.C.R. 444.

attempt to change it can effectively substitute another.[31] So dismissal for dishonesty may stand as a fair dismissal despite subsequent acquittal, on substantive grounds, of criminal charges arising therefrom. So far as the aspect of proof of reason goes, nothing that happens after the dismissal can affect the existence of that reason. Fairness is a wholly different consideration. What action could normally be taken in the light of the existence of that reason may well be changed by subsequent doubt cast on it.

United Kingdom law has always been clear that tribunals seek the reason which the employer believed—not necessarily the reason that actually existed. So clear is this proposition that it is in danger of being accepted as inevitable. If we are to ask whether a reasonable employer, in the light of the reason would have dismissed, however, there is no inevitability in the assumption that we can base that only on his reasonable belief. The thinking behind this approach appears to depend on some idea that the employer is at fault for acting unreasonably. It would be of great benefit to processes such as reinstatement if the feeling of fault were dispensed with. Why should we not ask what a reasonable employer would have done in the light of the reasons which actually existed? He may have come to the wrong conclusion as to those facts but now that it appears that he has why should he not be required to undo, or compensate for, what he has incorrectly done? It cannot be contended that tribunals are not equipped to find the true facts. Very often it is clear at the tribunal hearing that the employer's belief could not be sustained as such in the light of the facts he now should reasonably know. It can be argued that the way the law has gone is the way it was directed by the statutory requirement that the employer should show the reason for dismissal. How can the reason be other than that which was in his mind? If this were to be disallowed would the employer inevitably be left without a reason since, even if one existed, he did not have that one in his mind? Or, by disallowing his reason because it was wrong, must he be permitted to substitute the actual situation?

Unanswerable as these problems may seem, the courts have gone some way to discounting a reason actually in the employer's mind without permitting an alternative to be substituted. This arises from the rule, if it is a rule, that a reason, though a matter of the employer's belief, can only be advanced if it has been established in his mind by reasonable enquiry. In *British Home Stores Ltd.* v. *Burchell*[32] the applicant had been dismissed for, allegedly, being involved in dishonest counter-signing of fellow employees' purchases. She was implicated by another employee during the employer's investigation. Arnold J. held that the test of reason was whether the employer entertained a reasonable suspicion amounting to a belief and that, in order to amount to a reasonable belief it must be shown that the employer did indeed hold that belief, having in his mind reasonable grounds to sustain it. Thirdly, the belief must have been formed after the employer had carried out as much investigation as was reasonable in all the circumstances. There was no objective standard by which to judge as correct and justifiable an alleged reason and the process of reasonable investigation was distinct from the procedure of deciding what action to take after so establishing the reason. The Court of Appeal,

---

[31] *Monie* v. *Coral Racing Ltd.* [1980] I.R.L.R. 464.
[32] [1978] I.R.L.R. 379.

obiter, in *W. Weddel and Co. Ltd.* v. *Tepper*,[33] preferred this approach to the application of a test based on *St Anne's Board Mill Co. Ltd.* v. *Brien*[34] of whether the employer had acted on the basis of matters which he ought reasonably to have known. The remarks of the Court of Appeal are a good deal less satisfactory than the decision in *Burchell* since they undoubtedly confuse the test of reasonableness of dismissal with the establishment of the reason.

The question of what is a reasonable enquiry is, of course, a question of fact for the tribunal; but there are one or two standard problems which may be considered briefly. It often happens that an employer is unable to conduct a full enquiry in a case where criminal charges may be preferred because the police, for one reason or another, ask him not to do so. It was made clear by the Court of Appeal in *Pritchett and Dyjasek* v. *J. McIntyre Ltd.*[35] that this consideration is effectively dealt with by the *Burchell* requirement of such enquiry as can reasonably be expected. The Court of Appeal took the view that the tribunal were entitled to find that it would have been impossible for the employer to conduct a full enquiry in view of his obligation of confidentiality to the police. One wonders, however, how far this would extend to "impossibility" amounting to no more than breach of contractual obligations to other third parties. This situation must be distinguished from that in *Read* v. *Phoenix Preservation Ltd.*[36] where the presence of two policemen at the enquiry was held to have prevented the employee adequately presenting his side of the story. Presumably this turns on the assumption that there was nothing in practice to prevent an adequate enquiry being held otherwise than in the presence of the police. In *Royal Society for the Protection of Birds* v. *Croucher*[37] the employee admitted the charge for which he was dismissed. The E.A.T. held that the industrial tribunal had been wrong to regard the *Burchell* test as one to be applied automatically. There was, said the court, very little scope for the kind of investigation, referred to in that case, designed to affirm a suspicion or clear up a doubt as to whether or not a particular act of misconduct has occurred.

The *Burchell* test of the adequacy of the reason is admirably useful and, perhaps for that reason, largely unquestioned in reported decisions. It has the considerable merit of avoiding the problem experienced by the Court of Appeal in *Hindle* v. *Percival Boats Ltd.*[38] of having, in practice, to accept the assertion of belief in one reason when another seems more probable. Reasonable enquiry in such circumstances would, presumably, produce evidence that both possibilities were discussed, thus enabling a clearer view to be formed of whether the employer really did believe the less likely, but more convenient, reason. Apart from the usefulness of the test one may pause to wonder from where was derived the authority for the suggestion that proof of a reason could not succeed without such enquiry as was reasonable in the circumstances. An unreasonable employer may jump to a conclusion without adequate consideration. The end result will be the same since it will be held

---

[33] [1980] I.R.L.R. 96.
[34] *Supra.*
[35] [1987] I.R.L.R. 18.
[36] [1985] I.R.L.R. 93.
[37] [1984] I.R.L.R. 425.
[38] [1969] 1 W.L.R. 174.

that he has acted unfairly. But why should it be held that he has failed to show the reason for the dismissal when plainly he has shown his reason? Did Arnold J. also, though less obviously, confuse the two stages, despite saying that they were separate?

In *Monie* v. *Coral Racing Ltd.*[39] the E.A.T., it is submitted, made something of a mess of resolving the effect of proof of suspicion. The Court of Appeal, however, held that suspicion could be advanced as a reason for dismissal. This is obviously correct. Dismissal on suspicion not founded on reasonable enquiry will, under *Burchell*, be incapable of defence, since no reason can be shown. But if there has been reasonable enquiry which leaves only a suspicion then "suspicion" is the reason for the dismissal and the tribunal can move on to consider whether dismissal was the reaction of a reasonable employer. In *Burchell*, it will be remembered, Arnold J. spoke of "suspicion amounting to belief." But why should an employer who has said "I do not believe he did it, but I think he might have done and I cannot afford to take the risk" not advance that as his reason for dismissal and be entitled to have the reasonableness of his reaction considered?

In *Monie's* case only one of two employees had, almost certainly, stolen cash from the employer's safe. The enquiry, which may be presumed to have been reasonable, did not establish which of them was guilty. Both were dismissed for dishonesty although, on appeal, a discerning director had sought to alter this ground to misconduct in using unauthorised cash procedures. This attempt failed because it purported to substitute a different reason for that which had motivated the dismissal (although the E.A.T. had thought it more obvious that an employer should be able, on appeal, to confirm the dismissal for other reasons). Sir David Cairns considered that the industrial tribunal had asked the correct question in putting forward the requirement that there should be "solid and sensible grounds on which the employers could reasonably infer or suspect dishonesty."[40] Plainly, this goes further than the proposition of Arnold J. in *British Home Stores* v. *Burchell*[41] that the employer must show a "reasonable suspicion amounting to a belief." That, it is suggested, would require an employer actually to believe the conclusion whilst admitting the presence of circumstances justifying doubt in others. Sir David Cairns' formulation appears to acknowledge that an employer may admit that he is not sure; but still fairly dismiss on the ground that he has a reasonable suspicion. The qualification "reasonable" still indicates that the suspicion must exist after reasonable enquiry. Dunn L.J. makes this less strict view even clearer when he says "it is not necessary for the employer to believe that either of them acted dishonestly."[42] Stephenson L.J. confuses the issues by saying:

"When a single employee is suspected of dishonesty, it would clearly be unfair

---

[39] [1981] I.C.R. 109.

[40] At p. 121. This seems preferable to the requirement in *Whitbread and Co. p.l.c.* v. *Thomas* [1988] I.R.L.R. 43 that the tribunal should be satisfied that one or more of those dismissed did commit the offence.

[41] [1980] I.C.R. 303 at p. 304.

[42] At p. 124.

and unreasonable for an employer to dismiss him without belief in his guilt and reasonable grounds for that belief.''[43]

He had taken part in the decision in *Weddel and Co. Ltd.* v. *Tepper*[44] which has here been described as an unsatisfactory confusion of two different stages and it is plain from this passage that he is again confusing the need to establish reason with the test of fairness.[45]

It is submitted that the position of suspicion as a reason is, despite this confusion, now tolerably clear. The employer must put forward a reason in which he believes and he can only assert belief after reasonable enquiry. If such enquiries leave him with no more than a belief that it may, or may not, be so he can only assert belief in a possibility. In this sense he is putting forward only a well-founded suspicion but this is capable of being accepted as the reason for the dismissal. Lest this be thought an empty exercise in logic, if Stephenson L.J. is right that the entertainment of doubt necessarily renders subsequent dismissal unfair, it must be said, with respect, that that proposition cannot be correct. A reasonable employer may well come to the conclusion that he cannot retain an employee as to whose honesty he has a well founded suspicion, even though he accepts that those suspicions might ultimately fail to be substantiated if all the facts could be ascertained.

Reasonableness

Assuming that the complainant of unfair dismissal is qualified to make that claim, and has been actually or constructively dismissed and the respondent has established a reason, the question for an industrial tribunal is statutorily defined,[46] save where special provision is made for unfairness to be presumed in a specified case,[47] as:

" . . . the determination of the question whether the dismissal was fair or unfair, having regard to the reason shown by the employer, shall depend on whether in the circumstances (including the size and administrative resources of the employer's undertaking) the employer acted reasonably or unreasonably in treating it as a sufficient reason; and that question shall be determined in accordance with equity and the substantial merits of the case."

Despite the grammatical quibble, the question to be viewed in the light of equity and substantial merits is, as we shall see, that of the employer's reaction and not the fact of termination.[48] It will be observed that no burden of proof is specified. The industrial tribunal comes to a decision on the facts as presented to it without any initial supposition that the employer must justify his action. The fact that the employer is usually requested to present his case first, if it is not purely an historical survival, derives largely from the assumption that he is in the best position to give an initial account of his actions.

---

[43] At p. 126.
[44] *Supra.*
[45] In *Alidair* v. *Taylor* [1978] I.C.R. 44 it is clear that the remarks of Lord Denning at p. 45 are addressed to the question of fairness rather than the establishment of a reason.
[46] E.P.C.A. 1978, s.57(3) as amended by Employment Act 1980, s.6.
[47] See *e.g.* pp. 192 *et seq.*
[48] *D.G. Moncrieff (Farmers)* v. *MacDonald* [1978] I.R.L.R. 112.

Reasonableness "in all the circumstances" not only involves consideration of a number of factors such as the reason for the decision, the way that reason was established and the way in which the situation was handled thereafter; it also, necessarily, interlinks them.[49] The need for warnings depends on the nature of the offence, enquiry depends on the availability of the facts. The extent of the employee's chance to explain himself may be directly related to the nature of the investigation. The investigation in a case of sickness is a very different matter from that in the case of misconduct or redundancy. Redundancy itself produces a procedure, not only different in name, in which discussion replaces a hearing and, to some extent, enquiry. In any event, the procedure leading up to, and following, a dismissal—which can be lengthy—is not separated into individual episodes by the parties. It is incapable of division into the tidy little compartments which were once seen to spring from the guidance contained in the original code of dismissal practice issued in 1972. This code gave rise to a growth of sub-rules of procedure and, in the case of some writers, even an attempt to classify reasons into those which afforded justification and those which did not.[50]

Nevertheless, there is a stage in the consideration when individual factors have to be separately evaluated. It is not possible to lay down normal standards of enquiry since they will not take into account the fact, for instance, that a reasonable requirement of confidentiality may make some levels of enquiry unreasonable,[51] but it is necessary to be aware of a prima facie expectation of the nature of an enquiry stage and of its purpose. It is sometimes possible to detect unfairness after a full enquiry because the possibility of dismissal was not then in the mind of the employee who has, subsequently, had no adequate opportunity to defend his conduct in that light. Neither of these situations is particularly affected by any other aspect of the specific case. Such examples could be considerably multiplied.

In the following account of the question of the test of reasonableness, therefore, a particular aspect of the process of dismissal is likely to be considered as if it was isolated from other aspects. The reader must always remember that, having been analysed, it may have to be brought back into the general account before a conclusion in the particular case can be arrived at.

Although the words of the statute do not compel such a conclusion, we have seen that the standard is obviously that of the reasonable employer and not of the reasonable man. Courts applying the test of the reasonable man inevitably apply their own standard to judge that of the defendant. They will have to imagine themselves in the position of the defendant in the circumstances, but how he should reasonably react is, in the end, a matter of how a court would wish to see itself reacting. The test of a reasonable employer, on the other hand, necessarily involves an industrial tribunal viewing the actions of a similarly stylised person, but one with which it does not identify itself. It cannot purport to be a reasonable employer, as a court can purport to be the epitome of a reasonable man, so it cannot substitute its own judgment. In

---

[49] *Grundy* v. *Plummer and Salt* [1983] I.R.L.R. 98.

[50] See, *e.g.* McGlyne: *Unfair Dismissal Cases* (1st ed. 1976) Butterworth.

[51] *Pritchett and Dyjasek* v. *J. McIntyre Ltd.* [1987] I.R.L.R. 18—illustrates this point in connection with hearings.

other words, it must judge reasonableness against its view of how employers might reasonably be expected to react, and not against how its members would see themselves as reacting. It is suggested that this limitation is unavoidable once the test is seen as that of the reasonable employer and tribunals cannot, therefore, be criticised for refusing to substitute their own business judgment. Nevertheless, the disability is capable of producing some rather technical results. In *Gair* v. *Bevan Harris Ltd.*[52] the Court of Session held that a tribunal, which had said that a foreman dismissed for failure to carry out his duties should have been demoted, had seen only one course of action as reasonable. Had the tribunal been less forthcoming and confined itself to decision that dismissal was an unreasonably excessive penalty no appeal could have succeeded.

In *Vickers Ltd.* v. *Smith*[53] it was said that the test of reasonableness asks whether, on balance of probabilities, no reasonable management would have arrived at the conclusion reached by the respondent. That was a case involving selection for redundancy. In such a situation an industrial tribunal, as we have seen, normally accepts that money has to be saved, since that is a business judgment it cannot challenge. A very few decisions have asserted power to judge the business necessity of a managerial decision to create a redundancy.[54] But the only case where this argument seems to have succeeded[55] depends primarily on the obvious failure of local management adequately to enquire into the available courses of action. Even in the context of redundancy, the test, in *Vickers*, is unduly restrictive. Just as there will usually be alternatives in the case of a decision to save money so there will inevitably be at least one alternative in cases of misconduct, lack of qualification or sickness. It cannot be said to be unreasonable to dismiss just because more lenient employers, or those more able to carry a passenger, would not. If one includes a consideration of procedures, as well as alternative final resolutions of the question, there may well be a considerable range of conceivable responses. In all circumstances some may appear reasonable, others unreasonable. Phillips J. made this point in *Watling & Co. Ltd.* v. *Richardson*.[56] He also took the opportunity to point out that the approach tribunal members would have considered reasonable would only be one among the range of reasonable responses. Browne-Wilkinson J. produced a summary of the position in *Iceland Frozen Foods Ltd.* v. *Jones*[57]:

" . . . (1) the starting point should always be the words of section 57(3) themselves; (2) in applying the section an industrial tribunal must consider the reasonableness of the employer's conduct, not simply whether they (the members of the industrial tribunal) consider the dismissal to be fair; (3) in judging the reasonableness of the employer's conduct an industrial tribunal must not substitute its decision as to what was the right course to adopt for that of the employer; (4) in many, though not all, cases there is a band of reasonable responses to the employee's conduct within which one employer might reasonably take one view,

---

[52] [1983] I.R.L.R. 368.
[53] [1977] I.R.L.R. 11.
[54] *Banerjee* v. *City and East London AHA* [1979] I.R.L.R. 147; *Orr* v. *Vaughan* [1981] I.R.L.R. 63.
[55] *Ladbroke Courage Holidays Ltd.* v. *Asten* [1981] I.R.L.R. 59.
[56] [1978] I.C.R. 1049.
[57] [1983] I.C.R. 17 at p. 24.

another quite reasonably take another; (5) the function of an industrial tribunal, as an industrial jury, is to determine whether in the particular circumstances of each case the decision to dismiss the employee fell within the band of reasonable responses which a reasonable employer might have adopted. If the dismissal falls within the band the dismissal is fair: if the dismissal falls outside the band it is unfair."

The idea of a band of reasonable responses has caught on and is often referred to, but the student may be unsure how it differs from the *Vickers* test. Perhaps the difference is best explained in this way. If a tribunal permits a dismissal to be regarded as fair, unless on balance of probabilities no reasonable employer could be thought capable of arriving at that conclusion, one is patently moving the line of unreasonableness a long way down the scale. If, on the other hand, one imagines a range of responses, from the very generous to the intolerable, in practice it is likely that more of the fringe, where it is a strain to regard the reaction as reasonable, will be considered unreasonable. Although the *Iceland Frozen Foods* explanation does not say so, in practice the impression will be, as Davies and Freedland say[58] of a general consensus among employers as to what is reasonable, rather than the inclusion of remote possibilities. There seems no doubt that Browne-Wilkinson J. envisaged not one response as reasonable, but a variety of alternatives any one of which was acceptable. Since the tribunal is only considering the conclusion adopted in the case before it, it only has to say whether that choice comes within the "reasonable" category, or not. The whole point of the "band of reasonable responses" approach, therefore, is to emphasise that an alternative is not unreasonable just because it is clear that some employers would have adopted a different alternative, which the tribunal may prefer. It does not, in fact, tell us how, or where, a tribunal should draw the line between reasonableness and unreasonableness within the likely alternative courses of action.

The band can be seen to operate in *Saunders* v. *Scottish National Camps Association*.[59] The applicant was a homosexual, dismissed for that reason, from his employment as a maintenance handyman at the respondent's childrens' camp. Psychiatric evidence was presented to the effect that heterosexuals were as likely to interfere with children as homosexuals. The industrial tribunal appears to have been more in tune with the *Vickers* test, but the Scottish E.A.T. held that the conclusion that the dismissal was reasonable would accord generally with the less rigid test of a band of reasonable responses. It had been admitted that, though it had no scientific basis, a considerable body of opinion would regard homosexuals as constituting a particular danger to children. Dismissal was, therefore, a reasonable response even if many employers, on better authority, would not have resorted to it. The significance of this is very clear when one is dealing, for instance, with a decision that some policy should be adopted in a particular situation; such, for instance, as the dismissal of employees with AIDS.

The same approach applies to economic choices. In *Green* v. *A. & I. Fraser Ltd.*[60] a lorry driver, capable of doing the work of a mechanic but selected for

[58] At p. 477.
[59] [1980] I.R.L.R. 174.
[60] [1985] I.R.L.R. 55.

redundancy because he was the most junior among the lorry drivers, argued that it was unreasonable to have selected him rather than a more junior mechanic who occasionally drove lorries. The E.A.T. said that either choice would have been reasonable.

In *Moon* v. *Homeworthy Furniture (Northern) Ltd.*[61] Kilner Brown J. in the E.A.T. stated uncompromisingly that an industrial tribunal has no jurisdiction to investigate the reasons for creating redundancies. The same would be true of any "re-organisation." The learned judge based his decision on the unwisdom, demonstrated historically by the fate of the N.I.R.C., of entering into the merits of an industrial dispute. It can be said that the merits of any dismissal may become a matter of industrial dispute so that, by passing judgment, the tribunal is adjudicating upon the merits of that dispute. But the context of the statement of Kilner Brown J. is not one of a dispute arising from the dismissal but of a disputable issue leading to the dismissal. As with all unfair dismissal claims the employer can only establish a reason if he has reasonably satisfied himself that that reason exists. Once he has done so it has been said that the tribunal should avoid the danger of constituting itself a court to retry the charge. The same applies where "charge" would not be an appropriate way to describe the reason.[62]

Once established, the reason is accepted by the tribunals as constituting the circumstance against which to judge the fairness of dismissal. So in *Orr* v. *Vaughan*,[63] Slynn J. said that it was for the employer to decide what was to be done by way of re-organisation and whether that lead to a diminution in requirement for employees. It is, of course, still possible to challenge the very existence of such a decision[64] but once the employer has properly reached his conclusion it must follow that it is difficult to challenge it substantively as failing to provide sufficient reason to dismiss.

It is common to find criticism of this conclusion, based, for instance, on the argument that it is an unnecessary concession to management prerogative. It is, however, not a concession to management practice to hire and fire, but rather, to manage. It is difficult to see how industrial tribunals could impose a different managerial decision of their own, even if they were so inclined. If a frontal assault on the ultimate power of management to take such decisions is unlikely, a considerable inhibiting effect could be achieved by compelling consideration of the interests of employees as part of a reasonable process of decision making. In *Evans* v. *Elemeta Holdings Ltd.*[65] an employee was dismissed for continuing refusal to accept re-organisation involved in new overtime obligations expressed in these terms:

> " . . . you will be expected to work past your normal hours as requested by your manager during the evening and up to four hours on a Saturday. Your salary has been calculated taking this into account."

All other employees accepted these terms. The E.A.T. held that the ques-

---

[61] [1976] I.R.L.R. 298.

[62] *e.g. Parkers Bakeries Ltd.* v. *R.E. Palmer* [1977] I.R.L.R. 215.

[63] [1981] I.R.L.R. 63; see also *Bannerjee* v. *City and East London AHA* [1979] I.R.L.R. 147.

[64] As in *Orr* v. *Vaughan* itself and *Ladbroke Courage Holdings Ltd.* v. *Aston* [1981] I.R.L.R. 59 and *Oakley* v. *The Labour Party* [1988] I.R.C.R. 34.

[65] [1982] I.R.L.R. 143.

tion of whether dismissal was reasonable required consideration of whether it was reasonable for the employee to decline the new terms. If it would have been reasonable for the employee to refuse the new terms then it would be unreasonable to dismiss him for that refusal. Equally, in its context, the decision to allow the appeal in this case was almost certainly correct because the industrial tribunal had accepted the same proposition, and then arrived at the conclusion that the changes were not unreasonable without any indication of adequate grounds to support that conclusion. If more general consequences are attributed to the decision it can be seen to be unacceptably sweeping. It is easy to envisage circumstances in which it is unreasonable to expect a particular employee to accept a variation of his contractual terms but reasonable for management to seek to impose such a variation and employ someone else if the demand is rejected. Once that is conceded it must follow in principle that it may be reasonable to dismiss those who do not accept terms which no reasonable employee would accept unless compelled by economic necessity. Management which did not adequately consider the conflicting interests would, no doubt, act unfairly and the more unreasonable the demands the more careful must be the consideration of the necessity for them. In order to arrive at any other conclusion it would be necessary to displace the assumption that management are entitled to consider "business interests," that is to say, to apply the profit motive. Except ideologically, it would be difficult in a capitalist economy to support such an argument. But still, the right of management to manage could be curtailed by requiring a balance of conflicting interests. This was the conclusion of the E.A.T. under a new President, sixteen months later in *Chubb Fire Security Ltd.* v. *Harper.*[66] In that case the court announced that the correct approach was to consider whether the employers were acting reasonably in deciding (or, presumably, whether they had properly addressed their minds to the question at all) that the advantages of re-organisation outweighed any disadvantages which it was contemplated the employee would suffer. This suggests a more precise balance of interest than the E.A.T. in *Richmond Precision Engineering Ltd.* v. *Pearse*[67] was prepared to accept. Such a balancing by the employer was, in its view, only one of the circumstances of a dismissal which a tribunal should consider. The extent to which the employer had discussed the matter, pointed out its difficulties and been met by the employee were important factors. Logically, it is difficult to see why this should be so. Discussion is an important part of the process by which an employer would arrive at the balance of convenience. If that balance is in favour of the employee's objections, how is it that he cannot finally assert these objections and expect a reasonable employer to concede the argument? The answer can only be that it is not necessarily unreasonable for an employer to assert his own interest over what is recognised by the employer himself as the interest of the employee. Reference by the court to a range of reasonable responses seems, at first, out of place in this argument, but is significant. Clearly the court is implying that whereas some employers would give priority to the greater interest of the employee it is not unreasonable for others, after due consideration, to give priority to the lesser interest of the employer. In view of this it may be asked

---

[66] [1983] I.R.L.R. 311.
[67] [1985] I.R.L.R. 179.

whether the assertion by the Court of Appeal in *Dobie* v. *Burns International Security Services (U.K.) Ltd.*[68] that the extent of injustice to the employees occasioned by the dismissal is a very important factor is anything more than mere form. Sir John Donaldson M.R. said the employer would have to take account of the length of time during which the employee has been employed by him, the satisfactoriness, or otherwise, of the employee's service and the difficulties which may face the employee in obtaining other employment. All are "matters which affect the justice or injustice to the employee of being dismissed." One wonders, however, what these words mean, since that is not the question before the tribunal.

In the end, therefore, the range of reasonable responses, coupled with the long accepted view of management's right to manage in the interests of the business, will in practice lead to the view that to give predominance to these business interests over those of the employee is not unreasonable. There will, of course, be cases where a tribunal concludes that the imbalance is too great to permit the overriding of the employee's interest to be seen as reasonable. There will be other cases where unreasonableness will spring from failure properly to consider the matter. By and large, however, the reason for the dismissal is, in practice, likely to be viewed primarily as it reflects on business interests. Is it too much to say that the reasonable employer is one who looks after his business interest? Only if it is unreasonable to consider them significantly threatened will the interests of the employee necessarily be predominant in the minds of reasonable employers.

Here it may be appropriate to point out again that the employee's interest, derived from his contractual rights may reasonably be seen to yield to the employer's business interests. In *Horrigan* v. *Lewisham L.B.C.*[69] the employer might reasonably dismiss though the employee had no contractual obligation to work overtime and in *Woods* v. *W.M. Car Services (Peterborough) Ltd.*[70] Mrs. Woods was considered herself to be unreasonable in seeking to maintain her wage level. Lord Wedderburn[71] has presented this general result as substantially the fault of the dead hand of the common law. "It is," he says, "the very function of the common law to preserve subordination inherently within employment." This leads, for instance, to "the implicit duty of the worker to accept the employer's changes in search of 'improved business methods' so long as there is a 'sound business reason,' an implication which both in redundancy and in unfair dismissal (not least by manipulation of the magical 'some other substantial reason') has transformed the statutes." The preceding account would suggest that the dead hand of the common law was laid on the system by statute, rather than being adopted instinctively by industrial tribunals. Twenty years ago, the draftsmen failed to envisage developments which never occurred, but which we can now see as a lost opportunity. Was it really to be supposed that tribunals should consider unreasonable the actions of employers which were identical with those of most of their brethren and which the law, whether or not one calls it the common law, had consistently encouraged? The very fact that Wedderburn envis-

---

[68] [1984] I.R.L.R. 812.
[69] [1978] I.C.R. 15.
[70] [1982] I.R.L.R. 13 (C.A.).
[71] (1987) 16 I.L.J. 1, *Labour Law: From Here to Autonomy.*

ages a new regime of "autonomous" labour law as necessary to produce a relationship in place of a legal subservience is surely an acknowledgment that the courts did not subvert statutes which were themselves heavily influenced by the old regime. However that may be, if employers are to be required to behave no more than as reasonable employers no progress at all will be achieved under any regime which does not redefine the essential nature of the relationship between parties who could almost as well still be called master and servant. The political movements of the past ten years have not suggested the likelihood of such redefinition.

The employer's response, the reasonableness of which falls to be decided, is not, of course, comprised in an instant assessment, immediately followed by action. The employer's response is almost always a process and it would be ridiculous to seek to judge what he did but not how he did it. At one time it was thought that sub-rules could be laid down to govern the elements of that process. That is no longer so and the decision in *The County Council of Hereford and Worcester* v. *Neale*,[72] for example, shows why. A schoolmaster had been dismissed because, while invigilating an examination, he had advised one of the candidates of a point raised by a question. The examining body apparently did not take a serious view of the matter but the appropriate committee of the education authority took the decision to dismiss by a majority decided on political lines, although, as the tribunal found, not deciding the issue as a political caucus. The decision described his action as gross misconduct and a wilful disregard of professional propriety. The Industrial Tribunal noted defects in the procedure, indicated that it would not necessarily have decided to dismiss, but concluded that dismissal in this manner was still a reasonable response. The E.A.T. set aside this decision on the ground that the procedure revealed too much haste, stubbornness and secrecy and too little concern for the appearance and substance of fairness. The Court of Appeal restored the decision of the industrial tribunal as one which it could properly make. Clearly procedure and reason are here inextricably linked and the Court of Appeal rejected the analytical approach of the E.A.T. which would, at least, to an extent, have separated the mixture.

Immediately following the introduction of the statutory remedy for unfair dismissal in 1972 the National Industrial Relations Court, apparently influenced by the Code of Industrial Relations Practice promulgated under the Industrial Relations Act 1971, produced a "natural justice" style of thinking which demanded adherence to standards of fair procedure. In *Earl* v. *Slater and Wheeler (Airlyne) Ltd.*[73] the industrial tribunal had viewed the rule as one of injustice to the employee rather than unreasonableness by the employer. The N.I.R.C. firmly asserted that unfair procedure alone could render a dismissal for "good" reason unfair. This much is still true today. In practice, however, this instance led to over-emphasis of procedural requirements, the high point of which is *Budgen and Co.* v. *Thomas*[74] in which the enquiry stage was distinguished from the hearing stage and the latter held inadequate. The result was that employees were seen to be being awarded compensation for the dismissal they deserved solely because a procedural step

---

[72] [1986] I.R.L.R. 168.
[73] [1972] I.C.R. 508; see also *Clarkson International Tools Ltd.* v. *Short* [1973] I.C.R. 191.
[74] [1986] I.C.R. 344.

had not been followed properly. The conflict between the two views is plain in the judgments of the House of Lords in *W. Devis and Sons Ltd.* v. *Atkins.*[75] Viscount Dilhorne is often said to support the predominance of procedure. In fact all he said was that a procedural defect would render unfair an otherwise justified dismissal. The House was clearly most concerned to avoid awarding compensation to the undeserving for procedural error alone. Inevitably the courts reacted against this situation, reducing the significance of procedure in two main ways. In *Retarded Children's Aid Society Ltd.* v. *Day*[76] the E.A.T. had stated that there was a heavy burden on an employer who had dismissed for misconduct without a warning. The Court of Appeal was prepared to assume that the industrial tribunal which had described the case as "very special" had been willing to overlook the absence of warning. It had, of course, always been possible to conclude that a warning was not necessary where, for instance, gross misconduct had occurred. The significance of this decision is that it signified acknowledgment by the Court of Appeal of the single test of reasonableness in all the circumstances. Procedure ceased to be a set of rules to be disregarded at the employer's peril. Thereafter numerous procedural defects were overlooked. In *The Royal Naval School* v. *Hughes*[77] the organisational imperfections of the small employer were held to render reasonable what, in the abstract, would have been unreasonable procedure.

The present approach is well demonstrated in *Tower Hamlets Health Authority* v. *Anthony*[77a] where an employee entitled to the benefit of a disciplinary code normally requiring three warnings before dismissal had been dismissed whilst her appeal against the final warning was pending. The E.A.T. held that there was no rule that dismissal would be unfair in such circumstances but failure to take into account the fact that an appeal was pending could indicate unfairness.

More marked than this whittling away of rigid procedural requirements was the development which became known as "the rule in *British Labour Pump Co. Ltd.* v. *Byrne*." The decision[78] itself clarified a development that had been gathering support for some time. That process had produced the decision in *Charles Letts and Co. Ltd.* v. *Howard*[79] that a procedural defect would be overlooked if it could be shown that the same conclusion would inevitably have been reached had the proper procedure been followed. Not only would it normally be impossible to satisfy such a standard of proof, but such a standard is contrary to the normal civil standard of balance of probability. *Byrne's* case was primarily concerned to point this out. The most obvious conclusion was that the rule should be that a defect in procedure would not render a dismissal unfair, if, on balance of probabilities, the employer would have taken the same action after proper procedure. That has been the rule from 1979 to the end of 1987. With hindsight, it can be seen that the court in *Charles Letts* was being so cautious because it was aware of the fact that it was using illogicality to pursue a policy dictated by complaints of excessive severity.

---

[75] [1977] A.C. 931.
[76] [1978] I.C.R. 437. See also, *Bailey* v. *B.P. Oil* [1980] I.C.R. 642.
[77] [1979] I.R.L.R. 383.
[77a] [1988] I.R.L.R. 331.
[78] [1979] I.C.R. 347.
[79] [1976] I.R.L.R. 248.

In its enthusiasm correctly to state the standard of proof not only did the E.A.T. fail to notice this but it also failed to notice that it was not dealing with a form of procedure to which the standard of reasonableness in section 57(3) applied, but to the establishment of the reason under section 57(1) and (2). It is true that *British Home Stores Ltd.* v. *Burchell*[80] had not yet appeared to confirm the proposition that an employee cannot assert a reasonable belief in a reason which he has not established in his own mind by reasonable inquiry. It should have been obvious, however, that the self-implication of Byrne in the conspiracy into which the employer was enquiring was not sufficient to formulate the reason for dismissal with sufficient certainty. That being so the employer had simply failed to establish the reason for dismissal. Without such a reason unfairness is a necessary conclusion. There is no room to consider, as a matter of equity, what might have been had the employer proceeded to establish the reason which emerged as a possible proposition in the tribunal hearing. Strangely enough, the same criticism applies to the decision in *Siggs and Chapman (Contractors) Ltd.* v. *Knight*,[81] which is regarded as the high point of the rule since it held that application of the rule was to be presumed from consideration of the reasonableness of the decision. Beware of answering that this reasoning is a pedantic argument savouring of the days of rules of procedure and that support for the distinction between enquiry and hearing in *British Home Stores* itself[82] is only a late example of the same thing. The line is not being drawn between enquiry and hearing. It is, of course, clear that, in practice, the one develops into the other. The line is between two different functions. An enquiry can serve both to establish the reason and to commence the process of what to do about it. As *Budgen Ltd.* v. *Thomas*[83] held, however, the main purpose of the enquiry is to establish the reason. In satisfying that function it does not necessarily achieve the wholly separate purpose of considering what it is reasonable to do about it. But if it does not satisfy that function the defect is not one of procedure but a failure to comply with the requirement to show a reason.

More surprising than the fact that no one seems to have noticed this misapplication of the requirement of proof of the possession of a reason is the number of times that the rule in *British Labour Pump* was stated to be whether, on balance of probabilities, the employer would have been acting reasonably if he had dismissed after pursuing a proper procedure. No less an authority than Browne-Wilkinson J. so mistated the rule in *Sillifant* v. *Powell Duffryn Timber Ltd.*[84] which, though applying it, contains the most detailed and outspoken exposure of its flaws on record. This was the decision which the Lord Chancellor in *Polkey* v. *A.E. Dayton Ltd.*[85] adopted without qualification as his own reason for overruling it. If it is borne in mind that reasonableness is determined on a range of responses it will at once be apparent that wherever procedural defect is a significant issue in an application it is likely that the elimination of that defect will leave dismissal as a reasonable response.

---

[80] [1980] I.C.R. 303.
[81] [1984] I.R.L.R. 83.
[82] At p. 308.
[83] [1976] I.C.R. 344.
[84] [1983] I.R.L.R. 91.
[85] [1988] I.C.R. 142.

The statement of the rule is in this form:

> "In the first place, has the employer shown on the balance of probabilities that they would have taken the same course had they held an enquiry and had they received the information that that enquiry would have produced? Secondly, the employer must show . . . that in the light of the information they would have received had they gone through the proper procedure, then would they have been behaving reasonably in still deciding to dismiss."

The first limb is applied to enquiry because that was the aspect, wrongly thought of merely as procedural, with which the case was concerned. If the rule is extended to other aspects of procedure it asks whether, had they been proper the same result would—not "could reasonably"—have been arrived at. Only if the answer to that is in the affirmative is one to proceed to a consideration of whether the similar result would have been reasonable. That second limit is obvious. It is true that in most cases where the issue arises, once the procedural defect has been eliminated as irrelevant the answer will be that dismissal is within the range of reasonable response, but it is necessary to make it clear that the question still has to be asked where, for instance, the reason does not justify dismissal. Elias, therefore, correctly states the rule in its simple first limb form.[86] The second limb is no more than a reminder of the need, even if procedural defect is overlooked, to satisfy section 57(3).

The most severe criticism, and that most normally advanced, is that the rule allows the question as to reasonableness to be answered not at the time of dismissal but, with hindsight, at some later stage. The employer who had unreasonably neglected some aspect of procedure and had dismissed in the light of incomplete knowledge of arguments to the contrary was saved from the results of that unreasonableness by the fortuitous fact that it later appeared that possession of that knowledge would probably have made no difference to his decision. It is, of course, well established that fairness is to be judged at the moment of dismissal and in the light of that there can be no doubt that the reasoning in *British Labour Pump* is based on some wider idea of equity. Rather than the statutory question "did the employer act reasonably when he dismissed" it asks whether the eventual outcome is unfair. It is no real answer to point out that the critics of the rule contained a large number of people who would have been the first to contend that dismissal is a process. There may be a point of time when the employment relationship ends but that is usually different from the point of time at which the decision to end it is taken. Moreover, one has to be careful not to be too pernickety about the fact that an employer is not only the judge but also the prosecutor who will have come to a prima facie decision before he seeks the comments of the employee on that decision. Modification of the point of dismissal approach in favour of the employee—but not of the employer—is well established.[87]

Much of the force of criticism of *British Labour Pump* is that it permits consideration not only of what it is clear would have been established but of what would, on balance of probabilities, have been established. This is not a ques-

---

[86] (1981) 10 I.L.J. at p. 214.
[87] *e.g. West Midlands Co-operative Society* v. *Tipton* [1986] I.R.L.R. 112; *Greenall Whitley PLC* v. *Carr* [1985] I.R.L.R. 289; *Oakley* v. *The Labour Party* [1988] I.R.L.R. 34 (C.A.).

tion of looking back to *Charles Letts*, since the employer would, under such a rule still be free to show in the light of proved facts how he would probably have reacted. The rule allows him to show, in the light of facts which would probably have been established, how he would probably have reacted. As Waite J. said in *Lafferty Construction* v. *Duthie*[88] it is difficult to be sufficiently sure of such a speculative point.

The rule had few friends. It survived only because the Court of Appeal had affirmed it in *W. and J. Wass Ltd.* v. *Binns*[89] so that Browne-Wilkinson J.'s open disapproval could have no effect. Even in the modified form in which public law tends now to regard the necessity for natural justice it was an unjustified deviation. In *R.* v. *Chief Constable of Thames Valley Police ex parte Stevenson*[90] Mann J. said that, though it was unlikely that any representation of the applicant would have altered the result, breach of the requirements of fairness, even if devoid of practical consequences, was a serious matter. He then granted a declaration that there had been a procedural irregularity in dispensing with the services of a probationer under the 1979 Police Regulations.

The decision of the House of Lords in *Polkey* v. *A.E. Dayton Ltd.*[91] sweeps away the rule in *British Labour Pump*, using the arguments marshalled against it by Browne-Wilkinson J. in *Sillifant* v. *Powell Duffryn Timber Ltd.*[92] which were based upon the point that it asked whether the outcome, rather than the conduct of the employer, was reasonable. The only concession the House of Lords made to the likelihood of arrival at the same conclusion was that an employer might, at the time of the dismissal, reasonably come to the conclusion that further, or better, procedures would lead to no different results.

In passing, it may be remarked that the decision may not produce any startling advantage for the employee. It is likely, in misconduct and inability cases, that industrial tribunals, following *Polkey* will hold unfair a dismissal involving faulty procedure but conclude that the employee has so heavily contributed to his own dismissal that he should not be reinstated or re-engaged and should receive much reduced compensation.[92a]

Where then does this leave procedural requirements? In *Polkey* Lord Bridge said:

> "But an employer having *prima facie* grounds to dismiss for one of these reasons will in the great majority of cases not act rationally in treating the reason as a sufficient reason for dismissal unless and until he has taken the steps, conveniently classified in most of the authorities as "procedural," which are necessary in the circumstances of the case to justify that course of action. Thus, in the case of incapacity, the employer will not act reasonably unless he gives the employee fair warning and an opportunity to mend his ways and show that he can do the job; in the case of misconduct, the employer will normally not act reasonably unless he investigates the complaint of misconduct fully and fairly and hears whatever the employee wishes to say in his defence or in explanation or mitigation; in the case

---

[88] [1985] I.R.L.R. 486.
[89] [1982] I.R.L.R. 283.
[90] *The Times*, April 22, 1987.
[91] [1988] I.C.R. 142.
[92] [1983] I.R.L.R. 591.
[92a] But see, *Mining Supplies (Longwall) Ltd.* v. *Baker* [1988] I.R.L.R. 417.

of redundancy, the employer will normally not act reasonably unless he warns and consults any employees affected or their representative, adopts a fair basis on which to select for redundancy and takes such steps as may be reasonable to avoid or minimise redundancy by redeployment within his own organisation."

No one who remembers the rubbishing of the high hopes raised by the judgment of Browne-Wilkinson J. in *Williams* v. *Compair Maxam Ltd.*[93] will mistake this for the trumpet call of a new era of resurgent procedural requirements even if, on the question of redundancy procedures, it appears to be a restatement of those requirements. The chances are that its significance will be masked by the proposition for which *Polkey* will be better known. On the other hand, courts are continually drawn to the original, natural justice, base of a requirement for a hearing, apparently still on the blind assumption that this will, somehow, produce fairness. In *McLaren* v. *National Coal Board*,[93a] for instance, a colliery manager, feeling he would be biased, had left investigation of whether a striking miner had assaulted a working miner to the police. The striking miner was convicted and dismissed. The Court of Appeal, in setting aside the decision of an industrial tribunal that dismissal was not unfair concentrated more on the irrelevance of that tribunal's view that in a state of industrial warfare ordinary safeguards might be discarded but its decision seems to imply that the established disciplinary procedures ought not to be discarded in favour of substitutes.

Industrial tribunal methods

We shall consider later other aspects of unfair dismissal which involve more issues of law. Preliminary hearings deal with matters of qualification to claim.[94] The definition of redundancy, which becomes significant whenever statute uses that term, is almost pure contract.[95] Even what amounts to trade union activity can, amid a large measure of instinctive factual comprehension among industrial tribunal members, throw up something approaching rules of law.[96] The basic test of the action of a reasonable employer, however, is now firmly accepted as a straightforward proposition, shorn of sub-rules, single and indivisible.[97] The issue of reasonableness is, as the Court of Appeal has often said, one of fact.[98]

Law students, who are capable of reconciling their wish for rules of law with the concept of the reasonable man in the law of negligence seem, however, to find difficulty in knowing how they should handle the concept of the reasonable employer as expounded by an industrial tribunal. They, like applicants and employers, often, in despair, describe the adjudication on unfair dismissal as a lottery. Employers appear to put this feeling into practice by

---

[93] [1982] I.C.R. 156.
[93a] [1988] I.R.L.R. 215.
[94] *Infra*, pp. 192–197.
[95] *Infra*, pp. 181–189.
[96] *Infra*, pp. 305–308.
[97] See, *e.g. Grundy* v. *Plummer and Salt* [1983] I.R.L.R. 98.
[98] *Bailey* v. *B.P. Oil (Kent Refining) Ltd.* [1980] I.R.L.R. 287; See, *e.g. Anandarajah* v. *Lord Chancellor's Department* [1984] I.R.L.R. 130.

considerable extension, in recent years, of the practice of settlement, probably approved but very often not monitored, by ACAS conciliation officers. Yet every practitioner of experience in this field knows what are reasonable indications of the chance of success or failure, and of the matters which will most affect that chance. Is this a matching of the instinct, born of experience, applied by tribunal members with a similar instinct in those who appear before them; or has it, if not principles, guidelines which can be learnt?

It is beyond question that there is a strong element of impression governing the decision of tribunal members. But could it be denied that a similar element exists in the decision of a High Court judge deciding a negligence claim?[98a] Lawyers would probably like to believe that they are less influenced by subjective impression than others. This may well be true of the chairmen of industrial tribunals, not so much because they insist on proper evidence to support a conclusion as because they do not have such direct or immediate knowledge of the type of situation on which they are passing judgment. As to that knowledge, it has often been said, both by the E.A.T. and the Court of Appeal, that its possession is the reason for the tripartite composition of the tribunal so that members not only may, but should, use it. To a lawyer, for instance, failure to follow a certain procedure may appear as likely to be careless as deliberate and sinister. The tribunal member, from his experience as a personnel manager or a union official used to intervening in disciplinary matters, may be satisfied, on balance of probabilities, that it is unlikely that the defect is accidental. If that is the conclusion that member may well feel that "something funny was going on." This in turn, may lead him to view with some reserve, say, the proffered reasons for the dismissal. In the end he may say that the dismissal is unfair for failure to follow a proper procedure. The outside observer (or, indeed, the respondent, publicly) may regard this as something of a technicality and wonder whether the member has caught up with the fact that the age of procedural rules is past. The decision of the tribunal member cannot be said to rest upon defective procedure. What he feels is a sense of unfairness. It may be difficult to draft that test for statutory purposes but it is submitted that that somewhat subjective impression was the test the legislature intended, even if it took a few years of experimenting with rules to reach that realisation.

Suppose we apply this to a particular set of facts in which the employer seems to have furnished a sound enough reason. In the course or reorganising his management structure under considerable economic pressure an employer finds himself faced with two people, only one of whom can be appointed to the reorganised post. One of the candidates has a wider experience of the range of work in that post because he has occupied a post very like it in a location and at a time when considerable problems had to be faced. On the whole he has coped well but, perhaps inevitably, there have been defects in his handling of the situation. Perhaps his very competence has made him appear a little remote and lacking in some aspects of man-management. The other has occupied a rather easier position. Probably because of that his results, relatively speaking, have been better, he has been more popular with his subordinates. If he is less competent or as prone to mistakes (and when he gives evidence it certainly appears that this may be so) it has not shown. The second candidate is selected for the post and the first

---

[98a] See, *e.g.*, *Judging Judges*: Simon Lee (London: Faber and Faber, 1988).

dismissed because, according to the employer, recruitment, training and handling of the staff has been proved to be central to the success of the undertaking.

It can be objected that the tribunal system is not at its best when dealing with dismissals of management. It is sometimes said that the somewhat indefensibly low upper limit on awards of compensation was designed to make it clear that tribunals were not intended for higher management. Had we been talking in the above example of choice at a lower level we could almost have formulated rules[99] about criteria for selection and a careful enquiry as to whether they were satisfied. Without them, it could be said that a reasonable employer would not be in a position to make a choice. That is precisely why this example has been chosen. In this case the Director who made the choice, and the personnel officer he consulted before finalising it, knew the qualities of the candidates well. The Director should have known what he was looking for but it was actually left to the personnel officer in evidence before the tribunal to furnish a clear enough description of the man-management criteria for any member of the tribunal to accept that that was the test applied.

The outcome was that two members of the tribunal felt that they had no evidence to lead them to suppose that this criteria was not genuine. Both might, themselves, have paid more attention to the fact that the rejected candidate had been under a lot of pressure so that any faults he had showed up, but tribunals have been told often enough not to subsitute their judgment for that of the employer. Once the reason for the dismissal is accepted as sound it is easier to avoid the conclusion that the procedure is defective just because it might have been better.[99a] The reasons furnished by the minority member indicate that he clearly thought the decision on man-management ability open to such a degree of doubt that it was not a question of his judgment opposed to that of the employer so much as a doubt about whether the employer really believed it. He preferred to express this doubt by saying that the reasonable exercise of such a judgment required much more careful examination of the facts than had taken place. He saw the evidence as indicating that the Director who had not explained his decision in terms of selection criteria had taken that decision without such clear rationalisation and had merely sought confirmation from the personnel officer. The latter was more likely to have rationalised the position for his own satisfaction.

There is clearly no application of rules of law in either decision. Both can be justified even if it is accepted that it is not possible to say whether the supposed criteria were applied or were a later invention. Anyone advising a client in such a situation would be right to point to the fact that the strength of the employer's case lay in the existence of a reorganisation, forced by economic circumstance, which required selection of one of two employees for dismissal. The weakness of that case obviously lay in the informal way in which the choice was made and the question whether that informality meant that the criteria applied had never been sufficiently formulated to be clear to the employee. Examples of this type could be endlessly presented. A book of this nature is not the right medium for the presentation of second hand experience. All it is hoped to do by the above example is to indicate the purely factual situation which an industrial tribunal usually has to judge.

---

[99] See pp. 194–195, *infra.*
[99a] See, *e.g. Hereford and Worcester County Council* v. *Neale* [1986] I.R.L.R. 168.

Remedies

Statutory efforts have been made to ensure that the first remedy an industrial tribunal considers, if it finds a dismissal unfair, is reinstatement or re-engagement. The difference between the two is that reinstatement envisages return to the same job as if the dismissal had never occurred, and therefore with wages in the interval between dismissal and reinstatement. Re-engagement involves re-employment by the same employer, his successor or an associate employer, in comparable, or otherwise suitable, employment on terms specified by the tribunal and with such compensation as the tribunal considers just and equitable.[1] If the employee asks for such a remedy[2] it is provided that the tribunal shall first consider whether to make an order for reinstatement, taking into account the wishes of the applicant, whether it is practicable for the employer to comply with such an order and, if the applicant has contributed to the dismissal, whether it would be just to order reinstatement.[3] If the tribunal decides not to order reinstatement it is then required to consider whether to make an order for re-engagement and, if so, on what terms, taking into account considerations similar to those preceding an order for reinstatement.[4] If an order for reinstatement or re-engagement is made but not fully complied with, the tribunal may award such compensation as it thinks fit (subject to the statutory maximum limit). If the order is not complied with at all the tribunal shall make an award of compensation to which it shall add, unless the employer satisfies it that it was not practicable for him to comply, a sum equivalent to not less than 13 weeks, nor more than 26 weeks', pay up to the statutory limit of a countable week's pay.[5]

On average, orders for reinstatement are made in about 1 per cent. of all applications and 6 per cent. of successful claims. Whilst the normal remedy in an internally arbitrated dismissal case would be some form of re-engagement the normal remedy in industrial tribunals is a monetary award. The reason employers are reluctant to accept from a tribunal a remedy their own internal procedures would be most likely to provide, must be the psychological effect of judicial compulsion and the "loss of face" involved when set against an industrial relations procedure in which they appear to be agreeing a settlement. It is probable, however, that most industrial tribunals expect the employer to say that it is not reasonably practicable for him to reinstate and ask the question, if indeed they ask it at all, as something of a formality. There is no doubt that even a high monetary award is little disincentive to an employer intending to dismiss. The marked increase, in recent years, in employer readiness to settle claims indicates that employers are probably more worried by the likely cost of resisting a claim to an industrial tribunal. On the other hand, the reaction of employers to any suggestion that they should reinstate indicates dislike, if not fear, of this remedy. Tribunals, therefore, come under academic attack for not being more ready to apply the remedy most likely to preserve job security as distinct from acknowledging the

---

[1] E.P.C.A. 1978, s.69(2) and (4).
[2] *Sweetlove* v. *Redbridge and Waltham Forest A.H.A.* [1979] I.C.R. 477.
[3] s.69(5).
[4] s.69(6).
[5] If the reason for dismissal is an act of unlawful discrimination within the Sex Discrimination Act 1975 or the Race Relations Act 1976 these limits are extended to 26 and 52 weeks' pay.

freedom to buy the employee out. Some of this criticism is justified. In this, as in other respects, the attitude of members and chairmen of industrial tribunals is too much influenced by the impression of managerial prerogative. On the other hand, applicants to industrial tribunals certainly give the impression that their primary object is to secure a decision as to unfairness beside which even the amount of compensation seems to be of little significance. If they ask for reinstatement or re-engagement they seem more often intent on making their point than to have any expectation of any order being implemented. The author has experienced rejection of offers of re-engagement because of the expressed fear that the employer will soon manufacture a redundancy to make sure he does not have to put up with the returned employee for long. Most tribunals would be aware, therefore, of a strong possibility that an order would be no more than a prelude to increased compensation.[6] Virtually no guidance is furnished in reported cases as to what tribunals should consider in deciding on the practicability of such an order, beyond some generality such as "the industrial relations realities."[7]

Monetary compensation—the basic award

The common law was only capable of awarding damages for breach of contract representing the loss suffered as a result of dismissal. It took a very restricted view of causation, in that respect, and limited the effect of breach of contract to the difference between the situation thereby created and the position as it would have been had the employee been dismissed with proper notice. In most cases, therefore, the common law remedy would not have exceeded a sum equivalent to wages for a week or two. The contractual period of notice has been extended both by statute[8] and the results of the example set by that statutory provision, but amounts of compensation for wrongful dismissal will not be high and will not take into account either the loss of opportunity to use accumulated skills and benefit from security in a particular employment, or difficulty in replacing the lost employment.

Provision in 1965 of a remedy for dismissal for redundancy acknowledged the former by a formula linking the amount of compensation to the length of continuous employment. This formula approach was, in 1975 considered the best means of producing a minimum rate of compensation regardless of provable monetary loss in cases of unfair dismissal.[9] This element of compensation is called the basic award. The formula is precisely that applied to statutory redundancy compensation, namely; half a week's pay for each year of employment under the age of 22 (though, in the case of unfair dismissal calculation may begin at the age of 16), one week's pay for each year of employment between the ages of 22 and 40 and one and a half weeks' pay for each year of employment between the ages of 41 and 65. No more than 20 years' employment may be considered so that the maximum award a man can receive is 30 weeks' pay. The amount so calculated will be reduced if dismissal occurs during the last year of entitlement by one twelfth for every month of that year. There is an upper limit on the

---

[6] The effects of these remedies have been documented by Williams and Lewis: *The Aftermath of Tribunal Reinstatement and Re-engagement*, D.E. Research Paper No. 23 (June 1981).
[7] *Coleman* v. *Magnet Joinery Ltd.* [1975] I.C.R. 46.
[8] *Supra*, pp. 121–123.
[9] See now, E.P.C.A. 1978, s.73.

amount of weekly pay that may be taken into account.[10] In the case of the basic award the amount is the normal *gross* rate of pay and "pay" includes all items of remuneration which have a monetary value attached to them. A considerable amount of case law has developed on the question of what should be included. As a general rule it can be said that pay for the contractually obligatory hours will be taken into account. Overtime payments will be excluded unless the employer is contractually bound to offer overtime and the employee is bound to work—unless, in other words, "overtime pay" is in practice a premium for hours in the normal working week over a stated minimum.[11] Fringe benefits which have no assigned monetary value are not regarded as remuneration for this purpose.[12] The well known fact that some payment is expressed as "expenses," though it is accepted that the amount will provide the employee with a net profit, has led to the conclusion that any amount which, on an "ordinary common-sense approach" can be seen to be a profit may be taken into account.[13]

If the employee is unfairly dismissed by reason of redundancy he is entitled to a minimum basic award of two weeks' pay even if he would not, because of unreasonable refusal of a suitable alternative offer, be entitled to a redundancy payment. The only other minimum applies to dismissal by reason of trade union membership, non-membership or activities.[14] The amount of the award must be reduced by the amount of any redundancy payment made in respect of the same dismissal[15]; and may be reduced by such amount as the tribunal considers just and equitable if the employee has unreasonably refused an offer of total reinstatement[16] or where the tribunal considers any conduct of the complainant before the dismissal was such that it would be just and equitable to reduce the award. It will be noted that this final provision is not limited to conduct contributing to the dismissal.

The compensatory award

In addition to the basic award the tribunal may award such amount of compensation as it considers just and equitable in all the circumstances having regard to the loss sustained by the complainant in consequence of the dismissal and attributable to the employer's action. The history of the development of the law on compensation, not surprisingly, repeats the process apparent in the substantive law of the growth and gradual decay of detailed rules. Most tribunals these days would probably include in their calculations the discretionary element of an amount considered just and equitable after they had arrived at an assessment by more mathematical means.[17] In practice, the result may not differ much from simple mathematics since tribunals have always been able to regulate the amount of compensation by restricting or extending the projected period of loss beyond the date of the hearing.

---

[10] At the time of going to press it is £164 (S.I. 276/1988) taking effect on April 1, 1988.
[11] *Tarmac Roadstone Holdings Ltd.* v. *Peacock* [1973] I.C.R. 273; followed in *Lotus Cars Ltd.* v. *Sutcliffe and Stratton* [1982] I.R.L.R. 381.
[12] *Lyford* v. *Turquand* [1966] I.T.R. 544 free accommodation.
[13] *S. and U. Stores Ltd.* v. *Wilkes* [1974] I.C.R. 645.
[14] E.P.C.A. s.73(4A). *Infra*, pp. 305 *et seq.*
[15] E.P.C.A., s.73(a).
[16] E.P.C.A. 1978, s.73(7A).
[17] See *Townson* v. *The Northgate Group Ltd.* [1981] I.R.L.R. 382.

Whereas the basic award takes account of gross income the compensatory award is most likely to be based on net income.[18] To date, no power to award interest on lost wages has been granted. Appeal to the E.A.T. may delay payment by a year or more. No deduction from the award is made by reason of the fact that the applicant has been in receipt of unemployment or supplementary benefit. The tribunal is required, however, to notify the Department of Social Security immediately of the amount of compensation attributable to the period between dismissal and the date of the award. This amount, known as the "prescribed element" may then be reduced before payment to the claimant, by the amount of such benefits he has received. It could well be, therefore, that a claimant who had received unemployment benefit and whose award of compensation was, for instance, reduced by a substantial contributory factor[19] would actually receive none of the compensation awarded for the period up to the date of the decision.[20] The Regulations only apply to an award. If the parties settle compensation between themselves no such recoupment takes place. Sickness, or other similar, benefit received by the employee should be deducted from his loss and thus from the amount of compensation awarded.[21]

It is open to the tribunal to consider any items of loss upon which a monetary value can be placed, as distinct from the more limited concept of pay which has actually been quantified monetarily for the purpose of determining the amount of the basic award. It is for the claimant to prove his loss. It has been said that it is for the tribunal to raise for consideration each available head of loss[22] but this, in practice, will not mean that the tribunal asks the claimant whether he had a company car[23] or received luncheon vouchers. What it will mean is that the tribunal will consider loss up to the time of the hearing and then beyond the hearing if the claimant has not by then obtained fresh employment at at least the same level of remuneration as his previous employment. The tribunal will also, on its own initiative, add the element of compensation for "loss of statutory protection" brought out by the fact that the dismissal deprives the employee of his accumulated continuous employment which qualifies him to certain statutory rights.[24]

In *Ging* v. *Ellward Lancs Ltd.*[25] Arnold J. in the E.A.T. said that loss to the date of the assessment should consider what remuneration and other valuable benefits the claimant would have received had he not been dismissed, and deduct from that all earnings and benefits he did actually receive in that period. A claimant who, after a brief period of unemployment, found more remunerative employment, could well find himself disentitled to any compen-

---

[18] *Scottish Co-operative Wholesale Society Ltd.* v. *Lloyd* [1973] I.C.R. 137. But see *Secretary of State for Employment* v. *John Woodrow and Sons (Builders) Ltd.* [1983] I.R.L.R. 11. Net income refers to the employees' entitlement whether or not it is actually being received—*Kinzley* v. *Minories Finance Ltd.* [1987] I.R.L.R. 490.

[19] *Infra*, pp. 176–177.

[20] See The Employment Protection (Recoupment of Unemployment Benefit and Supplementary Benefit) Regulations 1977 (S.I. 1977 No. 674).

[21] *Sun and Sand Ltd.* v. *Fitzjohn* [1979] I.C.R. 268.

[22] *Tidman* v. *Aveling Marshall Ltd.* [1977] I.C.R. 506.

[23] *Tidman's* case itself mentioned only wages, pension, manner of dismissal and loss of protection.

[24] *Infra*, pp. 212–223.

[25] [1978] I.T.R. 265.

sation. In such a situation it could be beneficial to the respondent to delay the hearing whilst the claimant's profit accumulated, since it does not appear that potential profit after the hearing will do more than eliminate any further compensation for that subsequent period. There is, however, a well established exception to this deduction of receipts. In *Norton Tool Co. Ltd.* v. *Tewson*[26] the N.I.R.C. held that good industrial relations practice was to pay wages in lieu of notice (largely regardless of the existence of cause to dismiss) and not to require the employee to account for anything he earned elsewhere during the period covered by such payment. In consequence, earnings during the period of notice entitlement were not to be set-off against compensation. This principle was confirmed by the Court of Appeal in *Babcock F.A.T.A. Ltd.* v. *Addison* though possibly only because it had stood for so long.[27] The principle does not mean that compensation should be awarded for a period already covered by payment in lieu. The Court of Appeal made the point that deduction of earnings should occur, for instance, if the period of notice entitlement was so long that it would not be normal good practice to pay wages in lieu for the whole time. Somewhat carried away by the clarity of this proposition the present writer supported the members of a tribunal which, in *Isleworth Studios Ltd.* v. *Rickard*[28] awarded the maximum level of compensation to a highly paid manager, with almost six months of a contract for a year certain to run, disregarding the fact that he had more than made up his loss in that period, on the ground that it would indeed be normal practice to pay such a person in lieu until the end of the contractual period. In *Babcock* the Court of Appeal had advised against the approach of "a conscientious and skilled cost accountant" (a description the present writer had not thought applicable to himself) and suggested that the principle was compensation, not the award of a bonus. The E.A.T. in *Isleworth Studios*, in over-ruling the tribunal, obviously had this in mind, though it expressed its view, somewhat confusingly, as based on the "no loss" principle which is, of course, precisely the principle *Babcock* declines to apply to this situation. It seems, therefore, that a claimant who has earned some remuneration in his notice period need not account for it whilst a claimant who has completely made up his loss will be regarded as not entitled to a bonus.

In normal circumstances *ex gratia* payments made as a consequence of the dismissal should be deducted from compensation,[28a] although, in *Addison* v. *Babcock F.A.T.A. Ltd.* the E.A.T. had declined to make such a deduction where the employee would probably have been dismissed, in any event, within fifteen months and would then have received the same payment. This raises the question whether it is permissible to refuse to offset an *ex gratia* payment wherever the unfairness arises from a procedural defect such that dismissal, with the same payment, would have probably occurred in any event.[28b] This would be a very strange consequence of "technical" unfairness.

If, by the time of the hearing, the claimant has secured other equally well remunerated employment no further compensation will be awarded. Most

---

[26] [1972] I.C.R. 501.
[27] [1987] I.C.R. 805.
[28] [1988] I.R.L.R. 137.
[28a] See, *Horizon Holidays Ltd.* v. *Grassi* [1987] I.R.L.R. 371.
[28b] *Road Chef Ltd.* v. *Hastings* [1988] I.R.L.R. 142.

often the claimant either has not secured any regular alternative employment or has new employment at a lower rate of pay. The tribunal must then assess his prospects considering, in the first case, when he is likely to obtain further employment and how well that employment is likely to be remunerated. In former days when acknowledgment of discretions was considered less desirable, guidance was attempted[29] and it was said that a tribunal must set out its reasoning in sufficient detail to show how it arrived at each figure.[30] This must not, however, be taken to give the impression that the process is normally particularly scientific. In deciding to what extent the claimant should have mitigated his loss, the tribunal will, of course, take account of its local knowledge and knowledge, or even supposition, about the state of the industry involved. It may well (as *Fougere* said) consider the employee's personality, since the object is to compensate him and not to punish the employer for fault. In the end, however, the period covered is more likely to be determined by impression with even an element of "justice and equity" creeping in when the figure it will produce is considered. It is worth pointing out that, despite this, industrial tribunals pursue a more regulated and less discretionary approach in assessing compensation than most other judicial bodies.

The claimant is under a statutory duty to mitigate his loss.[31] But it has been held that a tribunal should consider mitigation even if it is not raised[32] and it is, therefore, proper for a tribunal to consider whether the claimant could reasonably have been expected to obtain alternative employment before the hearing or, if he has done so at a lower rate of pay, whether that rate might reasonably have been improved.[33] In practice tribunals have to behave as much like a jury in this area as in others. Quite often claimants seem to do relatively little in the way of job hunting before the hearing—often saying there is not much point with an unexplained dismissal hanging over them—whilst being unduly optimistic as to their chances thereafter.

The "no loss" principle referred to in *Isleworth Studios Ltd.* v. *Rickard*[34] is more often applied to deny compensation to a claimant who cannot be said to have lost by his unfair dismissal because he would, anyway, have been dismissed fairly. In *Polkey* v. *A.E. Dayton Services Ltd.*[35] the House of Lords said that a dismissal, unfair for failure to follow proper procedure, might result in a nominal, or even nil, award if the tribunal considered that a proper procedure would probably have produced dismissal in the same way.

The duty to mitigate and the no loss approach only apply to assessment of the compensatory element of the award. Statutory provision enabling the tribunal to take into account the complainant's contribution to his dismissal may reduce both the basic and the compensatory awards and should normally do so by the same percentage. Contribution is, however, not to be taken into account where dismissal is for trade union membership or activities.[36] This

---

[29] *e.g. Fougere* v. *Phoenix Motor Co. Ltd.* [1976] I.R.L.R. 259.
[30] *Blackwell* v. *GEC Elliott Process Automation Ltd.* [1976] I.R.L.R. 144.
[31] The burden of proof of failure in which is on the employer—*Bessenden Properties Ltd.* v. *Corness* [1974] I.R.L.R. 338.
[32] *Morganite Electrical Carbon Ltd.* v. *Donne* [1988] I.C.R. 18.
[33] *Peara* v. *Enderlin Ltd.* [1979] I.C.R. 804.
[34] [1988] I.R.L.R. 137, *supra.*
[35] [1988] I.C.R. 142.
[36] E.A. 1982, s.6.

element is normally referred to as contributory "fault." The question for the tribunal is one of causation. The necessary findings are that:

(a) the matters to which the complaint relates (that is to say the circumstances of the dismissal in general and not the particular source of unfairness)[37] were to some extent contributed to by some behaviour, conduct or lack of conduct, of the employee;

(b) that the conduct was culpable or blameworthy,[38] and

(c) that having regard to (a) and (b) it is just and equitable to reduce the award to the specified extent.[39]

In addition to these deductions all payments, including *ex gratia* payments, made by the employer as a result of the termination of employment must be taken into account. In particular the tribunals will normally deduct payment of wages in lieu of notice in this fashion rather than adopting the alternative of assuming that loss only arises after the end of the notice period. After considerable uncertainty it has been settled that deduction of such payments which go to the ascertainment of loss should be made before deduction for contribution and mitigation. This is very important in the case of contribution which is assessed as a percentage of the loss. Only after both sets of deductions have been made should the statutory maximum fixed for the total of the compensatory award (which, in 1988, was not raised and was £8500) be applied.[40] In the case of an employee likely to have large losses, for instance, because of high pay (there is no weekly limit to the amount of net wages taken into account in the assessment of the compensatory award) or a long period of inability to achieve previous earnings levels, an employer might be well advised not to make an *ex gratia* payment which will only go to reduce the loss over and above the maximum award.

There is no limit to the potential items of loss for which compensation may be awarded, provided only that they have a monetary value.[41] Although it has been held[42] that anticipated salary increases may be included, it is unlikely that most tribunals will add to a current award compensation for unspecified salary increases likely to occur in the normal course of collective negotiation. Company cars give rise to a highly variable response which may be said to be based on the Inland Revenue figure for income tax liability rather than the Automobile Association figure of real value but is usually a somewhat impressionistic compromise.

It will sometimes be the case that an employee is earning the same amount, or more, in new employment because he works harder or longer. A variant of this position occurs where paid holiday entitlement is less in the new employment. In both cases the employee may earn the same and it seems that the correct approach is that all he has suffered is inconvenience which is not

---

[37] See, *Courtaulds Northern Spinning Ltd.* v. *Moosa* [1984] I.C.R. 218.

[38] *Hoover Ltd.* v. *Forde* [1980] I.C.R. 239.

[39] *Nelson* v. *B.B.C. (No. 2)* [1980] I.C.R. 110.

[40] *UBAF Bank Ltd.* v. *Davis* [1978] I.R.L.R. 442; *Parker and Farr Ltd.* v. *Shelvey* [1979] I.C.R. 896; *McCarthy* v. *BICC p.l.c.* [1985] I.R.L.R. 94.

[41] So it is suggested that *Imperial London Hotels Ltd.* v. *Cooper* [1974] I.T.R. 312 is wrong to take account of discomfort.

[42] *York Trailer Co. Ltd.* v. *Sparks* [1973] I.C.R. 518 but compare *Gill* v. *Harold Andrews (Sheepbridge) Ltd.* [1974] I.R.L.R. 109 when the prospect was unlikely.

capable of expression in money terms. Some monetary compensation might be awarded, however, if, for instance, the need to work overtime did produce actual expense or if the employee could convince the tribunal that he would have to supplement his new, more meagre, paid holiday entitlement with unpaid holiday time so that his annual earnings would be less. The same confinement to monetary loss is applied to the item "manner of dismissal" which is specifically included but rarely results in any additional award. In *Vaughan* v. *Weighpack Ltd.*[43] it was held that compensation should only be awarded under this head on cogent evidence of actual financial loss. Most aspects of the manner of dismissal, in any event, go to the issue of unfairness.[44]

One standard item of loss known as "loss of statutory rights" is almost always included in an award. This is designed to compensate the dismissed employee for the fact that he will not be entitled to claim for unfair dismissal or redundancy payment again until he has completed two further years of continuous employment.[45] It tends, therefore, to be regarded as a nominal figure of a more or less fixed amount. For many years it had stood at £20 but in *Head* v. *Muffet Ltd.*[46] Kilner-Brown J. in the E.A.T., suggested it should be raised to £100 and that quickly became the newly established amount. In this case the E.A.T. said that only rarely should the suggestion in *Daley* v. *Dorsett (Almar Dolls) Ltd.*[47] be applied so as to award compensation for loss of statutory notice entitlement which that decision had set at an amount equivalent to half the wages for that period. On the other hand, this statutory right is a little different from the right to make claims for unfair dismissal and redundancy. It creates an implied term in the contract of employment and its value is predictable. Though it may be said to be part of the accrued seniority for which, presumably, the basic award provides compensation it could provide a sizeable sum which, in the case, for instance, of an employee of many years' service nearing retirement age could never be replaced.

By far the most problems in the assessment of compensation are created by loss of pension entitlement. Whereas industrial tribunals normally announce their decision orally on the final day of the hearing and usually then proceed immediately to the assessment of compensation it would be a rare tribunal that was prepared to announce a figure for this item without time for calm thought on a new day. Many tribunals, indeed, will invite the parties to settle the amount of compensation if they see that it contains an element of lost pension. There is something to be said for such a practice. Other judicial bodies do not normally attempt a mathematical calculation of such an item, and it is often questioned whether such evaluation will produce an accurate assessment of loss. On the other hand, there is little doubt that an impressionistic approach is most likely wildly to undervalue this element so that even lawyers acting for the applicant may fail to secure fair compensation. Greater familiarity of ordinary people with the statements of surrender value of pensions which employers are now required to supply to their employees will, no doubt, do a lot to provide applicants with a greater realisation of what they

---

[43] [1974] I.R.L.R. 105.
[44] See *Polkey* v. *A.E. Dayton Services Ltd.* [1988] I.C.R. 142 (H.L.).
[45] *Infra*, pp. 212–223.
[46] [1986] I.R.L.R. 488.
[47] [1982] I.C.R. 1.

have lost if new employment does not provide an equivalent pension scheme. At the present time it is suggested that few of them should be left to negotiate a settlement of a pension scheme even if the employer is also unrepresented.

This position was emphasised by the Government Actuary's advice that the somewhat simple methods suggested in early cases would lead to serious inaccuracy.[48] It is, however, still true to say that if the employee is close to retirement it is probably best to work out the sum necessary to purchase an annuity equivalent to the pension that he would have been entitled to on reaching retirement, reduce it to take account of accelerated payment and deduct from it any return of pension contributions he has actually received. The problem is that such an exercise is so likely to produce a sum far in excess of the statutory maximum award that it is frustrating to have to go through it knowing what the result will be. (A tribunal is, of course, not entitled simply to award the maximum amount on the ground that loss is obviously well in excess of that amount). In other cases the approach recommended by the government actuary assesses the amount of accumulated entitlement, offset by early payment, and the ongoing loss of employers' contributions to a continuing scheme. It is not feasible to embark on an explanation of the calculations necessary in a student textbook.[49] Since most parties approach the conclusion of an industrial tribunal hearing completely unprepared to prove this item of loss, it may be worth explaining to students, who may soon have to do so, with what information it is necessary to supply the tribunal or to approach the calculation of a possible settlement.[50] They are:

(a) the age, sex and past pensionable service of the applicant;
(b) The applicant's annual wage or salary;
(c) The employer's contribution rate;
(d) The benefits received under the pension scheme on dismissal;
(e) The accrued pension and the transfer value;
(f) Whether there is provision for a widow's pension and, if so, to what extent;
(g) The period of unemployment, and, if new employment has been secured whether it has an occupational pension scheme.

Provision is made[51] for payment of the basic award by the Secretary of State if the employer is insolvent. No similar provision applies to the compensatory award. The procedure for enforcement of payment is by action in the County Court. Most tribunals will take care to ensure that their decisions are so enforceable, but many parties prefer entitlement under a settlement also to be recorded as part of the decision so as to ensure this.

---

[48] See *Scottish Co-operative Wholesale Society Ltd.* v. *Lloyd* [1973] I.C.R. 137; *Cawthorne and Sinclair Ltd.* v. *Hedger* [1974] I.C.R. 146; *Gill* v. *Harold Andrews (Sheepbridge) Ltd.* [1974] I.C.R. 294; *Hilti Ltd.* v. *Windridge* [1974] I.C.R. 352; *Copson* v. *Eversure Accessories Ltd.* [1974] I.T.R. 406.

[49] They are admirably explained in IDS Handbook No. 40 (February 1988) although it may be well to heed the advice of one tribunal chairman that the examples given are considerably easier to understand than the words used by the Government Actuary to explain the scheme.

[50] Some industrial tribunal regions send to the parties a questionnaire designed to obtain this information.

[51] *Infra*, pp. 87–89.

CHAPTER VI

REDUNDANCY AND QUALIFICATION TO CLAIM

Signs of redundancy

The student may feel, upon discovering the law relating to redundancy, that he has stumbled into a clearing in the jungle of industrial tribunal discretion, much of which is never penetrated by an appeal ruling unless an unwary chairman fails to present the decision as one of fact. In the clearing he will find a structure of great technical beauty built by lawyers steeped in the contract law of their ancestors and anxious to create a legal concept as an explanation of a common feature of employment; namely, dismissal because the employee's job has been lost. The monument they have built has little relation to the situation it is designed to represent, but has proved an attractive marker for lawyers.

The definition of "redundancy" is of considerable importance since it is automatically applied whenever statute uses the word. "Redundancy" is actually only one form of economic reorganisation (though in its extreme form of complete closure it would not be popularly so called). The consequences of reorganisation upon the relationship of an employee to his employment vary in severity but the variation has little to do with whether the reorganisation fits into the narrow confines of redundancy. Nor is redundancy by any means the only form of reorganisation which may lead to dismissal. An employer planning the economic future of his business does not usually think principally of a choice between redundancy and other forms of reorganisation. He is most likely to think first of the need for economies, then of how to achieve as much saving as he needs, and only thirdly of the consequences if he chooses a method within, or outside the definition of redundancy. As we shall see in more detail shortly, "redundancy" requires a diminution in the employer's requirement for employees to do a particular job. So the consequences of a redundancy can be avoided by arranging that the saving should affect not the job but some costly feature accompanying it. We shall see also that the critical test of the job is most probably not provided by what the employee is doing, but by what he might be required to do. An apparently moribund or artificial contractual obligation, therefore, can be revived, producing a job requirement wholly new to the employee but not producing any alteration in the job "he is employed to do." The employee may well conclude that he cannot accept the change, even if the choice is available to him. Loss of a night shift premium by one transferred to the day shift will make a great difference to take-home pay. Introduction of computerisation may be taken in its stride by a generation educated to understand such techniques but be terrifying to an older employee, in turn less likely to find alternative work.

Not all reorganisations are obvious in themselves. In the last resort it is necessary to ask not whether there has been a reorganisation but whether there is dismissal by reason of redundancy. If there is no diminution in requirement for employees the conclusion can only be that dismissal is not due to redundancy. This is apparent in the facts of *North Yorkshire County Council* v. *Fay*.[1] The applicant had been employed, the tribunal found, not as a general teacher but to undertake, in succession, contracts to fill temporary gaps in the English Department. This does not necessarily mean that the tribunal categorised her contractual position as an English teacher. It was held to mean, however, that the reason for her dismissal was not a diminution in requirement because there had not been one in relation to her. As the Court of Appeal said this was a pure question of fact. She might have shown that she was displaced because of the redundancy of the replacement. The tribunal, however, held that she was displaced because the authority decided to replace her temporary position with a permanent appointment.

A system of statutory protection of the employee from the consequences of organisational change, therefore, is bound to fail to the extent that it is limited to a definition excluding much of that change. An employee faced with the risk of selection for the consequences of change may be encouraged by the thought that that selection must adhere to the terms of a collective agreement made by his trade union,[2] only to discover that the change does not constitute "redundancy" so that the statutory obligation does not apply. A recognised trade union may similarly be comforted by the thought that an employer contemplating redundancy must consult with it "at the earliest opportunity" before dismissals occur,[3] only to find that what is proposed is a reorganisation not amounting to "redundancy." Most obviously, the payment designed to provide some compensation for loss of the accumulated seniority and skills of employment in a particular job may not be available if that particular job is lost because one cannot adapt to new demands built into it. The statutory rights available to the employee who thinks he is redundant are, therefore, a lottery to a similar extent to the rights of those who suppose they have been unfairly dismissed, but on this occasion not because of the discretionary nature of the test. Rather, the problem is the excessive narrowness created by the relative certainty of a definition, the legalistic boundaries of which bear no resemblance to the boundaries formed by popular understanding of what was, after all, a popular concept before it became a legal one.

Statutory definition of "redundancy"

The statutory definition of redundancy reads as follows[4]:

> " . . . an employee who is dismissed shall be taken to be dismissed by reason of redundancy if the dismissal is attributable wholly or mainly to:
>   (a) the fact that his employer has ceased, or intends to cease, to carry on the business for the purposes of which the employee was employed by him, or has ceased or intends to cease, to carry on that business in the place where the employee was so employed, or

---

[1] [1985] I.R.L.R. (C.A.) 247.
[2] E.P.C.A. 1978, s.59.
[3] E.P.A. 1975, s.99.
[4] E.P.C.A. s.81(2).

(b) the fact that the requirements of that business for employees to carry out work of a particular kind, or for employees to carry out work of a particular kind in the place where he was so employed have ceased or diminished or are expected to cease or diminish.[5]

The first limb gives rise to few problems. It is usually fairly obvious that a business has closed down, or is about to close down. Even if it is not, the situation will simply transfer itself to the second limb if the changes amount to less than cessation of business. Cessation in the place where the employee was employed may raise the question whether the employee is employed to work in a wider geographic area than that in which he is currently operating. The same question arises under the second limb and will be dealt with in due course.

The second limb deals with job reduction falling short of complete closure and often requiring selection if a particular job category is not being wholly eliminated, but merely reduced. It must be noted that the definition does not, as is often supposed, require that the job in question should be that done, or contracted to be done, by the employee dismissed. An employee may be dismissed by reason of redundancy though the redundancy is that of someone else; as, for instance, someone moving into the job of the dismissed employee because their own job has gone.[6]

But what is "work of a particular kind"? It is submitted that the distinction between characteristics of the work and other terms of employment is now clearly established. In *Chapman* v. *Goonvean and Rostowrack China Clay Co. Ltd.*[7] employees were provided with transport to and from work. The number of employees using the transport dropped to seven and the employer decided to economise by withdrawing the service. It is likely that such a withdrawal was in breach of contract and when the seven employees left work because they could not economically make their own arrangements to travel they were entitled to claim to have been constructively dismissed. After 1971 their dismissal might well have been held to be unfair for want of consultation, but the statutory remedy of unfair dismissal had not been created at the time of termination of their contract. They claimed to have been dismissed by reason of redundancy or, more probably, by reason of expected redundancy. It had been held in two previous cases[8] that when existing terms and conditions have altered because it was anticipated that their uneconomic nature would lead to a redundancy, the alteration of terms could be said to be by reason of expected redundancy. The Court of Appeal rejected this argument. Whatever other reasoning might have been involved in this decision it is quite clear that the court accepted that a cessation of a requirement for employees on terms other than those relating to job content did not constitute a redundancy. The earlier decisions had achieved their result by extending the chain of causation so as to look beyond the immediate change of terms and to

---

[5] There is a presumption that a dismissal is by reason of redundancy if the employer is unable to prove that it is not. C.P.C.A. 1978, s.91(2). See *Wilcox* v. *Hastings* [1987] I.R.L.R. 298. The presumption operates only for the purposes of a claim for redundancy payment and does not supply a reason in a claim for unfair dismissal—*Midland Foot Comfort Centre* v. *Moppett* [1973] I.L.R. 219.

[6] This was decided as early as *Spurrett* v. *W. Gimber & Son Ltd.* [1966] I.T.R. 391.

[7] [1973] I.C.R. 310.

[8] *Dutton* v. *C.H. Bailey Ltd.* (1968) 3 I.T.R. 355; *Line* v. *C. E. White and Co.* [1969] I.T.R. 336.

conclude that that change would not have been made were it not for a longer-term objective of avoiding job losses. The reference to expectation was regarded by the Court of Appeal as requiring a more immediate and demonstrable anticipation. Neither proposition has since been seriously questioned, and there are many existing cases which illustrate that alteration in terms not relating to job content, though it may cause the requirement for a particular type of contract to cease, does not produce a cessation of requirement for employees to carry out the work involved. In *Johnston v. Nottinghamshire Combined Police Authority*[9] a change in shift pattern was held not to constitute a redundancy. Stephenson L.J. said[10]:

> "You look at the task or job which the employee did [the emphasis on what was done may now be incorrect] . . . I will assume that an alteration of method or hours or of the type of person employed or of status or responsibility—or even of remuneration—may alter the work done to such an extent that it would in common sense be regarded as a different task or job so that the change required by the employer and rejected by the employee would be a change in kind."

The next question is by which of two standards, (i) the contract or (ii) current practice, is job content to be decided.

It is submitted that authority now clearly favours the view that the job is that defined by the contract.[11] It is not entirely clear whether Wedderburn[12] intends to suggest that this may still be open to doubt or merely to warn that there is still room for flexibility in deciding the extent to which contract requires acceptance of change.[13] Certainly, it is true that the proposition could not have been put as clearly as it just has before 1979. In many instances, of course, the actual work done has been the same for years, or at least long enough to provide evidence of an established content. In the absence of express job definition what has thus been done will establish what the contract requires to be done. Where this is not so, however, adoption of a "job function" approach would necessitate a decision upon the period of time over which are accumulated job changes so as to form a pattern of what might be called the reasonable expectations of the employee. It might well be thought less uncertain to look at the contract than at a situation which, in the stress of economic decline, might have changed rapidly over a short period, although it should be realised that a test which looked at the function as it was at the time of dismissal is not so impracticable as it looks at first sight. That, after all, was the sticking point at which the parties' ability to agree change came to an end and it was that cessation which caused the dismissal. One of the features of the contract approach, however, is its ability to incorporate the functional approach. In other words, the courts often imply the contractual obligation from what has actually happened. One consequence of this is that a court applying the functional approach, as it probably did, for instance in

[9] [1974] I.C.R. 170.
[10] At p. 179.
[11] *Nelson v. B.B.C. (No. 2)* [1979] I.R.L.R. 346; *Haden Ltd. v. Cowan* [1982] I.R.L.R. 314; *Pink v. White* [1985] I.R.L.R. 489. The N.I.R.C. had held this to be so much earlier—*Runnals v. Richards and Osborne Ltd.* [1973] I.C.R. 225.
[12] 3rd ed. at p. 229.
[13] But see *Pink v. White* [1985] I.R.L.R. 489.

Vaux and Associated Breweries Ltd. v. *Ward*[14] could easily reach the same conclusion by using the existence of the function to create an implied term in the contract. Suppose in *Haden Ltd.* v. *Cowan*[15] for example, the contracts surveyor had been in the habit of undertaking work outside that job category one imagines the court might well have concluded that "within his capacity" extended to the work he had been doing. In *Murphy* v. *Epsom College*[16] also, the employee's functions and his contract are linked but the Court of Appeal, almost certainly, saw itself as deciding on the contractual job.

Though few commentators make this distinction, it is submitted that whether the contract or the functional approach is used, the courts have to decide whether the changes that are required in the job content are so extensive as to place the new job in a different category. Long ago, in *Smith* v. *G.K. Purdy Trawlers Ltd.*[17] the question arose whether a requirement for operating a diesel trawler involved a job different from that of operating a steam trawler. If "the function" might be said to be the question it has to be conceded that some functional aspects had changed. So they had, perhaps less tangibly, in *Vaux and Associated Breweries Ltd.* v. *Ward*[18] where a 57-year-old barmaid was replaced by two bright young girls. This was so regardless of whether they operated behind, or in front of, the bar. Again, in *North Riding Garages* v. *Butterwick*[19] the workshop manager had never estimated for repairs and it could scarcely have been claimed that such a function was within his contractual obligation. The case does not depend, therefore, on choice of the functional or the contractual approach but on how we entitle his job and whether the same title should be applied to his replacement. Stephenson L.J. in *Johnson* v. *Nottinghamshire O.P.A.*[20] was considering the distinction between job characteristics and other terms but his question, "Who is doing your job now?" still has to be asked when both that distinction and the choice between contract and function have been settled. Possibly that question is the only guidance that can be given on what might be called "common classification of the two contractual job contents." The scrambling may be even more complex when a number of packages are put in and emerge as a number of different packages. *Robinson* v. *British Island Airways Ltd.*[21] reveals the subjectivity of the decision as to whether the former job has changed sufficiently to produce a diminution in requirement for it as a job. The Flight Operations Manager had reported to the General Manager, Operations and Traffic. Both were replaced by one Operations Manager. Phillips J. in the E.A.T. held that all three were different "jobs of a particular kind" so that, despite the replacement, each of the two original employees was redundant. Much will depend, of course, on the readiness of the court to accept a wide range of different job categories. The evidence seems to suggest a desire to limit such categorisation. In *Arnold* v. *Thomas Harrington Ltd.*,[22]

---

[14] [1969] 7 K.I.R. 309.
[15] [1982] I.R.C.R. 314.
[16] (1984) I.R.L.R. 271; see *infra* p. 185.
[17] [1966] I.T.R. 508.
[18] *Supra.*
[19] (1967) I.T.R. 229. See also *A. W. Champion* v. *Scoble* (1967) I.T.R. 411.
[20] *Supra.*
[21] [1978] I.C.R. 304.
[22] [1967] 2 All E.R. 866.

for instance, the job was classified as that of a motor fitter. The category "resident fitter" was rejected, logically, perhaps, because of the absence of a function in the adjective. More to the point, the element of operating an emergency breakdown service was not considered to change the type of job. It will be appreciated, however, that the decision whether an employee is classified as a plumber working on gas fittings or as a gas fitter[23] is one of fact which tribunals are likely to decide as such, rather than to rely on throwing up their hands in despair and falling back on the presumption of dismissal by reason of redundancy in the absence of proof that the jobs are the same.[24] In consequence the student should not be too concerned if he differs, factually, on the decision in *Murphy* v. *Epsom College.*[25] Murphy was the school's assistant plumber doing maintenance plumbing and assisting with the central heating boilers. He pushed his luck somewhat when he placed limits on what he would do in respect of the modernised heating system and other work fit for a plumber and the school hired a "heating engineer," deciding that apart from that it only needed one plumber. The Court of Appeal concluded that a heating engineer was a different kind of tradesman with different qualifications performing more extensive, and more responsible, work than Murphy.

Although it has been suggested that this process of classification is wholly separate from the question whether the job content is found in the contract or in what is done, there seems little doubt that the contract approach has emphasised the control of the employer over the job content. *Cresswell* v. *Board of Inland Revenue*[26] is not a redundancy case but provides a good illustration of the point. Tax officers and clerical assistants were required to operate a new computerised system which would not only record information about the taxpayer but also issue postal communications to him. Largely from fear of resultant redundancy the employees refused to operate the new system and the question arose whether they were in breach of their contracts. Two different approaches could have been adopted in that, either it could have been held that employees were contractually obliged to accept reasonable change, or that the contractual statement of the job left the method of performance to the employer so that no change was involved. The Chancery Division preferred the view that the job had not changed. This would mean that no redundancy would arise from the change of method. A job function approach, it is suggested, would make such a conclusion much less easy since it would be necessary to establish that the functions had changed but that the change did not alter the overall classification. In other words, it is easier to conclude that clerical assistants remain clerical assistants by relying on their contract, from which is excluded the method of performance, than it is if one has to rely on their actual performance and then conclude that the undeniable differences therein are insufficient to produce a change of category.

The diminution or cessation must occur at the place of employment. This seems always to have had a contractual, rather than a functional, conno-

---

[23] *O'Neill* v. *Merseyside Plumbing Co. Ltd.* [1973] I.C.R. 96.
[24] E.P.C.A., s.91(2). See, on throwing up their hands, *London Carpet Cleaners* v. *Bell*, I.D.S. Report 131 p. 23 and, on the presumption generally, *Midland Foot Comfort Centre* v. *Moppett* [1973] I.C.R. 219.
[25] [1984] I.R.L.R. 271. (C.A.).
[26] [1984] I.C.R. 508.

tation,[27] although the contract is much less likely expressly to provide for the place of employment than for the content of the job so that the terms of the contract as to place are more likely to be implied from practice.[28] In some ways contradicting this, the courts seem to have been more ready to accept wide express terms as to place than wide terms as to function.[29] The effect of this has been to deter courts from contractualising wide requirements.[30] At an earlier stage they had avoided the consequence of wide movement requirements by construing a change of location as a dismissal rather than an invitation to move within the contract.[31]

In practice, the "place of work" provision operates differently from the "particular kind of work" requirement. Once it is shown that an employee has an obligation to move, his refusal to do so provides a reason for dismissal distinct from redundancy, and it is usually irrelevant to consider whether there is actually an overall diminution in requirement in the wider geographic area covered by the contract.[32] It is not that requirement that has caused his dismissal. As we have seen, there are, conversely, many situations in which the job content has not changed but the employee is, for other contractual reasons, entitled to refuse the development, and claim constructive dismissal. His remedy for dismissal then has to turn on redundancy or reorganisation.

"Place" is as imprecise a term as "job," although it is probably open to more common-sense application. Most people would intuitively accept that a move from one street to an adjacent one was not a change of place.[33] Contracts tend only to make specific provision where the move would otherwise seem unusually wide. In between, the matter will have to be resolved either by implied obligation or by a wide view of the meaning of "place" which, it is to be assumed, raises a question of law.

The requirement contained in the definition refers not to the need for work but to a requirement for employees to do the work. Some decisions would be easier to explain if the opposite were true[34] and it seems to be this that has caused some textbook writers in the past to doubt the point. Any other rule would be difficult to operate. Industrial tribunals usually reject any invitation to make business decisions, quite apart from the invidious position in which they would find themselves in having to decide by how many employees an employer was overmanned before he reduced his workforce. Dismissal to reduce overmanning, therefore, will usually be by reason of redundancy. So, rather technically, will be dismissal of employees in order to contract the

---

[27] Nevertheless, this has had to be confirmed from time to time; see, *Sutcliffe* v. *Hawker Siddeley Aviation Ltd.* [1973] I.R.L.R. 304.

[28] See *O'Brien* v. *Associated Fire Alarms Ltd.* [1968] 1 W.L.R. 1916.

[29] Compare: *U.K. Atomic Energy Authority* v. *Claydon* [1974] I.C.R. 128, with *Haden Ltd.* v. *Cowan* [1982] I.R.L.R. 314.

[30] As in *Jones* v. *Associated Tunnelling Ltd.* [1981] I.R.L.R. 477; *Hawker Siddeley Power Engineering Ltd.* v. *Rump* [1974] I.R.L.R. 429. But see now, *Rank Xerox Ltd.* v. *Churchill* [1988] I.R.L.R. 180.

[31] *McCullock Ltd.* v. *Moore* [1967] 2 All E.R. 290; *John Laing & Son Ltd.* v. *Best* [1968] I.T.R. 3.

[32] See *Murray* v. *Robert Rome and Son (Rotherglen) Ltd.* [1969] I.T.R. 20.

[33] See *Margiotta* v. *Mount Charlotte Investments Ltd.* [1966] I.T.R. 465 and compare *Buck* v. *Edward Everard Ltd.* [1968] I.T.R. 328.

[34] e.g. *O'Hare* v. *Rotaprint Ltd.* [1980] I.R.L.R. 47; *Ranson* v. *G. and W. Collins Ltd.* [1978] I.C.R. 765.

work to self-employed workers or outside contractors.[35] Much more difficult to settle is the scope to be given to "requirement." In *Brombey and Hoare Ltd.* v. *Evans*[36] it was said by the N.I.R.C. that it meant "need," so that an employer who only contracted out because he could not obtain a particular class of employee still required employees to do the job whilst one who decided that the self-employed were more economical no longer required employees. It is suggested that this view of "need" is wrong. It is true, as we shall see, that the employer has to have decided he can do without some employees previously contracted to do that job. Once he has so decided, however, his requirement has diminished. Consequently the fact that fewer employees remain in the job category and replacements are not being sought is strong evidence of a diminution in requirement which is not cast in doubt by evidence, for instance, that manning is dangerously below what is necessary, as objectively assessed. So, in *Brombey*, the presumption would be that there had been a diminution in requirement for employees unless the employer was trying to recruit replacements, regardless of the reason he had given up looking for them.

This was the point made by Kilner-Brown J. in the much misunderstood case of *O'Hare* v. *Rotaprint Ltd.*[37] The employer, anticipating an increase in demand for the product, had substantially increased his workforce. The demand did not materialise and a reduction in the workforce was regarded as essential. The workers themselves were asked to suggest the best way in which this could be done. They proposed a 20 per cent. reduction in every category of job. It is tempting to interpret the decision that there had been no dismissal by reason of redundancy as meaning that this was because no reduction in the amount of work required had occurred. That, as we have said, would contradict the statutory definition. The decision is an application of that in *Delanair Ltd.* v. *Mead*[38] that dismissal must be shown to be by reason of redundancy. The employer must convince the tribunal that he acted because he believed he required less employees. In this case, rarely, the employer had no relevant belief. He had simply done what his workforce suggested. This, however, has nothing to do with a choice between requirement and need. In *O'Hare*, before the dismissals the employer required an extra 20 per cent. of employees whether he had any need for them or not. After the dismissals he did not so require them. The diminution in requirement, however, was the outcome of the dismissals, not the reason for it. The same is true of *Ranson* v. *G. and W. Collins Ltd.*[39] where the takeover of one company by another meant that one of two general managers, kept on, largely at the request of the transferor, as assistant manager, was not really needed. It was everyone's intention that, if he fitted in well, the applicant would be considered for promotion to manager again. In practice he was never prepared for this post. Eventually, it was decided that the applicant's branch at Bolton could do without an assistant manager and he was declared redundant. The E.A.T. overruled the tribunal and held that the employee was not dismissed

---

[35] *Brombey and Hoare Ltd.* v. *Evans* [1972] I.C.R. 113.
[36] *Supra.*
[37] [1980] I.R.L.R. 47.
[38] [1976] I.C.R. 522.
[39] [1978] I.C.R. 765.

by reason of redundancy. Again, it is tempting to explain this on the ground that there never had been a need for an assistant manager so there was no diminution. The headnote falls into this trap. That conclusion is quite wrong. There was plainly a *requirement* for an assistant manager because the applicant occupied that post. The dismissal of the applicant without replacement obviously diminished that requirement. But the dismissal was not by reason of the diminution as it would have been if the employer had at last decided to implement his feeling that he did not need the post. Unusually, in *Ranson* the employer never suggested that he was dismissing for that reason. The fact that his recognised absence of need had existed for so long simply made it easier for him to establish that the reason for Ranson's dismissal was that the plans for his future development had not worked out. Both in *O'Hare* and in *Ranson*, therefore, the potential redundancy (sometimes called a "redundancy situation," though the E.A.T. criticised this in *Ranson*) which arises when a workforce is reduced could be shown to have been what motivated the employer to decide on dismissal. It is suggested that the decision in *AUT* v. *University of Newcastle on Tyne*[40] follows obviously from this well-established position. In that case there was a demand for places on a University course but the employer had no money to mount it. It was held that whatever the need might be the employer's requirement had ceased.

Looking back it is apparent that this possibility of a reason different from that suggested by the situation was behind the involved decision in *Hindle* v. *Percival Boats Ltd.*[41] The applicant in that case had been dismissed as an economy measure. The employer convinced the industrial tribunal that he intended to replace Hindle with someone who produced results faster, if not so well, and therefore more cheaply. Unless one could distinguish the two jobs it followed inevitably that the reason for dismissal could not be a diminution in requirement. It had to be a decision to employ someone cheaper. One suspects that the Court of Appeal did not really agree with this decision of fact. Hindle had not been replaced, which might seem surprising since the employers only wanted a carpenter of sorts. This seems to have induced Lord Denning, in particular, to try to argue for a difference between subjective motive and objective reason. That distinction is not sustainable. It follows that an employer contemplating a diminution in his need may dismiss and not replace, thus creating a diminution in his requirement, but do so for an immediate reason other than that diminution.[42] He may have difficulty convincing a tribunal that this is so, but that is another matter. As with any other reason for dismissal, the less he enquires the less he will be in a position to show that he believed in the existence of the less obvious reason such enquiry might have established. But it was the absence of any evidence of enquiry into the effects of economy in *O'Hare* which lay behind the decision that the employer had not acted by reason of any decision of his own as to requirement.

One final consideration sets a seal on the subjectivity of redundancy. Once the employer has established that he dismissed because his requirement for employees had diminished tribunals will not consider the soundness of his

---

[40] [1988] I.R.L.R. 11.
[41] [1969] 1 W.L.R. 174.
[42] *e.g. Sanders* v. *Ernest A. Neale Ltd.* [1974] I.C.R. 565.

judgment. In *Moon* v. *Homeworthy Furniture (Northern) Ltd.*[43] the not unique situation arose of employees disputing the employer's decision that an undertaking was not economically viable. The employees sought to argue that dismissal was unfair. As we have seen, it is difficult, if not impossible, to argue that dismissal is not justified once redundancy has been decided upon so, in this instance, they contended that the redundancy itself could be challenged on its merits. An industrial tribunal, straightforwardly, decided that there was no reason to challenge the validity of the decision to close down and that necessarily established redundancy as the reason. The E.A.T., in a burst of something approaching indiscretion, revealed a firm practical base for staying out of disputes on managerial decisions by stating that it was not going to run the risk of the same fate as the N.I.R.C.

Summary

There seems little doubt, from all that has gone before, that it is correct to say that redundancy is nothing but an exercise of managerial prerogative. It is open to management to decide to economise and no tribunal will consider whether such a decision is reasonable, let alone necessary. Economy can be effected in many ways although the relative proportion of labour to other costs in the majority of industrial situations is likely to mean that substantial economies have to be brought about by reduction of labour costs. Such reduction may be produced by reducing the number of employees, thus producing a redundancy, but many other forms of reorganisation outside the statutory definition are available. Some of them affect the employee's economic position to such an extent that in all but abnormal circumstances he is likely to seek other employment. The employer may well have calculated that this would be so. Whatever his situation, however, it is for the employer to formulate his reason for dismissal and the outcome of the dismissal is not necessarily the reason for it.

Alternative offers

There can be no doubt that the legislature in 1965 intended to encourage an employer who had made a decision to reduce his workforce in a particular job category to retain the individuals in his employment by offering them other jobs. If they accept such an offer no question of a claim for redundancy compensation will arise because they will not have been dismissed. This is part of the explanation of the decision in *Meek* v. *J. Allen Rubber Co. Ltd.*[44] where it was found as a fact that the employer intended to terminate employment and offer a new contract for a different job. Normally, however, an alternative offer which is accepted and which involves no break in employment will operate as a consensual variation of contract. It has to be said that this, like most other so-called consensual variation of the contract of employment, stretches the normal law of contract to some extent. In particular consensual variation requires consideration; although, if pressed, the courts would, no doubt, say that this was to be found in the continuation of employment which would otherwise have been terminated. The main areas of operation for the statutory provisions, therefore, are those in which there might be a doubt as to

---

[43] [1977] I.C.R. 117.
[44] [1980] I.R.L.R. 21.

whether the contract had been terminated and restarted (and statute is very specific as to which work situations are provided for in this respect) and those in which the offer is rejected, so that a dismissal by reason of redundancy has occurred and the employee's right depends on whether the employer can raise what amounts to a defence that he has made a suitable offer.

Whether one is speaking of consensual variation or the defence of an allegedly rejected offer it may be necessary to make a factual decision on acceptance or rejection. Over the 25 years in which this legislation has operated a greater understanding of the legal consequences of this situation has developed. In the early years the picture was confused by a tendency to assume that an employee still working must have accepted the terms on which he was working. In *Marriott* v. *Oxford and District Co-operative Society Ltd.*[45] the Court of Appeal had to work hard to produce the conclusion that an ultimatum destroyed the original terms and that an employee who constantly protested about the new terms could not be said to have accepted them just because he went on working under them for a few weeks. By 1984[46] the courts were taking long-term objection in their stride and raising no quibble about the exact content of the arrangement under which the parties were subsequently operating; so much so that it had begun to be asked whether all the employee had to do to keep alive a repudiatory breach was to register non-acceptance. Whatever the answer to this may be there will always be those too taken-aback, or unaware of their rights, to protest immediately. The courts had to decide on common law principles when to consider acceptance of the new offer to have occurred if there was no evidence of objection.[47] The outcome was rather more of a lottery than is usually the case before industrial tribunals. Those who knew what they were doing could achieve long, or as it would now seem almost indefinite, trial periods in the new job during which period they might at any time leave and claim the withdrawal of the original job as a dismissal by reason of redundancy. Those who did not might find that after two or three weeks of struggling to see if they could cope they were deemed to have accepted the new position, which if they now left they left of their own volition.

The legislature clearly intended to sort this out and produce a standard trial period of four weeks available to all those faced with an alternative job.[48] If that was the intention, however, it is difficult to understand the decision in *Air Canada* v. *Lee*[49] that despite the expiration of the statutory trial period it is open to the employee to continue to assert non-acceptance. It is even more difficult to comprehend *Turvey* v. *C.W. Cheyney and Son Ltd.*[50] which, in effect, decides that the trial period is available as an addition to any common law period of non-acceptance. Presumably, the argument is that the non-acceptance of change causes the previous contract to continue so that the statutory reference to a trial period commencing when the previous contract terminates refers to the time at which the employee accepted the repudiation.

---

[45] [1970] 1 Q.B. 186.
[46] *Burdett-Coutts* v. *Hertfordshire County Council* [1984] I.R.L.R. 91 and see also *Hawker Siddeley* v. *Rump* [1982] I.R.L.R. 425.
[47] See, *e.g. Sheet Metal Components Ltd.* v. *Plumridge* [1974] I.C.R. 373.
[48] Now in E.P.C.A., s.84.
[49] [1978] I.R.L.R. 392 (E.A.T.).
[50] [1979] I.R.L.R. 105 (E.A.T.)

That view has on its side the fact that the alternative offer provisions do not apply to a clear termination followed by new employment[51] but it suffers from the practical disadvantage of reopening all the uncertainty of the previous common law position. In practice, the problem is not likely to occur often, since employees will generally rely on the statutory period and not register a separate objection.

If an employer makes the employee an offer in any form,[52] before the ending of employment under the previous contract, to renew that contract or re-engage the employee with himself or an associated employer, within not more than four weeks after the ending of the previous contract, and the offer would not differ from the terms of the previous contract, or constitutes an offer of suitable employment in relation to the employee, the employee will be unable to claim a statutory redundancy payment if he unreasonably refuses that offer. Where any terms or conditions do differ as between the previous, and the offered, contract a trial period of four weeks begins with the ending of employment under the previous contract.[53] The four weeks can be extended by agreement in writing between the employer and the employee or his representative, made before the new, or second, contract starts, provided the agreement specifies the date of ending of the extended period and the terms and conditions which will then apply.[54] The employee may, for any reason, terminate the new contract at any time during the four weeks, whilst the employer may terminate it for a reason connected with or arising out of the change. If that happens the employee is treated as if he had been dismissed at the time the previous contract was terminated. The original claim for redundancy will, in effect, revive. If the employee has terminated the trial period, the employer is entitled to assert that a suitable offer was made which, as it turns out, has been rejected. Presumably the employer would not raise this defence if he himself had terminated the trial period since he would be unable to show that the offer had been rejected and his termination would tend to support the conclusion that, in any event, the job was not suitable in relation to that employee. The employer is free, of course, to terminate the new contract for any other reason. In that event any claim by the employee would seem to have to be for unfair dismissal based on that reason and the original redundancy claim will not revive.[55]

A great deal of reported case law has accumulated—though not so much recently—on what is suitable and what is a reasonable rejection. They are both questions of fact,[56] and it is for the employer to prove that the rejection was unreasonable.[57] There is little point in doing other than provide a few examples, which include loss of status,[58] but do not include fears of hypotheti-

---

[51] *Meek* v. *Allen Rubber Co. Ltd.* [1980] I.R.L.R. 21.

[52] Thus avoiding technicalities about what appeared in written offers—*e.g. Toolan* v. *Beck and Pollitzer Engineering Ltd.* [1975] I.R.L.R. 183—although it is still necessary to determine reasonable refusal on the basis of the offer as put—*Simpson* v. *Dickinson* [1972] I.C.R. 474.

[53] *Bolton* v. *Sanderson Kayser Ltd.* [1987] I.R.L.R. 237—non-working weeks do not count as part of the period.

[54] *McKindley* v. *William Hill (Scotland) Ltd.* [1985] I.R.L.R. 492.

[55] *Hempell* v. *W.H. Smith and Sons Ltd.* [1986] I.R.L.R. 95.

[56] *Williamson* v. *N.C.B.* [1970] I.T.R. 43; *Kerr* v. *N.C.B.* [1970] I.T.R. 48.

[57] *Jones* v. *Aston Cabinet Co. Ltd.* [1973] I.C.R. 292.

[58] *Taylor* v. *Kent County Council* [1969] 2 All E.R. 1080; but compare *Kane* v. *Raine and Co. Ltd.* [1979] I.C.R. 300.

cal insecurity.[59] Fear of underemployment has been accepted[60] though this seems better classified as reasonable ground for rejection.[61] Clearly, a significant reduction in wages will cause the offer to be regarded as unsuitable.[62] In *Hindes* v. *Supersine Ltd.*[63] the E.A.T. said that the test of suitability is whether the new job is substantially equivalent to the employment that has ceased, but this, it is suggested, is only correct in relation to terms such as pay. It must not be supposed that it refers to similarity. A certain amount of judicial inventiveness was at one time devoted to defining the difference between suitable offers and unreasonable refusals.[64] Though such matters as personal preference would seem to fall more comfortably within the second heading,[65] as would extraneous considerations such as the fact that the employee had found other apparently secure employment,[66] nothing is to be gained by assignment to one or the other. It is only necessary to note that the joint formula includes both circumstances personal to the employee and considerations of comparability with previous employment.

Unfair redundancy

As has been said before,[67] the refusal of tribunals to enquire into the business judgment of an employer leads to the acceptance of a managerial decision to create a redundancy by reducing staff.[68] Once that decision is taken it must inevitably be held that a reasonable employer is entitled to make some dismissals. There seems little reason to doubt that both industrial tribunals and courts begin with an assumption that it must be open to an employer to dismiss for redundancy, provided that he does so in a reasonable manner either hallowed by good industrial relations practice or a practice in accordance therewith. It may still be questioned, however, whether it was fair to choose a particular complainant. In this context statute has provided a presumption of unfairness when the choice is based on union membership or activities or where it is in breach of agreed procedure or customary arrangement. Procedural defects, and particularly absence of consultation, may also render dismissal, particularly selective dismissal, for redundancy unfair. In *Elliott* v. *Richard Stump Ltd.*[69] it was held that to deny a trial period might render the offer of an alternative job unreasonable so as to produce an unfair dismissal. There is[70] likely to be a financial advantage in a claim for unfair redundancy, as distinct merely from redundancy, since the basic award for unfair dismissal is equivalent to the statutory redundancy payment (and if that

---

[59] *Morganite Crucible Co. Ltd.* v. *Street* [1972] I.C.R. 110.
[60] *Hawkins* v. *Thomas Forman and Sons Ltd.* [1967] I.T.R. 59.
[61] *Spencer and Griffin* v. *Gloucester C.C.* [1985] I.R.L.R. 343 (C.A.).
[62] *Kennedy* v. *Werneth Ring Mills Ltd.* [1977] I.C.R. 206.
[63] [1979] I.R.L.R. 343.
[64] *e.g. Carson Company* v. *Robertson* [1967] 1 I.T.R. 484.
[65] See, *e.g. Fuller* v. *Stephanie Bowman (Sales) Ltd.* [1977] I.R.L.R. 81.
[66] *Paton Calvert and Co. Ltd.* v. *Westerside* [1979] I.R.L.R. 108.
[67] *Supra*, pp. 162 and 189.
[68] See *Hollister* v. *National Farmers Union* [1979] I.C.R. 542 (C.A.) But in *Forth Estuary Engineering Ltd.* v. *Lister* [1988] I.R.L.R. 289 the Scottish E.A.T. had held that a dismissal for redundancy was unfair because it was unnecessary. The reasons given by the Court of Session for overruling this decision seem to treat redundancy as an objective fact.
[69] [1988] I.R.L.R. 215.
[70] *Supra*, pp. 172–173.

payment has been made it will normally eliminate the basic award) and the compensatory award is additional thereto.

A dismissal for redundancy may be unfair on any of the following grounds:

(i) Theoretically, that there is no justification for redundancy but this is unlikely to be sustainable in view of the concessions made to the employer's right to take such business decisions.[71]

(ii) That the situation is not properly described as redundancy,[72] but this is quite likely to be no more than wrong labelling of an undisputed fact situation (usually amounting to some other form of reorganisation).[73]

(iii) That a procedural requirement, usually consultation, has been inadequately observed.[74]

In a selection case it is quite likely to be impossible to say that the employee would probably have been selected anyway, even after proper consultation, so this is a form of unfairness capable of leading to a meaningful compensatory award.[75]

(iv) That the alleged redundancy is a cloak for some other reason. This is obviously what the tribunal had thought in *Timex Corporation* v. *Thompson*,[76] although it was not prepared to commit itself beyond saying that the possibility of one or other of two reasons meant the employer had not proved the reason for dismissal. It is also the most likely way in which a tribunal could describe the situation in (i) if it wished to award compensation rather than confirming the managerial decision. In selection for redundancy there has to be a reason other than the redundancy for the selection, but the courts do not normally experience difficulty in presenting redundancy as the primary reason for dismissal.

(v) That selection has been made on the grounds of trade union membership, or non-membership, or trade union activities at an appropriate time.[77] This will make the dismissal automatically unfair. It is, of course, a difficult point for the employee to prove. Normally he can only expect to sow suspicion in the minds of the tribunal and the decision is likely to turn on the degree of suspicion its members entertain.

(vi) That selection has been in contravention of a customary arrangement or agreed procedure relating to redundancy and there were no special reasons justifying a departure from that arrangement or procedure in the instant case.[78] This too produces automatic unfairness however reasonable the procedures actually applied.

(vii) That, for some other reason, the criteria for selection, or the procedure, were unfair. In practice it will be difficult, where an agreed procedure is followed, to show that it is unfair. In theory, the automa-

---

[71] *Moon* v. *Homeworthy Furniture Ltd.* [1977] I.C.R. 117.
[72] See, *e.g. Nelson* v. *BBC (No. 2)* [1979] I.R.L.R. 346.
[73] See *Williamson* v. *Allcan Ltd.* [1977] I.R.L.R. 303.
[74] *Williams* v. *Compair Maxam Ltd.* [1982] I.C.R. 156 and Lord Bridge in *Polkey* v. *Dayton* [1988] I.C.R. 142.
[75] See *Howarth Timber Ltd.* v. *Biscomb* [1986] I.R.L.R. 52.
[76] [1981] I.R.L.R. 522.
[77] E.P.C.A., s.59(a).
[78] E.P.C.A., s.59(b).

tic unfairness of not following an agreed procedure does not produce the opposite conclusion that adherence to such a procedure is automatically fair. The general test of reasonableness in E.P.C.A., s.57(3) is available to challenge any procedure. In practice, it would be very difficult to persuade an industrial tribunal that an employer was acting unreasonably in adhering to a collectively agreed redundancy procedure.[79] The application of the general test of reasonableness to an allegedly unfair redundancy selection is, therefore, largely confined to situations where there is no collectively agreed procedure, or possibly, to a situation where no attempt has been made to use that procedure.[80]

It is not clear whether the same reluctance to interfere exists in the case of an employer following a purely customary procedure. In *Atkinson* v. *George Lindsay and Co.*[81] the Court of Session thought it would be difficult to find unfairness once the test in section 59 had been satisfied. The logic of that conclusion is less obvious than that applicable to agreed procedure, since representatives of the employees have not necessarily accepted a customary procedure as fair, and the same flaw in the reasoning exists in that section 59 raises no presumption of fairness.

A number of cases consider the existence of agreed procedure or custom. In *Henry* v. *Ellerman City Liners Ltd.*[82] the same criteria had been applied, without union objection, for five years and the Court of Appeal held that the industrial tribunal was entitled to consider this indicative of agreement. This same readiness to find established redundancy procedures is apparent in *Tillgate Pallets Ltd.* v. *Barras*[83] in which the union's supposition that a "last in-first out" policy had been abandoned was held not to destroy its existence as customary practice. On the other hand, it is obvious that a long-standing agreement can be displaced by a new agreement dealing specifically with the forthcoming redundancy only and altering past procedure and criteria. It will be observed that this represents an unusual statutory inducement to collective bargaining, since an employer who views the past procedure as inappropriate is likely to fall into automatic unfairness if he unilaterally replaces it with another, but is almost certainly protected from such a claim if he negotiates a substitute. An employer may wish to plead special circumstances to justify a departure from usual procedure. His desire to maintain a balanced workforce was held not to be such a circumstance in *Tillgate Pallets Ltd.* v. *Barras*.[84]

Courts have, recently, shown signs of requiring more definite establishment of customary selection procedures than hitherto. In *Rogers* v. *Vosper Thornycroft (U.K.) Ltd.*[85] it was said that, to fall within section 59, a customary arrangement must be capable of indicating the criteria and process so that a

---

[79] *e.g. Evans* v. *A.B. Electronic Components Ltd.* [1981] I.R.L.R. 111; *Valor Newhome Ltd.* v. *Hampson* [1987] I.C.R. 407.

[80] *McDowell* v. *Eastern British Road Services Ltd.* [1981] I.R.L.R. 482.

[81] [1980] I.R.L.R. 197; *Buchanan* v. *Tillcon Ltd.* [1983] I.R.L.R. 417.

[82] [1984] I.R.L.R. 409.

[83] [1983] I.R.L.R. 23. But in *Suflex Ltd.* v. *Thomas, supra* a "last in—first out" policy was held too uncertain to be customary.

[84] *Supra.*

[85] [1988] I.R.L.R. 229. See also *Suflex Ltd.* v. *Thomas,* [1987] I.R.L.R. 435.

tribunal is able to compare the dismissed employee with those who were not so selected.

A defect in procedure outside the scope of an agreement is most likely to occur in a failure to consult either the relevant union, or the individual if there is no union. Browne-Wilkinson J. in *Williams* v. *Compair Maxam Ltd.*[86] attached the procedural requirements in redundancy cases to a standard of good industrial relations practice. It has also been seen that this attempt to reintroduce a procedural obligation, which could not be side-tracked as easily as the "natural justice" standard, has had a chequered career but may have been revived by the express inclusion of its basic requirement in the speech of Lord Bridge in *Polkey* v. *Dayton.*[87] Such a requirement has serious limitations in practical effect, however, in a case involving a clearly justified reason for dismissal. It is true that, since the *Polkey* decision, industrial tribunals are unable to say that the decision is fair because it would probably have been the same after proper procedure. They are, however, entitled to limit compensation to a short period only during which, they may conclude, the employee would have remained employed pending the proper procedure. In fact the less precise among them may conclude that no compensation is payable. It can be argued that it ought to be difficult to decide, even on a balance of probabilities, what would be the outcome of consultation. Some tribunals have taken this line,[88] but the outcome may differ in practice between the conclusion that consultation would have made a difference to the need to dismiss at all, and the conclusion that if it was not the applicant who was selected it would have been someone else. Academically, of course, this latter consideration is not justified since each case should be looked at individually. A tribunal would be unwise, therefore, to give it as a reason for a finding of fairness.[89] It is, however, something that will probably figure in the consideration of the members.

Consultation, in the *Williams* v. *Compair Maxam*[90] sense, is usually thought of as collective consultation with trade unions. The requirement was extended to individuals in the immediate aftermath of that decision.[91] Despite the subsequent lack of enthusiasm for the *Williams* approach there are signs that the E.A.T. feels that if consultation is required with trade unions it ought, in fairness, to be available in respect of employees who are not members of a union.[92]

The other principal source of successful claims for unfair selection is the adequacy of the criteria which should be applied. Again, where an agreed procedure is observed which itself contains the criteria or provision for fixing them, the chances of a decision in favour of unfairness are small.[93] Management is likely to wish to include among the criteria more general, if disguised, discretion such as the need to maintain a balanced workforce. This was

---

[86] [1982] I.R.L.R. 83.
[87] [1987] I.R.L.R. 503.
[88] *e.g. Howarth Timber Co. Ltd.* v. *Biscomb* [1980] I.R.L.R. 52; *Holden* v. *Bradville* [1985] I.R.L.R. 483.
[89] But see the clever way of putting it in *Lafferty Construction Ltd.* v. *Duthie* [1985] I.R.L.R. 486.
[90] *Supra.*
[91] *Freud* v. *Bentalls Ltd.* [1982] I.R.L.R. 443.
[92] *Holden* v. *Bradville* [1985] I.R.L.R. 483.
[93] *Buchanan* v. *Tillcon Ltd.* [1983] I.R.L.R. 417.

included in *B.L. Cars Ltd.* v. *Lewis*[94] and it clearly overrode other criteria in the applicant's case. It was held, however, that there was no evidence that it was not a proper ground for selection or that it had not been fairly applied. Attempts were made to lay down standards of objectivity to be applied to the selection criteria but it is difficult to see that they will amount to much in practice in the light of the general tendency to accept business decisions. Suppose, for instance, two sales districts are combined. The junior, and much less experienced, sales representative is retained, it is said, because he has more expertise in that aspect of the trade which the combined district will mainly be concerned. The tribunal may note that he has always had lower sales figures and suspect that the real reason is that the more experienced sales representative is approaching the age when salesmen are assumed to lose their edge. Is it correct, on the other had, to say that the employer's criterion for choice was unreasonable? If any confidence had been felt in such criteria it was dispelled by the decision in *Graham* v. *A. B. F. Ltd.*[95] One of the criteria was "attitude to work." The applicant was selected despite the fact that a volunteer could have been found. The E.A.T. agreed that this criterion involved personal and subjective judgments and was dangerous, vague and ambiguous. Nevertheless, it concluded that a decision that the choice of the applicant was fair was not so startling as not to be open to a reasonable tribunal.[96] Whether the criteria include it or not, the performance of the individual selected is likely to influence management choice. No one likes to lose a "good worker"; most management would like to be rid of a troublesome, or unreliable, one. In *Gray* v. *Shetland Norse Ltd.*[97] the applicant was selected for poor attendance and claimed, unsuccessfully, that it was unfair to dismiss him without warning him that his conduct placed him at risk. However it is explained, such a conclusion seems inevitable. It is not feasible to request warnings to be given to those whose performance is unsatisfactory that, should a redundancy occur, they are likely to be selected. Indeed such apparent prejudging the issue itself seems unfair. That is, of course, a different matter from warning that redundancy is a possibility and that the employee is at risk of being selected.[98] Browne-Wilkinson J. underlined such warning in his list of good procedures in *Williams* v. *Compair Maxam Ltd.*,[99] at the same time pointing out that that warning has no direct connection with the statutory requirement[1] for warning recognised trade unions of anticipated redundancies.

Selection of an employee whose job continues to exist to make way for one whom the employer wishes to retain, but whose job has gone, might be thought to raise more concern despite the fact that statutory provisions are not directed to the diminution in demand for the employee dismissed. In *North Yorkshire County Council* v. *Fay*[2] Browne-Wilkinson L.J. quoted with approval the judgment of the tribunal that if this was a policy of "bumping" it

[94] [1983] I.R.L.R. 58.
[95] [1986] I.R.L.R. 90.
[96] Must one now startle the E.A.T. to succeed on appeal?—see *Isleworth Studios Ltd.* v. *Rickard* [1988] I.R.L.R. 137.
[97] [1985] I.R.L.R. 53.
[98] See *Pink* v. *White* [1985] I.R.L.R. 489.
[99] *Supra.*
[1] E.P.A., s.99. See pp. 200–204, *infra.*
[2] [1985] I.R.L.R. 247.

was a perfectly proper policy. The fact that the reason is also true and that an employer is entitled to confine selection within a single group[3] merely adds another illustration of the readiness to accept managerial business judgment. It is largely open to an employer to decide whether to re-employ a redundant person in someone else's position. In much the same way, an employer has selection freedom in respect of filling a vacancy by offer to an employee who will otherwise be dismissed for redundancy. The decision in *Vokes Ltd.* v. *Bear*[4] did no more than hold that it was unfair for a large company not to have considered the possibility. There is no satisfactory answer to the objection that all this means is that the employer should produce evidence of such consideration and suppress the fact that he knew all along what the decision would be. That is an evidential problem of a type found by all first-instance courts. In *Barratt Construction Ltd.* v. *Dalrymple*[5] the employer had paid scant regard to the possibility of a vacancy in a subordinate position, but the tribunal was satisfied that he had considered the question of alternative employment generally and had no reason to suppose that the employee would have accepted demotion. It may be on occasion, of course, that an employer would have difficulty in satisfying a tribunal that he had properly considered alternative employment, because the tribunal would be likely to consider that, if he had, he would have offered it. In *Stacey* v. *Babcock Power Ltd.*[6] a new contract containing the type of work done by the applicant came up shortly after he had been given notice of redundancy. He was not offered the job which was given to a new employee. The tribunal considered the dismissal unfair on the grounds that good industrial practice would require the offer to be put to a long-standing employee.[7] The fact that the dismissal has actually occurred before the possibility of an alternative arises may, however, have considerable significance in fixing the reason for the dismissal. In *Brown* v. *Stockton-on-Tees Borough Council*[8] an alternative job was not offered to an employee, who was already due to become redundant, because she was pregnant and would require maternity leave which, in the view of the personnel officer would mean she could not fulfil the contract. The Court of Appeal had held that the reason for dismissal was redundancy, not pregnancy. The House of Lords, however,[9] held that in this case the primary reason for dismissal was the employee's pregnancy. It pointed out that selection of a pregnant woman for redundancy would not be unfair if there was some other reason than pregnancy for her selection.

Misconduct excluding the right to redundancy compensation

Upon a claim for redundancy there arises a presumption that the dismissal is by reason of redundancy unless it is proved by some means, not necessarily by the employer, that redundancy was not the primary reason.[10] This situ-

---

[3] *Green* v. *A. and I. Fraser Ltd.* [1985] I.R.L.R. 55.
[4] [1983] I.C.R. 1.
[5] [1984] I.R.L.R. 385.
[6] [1986] I.R.L.R. 3.
[7] This approach was upheld by the Court of Appeal in *Oakley* v. *The Labour Party* [1988] I.R.L.R. 34.
[8] [1987] I.R.L.R. 230.
[9] *Stockton-on-Tees B.C.* v. *Brown* [1988] I.R.L.R. 263.
[10] E.P.C.A., s.91(2).

ation is, however, further affected by two statutory provisions of some complexity. In the first place:

> . . . an employee shall not be entitled to a redundancy payment by reason of dismissal where his employer, being entitled to terminate his contract of employment without notice by reason of the employee's conduct terminates it either:
> (a) without notice, or
> (b) by giving shorter notice than that which, in the absence of such conduct, the employer would be required to give . . . or
> (c) by giving notice (not being such shorter notice . . .) which includes or is accompanied by, a statement in writing that the employer would, by reason of the employee's conduct, be entitled to terminate the contract without notice.

It will be noted that provisions (a) and (b) do not require a dismissal for any stated reason other than redundancy. An employer might, therefore, dismiss intending that dismissal to be for redundancy, accidentally giving inadequate notice, and rely on the section to exclude a claim for redundancy compensation by alleging a pre-existing cause. On the other hand if the employer gives proper notice and does not comply with provision (c), as for instance by failing to state *in writing* the reservation, the employee is entitled to a redundancy payment provided, of course, that he is otherwise entitled. The section will, of course, permit a dismissal for subsequent cause to displace a previous dismissal for redundancy by notice.

An exception to the operation of this subsection is created by section 92. This applies to exclude the operation of the preceding provision where an employer has given notice of termination by reason of redundancy or the employee has given notice by reason of lay-off or short time and the employee takes part in a strike either during the *obligatory statutory period* of notice to which he is entitled or after himself giving notice. In such circumstances the employer may, *for that reason* terminate the contract in any of the ways mentioned in (a), (b) or (c) above. If the employer does so then the exclusion from redundancy payment entitlement provided by section 82(2) will not apply but instead an application can be made to a tribunal to decide what part of the redundancy payment it thinks fit to award. This partial restoration of the right to redundancy payment applies only where the strike follows the dismissal for redundancy and also only where the strike is given as the reason for the ultimate dismissal. In other words, for section 92(2) to apply there must be two dismissals whilst section 82(2) may apply either to a one, or a two, dismissal situation. If the employee is already on strike and is then dismissed for redundancy section 92(2) will not apply but section 82(2) might, depending on the manner of dismissal, so as to disentitle to redundancy payment. This assumes that a strike constitutes misconduct but that assumption is supported by the very lengthy consideration of the application of these provisions in *Simmons* v. *Hoover Ltd.*[11]

It is obvious that section 92 was intended to avoid a situation where a strike

---

[11] [1977] I.C.R. 61.

in protest at dismissal for redundancy would operate under section 82(2) to disentitle those participating from their redundancy payments. Unfortunately, section 92 only applies to strikes. Any other form of industrial action in protest would be caught by section 82(2) unless the argument of Mr. Sedley, which failed in *Simmons* v. *Hoover* in relation to strikes, could succeed in relation to lesser action allowing it to be regarded as constituting less than a repudiatory breach.

Time off upon redundancy

An employee with two years' continuous service who is given notice of dismissal by reason of redundancy is entitled before the expiration of his notice to be allowed by his employer reasonable time off work in order to look for new employment or make arrangements for training for future employment.[12] This entitlement is to paid time off of up to two-fifths of a week's pay.[13] The right only applies to an employee who on the date on which the notice is due to expire or would expire had he received the proper statutory minimum period of notice would have had two years' continuous service with that employer.[14] An employee may present a claim to an industrial tribunal within three months of the day on which it is alleged the paid time off should have been permitted that the employer has unreasonably refused such entitlement. The tribunal may award payment equal to the amount of any entitlement.[15]

It seems, from the way section 31 of the Employment Protection (Consolidation) Act 1978 is drafted, that the right is to reasonable time off work and that the limitation on the amount of pay to which the employee is entitled does not qualify this basic right. In other words, an employee is entitled to reasonable time off in excess of two-fifths of a week although this extra entitlement may be unpaid. The problem about this interpretation, however, would seem to be that no sanction exists since a tribunal may only award the amount of pay to which the employee would have been entitled had he been allowed the time off.

Collective procedure for dealing with redundancy

There has, for some time, been a considerable movement within the EEC to recommend special provisions for the method of dealing with collective dismissals. It is this movement which has, no doubt, inspired some relatively elementary proposals contained in the Employment Protection Act 1975 and which has led to further provisions relating to transfer of business.[16]

Consultation

These proposals centre upon two different requirements for notification and consultation. The first requires an employer to consult the authorised

---

[12] Now E.P.C.A. 1978, s.31. It is not a necessary precondition that an employee should supply details of the appointments he will keep—*Dutton* v. *Hawker Siddeley Aviation Ltd.* [1978] I.C.R. 1057.

[13] s.31(9).

[14] s.31(2).

[15] s.31(5)–(7).

[16] E.P.C.A. 1978, ss.99–107.

bargaining representatives of[17] an independent trade union recognised for the description of employees of which a potentially redundant employee is one. Recognition implies agreement.[18] If recognition is to be implied, the acts alleged to amount to recognition must be clear and unequivocal and involve a course of conduct over a period of time.[19] An isolated act which, of itself is clearly one of recognition, was treated in *Transport and General Workers Union* v. *Courtenham Products Ltd.*[20] as ineffective for that purpose since the employer had not realised its general significance and the union had clearly not regarded it as indicating general recognition. In *T.G.W.U.* v. *Andrew Dyer*[21] the E.A.T. said that recognition should only be inferred from acts which were clear and unequivocal. It may be objected that it is very unlikely in practice that the employer would not so consult in the absence of a legislative duty and that it would be more important to require consultation in other cases. The difficulty, so far as this country is concerned, as against other EEC countries, is that there does not exist here any such machinery as compulsory Works Councils which would be available for consultation in the absence of recognised trade unions. Provision could, of course, be made to consult "worker representatives," *i.e.* ad hoc delegates. It is probably true to say that this was not made because of the current strength of feeling that trade union membership and, subsequently, recognition is best encouraged by granting certain rights to recognised unions only.

The consultation that is required must begin *at the earliest opportunity*[22] *and in any event* not later than 90 days before the first of a series of dismissals of 100 or more employees within a period of 90 days; or 30 days before the first of a series of 10 or more dismissals within a period of 30 days within one establishment.[23]

Though the reference is to a series, it is clear that the series must spring from one decision. The total redundancy from one of two separate decisions is not aggregated.[24] Each group is to be treated separately so that once consultation has begun for one group others are not to be added to it. Only if the employer can show the existence of special circumstances justifying non-consultation will he be able to avoid the consequences of a failure to consult within the required time.[25] There will be a breach of the statutory require-

---

[17] *G.M.W.U.* v. *Wailes Dove Bitumastic Ltd.* [1977] I.R.L.R. 45.

[18] *National Union of Tailors and Garment Workers* v. *Charles Ingram & Co. Ltd.* [1977] I.C.R. 530.

[19] *National Union of Gold, Silver and Allied Trades* v. *Albury Bros.* [1979] I.C.R. 84 C.A.

[20] [1977] I.R.L.R. 8.

[21] [1977] I.R.L.R. 93.

[22] In *Union of Construction, Allied Trades and Technicians* v. *Ellison Carpentry Contractors Ltd.* [1976] I.R.L.R. 398 an industrial tribunal held that consultation becomes feasible as soon as it is clear that the next move will be a reduction of the workforce even if no definite proposals can yet be made. Ignorance of the obligation does not prevent compliance from being reasonably practicable. *UCATT* v. *H. Rooke and Son Ltd.* [1978] I.C.R. 818.

[23] These periods were amended by the Employment Protection (Handling of Redundancies) Variation Order 1979 (S.I. 1979 No. 958). On the meaning of establishment see *Barratt Developments (Bradford) Ltd.* v. *UCATT* [1978] I.C.R. 319.

[24] *T.G.W.U.* v. *Nationwide Haulage Ltd.* [1978] I.R.L.R. 143.

[25] As to what constitutes special circumstances see *Bakers Union* v. *Clarks of Hove* [1978] I.R.L.R. 366.

ment even if, as a result of the consultations the termination date is brought forward so as to have the effect of reducing the consultative period below the minimum required.[26]

Information

The employer must disclose, in writing, to the representatives the reasons for the redundancy, the number it is proposed to dismiss and the number of employees of that description at the establishment in question, the proposed method of selection and the proposed method and period for carrying out the dismissals. It should be noted that he does not have to disclose the precise identity of those it is proposed to dismiss. The employer must consider the representations of the union and give reasons if he rejects any of them. If he cannot reasonably practicably comply with any of the requirements as to consultation he must take such steps towards compliance as are reasonably practicable in the circumstances. Should he be challenged on this point it is for him to prove the reasonableness of his alternative steps. Discussion must conform with any agreed procedure.

A company or industry with its own adequate consultation scheme may seek exemption on the ground that it is at least as favourable.

There were a number of decisions holding that failure to consult in accordance with the statutory provisions constitutes a factor in unfair dismissal. In *Forman Construction Ltd.* v. *Kelly*[27] however, the Scottish division of the E.A.T. held that the statutory provisions constituted a separate procedure with its own penalty, and did not infer any right other than those specifically contained in it. This was affirmed in *Williams* v. *Compair Maxam Ltd.*[28] but it was pointed out that absence of consultation would tend towards an unfair procedure regardless of any statutory provision.

Protective award

A recognised trade union may present to an industrial tribunal a complaint of non-compliance with any of these requirements after the failure of conciliation. If the tribunal finds the complaint well-founded it may[29] make a "protective award" under which every employee to whom the award relates is entitled to be paid remuneration by his employer of a week's pay for each week up to the limit of a 90 day or 30 day period according to the length of consultation due and 28 days in all other cases. This liability to pay remuneration will be reduced by any payment under the contract of employment or by way of damages for breach of that contract, and vice versa. It should be noted that compensation for unfair dismissal is not capable of being set off in this way. The actual length of the protective award in any situation is for the industrial tribunal to fix. In *Talke Fashions Ltd.* v. *Amalgamated Society of Textile Workers and Kindred Trades*[30]; the E.A.T. held that the award should

---

[26] *ASTMS* v. *Hawker Siddeley Aviation Ltd.* [1977] I.R.L.R. 418.

[27] [1977] I.R.L.R. 468.

[28] *Supra.*

[29] The tribunal has the right to make no protective award—see, *e.g. ASTMS* v. *Hawker Siddeley Aviation Ltd. supra.*

[30] [1977] I.C.R. 833.

be commensurate with the loss suffered by the employee; the seriousness of the employer's default should not be considered. On the other hand there is no ground for saying that the original period can ever be longer than the specified statutory periods.[31] The entitlement ceases if a suitable alternative offer is made which is unreasonably rejected or which is accepted and later unreasonably terminated by the employee in respect of any period when, but for that rejection or termination, the employee would have been employed. An employee may complain to an industrial tribunal of non-observance of a protective award within three months of the last of the days to which the complaint relates.

Notification

The second type of obligation is one, in the same circumstances, but whether or not there are recognised unions, to notify the Secretary of State in writing of dismissal proposals within 90 or 30 days and to give a copy of the notice to any recognised union. The Secretary of State may subsequently call for any further specified information. The sanction for failure to take this step is a fine, on summary conviction, not exceeding £400.

Consultation preceding a transfer of undertaking

The elementary nature of the requirements for consultation preceding redundancy just considered is clearly revealed by the more advanced requirements contained even within the somewhat generalised requirements of the EEC Council Directive No. 77/187 upon transfer of employee's rights. In turn, the way in which those requirements are enacted in the Transfer of Undertakings (Protection of Employment) Regulations 1981 reveals the reluctance of British thinking to comprehend more extensive obligations. The Regulations apply upon a transfer of business.[32]

Article 6 of the Directive requires both the transferor and the transferee employer to inform *the representatives of their respective employees affected by the transfer* in *good time*, before the transfer is carried out and before the employees are directly affected as regards conditions of work, of the reasons for the transfer, the *legal, economic and social implications* of the transfer for the employees and the measures envisaged in relation to the employees. Where such measures are envisaged the Directive requires the transferor or the transferee to consult his employee representatives in good time and *with a view to seeking agreement.* The United Kingdom Regulations[33] require the giving of information only to representatives of an independent recognised trade union and only "long enough" before the relevant transfer to enable consultations to take place. It is probably correct to say that this will be interpreted to mean that there must be time for effective consultations. It is clear that there need be no intention to agree since paragraph 6(6) only requires the employer to consider and reply to any union representations stating his reasons for rejecting any of them. Even then a let-out clause is provided typical of similar United Kingdom legislation but

---

[31] *National Union of Teachers* v. *Avon County Council* [1978] I.C.R. 626.
[32] *Supra* p. 108.
[33] Para. 10.

such as would not be found in many other EEC member countries. It is provided[34] that if there are special circumstances which render it not reasonably practicable for an employer to perform the duties of informing and
consulting he must take all such steps towards performing these duties as
are reasonably practicable. If the same reasoning as to the application of
this escape clause is applied as has been applied to that in section 99 of the
Employment Protection Act 1975, then, as we have seen, an employer may
postpone the giving of information in the hope of an improvement,[35] so
long as he does not shut his eyes to the obvious,[36] until sudden disaster
forces a transfer.[37] It will, however, be for the employer to prove the
special circumstances.

It may be noted that in other respects the Regulations have followed and
even slightly extended the Directive. The employer must inform the representatives of approximately when the transfer is to take place and a transferee
employer must inform the transferor employer of the measures the former
proposes to apply to the employees he takes over. The restriction of the obligations to recognised unions is, however, very significant. There is no reason
why the employer should not be required to inform and consult even ad hoc
employee representatives. But this, like the obligation to consult with a view
to agreement, would break new ground in the United Kingdom. The fact that
it might be very beneficial to explore such new ground in this limited way may
have to be forcibly brought home by EEC pressure to a legislature and civil
service more interested in the political advantages of inertia.

The remedy for failure in either of these duties is, as might be expected,
complaint to an industrial tribunal within three months of the date of completion of the transfer. If the complaint is made by the union involved the
tribunal may declare the complaint to be well-founded and order "compensation" not exceeding an amount equivalent to two weeks' wages to be paid
to any of the affected employees specified in the award. If the complaint is
made by an individually affected employee the tribunal may only award him
that compensation. Even this limited compensation goes towards discharging any liability of the employer for breach of contract in respect of any
period falling within the protected period. It seems that it would not detract
from the amount of a protective award. Appeal lies on a point of law to the
E.A.T.

Special circumstances

If the employer wishes to establish a defence to a claim for failure to consult
in time that it was not reasonably practicable for him to do so he must show:

  (i) that there were special circumstances applicable to him;
 (ii) that they did, in fact, render compliance not reasonably practicable;
      and,
(iii) that he took all such steps as were reasonably practicable to comply.

[34] Para. 6(7).
[35] *Hamish Armour* v. *ASTMS* [1979] I.R.L.R. 24.
[36] *APAC* v. *Kirvin Ltd.* [1978] I.R.L.R. 318.
[37] *Clarks of Hove Ltd.* v. *The Bakers' Union* [1978] I.C.R. 1076.

The Court of Appeal in *Clarks of Hove Ltd.* v. *The Bakers' Union*[38] defined special circumstances as "something out of the ordinary run of events, such as, for example, a general trading boycott." An insolvency is not on its own a special circumstance even if it is convenient for business purposes to conceal a gradual run-down until the last minute. On the other hand, the general reluctance to question management decisions suggests that this requirement may be less restrictive than it appears at first sight. In *Hamish Armour* v. *A.S.T.M.S.*[39] Lord McDonald, in the Scottish E.A.T., said that a tribunal should not seek to substitute its own business judgment for that of management in order to decide whether alleged hopes of recovery were sufficiently substantial to be justified. In that case uncertainty about the prospects of a continuing government loan were held to be a special circumstance. So was the uncertain state of a construction project in *A.S.B.S.B.S.W.* v. *George Wimpey (ME and C) Ltd.*[40] It is suggested that it is more realistic to say that uncertainty is usual[41] so that only an especial degree of uncertainty, or unusual consequences of anticipating the outcome should excuse compliance with the consultation requirements.

Redundancy payment

The amount of statutory compensation is based on the period of continuous employment. The scale of payment is half a week's pay for each year of employment between the ages of 18 and 21; one week's pay for each year of employment between the ages of 22 and 40, and one-and-a-half weeks' pay for each year of employment from the age of 41. This is subject to a maximum of 20 years' accountable employment and to a maximum week's pay, currently, £164. Thus a man of 61 or more who had worked with the same firm for the past 20 years or more and who was then earning £135 or more before he left, would be entitled to the maximum payment of £4,050.[42] Remembering that, in practice, there will be little examination of the details of these years of work to see whether they were continuous, few problems will be raised at this stage. The calculation which causes most difficulty is that of the week's pay which is to form the basic unit of calculation.

Calculation of a week's pay

Normally, where a worker is employed on a fixed rate, the week that is taken is the last one in which he is employed. The normal rate of pay will be adopted. Where there are a fixed number of hours in a working week or other period, that fixed number constitutes the "normal working hours" even if some of these fixed hours are treated as overtime.[43] On the other hand, in the absence of a specified minimum number, the fact that overtime is paid after a given number of hours has been worked may imply that that given number is

---

[38] [1978] I.C.R. 1076.
[39] [1979] I.R.L.R. 24.
[40] [1977] I.R.L.R. 95.
[41] *G.M.W.U. (MATSA)* v. *British Uralite Ltd.* [1979] I.R.L.R. 409, I.T.
[42] *Ibid.* Sched. 4.
[43] *Ibid.* Sched. 14, paras. 1 and 2.

the fixed number.[44] Overtime hours over and above a basic working week are only counted if it is obligatory upon the employer to provide the hours and upon the employee to work them and that obligation is contractual.[45] If the employee's remuneration in normal working hours does not vary with the amount of work done then the week's pay will be the amount due if the employee works throughout the normal week. In cases where remuneration does vary, the amount of a week's pay will be the average hourly rate over the period of 12 weeks preceding the calculation date, multiplied by the number of normal working hours in the week. If there are no normal hours or the rate of remuneration varies according to the time at which the work is done similar provision is made for determining an average.[46]

The effect of this provision is to concentrate attention on the contract, rather than the period actually worked. If work is, for instance, running down, unless the contract has been consensually varied,[47] the calculation will be unaffected. Even where an employee regularly works less than the number of hours specified in the contract, calculation is based on the contractual hours.[48]

"Remuneration"

All regular payment will be taken into account. So a regularly paid bonus, even if not strictly contractual, will be included.[49] A pay rise awarded after the date of dismissal but payable retrospectively to a date before the dismissal will be taken into account and a fresh claim entertained if necessary.[50] On the other hand provision is only made for "remuneration." Accordingly such benefits as free accommodation will not be given a weekly monetary value unless the contract so quantifies them.[51] A service charge paid by customers to management and subsequently divided among the staff has been held to be part of remuneration.[52] This situation is distinguishable from one in which tips are paid by the customer directly to the employee, since that is not remuneration from the employer.[53] Commission is also included.[54] In other

---

[44] Fox v. C. Wright (Farmers) Ltd. [1978] I.C.R. 98.

[45] Tarmac Roadstone Holdings Ltd. v. Peacock [1973] I.C.R. 273; followed in Lotus Cars Ltd. v. Sutcliffe and Stratton [1982] I.R.L.R. 381.

[46] E.P.C.A. 1978, Sched. 14, paras. 4–6.

[47] Saxton v. National Coal Board (1970) 8 K.I.R. 893, Basted v. Pell Footwear [1978] I.R.L.R. 117.

[48] Truelove v. Mathew Hall Mechanical Services Ltd. [1978] I.T.R. 65; Saxton v. National Coal Board, supra; Allied Ironfounders Ltd. v. Macken [1971] I.T.R. 109; Mole Mining Ltd. v. Jenkins [1972] I.C.R. 282.

[49] A. and B. Marcusfield Ltd. v. Melhuish [1977] I.R.L.R. 484.

[50] Carron v. Pullman Spring-Filled Co. Ltd. [1967] I.T.R. 650.

[51] Lyford v. Turquand [1966] I.T.R. 544.

[52] Tsoukka v. Potomac Restaurants Ltd. [1968] I.T.R. 259.

[53] Wrottesley v. Regent Street Florida Restaurant [1951] 2 K.B. 277 at 283.

[54] Weersmay Ltd. v. King [1977] I.C.R. 244. As to the method of calculation see Bickley (J. and S.) Ltd. v. Washer [1977] I.C.R. 425.

respects also the calculations follow those for the basic award in unfair dismissal cases (or rather, vice versa)[55]

The amount of redundancy payment is reduced by one-twelfth for each month of a year after the employee has reached the age of 64, or 59 in the case of a woman.[56]

The Secretary of State has power by regulation to exclude, or reduce the amount of, a redundancy payment in prescribed cases in which the employee has a right or claim (whether legally enforceable or not) to a periodical payment or lump sum by way of pension gratuity or superannuation allowance payable by reference to his employment by a particular employer from the time he leaves that employment or within such period as may be prescribed.[57]

On making a redundancy payment, otherwise than in pursuance of a tribunal decision which itself specifies the amount, the employer must give the employee a written statement indicating how the amount has been calculated. Failure to comply is an offence punishable by fine.[58]

QUALIFICATIONS TO ENFORCE STATUTORY RIGHTS

We have now considered the statutory rights of an employee. In United Kingdom labour law, however, not all workers are entitled to the same statutory rights. Most obviously, as we have already seen,[59] many statutory rights are limited to those working under a contract of employment. As the definition of employment changes, or perhaps one should say, develops, concentrating more on continuous obligation, categories such as long-term casuals are less assured of protection. This may be thought no more than an unfortunate detailed consequence of a perfectly justified policy as is also the case with the somewhat startling effect of an illegal contract of service.[60] Lines of protection must be drawn somewhere. It is inconceivable that termination of a contract for services should be assimilated to dismissal so as, for instance, to give the domestic plumber a right to complain of unfairness. In turn limitation periods are usually understood as justified by the unfairness of subjecting the respondent to judicial process excessively long after the event. In the case of unfair dismissal, by seeking to ensure early adjudication whilst recollection of facts is clear, it was hoped to avoid uncertainty and expense. It may also have been hoped that reinstatement of re-engagement would prove realistic remedies if the time elapsed since dismissal was short, but his was never a real hope once the employee had left the workplace and walked through the doors of an industrial tribunal.

---

[55] See, e.g. S. and U. Stores Ltd. v. Lee [1969] I.T.R. 227; N.G. Bailey and Co. Ltd. v. Preddy [1971] 1 W.L.R. 796; Barclay v. Richard Crittal (Electrical) [1978] I.T.R. 173, and pp. 172–3, supra.

[56] Ibid. Sched. 4, para. 4.

[57] Ibid. s.98(1).

[58] Ibid. s.102.

[59] Supra p. 4.

[60] Supra pp. 14–16.

Many other qualifications imposed by statute are, it is suggested, unnecessary. They produce a degree of legal technicality far in excess of that raised by substantive issues and they lack any rational basis. If an employee is entitled to protection against unreasonable dismissal why should that protection not be available as soon as he commences employment? Inevitably, it may be more likely that termination would be considered reasonable in the early days of his employment, whilst he has little seniority to protect and whilst he is likely to be regarded as on probation. That is a matter totally different from permitting the employer freedom, for a period which is now as long as two years, to dismiss with virtual impunity. As academics who have produced for foreign jurists learned papers on the assessment of continuity of employment have discovered, such limitations are beyond the comprehension of systems where employment and rights go together. Some of those who advised the Department of Employment during the drafting of the original provisions for unfair dismissal claims in 1971 said that the real reason was a supposed need to limit the number of potential claims within the calculated capacity of a tribunal system. If that was the explanation such caution was proved excessive when the limit was reduced to six months without serious consequences to the overloading of industrial tribunals. Such a limit may, of course, be more justified if compensation is considered to be for accumulated experience and seniority, as in the case of the statutory claim for redundancy compensation. It is all too easy to transfer, without much thought, from one provision where there was a rational explanation, a qualification requirement which has no logical application elsewhere. In the case of age limits the transfer from redundancy to unfair dismissal seems to have occurred after enough thought to vary significantly the date of the limit— but apparently without any realisation that such a limit was not necessary at all in the latter case.

Much of this section, therefore, is an artificial exercise in the formulation of rules. Law students, in their unremitting search for certainty, will approach it with a sense of relief after the vagueness of the common law contract and the factual discretion which characterises the majority of the decisions of industrial tribunals. That does not alter the fact that if we are looking for employment protection it would be a good deal more obvious without these limitations, the absence of many of which would cause no ill effects, save to the employer seeking a free hand.

(a) *Qualifying age*

There is no minimum age for a claim for unfair dismissal and compensation is available in respect of any period of employment. In the case of a claim for redundancy compensation, however, no account is to be taken of employment during any period before the applicant attained the age of 18.[61]

The upper limit for statutory redundancy compensation is 60 in the case of a woman and 65 in the case of a man with provision for reducing the amount due by one-twelfth for each completed month of the final year after 59 and 64

---

[61] This limit does not apply to the assessment of the basic award for unfair dismissal which, in other respects, is based on the same rules as assessment of redundancy compensation.

respectively.[62] Plainly, in origin, this limit related to the availability of state pensions. European Community policy now envisages the elimination of such inequality even if it derives from national social security schemes. In the United Kingdom reliance on private pension schemes has developed extensively, particularly in the past 10 years, and account has been taken of these, for instance in offsetting their benefits against statutory redundancy compensation.[63] Such private schemes will not generally contain discriminatory retirement ages.

No application for unfair dismissal will lie, however, if, on or before the effective date of termination, the applicant had passed the normal retirement age for employees holding the position he held in the establishment in which he was employed; or has attained 65.[64] The cut-off at normal retirement age is, since 1986, only effective if the retirement age is the same for men and for women. The House of Lords, in *London Borough of Barnet* v. *Nothman*[65] had given the retirement age priority even if the fixed age had been reached. It is, of course, unlikely now that a normal retirement age will exceed 65.

The contractual statement of a retirement age is not conclusive, although there is a presumption that it is the normal retirement age.[66] If evidence is adduced of a regular practice for the group of employees[67] in question to retire at a different age an industrial tribunal must inquire, not merely statistically, but as to the reasonable understanding of employees in that group at the relevant time. A minimum age, therefore, is open to evidence of what is the actual expectation. If the evidence is that the contractual retirement age has been abandoned without any regular practice taking its place there is no normal retirement age and the fixed age of 65 will operate.[68] The normal age must be definitive. If there is a range of ages then there is no normal retirement age and an employee, even if he has reached the highest age in that range, is entitled to rely on the fixed age of 65.[69]

This unusual departure from contract into expectation produces the somewhat surprising consequence that an employee's rights can be affected adversely by the unilateral action of the employer. Since the earlier norm may be no more than an expectation it can be altered without the contractual requirement of consent to the variation. So long as the employee may reasonably be expected to know of the change, his expectation will have altered. A change of policy communicated to the affected employees, therefore, is capable of altering their normal retirement age without their consent.[70] In

---

[62] E.P.C.A., s.82(1).

[63] *e.g.* The Redundancy Payments Pensions Regulations (S.I. 1965/1932.)

[64] E.P.C.A., s.64(1)(*b*) as amended by Sex Discrimination Act 1986, s.3. The set-off only applies to the *right* to claim. Compensation is not limited to loss sustained before that date—*Barrell Plating and Phosphating Co. Ltd.* v. *Danks* [1976] I.R.L.R. 262 (E.A.T.).

[65] [1979] I.C.R. 111, affirming the decision of the Court of Appeal.

[66] *Waite* v. *Government Communications Headquarters* [1983] I.R.L.R. 341 (H.L.).

[67] As to what comprises a group see *Highlands and Islands D.B.* v. *MacGillivray* [1986] I.R.L.R. 210.

[68] *Mauldon* v. *British Telecommunications plc* [1987] I.C.R. 450 (E.A.T.).

[69] *Swaine* v. *Health and Safety Executive* [1986] I.C.R. 498.

[70] *Hughes* v. *DHSS, Coy* v. *DHSS,* [1985] I.C.R. 419 (H.L.)

Whittle v. *Manpower Services Commission*[71] the implication is clearly made that an expectation is destroyed immediately a new policy is notified. Although expectation is said to arise from regular practice it seems likely that notification of an intention to pursue a regular practice in future will establish the new expectation immediately.

The age disqualification does not apply to a claim for unfair dismissal if the alleged reason for the dismissal was that the employee was, or proposed to become, a member of an independent trade union, had refused, or proposed to refuse to become, or remain, a member of any trade union, or had taken, or proposed to take, part at any appropriate time in the activities of an independent trade union.[72]

(b) *Time for making a claim*

The following limitation periods apply to the presentation of employment claims in industrial tribunals.

* *Unfair dismissal*—three months from the effective date of termination.[73]

 Redundancy payments—six months from the relevant date of termination unless within that time the employee has presented the claim to his employer in writing.[74]

 Guarantee payment—three months from the date for which the payment is due.[75]

* *Payment during suspension on medical grounds*—three months from the date for which the payment is due.[76]

* *Action short of dismissal for the purpose of interfering with union activity or membership*—three months from the day, or last of the days, on which the action complained of occurred.[77]

* *Time off work*—three months from the date when failure to comply with the statutory requirement occurred.[78]

* *Failure of Secretary of State to make payments arising from employee's redundancy*—three months from date of communication of decision.[79]

 Written statement of reasons for dismissal—at any time during the employment or within the time permitted for a complaint of unfair dismissal.[80]

 Written statement of terms of employment and itemised pay state-

---

[71] [1987] I.R.L.R. 441.
[72] E.P.C.A. 1978, s.64(3).
[73] E.P.C.A. 1978, s.67(2). See also E.A. 1982, s.10.
[74] E.P.C.A. 1978, s.101(1). The reference to "effective date" and "relevant date" is defined respectively in ss.55(4) and 90(1). The two dates are *not* subject to notional extension so as to affect the limitation period to include a statutory period of notice which has not actually been given. Where notice is given, there will be a presumption that the date of termination is the date of expiry of the notice but this will be rebutted by the commonly specified provision for immediate termination.
[75] E.P.C.A. 1978, s.17(2).
[76] E.P.C.A. 1978, s.22(2).
[77] E.P.C.A. 1978, s.24(2).
[78] E.P.C.A. 1978, ss.30(2) and 31A.
[79] E.P.C.A. 1978, s.124(2).
[80] E.P.C.A. 1978, s.53(5).

ments—at any time during the employment or within three months from the date on which the employment ceased.[81]

Equal pay claims—any time before the expiration of six months after the applicant has left the employment in question.[82]

Sex and Race Discrimination—three months from the act of discrimination.

Non-discrimination notices—within six weeks of the issue of the notice.

Appeals

* *Appeals against Improvement and Prohibition Notices issued under the Health and Safety at Work, etc., Act*—within 21 days from the date of service upon the appellant of the notice in question.

* *Appeals from failure of Secretary of State to pay redundancy on employer's insolvency or failure to comply with order to pay*—three months from date of communication of Secretary of State's decision.

* *Appeal from rejection by Secretary of State of application for payment upon an employer's insolvency*—three months from date of communication of Secretary of State's decision.

The question of time limit is jurisdictional[83] and, in practice, attention will normally be drawn to an apparent lack of jurisdiction by the Regional Office of Industrial Tribunals. It may, however, be raised at any time.[84]

Appeals to the Employment Appeal Tribunal

In all cases, within 42 days of the date on which the document recording the decision or order appealed against was sent to the appellant.[85]

Extension of time limits

In the case of claims for redundancy payment there is power to extend the time limit by up to a further six months if the tribunal is satisfied that it is just and equitable that the employee should receive a redundancy payment.[86] The same test is applied to anti-discrimination legislation. In all the situations marked with an asterisk, there is power to extend the time limit indefinitely for such time as the tribunal considers reasonable if the tribunal is satisfied that it was not reasonably practicable for the complaint to have been presented within the permitted time. The principles governing what is to be regarded as reasonably practicable laid down in *British Building and Engineering Appliances Ltd.* v. *Dedman*[87] continue to be applicable. In this case Lord Denning M.R. stated the proper approach thus:

"If in the circumstances the man knew or was put on inquiry as to his rights, and as to the time limit, then it was 'practicable' for him to have presented his complaint within the [appropriate time], and he ought to have done so. But if he did not know and there was nothing to put him on inquiry, then it was 'not practicable' and he should be excused. But what is the position if he goes to skilled

---

[81] E.P.C.A. 1978, s.11(9).
[82] E.P.A. 1970, s.2(4).
[83] *Westward Circuits Ltd.* v. *Read* [1973] I.R.L.R. 138.
[84] *Rogers* v. *Bodfari (Transport) Ltd.* [1973] I.C.R. 325.
[85] E.A.T. Practice Direction, March 3, 1978.
[86] E.P.C.A. 1978, s.101(2).
[87] [1974] I.C.R. 53.

advisers and they make a mistake? The English court has taken the view that the man must abide by their mistake."

The *Dedman* approach was confirmed in *Porter* v. *Bandbridge Ltd.*[88] despite addition to the test of practicability of the word "reasonably." The test involves a finding of fact and has been said to depend on the good sense of the industrial tribunal.[89] An appeal will, therefore, rarely succeed.[90]

In *Churchill* v. *Yeates and Son Ltd.*[91] it was held that ignorance of facts fundamental to the prospects of success might make it not reasonably practicable to complain. It was said, however, that it would be rare for discovery of new facts to make a crucial difference and ignorance of less significant facts was irrelevant. The applicant must establish that it was reasonable for him not to be aware of the factual basis for an application within the three months.[92]

Dedman referred to skilled advice and this produced a distinction between "professional," and other, advice. The Court of Appeal rejected this distinction in *Riley* v. *Tesco Stores Ltd.*[93] holding that reasonable practicability must be assessed in the light of whatever advice was available. *Riley*, in turn, said that failure by the adviser to act on, or give, advice in time would be an excuse, but in *Papparis* v. *Charles Fulton and Co. Ltd.*[94] solicitors failed to present a claim in time because they had not received advance payment on account of their costs and the E.A.T. confirmed the industrial tribunal decision that it had been reasonably practicable to present the claim in time.

It is quite common for a trade union to seek to negotiate reinstatement, or some other remedy, for a dismissed employee and it is understandable that an applicant may not wish to appear to adopt a threatening position during this process. In *Palmer and Saunders* v. *Southend on Sea BC*[95] the Court of Appeal, suggesting that "reasonably feasible" was a better way of expressing the meaning of "reasonably practicable," held that the fact that internal appeals were being pursued does not necessarily make it not reasonably practicable to present a claim. The Court of Appeal made it quite clear, however, that it was not laying down a rule of law and that the question was one of fact for the tribunal. It is suggested that there are many situations where internal negotiations make it impracticable to complain to an industrial tribunal although, with respect, it is feasible to do so.

This book is not concerned with rules of procedure of industrial tribunals but the relative strictness of the approach outlined above will be better appreciated when combined with the strictness of the rules relating to presentation of a complaint. It appears sufficient to have despatched a claim for redundancy compensation within the limitation period.[96] An unfair dismissal claim must be received at the office of an industrial tribunal by 12 midnight on the day before the day of the third month corresponding with the date of the dis-

---

[88] [1978] I.C.R. 943.
[89] *Walls Meat Co. Ltd.* v. *Khan* [1979] I.C.R. 52.
[90] *Palmer and Saunders* v. *Southend on Sea BC* [1984] I.R.L.R. 119.
[91] [1983] I.C.R. 380 (E.A.T.).
[92] *The Machine Tool Industry Research Association* v. *Simpson* [1988] I.R.L.R. 212 (C.A.).
[93] [1980] I.C.R. 323.
[94] [1981] I.R.L.R. 104.
[95] [1984] I.R.L.R. 119.
[96] *Nash* v. *Ryan Plant International Ltd.* [1978] 1 All E.R. 692.

missal. A Practice Direction[97] presumes that first class mail will be delivered on the second working day after posting and second class mail on the fourth day. This reference to working days applies to the postal system. It does not infer that non-working days may be ignored when calculating the limitation period. If there is a way of presenting a complaint to the tribunal office on a Sunday, as the last day in the three-month period, it must be so presented.[98] This does not apply, however, if there is no "acceptable channel" for delivery to the office on that day as, for instance, no letter box.[99] The effect of these requirements can, sometimes, be avoided by constituting an earlier communication as the application. It is not necessary for the application to have been registered by the tribunal office,[1] and so a letter giving the name and address of the applicant, the name and address of the respondent and stating the ground of complaint may well suffice.[2]

(c) *Continuous employment*

Most of the statutory employment protection rights accrue only after a minimum qualifying period of continuous employment with the same employer, a successor or transferee of the business. In practice, the only rights seriously affected by this are the rights to claim unfair dismissal, redundancy compensation, the higher rate of sick pay applicable to maternity or the right to return to work after maternity leave. In each of these cases the qualifying period is two years. The rules for calculation of the period of continuous employment are contained in Schedule 13 of E.P.C.A. 1978 although it should be observed that an employee of the transferor immediately before the transfer of a business to which the Transfer of Undertakings Regulations applies[3] will automatically have all his contractual, and related statutory, rights transferred to the transferee. Otherwise, the provisions of Schedule 13 are the sole source of continuity. No agreement between the parties, nor any estoppel can create continuity where none exists under that Schedule.[4] An express term excluding continuity is void.[5]

The continuity period is not determined by a single contract and the tribunal is not concerned with whether one contract has been terminated and another begun. The question is simply whether employment has lasted sufficiently long.[6] Once an employee has shown employment lasting for a week which counts under Schedule 13 there is a presumption of continuity[7] in relation to all subsequent weeks, unless the contrary appears from the evidence. The presumption cannot be applied, however, to assume a transfer of employment. It applies only to the period with one employer.[8]

---

[97] See *New Law Journal* March 25, 1985 at p. 296.
[98] *Swainston* v. *Hetton Victory Club Ltd.* [1983] I.R.L.R. 164 (C.A.).
[99] *Ford* v. *Stakis Hotels and Inns Ltd.* [1988] I.R.L.R. 46.
[1] *Dodd* v. *British Telecom plc* [1988] I.R.L.R. 16.
[2] *Allen Munro (Butchers) Ltd.* v. *Nicol* [1988] I.R.L.R. 49. In this instance a statement that the applicant had been constructively dismissed was held not to state the ground of application.
[3] *Supra* pp. 108–111.
[4] *Secretary of State for Employment* v. *Globe Elastic Thread Co. Ltd.* [1979] I.C.R. 706.
[5] E.P.C.A. 1987, s.140.
[6] *Rowan* v. *Machinery Installations (South Wales) Ltd.* [1981] I.C.R. 386.
[7] Sched. 13, para. 1(3).
[8] *Secretary of State for Employment* v. *Cohen and Bean Press Ltd.* [1987] I.R.L.R. 169 (E.A.T.).

The period is calculated week by week and compiled in months and years. Basically, each week during which there is in existence a contract of employment which would normally involve employment for 16 hours or more counts as a week of continuous employment[9] whether the employee is actually at work in any part of that week or not.[10] It follows that periods of absence from work by reason, for instance, of sickness or pregnancy will count as periods of continuous employment, without reliance on any other provision, so long as the contract of employment has not been terminated either by the employer or the employee. The only exception to this rule is that weeks on strike do not count for continuity even if there is in existence a contract of employment. The beginning of the period of continuous employment is deemed to be postponed by the number of days which do not count.[11] A period of employment outside Great Britain counts for purposes of continuity.[12]

The need for a contract providing for 16 hours' employment per week is reduced in the following circumstances:

(i) If an employee has once had such a contract but this has been reduced to a contract normally involving employment for more than eight hours but less than 16, so long as that reduction does not last more than 26 weeks at a time.[13]

(ii) If the employee has been continuously employed for a period of five years under a contract normally involving more than eight hours' employment.[14]

(iii) So far as any particular right is concerned, if the employee has once qualified for the right in question and has not subsequently had a week in which he has a contract normally involving both less than eight hours' employment and actual employment of less than 16 hours.[15]

In such a situation not only is the right retained but the entire period covered is to be regarded as one of continuous employment. In ascertaining the number of contractual hours of employment in any week averaging over any number of weeks is not permitted unless that is the proper way to decide what the contract normally requires.[16]

Reckonable hours

The weekly hours are specified as those under a contract. It is, therefore, not permissible for this purpose to aggregate different contracts, even with the same employer, so as to produce the required weekly hours.[17] In *Suffolk County Council* v. *Secretary of State for the Environment*[18] it was held that a period when the employee remains on call is not within the meaning of hours of employment. Unless he were called out regularly he would not be able to

---

[9] Para. 4.
[10] So far as redundancy is concerned the period of calculation begins on the employee's 18th birthday.
[11] E.A. 1982, Sched. 2.
[12] Para. 1(2).
[13] Para. 5.
[14] Para. 6.
[15] Para. 7.
[16] *ITT Components (Europe) Ltd.* v. *Kolah* [1977] IC.R. 740.
[17] *Lewis* v. *Surrey County Council* [1987] I.C.R. 982 (H.L.).
[18] [1985] I.R.L.R. 24 (H.L.).

produce any lengthy continuity, even if he were able to add hours in which he actually did work. This decision seems to suggest that the old case of *Kincey* v. *Pardey and Johnson Ltd.*[19] decided by the President of Tribunals in the days before a separate appeal system, may be reliable. It was there held that lunch and tea breaks, though contractual, were not hours of employment.

Where there is no indication in the express contract of the hours to be worked. These will have to be implied, possibly from practice.[20] It is uncertain what the rule is where the contract does contain express reference to a certain number of hours, but more are regularly worked. In *Lake* v. *Essex County Council*[21] there was no room for implication of hours spent in preparation at home into the contractual obligation time. The most likely basis of decision will be to consider whether the regular extra working has varied the contract or, as in *Horrigan* v. *Lewisham LBC*,[22] involves no contractual obligation.

Interruptions

In *Ford* v. *Warwickshire County Council*[23] the House of Lords dealt with the provisions of paragraph 9 of the Schedule which has a marginal reference, "Periods in which there is no contract of employment." The paragraph itself does not mention absence of a contract but provides for four situations where the employee is absent from work. The House held the paragraph had no application unless there was no contract of employment in existence. It seems, therefore, that if contractual employment is actually reduced below the number of hours required to produce continuity, as it might be for instance during a long period of disability to do a full week's work, paragraph 9 affords no protection. Paragraph 9 only refers to an interval between termination of one contract of employment and re-engagement under another.

The specified periods of interruption are:

(i) Up to 26 weeks without a sufficient contract where the employee is incapable of work in consequence of sickness or injury. It follows that the employee must resume a sufficient contract with the employer in the first week in which he does again become capable of work. It has been held, however, that "capable of work" means capable of the work he was previously engaged to perform.

(ii) Up to 26 weeks' absence wholly or partly because of pregnancy or confinement.

(iii) The whole of the statutorily permitted absence for maternity provided the employee returns to her former employer in accordance with the statutory provisions.

It will be noted that (iii) will absorb (ii) but that (ii) is available, for example, to the woman who does not qualify by two years' continuous employment for the statutory maternity rights. On the other hand (ii) does not cover the period of maternity after confinement. Very often, of course,

---

[19] [1966] 1 I.T.R. 182.
[20] *ITT Components (Europe) Ltd.* v. *Kolah* [1977] I.C.R. 740.
[21] [1979] I.C.R. 577.
[22] [1978] I.C.R. 15 (E.A.T.).
[23] [1983] I.R.L.R. 126.

the contract will subsist during such absences so that there will be no need to rely on these provisions.

(iv) Any period of absence from work will count as a period of continuous employment if it is:
(a) on account of a temporary cessation of work, or
(b) in circumstances such that, by arrangement or custom, the employee is regarded as continuing in the employment of his employer for all or any purposes.

The provision of temporary cessation was introduced because of a number of perceived instances, such as seasonal employment, where continuity otherwise would not run. It looks, however, as if the draftsmen could not decide how to define such situations in more general terms and, instead, hit upon the title "temporary cessation," leaving it to the courts to decide what it meant. To be fair, the courts have not done a noticeably successful job.

In *Ford* v. *Warwickshire County Council*[24] Lord Brightman confirmed the view in *Fitzgerald* v. *Hall, Russell and Co. Ltd.*[25] that the absence of work referred to was the employee's individual work and not absence of the type of work he did. The House of Lords, by a majority, held that a cessation of work required that the employer should have ceased to make work available. This is an obvious limitation since, without it, the employee who was able to return from absence could take advantage of the provision even though he had caused the contractual gap as, for instance, by his own repudiatory breach. What was not clear from *Fitzgerald* was whether the absence of work must be because the employer had no work to offer or could include a situation in which the employer chose to offer no work.

In *Byrne* v. *City of Birmingham DC*,[26] however, the Court of Appeal held that the expression "absence of work" must denote that some quantum of work had, for the time being, ceased to exist and was no longer available for the employer to give. In that case, therefore, where a constant amount of work was assigned, variously, to a pool of casual cleansing operatives those who did not receive such work for certain periods could not be said to experience a temporary cessation. Although the court asserted that this was consistent with *Fitzgerald*, it is submitted that it is not. It is true, as the court said, that *Fitzgerald* did not establish that any employer initiated absence of work would suffice. Nor did *Ford* expressly say so at any point. The fact remains, however, that to make *Byrne* practicably workable one has to find an absence of work in general (which *Byrne* calls "the quantum of work") rather than an absence of work for the employee. Both *Fitzgerald* and *Ford* indicate the latter as the correct standard.

The conflict becomes clear if we consider two contrasted situations:

(a) An employer with plenty of work sends an employee on a period of study leave, terminating his contract but indicating that he will re-engage him on completion of the study. According to *Byrne*, this is not a temporary cessation of work although it is clear that, so far as the employee is concerned, work is not available.

---

[24] [1983] I.R.L.R. 126.
[25] [1970] A.C. 984.
[26] [1987] I.R.L.R. 191.

  (b) An employer envisages a shortage of new work and lays off some of his workers, assuming the remaining workforce can spin out those jobs still to be completed. In fact, fresh orders come in within a week or two so that, as it turns out, there was always enough work to keep the whole force busy. The whole force is re-engaged. Again, according to *Byrne*, there is no temporary cessation unless we are to rely on employer belief in a reduction in quantum.

    If we are to rely on employer belief, the existence of a temporary cessation on the *Byrne* test will depend on whether the employer is prepared to admit that work has fallen off, or whether he asserts that he was overmanned. This would be totally inconsistent with the definition of redundancy, and it might seem surprising that the legislature should have intended such a different standard without saying so.

It is submitted, despite the reference by Lord Diplock in *Ford* to unavailability of work, that the test has to be either whether work in general has ceased (which was rejected by all save Lord Guest in *Fitzgerald*), or whether work is in fact not made available to the employee. The half-way stage suggested in *Byrne* where it has to be shown both that there has been a decline (or belief in a decline), and that the individual's contract has been selectively terminated for that reason, leaves many employees whose contracts are temporarily terminated at the initiative of the employer, unable to claim the benefit of this exception.[27]

The House of Lords, in *Ford*, also considered the temporary nature of the cessation. Lord Diplock proposed a formula approach in which the period of cessation is tested for "transience" in relation to the periods of employment on either side. Whether the interval can be characterised as "short" in relation to the two periods of employment is a question of fact. Despite the clarity of this statement the Court of Appeal in *Flack* v. *Kodak Ltd.*[28] stated that this was not the correct approach which, in its view, was to take into account all the circumstances but, in particular, the length of the absence in the context of the entire period covered. The implication of this decision is that determination of the temporary nature of the gap is much more a matter of impression than mathematical calculation.

On one point there does seem to have been general agreement. The temporary nature of the cessation is to be assessed with hindsight[29] and not, for instance, according to the foresight, or intention, of the parties. The decision in *Ford* also settled an argument about foresight of the cessation. It was contended that the intervals between a series of fixed-term contracts could not be regarded as on account of a temporary cessation of work because they were on account of the expiration of the contract. In other words, the provision

---

[27] In *University of Aston* v. *Malik* [1984] I.C.R. 492 (E.A.T.), Balcombe J. said it mattered not whether it was the work or the employer's ability to pay for it that was absent.

[28] [1986] I.R.L.R. 255. In *Sillars* v. *Charringtons Fuels Ltd.* [1988] I.R.L.R. 180 Popplewell J. in the E.A.T. said that the Court of Appeal in *Flack* v. *Kodak Ltd.* had not rejected the mathematical approach in *Ford* v. *Warwickshire C.C.* but had rejected its universal application, especially to irregular employment. The Court of Appeal described it as the proper test, *The Times*, February 16, 1989.

[29] *Hunter* v. *Smiths Dock Co. Ltd.* [1968] I.W.L.R. 1865, approved in *Fitzgerald* v. *Hall, Russell and Co. Ltd.* [1970] A.C. 984 and, *per* Lord Brightman, in *Ford* v. *Warwickshire CC*, *supra*, at pp. 131–2.

would not apply where the cessation was not only foreseen but provided for in advance in the contractual arrangements. As Lord Brightman said, the immediate cause of the absence from work is the expiration of the contract just as, in the case of termination by notice, it is the running out of the notice period. The effective cause, however, is the anticipated cessation of work.

The problem will often arise of a possible difference between employment punctuated by temporary breaks and periods of temporary employment. Just as the Court of Appeal was reluctant to create a continuing employment situation from a series of individual contracts in *McLeod* v. *Hellyer Brothers Ltd.*[30] so courts may hesitate to deem there to be continuity for statutory purposes when it seems to them more apparent that the parties envisaged only intermittent obligation.[31]

The existence of an arrangement or custom by which employment is regarded as wholly or partly continuing[32] may, in some cases, be an alternative to "temporary cessation" but this must not conceal the difference in the characteristics of each category. In the case of arrangement the requirement is that the employment, or some aspects of it, is regarded as continuing. In *Wishart* v. *National Coal Board*[33] the practice when seconding employees to contractors was to agree to restore them to the NCB payroll and to regard them as not having permanently left the industry. It is not clear whether that alone would have sufficed but the employee in that instance was also, erroneously, retained as a member of the Mineworkers' Pension Scheme.[34]

In *Murphy* v. *A. Birrell and Sons Ltd.*[35] the Scottish E.A.T. held that the agreement in question must have existed at the time the absence commenced; but the English E.A.T. distinguished this in *Ingram* v. *Foxon*[36] where an agreed reinstatement had followed dismissal without payment of wages for the interval. No possibility of fraud existed in this latter situation and it was pointed out that it could not be the case that continuity would be lost by a settlement, as distinct from an order for reinstatement.

A week does not count for the purpose of computing continuity of employment if the employee takes part in a strike in any part of that week.[37] In all other cases save that of weeks of lock-out the effect of discounting a week would be irretrievably to break the continuity of employment so that computation would have to start afresh on resumption of work. It is provided, however, that this consequence does not follow a week in which there is a strike or lock-out.[38] The period of interruption is deducted from the beginning of the period of employment.

The Schedule contains a number of more particular provisions:

   (i) Where in the case of a redundancy an employee accepts alternative employment which has the effect of his not being dismissed by reason

---

[30] [1987] I.R.L.R. 232.
[31] See *Barry* v. *D. Murphy and Son Ltd.* [1967] I.T.R. 134.
[32] Sched. 13, para. 9(1)(*c*).
[33] [1974] I.C.R. 460.
[34] See *MSA (Britain) Ltd.* v. *Docherty*, unreported August 18, 1982 (E.A.T. Sc.).
[35] [1978] I.R.L.R. 458.
[36] [1985] I.R.L.R. 5 (Balcombe J.).
[37] Para. 15(1).
[38] Para. 15(2) and (3).

of the operation of section 84(1) any interval between the two jobs is treated as a period of continuous employment.[39]

(ii) Where an employee's previous contract is renewed or he is re-engaged by the same or another employer in circumstances where he would otherwise be treated as continuously employed but a redundancy payment is made then no account shall be taken of any time before the relevant date for that payment so far as redundancy rights are concerned.[40]

(iii) For the purpose of qualification by 26 weeks' continuous employment to claim for unfair dismissal or the calculation of the basic award the period between the actual date of termination of the contract and the date deemed to be the effective date of termination by adding the statutorily required period of notice will be regarded as a period of continuous employment.[41]

Transfer of business

Prima facie the employment to which Schedule 13 of the 1978 Act refers is employment with a single employer.[42] The Schedule provides for several exceptional cases where employment with two or more different employers may be considered continuous. These cases are:

(a) where a trade business or undertaking is transferred from one person to another;

(b) where under Act of Parliament a contract of employment with a body corporate is modified so as to substitute some other body corporate as the employer;

(c) where on the death of an employer the employee is taken into the employment of personal representatives or trustees of the deceased;

(d) where there is a change of employing partners, personal representatives or trustees;

(e) where an employee is taken into the employment of an associated employer of his previous employer.

We will here discuss in detail only the first and last of these special cases.

The original provision in the Redundancy Payments Act 1965[43] specifically included the transfer of a part of the business. The same is true of the latest provision made to satisfy the requirements of an EEC Directive guaranteeing continuation of the accrued rights of transferred employees.[44] In practice the courts have insisted that to satisfy this extension the part of a business must also be transferred as a going concern. They concluded, therefore, that the section transferred must have been operating as a separate business before the transfer.[45] The 1981 Regulations add to the express mention of transfer of

---

[39] Para. 11(2).
[40] Para. 12. Similar provision is made in respect of payment under the Superannuation Act 1972.
[41] Para. 11(1).
[42] See *Lee* v. *Barry High Ltd.* [1970] 1 W.L.R. 1549.
[43] s.13.
[44] Transfer of Undertakings (Protection of Employment) Regulations 1981.
[45] *Macleod* v. *John Rostron and Sons Ltd.* (N.I.R.C.) (1972) I.T.R. 144; *Meadows* v. *J. Stanbury Ltd.* [1970] I.T.R. 57; *G. D. Ault Ltd.* v. *Gregory* (1967) 3 K.I.R. 590 followed in *Newlin Oil Co. Ltd.* v. *Trafford* [1974] I.T.R. 324 (N.I.R.C.); *Secretary of State* v. *Rooney* [1977] I.T.R. 177.

part of a business the words "so long as the part is transferred as a business." Although this is probably meant to represent the outcome of the judicial approach to partial transfer these words appear to open up the possibility not considered by the courts that a part which had not been carried on as a business could be transferred in order to run it as a separate business.

If any one of the exceptions applies there will be continuity of employment notwithstanding a change in the nature of the job the employee undertakes.[46]

The provisions for continuity spanning a transfer are not capable of extension to cover an intervening period of non-employment. At one time it was held that the two periods must abut precisely.[47] This application of the rule could operate harshly in a redundancy situation where the previous employer had given notice to terminate employment on Friday so that the employee was not actually in employment again until the Monday—the transfer having taken place during the interval. So far as redundancy rights were concerned this situation was covered by later statutory provision.[48] The problem, however, was solved more generally by the decision of the Court of Appeal in *Teeside Times Ltd.* v. *Drury*.[49] The Receiver of the former employer reached agreement for the transfer of its business and before the final transfer informed the employees that their employment terminated forthwith. The Board of the transferee company resolved to dismiss the general manager of the transferor company and argued that his brief period of employment by it was not continuous since he had not been employed by the transferor at the time of the transfer. The members of the Court of Appeal differed in their method of arriving at the conclusion that the two periods of employment were continuous. Stephenson L.J. took the view that transfer did not take place at a precise moment but extended over a period of time. Goff L.J. did not agree with this. Eveleigh L.J. took the view that there was a period of employment and that all that was necessary was for the two periods to abut. A small gap at the end of a week in which there had been sufficient employment for continuity purposes would not, in his view, operate to break continuity. All of them, however, concluded that, as continuity was measured by the week, one week with sufficient employment followed by another in which a contract existed which would normally produce sufficient employment represented no break in continuity.[50]

In *Allen and Son* v. *Coventry*[51] it was held that the transfer to one partner of the entire equity of the partnership could amount to transfer of the business. It must be carefully noted that this situation differs from that of transfer of control of a company by means of shareholding. In the latter case there is no transfer of the business from one person to another.[52] In such a case, of

---

[46] *Lord Advocate* v. *De Rosa* [1974] I.C.R. 480. This decision was not cited in the contrary judgment of O'Connor J. in *Allman* v. *Rowland* [1977] I.C.R. 201 which must, therefore, be regarded as incorrect. In *Lloyd* v. *Brassey* [1969] 2 Q.B. 98 Lord Denning had incidentally referred to the employee keeping the same job.

[47] *Logan* v. *G.U.S. Transport Ltd.* [1969] I.T.R. 287.

[48] Now the E.P.C.A. 1978, s.84(2).

[49] [1980] I.C.R. 338.

[50] The decision in *Secretary of State* v. *Spence* [1986] I.R.L.R. 248 that transfer, for the purposes of the Transfer of Undertakings Regulations, refers to a point of time, may cast doubt on the reason advanced by Stephenson L.J. but this final, agreed, position seems beyond doubt.

[51] [1980] I.C.R. 9.

[52] See, *e.g. Winter* v. *Deepswain Garages Ltd.* [1969] I.T.R. 162 (I.T. only).

course, employment by the same company will normally remain unbroken so that there is no need to make special provision for continuity.

Authority upon what is meant by transfer of a business appears to begin with the English decision in *Dallow Industrial Properties Ltd.* v. *Else*[53] and the Scottish decision in *Rencoole (Joiner and Shopfitters) Ltd.* v. *Hunt.*[54] In the former Diplock L.J. said:

> "In order to come within section 13(1) of the Act of 1965 there must be a change of ownership, not merely in an asset of a business as in this case, but a change of ownership in the combination of operations carried on by the trader or by the non-trading body of persons, and there can only be a change of ownership in a business or part of a business . . . if what is transferred is a separate and self-contained part of the operations of the transferor in which assets, stock-in-trade and the like are engaged, or the corresponding expression which would apply to a body of persons which was carrying on operations not for profit."

The tendency to seek a single critical element such as the transfer of goodwill was resisted in *Kenmir Ltd.* v. *Frizzell*[55] although it was said that the presence or absence of this element would be strong evidence. Widgery J. said:

> "In the end the vital consideration is whether the effect of the transaction was to put the transferee in possession of a going concern the activities of which he could carry on without interruption."

Lord Denning M.R. took up this reference to transfer of a going concern in *Lloyd* v. *Brassey.*[56] The subject matter of the business was farming, in the transfer of which goodwill does not tend to play a signficant part. Very often, indeed, the farmland is held on a lease and this factor had prompted Lord Parker C.J. to follow his own earlier decision[57] and to conclude that the essence of the transaction was simply the transfer of a lease. Though there was some difference in the Court of Appeal on what exactly was the nature of the business all the members agreed that sale of the farm and buildings, the new owner intending to continue the same type of farming, would constitute a transfer of the business. Salmon L.J. proposed that two questions be asked of the reasonable man, namely; what was the nature of the business before the transfer and what was the nature of the business after the transfer. Even so useful a concept as "going concern" can be perverted by treating it as if it constituted the statutory requirement. In *Dhami* v. *Top Spot Night Club*,[58] for instance, the E.A.T. suggested that a deliberate termination of contracts of employment might mean that the whole complex of activities had not been transferred.[59]

The most significant of the authorities is, however, *Woodhouse* v. *Peter Brotherhood Ltd.*[60] The transferor employers were manufacturers of large

---

[53] [1967] 2 Q.B. 449.
[54] (1967) S.L.T. 218.
[55] [1968] 1 W.L.R. 329.
[56] [1969] 2 Q.B. 98.
[57] *Bandey* v. *Penn* [1968] 1 W.L.R. 670.
[58] [1977] I.R.L.R. 231.
[59] More obviously incorrect is the tribunal decision in *Whiterod* v. *Safety Fast Ltd.* (1975) COIT. 306/96 that a business which is not independently viable is not a going concern.
[60] [1972] I.C.R. 196.

diesel engines. They sold one of their factories to the transferees who took on almost all the previous employees. Those employees continued to operate the same machines but after the completion of four or five large diesel engines for the former employers they were engaged in the manufacture of spinning machines, compressors and steam turbines. There was no transfer of goodwill or restriction on competition, no transfer of business name, and no transfer of customers or the benefit of contracts. The N.I.R.C. held that the object of the legislation was to avoid prejudice to an employee by change in ownership of the business. This, in the opinion of Sir John Donaldson involved the transfer of the whole working environment. In his view only if failure to transfer the goodwill effected no change in that environment would it prevent the conclusion that there had been a transfer of the business. Inevitably concentration on the business of the employee rather than that of the employer produced a fundamentally different result. The Court of Appeal firmly returned to the former concept of the employer's business. Lord Denning asked the questions proposed by Salmon L.J. in *Lloyd* v. *Brassey*[61]:

> "It seems to me that this factory is quite different from the farm in *Lloyd* v. *Brassey*. In that case there was the same business being carried on both before and after the transfer. Here it was a different business. I would ask a similar question to that asked by Salmon L.J. in *Lloyd* v. *Brassey*: if anyone had been asked prior to August 1965: 'What business is being carried on in the factory at Sandiacre?,' his answer would have been 'The manufacture of diesel engines.' And if he had been asked the same question in January 1966, his answer would have been 'The manufacture of spinning machines, compressors and steam turbines.' If he had been asked 'Is it the same business?'; he would have said 'No. The manufacture of diesel engines has now gone to Manchester. All that is being done at Sandiacre is the manufacture of spinning machines etc.' True the same men are employed using the same tools: but the business is different.
> That is how the majority of the tribunal looked at it. The Industrial Court looked at it differently. They seem to have asked themselves the question; was there a change in the working environment of the men? It seems to me that that was not the right question. The statute requires the tribunal to see whether there was a transfer of the 'business' of the employer. So you look at the nature of the business of the employer and not at the actual work being done by the men. Looking at it in that way, I am quite satisfied that in 1965 Crossleys did *not* transfer their business at Sandiacre to Peter Brotherhood Ltd. They took it off to Manchester. They only transferred the physical assets to Peter Brotherhood Ltd. The result is that, as from 1965, the men were employed in a different business, namely, that of Peter Brotherhood Ltd.: and are only entitled from Peter Brotherhood to redundancy payment for the period of their service with Peter Brotherhood. So I think the majority of the tribunal were right. I would therefore allow the appeal and restore their decision."

Up to this point the reader may reasonably have assumed that the business was comprised of the essential elements of producing goods or services and marketing them. This is true, but the industrial tribunal which first heard the case of *Melon* v. *Hector Powe Ltd.* and whose decision was subsequently upheld by both the Court of Session and the House of Lords gave the package

---

[61] [1969] 2 Q.B. 98.

an unexpectedly limited content.[62] The transferor employer had manufactured suits for their own retail outlets, and for one other retailer, at two factories. The factory at Dagenham supplied the factory at Blantyre with all its requirement of cloth save that used in products for the other retailer. Decisions as to apportionment of work were made at Dagenham. Due to a decline in demand the Blantyre factory was sold to another company which, apart from finishing off work in hand, did not intend to limit its customers in the same way. The employees, with the exception of the general manager, were taken on by the transferee and subsequently claimed redundancy compensation from the transferor. The Redundancy Payments Act 1965[63] provided that where a business or part of a business is transferred employees who continue to work for the transferee shall be treated as if their contracts had been varied by agreement rather than terminated by dismissal. The Court of Session and the House of Lords concluded that there had been no transfer of business. The clearest example of the reasoning of these two courts is contained in the judgment of Lord Emslie in the Court of Session:

> "[I]n looking at what happened on and after the take-over as the result of the contract [the industrial tribunal] were, it seems to me, quite entitled to notice that in considering whether or not to take over the Blantyre factory Executex clearly had in mind the necessity of guaranteeing continuity of work there until such time as they had established themselves as manufacturers of suits and clothing for all comers. They were entitled, too, not to ignore the facts that before the take-over the main function of the Blantyre factory was the production of made-to-measure suits, and that the business of Executex at Blantyre was, at least after 31.8.77, to be the manufacture of garments of a quality different from those formerly made there by Hector Powe."

Both higher courts carefully avoid the inference that it would have been wrong to hold that the business was the making and selling of suits. Very few transfers of companies with established and limited custom are likely to operate to transfer that custom. Indeed it may be the loss of such custom that precipitates the transfer. The employee is quite likely to know what customers his employer serves but he is unlikely to appreciate that absence of any change in either his environment or the product has nonetheless resulted in a change in the nature of the business. The issue may be defined as a question of fact for the tribunal but that cannot permit a tribunal to apply an incorrect definition of business to the facts. It is submitted that there is a considerable case for legislation effectively to reverse the permission given in *Melon's* case to apply a narrow technical definition having no connection with any logical purpose of continuity and which is likely to exclude most transfers from providing continuity of employment. It cannot be pretended that this complexity is tolerable when it is borne in mind that an employee who is retained when the business is not transferred will lose his accumulated redundancy entitlement against his former employer if he neglects to claim within six months.

It should be observed that continuity of employment will arise automatically from the operation of the Transfer of Undertakings Regulations.[64] So

---

[62] [1978] I.R.L.R. 258 (E.A.T.); [1980] I.R.L.R. 80—Court of Session [1980] I.R.L.R. 477 (H.L.).

[63] s.13. Now, The E.P.C.A. 1978, s.94.

[64] *Supra* pp. 107–112.

long as the undertakings are commercial ventures and the employee in question is employed by the transferor at the moment of transfer, Regulation 5 will operate to transfer all his existing contractual and statutory rights and obligations. The principles for determining whether the business, or only its assets, has been transferred would seem to be the same in both cases.

Associated employers

Continuity of employment will exist when an employee transfers from one employer to an "associated employer." This term replaces the earlier "associated company" and the amended definition states that;

" . . . any two employers are to be treated as associated if one is a company of which the other (directly or indirectly) has control or if both are companies of which a third person (directly or indirectly) has control . . . [65]"

The controlled organisation must be a company[66] and this lends some support to the view that, despite the reference to direct or indirect control, the control in question is meant to be confined to control by majority shareholding. Whatever the justification for that view it does now seem to be established that it is the test.[67] In *Hair Colour Consultants Ltd.* v. *Mena*[68] it was held that where the shares were equally split between two persons, neither controlled the company. There is, however, some suggestion that if one of those persons, *de facto*, controlled the voting of the other a single control might be established.[69] Although, on the facts of the case in question, that suggestion seems to depend on the chauvinistic assumption that a wife is a nominal shareholder controlled by her husband it would give some meaning to the word "indirectly" and, unlike the rest of the case law, would consider the reality of the situation; although "reality" may seem an unconvincing justification in this artificial world of unnecessary qualifications. When control is exercised on both employers by the same group of shareholders the two have been held to be associated.[70] But this is not the case if the group is not identical.[71]

---

[65] E.P.C.A. 178, s.153(4).

[66] *London Borough of Merton* v. *Gardiner* [1980] I.R.L.R. 302 (E.A.T.), overruling *Hillington AHA* v. *Kauders* [1979] I.C.R. 472.

[67] *Umar* v. *Pliastar Ltd.* [1981] I.C.R. 727; *Secretary of State* v. *Newbold* [1981] I.R.L.R. 305. But earlier decisions such as *Southwood Hostel Management Committee* v. *Taylor* [1979] I.C.R. 813 clearly assume the tribunal to be looking for *de facto* control. Bowers (1982) 11 I.L.J. 190 points out that most employees will not be in a position to know who holds a controlling interest in the shares. On the other hand it would be difficult for tribunals to decide a dispute as to *de facto* control.

[68] [1984] I.R.L.R. 386 (E.A.T.)—confirmed by Court of Appeal in *South West Launderettes Ltd.* v. *Laidler* [1986] I.R.L.R. 305.

[69] *South West Launderettes Ltd.* v. *Laidler, supra.*

[70] *Zarb and Samuels* v. *British and Brazilian Produce Co. (Sales) Ltd.* [1978] I.R.L.R. 78. Mustill L.J. (*obiter*) doubted the validity of this composite person in *South West Launderettes Ltd.* v. *Laidler, supra,* but Popplewell J. in the E.A.T. in *Harford* v. *Swiftrim Ltd.* [1987] I.R.L.R. 360 refused to disturb *Zarb* on that account. He pointed out that it would be easy for the company to prove that the group voted independently, if this was so.

[71] *Poparm Ltd.* v. *Weekes* [1984] I.R.L.R. 388.

(d) *Employment in Great Britain*

Partly because the various rights to which they apply were enacted at different times, qualification requirements are apt to vary in small details. This is particularly noticeable in relation to the requirement that employment should be in Great Britain.[72]

(i) The statutory right to statements of terms and conditions of employment and the minimum notice provisions which stem from the Contracts of Employment Act 1963 do not apply during any period when the employee is engaged in work wholly or mainly outside Great Britain unless the employee ordinarily works in Great Britain and the work outside Great Britain is for the same employer.
(ii) The statutory rights to an itemised pay statement, to written reasons for dismissal, guarantee payments, protection from action short of dismissal, time off work, maternity leave, protection from unfair dismissal and protection upon insolvency of an employer do not apply to employment where under his contract of employment the employer ordinarily works outside Great Britain.
(iii) The statutory right to payment upon redundancy does not apply to an employee who is outside Great Britain on the relevant date unless under his contract he ordinarily worked in Great Britain or, conversely, to an employee who under his contract ordinarily works outside Great Britain unless on the relevant date he is in Great Britain in accordance with instructions given to him by his employer.[73]

But a person employed to work on board a ship registered in the United Kingdom shall be regarded as one who under his contract ordinarily works in Great Britain unless the employment is wholly outside Great Britain or he is not ordinarily resident in Great Britain.[74]

In *Portec (U.K.) Ltd.* v. *Mogensen*[75] the E.A.T. had held that the second of these provisions applied to everyone who ordinarily worked under a contract of employment outside Great Britain even if that person also ordinarily worked under that contract inside Great Britain. This decision was overruled by the Court of Appeal in *Wilson* v. *Maynard Shipbuilding Consultants Ab*.[76] The court said that a person could not ordinarily be working both inside and outside Great Britain. Since one venue had to be selected the question was not simply what happened in practice, it must be ascertained from the contract where the base was to be. Subsequently this test was applied by Lord Denning M.R.[77] but Eveleigh L.J. doubted that it had great significance since, in his view, it was only intended to exclude those who worked almost exclusively outside Great Britain. In *Scott, Brownrigg and Turner* v. *Dance*[78] the E.A.T. said that in cases where employment was of brief duration

---

[72] E.P.C.A. 1978, s.141.
[73] See *Costain Civil Engineering Ltd.* v. *Draycott* [1977] I.C.R. 335.
[74] See *Royle* v. *Globtik Management Ltd.* [1977] I.C.R. 552.
[75] [1976] I.C.R. 396.
[76] [1978] I.C.R. 376.
[77] *Todd* v. *British Midland Airways Ltd.* [1978] I.C.R. 959.
[78] [1977] I.R.L.R. 141.

"ordinary course" would have to be established by reference to the contract, the circumstances under which it was entered into and what could reasonably be contemplated at that time.

It is for the employee in this, as in every other case, to prove his qualification. In *Claisse* v. *Hostetter, Stewart and Keydrill Ltd.*[79] the E.A.T. held that he failed to do so when his place of employment—a floating oil rig in the North Sea—moved across national boundaries so that it was impossible to say whether or not it was ordinarily in Great Britain. In *Todd* v. *British Midland Airways Ltd.*[80] however, Lord Denning M.R. pointed out that the base is not necessarily at the same location as one normally works. The base in *Claisse's* case is most likely to have been the port from which the rig was administered.

(e) *Fixed term contracts*

The right to claim an unfair dismissal upon the expiration of the term of a fixed-term contract for a period of one year or more[81] may be excluded by a written agreement to that effect between the employer and the employee entered into at any time before the expiration of that term. The right to claim a redundancy payment may, similarly, be excluded provided that the fixed term is for two years or more.

A fixed-term requires a defined beginning and a defined ending. A contract to terminate on the happening of a future uncertain event is not a fixed-term contract. But in *Wiltshire County Council* v. *N.A.T.F.H.E.*[82] employment for an academic year was held to be for a fixed term, notwithstanding that the obligation to teach might end earlier, so long as the contractual obligations would continue. A fixed-term contract is not confined to one that cannot properly be terminated before the expiration of the term. Provision for earlier termination by notice of a fixed term will not destroy its character as such.[83]

Despite the introduction in 1963 of the statutory concept of continuity of employment it was held in *The Open University* v. *Triesman*[84] that when deciding whether a fixed term was for the necessary one or two years one must look only at the current contractual period. It follows, therefore, that an exclusion clause inserted in the very common case of a fixed-term contract for three years, renewal thereafter for a year at a time, will cease to be effective to exclude a claim for unfair dismissal if the contract is terminated at the end of any year succeeding the first three.

It should be noted that the exclusions only refer to termination at the end of a fixed term. Dismissal for any reason during the course of a term will not be affected by the exclusion clause.

(f) *Miscellaneous exclusions*

Employees of the Crown are excluded from claiming in respect of statutory statements of terms and conditions (though they may claim an itemised pay

---

[79] [1978] I.C.R. 812.
[80] [1978] I.C.R. 959.
[81] E.A. 1980, s.8(2) amending E.P.C.A. 1978, s.142(1).
[82] [1980] I.C.R. 455.
[83] *British Broadcasting Corporation* v. *Dixon* [1979] I.C.R. 281.
[84] [1978] I.C.R. 524.

statement), minimum notice rights and the right to redundancy payment. None of the statutory rights applies to the armed forces.[85]

A number of specific detailed exclusions apply to seamen,[86] shore fishermen[87] and dock workers.[88] Statutory remedies for unfair dismissal are not available to the police or, it seems, to prison officers.[89]

---

[85] E.P.C.A. 1978, s.138.
[86] E.P.C.A. 1978, s.144.
[87] E.P.C.A. 1978, s.144.
[88] E.P.C.A. 1978, s.145.
[89] *Home Office* v. *Robinson* [1981] I.R.L.R. 524.

Chapter VII

DISCRIMINATION

Legislative Prohibition

Three main areas of discrimination are immediately apparent: sex, race and religion. In this country, apart from Northern Ireland, where religious barriers may be an excuse for entirely different types of fear, the battle against the last was fought in the nineteenth century, skirmishing continued into the twentieth, but did not survive the social revolution after the Second World War. Sex discrimination in employment is, more often than not, a product, direct or indirect, of a social system based on assumptions about the proper role of each sex. The fact that a night shift is likely to be all male has little to do with strange ideas about what might happen to women at night which would not happen in the day-time, and much to do with the assumption shared by both sexes that women, with or without children whom someone must look after, should then be at home. These assumptions may in turn be linked to a common factor of inequality. In that respect sex discrimination shares origins with race discrimination. Race discrimination seems more intractable. Both race and sex discrimination can still be said to be rife in employment but there can be little doubt that the woman who is prepared to break the social mould now has a lot more chance than the black. Whilst most employers would now consider it necessary to advance a reason, however it might be founded on sexist assumptions, against employing or promoting a woman, the same employers would reject a member of a racial minority without formulating an explanation.

Anti-discrimination legislation is the product of awareness of the unjustifiability of the assumptions on which discrimination is founded and inevitably, therefore, primarily seeks to achieve its purpose by attempting to extend that awareness. More than almost any other example of legislation, it relies for success on acceptance of its objectives rather than on measures of enforcement. Criticism of it cannot be that it has not succeeded. It would be too much to hope for that in a mere 15 years. But concern must grow, if signs of awareness seem actually to be diminishing, or lessons learned about causes of its ineffectiveness are not implemented by change.

Because the situation was accepted without widespread question, or even awareness that it was other than normal, little was done in the United Kingdom about either race or sex discrimination until the 1970s. The Equal Pay Act 1970, which for the first time seriously sought to equalise opportunity of the sexes in employment, was given five years in which its concept could be accepted before enforcement. In those five years it became clear, if it had not been so before, that comparison on the basis of like work or job evaluation would deny a remedy to most women in employment. Yet the opportunity in 1975 to amend it, before its enforcement, did not lead to its obvious extension to allow equal terms for work of equal value. When such a step was forced on an unwilling Government by European Community pressure in the early 1980s a remedial procedure was devised of such cumbrous complexity that it is difficult to believe it was ever intended to work for all save the hardiest campaigner.

Sex and race discrimination

The Sex Discrimination Act 1975, and its companion the Race Relations Act of 1976, applying a single pattern of prohibition, are of a different order. Experience of the failure of many to understand, or if understanding to accord with, their intention now reveals need for extension and reform but, when passed, they were the product of an advanced realisation of the problem and how it might be solved. True, the legislature could not be persuaded to embark on encouragement for positive discrimination to redress the balance, which may, without it, now be seen as inherently resistant to rectification. It was also too much to expect that the barrier to successful claims formed by the burden of proof could be surmounted in a single step, though, as we shall see, it has been lowered subsequently. Nevertheless, the concept of indirect discrimination has proved enlightened and effective in the hands of those similarly enlightened.

It is the course of enlightenment following this legislation which we must now chart. If one is in a hurry it will seem that the light is painfully slow to dawn. By now we should, by any standards of experimental steps to deal with a serious problem, have taken the further legislative steps which experience suggests would improve effectiveness. Early pioneers, and particularly Phillips J., who set out consciously to further the legislative purpose they clearly appreciated have given place to those alarmed by the changes in thinking demanded of the new approach. Sweeping propositions such as, for instance, the dependence of the defence of justification on proof of necessity, have been watered down to what reasonable people would consider right and proper. But judges have emerged to express disquiet at this and the process of acclimatisation, if depressingly slow, clearly continues.

The definition of unlawful discrimination

Apart from Northern Ireland where discrimination on grounds of religion is also proscribed, the sex and race legislation declares illegal direct and indirect discrimination on grounds of sex, married (not marital) status, colour, race, nationality or ethnic or national origins. Of these headings "ethnic origin" has proved the most difficult to define, although the House of Lords has seized the opportunity it was given in 1983[1] to produce authoritative criteria. A Sikh had been refused admission to a school unless he removed his turban, cut his hair and complied with the uniform regulations of the school. Lord Frazer said that there were two essential conditions for an ethnic group:

(a) its members must have a long shared history of which the group is con-

---

[1] *Mandla* v. *Dowell Lee* [1983] I.C.R. 385.

scious as a distinguishing factor, the memory of which keeps it alive; and

(b) it must have a cultural tradition of its own, which is often, though not necessarily, associated with religious observance.

   Other relevant considerations were:

   (i) either a common geographical origin or descent from a small number of common ancestors;

   (ii) a common language, not necessarily peculiar to the group;

   (iii) a common literature peculiar to the group;

   (iv) a common religion different from that of neighbouring groups, or the community surrounding it;

and, he added, perhaps more as an example than a test,

   (v) being a minority, an oppressed or a dominant group as, for instance, the Saxons and the Normans after the conquest.

That the Welsh are an ethnic and a national group is clear but the single factor of language was held[2] not sufficient to create separate ethnic groups of Welsh and non-Welsh speakers among them.

At this early stage the reader ought to be reminded that the operation of this legislation depends on establishing the reason for the difference. Someone who is treated differently may be different on one of the stated grounds but, to succeed in a complaint under this legislation will have to show (if perhaps only by necessary inference) that that difference was the cause of the different treatment or effect.[3] We shall return to this problem of causation later when we have seen something of the questions it has to answer.

Direct discrimination

(a) Intention

The straightforward conscious form of discrimination is dealt with by what has become known as the definition of direct discrimination.[4] A person discriminates against another if, on one of the specified grounds, he treats that other "less favourably" than he would treat a person to whom that ground did not apply. A deliberate intention to differentiate is essential to this form of discrimination. So, in De Souza v. Automobile Association[5] the Court of Appeal considered that an insult could not be described as treatment unless it was intended to come to the notice of the applicant. In the absence of provision for vicarious liability even the foreseeable discrimination of a third party will not fix an alleged discriminator with liability for direct discrimination.[6] It would, of course, be otherwise if the decision had been left to the third party with the probable intention that the result should be discriminatory. Motive, on the other hand, is irrelevant.[6a] The statutes ask whether the

---

[2] Gwynedd County Council v. Jones [1986] I.C.R. 833.
[3] Tejani v. Superintendent Registrar for Peterborough [1986] I.R.L.R. 502.
[4] R.R.A. 1(1)(a); S.D.A. 1(1)(a).
[5] [1986] I.R.L.R. 103.
[6] Armagh District Council v. Fair Employment Agency of Northern Ireland [1984] I.R.L.R. 234 (N.I. Court of Appeal).
[6a] Birmingham City Council v. Equal Opportunities Commission, The Times, February 24, 1989 (H.L.).

person discriminated against was intentionally treated less favourably, because he was a member of a specified group—not why. In *Peake* v. *Automotive Products Ltd.*[7] the Court of Appeal failed to understand this; they held that the motive, desirable in their opinion, of being courteous to women, prevented the deliberate disadvantage of restricting men, leaving work for a further five minutes after women were allowed to go, from being discriminatory. Shaw L.J. was particularly convinced of the need for an improper motive. He, at least, had become totally convinced that this was wrong by 1979[8] when men examiners in munitions factories complained of discrimination arising from the fact that they, but not women, having volunteered for overtime, might be assigned to the particularly unpleasant sections where colour bursting shells were made. Women's hair was adversely affected by dust in the atmosphere of these shops and there were no separate shower facilities, where they might wash.[9] In *R.* v. *Commission for Racial Equality ex p. Westminster City Council*[10] an official of the council, with the intention of eliminating racial discrimination among the wholly white force of rubbish collectors in its northern section, had temporarily appointed a road sweeper as a refuse collector. The appointment was revoked by the same official in face of a threat of industrial action by the white refuse collectors, ostensibly on the ground of the appointee's bad attendance record. As Woolf J. appreciated in the lower court, the existence of a particular motivation may affect the reason for the differentiation. Dismissal of a black employee because white customers will not deal with him and the business cannot survive without their custom is discriminatory. However understandable, the dismissal is because the employee is black. Dismissal of a black employee because a white employee complains of his incompetence may lead to the conclusion that the reason for the dismissal is not that the employee is black. It was on this line of distinction that Sir Denys Buckley in the Court of Appeal dissented, holding that the official's reason for withdrawing the appointment was the threat of strike action. The majority of the Court of Appeal, however, felt unable to draw a line between the industrial action and the reason for it and concluded that the appointment had been withdrawn because the employee was black. The absence of any hostility on the part of the official could not alter the fact that he had subjected the employee to a disadvantage because he was black.

The intentional element in direct discrimination is most likely to arise in reported cases from deliberate assumptions. The irrelevance of motive makes in unnecessary to appreciate the discriminatory effect.[11] It is worth considering a few examples. One of the earliest arose in *Shields* v. *E. Coomes (Holdings) Ltd.*[12] in which an assumption that male employees would perform security duties more effectively than women was ridiculed by Lord Denning. It is not normally necessary to go that far. It will be very difficult to show that any such generalised assumption is so rarely wrong that it can be relied upon as the actual reason for the differentiation. If it is open to doubt then it must

---

[7] [1977] I.C.R. 968.
[8] *Ministry of Defence* v. *Jeremiah* [1980] I.C.R. 13.
[9] Slightly earlier—*Greig* v. *Community Industry and Ahearn* [1979] I.R.L.R. 158, the E.A.T. had contrived to distinguish *Peake* so as to arrive at the same conclusion.
[10] [1984] I.C.R. 770 (Q.B.).
[11] As, for instance, by Lord Denning M.R. in *Peake*, *supra*.
[12] [1978] I.C.R. 1159.

follow that the differentiation is being made by reason of the fact that the applicant falls into a particular class. In *Hurley* v. *Mustoe*,[13] for example, no inquiry had been made to establish whether a woman applicant for the post of waitress, who had young children to look after, would prove unreliable. The employer did not seek to dispute the fact that he had a policy of not engaging those in this group. As the E.A.T. pointed out, the only effect of showing that he adopted the same policy towards men would be to disclose that he was discriminating against married men and women. Assumptions that married women are subordinate to their husbands have proved particularly dangerous, whether they presume that the husband is the principal support of the family[14] or that the woman will follow the man, rather than vice versa, in a change of job.[15]

(b) *Disadvantage, detriment and less favourable treatment*

The definition of direct discrimination requires that it produce less favourable treatment. Indirect discrimination is required to be detrimental and this same concept of detriment appears, expressly and by implication, in the application of both definitions to employment situations. "Detriment" has been said to mean "disadvantage."[16] Can one go further and say that unfavourable consequences are disadvantageous and detrimental? In *Gill and Coote* v. *El Vinos Co. Ltd.*[17] denial to women of a facility—namely the right to purchase drinks at the bar, which was "greatly prized" by men—was held to be unfavourable treatment. This is in tune with the view of detriment in *Porcelli* in which the Court of Session equated detriment with disadvantage. This is the same view as was taken by Brandon L.J. in *Ministry of Defence* v. *Jeremiah*.[18] But in *Porcelli* a programme of suggestive comment and other offensive conduct, mounted by two male employees, was considered to produce a detriment not in itself but because it forced the women concerned to seek a transfer. Similarly, in *De Souza* v. *Automobile Association*[19] the Court of Appeal considered that the racial insult in the advice to another secretary to give certain typing to "the wog" was not, in itself, disadvantageous, even if it caused distress. In the view of the court there would have been a detriment if a complaint about working conditions could arise as a result of the insult. The distinction between a situation which causes distress and one which makes the applicant feel at a disadvantage—the latter having been held to constitute a detriment[20]—may be difficult to envisage in practice. The most obvious problem for the applicant is to know what evidence is sufficient to induce a court to conclude that the barrier between mere feelings and positive disadvantage, arising from those feelings, has been passed.

Browne-Wilkinson J., it is submitted, was clearly correct to hold that those sections which apply the definition of discrimination to the employment situation, by "detriment" as well as more specific disadvantages, refer to the out-

---

[13] [1981] I.C.R. 490.
[14] *Coleman* v. *Skyrail Oceanic Ltd.* [1981] I.C.R. 864.
[15] *Horsey* v. *Dyfed C.C.* [1982] I.R.L.R. 395.
[16] *Strathclyde Regional Council* v. *Porcelli* [1986] I.R.L.R. 134 (C.Sess.)
[17] [1983] I.R.L.R. 206. See now, *Birmingham City Council* v. *Equal Opportunities Commission*, *The Times*, February 14, 1989 (H.L.).
[18] [1980] I.C.R. 13 at 26.
[19] [1986] I.R.L.R. 105.
[20] *Snowball* v. *Gardner Merchant Ltd.* ([1987] I.R.L.R. 397).

come of the situation created by the alleged discrimination.[21] It would appear to follow, therefore, that there is no detriment if an action has no outcome so far as the applicant is concerned. In this respect "less favourable treatment" does differ from "detriment." In *F.T.A.T.U.* v. *Modgill*[22] the minority group suffered more than others and so, in outcome may well have suffered a detriment. It had not, however, been treated less favourably since the majority would have been served equally badly, though it would have had less effect on them.

A detriment may be overlooked if *de minimis*. Lord Denning M.R. accepted[23] that this was the only ground upon which the decision in *Peake* v. *Automotive Products Ltd.*[24] holding five minutes' difference between the time men and women left work not to be discrimination, could be upheld. Phillips J. had followed this aspect of that decision in holding that there was nothing serious or important about a requirement that a woman should wear a skirt.[25] It might be better to treat the example given by Brightman L.J. in *Jeremiah's* case of the loss to men of the choice of entering a "Ladies Only" railway compartment as an example *de minimis*. There is obviously a detriment in a restriction of freedom.

(c) *Similar circumstances*

Clearly, like must be compared with like, and statute so provides by requiring that the relevant circumstances in the one case are the same, or not materially different, in the other.[26] The relevant circumstances obviously depend upon the reason the difference has occurred. Care has to be taken in understanding this situation. Circumstance is a more generalised factor than reason. It cannot, for instance, be said that the relevant circumstances differ because the applicant's skin is black whilst he is seeking to compare himself with those whose skins are white. The relevant circumstance in such a case is the factor of colour, not a particular colour. In *Turley* v. *Alders Department Stores Ltd.*[27] the E.A.T. had difficulty in thus getting round the argument that dismissal had occurred because the applicant was pregnant. It concluded that no comparison could be made with men on this basis. It is suggested that a later E.A.T., in *Hayes* v. *Malleable Working Mens' Club*[28] was doing no more than broadening the specific reason into its general circumstance when it concluded that pregnancy in a woman could be compared to sickness in a man. The problem is that that may be the wrong analogy, and the possibility that it is wrong serves to indicate how important it is to be right in assimilating specific reason and general circumstance. It is the basis for a comparison and if one asks whether an employer would have dismissed a man who announced that he would be off sick for six months, and receives an affirmative answer, does this really mean that there is no discrimination against a woman who makes a similar announcement by reason of pregnancy. It would scarcely have been

---

[21] *Brennan* v. *J. H. Dewhurst Ltd.* [1983] I.R.L.R. 357.
[22] [1980] I.R.L.R. 142.
[23] *Ministry of Defence* v. *Jeremiah* [1980] I.C.R. 13.
[24] [1977] I.R.L.R. 365.
[25] *Schmidt* v. *Austicks Bookshops Ltd.* [1977] I.R.L.R. 360.
[26] S.D.A., s.5(3); R.R.A., s.3(4).
[27] [1980] I.R.L.R. 4.
[28] [1985] I.R.L.R. 367.

better to speak of comparison with a man seeking six months' leave to look after his family. The difficult choice of analogy cannot be avoided by considering the matter as one of indirect discrimination as it is still necessary to show disadvantage as against a similarly placed member of the comparator group. It would, of course, be possible to deal with a specific problem such as this by placing pregnancy among the list of prohibited grounds of discrimination, but this would override, rather than solve, the problem of a correct basis for determination of comparative disadvantage. The alternative is effectively to ignore the element—for example, pregnancy—by regarding it as a characteristic of women and not a relevant circumstance at all. The comparison is then made between a normal woman, whether she is pregnant or not, and a normal man. That, after all, is what one is doing by comparing a normal black man with a normal white man.

By excluding cases where relevant circumstances differ legislation is effectively deeming the circumstance to be the reason. It is always open to one accused of discrimination to show that he has acted because of the existence of a circumstance which is not among the listed prohibitions. The argument will have to be supported by establishment of the fact that the individual concerned is subject to that different circumstance. If then, others in the comparator group would have been treated similarly had those circumstances applied to them, it follows that the reason for discrimination is the circumstance and not the grouping. The fact that the circumstance is associated with one group rather than another, does not alter the conclusion that differentiation has occurred because of the different circumstance and not the group. The position is exactly that in *Perera* v. *Civil Service Commission*,[29] where the Court of Appeal said that a finding that the alleged discrimination was based on the applicant's personal characteristics is fatal to a claim for direct discrimination under section 1(1)(*a*).

In *Perera* the applicant was said to be lacking in experience of the United Kingdom and command of English. These deficiencies arose because he came from Sri Lanka but, so long as they were the reason for treating him differently, his origin was not the reason and a claim for direct discrimination failed. It is suggested therefore, that the "circumstance" exclusion is unnecessary. If a different circumstance, though relevant, is not part of the reason for the discrimination why should it not be ignored? If it is part of the reason it can be dealt with accordingly.

(d) *Assumptions*

That situation is easily distinguishable from one in which the characteristic is not established in the individual but is assumed to exist because of that individual's membership of one of the specified groups. The circumstances are then, in fact, similar and the reason for different treatment is seen to be membership of the group. If an employer does not engage a woman because they chatter too much, it is women he objects to. He is at liberty to apply his preference for non-chatterers but he cannot make a selection on group assumptions without discriminating against that group. *Hurley* v. *Mustoe*[30] furnishes a clear example. The owner of a restaurant knew that a woman who was

---

[29] [1983] I.C.R. 428.
[30] [1981] I.C.R. 490.

applying for a job as a waitress had the care of young children. He instructed
the manager, who had just taken her on, to dismiss her on the ground that
women with young children were unreliable. If, as he argued, he would have
made the same decision about men with young children, he could be said to
be making an assumption about married people or, at least, one which would
affect a higher proportion of married people. He was entitled to reject the
unreliable, even those he decided would be unreliable, but he was rejecting a
group, as such. In the earlier case of *Shields* v. *E. Coomes (Holdings) Ltd.*[31]
men were paid more because they were expected to undertake security
duties. Such a decision assumes that women are less able to undertake such
duties and is discriminatory. In *Skyrail Oceanic Ltd.* v. *Coleman*[32] two travel
agents had decided that a situation in which a man employed by one had married a woman employed by the other constituted a security risk and that the
woman should be dismissed because the man was the breadwinner. A similar
assumption was made in *Horsey* v. *Dyfed C.C.*[33] that a woman would accompany her husband should he move job location. The distinction drawn by the
Court of Appeal between an impressionistic assumption and the exercise of
judgment[34] presents considerable difficulties of proof.

The concept of less favourable treatment on one of the specified grounds is
wide enough to cover unfavourable treatment of a person because of the
grouping of someone else. In *Showboat Entertainments Centre Ltd.* v.
Owens[35] a white manager of an amusement centre alleged that he had been
dismissed because he refused to comply with an instruction to exclude young
blacks. The E.A.T pointed out the fact that the giving of racist instructions,
dealt with by section 30, which gives the C.R.E. a right to take action, does
not justify the conclusion that someone who has suffered as a result of such an
instruction has no remedy. (This extension does not apply to indirect discrimination where statute says that the unequal condition must disadvantage the
racial group of "that other.")

(e) *Proof*

Whilst the legislature has declined several invitations to impose the burden
of proving an absence of discrimination upon the respondent, the courts have
recognised the peculiar difficulty of proving the existence of discrimination. It
is not sufficient that race or sex has something to do with the background of
the case or that it is a *causa sine qua non*. What has to be proved is the reason
for the action. In *Seide* v. *Gillette Industries Ltd.*[36] a Jewish toolmaker suffered anti-Semitic remarks from another employee and left work without permission because of this. Both received written warnings and the Jew was
transferred to another shift. The man he then worked with asked to be moved
because he was being drawn into the dispute. Management decided to move
the Jew to the day shift, where he would be more closely supervised, and he
complained of racial discrimination. It was held by the E.A.T. that the reason
for the moves was not the applicant's ethnic group but the industrial situation

[31] [1978] I.C.R. 1159.
[32] [1981] I.C.R. 864.
[33] [1982] I.R.L.R. 345.
[34] *Noble* v. *David Gold and Son (Holdings) Ltd.* [1980] I.R.L.R. 253.
[35] [1984] I.R.L.R. 7; see also *Zarcynska* v. *Levy* [1978] I.R.L.R. 532.
[36] [1980] I.R.L.R. 427.

created by the bad relations. There was no evidence that any, save the perpetrator of the original insult, was motivated by racism and the very fact that the applicant had first used the internal grievance procedure tended to show that he did not think such feeling existed. In proving a discriminatory reason the courts have often indicated that they will draw inferences from surrounding facts, and even from facts occurring after the acts of illegal discrimination.[37] In *Moberly* v. *Commonwealth Hall (University of London)*[38] the E.A.T. went so far as to say that where a difference of treatment between two groups is established a prima facie case of discrimination is raised which the respondent must seek to disprove. In the case in point, however, it was held that there was sufficient evidence to show that the difference had nothing to do with the race of the applicant. Inferences may be matched by counter-inferences as in *Owen and Briggs* v. *James*[39] where a coloured applicant was twice unsuccessfully interviewed by the same partner for similar jobs as a shorthand typist. There was evidence that the partner had expressed surprise to a white, and successful, applicant, with a shorthand speed of 55 words per minute against the applicant's 80, that any employer should wish to take on a coloured applicant when an English (sic) girl was available. There was also evidence that the firm did employ coloured staff. The Court of Appeal confirmed both previous tribunals and held that the industrial tribunal was entitled to conclude that there was a significant element in the decision amounting to unlawful discrimination. Obviously not every inference is conclusive. In *Saunders* v. *Richmond L.B.C.*[40] the question "are there any women golf professionals in clubs?" put to a female applicant for such a position, though held not to amount to discrimination itself was considered to provide evidence of it, which, however, the tribunal was entitled to reject.[41] One of the most detailed situations of this type was considered in *Khanna* v. *Ministry of Defence*.[42] The applicant, born in India, was employed as a "senior photographer" for almost 10 years, during which time he made 22 unsuccessful applications for promotion to "principal photographer." For some months he ran his section after the principal photographer left. He was shortlisted for permanent appointment to this vacancy and placed third, although the successful applicant did not have some of the requisite experience which the applicant possessed. The tribunal held that there was an "unavoidable inference" of discrimination but that this was disproved by the fact that the members of the board had given sworn evidence that they were not acting for discriminatory reasons. The E.A.T. referred the matter back to the tribunal to make it clear whether it accepted this evidence or not. The E.A.T. said that, in future, tribunals might find it better to forget about shifts in the evidential burden in favour of the simple question whether the claim had been established. It added that affirmative evidence of discrimination will usually derive from inferences based on primary facts. An inference of discrimi-

---

[37] *Chattopohadhyay* v. *Headmaster of Holloway School* [1982] I.C.R. 132.
[38] [1977] I.C.R. 791; see also *Wallace* v. *S.E. Education and Library Board* [1980] I.R.L.R. 193.
[39] [1982] I.R.L.R. 502.
[40] [1978] I.C.R. 75.
[41] Consider, in this context, the question "will you be able to get home in time to get your husband's tea?"
[42] [1981] I.C.R. 653.

nation, arising from those facts which is not satisfactorily explained, should result in a decision that the claim succeeds.[43]

Balcombe L.J., in *West Midlands Passenger Transport Executive* v. *Singh*[44] accepted the following propositions concerning burden of proof in racial discrimination:

  (i) If the applicant could show that he had been treated less favourably than others in circumstances consistent with racial discrimination a tribunal should infer the presence of racial discrimination unless the respondent (employer) could show the opposite.[45]

  (ii) evidence in such cases was required only to tend to prove the case. (Though it is doubtful what this means if the case is one relying on inference and the evidence is not likely to be aimed at disproving the case);

  (iii) "statistical" evidence might establish a discernible pattern giving rise to an inference of discrimination;

  (iv) a practice operated against a group makes it reasonable to infer, in the absence of satisfactory explanation, that a member of the group is being discriminated against;

  (v) there was an approved practice for employers to provide evidence of a non-discriminatory attitude and in consequence any evidence of a discriminatory attitude would have probative effect;

  (vi) suitability for appointment was rarely measured objectively and evidence of a high percentage of failure by members of a particular group might indicate conscious, or unconscious, racial attitudes.

Both Acts[46] make provision for a person, against whom discrimination is considered to have occurred, to require the alleged discriminator to answer questions designed to clarify the position. In *Virdee* v. *E.C.C. Quarries Ltd.*[46a] an industrial tribunal considered "equivocal and evasive" the failure to answer all but one of nine questions, making it "just and equitable" to infer discrimination.

Discovery

It will be apparent that in so difficult an area of proof as that involved in discovering which facts actually did influence a decision the applicant will be at a disadvantage, despite the ready shift of the burden, if he is unable to secure certain evidence. If, for instance, it is asserted that it was not the fact that he was black but the fact of inferior qualification which produced rejection he cannot be in a position to challenge the relevance of the alleged differences unless he can examine them in detail. For this reason the development

---

[43] Although May L.J. in *North West Thames R.H.A.* v. *Noone* [1988] I.C.R. 813, said that he did not find this decision altogether satisfactory he seems to agree with the proposition stated, although he emphasised that it is always for the applicant to prove the allegation. In *London Borough of Barking and Dagenham* v. *Camera* [1988] I.R.L.R. 373 Wood J. in the E.A.T. said that the burden of proof could not be shifted by any such presumption but that a tribunal might reasonably draw inferences bearing in mind the difficulty of positive proof of discrimination.

[44] [1988] I.C.R. 614.

[45] *Chattopohadhyay* v. *Headmaster of Holloway School*, [1982] I.C.R. 132.

[46] S.D.A., s.74; R.R.A., s.65.

[46a] [1978] I.R.L.R. 295.

of the law relating to disclosure of documents in this field is most significant. In *Science Research Council* v. *Nassé*[47] the House of Lords confirmed the view of the Court of Appeal there there is no rule barring disclosure of confidential documents although Lord Edmund-Davies was careful to point out that confidentiality is a relevant consideration. On the other hand there is no general right of discovery in industrial tribunals. Lord Scarman said[48]:

"The criterion is not relevance alone, nor are general orders for discovery appropriate in this class of litigation. The true test, as formulated by the rules of court, is whether discovery is necessary either to save costs or for the fair disposal of the case. Where speed and cheapness of legal process are essential, as they are in county courts and industrial tribunals, general orders should ordinarily be avoided. And where, as will be frequent in this class of litigation, confidential records about other people are relevant, the court must honour the confidence to this extent: that it will not order production unless the interest of justice requires that they be disclosed. No hard and fast rules can be laid down: but I agree with others of your Lordships in thinking that the Employment Appeal Tribunal gave very useful guidance on the appropriate practice in *British Railways Board* v. *Natarajan*."

The House of Lords expressed approval of the approach adopted by the E.A.T. under Arnold J. in *British Railways Board* v. *Natarajan*.[49] Referring to the Court of Appeal decision in *Nassé*[50] he said[51]:

"Now the way in which the decision whether disclosure is essential in the interests of justice is to be made in a particular case is plainly spelled out in the decision of the Court of Appeal. The proper procedure is for the documents in question to be looked at by the judge in the county court or chairman of the industrial tribunal in order to see whether it is essential, in the interests of justice and with regard of course to the claims relevant in the cases before them, that disclosure should take place.

What does not emerge with any clarity as embodying any general principle, and what it would perhaps be impossible to embody in a general principle, is, first of all, what degree of probability has to be demonstrated before the judge or chairman performs the exercise of examination, and, secondly, at what stage in the litigious process the examination should take place. We must deal as best we can with those two matters.

We think that before deciding whether an examination is necessary, the judge or chairman of the tribunal in a case in which the matter is dealt with at first instance, or the appellate court, where the matter comes before it on review, must decide whether there is any prima facie prospect of relevance of the confidential material to an issue which arises in the litigation; put another way, whether it is reasonable to expect that there is any real likelihood of such relevance emerging from the examination. If there is not, we do not think that the exercise of examination is necessary or should take place. If there is, then to come to the second matter which we have mentioned, it is, we think, a matter of convenience in each case whether the examination should take place at the interlocutory stage of dis-

---

[47] [1979] I.C.R. 921. See also *West Midlands Passenger Transport Executive* v. *Singh*, [1988] I.C.R. 614.
[48] At p. 952.
[49] [1979] 2 All E.R. 794.
[50] [1979] Q.B. 144.
[51] At p. 799.

covery or immediately the matter arises at the trial. We can conceive that there would be many cases in which, having regard to the probable way in which the material, if found relevant, would have to be treated, that it would be essential for the decision to be made at the interlocutory stage of discovery. But there are also cases where, having regard to the way in which the material would have to be dealt with, such an early examination would not be necessary. That is a matter which we think must be decided in relation to each case in which the point is relevant."[52]

An applicant cannot launch an action without a prima facie case and rely on discovery to ferret out enough documents to raise one. On the other hand, the existence of a prima facie case is easier to establish than an implication which will shift the burden of proof. In *Clwyd County Council* v. *Leverton*[53] the applicant was allowed to rely on a joint statement by employers and unions asserting disparity of treatment between nursing and clerical staff.

Indirect discrimination

Indirect discrimination is defined as involving the application of a requirement or condition which applies, or would apply, to one of the other sex, married status, colour, race, nationality or ethnic or national origin but which:

(a) is such that the proportion of persons of the same sex, etc., who can comply with the condition is considerably smaller than the proportion of corresponding persons not of that group who can comply with it; and

(b) cannot be shown to be justified irrespective of the sex, etc., of the person to whom it is applied; and

(c) is to the detriment of that other because he or she cannot comply with it.

It is necessary to consider, therefore, what amounts to a "requirement or condition," what constitutes a considerably smaller proportion in relation to what other groups, what is justification and, what constitutes ability to comply with the requirement or condition.

(a) *Requirement or condition*

In *Perera* v. *Civil Service Commission*[54] the applicant contended that a combination of factors taken into account by an interviewer, towards considering appointment of applicants to the post of legal assistant in the Civil Service, amounted to a condition for that appointment. The factors included command of the English language, experience of the United Kingdom, British nationality and age. The appropriate comparator groups were qualified lawyers from Sri Lanka and the United Kingdom. The chairman of the

---

[52] The way in which these principles can be applied to sift out the relevant evidence appears clearly in *Perera* v. *Civil Service Commission* [1980] I.C.R. 699 (E.A.T.) affirmed [1982] I.R.L.R. 147 (C.A.). See also, *The British Library* v. *Palyzo and Mukherjee* [1984] I.R.L.R. 308.

[53] [1985] I.R.L.R. 197. The House of Lords did not deal with this point.

[54] [1983] I.C.R. 428. The Court of Appeal confirmed that this decision established that a 'requirement or condition' must be mandatory in *Meer* v. *Tower Hamlets L.B.C.* [1988] I.R.L.R. 399.

interview board had said that the applicant was "clearly short of the minimum recruitment standard," but the Court of Appeal held that the evidence showed that a sub-standard person might have passed the board so that there was no individual, or cumulative, *requirement*. In *Home Office* v. *Holmes*[55] the E.A.T., whilst accepting that a requirement or condition must be mandatory, concluded that an inflexible policy that the grade of executive officer in the immigration department would only be occupied by full-time staff, amounted to a requirement of full-time availability. The flexibility referred to lies in the application of the criteria, not in the criteria themselves. A promotion procedure requiring the satisfaction of vague criteria and lacking a mechanism to stop unconscious bias was held to amount to a requirement in *Watches of Switzerland Ltd.* v. *Savell*.[56] Apart from the obvious requirements of allegedly appropriate qualifications,[57] requirements may include residence,[58] age range,[59] full-time availability,[60] marriage,[61] various dress and sartorial regulations,[62] and seniority.[63]

(b) *Considerably smaller proportion*

The determination of the requisite proportion is a matter of great difficulty because of the variation that can be achieved by selecting one pool of comparison rather than another. It was pointed out in *Orphanos* v. *Queen Mary College*,[64] in which a Greek Cypriot complained of discrimination between the fees charged to an overseas student and those charged to a "home-based" student, that a number of different groupings might easily have been compared but that the pool must be those seeking admission. In *Home Office* v. *Holmes*[65] it seems that the E.A.T. adopted a straightforward comparison between the proportions of men and women available to work full-time. A year later under the same chairman, the court held in *Kidd* v. *D.R.G. (U.K.) Ltd.*[66] that choice of what has come to be called the "pool"—the appropriate section of the population—is not a matter of law and that the tribunal had acted "fairly" in limiting the range of comparison to the section of the population for whom the need to provide care for children at home represents a barrier to work. The effect of the difference is startling since the *Kidd* pool excludes entirely the effect of social sex discrimination by selecting a pool of the disadvantaged in which women are already in the majority. It may reasonably be assumed (though whether assumptions are to be accepted as evidence in place of statistics has not been satisfactorily decided) that a far higher proportion of women than men were subject to such a need. Suppose, for the sake of argument, that 30 per cent. of all women in employment are subject to

---

[55] [1984] I.C.R. 678.
[56] [1983] I.R.L.R. 141.
[57] *e.g. Hampson* v. *D.E.S.* [1988] I.R.L.R. 87.
[58] *Orphanos* v. *Queen Mary College* [1985] I.R.L.R. 349.
[59] *Price* v. *Civil Service Commission* [1978] I.C.R. 27.
[60] *Home Office* v. *Holmes, supra; Clarke* v. *Eley (I.M.I.) Kynoch Ltd.* [1983] I.C.R. 165; *Kidd* v. *D.R.G. (U.K.) Ltd.* [1985] I.C.R. 405.
[61] *R.* v. *Secretary of State for Education ex p. Schaffer* [1987] I.R.L.R. 53.
[62] *Mandla* v. *Lee* [1983] I.C.R. 385; *Singh* v. *Rowntree Mackintosh Ltd.* [1978] I.C.R. 554.
[63] *Steel* v. *Union of Post Office Workers* [1978] I.C.R. 181.
[64] [1985] I.R.L.R. 349.
[65] *Supra.*
[66] [1985] I.C.R. 405. See also, *Pearse* v. *City of Bradford MDC.* [1988] I.R.L.R. 379.

such need but only 10 per cent. of men. Then 70 per cent. of the women who
can comply with a requirement for full-time work is considerably smaller than
the 90 per cent. of men. If, however, we take as comparative groups the 30
per cent. of women and 10 per cent. of men, the proportions of such groups
whose obligations prevent availability for full-time work is likely to be more
or less equivalent.[67] Worse still, there will probably be an absence of statistical evidence to prove the point, so the tribunal is quite likely to conclude that
it cannot make a guess, let alone a guess contrary to what it is inclined to
assume. One is bound to ask whether it is logical to define the pool by the
very factor said to produce the disadvantage. The E.A.T. observed that the
parties might be surprised by the tribunal's factual choice of pool which might
deprive the comparative evidence they had amassed of any relevance, but
added that industrial tribunals could be relied on to see that this decision produced no unfair disadvantage.[68] It would be of interest to know how industrial
tribunals would do this. One can, however, appreciate the difficulty of laying
down criteria for selection of the pool. It is, of course, clear that it cannot be
everyone in the race or sex. The very fact of the need to compare like circumstances means, for instance, that if the requirement is the possession of a
qualification one compares those in both groups who possess the qualification.[69] Not since the days of Phillips J.[70] is there any reported consideration
of how to determine what proportion is "considerable." Wisely he too, in that
respect, laid down no tests.

(c) *Ability to comply*

In contrast to this uncertainty the courts have settled the meaning of "can
comply." It clearly does not mean "can possibly comply." A Sikh could cut
his hair and dispense with a turban, but is not required to do so.[71] In *Price* v.
Civil Service Commission[72] Phillips J. said that "can comply" referred not to
the theoretical possibility but to what happens in practice. In practice, considerably more women than men are absent from the labour market between
the ages of $17\frac{1}{2}$ and 28, although they could be available if they chose not to
have, and care for, children. In *Clark and Powell* v. *Eley (IMI) Kynoch Ltd.*[73]
in which women employed part-time were selected for redundancy, it was
argued that one of the employees could have become full-time at some earlier
date. The E.A.T. held that the question whether a condition can be satisfied
arises for decision at the time at which the condition is imposed. In other
words, it arises at the time the applicant alleges a detriment from her failure
to satisfy it. The employee could not comply with the requirement that she
was a full-time worker, because she was not. The industrial tribunal in *Raval*
v. *DHSS*[74] felt that ability in practice ought to refer to an obviously existing

---

[67] See *Price* v. *Civil Service Commission* [1978] I.C.R. 27, which case was referred back to tribunal to decide on statistical evidence, because knowledge and experience were unreliable.
The tribunal does not appear to have done so [1978] I.R.L.R. 3.
[68] As to the effect of choosing the wrong pool see *Pearse* v. *City of Bradford MDC, supra.*
[69] *Perera* v. *Civil Service Commission* [1983] I.C.R. 428; *Raval* v. *DHSS* [1985] I.R.L.R. 370;
Bohun-Mitchell v. *Common Professional Examination Board* [1978] I.R.L.R. 525 (I.T.).
[70] *Price* v. *Civil Service Commission* [1978] I.C.R. 27.
[71] *Mandla* v. *Lee* [1983] I.C.R. 385.
[72] [1978] I.C.R. 27.
[73] [1983] I.C.R. 165.
[74] [1985] I.R.L.R. 370.

ability even if it had not been exercised. In that case the applicant lacked the requisite "O" level pass in English Language although there was no dispute that she could have done the job and little doubt that she could obtain the pass. Again, the E.A.T. held that the question was whether, at the time when satisfaction was required, she was in a position to provide it. The proportion of Asians capable of obtaining an "O" level in English must be significantly less than that of those born in England. The applicant might have overcome that disadvantage but had not done so. It seems obvious that she should be treated as still subject to it and if "can comply" had produced a different result it would have seemed the wrong test. The possibility of future compliance in relation to a pension scheme which contained an advantage for married women arose in *Turner* v. *The Labour Party*.[75] Two members of the Court of Appeal concluded that a single woman could comply in future. The dissenting member did not dispute this date of application since the scheme provided an alternative benefit.

(d) *Justification*

It would be burdensome, if not unworkable, to insist that those not qualified could not be excluded simply because their group contained a smaller proportion of those qualified. Consequently, statute permits proof of justification irrespective of its disadvantage to membership of the specified group. Originally a strict view of justification as requiring necessity was put forward.[76] This was, in part, explained by the intention that it should be assimilated with the test of "genuine material difference" in the Equal Pay Act 1970, s.1(3). The E.A.T. added this important note on method of determination[77]:

> "The question is what considerations are relevant and proper to be taken into account when determining whether the requirement or condition was justifiable, in particular, is it sufficient merely to take into account the needs of the enterprise for the purpose of which the requirement or condition has been imposed, or is it necessary to the requirement or condition? We are satisfied that the latter is the case and that the industrial tribunal has to weigh up the needs of the enterprise against the discriminatory effect of the requirement or condition. Were it not so, many acts *prima facie* discriminatory would be allowed when there was no overriding need."

This "overriding necessity" has been watered down through a series of decisions. In *Singh* v. *Rowntree Mackintosh Ltd.*[78] it was said that it should be applied reasonably and with common sense and in *Panasar* v. *Nestlé Co. Ltd.*[79] the E.A.T. said that though the reason must be genuine and more than a matter of convenience, "necessity" as used in *Steel* was not to be rigidly construed. It used the passage quoted above as indicating a modification of necessity in the light of a balance of the reasons whereas, it is submitted, that passage, if anything, strengthens necessity by suggesting that even a necessary requirement must be justified as overriding its discriminatory effect. The test,

---

[75] [1987] I.R.L.R. 101.
[76] *Steel* v. *Union of Post Office Workers* [1978] I.C.R. 181.
[77] At p. 186.
[78] [1979] I.C.R. 554.
[79] [1980] I.R.L.R. 60, affirmed without detailed discussion by C.A. [1980] I.C.R. 144.

it said, was whether the condition would be thought "right and proper." The Court of Appeal did not cite this decision in *Ojutiku* v. *Manpower Services Commission*[80] but expressed the test of justification as whether it would be acceptable to right-thinking people as sound and tolerable. The Court of Appeal here admitted that this was not what *Steel* had intended but thought that *Steel* went too far. Kerr J. described it as placing a gloss on "justifiable" and suggested that "advancing good grounds" for the condition would not be a bad approach.

So, in *Greater Glasgow Health Authority Board* v. *Carey*[81] the court held that the administrative efficiency of the service could provide justification for the requirement of a five-day week. Conditions as to the wearing of a uniform by nurses, held reasonable by the industrial tribunal, were considered justified in *Kingston and Richmond Health Authority* v. *Kaur*.[82] On the other hand, the application of the test of sound and tolerable reasons acceptable to right-thinking people in *Kidd* v. *D.R.G. (U.K.) Ltd.*[83] seems totally to ignore the need to balance the condition against its discriminatory effect. Even the respondent had admitted that there was only a marginal advantage to the employer of operating one full-time shift rather than two part-time shifts. With respect, it seems that the tribunal was confusing what a reasonable employer might do in the management of his business, which might in turn produce dismissal, with the justification necessary to exercise discrimination.

The House of Lords in *Rainey* v. *Greater Glasgow Health Board*[84] accepted the proposition that justification in the discrimination legislation should be assimilated with "material difference" in the Equal Pay Act. In that case it was held that the Equal Pay expression required proof of objectively justified grounds of difference,[84a] following the same view as the European Court of Justice in relation to Article 119 of the Treaty of Rome expressed in *Bilka-Kafhaus GmbH* v. *Weber von Harz*.[85] The effect of these decisions is to allow the consideration of economic reasons as well as personal circumstances, but the House of Lords in *Rainey* held that administrative efficiency would not be excluded simply because it had no commercial or business connotation. The need to attract certain people in the interests of providing a viable service within a given time was considered justification for the payment of more money to men recruited from the private sector than to women taken on from the National Health Service. The European Court in *Bilka-Kafhaus*, however, considered that justification has to be based on satisfaction of a real need pursued by appropriate means necessary to achieve that end.

Victimisation

It is not the sex or race of the complainant which is the determining factor in victimisation but whether the complainant's conduct, in one of the ways

---

[80] [1982] I.C.R. 661.
[81] [1987] I.R.L.R. 484 (E.A.T. Scotland).
[82] [1981] I.R.L.R. 337.
[83] [1985] I.C.R. 405.
[84] [1986] I.R.L.R. 26.
[84a] Which Balcombe L.J. in *Hampson* v. *Department of Education and Science, The Times* 15 December, 1988, expressed as objective balance between the discriminatory effect of the requirement and the reasonable needs of the party who applied it.
[85] [1986] I.R.L.R. 317.

specified, has brought the disadvantage upon him. So anyone who falls into one of the protected list of actions can make a claim.[86] The claimant must prove that he has done one of the actions specified, that he has been treated less favourably than others in the same circumstance and that that treatment was by reason of the specified action.[87]

The list of specified actions includes any proceedings under the Act against any person, so that a third person responding to such action may be held to have victimised the claimant. The giving of any information, whether before or during proceedings, will be covered by the second head, but it was held in *Kirby* v. *Manpower Services Commission*[88] that the protection does not arise if no proceedings actually ensued. This decision also took a restrictive view of the general provision in relation to any other act under the legislation, holding that the action must relate to an express provision of that legislation. The E.A.T. held, however, that addition of the words "by reference to" would cover a report alleging discrimination made to a local Community Relations Council. In *Aziz* v. *Trinity Street Taxis Ltd.*[89] the recording of conversations, intended to provide evidence to support the applicant's feeling that he was being discriminated against, was held to be covered by this third category. Even an allegation that an incident may be within the legislative prohibition of discrimination will suffice under the final head.

The comparison which has to be made in a victimisation claim in order to establish less favourable treatment cannot be with anyone else who has committed the specified act because this would be to allow victimisation to justify victimisation. In *Kirby* v. *Manpower Services Commission* the E.A.T. said that one should look at the potential treatment of one to whom applied the same reason as was asserted by the respondent for the treatment of the applicant. An employee who had leaked information to the Community Relations Council was, therefore, to be compared to an employee who had leaked similar information not in connection with any allegations of discrimination. This, of course, would allow the employer to choose the ground of comparison and to choose narrowly so that an answer in his favour was more likely. In *Aziz* Slade L.J. said that the correct comparison was with the treatment of someone who had not done the protected act. This, in turn, seems rather wide since an action such as leaking confidential information might be regarded as punishable regardless of any discriminatory element; but such punishment would obviously involve less favourable treatment in relation to someone who had not broken the duty of confidentiality.

It is always possible to eliminate the effect of this problem, however, by considering whether it is indeed the specified action which is the reason for the disadvantage. If the tribunal is satisfied that the penalty was imposed because of, say, breach of confidentiality, then it follows that it is not victimisation contrary to section 2, even if this does produce a disadvantage as compared to someone who had not taken such action. It must be borne in mind, however, that this is not a complete answer. We have already noted that the

---

[86] *Cornelius* v. *University College Swansea* [1987] I.R.L.R. 141.
[87] *Aziz* v. *Trinity Street Taxis Ltd.* [1980] I.R.L.R. 435 E.A.T; the Court of Appeal decision did not affect this classification.
[88] [1980] I.R.L.R. 229 (E.A.T.).
[89] Confirmed by Court of Appeal in *Aziz* v. *Trinity Street Taxis Ltd.*, [1988] I.R.L.R. 204.

difficulty of obtaining evidence of discrimination necessitates reliance on implication. It is possible to envisage circumstances in which it would be difficult to rebut a presumption that the cause of the disadvantage was the specified conduct.

Anti-discrimination legislation[90] also prohibits discrimination by less favourable treatment aimed at victimising a person for bringing discrimination proceedings, or giving evidence, or information in connection with proceedings brought by any person against any other person under the anti-discrimination legislation (including the Equal Pay Act); or for doing anything else under that legislation, or alleging a contravention of those legislative requirements in relation to any person.

Vicarious liability and inducement

Save as regards offences under the Acts, anything done by a person in the course of his employment shall be treated, for the purpose of the discrimination legislation, as done by his employer as well as by him, whether or not it was done with the employer's knowledge or approval, unless the employer proves that he took such steps as were reasonably practicable to prevent the employee from doing the act or from doing acts of that description in the course of his employment. A principal is similarly liable for the authorised acts of his agents.[91] Supervision and a known policy of equal opportunities were held capable of constituting reasonably practicable steps to prevent alleged sexual harassment in *Balgobin and Francis* v. *London Borough of Tower Hamlets*[92] despite the fact that the E.A.T. described as intolerable the continuing requirement that the women should work in proximity to the man involved in the allegation. "Course of employment" appears to involve the same type of consideration as in other areas of vicarious liability.[93] It is unlawful to induce or attempt to induce (by direct or indirect means) any unlawful act of discrimination[94] although the Sex Discrimination Act is more narrowly qualified than the Race Relations Act.

Exceptions to liability

(a) *Genuine occupational qualification*

Both Acts contain provisions applicable to discrimination in employment and somewhat similar to section 1(3) of the Equal Pay Act exempting from prohibition the imposition of certain "Genuine Occupational Qualifications." The exemption is, however, not as large as in the earlier Act but consists of specific situations which, in the case of the Race Relations Act at least, are few and narrow.

The list in the Sex Discrimination Act[95] is as follows:

7. (1) In relation to sex discrimination:

---

[90] S.D.A., s.4; R.R.A., s.2.
[91] S.D.A., s.41; R.R.A., s.32.
[92] [1987] I.R.L.R. 401.
[93] *Irving* v. *The Post Office* [1987] I.R.L.R. 289.
[94] S.D.A., s.40; R.R.A., s.31; *Commission for Racial Equality* v. *Imperial Society of Teachers of Dancing* [1983] I.R.L.R. 315.
[95] s.7.

(a) section 6(1)(a) or (c) does not apply to any employment where being a man is a genuine occupational qualification for the job, and

(b) section 6(2)(a) does not apply to opportunities for promotion or transfer to, or training for, such employment.

(2) Being a man is a genuine occupational qualification for a job only where:

(a) the essential nature of the job calls for a man for reasons of physiology (excluding physical strength or stamina) or, in dramatic performances or other entertainment, for reasons of authenticity, so that the essential nature of the job would be materially different if carried out by a woman; or

(b) the job needs to be held by a man to preserve decency or privacy because:

   (i) it is likely to involve physical contact with men in circumstances where they might reasonably object to its being carried out by a woman, or

   (ii) the holder of the job is likely to do his work in circumstances where men might reasonably object to the presence of a woman because they are in a state of undress or are using sanitary facilities; or

(c) the nature or location of the establishment makes it impracticable for the holder of the job to live elsewhere than in premises provided by the employer, and:

   (i) the only such premises which are available for persons holding that kind of job are lived in, or normally lived in, by men and are not equipped with separate sleeping accommodation for women and sanitary facilities which could be used by women in privacy from men, and

   (ii) it is not reasonable to expect the employer either to equip those premises with such accommodation and facilities or to provide other premises for women; or

(d) the nature of the establishment, or of the part of it within which the work is done, requires the job to be held by a man because—

   (i) it is, or is part of, a hospital prison or other establishment for persons requiring special care, supervision or attention, and

   (ii) those persons are all men (disregarding any woman whose presence is exceptional), and

   (iii) it is reasonable, having regard to the essential character of the establishment or that part, that the job should not be held by a woman; or

(e) the holder of the job provides individuals with personal services promoting their welfare or education, or similar personal services, and those services can most effectively be provided by a man, or

(f) the job needs to be held by a man because of restrictions imposed by the laws regulating the employment of women, or

(g) the job needs to be held by a man because it is likely to involve the performance of duties outside the United Kingdom in a country whose laws or customs are such that the duties could not, or could not effectively, be performed by a woman, or (*h*) the job is one of two to be held by a married couple.[96]

(3) Subsection (2) applies where some only of the duties of the job fall within paragraphs (*a*) to (*g*) as well as where all of them do.

(4) Paragraphs (*a*), (*b*), (*c*), (*d*), (*e*), (*f*) or (*g*) of subsection (2) do not apply in relation to the filling of a vacancy at a time when the employer already has male employees:

(*a*) who are capable of carrying out the duties falling within that paragraph, and

(*b*) whom it would be reasonable to employ on those duties, and

(*c*) whose numbers are sufficient to meet the employer's likely requirements in respect of those duties without undue inconvenience.

That in the Race Relations Act is much shorter[97]:

5. (1) In relation to racial discrimination:

(*a*) section 4(1)(*a*) or (*c*) does not apply to any employment where being of a particular racial group is a genuine occupational qualification for the job; and

(*b*) section 4(2)(*b*) does not apply to opportunities for promotion or transfer to, or training for, such employment.

(2) Being of a particular racial group is a genuine occupational qualification for a job only where:

(*a*) the job involves participation in a dramatic performance or other entertainment in a capacity for which a person of that racial group is required for reasons of authenticity; or

(*b*) the job involves participation as an artist's or photographic model in the production of a work of art, visual image or sequence of visual images for which a person of that racial group is required by reasons of authenticity; or

(*c*) the job involves working in a place where food and drink is (for payment or not) provided to and consumed by members of the public or a section of the public in a particular setting for which in that job, a person of that racial group is required for reasons of authenticity; or

(*d*) the holder of the job provides persons of that racial group with personal services promoting their welfare, and those services can most effectively be provided by a person of that racial group.

(3) Subsection (2) applies where some only of the duties of the job fall within paragraphs (*a*), (*b*), (*c*) or (*d*) as well as where all of them do.

(4) Paragraphs (*a*), (*b*), (*c*) or (*d*) of subsection (2) do not apply in relation to the filling of a vacancy at a time when the employer already has employees of the racial group in question:

---

[96] [1983] I.R.L.R. 404. In *Sisley* v. *Britannia Security Systems Ltd.* [1983] I.R.L.R. 404 only women were engaged to work a shift up to twelve hours at a security control station because the women were in the habit of taking extended rests in their underwear. It was held that the fact that beds were provided for them did not produce a residence, but the fact that the women, of their own choice, conducted themselves in a way reasonably incidental to their need for a rest did not exclude the situation from s.7(2)(b)(i).

[97] s.5.

(*a*) who are capable of carrying out the duties falling within that paragraph; and

(*b*) whom it would be reasonable to employ on those duties; and

(*c*) whose numbers are sufficient to meet the employer's likely requirements in respect of those duties without undue inconvenience.

It is often said that there are no grounds apart from this limited group which will excuse unlawful discrimination. That is strictly true. As we have noted, however, the enquiry may never reach this point because a decision resulting in discrimination is based on some established fact other than sex or race or because a discriminatory condition is justified. In *Ojutiku* v. *Manpower Services Commission*[98] for example the state of the job market effectively excused discrimination, or if one wishes to put it that way, removed the unlawful element from discrimination.

There is singularly little case law on the meaning of either of these two sections. Some of the loosest wording in either is contained in section 7(2)(*b*) which is replete with "likely" and "might reasonably object." Nevertheless in *Wylie* v. *Dee and Co. (Menswear) Ltd.*[99] an industrial tribunal interpreted them more nearly as "probably" when accepting evidence of six different ways in which a woman employed in a gents' outfitters might avoid causing objection to her taking inside leg measurements. The employer appears only to have provided an answer to one of these.

One of the most far-reaching of the exceptions is contained in section 7(1)(*f*) of the Sex Discrimination Act referring to the imposition of restrictions necessary to comply with laws regulating the employment of women.[1] One of the principal examples of such statutory requirement is the provisions of the Factories Act 1961.[2] Originally the Equal Opportunities Commission took the view that it might be argued that compliance with this did not become necessary unless the employer had tried and failed to obtain a certificate of exemption.[3] The Sex Discrimination Act does not permit complaints in respect of benefits consisting of the payment of money regulated by the contract of employment.[3a]

(b) *Statutory authorisation*

Acts of racial discrimination done in pursuance of statute, Order in Council or statutory instrument, or in order to comply with any conditions or requirement imposed by a Ministry of the Crown by virtue of any enactment are not unlawful discrimination.[4] The exclusion in the case of sex discrimination only

---

[98] [1982] I.R.L.R. 418 (C.A.).

[99] [1978] I.R.L.R. 103.

[1] Despite the alleged exclusiveness of s.7, s.51 contains a similar but slightly wider provision. E.P.A. 1975, s.6(1)(*a*) has the same effect as S.D.A. 1975, s.7. A number of these restrictions were repealed by the Sex Discrimination Act 1986 and most of the rest of them are likely to be repealed in 1989.

[2] s.93.

[3] The industrial tribunal in *White* v. *British Sugar Corporation Ltd.* [1977] I.R.L.R. 121 thought that the dismissal of Ted White upon the discovery that she was a woman was justified by the fact that an exemption certificate would have been needed to employ her on Sundays and this would have taken time to acquire.

[3a] SDA, s.6(b).

[4] R.R.A., s.41.

applies to Acts passed before the 1975 Act, or to provisions of such Acts re-
enacted, with or without modification, thereafter or to statutory instruments
made at any time under the authority of such Acts or re-enactments.[5] The
width of this exclusion was considered by the Court of Appeal in *Hampson* v.
Department of Education and Science.[5a] A majority rejected the "wide" construction which would cover everything done *intra vires* by a body which owed
its existence to an enactment. They stated, however, that it was not desirable
to formulate a universal test but concluded that the exception applied when
the individuals right was a public one stemming from regulations authorised
by legislation so that the decision maker had a public duty to consider the
matter in accordance with the regulations.

The statutory requirements most frequently relevant to these exclusions in
the law of employment were those in the Factories Acts and similar legislation
which restricted hours of work of women. Many of them were repealed in
1986[6] in response to persistent representation from groups representing the
interests of women that this form of protection was either itself discriminatory
or caused or excused other discrimination.

In *Page* v. *Freight Hire (Tank Haulage) Ltd.*[7] Mrs. Page, a divorcee of 23,
was engaged on a casual daily basis as a heavy goods vehicle driver. She
delivered a load of dimethyl-formamide to ICI who subsequently instructed
her employers not to use her again on such work because of danger to a
woman of child-bearing age. Although the E.A.T. held that, since the
decision in *Ministry of Defence* v. *Jeremiah,*[8] the pursuit of safety was not an
excuse for discrimination, the Health and Safety at Work Act had been
passed before the Sex Discrimination Act and required an employer to take
reasonably practicable steps to ensure the health of his employees. He would
be complying with this requirement if he showed that he thought it appropriate to prevent an employee doing the job at all. He did not have to show that
that step was the only way in which he could comply.

(c) *Work outside Great Britain*

Work done wholly or mainly outside Great Britain is excluded from the
operation of anti-discrimination legislation unless it is work (other than work
wholly outside Great Britain) on board a ship registered in the United Kingdom and operated by a person having his principal place of business, or being
ordinarily resident, in Great Britain.[9]

(d) *Provisions relating to death or retirement*

These will be considered when the effect of the Equal Pay Act is considered.[10]

---

[5] S.D.A., s.51.
[5a] *Times* 15 December, 1988. See also *General Medical Council* v. *Goba* [1988] I.R.L.R. 425.
[6] S.D.A. 1986, s.7. The government has announced its intention to repeal most of those remaining.
[7] [1981] 1 All E.R. 394.
[8] [1980] I.C.R. 13.
[9] S.D.A., s.10; R.R.A., s.8; *Devia* v. *General Council of British Shipping* [1986] I.R.L.R. 108;
Houghton v. *Olav Line (U.K.) Ltd.* [1986] I.R.L.R. 465.
[10] *Infra*, pp. 262–264.

(e) *National security*

It is provided in the Sex Discrimination Act that nothing in the prohibitions of that Act shall render unlawful an act done for the purpose of safeguarding national security. Conclusive evidence of that situation is provided by a certificate to that effect purporting to be signed by or on behalf of a Minister of the Crown.[11] The same immunity is provided by the Race Relations Act[12] which does not, however, contain the provision as to evidence by Ministerial certificate. In *Johnston* v. *Chief Constable of the Royal Ulster Constabulary*[13] a woman member of the Royal Ulster Constabulary complained to the European Court of breach of the Equal Opportunities Directive[14] in the refusal to offer her renewal of a contract for full-time service in the reserve on the ground that it would be necessary to carry firearms at times during such service and it was not the policy to issue women with guns. The Secretary of State issued a certificate that refusal of full-time engagement was for the purpose of safeguarding national security. The European Court refused to accept this as conclusive and held that the interests of public safety must be examined in the light of their derogation from the principle of equal treatment. It was for the national courts to decide whether the reasons were well-founded and justified and whether the applicant's contract could have been operated without requiring her to carry firearms. It pointed out that Article 2(3) permits exceptions designed to protect a woman's biological condition, especially in the relation between her and her child, so that an exception could not be made on the general ground that women should be given greater protection than men.

(f) *Reverse discrimination*

Discrimination in favour of a normally disadvantaged group producing detriment to other groups will normally be prohibited. Some reverse discrimination is, however, expressly permitted by statute in connection with training[15] to fit members of a group for work in which no such members have been engaged in the 12 months preceding the doing of the act, or the proportion of such persons was comparatively small. In the case of positive racial discrimination acts are permitted if done to afford members of a particular racial group access to facilities or services to meet the special needs of persons of that group in regard to their education, training, welfare or ancillary benefits,[16] or where it appears to the person doing the act that those for whom it is done do not intend to remain in Great Britain after their period of education or training there.[17]

Enforcement

An individual may complain of discrimination in any of the areas covered by Part II of the Sex Discrimination Act or of the Race Relations Act to an

---

[11] s.52.
[12] s.42.
[13] [1986] I.R.L.R. 263.
[14] 76/207 of February 9, 1976.
[15] S.D.A., ss.47 and 48, R.R.A. ss.37 and 38.
[16] R.R.A., s.35.
[17] R.R.A., s.36.

industrial tribunal[18] normally within three months of the act of discrimination or the last date of a continuing discrimination.[19] When such a complaint is made an ACAS conciliation officer must be notified[20] and he may endeavour to promote a settlement wherever requested to do so by both parties or of the opinion that he could act with a reasonable prospect of success.

If a tribunal finds a complaint well-founded it may make such of the following as it considers just and equitable[21]:

(*a*) an order declaring the rights of the complainant and the respondent in relation to the act complained of;

(*b*) an order for compensation corresponding to county court or sheriff court rules subject to the upper limit currently applicable to unfair dismissal claims but including any element for injury to feelings.[22] The amount of compensation for injured feelings should be moderate in accordance with the guidance given in defamation cases.[23] No award of compensation may be made, however, where the respondent proves that indirect discrimination was not intended to result in unfavourable treatment;

(*c*) a recommendation that the respondent take within a specified period action appearing to the tribunal to be practicable for the purpose of obviating or reducing the adverse effect on the complainant of the discrimination to which the complaint relates.[24]

A failure without reasonable justification to comply with a recommendation may lead to an award of increased compensation. In *Prestcold* v. *Irvine*[25] the Court of Appeal held that the power to make a recommendation does not permit a recommendation that wages should be paid or that an employer shall seriously consider the complainant for appointment to the next available vacancy and provide an opportunity for career development in the meantime. In its view, the wording of the legislation did not suggest that an award could cover an indefinite period.

Complaint may be made of discrimination by an employer as a company but it is important to note that such complaint can be made against any person. Any person who knowingly aids another person to do an unlawful act shall himself be treated as having done an unlawful act of like description and the act of an employee or agent for whose act an employer or principal is liable shall be deemed to aid the act of the employer or principal.[26]

---

[18] S.D.A. 1975, s.63; R.R.A. 1976, s.54.

[19] The test of "just and equitable" for permitting claims out of time is somewhat more lenient than that applicable to complaints for unfair dismissal. See *Hutchison* v. *Westward Television Ltd.* [1977] I.C.R. 279.

[20] S.D.A. 1975, s.64; R.R.A. 1976, s.55.

[21] S.D.A. 1975, s.65; R.R.A. 1976, s.56.

[22] S.D.A. 1975, s.66(4); R.R.A. 1976, s.57(4).

[23] *Skyrail Oceanic Ltd.* v. *Coleman* [1980] I.C.R. 596.

[24] In *Jeremiah* v. *Ministry of Defence* [1980] Q.B. 87 it was held that this did not confer power to make an order to instal showers for women.

[25] [1981] I.C.R. 177.

[26] S.D.A. 1975, s.42; R.R.A. 1976, s.33.

The Commissions

The Equal Opportunities Commission was established under the Sex Discrimination Act and the Race Relations Commission under the Race Relations Act with identical power primarily to exercise a more general function of detection and removal of discrimination than would be achieved merely by reliance on individual complaint. The Commissioners have powers to promote research and education to this end.

In one particular the Commissions provide the only enforcing body. The publication of advertisements *which might reasonably be understood* as indicating an intention unlawfully to discriminate is itself unlawful: in the case of the Sex Discrimination Act only if the discrimination intended would be unlawful[27] but in the case of the Race Relations Act whether that is so or not.[28] The test is the likely response of the ordinary reader.[29] If the act complained of itself constitutes discrimination within the scope of an industrial tribunal the Commission must first secure a decision from such a tribunal that the act was unlawful before seeking an injunction from a county court. Otherwise the Commission may immediately seek such an order.

The power to conduct formal investigations on relevant matters at its own initiative or at the request of the Secretary of State into matters within its scope was, no doubt, intended as the principal effective function of each Commission. The E.O.C., however, has taken the view that the safeguards preceding the carrying out of its function render such powers of little practical value. The Commission for Racial Equality, however, habitually uses evidence of discrimination from which no individual complaint arises to guide it in the establishment of formal inquiries. It has indicated[30] that as a matter of policy it will initiate investigations in areas where equal opportunities are of proportionately high importance for the establishment of good race relations and the extent to which unlawful discrimination is a cause of significant disadvantage to ethnic minorities is itself considerable. It will also have regard to the appropriateness and effectiveness of formal investigation to eliminate discrimination and to the work being done by other agencies. It regards employment as a particularly suitable area for investigation.

It is intended that the power of the Commissions to issue non-discrimination notices shall provide the sanction, if such is necessary, after a formal investigation. A non-discrimination notice may require the person on whom it is served not to commit the acts in question and to inform the Commission of changes he has made which are necessary to comply with the order. He may also be required to take reasonable steps to inform other persons concerned of those steps.[31] But the Commission must first give such person notice that it is minded to issue such a notice, specifying the grounds upon which such issue is contemplated.[32] Such person must be given an opportunity within a period

---

[27] s.38.

[28] s.29.

[29] *Commission for Racial Equality* v. *Associated Newspapers Group Ltd.* [1978] 1 W.L.R. 905.

[30] Annual Report 1978.

[31] S.D.A. 1975, s.67(2); R.R.A. 1976, s.58(2).

[32] See *R.* v. *Commission for Racial Equality ex p. Westminster City Council* [1985] I.R.L.R. 426 on the observance of natural justice in such proceedings. A non-discrimination notice must, however, be based on findings of fact—*Commission for Racial Equality* v. *Amari Plastics Ltd.* [1982] I.R.L.R. 252.

of not less than 28 days specified in the notice to make representations and those representations must be taken account of. Not later than six weeks after the non-discrimination notice is served the person on whom it is served may appeal, in the case of employment matters, to an industrial tribunal which may quash any requirement which it considers to be unreasonable and substitute some other requirement in its place. A public register of final discrimination notices is kept.[33]

The Commissions may seek an injunction to prevent repeated discrimination within five years of a non-discrimination notice becoming final.[34]

Finally, it is within the powers of the Commissions to give advice and assistance to those who are actual or prospective claimants against discrimination.[35] The Commission may give advice, seek to procure a settlement, arrange for legal advice or representation or give any other assistance it considers appropriate. It has, however, no obligation, having considered the application for assistance, to grant it.

Compensation

The question of the amount of monetary compensation to award for injury to feelings has given rise to considerable discussion in the courts. The outcome can best be illustrated by example and two recent decisions of the Court of Appeal are here selected for that purpose.

In *Alexander* v. *Home Office*[36] the Court of Appeal held that the object of damages for discrimination was restitution. General damages for injury to feelings should be restrained, but not nominal or minimal. A serving prisoner had clearly been discriminated against on several grounds in comments made by prison officers in reports concerning him. As a result he had been denied higher pay for employment within the prison and he was awarded £68 for loss of this higher rate. Taking into account the fact that he had been vindicated by the proceedings a county court judge awarded him £50 for injury to feelings. The Court of Appeal said that it was impossible to say what was restitution in such a case and that must rely on the good sense of the judge. Injury to feelings was likely to be of short duration and less serious than physical injury. Nevertheless compensatory damages might include an element of aggravated damage for high-handed, malicious, insulting or oppressive conduct. The claimants' knowledge of the discrimination, holding him up to ridicule or contempt was also a relevant factor. So far as the compensatory element was concerned, however, the mere facts of deliberately detrimental treatment or the failure to treat the claimant as an individual were not themselves factors which should be taken into account. In the present case, the defendant's high-handed conduct, persistent abuse of power and conspicuous want of apology or withdrawal would all be taken into account, but the plaintiff's conduct could also affect the issue. In the end the Court of Appeal concluded that the original award had been nominal and an award of £500 should be substituted. In *North West Thames Regional Health Authority* v. *Noone*[37] the Court of Appeal concluded that £3,000 was a proper sum to compensate

---

[33] S.D.A. 1975, s.70; R.R.A. 1976, s.61.
[34] S.D.A. 1975, s.71; R.R.A. 1976, s.62.
[35] S.D.A. 1975, s.75; R.R.A. 1976, s.66.
[36] *The Times*, February 22, 1988.
[37] *The Times*, March 23, 1988.

for severe injury to the feelings of a doctor who, by inference, had been discriminated against by non-appointment as a consultant microbiologist. The industrial tribunal had awarded £5,000 which the E.A.T. had reduced to £1,000. No actual loss was alleged and no claim was made for aggravated damages.

In *Marshall* v. *Southampton and South West Hampshire A.H.A.*[37a] an industrial tribunal awarded £19,405 compensation for discrimination contrary to the E.C. Equal Treatment Directive on the ground that the limit imposed by the Sex Discrimination Act failed to provide an adequate remedy as required by Article 6.

EQUAL OPPORTUNITIES

The principle of equal opportunities between men and women as regards terms of employment—particularly pay—and access to employment and employment opportunities is treated by United Kingdom legislation as an aspect of a wider attack on discrimination. It a quires particular prominence because it is enshrined in the Treaty of Rome of March 25, 1957 establishing the European Economic Community. Article 119 provides:

"Each Member State shall during the first stage ensure and subsequently maintain the application of the principle that men and women should receive equal pay for equal work.

For the purpose of this Article, 'pay' means the ordinary basic or minimum wage or salary and any other consideration, whether in cash or in kind, which the worker receives, directly or indirectly, in respect of his employment from his employer.

Equal pay without discrimination based on sex means:
(a) that pay for the same work at piece rates shall be calculated on the basis of the same unit of measurement;
(b) that pay for work at time rates shall be the same for the same job."

Narrowly construed this could be rendered as equal pay for like work. Implementation of that principle would leave a great deal of sex discrimination unremedied, since much of it consists in assumptions about "women's work" and "men's work." Consequently, Article 119 was "explained" in Council Directive 75/117 of February 10, 1975 as requiring "for the same work *or for work to which equal value is attributed*, the elimination of all discrimination on grounds of sex with regard to all aspects and conditions of remuneration."[38]

The principle of "equal pay" was rendered as the principle of equal treatment by Directive 76/207 of February 9, 1986 and extends to access to employment and promotion, vocational training and working conditions.

Interaction of United Kingdom and European community provisions

It is against this background that the various stages of the United Kingdom's Equal Pay Act can best be appreciated. It must first be noted that the

---

[37a] [1988] I.R.L.R. 325. See also *Dowuona* v. *John Lewis p.l.c.* [1987] I.R.L.R. 310.
[38] Art. 1.

Equal Pay Act was never limited to comparison of remuneration and that Directive 76/207 extends beyond pay to equal treatment in working conditions. In *Worringham and Humphreys* v. *Lloyds Bank Ltd.*[39] the European Court of Justice ruled that even as regards Article 119 "pay" included contributions by an employer to a private pension scheme.[40] As this decision reveals, the variation in scope between these provisions is significant. The United Kingdom legislation may be invoked by any employee, male or female, employed under a contract of service or of apprenticeship or a contract personally to execute any work or labour at an establishment in Great Britain. Article 119 is directly enforceable by any worker.[41] Directives, however, are addressed to governments. They grant no rights to workers save against that government. In *Marshall* v. *Southampton and South West Hampshire A.H.A.*[42] the European Court of Justice ruled that this permitted their enforcement against an "organ of the state." Directives, therefore, may be said generally, if imprecisely, to be directly enforceable by those employed in public services administered through the national government.[43] As if to complete the range of issues and jurisdictions the Divisional Court decided that public authorities, such as the Secretary of State for Social Services, were subject to judicial review if carrying out their obligations contrary to EEC law.[44]

Method of operation of the Equal Pay Act

The Equal Pay Act permits a worker of one sex to compare his or her terms of employment with those of a worker of the other sex employed at the same establishment, or by the same employer or an associated employer at the same or another establishment, at which common terms and conditions of employment are observed. In *Leverton* v. *Clywd County Council*[45] the House of Lords confirmed the view of the Court of Appeal that only broad similarity of terms is required to warrant comparison. In its view it could not have been the intention of Parliament to require the claimant to prove an undefined substratum of similarity in the particular terms applicable to herself and her comparator. The issue was one of fact so long as the appropriate broad comparison was made. In *Thomas* v. *National Coal Board*[46] the E.A.T. held that national negotiations established common terms even though the amounts of bonus and concessionary entitlements varied by location. Common terms are not required where comparison is made within the same establishment.[47] It is for the applicant to select the comparator[48] and there is no power in the tribunal to substitute one of its choice. In *Dennehy* v. *Sealink (U.K.) Ltd.*[49] the

---

[39] [1981] E.C.R. 767 applied by the Court of Appeal [1982] I.R.L.R. 74.
[40] See also *Hammersmith and Queen Charlotte's Special H.A.* v. *Cato* [1987] I.R.L.R. 483.
[41] *Defrenne* v. *Sabena (No. 2)* [1976] E.C.R. 455 [1976] I.C.R. 547.
[42] [1986] I.C.R. 335.
[43] See, *e.g. Hammersmith and Queen Charlotte's Special A.H.* v. *Cato* [1987] I.R.L.R. 483. Public corporations operating nationalised industries are not organs of the state for this purpose—*Foster* v. *British Gas p.l.c.* [1988] I.R.L.R. 354.
[44] *R.* v. *Secretary of State for Social Services ex p. Clarke* [1988] I.R.L.R. 22.
[45] *The Times*, December 16, 1988.
[46] [1987] I.R.L.R. 451.
[47] *Lawson* v. *Britfish Ltd.* [1987] I.C.R. 726 E.A.T.
[48] *Ainsworth* v. *Glass Tubes Ltd.* [1977] I.C.R. 347.
[49] [1987] I.R.L.R. 120.

application did not identify a particular comparator in an equal value claim, but the E.A.T. held that the tribunal should have considered whether on the evidence, there was a reasonable basis for a claim in respect of the class referred to. If the comparator is the predecessor or successor of the applicant, the claim will have to invoke Article 119, since the Court of Appeal has held that the working of the Equal Pay Act clearly refers to one in the same employment at the same time.[50]

The basis of the claim is a statutorily implied term in all workers' contracts that terms and conditions should be equal as between men and women in the three categories referred to. It is clear, therefore, that the alleged inequality must be found in contractual terms and not in working conditions outside the contract. In *Pointon* v. *University of Sussex*[51] a female lecturer argued that, though she was receiving more pay, she should have been on a higher point in the salary scale than a recently appointed man because she was older and better qualified. It was the normal practice of the University to grant higher salary scale points the older the employee, but the Court of Appeal held that this was only a practice. The contract itself, therefore, revealed no inequality. On the other hand in *Benveniste* v. *University of Southampton*[51a] the Court of Appeal accepted evidence that the applicant would have been placed at the same point in a discretionary salary scale but for the fact that the employer could not afford it as indicating that there was a less beneficial term in her contract.

Comparison may be based either on the contention that the comparators are doing like work, or that their work has actually been rated (*i.e.* by a job evaluation exercise) as equivalent, or that their work is of equal value. This last basis of comparison was added in 1983[52] and it is provided that it shall not be applied if either of the other two bases is available.[53]

The Equal Pay Act refers to "any term" of the contract which "is or becomes less favourable." This had, until 1986, been assumed to permit comparison term by term. So, for instance, an unequal rate of pay might be equalised despite the fact that it was obviously meant to take account of reverse inequality in, say, paid holiday entitlement, which, in turn, could be equalised in favour of the sufferer. Since the Act requires modification so that the less beneficial term becomes not less favourable than the more beneficial, it is clear that equalisation is required to be upwards. It follows, therefore, that a series of compensating inequalities could be equalised in favour of the most beneficial position in each case in a series of leapfrogging complaints. The answer to the allegation that such a process is not justified where the overall benefit is more or less balanced lies, as we shall see, in the provision allowing a tribunal to dismiss the claim where the employer proves the existence of a "genuine material difference/factor."[54] He can argue, thereby, that the existence of the more beneficial holiday entitlement is a genuine material differ-

---

[50] *Macarthy's Ltd.* v. *Smith* [1979] I.R.L.R. 316. The decision of the European Court allowing such a claim under Art. 119 is reported in [1986] I.C.R. 672.

[51] [1979] I.R.L.R. 119 (C.A.).

[51a] *The Times*, December 17, 1988.

[52] Equal Pay (Equal Value) Amendment Regs. 1983; S.1 1983 No. 1797.

[53] s.1(2)(c) " . . . which, not being work in relation to which paragraph (a) or (b) above applies. . . . " But Art. 119 of the Treaty of Rome is not so limited.

[54] s.1(3).

ence between the man and the woman in turn justifying the less beneficial wage rate. Nevertheless, in *Hayward* v. *Cammell Laird Shipbuilders Ltd.*[55] every court up to the House of Lords took the view that comparison should be made with a package of terms. It seems that the Court of Appeal envisaged that the package should not include the entire contract but that where an aspect of remuneration was in issue, for instance, it should include all aspects of remuneration. As the Lord Chancellor pointed out, this involves reading the reference to a term as a reference to a package of terms and this makes nonsense of the express statutory provision for including "a term" in a contract which had not previously included that term found in the comparator. The House of Lords, accordingly, confirmed the former view that the statutory intention was to compare each term with its equivalent, or lack of it.

(a) *Like Work*

> "A woman is to be regarded as employed on like work with men if, but only if, her work and theirs is of the same or a broadly similar nature, and the differences (if any) between the things she does and the things they do are not of practical importance in relation to terms and conditions of employment; and accordingly, in comparing her work with theirs, regard should be had to the frequency or otherwise with which any such differences occur in practice as well as at the rates and extent of the differences."[55a]

There are several indications in this definition of intention to compare jobs somewhat broadly rather than by requiring precise similarity. In *Capper Pass Ltd.* v. *Lawton*[56] the E.A.T. held that a tribunal was to make a broad judgment without too minute an examination of differences. It suggested the inquiry should be in two stages. The first stage would pose the somewhat impressionistic question—said in *Dorothy Perkins Ltd.* v. *Dance*[57] to be based on the nature of the contract—whether the jobs were broadly similar. The second stage would examine actual differences, but even then only those of practical importance. A good example of a difference, excluded by this approach, would be an obligation on the comparator to perform a task that was rarely required, such as the occasional lifting of heavy loads.[58] In *Shields* v. *E. Coomes (Holdings) Ltd.*[59] male counter-hands were paid a higher hourly rate than females. The employer sought to establish that they were doing different work because they were required to act as a deterrent to rowdyism among the customers. Apart from the obviously discriminatory assumption that men do this better than women[60] this was clearly not a significant part of their job and the Court of Appeal so held.[61] In *Maidment and Hardacre* v. *Cooper and Co. (Birmingham) Ltd.*[62] Mrs. Hardacre did not set

---

[55] [1988] I.C.R. 464, (H.L.); [1987] I.R.L.R. 186 (C.A.); [1986] I.R.L.R. 287 (E.A.T.); [1984] I.R.L.R. 463.

[55a] E.P.A., s.1(4).

[56] [1977] I.C.R. 83.

[57] [1978] I.C.R. 760.

[58] See, *e.g. Electrolux Ltd.* v. *Hutchinson* [1977] I.C.R. 252.

[59] [1978] I.C.R. 1159.

[60] *Supra*, pp. 233–234.

[61] Lighter work can be held to be work of a different kind—*Noble* v. *David Gold and Son Ltd.* [1980] I.C.R. 543.

[62] [1978] I.R.L.R. 462.

her own machine whilst her comparator did. It was held that, though this took little time, it significantly added to the responsibility of the job. So far as Mrs. Maidment was concerned, the court held that normally it was not permissible to separate two jobs done by one person, even if separately remunerated, so as to equate a claimant performing only one of those jobs.

This decision raises the question of the extent of the aspects that can be taken into account. The definition quoted above speaks of what is done and this has been held to exclude the time at which it is done.[63] On the face of it, this would seem to exclude intangible factors such as experience, but the E.A.T. held at an early stage[64] that responsibility, if actually exercised, could produce a difference in the work done. Similarly, a trainee could not compare his work to that of a fully-qualified woman.[65] Mere experience not affecting what is actually done, therefore, does not distinguish the work[66] but qualification, experience and responsibility could all be taken into account as genuine material differences under subsection (3), even if they did not produce unlike work.

In deciding what degree of difference is significant it may be helpful to consider whether such a difference could reasonably be expected to produce different terms and conditions.[67] This actually is the question asked in the definition and, though it may seem no more than another way of asking if the job is the same,[68] it does provide a test, albeit an impressionistic one apart from the content of the job itself. An interesting device was adopted for dealing with minor differences not going to the nature of the job in *Electrolux Ltd.* v. *Hutchinson*[69] whereby it was suggested that terms could be amended rather than equated. This seems clearly outside the power conferred by the Equal Pay Act and, in any event, purports to take account of a difference which, by definition, does not activate the equality clause.

(b) *Work rated as equivalent*

The second basis of comparison refers to a situation in which the two jobs to be compared have been "given an equal value in terms of the demand made on a worker under various headings (for instance effort, skill, decision), on a study undertaken with a view to evaluating in those terms the jobs to be done," or which would have been given an equal value but for the setting of different weightings for men and women. This final qualification is interesting. Faults such as that referred to would normally invalidate the evaluation exercise so that it would not be used as a basis for comparison. Direct discrimination on grounds of sex does not, by reason of the qualification, have that effect.

It will be observed that the Act imposes no requirement for such evaluation to take place. The provision is an obvious compromise between acceptance of

---

[63] *Dugdale* v. *Kraft Foods Ltd.* [1976] I.R.L.R. 368.

[64] *Eaton Ltd.* v. *Nuttall* [1977] I.C.R. 272; *Edmunds* v. *Computer Services (South West) Ltd.* [1977] I.R.L.R. 359.

[65] *De Brito* v. *Standard Chartered Bank Ltd.* [1978] I.C.R. 650.

[66] See, *e.g. Pointon* v. *University of Sussex* [1974] I.R.L.R. 119.

[67] *Capper Pass Ltd.* v. *Lawton* [1977] I.C.R. 83. In *British Leyland Ltd.* v. *Powell* [1978] I.R.L.R. 57 it was suggested that it be asked whether the difference would affect a job evaluation. To most people, however, this would be a meaningless test.

[68] See *Capper Pass Ltd.* v. *Allan* [1980] I.C.R. 194.

[69] [1976] I.R.L.R. 410.

equal value as a basis for comparison and reliance solely on like work. In terms of eliminating sex discrimination "like work" is a relatively ineffective standard. It is a well-established fact that the industrial scene is full of jobs regarded either as men's, or women's, work. A particular job may be more demanding intellectually than another but be lower paid. No comparison on the basis of like work is possible, however, if one is solely done by men and the other solely by women. The National Coal Board (and the industrial tribunal which had to cope with the procedural problem) must have regretted the employment of a single male canteen assistant on night work at a higher rate than women which gave rise to the claim in *Sherwin* v. *N.C.B.*[70] but which, far more significantly, allowed 1,500 women canteen assistants to claim in *Thomas* v. *N.C.B.*[71] It should also be noted that no claim can proceed if the jobs are rated differently but the disparity in terms is out of all proportion to the difference.

There has been relatively little litigation on this standard but in what has occurred the question of what amounts to a valid job evaluation study has usually figured. There is no science of job evaluation and not only method, but factors tested and the weight given to them, may differ more or less according to the choice of the individual evaluator. This is no place to describe methods of evaluation, but a good idea of how the system might work is to be derived from *Bromley* v. *H. and J. Quick Ltd.*[72] Five assessment factors and 74 representative jobs were selected. Each of the jobs was separately assessed on all five factors, rather than comparing each factor separately across all the jobs. Twenty-three benchmark jobs were then selected and ranked in five grades. All jobs were then equated to a benchmark and so assigned to a grade. Two main objections were raised to this. The job of any particular individual may not be valued at all in the process but merely assigned to a grade because it equates with a benchmark. Secondly, as the Court of Appeal noted, there were no universally accepted criteria apart from the jobs themselves for measuring how much of a particular quality was involved, nor for deciding what weight ought to be attached to any such quality in any given job. If one took physical effort, for instance, the decision to give it six out of 10 in one job and eight out of 10 in another depended to a considerable extent on subjective judgment as did the question of the extent to which physical effort should compensate for the absence of significant quantities of some other qualities. The Court of Appeal acknowledged that the European Court, in *Rummler* v. *Dato Druck GmbH*[73] had required objective consideration of the job and its qualities. Dillon L.J. said, however, that every job evaluation was bound to involve value judgments which were subjective, or felt to be fair, so that within a generally objective assessment there would always be subjective elements. It seems that he thought these would be kept within tolerable limits if care was taken to ensure that they did not let in discrimination. He thought, nevertheless, that the evaluation process could conveniently be regarded as having to be "analytical" so that each job was assessed on the basis of the demand it made on the worker. Although Woolf

---

[70] [1978] I.R.L.R. 122.
[71] [1987] I.R.L.R. 451.
[72] [1988] I.C.R. 623.
[73] [1987] I.C.R. 774.

L.J. considered that the situation of benchmark jobs was not only acceptable but necessary to avoid the exercise becoming intolerably burdensome, all members of the Court of Appeal took the view that the jobs actually in question had not been factorised, at least before the appeal stage, sufficiently for it to be said that they had been analysed.

Care must be taken that a selected factor does not unjustifiably benefit one sex. In *Rummler* the European Court had considered unobjectionable a factor such as muscular effort or physical heaviness, provided that the job actually contained such an element. There was a chance, it acknowledged, of discrimination in the use of criteria based on the values of one sex, but the significant defect to avoid was valuation of the job in relation to its effect on men or women, rather than according to its nature whoever performed it. There is, incidentally, no specific limit on the qualities that are assessed. Those specified in the Act are merely examples.

With a bit of luck, this development will provide some impetus to tighten up the practice of job evaluation, even though it must be accepted that Dillon L.J. is right and that it will always contain subjective judgments. Before this development United Kingdom courts seem to have been satisfied if the exercise was a joint one, as it usually would be, and both sides had agreed to it as carried out, whether or not they had put it into practice.[74] In *Arnold* v. *Beecham Group Ltd.*[75] Browne-Wilkinson J. held that the evaluation exercise was only completed when both parties had accepted its conclusions.

(c) *Work of equal value*

It is not really surprising that the European Court was not satisfied with the compromise embodied in the second basis of comparison. It is clear that Article 119 was intended to achieve equality as a matter of right and was not satisfied by a standard which depended on whether third parties chose to carry out the assessment from which that right to equality sprang. In *Commission of the European Communities* v. *United Kingdom*[76] it upheld a complaint that the Equal Pay Act did not comply with the Equal Pay Directive[77] in that it did not entitle an employee to claim that her work was of equal value. Something approaching an equal value test could have been applied if "like work" had compared elements such as skill, rather than looking narrowly at the job content.[78] In consequence the Equal Pay Act was amended by statutory instrument to permit an individual worker to claim that her work is "in terms of the demands made on her (for instance under such headings as effort, skill and decision)" of equal value to that of a man in the same employment. Section 1(2)(c) appears to preclude this claim if the claim could be based on one of the other two grounds but the House of Lords held that this only applied if the actual comparator selected fell within the other heads.[79] Presumably the tribunal, in determining whether there is a prima facie case and in ultimately assessing the validity of the evaluation, should apply the

---

[74] *O'Brien* v. *Sim-Chem Ltd.* [1980] I.R.L.R. 373 (H.L.).
[75] [1982] I.R.L.R. 307.
[76] [1982] I.C.R. 578.
[77] Directive 75/117.
[78] See Lord Denning M.R. in *Shields* v. *E. Coomes (Holdings) Ltd.* [1978] I.C.R. 1159; compare *Macarthy's Ltd.* v. *Smith* [1979] I.C.R. 785, and see Simpson, (1980) 43 M.L.R. 209.
[79] *Pickstone* v. *Freemans plc* [1988] I.R.L.R. 357.

considerations set out by the Court of Appeal in *Bromley* v. *Quick*.[80] If a job evaluation exercise produces a job value for the claimant higher than that for the comparator it is unlikely, in practice, that the claimant will be subjected to a contractual disadvantage. Therefore, the question whether a claim could be made if the evaluation was not equal was unlikely to be raised. Had it been the answer seems likely to have been that it could not. This question is much more likely in the case of a claim for equality where there has been no evaluation but it appears to the tribunal likely that the result of an evaluation will be to place a higher value on the job of the claimant than of the comparator (or, the evaluation ordered by the tribunal has actually produced that result and the tribunal has to decide the success of the application). The European Court has decided, however, that Article 119 requires equalisation of terms in favour of a job of unequal, but higher, value.[81] This would seem likely to produce the same conclusion in respect of section 1(2)(c) of the Equal Pay Act in view of the principle that ambiguity should be interpreted in accordance with Community Law.

The Equal Pay (Amendment) Regulations 1983[82] came into effect on January 1, 1984. They had actually been approved by the House of Commons before the decision of the E.C.J. in *Commission of the European Communities* v. *United Kingdom*[83] but had been withdrawn for amendment thereafter. The House of Lords accepted a motion that they be approved "but this House believes that the regulations do not adequately reflect the 1982 decision of the European Court of Justice and Article 1 of the EEC Equal Pay Directive of 1975." The regulations were accompanied by changes in industrial tribunal procedure rules to accommodate the new system.[84] The resultant procedure for dealing with equal value claims is slow and clumsy. This may not be entirely the fault of the legislation. Assignment of the work to the Central Arbitration Committee had been considered but rejected, no doubt partly because the Chairman of the C.A.C. argued that its function was properly confined to collective applications and partly because the system of C.A.C. arbitration had been regarded as inflationary. The result of this rejection, however, has been to emphasise the exclusion from consideration of collective implications on the wider industrial relations situation. With the repeal of section 3 of the Equal Pay Act there is no scope for collective application to amend collective agreements. The European Court of Justice had, anyway, ruled[85] that the United Kingdom was in breach of its obligation to provide mechanism for individual application to amend collective agreements. This shortcoming was dealt with, unsatisfactorily and inadequately in the Sex Discrimination Act 1986.[86]

Equal value claims are taken to industrial tribunals in the same way as any other equal pay claim, and ACAS may provide conciliation. If this fails the tribunal may grant an adjournment if the parties agree, so that they may seek

---

[80] *Supra.* But see *McGregor* v. *GMBATU* [1987] I.C.R. 505.
[81] *Murphy and Others* v. *Bord Telecom Eireann* [1988] I.R.L.R. 267.
[82] (S.I. 1983 No. 1794).
[83] *Supra.*
[84] The Industrial Tribunals (Rules of Procedure) (Equal Value Amendment) Regulations 1983 (S.I. 1983 No. 1807).
[85] *Commission of the European Communities (No. 2)* v. *United Kingdom* [1984] I.R.L.R.29.
[86] s.6. *infra*, p. 268.

a settlement. Whether this takes place or not, either party may apply for the tribunal to consider the likelihood of success of a defence of "genuine material factor."[87] The tribunal may hear such an application if it considers that it is appropriate to do so, having regard to the duty to clarify the issues and conduct the hearing informally.[88]

The intention was that tribunals should only use this stage to reject a claim on the basis of this defence in clear-cut cases.[89] In somewhat the same way, in a clear case where it is able to consider at this preliminary stage that there are no reasonable grounds for determining that the work is of equal value the tribunal may so determine.[90] It is bound to dismiss the application if a non-discriminatory job evaluation has given the job a different value.[91] There is, of course, a right to appeal to the E.A.T. from dismissal of a claim at this stage, although the decision would usually be one of fact so that the appeal would only succeed on the ground of perversity.

If the tribunal does not dispose of the claim at this stage it is referred to an independent expert who is a member of a panel maintained by ACAS. This panel was originally compiled after interview, following advertisement. Its best members are normally far too busy to afford the surprising amount of time necessary to conduct each assessment and, accordingly, this stage is a slow one.[92] The tribunal may give the expert instructions on how to act. The expert must consider all information supplied and all relevant representations and must send the parties a written summary thereof for comment before drawing up his report. The expert must then report to the tribunal, including a copy of this summary and giving his reason for his conclusions.

The tribunal may reject the expert's report on the grounds:

(a) that the expert has not complied with a stipulation in the requirement to him; or

(b) that the conclusion is one that he could not reasonably have arrived at; or,

(c) for some other reason (other than its disagreement with the report) it is unsatisfactory.

Christopher McCrudden[93] concludes that a report may also be rejected on the grounds that it is discriminatory.

To assist in this process the tribunal may, at any time after receiving the report, require the expert to confirm in writing any matter contained in his report. The tribunal may also permit the parties to call evidence and cross-examine on any matter relevant to the admission of the report. Either party, or the tribunal, may call the expert who may be cross-examined and, after

---

[87] *Infra*; see, *Reed Packaging Ltd.* v. *Boozer* [1988] I.R.L.R. 333, pp. 264–266.

[88] But the tribunal may not, as a preliminary point, determine whether subs. 1(3) has been satisfied *R.* v. *Secretary of State for Social Services ex p. Clarke* [1988] I.R.L.R. 22.

[89] But see *Forex Neptune Ltd.* v. *Miller* [1987] I.C.R. 170.

[90] See *Neil* v. *Ford Motor Co. Ltd.* [1984] I.R.L.R. 339 (I.T.).

[91] *Bromley* v. *H. and J. Quick Ltd.* [1988] I.C.R. 623; see E.A.T. [1987] I.R.L.R. 456. But, query if the applicant's job had been given a higher value.

[92] Although either party may apply to the tribunal if the report of the expert has not been received in six weeks(!) and the tribunal may ask for an explanation if of the opinion that there is likely to have been undue delay. In the light of that explanation the tribunal may replace that expert with another.

[93] [1984] 13 I.L.J. at p. 55.

notice, may call one expert witness on the question upon which the expert was asked to report.

If the report, or a substitute for a rejected report, is admitted the tribunal must then determine, if relevant, the evidence of "a genuine material factor" defence. In *Forex Neptune (Overseas) Ltd.* v. *Miller*[94] the defence was considered at the preliminary stage in respect of one of three applicants whom the employer conceded to be employed on like work and to two whose claims were for equal value. The defence was rejected and the two equal value claims were referred to an independent expert. The E.A.T. held that this procedure was within the tribunal's procedural discretion. Presumably the same question could have been raised again when the report was received. In finally deciding the question no evidence or cross-examination may be addressed to matters of fact upon which the expert's report is based, unless that evidence is relevant to the material factor defence or the expert has been prevented by a party's refusal to supply information from reaching a conclusion.

Defences to equal pay claims

An equality clause in the contract of employment shall not operate:

(a) in relation to terms affected by compliance with the laws regulating the employment of women; or,

(b) in relation to terms affecting special treatment in connection with pregnancy or childbirth; or

(c) in relation to terms related to death or retirement, or to any decision made in connection with retirement.[95]

Death or retirement

The exclusion of terms relating to death or retirement has caused most problems because of its potential to conflict with European Community Law. As we have seen, Article 119 of the Treaty of Rome requires equal pay and it has been held that this applies to the benefits of a private pension scheme. The benefits of a State social security pension scheme are, however, not remuneration within the meaning of the Article.[96] The actual benefits of a private pension scheme, therefore, must be non-discriminatory. Access to the pension scheme, however, will normally be by way of retirement so as to be excluded from the Equal Pay Act. The Equal Treatment Directive[97] requires equal treatment of men and women as regards access to employment, including promotion, vocational training, and working conditions. It is envisaged that Social Security arrangements will be included, subject to definition which has not yet occurred. Specifically, the Directive includes a guarantee of non-discrimination in provisions relating to dismissal. In *Marshall* v. *Southampton and South West Hampshire Area Health Authority*[98] the European Court held that compulsory retirement was a form of dismissal within Article 5 of the Directive.

---

[94] [1987] I.C.R. 170.
[95] E.P.A. 1970, s.6 (1A); and see S.D.A. 1975, s.6(4).
[96] *Bilka-Kaufhaus GmbH* v. *Weber von Hartz* [1987] I.C.R. 110.
[97] 76/207 of February 9, 1976.
[98] [1986] I.R.L.R. 140.

Article 119 is directly enforceable by any employee so that an aspect of retirement amounting to remuneration falls within it and must be equal. The Directive is, however, addressed to the Government of the State and binds only that Government. In *Marshall* v. *Southampton and South West Hampshire Area Health Authority*[99] the European Court held that the State was bound as an employer so that employees of state authorities, among which the Court of Appeal had accepted the National Health Service, were entitled to enforce the Directive. In that case a retirement scheme provided for women to retire at 60 and men at 65. The applicant, accordingly, could successfully claim that this was discrimination contrary to Article 5 of the Directive regardless of any exclusionary effect in United Kingdom statute law. The problem for United Kingdom courts has been to decide how far to go in interpreting the exclusion in respect of death and retirement so as to avoid a conflict with Community law. The problem is not acute if the applicant may rely on both United Kingdom and Community law, since the court may say that, whereas United Kingdom legislation grants no right, Community law does.[1] The courts would clearly prefer not to find a conflict. In *Garland* v. *British Rail Engineering Ltd.*[2] the Court of Appeal had held that differences in travel concessions between retired male and female employees were excluded from the operation of the Equal Pay Act by the retirement exception. The European Court[3] held that the differences were discrimination in pay contrary to Article 119. It commented that United Kingdom legislation should be construed, so far as possible, so as not to be inconsistent with the Treaty of Rome. In its view, section 6 referred only to provisions *consequent on* retirement and not *about* retirement. The House of Lords[4] accepted that view and construed section 61(4) of the Sex Discrimination Act in that limited fashion.[5] In *Roberts* v. *Cleveland Area Health Authority*,[6] however, the Court of Appeal had taken the opposite view holding that the words "in relation to" clearly meant "about." The House of Lords adopted the latter view in *Duke* v. *Reliance Systems Ltd.*[7] in which the applicant was unable to rely on Community law. In the view of the House of Lords the Equal Pay Act was not drafted to comply with the terms of the Directive and it was not open to a British court to distort its provisions so that it should apply. It held that a policy of dismissing women at 60 and men at 65 was clearly discriminatory within the Sex Discrimination Act but that Act did not apply to it because it was a "provision in relation to . . . retirement" within section 6(4). In its view, the same would be true of discriminatory benefits under a retirement scheme. Although it did not say so it presumably intended that the interpret-

---

[99] [1986] I.R.L.R. 140.

[1] *Pickstone* v. *Freemans plc* [1987] I.R.L.R. 218 (C.A.). The House of Lords construed U.K. law as consistent with EC law [1988] I.R.L.R. 357.

[2] [1979] I.R.L.R. 244.

[3] [1982] I.C.R. 420.

[4] [1982] I.R.L.R. 257.

[5] See also *Worringham and Humphreys* v. *Lloyds Bank Ltd.* [1981] I.R.L.R. 178 (E.C.J.); [1982] I.R.L.R. 74 (C.A.).

[6] [1979] I.L.R. 558, and see *Roberts* v. *Tate and Lyle Industries Ltd.* [1983] I.L.R. 521 (E.A.T.), with which, for other reasons, the European Court did not interfere—[1986] I.R.L.R. 150.

[7] [1988] I.C.R. 339 upholding the Court of Appeal [1987] I.R.L.R. 139.

ation could not vary because, in the second situation, there would be a right of complaint under Article 119. It seems, therefore, that current authority favours a wide interpretation of the exclusion in the United Kingdom statute law so that discrimination relating to retirement is best challenged under Community law, bearing in mind that the right to challenge unequal opportunity, other than remuneration, is confined to the employees of State agencies.

A statutory exception to the retirement exclusion, both in the Equal Pay Act and the Sex Discrimination Act, was made in 1986, in terms similar to the Directive, as a result of the decision in *Marshall* v. *Southampton A.H.A.*[8] Section 6 of the Equal Pay Act is now in the following terms:

> "An equality clause
>   (a) shall operate in relation to terms relating to membership of an occupational pension scheme (within the meaning of the Social Security Act 1975) so far as those terms relate to any matter in respect of which the scheme has to conform with the equal access requirement of Part II of that Act; but
>   (b) subject to this, shall not operate in relation to terms related to death or retirement, or to any provisions made in connection with death or retirement *other than a term or provision which, in relation to retirement, affords access to opportunities for promotion, transfer or training or provides for a woman's dismissal or demotion*"

(The corresponding qualification to the exclusion in (b) in the Sex Discrimination Act is similar though it uses considerably more words.)

The portion in italics clearly is intended to comply with the terms of the Equal Treatment Directive and should be construed accordingly. "Dismissal," for instance, should include compulsory retirement. This application is, of course, available to all claimants and not merely those entitled to direct application of the Directive.

Genuine material factor

All differences falling within the scope of the Equal Pay Act may be justified on proof by the respondent that the difference is genuinely due to a material factor which is not a difference of sex. The Act provides that in claims based on like work and job evaluation the factor must be a material *difference*. The distinction that this seemed likely to create has, however, disappeared.[9] The burden of proof rests upon the balance of probabilities.[10] The employer must justify the variation which actually exists, not merely some variation[11] and the reason must be genuine in the sense of not being a pretext.[12]

---

[8] *Supra.*
[9] *Infra.*
[10] *National Vulcan, etc. Group* v. *Wade* [1978] I.C.R. 800 (C.A.); *Methuen* v. *Cow Industrial Polymers Ltd.* (1980) I.R.L.R. 289 (C.A.); *McGregor* v. *GMBATU* [1987] I.C.R. 505. The matter should not be taken as a preliminary issue—*R.* v. *Secretary of State for Social Services ex p. Clarke* [1988] I.R.L.R. 22.
[11] *National Coal Board* v. *Sherwin* [1978] I.C.R. 700 (E.A.T.).
[12] See, *e.g. NAAFI* v. *Varley* [1977] I.C.R. 11.

Justification requires that the means chosen and constituting the difference:

(a) correspond to the real need of the undertaking;
(b) are appropriate to (and, now, actually) achieve the objective; and
(c) are necessary.[13]

In *Rainey* v. *Greater Glasgow Health Board*[14] Lord Keith of Kinkel, delivering the judgment of the House of Lords, said that there was no significant distinction of principle between the need to demonstrate objectively justified grounds of difference and the need to justify a requirement or condition in order to avoid a claim of indirect discrimination. This decision also added the requirement, in addition to necessity, that the difference must be shown actually to achieve its objective. Very similarly, in *Bilka-Kaufhaus GmbH* v. *Weber von Hartz*[15] the European Court, considering justification, on economic grounds, for departure from the obligation imposed by Article 119, said that objective economic grounds relating to the management of the undertaking must exist, which, in practice, are necessary and in proportion to the objectives pursued by the employer. The means must correspond to a real need, be appropriate to the objective and necessary to achieve it.

In *Clay Cross (Quarry Services) Ltd.* v. *Fletcher*[16] the Court of Appeal, considering what was then required to be a material *difference*, (the formal insistence on a "difference" remains in the Act, as it then did, in respect of the work and job evaluation claims, but not as regards equal value claims) held that the difference must relate to the "personal equation" of the worker. In *Rainey* v. *Greater Glasgow Health Board*,[17] however, the House of Lords held that this was unduly restrictive. Its view relied heavily on *Bilka-Kaufhaus*[18] to conclude that the difference may go beyond purely personal factors, such as skill, experience or training, to take account of the economic objectives affecting efficient conduct of the business or other activity. It went even further than this, however, to hold that though *Bilka-Kaufhaus* referred to "economic grounds" it did not mean thereby to exclude other grounds such as administrative efficiency in a concern not engaged in commerce or business. It seems likely that use of the word "factor" had been intended to broaden the scope of justification to the same extent in equal value claims and it must now follow that "material difference" and "material factor" have the same meaning.

In *Rainey* the factor which the House of Lords was prepared to take into account was the need, if the service was to be maintained at a viable level, of attracting to it employees currently enjoying higher rates of pay than those already in the service. This was precisely the difference which had been excluded from consideration in *Clay Cross* v. *Fletcher*. It has also been held that a material difference may be found between full and part-time employment justifying a different hourly rate on the ground that there is less eco-

---

[13] *Jenkins* v. *Kingsgate (Clothing Productions) Ltd. (No. 2)* [1981] I.C.R. 715.
[14] [1987] I.R.L.R. 26 (H.L.).
[15] [1987] I.C.R. 110.
[16] [1979] I.C.R. 1.
[17] *Supra.*
[18] *Supra.*

nomic advantage in the part-time use of equipment.[19] It was held in *ARW Transformers Ltd.* v. *Cupples*[20] that length of experience can constitute a material difference if there is a system for its recognition—that is to say, sufficient to make it both genuine and material. Differences often arise from a desire to maintain a particular employee's former advantages in a new job and this may be institutionalised by collective agreement, adopting a device known as "red-circling." In this situation a group of employees may be separately defined as enjoying rates of pay in excess of those paid to others in their job grade. The need to do this usually arises when a job regrading has abolished a high grade. The need is, of course, to ensure not merely that current differentials are retained but that when, in future, the new grade receives an increase those in the red circle receive a commensurate rise to maintain the differential.[21] The justification will fail if it is possible to include new members in the red circle,[22] or if the reason for the former differential was itself discriminatory. The justifying factor must not itself be a difference of sex, either directly or indirectly.[23]

In *Jenkins* v. *Kingsgate (Clothing Productions) Ltd.*[24] the European Court appeared to limit the scope of Article 119 by excluding unintentional indirect discrimination without expressly mentioning intentional indirect discrimination. The E.A.T.[25] considered that the Equal Pay Act should be viewed as part of a package of anti-discrimination legislation intended to outlaw all types of indirect discrimination. It is submitted that if objectively necessary factors constitute justification on economic grounds and this permits, for instance, a policy of discouraging part-time employees it is hardly feasible to extend the prohibition on discrimination to unintentional indirect discrimination.[26]

Time limits

Claims may be made either by a disadvantaged employee, an employer or the Secretary of State for Employment.[27] The claim must normally be made within six months of the applicant having been in the employment to which it relates,[28] but this does not apply to a claim arising from contraventions of a term modified by the equality clause or a dispute as to the effect of an equality clause. No payment in respect of arrears of remuneration or damages may be awarded in respect of a period more than two years before the date when proceedings were instituted, but this does not prevent a tribunal hearing a com-

---

[19] *Jenkins* v. *Kingsgate (Clothing Products) Ltd.* [1981] I.R.L.R. 228; *Handley* v. *H. Mono Ltd.* [1978] I.R.L.R. 534. But see *Durrant* v. *North Yorkshire A.H.A.* [1979] I.R.L.R. 401 where a comparison between full- and part-time employees failed on the basis of dissimilarity. Consider also the possibility of a claim for indirect discrimination—though not in respect of remuneration—in such a case.

[20] [1977] I.R.L.R. 227, see also *De Brito* v. *Standard Chartered Bank Ltd.* [1978] I.C.R. 650.

[21] *Snoxell* v. *Vauxhall Motors* [1977] I.C.R. 700; *Farthing* v. *Ministry of Defence* [1980] I.R.L.R. 402.

[22] *United Biscuits Ltd.* v. *Young* [1978] I.R.L.R. 15.

[23] *Sun Alliance and London Insurance Ltd.* v. *Dudman* [1978] I.C.R. 551.

[24] [1981] I.C.R. 592.

[25] [1981] I.R.L.R. 388.

[26] See *Bilka-Kaufhaus GmbH* v. *Weber von Hartz, supra.* A material difference or factor ceases to justify a difference when the factor ceases to exist—*Benveniste* v. *University of Southampton, Times,* December 17, 1988.

[27] s.2.

[28] s.2(4).

plaint relating to a situation before that time.[29] The effect of this is that there is no time limit on a claim under the Equal Pay Act by an employee still in the employment to which the claim relates.

Discrimination in collective agreements

Before its repeal in 1986 section 3 of the Equal Pay Act permitted application by a party to a collective agreement (or the Secretary of State in the case of a Wages Council award), to the Central Arbitration Committee, for rectification of any provision applying specifically to men only, or to women only. Initially, the C.A.C. rectified an agreement whenever it produced such discrimination in practice, but in *R. v. Central Arbitration Committee ex p. Hy-Mac Ltd.*[30] a Divisional Court held that "specifically to men only or to women only" could only refer to an agreement containing overt discrimination. It must follow also that the section could not apply even to overt, but indirect, discrimination. That decision reduced the usefulness of the jurisdiction almost to non-existence and it was repealed by the Sex Discrimination Act 1986. Just before that repeal took effect the C.A.C., by a majority, held[31] that Article 119, the effect of which had not been considered in *Hy-Mac*, applied to a claim in respect of indirect discrimination against women by the denial of a mortgage relief scheme to part-time employees. That is, of course, plainly so. The real question is whether the C.A.C. had jurisdiction to apply Article 119. The view of the C.A.C. was that it had jurisdiction to deal with the rectification of collective agreements producing inequality between men and women and, indeed, since the 1986 Act had not taken effect, the only jurisdiction. *Hy-Mac* had not excluded the jurisdiction to apply Article 119 because it had never considered the effect of that Article. The contrary argument is that the jurisdiction of the C.A.C. is derived from statute and cannot be extended. The problem with this is that there would be no jurisdiction to apply Article 119 to any more confined statutory definition of the powers of a tribunal. A higher court, on appeal, would be bound to consider that the tribunal had no jurisdiction and would not be entitled, of its own appellate jurisdiction to extend the initial jurisdiction. Browne-Wilkinson J. in *Albion Shipping Agency v. Arnold*[32] had pointed out the chaotic result if an applicant to an industrial tribunal had to alternate between it and the High Court in order to secure a point of Community law, not included in the statutory tribunal's jurisdiction. The Divisional Court, in *R. v. Central Arbitration Committee ex p. Norwich Union Insurance Group plc*[33] eventually seems to have held that a trade union does not acquire rights under Article 119, ignoring the possibility that it may be acting on behalf of individuals who do, or, alternatively, that it is normal for Community law to leave to national law the procedure by which individual rights are enforced. The Court otherwise seems, tentatively to accept that a tribunal such as the C.A.C. might apply the

---

[29] *British Railways Board v. Paul* [1988] I.R.L.R. 20.
[30] [1979] I.R.L.R. 461.
[31] *Norwich Union Insurance Group and ASTMS*, (Award No. 87/2). The author must declare an interest in the argument that follows.
[32] [1982] I.C.R. 22 at 30.
[33] Unreported. Subsequently employer and union agreed to extend the scheme to part-time employees.

article. The decision is of little value as a precedent since the judge indicated that he had not known much about Community law before the arguments in the case.

This jurisdiction was replaced by an individual's right to complain to an industrial tribunal.[34] The change came about as a result of the decision of the European Court in *Commission of the European Communities* v. *United Kingdom*[35] that the United Kingdom had failed to comply with Directive 76/207 within the time prescribed, *inter alia*, because there was no legislative provision by which an individual could seek to have a collective agreement declared void on the ground that it failed to provide equal treatment for men and women as regards access to employment, vocational training, promotion and working conditions. It is unfortunate that, in seeking to prescribe a right of individual complaint, the United Kingdom found it desirable to abolish the right of collective complaint. In the *Norwich Union* case, for instance, the trade union had pointed out that individual women could then have complained of indirect sex discrimination under the Sex Discrimination Act but were afraid to do so because they understood that if they were successful the cost of admitting them to the scheme would be recovered by reducing the benefits available to those currently entitled to participate. The system introduced in 1986[36] extends to collective agreements the provisions of the Sex Discrimination Act 1975[37] rendering void any term of a contract, the inclusion of which renders the making of the contract unlawful unless the discrimination is against a party to the contract, in which circumstance the term is unenforceable against that party. This is extended to the terms of a collective agreement whether or not the agreement is intended to be legally enforceable; to any rule made by an employer for application to all or any of his employees or applicants for employment; and to any rule by any organisation of workers, or employers or those who carry out a profession or trade or which grants authorisation or qualification for a profession or trade for application to its members, prospective members or those upon whom it confers authorisation or qualification.

There is power to amend a contract and, therefore, in theory now, a collective agreement where the term is unenforceable, but not where it is void. The term is only unenforceable where it discriminates against a party to the contract or collective agreement. In the case of a collective agreement it is the trade union which is the party to the agreement and the trade union cannot, of course, be subject to discrimination. Perhaps this disability could be avoided by declaring the individual worker party to it since this would have no effect on the absence of its legal enforceability. It is unlikely to occur in practice if only because employers are unlikely to agree to it and trade unions are unlikely to desire expressly to confer individual rights to seek amendments of collective agreements. It seems clear, therefore, that power to amend collective agreements has, in practice, disappeared. The only right is to seek to render the discriminatory term entirely void which would seem to enhance the

---

[34] S.D.A. 1986, s.6. s.77(5) of the S.D.A. 1975 speaks of a right for any person interested in the contract and this, presumably, now extends to any person interested in the collective agreement. But a trade union is not a person and its officials are not "interested."
[35] [1984] I.R.L.R. 29.
[36] S.D.A. 1986, s.6.
[37] s.77.

deterrent effect upon individual action. It must be assumed that the United Kingdom Government has interpreted the words "shall be, or may be declared, null and void or may be amended" in Directive 76/207 as permitting an alternative, but it should have realised that the choice of declaring an unenforceable agreement void was not likely to be readily understood by individual applicants. It can still be argued, therefore, that the 1986 amendment does not fulfil the obligation in Article 5(2)(c) of the Directive since no steps have been taken to ensure that labour and management shall be requested to undertake revision of a collective agreement. It is unlikely that the European Court would hold a collective agreement not to be a provision "similar" to a "law, regulation [or] administrative provision" simply because it was unenforceable.

Pregnancy

(a) *Dismissal*

If the reason, or principal reason, for dismissal is that the employee is pregnant, or any other reason connected with her pregnancy, the dismissal will be unfair unless one of two statutory situations pertains. These are:

(a) that the reason for the dismissal is that at the effective date of termination the employee is or will have become, because of her pregnancy, incapable of adequately doing the work which she was employed to do;

(b) that because of her pregnancy she cannot or will not be able to continue after that date to do that work without contravention (either by her or by her employer) of a duty or restriction imposed by or under any enactment.[38]

In *Brown* v. *Stockton Borough Council*[39] the employee was selected for dismissal for redundancy when the job in which she was employed ended. She was not retained to participate in a new job scheme because she was pregnant and it was anticipated that she would take maternity leave shortly after the start of that scheme. The House of Lords, reversing the Court of Appeal, held that the reason for the dismissal was directly connected with pregnancy. Pregnancy, it was said, was the real reason for the selection.

The exceptions are remarkably widely phrased. In *Martin* v. *B.S.C. Footwear (Supplies) Ltd.*[40] an industrial tribunal held that "suitable" related to the woman's pregnant condition and health as well as to skill, experience and qualifications. "Available" means the job should exist or be made to exist within the given staffing complement. An employer, it was said, is under no obligation to modify a woman's existing job to meet her requirements, nor to create a job. The first was subject to an interesting industrial tribunal decision in *Elegbede* v. *The Wellcome Foundation Limited*.[41] The employee had been dismissed on grounds of unfitness for work due to hypertension brought on by pregnancy. The industrial tribunal held that the dismissal was due to incapacity because of hypertension and was not "because of her pregnancy" within

---

[38] s.60(1)(*a*) and (*b*). Incapacity may arise from any reason, e.g. sickness connected with pregnancy—*Grimsby Carpet Co.* v. *Bedford* [1987] I.R.L.R. 438.

[39] [1988] I.C.R. 413 (H.L.).

[40] [1978] I.R.L.R. 95.

[41] [1977] I.R.L.R. 383.

the meaning of exception (a) above. On the other hand, the tribunal held, the dismissal was by reason of something connected with her pregnancy within the meaning of the initial provision rendering the dismissal unfair. In other words, a dismissal can be connected with pregnancy but not be because of pregnancy.

The width of the exceptions, though surprising, may well not have any very considerable effect because if they are invoked statute provides substantial protection for the employee. In the first place, even if the reason for the dismissal falls within one of the exceptions, the dismissal will still be unfair if the employer or any successor of his has a suitable available vacancy and neglects to engage the dismissed employee under a new contract of employment in that vacant post before, or on, the effective date of termination. Secondly, a dismissal, connected with the employee's pregnancy but rendered fair because it falls within one of the two exceptions mentioned, will not deprive the employee of her maternity rights, including the right to return to work, whatever the date at which the dismissal took place.[42]

Where an employee is absent because of pregnancy or confinement a replacement will often have to be provided. The employee so absent will normally now have a statutory right to return to her former employment after the permitted period of absence.[43] It is more than ever likely that such a replacement will be regarded as temporary. If the temporary does not remain in continuous employment for two years he or she will, of course, acquire no statutory right to claim an unfair dismissal. In other cases certain modifications apply to the normal process of determination of the nature of the dismissal.[44]

Where an employer informs an employee in writing, upon engagement, that his or her employment will be terminated on the return to work of another employee who is, or will be, absent wholly or partly because of pregnancy or confinement and dismisses the first-mentioned employee in order to give work to the other, then the dismissal will be regarded as having been for a substantial reason such as to justify the dismissal. This means that a claim for unfair dismissal could still succeed on the basis that, though such a substantial reason existed, it was not reasonable in all the circumstances for the employer to have treated it as a reason for dismissal. It may be suggested, for instance, that an employer with a large number of female employees might reasonably be expected to take steps to see whether another temporary vacancy which the replacement might fill in turn was imminent.

Similar provisions apply to dismissal of a temporary replacement for an employee compulsorily suspended for medical reasons.[45]

(b) *Time off work*

In addition to any contractual rights in this respect an employee who is pregnant and who has, on the advice of a doctor, midwife or registered health visitor, made an appointment to attend for ante-natal care has the right not unreasonably to be refused paid time off during working hours to enable her

---

[42] 1978 Act, s.33(4).

[43] *Infra*, pp. 272–273.

[44] 1978 Act, s.61. These will, of course, only apply to a temporary replacing several pregnant women in succession.

[45] 1978 Act, s.61(2).

to keep the appointment. In the case of appointments after the first one the employer is entitled to request a certificate of pregnancy and documentary evidence of the appointment. The employee is entitled to complain to an industrial tribunal within three months of the date of the appointment of an unreasonable refusal of time off and the tribunal may order payment of the amount which would have been due had permission been granted.[46]

Maternity leave and payment

An employee with not less than two years' continuous employment[47] who is absent from work wholly or partly because of pregnancy or confinement is entitled to full maternity payment and, within a specified time, to return to work[48] provided she remains *in employment* until immediately before the beginning of the eleventh week before the expected week of confinement.[49] There is no need for her actually to remain at work until that time.[50]

In order to qualify the employee should inform her employer in writing, at least 21 days before her absence begins or, if this is not reasonably practicable, as soon as is reasonably practicable, that she will be, or is, absent from work wholly or partly because of pregnancy or confinement and, in the case of the right to return to work, that she intends to return to work with her employer.[51] This information is not in itself to be construed as a resignation by the employee.[52] In addition, she must, if requested by her employer to do so, produce for his inspection a certificate from a registered medical practitioner or a certified midwife indicating the expected week of her confinement.[53] An employee who terminates her own employment, or who is dismissed before the beginning of the eleventh week before the expected week of confinement, will normally lose her claim under these provisions unless the dismissal is for a reason falling within section 60.[54]

Maternity Payment

As from April 6, 1987 maternity payment is administered by the employer and time limits and qualifications for benefit have been amended.[55] Payment is normally due for a period not exceeding 18 weeks nor continuing beyond the eleventh week following the expected week of confinement. The period of payment normally starts at the beginning of the eleventh week before the expected week of confinement. It will commence later than this where the woman gave notice that she would stop work, and did stop work, later than that week, or having given such notice, is confined before it expires. It will

---

[46] s.31A inserted by E.A. 1980, s.13.

[47] E.P.C.A., s.33(3)(*b*).

[48] s.33(1).

[49] s.33(3)(*b*).

[50] *Satchwell Sunvic Ltd.* v. *Secretary of State for Employment* ([1979] I.R.L.R. 455; *Secretary of State for Employment* v. *Doulton Sanitary Ware Ltd.* [1981] I.R.L.R. 477).

[51] s.33(3)(*c*). As to what is reasonably practicable see *Nu-Swift International Ltd.* v. *Mallison* [1978] I.C.R. 157. In respect of maternity pay alone the notice may be oral unless the employer requires it in writing.

[52] *Hughes* v. *Gwynedd A.H.A.* [1978] I.C.R. 161.

[53] s.33(5).

[54] See *supra*, p. 269.

[55] Social Security Act 1986 and Statutory Maternity Pay (General) Regulations 1986 (S.I. 86/1960).

never start later than the sixth week before confinement. Payment may start earlier than the eleventh week if the woman is actually confined at an earlier date.

There are two rates of maternity payment. The higher rate is nine-tenths of normal weekly earnings for the period of eight weeks immediately preceding the fourteenth week before the expected date of confinement. This is payable to a woman with two years' continuous employment with any employer liable to make the payment to her.[56] In all other circumstances a woman entitled to statutory maternity payment is entitled to the lower rate specified by statutory instrument from time to time and which, in 1986, was £32.85 per week. Payment is made by the employer who may recover a specified proportion of it in the same way as recovery of sick pay under the Statutory Sick Pay Scheme. No day falling within the maternity pay period shall be treated as a day of unemployment or incapacity for work for the purpose of determining Social Security benefits.[57]

If an employer is adjudicated liable to make maternity payments and fails to do so the liability becomes that of the Secretary of State.[58] The same applies from the first week in which an employer becomes insolvent.

Right to return

The second of the statutory maternity rights is the right for the employee to return to work at the conclusion of the statutorily permitted period of absence. Section 45(1) provides that the employee has a right to return to work with her original employer or his successor at any time before the end of the period of 29 weeks, beginning with the week in which the date of confinement falls, in the job in which she was employed under the original contract of employment, and on terms and conditions not less favourable than those which would have been applicable to her if she had not been so absent. If the employee also had a contractual right to return she may take advantage of whichever of the statutory or contractual rights is in any particular respect the more favourable. The E.A.T. held, however, in *Bovey* v. *Board of Governors of the Hospital for Sick Children*[59] that this did not mean that statutory and contractual rights could be intermingled in any favourable permutation.[60] Nevertheless, this provision has an effect not anticipated by the legislation in 1978, accustomed as it was to the concept of statutory provisions steadily improving the rights of the employee. Some employees will still possess contractual statements of terms and conditions of employment indicating that their maternity rights are as stated in either the 1975 or 1978 Acts. Employees who reject any attempt to reissue these statements amending the reference to the Employment Act 1980 will be entitled to rely on the contractually entrenched and more beneficial provisions of the earlier legislation.

It is suggested that it may be assumed that the use of the word "original" means that the employee who has accepted a suitable alternative offer of employment—made in a situation where she cannot adequately continue to

---

[56] Social Security Act 1986, s.48.
[57] *Ibid.*, Sched. IV, para. 11.
[58] S.I. 1986 No. 1960, Reg. 7.
[59] [1978] I.C.R. 934.
[60] A point apparently not noticed in *Kolfor Plant Ltd.* v. *Wright* [1982] I.R.L.R. 311 (E.A.T. Scotland) when it was said that contract might alter the requirement for giving notice.

perform her original work or such continuous performance would be a breach of a statutory obligation is entitled to return to the job she had before the acceptance of such an alternative. The Act states specifically that "terms and conditions not less favourable than those which would have been applicable to her if she had not been so absent" means, as regards seniority, pension rights and other similar rights, that the period or periods of employment prior to the employee's absence shall be regarded as continuous with her employment following that absence.[61] In fact, there is rather more to be said on the subject than this. "Job" refers to the nature of the work and the capacity in which she is employed and the place of her employment.[62] It is provided that for purposes of calculating continuity for statutory entitlement such as redundancy payment and entitlement to claim unfair dismissal, the period of absence for maternity reasons shall count as a period of continuous employment provided that the employee returns in accordance with the statutory right contained in section 45(1). So we may say that for many statutory entitlements the period before the absence, the period of the absence and the period following return to work all count towards the entitlement. For the purpose of many purely contractual rights section 45(2) ensures that rights similar to seniority and pension rights shall continue where the employee left them when she left work because of her impending maternity. There is of course no reason why the period of absence should not also be included if the contracting parties agree. In the case of all rights other than those specifically mentioned the effect of section 45(1) is to entitle the employee to their continuing accrual throughout the period of absence. It is not at all clear that these statutory provisions are necessary in most cases. In most cases, it will be unlikely (or at least unwise) for the employer to attempt to terminate the contract of employment. If the employee does not do so either before or after the eleventh week preceding the expected week of confinement, then the contract subsists throughout. It would follow that employment is continuous not only for statutory purposes, but also at common law.[63] Unless the contract made it clear that rights only accrued while the employee was at work, as distinct from being in employment, all other rights would continue to accrue throughout the absence period. It seems possible, for instance, that an employee absent for maternity reasons but possessing a subsisting contract of employment might in certain circumstances be able to argue that the wording of her contract entitled her, for instance, to sickness benefit during that period should she fall ill for some reason not connected with her pregnancy.

Exclusions

The basic right to return to her original employment is now subject to four significant limitations[64]:

(i) An employer of five employees or less (the Act does not indicate whether this is to include part-time employees) is relieved of the obligation wherever he can show that it is not reasonably practicable to

---

[61] s.45(2).

[62] E.P.C.A., s.153(1). See *McFadden* v. *Greater Glasgow P.T.E.* [1977] I.R.L.R. 327.

[63] But see *Lavery* v. *Plessey Telecommunications Ltd.* [1982] I.R.L.R. 180; *Kolfor Plant Ltd.* v. *Wright* [1982] I.R.L.R. 311.

[64] E.P.C.A. 1978, s.45(4) as amended by the E.A. 1980, s.12.

reinstate the absent employee, whatever the reason and whether or not he has, or offers, suitable alternative employment.

(ii) An employer of more than five employees who can show that it is not reasonably practicable *by reason of redundancy* to reinstate the employee is relieved of the obligation either if there is no suitable available vacancy in his own employment or that of any associated employer or successor or, if there is such suitable alternative, one such vacancy is offered and unreasonably rejected. There is a suitable available vacancy regardless of the consequences of giving the job to the employee. In *Community Task Force* v. *Rimmer*[65] the E.A.T. held an industrial tribunal entitled, as a question of fact, to find such a vacancy to exist even though the employer would have lost funding from the Manpower Services Commission had he reinstated the employee.

(iii) An employer of more than five employees who can show that it is not reasonably practicable, for a reason other than redundancy, to reinstate the employee is relieved of the obligation provided that he does offer a suitable alternative which is unreasonably rejected.

(iv) All employers are relieved of the obligation to reinstate if the employee fails, within 14 days of receipt of their intermediate inquiry referred to below, to indicate her continuing intention to return.

A suitable alternative is one in which the work to be done under the new contract is of a kind which is both suitable in relation to the employee and appropriate for her to do in the circumstances and the terms and conditions are not less favourable to her than if she had returned under her original contract.[66] Because the absence of a suitable alternative under (ii) above means that the employer needs to make no offer at all it is probably the employer in these circumstances who will be seeking to show that alternatives are unsuitable, whereas under (iii) it will be the employee seeking her original job or compensation who will wish to justify rejection of an offer on the ground that it is not suitable.

It is provided[67] that in a redundancy situation under (ii) above failure to offer a suitable alternative that is available will operate as an unfair dismissal. In fact this provision only brings the redundancy situation in line with all other failures to comply with the unrelieved obligation to reinstate. All count as a dismissal and apparently, therefore, complaint has to be made of unfair dismissal. This enables the tribunal to limit the right of return both by the statutory preconditions and by the fact that reasonable grounds for refusal to re-employ may be pleaded.[68] It seems to follow that despite the rather complicated provisions just discussed an employer who simply refuses to reinstate will only have to show that it was reasonable for him so to do. Suppose for instance that during the absence of a part-time employee who has qualified to exercise maternity rights the (large) employer decides to upgrade her job to full-time status. Suppose further that she is unwilling to undertake the full-time work. She is not redundant and the employer is, therefore, under an obligation to offer her suitable alternative employment or to reinstate her. If

[65] [1986] I.C.R. 491.
[66] E.P.C.A. 1978, s.45(4).
[67] *Ibid.*, Sched. 2, para. 2(2).
[68] *Lavery* v. *Plessey Telecommunications Ltd.* [1982] I.R.L.R. 180.

he does neither he faces a claim for unfair dismissal but only has to show that his decision to upgrade the job was a reasonable one and that he behaved reasonably in offering the job to her. If he has no alternative to offer he is relieved of all other liability. This appears to make nonsense of the careful provisions of the Act. The obvious solution is to hold that the statute confers an absolute right refusal of which leads to automatic unfairness. Unfortunately for this argument the Act could easily have so provided but it does not do so. The employee seems to have the worst of both worlds because it has been held[69] that a failure to satisfy the statutory conditions for an entitlement to return to work disentitles the employee to any remedy for unfair dismissal, notwithstanding that the contract subsists until the employer terminates it by his refusal to reinstate.

At any time later than 49 days from the expected date of confinement the employer may make an intermediate inquiry in writing of the employee as to whether she still intends to return to work. The inquiry must notify her that if she does not indicate such continuing intention within 14 days she will forfeit her right to return.[70] The employee must exercise her right to return to work by written notification to her original employer or, if appropriate, his successor, at least 21 days before the date on which she proposes to return.[71] The employer may postpone such a return for not more than four weeks from that notified day of return provided that he informs the employee before that notified day of return and furnishes her with specified reasons for the postponement.[72]

The employee may extend the permitted period of 29 weeks' absence from the week of confinement, once, for a maximum of four weeks upon production of a certificate from a registered medical practitioner stating that by reason of disease or bodily or mental disablement she will be incapable of work on the notified day of return or, if no such date has been notified, the expiration of the permitted period of 29 weeks.[73] In *Kelly* v. *Liverpool Maritime Terminals Ltd.*[73a] it was held that employment comes to an end if the employee fails to return on the due date, whether it be the original or the extended date. Submission of subsequent medical certificates merely indicated an inability to return and could not be construed as a request for sick leave. Certain provisions are made to deal with circumstances such as the existence of industrial action which makes it unreasonable to expect the employee to return to work on the notified day.[74]

Dismissal during absence

It is provided[75] that if in any proceedings arising out of a failure to permit an employee to return to work the employer shows that the reason for the failure is that the employee is redundant and that the employee was in fact

---

[69] *Lavery* v. *Plessey Communications Ltd.* [1982] I.R.L.R. 180; *Kolfor Plant Ltd.* v. *Wright* [1982] I.R.L.R. 311.
[70] E.A. 1980, s.11(2) inserting a new s.33(3A) into E.P.C.A.
[71] s.47(1).
[72] s.47(2).
[73] s.47(3).
[73a] [1988] I.R.L.R. 310.
[74] s.47(5) and (6).
[75] Sched. 2, para. 5.

dismissed or, had she continued to be employed by him, would have been dismissed, by reason of redundancy at some earlier date during her absence than the notified date of return but falling after the beginning of the eleventh week before the expected week of confinement, then for the purposes of "the statutory right to a redundancy payment" the employee shall be treated as having been dismissed with effect from that earlier date. Her continuity of employment will only run to that earlier date. It will be observed that this provision clearly anticipates that an employee who has already been dismissed for redundancy may nonetheless exercise her right to seek to return to work at the completion of her absence for reasons connected with her pregnancy. The fact that she has been dismissed at some earlier date, therefore, will apparently not deprive her of the chance of a suitable available vacancy upon the expiration of her statutory permitted period of absence. It also appears that the substitution of an earlier date than the date of return cannot be made if the employee has remained in employment without dismissal until the notified day of return even if the employer can show that she could have been dismissed for redundancy at an earlier date. The substitution provision only applies, in other words, to two situations: that in which the employee has actually been dismissed at an earlier date and that in which she has for some reason not continued in employment and so could not be dismissed at the earlier date when it became apparent that she was redundant.

Surprisingly little provision is made for dismissal, for any other reason than redundancy, during the permitted period of absence. It is briefly provided[76] that any cessation of the contract of employment after the beginning of the eleventh week before the expected week of confinement will not affect the employee's right to return to work. It is also provided that, should she bring any proceeding for unfair dismissal based upon this earlier dismissal compensation will be assessed without regard to her right to return to work but, if she does exercise her right to return to work, it shall be upon the condition that she repays any compensation in respect of such dismissal if the employer so requests.[77] No provision is made, however, for a situation in which, for instance, facts are discovered during the employee's absence which justify a dismissal and she is so dismissed. She would appear to be able to exercise her right to work within the statutory provisions. It would seem from the fact that the employee's remedy is for unfair dismissal that the employer would be entitled to refuse to reinstate her and to defend his refusal in any subsequent tribunal proceedings by arguing the earlier substantial reason for dismissal. This would not seem to cause a problem in respect of section 56. This section provides that where an employee who is entitled to return to work is not permitted to return to work, her rights in respect of unfair dismissal and redundancy payment shall apply as if she had been employed until the notified day of return. All this seems to mean is that an employee who has been dismissed on an earlier date would not be out of time in making a claim for unfair dismissal within three months of her notified day of return. It also seems to mean that she could not claim that any compensation should begin earlier than that notified day of return but this does not appear to be unfair since it can be shown that she would not have been at work during that period in any case.

---

[76] s.33(3).
[77] Sched. 2, para. 6(4).

There is a very ambiguous provision in Schedule 2,[78] the best interpretation of which seems to be that any attempt to dismiss an employee during the period after she has notified the employer of her specific intention to return to work, but before she actually does return to work, will be totally ineffective as a dismissal. Strictly read, the sub-paragraph might appear actually to deprive such an employee of her right to return to work by suggesting that the dismissal must be deemed to have occurred after her return to work, but that cannot be the correct interpretation.

Complaint to tribunal

An employee may complain to an industrial tribunal within three months beginning with the last day of the period of payment of maternity pay that her employer has failed to pay her the whole or any part of the maternity pay to which she is entitled.[79] Provision is made for an employee who has taken all reasonable steps other than proceedings to enforce the award of an industrial tribunal to secure her maternity payment, or for an employee whose employer is insolvent to claim payment from the Secretary of State.[80] The Secretary of State may seek to secure the amount so paid from the employer if satisfied that the employer's default is without reasonable excuse.[81] Section 54 makes it clear that an employee who is not permitted to return to work in accordance with the statutory rights may substantiate her claim in an ordinary proceeding for unfair dismissal. Either the failure to allow her to return will constitute a dismissal or she will have been dismissed at some earlier date. Care must be taken to distinguish between a woman who has established her right to return and may claim unfair dismissal; a woman who has not sought to rely on maternity rights at all but whose contract subsists until she is denied the opportunity to return and who also may seek to claim an unfair dismissal[82]; and a woman who has failed to establish her statutory rights, as, for instance, by giving inadequate notice to return.[83] In every case where the employee has acquired a right to return to work, whether or not she has been dismissed during her absence, it is provided[84] that she is to be treated as having been continuously employed until "dismissed" on the notified day of return. The reason for the "dismissal" will be the reason for which she was denied the right to return.

---

[78] Para. 6(2).
[79] s.36.
[80] s.40.
[81] s.41.
[82] *Lucas* v. *Norton of London Ltd.* [1984] I.R.L.R. 86.
[83] *Lavery* v. *Plessey, supra.*
[84] ss.56 and 86.

CHAPTER VIII

TRADE UNION ACTIVITY

"Sir, We the Operative Wire Drawers and Cardmakers are greatly surprised to
hear that you have signified your intention to lower the wages of your journemen
cardmakers . . . and at the same time we greatley regreet that you shold so act,
because it will call fourth such measures as may paraps be dissagreeable to boath
partys you know sir, that labour is the working man's property, and that he ought
at all times to have a faire remuneration for that labour."[1]

Thus, in 1833, did a Trade Union announce its involvement in the employment relationship.

Trade unions seek to recruit members at the workplace primarily to be in a
position of collective strength to enable them to negotiate terms and conditions of employment with the employer on behalf of those members. In
practice, such negotiations normally affect terms and conditions of non-
members similarly. The collective response of the members, however it is co-
ordinated, enables the union to present the employer with the threat, implicit
or open, that some form of restriction will be imposed on the willingness of
members to work if, ultimately, no proposal satisfactory to the union is made
by him to resolve a dispute or meet a claim. That restriction may go so far as
total withdrawal of labour but, initially, will often take some form less damaging to both sides. We shall consider legal control of forms of industrial action
in Chapter 9. This chapter is concerned with the activities of trade unions,
within the broad head of industrial relations, which take place at, or in connection with, the workplace. Historically, in the United Kingdom the legislature has preferred not to interfere with these activities, either by the grant of
rights or the imposition of restrictions. For a hundred years, until the 1980s,
the policy of successive governments had been to permit the collective power
of labour to meet, and bargain if it could, with the collective power of capital.
As we shall see, when judicial development of civil liability threatened the
balance of this confrontation—particularly by restrictions on industrial action
as labour's ultimate inducement to bargain—statutory protection from that
liability was granted, so as to leave the two sides free to match their strength.
Little else was attempted; save where the power of labour was so poorly
organised that it was felt necessary to provide some formal procedure within
which negotiation might proceed. The Wages Council was devised initially to
set a minimum wage in sections of industry where exploitation of the individual worker was considered intolerable. It was quickly extended into other
areas where, without it, collective negotiation would have been non-existent.
In the 1970s briefly, and largely ineffectively, its powers were increased to

---

[1] Malcolm Spiers, *One Hundred Years of a Small Trade Union* (1972).

deal with other terms. Yet the Royal Commission in 1965 declared it an unpopular institution tending to produce apathy and low wages.

The Government declared its position as a contractor in the Fair Wages Resolution of the House of Commons, which imposed on government contractors obligations to recognise the right of their employees to join a trade union and to adhere to standards of terms and conditions which had been established in their section of industry and locality. The device was adopted, by analogy, by a variety of other, public sector, employers. Again, briefly in the 1970s, this was extended by enabling trade unions to complain of the failure of any employer to meet such established standards. Trade unions found an indication that they were considering such a complaint a useful inducement to negotiation.[2]

This support machinery has been devastated in the 1980s. We shall, briefly, consider the remnant later in this chapter. Its existence did not affect the basic legislative policy of non-intervention. British trade unions were successful in using the freedom to form trade unions independent of employer domination and, in the public sector and the majority of private industry, to induce employers to negotiate with them. So, for many years, the United Kingdom answer to international calls for establishment of such rights was that given in the Report of the Royal Commission on Trade Unions in 1965, that the trade union movement was sufficiently strong not to need legislative protection.

The United Kingdom government was able to satisfy a number of international conventions[3] on the assumption that practice, rather than law, guaranteed such rights.

The Nature of Collective Bargaining

In the nature of things few individual employees will be able to negotiate more than minor variations in the terms offered by an employer and currently applicable to their employment. Quite apart from lack of bargaining strength the individual employee engaged in the same job as a number of other people at the workplace could not easily persuade the employer to depart from the common standards applicable to that grade. If there were no trade unions collective, rather than individual, negotiation would have to be invented if common changes in common terms were to be achieved other than at the employer's preferred pace. Most employers do not expect the employment relationship to stand still. Some may assume that group change can satisfactorily be maintained on the initiative of management. Most will realise that this, ultimately, will produce dissatisfaction among the workforce and that a grumbling worker is less productive than one who feels he can influence the situation in which he works. If there were no unions most large employers, at least, would have to look for some representative of each group with whom to discuss change. Collective bargaining, therefore, is the vehicle for the involvement of all but the lucky few strong enough, and sufficiently differentiated from their fellows to be able to negotiate their own terms. Without it

---

[2] E.P.C.A. 1987, Sched. 11.

[3] *e.g.* ILO Convention 87 of 1948 on the right to organise without interference from public authorities; ILO Convention 98 of 1949 forbidding discrimination against workers for trade union activity.

categories of worker will have to make their views known informally and hope for change or put up with the unchallenged exercise of managerial initiatives. It follows, therefore, that though the law assumes an individual contract the reality is that the workers' part in making and changing that contract, if it exists at all, will be undertaken on his behalf by trade unions through the process known as collective bargaining.

This process may be well-organised by the operation of national laws. In the United States of America, for instance, unions seeking bargaining status are entitled to ask for a ballot at the workplace to establish a single union as the representative of a bargaining unit. British governments have not denied the organisational value of collective representation but, save in 1971, have not seen the need to become involved either by guaranteeing that it occurs or by regulating its operation. British trade unions have asked no more than that legislative intervention should be confined to restraining the effect of judicial intrusion into the process, particularly by way of inhibiting industrial action as the ultimate sanction deployed by labour in answer to the power of capital.

In consequence, systems of bargaining in the United Kingdom vary according to the *de facto* manner in which an industry and its trade unions is organised. In some industries a single union, or a small group of specialised unions, will have developed to the exclusion of all others. There is no point, save the ease of classification, in saying that this is typically so in the public sector for such organisation mostly occurred whilst those industries were in the private sector. Coal mining and the railways afford good examples whilst British Telecom and what was formerly its other branch—the Post Office—is an example of single-union domination in an industry which was public and has been privatised. Single-union domination can develop among a multiplicity of employers, therefore, and will be found in some of the private sector. Save for the lost and peculiar world of Rossendale, the boot and shoe industry is in this position. Sometimes the achievement can be surprising. In the retail trade the Union of Shop Distributive and Allied Workers is not alone but has had a predominant position despite the unparalleled fragmentation of that industry and the fact that that union might never have obtained a foothold without the initial support of the Co-operative movement. More typical of the private sector, however, is a pattern of two or three large unions bargaining jointly with a large number of small unions. Such small unions have often been formed by particular crafts seeing themselves, usually incorrectly, as having an interest different from that of other workers. Vehicle Building, for instance, is dominated by the Transport and General Workers' Union and the Engineers, but joint negotiating committees have, in the past, contained representatives of a dozen other unions, some with only one or two members employed at the workplace. Some small unions, particularly confined to a small industry like lock making, or a locality like the Rossendale Union of Boot Shoe and Slipper Operatives, are very effective. Spread thinly across industry, however, a small union may, at best, trail along behind the unions which dominate the joint machinery or, at worst, be an irritant. Spread thus, or localised, small unions are doomed unless employers actively sustain them as a barrier to large unions. If a new craft develops its members are likely to join big unions in which they see strength. No one these days would, as in 1872, create a union of Card Setting Machine Tenters. Its membership has never exceeded 313. One day the demand which now keeps open the two factories where it operates will cease and it, and the craft it represents, will disappear. Many do not wait for this but amalgamate for greater strength, or perhaps a pension scheme for their paid officials, as did the Roofing Operatives and the National Association of Brushmakers. The Construction Industry once had a multiplicity of large and small unions and only in Civil Engineering could it be said that two were dominant. Most have now amalgamated, not always rationally. The Plumbers, for instance, joined the Electricians, but perhaps this was far-sighted since now new generalised "crafts," such as kitchen fitter, involve both electrical and plumbing work. Economic circumstances accelerate such unification. As membership figures declined in the 1980s many small unions ceased to be financially viable. Not all disappear with their craft. The Society of Lithographic Artists, Designers and Engravers saw its craft skill eroded in the printing industry and perpetuated itself first by absorbing the Wallpaper Workers and then by forcibly recruiting employees in a large number of small firms which originated art work.

The considerable increase in amalgamation and the desire of large unions to avoid, in new establishments, the complication caused by small unions would anyway mean that the trend was to smaller numbers of unions as members of joint negotiating panels. Recently, however, this somewhat stately process has been overtaken by a startling employer initiative in developing the single-union agreement. This is unlikely to occur in established bargaining units where the employer would need to rescind his agreements with other unions and face the prospect of industrial action by their members. It is most likely to occur on "greenfields sites." Like everything else in industrial relations this term applies to various situations. It may involve a transfer of employees from other establishments where they were organised in numerous unions, or it may lead to the recruitment of a wholly fresh workforce. Because of the facility with which transfers may be made in the name of a subsidiary, it can be argued that some transfers constitute wholly new operations. From the employer's point of view the engagement of a new labour force under the name of a new company may not seem to involve any commitment to unions which had organised the workforce at another place for an associated company. None of this variety is, of course, new. The radical change in the past few years derives from the willingness of employers, who take the initiative in the offer of recognition made in the new plant, to lay down much more restrictive terms, on a "take it or leave it" basis, for that recognition. The "Wapping" arrangement is only the most startling exercise of this initiative because of the extreme secrecy in which the move of production of *The Times* newspaper was conducted, a largely new workforce recruited and an agreement made for recognition of only one trade union—the E.E.P.T.U.—the craft specialisation of which lay more in new technology than traditional printing skills.

In fact, other trade unions, publicly vociferously critical of the "single-union agreement," have entered into such arrangements in less spectacular, and therefore less publicised, circumstances. If single unionism is the objection, as it usually appears to be before the TUC, which is asked to apply the Bridlington principles, the obvious answer will be that the employer often makes it clear that it is a choice between that and no recognition at all. Plenty of examples exist, frequently involving Japanese companies which have well-established working arrangements with trade unions in Japan, where TUC opposition, forcing the chosen union to withdraw, results in no bargaining structure, and, incidentally but not coincidentally, little union membership. The real opposition may derive from the fact that single-union agreements have been associated with "no strike" clauses. This term has no fixed meaning save, as section 18 of T.U.L.R.A. 1974 puts it, that it implies some restriction on freedom to strike. In practice virtually all procedure agreements will at least imply some restriction by expecting exhaustion of the agreed procedure before either party resorts to industrial action. In the past many have gone further than this, where a final arbitration stage is involved, by indicating that such arbitration should be regarded as binding. The difference between this and the type of agreement recently entered into, particularly by the E.E.P.T.U., is that, in the latter, resort to arbitration may be at the instance of either party without the particular agreement of the other in the instant case. In other words, resort, as well as the result, is compulsory. It is argued by those unions entering into this type of agreement that the difference is not one of principle. It seems unlikely that employers would, at present, go so far as to demand a clause in the agreement providing for its intended incorporation in the contract of employment. Even if they did it is doubtful, in view of the fact that most industrial action is in breach of the contract of employment in any event, that such a clause would make much more than psychological difference in practice. This argument would seek to point out, therefore, that even provision for unilateral resort to arbitration had no legally binding effect so that the "right" to resort to industrial action as a last resort was unimpaired. This last point is specious. Unions do not enter into such agreements with the intention of breaking them. The price—de-recognition—would be too high. But it remains true that no exception has been taken in principle by unions hitherto to provision for binding arbitration and in most cases where joint agreement to go to arbitration on each issue was necessary it would have been assumed that that agreement would be forthcoming. Binding arbitration cannot really be the stumbling block for this new type of single-union agreement; the more so because evidence suggests that employers have less faith in arbitration than trade unions.

To digress a little while on the subject of arbitration, employers would probably prefer to confine the arbitration function to a choice between their offer and the unions' demand; the, so-called, "pendulum." Such a restriction is likely to appear frequently in future in binding arbitration clauses. It has the beneficial tendency of eliminating extreme positions since a party making an unrealistic stand will run a high risk of the arbitrator favouring the other position. Open-ended arbitration is viewed with some suspicion on both sides. This may, in turn, have the beneficial effect of producing pressure for an agreed settlement. It is significant that, in the outcome, few major matters are referred to binding arbitration.

The truth about the opposition to single-union agreements is probably that the practice would not produce fairly equal benefit for the big unions, on a knock-for-knock principle, tending also to eliminate small unions, as a model situation would suggest. Employers, at present having the initiative, choose the union to which the offer is made. They are likely to choose the union with which they think they will get on best. Many would say this means the least militant. It may, incidentally, mean the smaller. There is plenty of evidence to suggest that employers in the furniture trade were anxious to sustain the

Furniture Trades Union against the T.G.W.U. and the lock-making industry goes to some lengths to support the Lock and Metal Workers. Hitherto, however, it has not been the employer who has, initially, selected one union or another. He either recognised or rejected the request for bargaining status. It is not difficult to understand union suspicion of this new phenomenon of the employer not only shopping for the most acceptable one of a number of alternative unions but also, in return for "awarding the contract" to bargain, imposing terms beneficial to him.

The unit for which bargaining is done is as various as trade union structure. Bargaining may take place on a national scale; indeed, before the Second World War national bargaining was the ultimate ambition of many unions which had painfully achieved regional bargaining out of plant bargaining. The trade union leaders, turned Government, who in 1946 inspired a revised Fair Wages Resolution[4] still thought in regional and national terms.[5] But the demands of the Second World War had already ensured that most effective wage settlement took place at the plant. This, of course, is not true of single-employer industries like the Civil Service, the Railways, the British Steel Corporation or the National Coal Board. Nor did local bargaining eliminate national bargaining. Even the diffuse and vast engineering industry still has in force a national agreement fixing a national minimum wage. It is sometimes said that no one receives a wage as low as the national minimum but the author found, in cases brought before the Central Arbitration Committee in the late 1970s, small employers who were paying that rate. National agreements are more likely to establish disputes and grievance procedures, but they may control substantive issues such as holiday entitlement. Even the national minimum pay rate may fix the rate on which overtime premiums are paid so that it is possible for workers paid "time and a half" for overtime to receive less for those hours than for standard hours paid at the local time rate. Between national and plant bargaining lie a number of other options which may co-exist in different plants and divisions of the same employer.[6] The move to plant bargaining naturally greatly enhanced the power of the unions' plant organisation, usually called "shop stewards" and reduced the influence of the full-time District official. The Royal Commission on Trade Unions which reported in 1968[7] accepted the evidence of Allan Flanders that workplace bargaining is "largely informal, largely fragmented and largely autonomous." It allowed that "the shift in authority from industry to the factory has been accompanied by decentralisation of authority in industrial relations within the factory itself." Some regarded this as a polite way of saying that management at that time had lost control of bargaining procedures. It is certainly true that between established anniversary dates for agreements there would often occur a bewildering drift in rates of pay and other working practices. As the Commission said: "minor revision takes place intermittently throughout this period." The minor revision was attributable to the influence of the shop stewards and was likely to be preceded by minor stoppages. Typically, if a worker objected to the state of a machine and the shop steward who

---

[4] Rescinded December 16, 1982, to take effect after 12 months.
[5] See *Racal Communications Ltd.* v. *The Pay Board* [1974] I.C.R. 590.
[6] See *Beal* v. *The Beecham Group* [1982] I.R.L.R. 192.
[7] Cmnd. 3623, para. 65.

decided to take the matter up did not quickly find himself in discussion with management, he would call out those working that type of machine until he did. The Royal Commission was, however, at pains to see the shop steward less as an irritant than as an oiler of the machinery. The evidence supports that conclusion. If the system was out of control it was more likely to be because the machinery was crazy than that those operating it were.

Since the mid-1970s management has strenuously reasserted its control. In many instances local bargaining was displaced by company-wide bargaining, and this was achieved in direct negotiation with trade unions bypassing the shop steward. Such moves have not been easy. In the former British Leyland Motor Company, for instance, those at the "Jaguar" plant were paid far more under local bargaining than at the "MG" plant at Abingdon. "Coventry" rates in the Engineering industry were likely to be higher than at factories of the same company outside the area they covered. Assimilation upwards would often have been economically disastrous. The effort put in to achieve the desired end indicates the determination that it should be obtained and suggested, long before "Wapping," that management of larger undertakings were back in control of the structuring of procedures. For all that, the shop steward remains crucial to the employment situation. As the Royal Commission recognised, he is the first to observe a problem. He is usually the only union official to do so unless the problem gets out of hand. No sensible management would ignore his representations or fail to discuss the problem with him.

This then, briefly, is the situation in which much of the working relationship, and the terms of the contract of employment, is worked out. The agreements reached may range from formal signed documents to mere alleged precedents arising from the handling of an individual grievance. We have seen[8] that courts construct contracts in straight lines rather than triangles. The situation we have described is one comprising two straight lines, one from bargainer to constituent, the other from bargainer to management. The third side which would form the triangle—the relationship between the worker and his union—is rarely part of this structure. (Though it is, for instance, in printing unions.) That is partly why the shop steward was autonomous and powerful. The unions' own internal organisation often fails to mention him and seldom incorporates him. Shop floor relations are the job of the one. Government of the union is the job of the other. One can readily appreciate why members look to shop stewards as more significant than branch secretaries.

LEGAL EFFECT OF COLLECTIVE AGREEMENTS

Courts sometimes understand the nature of collective agreements very clearly. In *Burroughs Machines Ltd.* v. *Timmoney*[9] the court understood that the agreement involved mutually dependent concessions by each side. It would have been nonsense to eliminate one side of the concession whilst enforcing the other. In *R.* v. *C.A.C. ex p. Deltaflow Ltd.*[10] the significance of written national agreements was unrealistically allowed to predominate over

---

[8] *Supra*, p. 40.
[9] [1977] I.R.L.R. 404.
[10] [1977] I.R.L.R. 486.

consistent contrary formal and informal local bargaining. In *Gascol Conversions Ltd.* v. *Mercer*[11] the Court of Appeal struggled with the difference between national and local agreements apparently without appreciating that it was the latter which was the more significant in the formulation of the individual contract of employment. *Gallagher* v. *The Post Office*[12] discloses an appreciation of one of the major problems of judicial application of collective agreements; that is, the language in which they are cast. Union negotiators can, and do, make use of arguments that lawyers give them but a lawyer must forget his expertise as such if he is to act as an industrial relations negotiator. No lawyer would accept a form of words he knew meant different things to each party. Settlement of industrial disputes may well be achieved precisely because of this lack of precision. Statements of intention may be more than the pious hopes they were supposed to be in *Gallagher*. The Industrial Relations Act 1971, perhaps unfortunately, adopted the device of seeking to ensure particular interpretations of its substantive provisions by an initial statement of what it intended to achieve. Such a device is common in collective agreements.

Perhaps because they realise they are speaking a different language, negotiators on both sides of industrial relations prefer to keep their agreements out of the courts. In any event, their position, like that of the arbitrator, differs from the judicial in that they are primarily concerned to settle disputes rather than applying rules to ascertain rights. They cannot, of course, deny the fact that substantive agreements will fix the conditions of the individual employment relationship and they know that the lawyer will call these the terms of the contract of employment and enforce them between the parties to that contract.[13] As between themselves, they do not see their settlement as establishing an enforceable rule to deal with the next dispute, but rather as a reference point from which to approach the next dispute. Why this is so in the United Kingdom whereas, in most other industrialised countries, the collective agreement is treated as an enforceable contract between the parties who made it, is a matter of history and the product of the attitude of mind it creates. In the United States, for instance, an employer who has an agreement on individual disciplinary disputes will be bound to the union to adhere to it. In many respects, the individual's rights are thereby transferred to his union, or even to a trade union of which he is not a member, acting as bargaining agent. In the United Kingdom, save for a brief statutorily produced interval, the supposition has always been that collective agreements are not intended to be enforceable as between the parties to them. The judicial authority for this proposition, which was reviewed in *Ford Motor Co. Ltd.* v. *Amalgamated Union of Engineering and Foundry Workers*[14] is tenuous and unconvincing. Geoffrey Lane J. (as he then as) professed to base his decision in favour of the non-enforceability of the agreement before him on the nature of the language used, and particularly its frequent resort to aspirational comment, the practical problems that would arise from such enforcement, and the

---

[11] [1974] I.C.R. 420.
[12] [1970] 2 All E.R. 112.
[13] See pp. 61–68 *supra*.
[14] [1969] 2 Q.B. 303. See Selwyn, *Collective Agreements and the Law* (1969) 32 M.L.R. 377, and Clark in reply (1970) 33 M.L.R. 117.

climate of opinion in favour of unenforceability. Subsequent events proved him right as to the third factor, at least. The Industrial Relations Act 1971 introduced a presumption of enforceability unless the contrary intention was expressed. The result was that most established trade unions insisted on the inclusion in each agreement of a statement that it was intended to be binding in honour alone and employers saw insufficient advantage in enforceability to persuade them to offer concessions to buy out this exclusion clause. The presumption was repealed in 1974[15] in favour of a conclusive presumption of non-enforceability unless the agreement was in writing and contained an express provision that the parties intended it to be legally binding.

This history was explained to the E.A.T. in *Marley* v. *Forward Trust Group Ltd.*[16] and that court properly separated the question of direct enforceability between the parties from incorporation of clauses from agreements into individual contracts of employment.[17] The E.A.T., nevertheless, held that a survivor of the standard exclusion clause of the 1970s should be taken to mean that the agreement was to have no legal significance collectively or individually. The Court of Appeal[18] made it clear that these were quite different issues. It would be difficult to distinguish a situation created by an express exclusion clause from that created by implied intention to the same effect. As the Court of Appeal pointed out[19] collective agreements can be incorporated into individual contracts. It might have gone much further so as to indicate that they normally are so incorporated so that denial of such a process where the agreement is intended not to be enforceable would make a nonsense both of accepted practice and of the law. Trade unions, which are generally still anxious to exclude direct enforceability, are usually equally anxious to bind individuals to the effect of collective agreements and, one suspects, welcome implication into the contract of employment.

There is, however, a hidden trap in implication into the individual contract. If a collective agreement contains a clause restricting freedom to take industrial action until exhaustion of procedure (or, more recently and more significantly, excluding it altogether in favour of final resort to binding arbitration) and that clause is incorporated into the contract of employment, procedure agreements effectively become binding on the individuals upon whom the union would wish to call for industrial action to back demands for revision of substantive agreements. The substantive agreements thereby become linked to the individual contractual enforceability of the procedure agreements. It may be said, in reply, that the extra contractual liability imposed on the individual for resorting to industrial action in breach of procedure agreements makes little difference because the industrial action is likely to be a breach of the contract of employment anyway.

In 1974, perhaps, the effect of a "peace clause" on the decision in *Rookes* v. *Barnard*[20] was more clearly remembered. Perhaps it was felt that the inevitable contractual breach involved in industrial action was still in question and

---

[15] T.U.L.R.A. 1974, s.18.

[16] [1986] I.R.L.R. 43.

[17] See p. 42 *supra.*

[18] [1986] I.R.L.R. 370.

[19] Although it is difficult to understand why it should have relied on *Robertson* v. *British Gas Corporation* [1983] I.R.L.R. 302, for the proposition.

[20] [1964] A.C. 1129.

that the courts should not be furnished with another source for it. Whatever the explanation, the T.U.L.R.A. of that year provides[21] that agreements restricting the "right" to strike or take other industrial action shall not be incorporated into individual contracts unless the collective agreement is in writing, expressly states that the restriction shall, or may, be incorporated, is reasonably accessible to the workers to whom it applies at their workplace, is made by independent trade unions only and is so incorporated expressly or impliedly. The trouble with this type of machinery is that, if it actually is used, it tends to be regarded as settling the issue of incorporation and enhancing the practical effect of acceptance of obligations. Such will, undoubtedly, be the effect of clauses in "single-union agreements" requiring resort to binding arbitration.

The issue of directly enforceable collective agreements is likely to arise again and it is far from impossible that legislation will return to a presumption of enforceability, possibly less readily set aside than in 1971. A foretaste of the theoretical effects of legal enforceability will be provided by the operation of single-union agreements and future legislative action will, no doubt, be influenced by that experience. At the moment, since the 1971 agreement was only implemented in isolated cases, and usually by "house" associations, only speculation is possible. It can be suggested with some good reason that enforceability could alter the pattern of collective bargaining. It is, for the reason just mentioned, likely only to have a psychological effect on readiness to resort to industrial action in breach of such agreements. The more formal collective agreements tend to be assumed to operate either indefinitely or for a year. Procedure, disciplinary and redundancy agreements fall into the first category. Wage agreements fall into the second. If they were legally enforceable no legal industrial action could be taken to amend them, without the consent of both parties, until that period had expired. Employers would undoubtedly use the psychological persuasion of the legal position to resist demands for negotiation. It would follow naturally that agreements would have to be negotiated with more care since the present practice of sorting out their meaning later by a series of disputes would be difficult for a union to maintain. It would also follow that more matters would tend to be included in any agreement intended to last any length of time. Employers, no doubt, would take the opportunity to seek to negotiate agreements to serve for longer periods than at present. All this would make negotiation more difficult and time-consuming. This would be offset by the reduction, at least in theory, of disputes during the currency of the agreement.[22]

Transfer of collective agreements

The Transfer of Undertakings (Protection of Employment) Regulations 1981[23] make provision for the transfer of collective agreements, and for consultation with recognised independent trade unions, upon the transfer to another of the whole or part of a business situated immediately before the

---

[21] s.18(4).
[22] See, on the possible effects of enforceability, Wilson, *Contract and Prerogative: A Reconsideration of the Legal Enforcement of Collective Agreements* (1984) 13 I.L.J. 1.
[23] (S.I. 1981 No. 1984). See pp. 107–112 and 202–204 for discussion of other aspects of these Regulations.

transfer in the United Kingdom, whether the transfer is by sale or by some other form of disposition.[23a]

Wherever the transferred undertaking maintains, after the transfer, "an identity distinct from the remainder of the transferee's undertaking"[24] any independent trade union recognised to any extent by the transferor in respect of any description of transferred employees shall be deemed to have been recognised by the transferee to the same extent.[25] The Regulations provide enigmatically that "any agreement for recognition may be varied or rescinded" [according to existing legal principles]. United Kingdom law, as we have seen, would allow most recognition agreements to be varied or rescinded at will. The agreement itself might provide for unilateral termination by notice or, alternatively, not envisage such termination. The critical question is whether the Regulations intended to provide as a matter of law that the agreement could only be terminated according to its own terms or, in other words, to make it contractually enforceable. On the one hand it is clearly the intention of the EEC Directive that such agreements should not be compulsorily transferred merely to be rescinded at will. On the other hand it would be a little surprising if United Kingdom law permitted most recognition agreements to be terminated at will but entrenched those recognition agreements which had passed a barrier of transfer of business.

There can be no doubt that it is permissible for legislation to provide for the contractual enforceability of a class of collective agreements even if these agreements already exist as non-binding agreements.[26] Even if the words of the Regulations were clearer, however, it is obvious that the intention to give binding effect to certain collective agreements is not apparent by any normal standard of statutory construction. It is an open question whether the obvious intention of the EEC will persuade British courts to confer that effect on these Regulations in the light of the anomalous situation in relation to other agreements which such an interpretation would produce.

The provisions relating to the transfer of other collective agreements[27] are no more clear. It is provided that wherever there is in existence in relation to any employee whose contract is transferred by reason of these Regulations a collective agreement with a recognised trade union that agreement shall have effect after the transfer as if made by or on behalf of the transferee with that trade union. Anything done in relation to that agreement by or in relation to the transferor before the transfer shall be deemed to have been done by the transferee. Any order[28] shall have effect as if the transferee were a party to the agreement.

"Long enough before a relevant transfer to enable consultations to take place between the employer," whether the transferor or the transferee, and any employee who may be affected by the transfer or measures taken in con-

---

[23a] This provision does not apply to transfer of control by means of acquisition of a controlling interest in the shares of a company.

[24] The EEC Council Directive 77/197 from which the Regulations spring refers to "maintenance of autonomy."

[25] Reg. 9.

[26] Restoration of Pre-War Trade Practices Acts 1942 and 1950.

[27] Reg. 6.

[28] For instance one made by the C.A.C. Most of the machinery for amendment of collective agreements—*e.g.* E.P.A., s.3—has now been abolished.

nection with it the employer must convey certain information, directly or by post, to representatives of any recognised independent trade union. The information must include:

(a) the fact that the transfer is to take place, approximately when and the reasons for it;

(b) the legal, economic and social implications of the transfer for the affected employees;

(c) the measures which the employer envisages he will take in connection with the transfer and in relation to those employees, or a statement that no measures will be taken;

(d) if the employer is the transferor, the measures which the transferee envisages he will take in relation to the transfer and those employees whose rights are transferred under Regulation 5,[29] or the fact that no measures are envisaged. The transferee must give the transferor such information in time to enable him to perform this duty.

In addition, an employer envisaging measures in connection with the transfer in relation to employees of a description for which an independent union is recognised by him, shall enter into consultations with the representatives of that union, consider and reply to any representations made by them and state his reasons if he rejects any of those representations. In *I.P.C.S.* v. *Secretary of State for Defence*[30] Millett J. considered that the provision for consultation was an open-ended one not limited to the matters to be notified. It was something the union might ask for when it had received that information. If in any case special circumstances made it not reasonably practicable for an employer to perform any of these duties he shall take such steps as are reasonably practicable in the circumstances.[31] The employer need only communicate some definite plan or proposal which it planned to implement and the information need not include the calculations and assumptions on which an appraisal, for instance of manpower forecasts, was based. Millett J. also held that the transferee was not obliged to envisage measures in time to allow them to be communicated, especially if it had not been given sufficient information by the transferor to enable it to do so. The learned judge also pointed out that such measures as were envisaged and communicated might be changed. "Envisage" suggested even less commitment than "intends."

A complaint of failure in any of these requirements may be presented by the union concerned to an industrial tribunal. If the tribunal finds the complaint well founded it must make a declaration to that effect and may award "appropriate compensation" which must be set off against any compensation secured, or complaint made, under E.P.A. 1985, s.99.[32] The shortcomings of these consultation and information provisions are often obvious in the uncertainty of the language used. The principal defect, however, is that the obligation is only owed to recognised trade unions which provide, of course, the least likely circumstance in which communication will fail to take place.

---

[29] See p. 110, *supra*.
[30] [1987] I.R.L.R. 373.
[31] Reg. 10.
[32] Reg. 11.

RECOGNITION OF TRADE UNIONS FOR BARGAINING PURPOSES

In line with the previous policy of non-intervention little legislative provision has been made to regulate the recognition of trade unions as entitled to bargain on behalf of groups of workers. Collective bargaining is not normally a one-off operation, if only because a trade union, once admitted to bargain, will cite this admission as a precedent when it wishes again to negotiate. Terms and conditions of employment are bound continually to change even if only because wage rates in the last fifty years have never been stable. There is, therefore, always likely to be something for a union to wish to discuss. An employer who is inclined to discuss anything with trade unions will tend to wish for the stability produced by discussion with the same union or group of unions. Those unions, in any event, will have recruited at least some of his employees and will have some power to control them. It would be pointless to consult with other non-representative unions and many employers would accept that it would be short-sighted to have no dealings with unions once they had obtained reasonable representation among the workforce. So "recognition" comes about.

It is, of course, open to argument that a situation in which trade unions are free to carry out their normal primary function of negotiation, if they are strong enough to maintain it by industrial pressure, is not as good as the imposition of an obligation upon an employer to bargain. In the United States, for example, the National Labour Relations Board will organise a ballot of employees in an industrial unit which, if successful, imposes on the employer an enforceable duty to bargain in good faith. A similar duty to "recognise" a trade union for bargaining purposes was imposed by the Industrial Relations Act 1971 (which relied heavily on the importation of the United States system) and was largely saved from the mass destruction of that experiment in 1975.[33] The 1971 system had been open to what the trade union movement considered an abuse in that the employer was at liberty to grant bargaining rights to an organisation of workers which either he had established or he had dominated. The 1975 legislation confined the right to independent trade unions and also freed the system of the somewhat rigid balloting provisions which had accompanied its predecessor. It allowed a trade union to complain to the Central Arbitration Committee if an employer failed to recognise it when the Advisory Conciliation and Arbitration Service had recommended that he should do so. In practice, the C.A.C. operated its sanction more by way of inducement, making an award of terms and conditions in respect of the particular dispute which the employer had failed to negotiate and intending, thereby, to indicate that this form of unilateral arbitration would continue to be available if the default continued. Although the present writer had, on occasion, to be talked out of interpreting the statutory provisions as enabling the Committee to make a direct order for recognition, the attitude generally adopted by the C.A.C. was the only one practicably available to it. It would not have been possible to draft a meaningful obligation to negotiate and the imposition of the obligation in general terms would have advanced it no further than the original ACAS decision. The Advisory Conciliation and Arbitration Service was also having difficulty, particularly in agreeing a level

---

[33] E.P.A. 1975, ss.11–16.

of support within the workplace which would justify compulsory recognition. Its Chairman concluded that it would not be possible for a body representing both employers and workers to agree upon a standard of support and, ultimately, he advised the Secretary of State for Employment that the statutory machinery for compulsory recognition should be repealed.[34]

No doubt, the failure of this provision will mean that no similar step will be attempted in the foreseeable future. Yet too much should not be made of this. Success or failure depends on attitudes of mind. ACAS had some notable successes in the early years backed by a general public impression that a certain level of unionisation should compel an employer to negotiate. Both statistics show that from 610 claims recommendations only applied to 16,000 workers. A further 49,000 were included by voluntary settlements.

Such compulsion works elsewhere. But then, similarly, schemes of consultation, for instance through Works Councils, which are imposed in the Federal German Republic, would be regarded on past experience as unlikely to be effective in the United Kingdom. Compulsory recognition, not surprisingly, had always provoked a hard core of opposition,[35] which came to the surface in the "Grunwick affair."[36] The fact that the employer in this situation was able to refuse to co-operate with ACAS, refuse to obey its recommendation for recognition, dismiss employees who had taken industrial action in an attempt to secure recognition, refuse to reinstate them and, ultimately, obtain a decision of the House of Lords that the ACAS recommendation was void for failure to consult workers to whom ACAS had been allowed no access, demonstrated the end of any assumption of acceptance of the compulsory recognition process. A new concept of "partnership" will have to develop if recognition is again to be enforceable.

Since 1982[37] a positive restriction has been imposed on certain indirect pressure to secure recognition. Any term or condition of a contract for the supply of goods or services is void in so far as it purports to require a party to the contract to recognise for negotiating purposes, or to negotiate or consult with any official of, one or more trade unions. Any person against whom action is taken, or who is adversely affected by a failure to include him in a list of suppliers, or by termination of contract, or by exclusion from a group of those invited to tender, or by failure to permit such a tender, or by any other determination not to enter into a contract because of such failure to recognise, negotiate or consult, has an action for breach of statutory duty.

Despite the collapse of compulsion recognition retains a few legislatively granted advantages:

(a) Only the representatives of independent recognised trade unions are entitled to paid time off to perform their bargaining duties and receive training therein.[38]

---

[34] The recommendation was implemented in the E.A. 1980, s.19. But compulsory recognition continues in Northern Ireland. (S.I. 1982 No. 528), para. 22.

[35] In all 100 employers failed to comply with the 158 recognition recommendations that were made.

[36] The series of events and judicial considerations arising from this event were fully considered by Elias, Napier and Wallington, *Labour Law*, and see *Grunwick Processing Laboratories Ltd.* v. *ACAS* [1978] A.C. 655.

[37] E.A. 1982, s.13.

[38] See pp. 310–313.

But the members of any independent trade union are entitled to unpaid time off for trade union activities.[39]

(b) Only an independent recognised trade union is entitled to appoint safety representatives under section 1 of the Health and Safety at Work, etc., Act 1975.

(c) Only the representatives of an independent recognised trade union are entitled to receive pre-redundancy information under section 99 of the E.P.A.[40] This limitation also applies to the information both transferor and transferee employers are required to provide upon the transfer of a business.[41]

(d) Only the representatives of an independent recognised trade union are entitled to avail themselves of the statutory right to seek from an employer information without which they would be materially impeded in collective bargaining.[42]

(e) Only the representatives of recognised trade unions are entitled to be consulted in respect of contracting out of occupational pension schemes.[43]

If the practice of conferring statutory rights to information, consultation and action only upon recognised trade unions continues the gap between such practices in the United Kingdom and such practices elsewhere in the EEC will widen. In other EEC countries it is common to provide (sometimes primarily) an alternative system of employee representation by way of joint Works Councils. Where this occurs the obligation to establish such Works Councils is irrespective of recognition, let alone voluntary recognition, of trade unions. It is also common to confer on these considerably more widespread Works Councils the rights which, in the United Kingdom, are only conferred on recognised trade unions.

Definition of recognition

The definition, such as it is, of recognition[44] is linked to the definition of collective bargaining which in turn refers to a list of matters originally designed to define the limits of a trade dispute.[45]

Most of the case law on the existence of recognition has been concerned, not with any matter in this definition but with the question whether the actions and attitudes of the employer amount to a sufficient acknowledgment of the bargaining function of the union. The bulk of them have arisen in relation to the duty to consult before redundancy. In *National Union of Gold, Silver and Allied Trades* v. *Albury Brothers Ltd.*[46] the employer was a member of an employers' federation which negotiated with the union and the employer had recently discussed the rates of pay of one employee with the

---

[39] See p. 314, *infra*.
[40] See p. 201, *supra*.
[41] Transfer of Undertakings (Protection of Employment) Regulations 1981 (S.I. 1981 No. 1794), reg. 10.
[42] E.P.A. 1975, s.17.
[43] Occupational Pensions Certification of Employments Regulations 1975 (S.I. 1975 No. 1927) reg. 4.
[44] E.P.A. 1975, s.126.
[45] See T.U.L.R.A. 1974, s.29(1).
[46] [1979] I.C.R. 84.

union's district secretary. The Court of Appeal held that there must be clear evidence of the establishment of recognition by agreement, oral or in writing, or clear and distinct conduct revealing an implied agreement. Discussion of industrial relations matters was not enough to constitute recognition by an employer, nor was membership of an employers' organisation which itself recognised the union. Eveleigh L.J. said that recognition involved not merely willingness to discuss but also to negotiate with a view to striking a bargain. Sir David Cairns obscured this attempted distinction between consultation and negotiation by saying that "recognition" means recognition that the union is to be consulted about some of the matters listed in the 1974 Act. There are thus clearly two separate aspects of the concept; namely, that of agreement and that of the purpose of the contact between union and employer. It is submitted that the requirement of agreement is established. It is clear that the element of agreement must derive from a conscious decision of the employer to recognise the union.[47] This decision may however be inferred from a course of conduct not necessarily entirely confined to the function of bargaining.[48] In *Cleveland County Council* v. *Springett*[49] it was held that recognition requires proof of intent to recognise but that, as the judgment accepted, prompts a question of the factors which will provide evidence of that intent. Recognition for the purpose of collective bargaining may come from a wider and more popular concept of recognition, although recognition of safety representatives was, in *Springett*, considered not to be relevant for this purpose. Some discussion of this had occurred, however, in *Union of Shop, Distributive and Allied Workers* v. *Sketchley Ltd.*[50] The company granted what was called "recognition" for representation purposes in respect of employees who were union members wherever the union secured a membership of 50 per cent. of the company's employees in any union District. The company allowed the appointment of shop stewards and gave them unpaid time off work. It refused to pay them for this time on the ground that no right to negotiate terms and conditions of employment had been conferred. When in January 1980 it agreed to a meeting with the union to discuss pay, it insisted that only discussion and not negotiation was to be undertaken. Subsequently a redundancy situation arose and the company's relations with the union on this question fell short of the statutory requirements in relation to a recognised union. It is well established that recognition includes partial recognition so the question before the E.A.T. was whether any recognition at all existed. Because the items listed in section 29(1) of the 1974 Act were designed to define the limits of a trade dispute and not, originally, the limits of recognition it is possible to find a number of them which would be covered by a grievance procedure. Indeed a grievance procedure involving negotiation is undoubtedly partial recognition. The decision of the E.A.T. turns, therefore, solely on the undefined meaning of the word "recognition." It held that there was a clear distinction between one who is entitled to make representations and one who may negotiate, and that it would be contrary to

---

[47] *Transport and General Workers' Union* v. *Andrew Dyer* [1977] I.R.L.R. 93; *National Union of Tailors and Garment Workers* v. *Charles Ingram and Co. Ltd.* [1978] 1 All E.R. 1271.

[48] *N.U.T.G.W.* v. *Charles Ingram and Co. Ltd.* [1977] I.C.R. 530; *Joshua Wilson and Bros. Ltd.* v. *Union of Shop, Distributive and Allied Workers* [1978] I.C.R. 614.

[49] [1985] I.R.L.R. 131.

[50] [1981] I.R.L.R. 291.

industrial relations practice to conclude that the first step towards recognition constituted such recognition. The court might have been nearer the truth to say that there may only sometimes be such clear distinction between consultation and negotiation, and the remainder of its judgment demonstrates the abnormality of such a situation. It stated that the employer's later actions came close to negotiation but were saved therefrom by his insistence that no negotiation was intended. It will be much more normal to find no such careful distinction drawn and what begins as consultation will edge towards negotiation.

If conscious agreement to bargain is necessary then it is open to the employer, as in the *Sketchley* case, effectively to deny his intention to negotiate even if the evidence suggests that that is what is happening in practice. Where intention must be deduced from practice it is unlikely that any single practice will so clearly fall on one side or the other of the line between consultation and negotiation as to make any list of practices a useful guide to the distinction.

The C.A.C., which has had to consider the meaning of recognition in relation to the duty to supply information, has shown itself more aware of the uncertain line which may divide recognition from the steps leading to it. In the light of this awareness it has been more ready to accept earlier steps as conclusive. In *Greater London Council and GLC Staff Association*[51] a tribunal chaired by Sir John Wood said:

> "We do not accept the argument put forward by the Employer's Counsel that collective bargaining only arises once there has been a formal offer or request. Bargaining is a more ongoing process than such a definition would allow. In this case it is clear that since 1977, when the rundown of the Department in question occurred, the parties have been in continuous (though obviously spasmodic) negotiation."

In *B.L. Cars Ltd. and General and Municipal Workers Union*[52] the employer argued that he did not recognise any union for the purpose of negotiation on the decision to cease production and that, accordingly, refusal of information on that matter could not impede the union in its negotiations. In fact, however, a great deal of information had been given to the Confederation of Shipbuilding and Engineering Unions and the Union's national officer for the Engineering Industry had been heavily involved in talks with the company and had regarded them as part of a bargaining process. The Committee concluded that discussions within the context of an agreed bargaining procedure could not be meaningfully separated into consultation on the one hand and negotiation on the other. The Committee said:

> "No doubt [the local officials of the union] understood that the existence of the [employer's plan for survival of the company] . . . would heavily influence any subsequent negotiation; but we are satisfied that the local officials did not intend to abdicate their bargaining function. Nor, we think, did the Employer assume that intention to exist. The Unions pointed out that after the adoption of the plan they were given a week to come up with alternative proposals. Had the Unions been able to do so in such a time and without adequate information negotiation

---

[51] Award No. 79/470.
[52] Award No. 80/65.

upon their proposals, even if it took the form of a brief meeting in which Management made it clear that the alternative proposals were not feasible, would have been inevitable. For the reason already mentioned we do not think that such a situation could reasonably be labelled "consultation" so as to distinguish it from bargaining. It would be a use of the collective bargaining procedure agreement and not of any more limited procedure."

Trade Union attempts to control recognition—the Bridlington Agreement

The TUC is aware, of course, that the initiative to grant recognition for bargaining purposes lies with the employer. One of its major activities, at least since 1924 when guidelines were first adopted at its Hull conference, has been to restrict the chances of unions jockeying for both membership and bargaining rights to each other's disadvantage. In 1939 certain principles were reformulated in what became known as the Bridlington Agreement. Many of them deal with procedures for recruiting members centred around the anti-poaching provision of paragraph 5 which states that "no union shall commence organising activities at any establishment or undertaking in respect of any grade or grades of workers in which another union has the majority of workers employed and negotiates wages and conditions, unless by arrangement with that union." The effect of this on the legal provisions relating to membership of a trade union will be dealt with later.[53]

"Bridlington" also provided for disputes about negotiating rights to be referred to the TUC Disputes Committee. The conflict between the "joint interest" approach of the TUC and recent employer initiatives favouring a choice of a single union is apparent in the wording of the first principle:

"Each Union shall consider developing joint working agreements with unions with whom they are in frequent contact, and in particular developing (a) procedures for resolving particular issues and (b) specific arrangements concerning spheres of influence, transfers of members and benefit rights, recognition of and demarcation of work . . . "

Note (e) to this, as amended in December 1985, (specifically said to have equal status with the main principle) adds:

"When making sole negotiating rights or union membership agreements affiliated unions should have regard to the interests of other unions which may be affected and should consider their position in the drafting of such agreements. No union shall enter into a sole negotiating agreement, union membership agreement or any other form of agreement in any circumstances, including a takeover or change of ownership or some other reason where another union(s) would be deprived of their existing rights of recognition or negotiation except by prior consultation and agreement of the other union(s) concerned. Where agreement cannot be reached through consultation between the unions concerned the issue will be referred to the TUC for advice and conciliation and if necessary a Disputes Committee adjudication."

The addition, in 1985, of the second sentence indicates hardening opposition to the signing of single-union agreements. Without it it was easy to

---

[53] *Infra*, p. 300 *et seq.*

argue that the main principle did not apply to "greenfields sites."[54] Conversely, however, the second sentence seems to indicate that whenever an employer brings to a new site employees from elsewhere, where unions were recognised, no union may sign a recognition agreement unless, either the previously recognised unions all agree to resign their claims, or the employer is prepared to continue to deal with all of them. In a number of decisions after 1985 the Disputes Committee ordered a union which had agreed in breach of this principle forthwith to terminate the agreement (although that would presumably be to break it rather than withdrawing from it) notwithstanding that it was obvious that the employer would not thereafter recognise any union. In one recent decision it even ordered a union which had secured a single-union agreement on a new site with a newly recruited workforce to exclude members it had recruited at that site after the agreement, even though they had not necessarily previously been members of another union.

It must have been obvious that sooner or later a union offered sole recognition, which it was forced to refuse because of the interest of other unions, would defy the order of the Disputes Committee. Plainly, the practically complete block on single-union agreements imposed by the 1985 amendment was not going to induce employers to enter into multi-union agreements. In 1987 the TUC established a Special Review Body to report upon the developing competitive hostility between member unions. Different parties expected different things from this review ranging from clear condemnation of "no-strike" agreements[55] to recognition that, in one form or another, they were normal and should be encouraged if they were, in fact, the way to secure recruiting rights.

It seems unlikely that the final report of the S.R.B. will recommend any change in either the principle or its extending notes. One way out of some of the problems would be to allow the TUC Disputes Committee to consider the prospects of success of the complainant unions in securing recognition. The alternative is for the TUC to take a more active part in securing agreement between the contestant unions whilst the discussions on a single-union agreement are continuing. Whatever the solution the question of "spheres of bargaining influence" has clearly, and suddenly, moved into a wholly different area where the employer no longer accepts or rejects the package of unions presented to him. A market-place approach in which individual unions try to purchase the preference seems inevitable.

DISCLOSURE OF INFORMATION FOR BARGAINING PURPOSES

It may be thought obvious that without reliable information on such matters as the employer's future plans, the negotiator is in a weak position as against whoever has that information. This conclusion is, in practice, not as inevitable as it looks. Many union officials would contend that they would be inhibited by too much information on the employer's financial position. They would say that what should interest them most is the employees' financial position relative to other employees, the change in the cost of living and so on. Their case is that if the employer is in business he should offer terms and conditions com-

---

[54] *e.g.* TUC Disputes Committee Report 85/583.
[55] Arthur Scargill, TUC Report 1987, p. 422.

parable to others and adequate for his employees. It is for him, not the union, to worry about how he will do this and satisfy his targets for profit margins. In any case, they would say, information the source of which is in the control of one party has a tendency to support that party's case. Nevertheless it is clear that there is a considerable amount of information known to an employer which it is essential for a trade union to know if it is to present an effective case. Comparisons with other groups of employees and the state of the pension fund are typical examples. It must be that if the union has to be in the position of challenging a decision formulated by the Board of Directors it should have at least certain pieces of information about that decision.

The Central Arbitration Committee still has a function in respect of the supply of information necessary for effective bargaining. The Employment Protection Act 1975 deals with the question of provision of information from an employer to the representatives of his employees with whom he negotiates terms and conditions of employment. This need for information has been recognised for some time and, indeed, provision was made for it in the Industrial Relations Act 1971. The provisions of that Act never became practically operational partly for the reason that the Commission on Industrial Relations, which was charged with investigating and reporting upon the best way of making detailed provision for the supply of such information, though it did in fact report, did not really resolve the difficulties which lie in the way of the practical operation of such a scheme.

The proposals in the 1975 Act appear on the face of it once more to delegate the resolution of these difficulties, since it is provided that the ACAS shall prepare a code of practice upon the disclosure of information. The Act provides that it shall be the duty of the employer, subject to certain exceptions, to disclose to the representatives of independent trade unions which he recognises all such information relating to his undertaking as is in his possession, or that of any associated employer, and is both information without which the trade union representatives would be to a material extent impeded in carrying on with him such collective bargaining, and information which it would be in accordance with good industrial relations practice that he should disclose to them for the purposes of collective bargaining.[56] The collective bargaining to which this applies is that with the recognised independent unions in respect of those employees for which the unions are recognised,[57] or originally, that falling within the scope of a recognition recommendation within the meaning of the 1975 legislation.

The employer is exempt from the obligation to supply information where the information:

(a) would adversely affect national security if disclosed;
(b) could not be disclosed without contravention of a statutory prohibition;
(c) has been communicated to the employer in confidence or has been obtained by him in consequence of the confidence reposed in him by another person;

---

[56] s.17(1).
[57] s.17(2).

(d) relates specifically to an individual who has not consented to disclosure;

(e) would, if disclosed, cause substantial injury to the employer's undertaking for reasons other than its effect on collective bargaining; or,

(f) has been obtained by the employer for the purpose of bringing, prosecuting or defending any legal proceedings.

The employer also has no duty to produce or allow inspection of any document other than a document prepared for the purpose of conveying or confirming the information, or to make a copy of or extracts from any document. Nor is he required to compile or assemble any information where that would involve an amount of work or expenditure out of reasonable proportion to the value of the information in the conduct of collective bargaining. One or two obvious points may be made about this list of exemptions. In the first place, it should be noticed that the important exemption contained in (e) is qualified by the word "substantial." It seems likely that this would have a very restrictive effect on the operation of that exemption and, indeed, in the few cases that come before the C.A.C., it is infrequently raised. It may also be inferred from the exemption provided for expensive compilation of information that it is not open to an employer to avoid his obligation to supply information by arguing that the information does not exist because it has not been collated or in some other way brought together. It would appear that information refers to known facts and not to any particular tangible source.

The ACAS Code of Practice gives certain examples of information relating to an undertaking which "could be relevant in certain collective bargaining situations" but admits that the list is neither exhaustive nor indicative of the fact that such information should be supplied in a given situation. It makes a similar attempt to list information which might cause substantial injury such as cost information on individual products, detailed analysis of proposed investments, marketing or pricing policies and price quotas or the make-up of tender prices. In general it states that substantial injury may occur if, for example, certain customers would be lost to competitors, or suppliers would refuse to supply necessary materials, or the ability to raise funds to finance the company would be seriously impaired. This type of guidance may be of some assistance but it must be borne in mind that the financial forecasts of a company's business are often the most useful pieces of information both a trade union and its business rivals could have.

The Code suggests that trade unions should make clear reasoned requests for specific information. In other words a fishing inquiry should not be resorted to. In turn it suggests that the aim of an employer should be to be as open and helpful as possible in meeting the request. A refusal should be explained and be capable of being supported should a claim be made to the C.A.C.

Where a trade union wishes to complain that it has not been supplied with information to which it is entitled under the statutory provisions that complaint must be made in writing to the C.A.C.[58] If the Committee is of the opinion that the complaint is reasonably likely to be settled by conciliation, it must refer it to the ACAS for this purpose. It will be observed that in this

---

[58] s.19.

instance the C.A.C. is the initial referee rather than an arbitrator of last resort. The C.A.C. has, therefore, developed the practice of holding a preliminary hearing before a chairman alone to ascertain whether the matter must go for hearing or whether there is a chance of settlement by conciliation. If the complaint is not settled or withdrawn, and ACAS is of the opinion that further attempts at conciliation are unlikely to result in a settlement, ACAS must inform the Committee of this opinion. Where conciliation has failed, or not been resorted to, the C.A.C. shall hear and determine the complaint and make a declaration stating whether it finds the complaint well founded wholly or in part and the reasons for its finding.[59] Any person whom the Committee considers has a proper interest in the complaint is entitled to be heard but only failure to hear the trade union and the employer directly concerned will invalidate the proceedings. The declaration must specify the information in respect of whch the Committee finds that the complaint is well founded, the date on which the employer refused or failed to disclose the information, and a period of not less than one week from the date of the declaration within which the employer ought to disclose such information. At any time after that specified period, the trade union may return to the C.A.C. and present to it in writing a complaint that the employer still fails to disclose or confirm in writing information specified in the declaration.[60] At the same time, or at any time after the presentation of this further complaint, the trade union may claim in writing, in respect of one or more descriptions of employees specified in the claim, that their contract should include the terms and conditions specified in the claim.[61] Apparently the Committee's award may deal with either or both of these aspects.[62] In practice the view of the C.A.C. is that since the award becomes operative as a term of the contracts of employment it affects, it is more appropriate that it should deal with the actual terms and conditions in dispute. Generally the C.A.C. would not regard an obligation to supply bargaining information as appropriate to the contract of employment and would tend not to seek to imply such a term.[63]

Section 16 of the Companies Act 1967 dealing with additional material to be included in the directors' annual report has been extended[64] so as to require, in the case of companies which have during the financial year employed an average of 250 persons each week, that that report should contain certain information as to the supply of bargaining information and the availability of consultation. The matters to be dealt with concern the action taken during the financial year: to introduce, maintain, or develop arrangements aimed at:

(a) providing employees systematically with information on matters of concern to them as employees,

(b) consulting employees or their representatives on a regular basis so that

---

[59] s.19(4).
[60] s.20(1).
[61] s.21(1).
[62] s.21(3).
[63] The provision for compulsory effect does not apply to Crown employment. It is proposed to refer any such dispute to an independent ACAS inquiry having no binding effect and without any element of C.A.C. intervention.
[64] E.A. 1982, s.1.

the views of employees can be taken into account in making decisions
which are likely to affect their interests,

(c) encouraging the involvement of employees in the company's performance through an employees' share scheme or by some other means,

(d) achieving a common awareness on the part of all employees of the
financial and economic factors affecting the performance of the company.

RECRUITING AND MAINTENANCE OF UNION MEMBERSHIP—THE CLOSED SHOP

It goes without saying that the bargaining strength of a trade union depends
on its support among the workforce. There is no point in threatening an
employer with industrial action if he knows that his workforce, or a significant
enough proportion of it to enable him to continue some production, will not
respond. Generally, at least until 1988, a union could assume that its members, once they had indicated their support for a course of action, would continue that support. The union will, of course, have means of securing such
support from a wavering minority and its disciplinary rules have been the
most obvious of these means. The effect of such discipline is enormously
enhanced if union membership is necessary to enable the worker to retain
employment. Briefly, the greater the proportion of the workforce in membership and the more effective the sanction against those not obeying its instructions, the stronger the union's bargaining position. So the union will seek to
recruit members (which in turn depends on its effectiveness) and, having recruited them, to retain them. What has long been known as the "closed shop,"
under which the employer agrees, or is at least expected, to dismiss any
employee not acquiring or retaining union membership, is the most effective
support both for recruiting and for sanctions against indiscipline.

Until 1982 no legal provision was made to regulate a union's recruiting
activities, whereas an employer who responded to recruitment campaigns by
dismissing those involved or otherwise discriminating against them might[65]
incur penalties for unfair dismissal or action short of dismissal. The Employment Act 1982[66] rendered void any term or condition of a contract for the
supply of goods or services which purported to require part, or all, of the
work to be done wholly by persons who are (or by persons who are not) members of a particular trade union. A statutory duty was enacted, actionable by
the supplier, not to fail to include in any list of approved suppliers any person
on the ground that the work would, or would be likely to, be done by non-
union workers or by union workers. Similarly actionable by the supplier is a
termination, or the exclusion of a person from a group of those invited to tender, or failure to permit such a person to tender for, or otherwise determining
not to enter into, a contract on the ground that the workers involved would
(or would not) be, or be likely to, be, trade union members.

The primary purpose of this prohibition is to prevent a trade union using its
influence with a main contractor to impose upon a subcontractor an obligation to employ union members, thus using union strength in one place to
secure membership in another. The reverse situation in which pressure is

---

[65] *Infra*, p. 305 *et seq*.
[66] s.12.

imposed on the subcontractor not to employ union members is much less likely to arise in practice. Apart from this situation the law had not intervened in the efforts of trade unions to ensure that only those who are, or intend to become, union members are recruited to employment; any more than it restricts the freedom of an employer to refuse to engage trade unionists.

As we shall see, however, it is now no longer open to an employer, without risk of an action for unfair dismissal, to dismiss an employee who does not honour his undertaking on engagement to join a trade union. Strangely, for the first would seem less supportable than the second, a trade union is free to seek to induce an employer to operate a pre-entry closed shop in which all those engaged must already be union members (though they are free to leave thereafter without fear of fair dismissal) but is not free, without the risk of involvement in an action for unfair dismissal, to seek enforcement of a post-entry closed shop whereby non-unionists are required, within a few months of engagement, to join a specified trade union or one of a number of trade unions.

The institution of the "closed shop" has appeared, since the modern trade union movement began in the United Kingdom, in a great variety of forms. The two clearest divisions are the pre-entry and the post-entry closed shops just mentioned. The pre-entry closed shop may, in extreme situations, take the form of a "union hiring hall" when agreement is reached with an employer, or, occasionally, an entire section of industry, that vacancies shall be notified to a local office of a trade union which will then provide a suitable employee from the list of its members seeking employment. Often, priority is given to such members according to the length of their membership of the union. At the other end of the range of post-entry closed shops there are many situations in which an employer is able to deny the existence of any closed-shop agreement but will agree that he has given the relevant union to understand that he will use his best endeavours to see that all employees, or all employees in a particular section of his undertaking, join the union. Practice varies as to the strictness with which closed-shop agreements will be enforced. Trade union officials are likely to wish to remove one or two workers actively opposed to the union but to take a more relaxed view of a larger group asserting a principle which precludes union membership for themselves, but not actively opposed to the activities of the union.

The principal justification for the closed shop is that it ensures that all those who will benefit from the union's negotiating strength share the cost of maintaining that strength, both in terms of payment of union dues and loss of wages and job security as a result of participation in industrial action. Various devices have been tried whereby the freedom of an individual not to join a union can be maintained without him enjoying a direct financial advantage, but none succeed in subjecting him to obligations equivalent to those of union membership. It is often contended that, since union membership in the United Kingdom implies no political commitment, there should be no objection to insistence on group solidarity in face of the power of organised capital.

There have been notable examples in the past of trade unions refusing, as a matter of policy, to bargain for closed shops on the ground that they produce an atmosphere of false security in which local organisation and responsiveness to the wishes of members suffers. It seems likely that there comes a point of organisation at which the employer prepared to deal with a trade union may well move from neutrality as regards recruitment to membership to active support. Provision in the Industrial Relations Act 1971, requiring certain majorities in ballots for closed-shop agreements, tended to destroy an earlier practice by which an employer faced with an achieved level of around 80 per cent. of union membership in a defined group of employees would make efforts to enable himself to accept 100 per cent. membership. This he might do by moving adamant non-unionists to other groups, or by seeking specifically to exclude from the obligation of membership existing employee non-members.

From the point of view of the affected employee it could be said that no widespread problem arose since trade unions in the United Kingdom were normally open to all applicants. It is true that there is less exclusiveness in the British trade union movement than, for instance, in some trade unions in the United States. On the other hand, in the past, craft unions have excluded applicants who had not served an apprenticeship by a certain age; thus effectively requiring early commitment to a chosen occupation if the union operated closed-shop agreements on any significant scale. Some untypical, but nonetheless highly exclusive, practices have existed such as that in the London Docks which denied employment to all but close relatives of existing dockworkers. Perhaps more worrying at the present time is the fact that those controlling the union will inevitably see certain types of vehement opposition as an attempt to destroy the union and visit it with expulsion, thus denying the opposition the freedom to work in the trade, or a section of it.

A closed-shop trade union cannot be equated to other voluntary associations whose members are free to decide with whom they associate. In such a case the effect of non-association of an individual is usually social. The question of the relative seriousness of disassociation is inextricably linked to the issue of whether a converse right not to associate springs inevitably from recognition of the right of workers to associate for their own protection. On the one hand the individual is forced into non-association, on the other he chooses it; but the effects and the questions of principle are the same. Wedderburn[67] discusses the arguments at length. He points out that some modern English judges have marshalled in favour of freedom of non-association a supposed "right to work."[68] Professor Hepple[69] has revealed a number of fundamentally different connotations for the term, none of which contain any definitive limits. If there is to be a right to offer oneself on the labour market it certainly is not matched by any reduction of management prerogative to reject whom it pleases. The development of such a right would contrast with the increasing perception, if not increasing reality, of lack of job protection. The real strength of the attack on the closed shop is that it interferes with the freedom of the individual to make and maintain the relationship with the employer which each desire. But in an industrial situation not designed to encourage individualism is there much substance in that freedom?

The rise and fall of the practice of union membership agreements in the space of 20 years has been startling. In 1964 McCarthy[70] estimated, largely by

---

[67] *The Worker and the Law*, (3rd ed.), pp. 362 *et seq.*
[68] See, *e.g. Langston* v. *A.U.E.W.* [1974] I.C.R. 180 at 190.
[69] *A Right to Work* (1981) 10 I.L.J. 65.
[70] W. E. J. McCarthy: *The Closed Shop in Britain* (Blackwell 1964).

informed impression, that one worker in six was covered by some form of union membership agreement. At its high point in the mid-1970s it was more like one in four. A dramatic rise, particularly in the incidence of formal agreements took place immediately after the repeal of the Industrial Relations Act. It has been suggested that a high point figure of 5.2 million workers in closed shops[71] at one time understated the numbers involved. This number had fallen by about a million in 1982, however, and, with the aid of legislative disincentives, has continued to fall. Evidence of employers, some in the public sector, announcing rescission of closed-shop agreements without waiting for evidence of declining support would not have been believable a few years earlier.

Symptomatic of the awareness of an opportunity to challenge what had been accepted tacitly as a feature of British industrial relations was the complaint taken to the European Court of Human Rights in *Young and James* v. *The United Kingdom* and *Webster* v. *The United Kingdom.*[72] The applicants were all employees of British Rail who had commenced their employment when no closed-shop requirement applied to them. British Rail had concluded a closed-shop agreement with the three railway unions in 1970 but had not implemented it because of the prohibition contained in the Industrial Relations Act 1971. Following the repeal of that prohibition a further agreement was concluded imposing a closed shop on specified categories of employees from August 1, 1975. That agreement incorporated what was then the sole statutory exception to permission to dismiss a non-unionist in a closed-shop situation by excepting an existing employee who genuinely objected on grounds of religious belief. None of the three objected to union membership on religious grounds, but all refused to join the appropriate union on other grounds. They based their claim primarily on Article 11 of the European Human Rights Convention. This provides for freedom of association and it was argued by the applicants that this should imply a negative right of non-association. A majority of the European Court held that compulsion upon those who had become employed before the imposition of a closed shop to join a particular trade union or face dismissal was contrary to the freedom guaranteed by Article 11. Some members of the court considered that the negative right was a necessary corollary of the positive freedom of association, but the majority of the court did not make this an essential aspect of its decision. In the view of the majority it was the element of compulsion, enforced by the sanction of dismissal on those who had not been employed subject to the obligation to join a union, which produced the breach of Article 11. The majority also held that this compulsion would have continued to be applied had the applicants sought to exercise a freedom to join other than the specified trade unions. It is, of course, similarly arguable that, in practice, the option open to those seeking employment to select some other trade amounted to compulsion on those wishing to become railwaymen. Such a conclusion, however, would suggest a freedom to choose one's trade which could operate against a trade union but not against an employer. The majority of the court also concluded that Article 11 was part of a pattern of protec-

---

[71] See Dunn and Gerrard: *The Closed Shop in British Industry* (1984).
[72] Applications 7601/76 and 7806/77 reported in [1981] I.R.L.R. 408.

tion of freedom of thought, conscience and expression which was threatened by compulsion to join an association contrary to one's convictions.

Meanwhile, United Kingdom legislation had continued to restrict the enforceability of the closed shop. It is worth remembering that closed-shop agreements were enforceable before 1971 simply because employment was largely unprotected. It was only necessary at common law for an employer to pay wages in lieu of notice to deprive the non-union employee of any remedy for dismissal. An employer, therefore, had little incentive to resist a union request for dismissal. This situation was sustained in 1976 by the provision that dismissal should be automatically fair if it had occurred in accordance with a union membership agreement. Not only did the collective agreement remove the sanction of unfairness from the reason for dismissal but it also provided the procedure that was automatically to be regarded as fair.[73] Even in the early 1980s the scope of this permission to dismiss was widely construed by the courts. In *Taylor* v. *Co-operative Retail Services Ltd.*[74] the Court of Appeal held that the existence of 10 per cent. of employees who were not union members did not eliminate a practice of joining so that, despite their presence, a union membership agreement existed. In *Gayle* v. *John Wilkinson and Sons (Saltley) Ltd.*[75] an employer who honestly believed an employee not to be a trade union member, because he had been misinformed by the union, was held to have dismissed fairly.[76]

At the same time, however, legislative restriction was increasing. The Employment Act 1982,[77] added a number of grounds of exception from enforceability to the "deeply-held personal conviction" which had, earlier, replaced religious objection. The most effective was the requirement that no closed-shop agreement should be enforceable unless approved by ballot of those affected within five years before the enforcement in question. Other exceptions covered those who objected to union membership on the ground that it might involve them in industrial action contrary to a code of conduct governing the conduct of persons holding qualifications relevant to the employment in question. This provision was designed to encourage professional associations opposed to industrial action on the ground that the nature of their work incorporated an obligation not to deny their services to those dependent on them.

A number of well-publicised cases of closed shops being renewed after ballots approving them, indicated that even the high-level support demanded of 80 per cent. of those entitled to vote, or 85 per cent. of those voting, would normally be achieved. That is predictable. Union members are not likely to vote against the interests of their union in any substantial number, save in a situation such as arose at the glass manufacturers Pilkingtons in 1970 when a revolt of 8,000 employees against the General and Municipal Workers Union occurred because the local officials had become too involved with management to respond to the wishes of union members. Members of professions

---

[73] *Jeffrey* v. *Lawrence Scott and Electromotors Ltd.* [1977] I.R.L.R. 466; *Curry* v. *Harlow District Council* [1979] I.C.R. 769.

[74] [1982] I.R.L.R. 354.

[75] 1978 I.C.R. 154. But compare *Blue Star Ship Management Ltd.* v. *Williams* [1978] I.C.R. 770.

[76] See also *McGhee* v. *Midland British Road Services Ltd. and T.G.W.U.* [1985] I.R.L.R. 198; *Sakals* v. *United Counties Omnibus Co. Ltd.* [1984] I.R.L.R. 474.

[77] s.3 providing a new s.58 to the E.P.C.A. 1978.

who objected to obeying a strike call were often able to remain within associations like the Royal College of Nursing which, whilst fulfilling bargaining functions on behalf of their members, eschewed industrial action so that that legislative exception produced little visible effect.

All in all, although the coverage of closed-shop agreements had declined it had done so from a quite exceptional peak at a time when trade unionism was under severe pressure and against a background requirement that support for it be regularly reaffirmed. The closed shop, until 1988, had proved one of the most durable institutions in British industrial relations.

Running parallel with legislative permission, however it might be restricted, was a corresponding provision that dismissal, or action short of dismissal, for non-union membership in the absence of a union membership agreement should be automatically unfair or give rise to a claim for compensation. Originally, this provision had been designed to protect those who adhered to independent trade unions and refused to join employer-dominated trade unions. It was only necessary to delete the reference to a non-independent union to reverse the effect of what had been a pro-trade-union provision. It was only necessary in 1988 to repeal the provision of section 58(3)–(12) (and of s.23(2A) and (2B) which permitted action short of dismissal against non-unionists in a closed-shop situation) of the Employment Protection (Consolidation) Act 1978 to alter a situation in which there could be no claim for unfair dismissal for non-union membership arising from enforcement of a union membership agreement for the remaining statutory provisions to make all dismissal on grounds of membership or non-membership of a union automatically unfair.[78] From July 26, 1988 an employer cannot enforce a closed-shop agreement without rendering himself, and a union inducing him to do so, liable to a financial penalty greatly in excess of the compensation rates normally available for unfair dismissal.[79] All the closed-shop provisions of the 1978 Act become ineffective and are repealed.[80] There is no point in insisting on approval by ballot. Closed-shop agreements are not unlawful, unless common law courts are again invited to consider whether they might be regarded as in unreasonable restraint of trade, but they now carry no legal privileges to make them enforceable or induce attack by those opposed to them. Time will tell whether the view of some British and most Continental European trade unionists that union officials and union organisation will be livelier without them is justified.

VICTIMISATION OF UNION MEMBERS, THOSE ENGAGED IN UNION ACTIVITY AND NON-MEMBERS

Statutory protection is provided from dismissal[81] where the dismissal is by reason of membership, or proposed membership, of an independent trade union, non-membership, or proposed refusal to join or remain a member, of any trade union, or participation, or proposed participation, in the activities of an independent trade union at an appropriate time. Dismissal for such

---

[78] E.A. 1988, s.11.
[79] *Infra*, pp. 309–310.
[80] That is to say, E.P.C.A. 1978, s.58(3)–(12) and s.23(2A) and 23(2B).
[81] E.P.C.A. 1978, s.58(1) and (2).

reason, or principal reason, will be automatically unfair. A right to compensation is similarly provided for "action short of dismissal" with the intention of preventing or deterring an employee from membership of an independent trade union or from taking part in its activities at an appropriate time or compelling an employee to be a member of any trade union.[82] Action short of dismissal is also prohibited if its purpose is to require an employee to make payments as an alternative to union membership.[83] Unusually, the applicant has, in these situations, to prove the reason for his dismissal,[84] although it is perhaps less clear that this should be so when the tribunal would have jurisdiction whatever the reason. The scope of "action short of dismissal" has been reviewed recently by the Court of Appeal in *National Coal Board* v. *Ridgway*.[85] Members of the National Union of Mineworkers were employed at a colliery alongside members of the breakaway Union of Democratic Mineworkers. The N.C.B. reached agreement with the U.D.M. on increased wages in January 1986 and commenced payment of the increase. No agreement had then been reached with the N.U.M. and the increase was not paid to its members. Some of them complained of action short of dismissal. The Court of appeal noted that "action" included omission to act[86] so that failure to pay a wage increase was action short of dismissal even if the complainants had no reasonable expectation that they would receive a rise.

The rather surprising decision of the E.A.T. that complaint could only be made if the employer was seeking to attack membership of all independent trade unions, rather than a particular independent trade union, was overruled.[87] The Court of Appeal held, however, that the statute referred to action against the applicant as an individual. There was a difference between this and the incidental effect upon such a person of action against a trade union. In *Post Office* v. *Crouch*[88] the House of Lords had held that a similar provision in the Industrial Relations Act 1971, which, however, did not contain the words "as an individual," meant that discrimination against a union was also discrimination against its members. In that case, the withdrawal of facilities for a trade union at the workplace was held to be action short of dismissal against its members, but in *Ridgway* the Court of Appeal concluded that that could no longer be so. May L.J. thought that refusal of a pay increase to all members of a union was properly regarded as action against the union and not the individual, but the majority held that since the "action" affected the individual not merely as a union member or official it should be regarded as action affecting him as an individual. The mere fact that a pay increase was made as a result of negotiation with the union did not mean that its denial affected a person only because of his membership of the union. The distinction is made, therefore, not on the basis of whether it is the individual or the union which is the subject of attack, nor by asking whether the effect

---

[82] E.P.C.A. 1978, s.23.

[83] E.P.C.A. 1978, s.23(1A).

[84] *Maund* v. *Penwith D.C.* [1984] I.R.L.R. 24. s.57 E.P.C.A. imposes the burden in other cases on the employer.

[85] [1987] I.C.R. 64.

[86] See E.P.C.A. 1978, s.153(1).

[87] Compare: *Rath* v. *Cruden Construction Ltd.* [1982] I.C.R. 60 with *Carlson* v. *The Post Office* [1981] I.C.R. 343.

[88] [1974] I.C.R. 378.

on the individual is direct or indirect. Action against an individual may arise from the effects of collective action against the union. The question is, does the action affect the applicant as an individual rather than merely as part of the union organisation?

Membership or non-membership of a union, even if only projected, is a reasonably clear concept. "Trade union activity" is not. Individuals often take action which might be taken by a union official in his capacity as such. In *Chant* v. *Aquaboats Ltd.*[89] the employee had organised a petition among his fellow workers against unsafe machinery. He had taken the draft petition to the local union official for comment. He was dismissed for "incapability," but the E.A.T. held that what he had done could not be described as a union activity even if he could show it to be the real cause of his dismissal.

On the other hand in *Brennan* v. *Ellward (Lancs.) Ltd.*[90] it was held to be too wide to say that the activities must be those of an authorised representative. The E.A.T. gave recruiting of union members by existing rank and file members during lunch breaks as an obvious union activity. In *Dixon and Shaw* v. *West Ella Developments Ltd.*[91] the E.A.T. sought to define the characteristics of trade union activity by pointing out that the provision did not say "activities of a trade union." So it was said to be strongly arguable that to contact one's union representative with a complaint about safety constituted a trade union activity. The difference between the situation in this case and that in *Chant* is that the individual sought to transfer his complaint to the normal industrial relations machinery operated by the union whereas in *Chant* the complaint remained an individual one outside that system. This seems to suggest that there is an area, admittedly not defined with precision, in which it is commonly acknowledged trade unions normally operate various procedures. Resort to that type of procedure in such a situation is likely to be regarded as a union activity. It is the conjunction of use of trade union procedures to deal with trade-union-type problems which creates a trade union activity. Such procedures are, however, themselves loosely defined. A union official may present a safety complaint to an employer in much the same way as an individual. The official's action is a union procedure because he is acting as a union official and not an individual. His action may be unauthorised but nonetheless he uses an authority to make the approach inherent in his office. It is correct to conclude from this that in doubtful cases it is more likely that a union official will be regarded as undertaking a union activity than will an individual pursuing the same end. The official, provided he acts as such, implies that the union machinery is functioning. An example of the lengths to which this can be taken is contained in *British Airways Engine Overhaul Ltd.* v. *Francis.*[92] An aircraft component worker who had been a A.U.E.W. shop steward for some three years was instructed to try to get a statement published in the local Press expressing the dissatisfaction of those she represented with the union's actions to secure equal pay. She succeeded in having such a statement published and was reprimanded by her employer for making a public statement requiring his permission. The E.A.T. held that an industrial tri-

---

[89] [1978] I.C.R. 643.
[90] [1976] I.R.L.R. 378.
[91] [1978] I.C.R. 856.
[92] [1981] I.C.R. 278.

bunal was entitled to regard hers as a union activity. In *Marley Tile Co. Ltd.*
v. *Shaw*[93] both Goff and Stephenson L.JJ. expressed doubts as to whether the
action of an individual in calling a meeting to protest at his non-recognition by
the employer as a shop steward was a union activity. The difficulty lay in the
fact that not only was the individual's action not positively authorised by the
union but might be said to have been positively unauthorised since consultation and negotiation procedures would normally be used between the union
and the employer to deal with disputes over such recognition. The method of
protest adopted by Shaw might, therefore, be seen as a private ventilation of
grievances.

A considerable loophole in the protection available has been opened by the
decision of the Court of Appeal in *Carrington* v. *Therm a Stor*[94] in which collective retaliation against individuals because of the activity of their union was
held not to arise from their union activities. The respondents were a non-
union employer. A small group of employees recruited about 60 of the 70
employees into the T.G.W.U. Chargehands were told by management to
select any 20 workers for dismissal on grounds of redundancy. The Court of
Appeal held that no individual membership or activity was thereby attacked.
An indiscriminate reign of terror thereby escapes the statutory protection
even though its purpose is to deter both trade union activities and membership.

It seems to be clearly established that industrial action cannot be regarded
as a trade union activity for the purposes of this section.[95] Tribunals will have
to decide, as a question of fact, whether the activity in question, as, for
instance, a union meeting, is industrial action.[96]

Employer consent during working hours

In the *Marley Tile* case[97] the E.A.T. had upheld the view of the industrial
tribunal[98] that employer consent to union activities in working hours could be
implied and that the existence of a normal bargaining and industrial relations
system might be sufficient to imply such consent. In overruling the finding
that such consent could be implied in the instant case the Court of Appeal did
not deny the possibility of implied consent. The court felt that such consent
could not be implied from the employer's silence when the activity in question
was an interference with production wholly unincorporated into the normal
industrial relations machinery. This leaves entirely open the situations in
which consent can be implied for some unusual or unexpected activity. In
between the decisions of the E.A.T. and the Court of Appeal in this case the
E.A.T. had considerably extended the concept of implied consent in *Zucker*
v. *Astrid Jewels Ltd.*[99] The court was prepared to imply consent to certain
union activities from the fact that they were normal human conduct which
might be expected in any employment situation. For example, few employers

---

[93] [1980] I.C.R. 72.
[94] [1983] I.C.R. 208.
[95] *Drew* v. *St. Edmundsbury Borough Council* [1980] I.C.R. 513; *Brennan* v. *Ellward (Lancs) Ltd.* [1976] I.R.L.R. 378.
[96] See *Winnett* v. *Seamarks Bros. Ltd.* [1978] I.C.R. 1240.
[97] *Supra.*
[98] [1978] I.R.L.R. 238.
[99] [1978] I.C.R. 1088.

would seek to deny that they consented to their employees talking to each other during a tea-break on any matter which the employees chose. The tea-break, therefore, is likely to be a time during working hours when the employer might be taken to have consented to employees discussing the advantages, or otherwise, of union membership. This is the essential element of an effort to recruit union members and the E.A.T. obviously did not think that consent to a particular activity should vary by reference to the purpose of that activity. Alternatively the E.A.T. took the view that not all the time during which an employee is on the employer's premises is "working hours." A tea-break is not a time when an employee is required to be at work and, therefore, it may be unnecessary to require an employer's consent to the use of such time for union activities.

In *N.C.B.* v. *Ridgway*[1] Bingham L.J. again emphasised that the statutory protection referred to activities on the employer's premises.[2]

Where the employer had a union membership agreement the right of participation in union activities was confined to the activities of one of the specified unions, but this limitation was repealed in 1988.[3] The main effect of leaving it in force would have been to allow a trade union, by a union membership agreement, to protect its position from the intrusion of activities in support of rival unions. Employees who most generally prefer absence of such intrusive organisation presumably also have to put up with the logical consequence of the new legislative supposition that the employment relationship is to be regulated by principles of individualism.

Remedies

The remedy for a complaint of action short of dismissal lies to an industrial tribunal within three months of the cause of the complaint. The tribunal may make a declaration that the action is well founded and may award such compensation as it considers just and equitable, taking into account the applicant's contribution and duty to mitigate.[4]

Unfair dismissal is visited with a punitive award. A minimum basic award is fixed[5] at £2,400 at time of going to press. Where the applicant applies for reinstatement or re-engagement, the tribunal may make a "special award" in addition to the basic and compensatory awards of 104 times a week's pay, up to a maximum of £23,850, or the sum of £11,950, whichever is greater. If the award of compensation is made following a failure to comply with an order for reinstatement or re-engagement, the amount of the special award is increased to 156 times a week's pay, or £17,900, whichever is greater. The special award may be reduced by such amount as the tribunal considers just and equitable if the complainant has unreasonably prevented an order for reinstatement or re-engagement from being complied with, or has unreasonably refused an offer by the employer which would have had the effect of reinstatement in employment in all respects as if he had not been dismissed.

If the employer or the complainant claims that the employer was induced to dismiss the complainant by trade union pressure on the employer by calling,

---

[1] [1987] I.C.R. 64.
[2] See also Denning M.R. in *Post Office* v. *Crouch* [1973] I.C.R. 366 at 378.
[3] E.A. 1988, s.11.
[4] E.P.C.A. 1978, s.26.
[5] E.A. 1982, ss.4 and 5 introducing s.75A into the E.P.A. 1978.

organising, procuring or financing industrial action, or threatening to do so, because the complainant was not a member of any trade union or of one of a number of trade unions, the employer or the complainant may, before the hearing of the complaint begins, require the person claimed to have exercised the pressure to be joined as a party to the proceedings. After the commencement of the hearing but before an award has been made the tribunal may be asked, in its discretion, to make such an order. Where such joinder is ordered any award may be apportioned between the employer and the inducer as the tribunal considers just and equitable.[6]

An employee complaining of unfair dismissal on grounds of union membership, non-membership or trade union activity may, within seven days of the effective date of termination, seek interim relief. Where the dismissal is by reason of union membership or activities a written certificate signed by an authorised official of the union concerned and stating that there appear to be reasonable grounds for supposing either to be the reason, or the principal reason, must be submitted within the same period. If, on hearing the application, the tribunal concludes that it is likely that the complainant will be found to have been unfairly dismissed for one of these reasons it must ask the employer whether he is willing to reinstate, or re-engage, on terms not less favourable. If he is, it must make an order to that effect unless, in the case of re-engagement the employee reasonably refuses to accept the offer. In the event of such reasonable refusal, or where the employer is not willing to reinstate or re-engage[7] the tribunal shall order continuation of the contract of employment, so far as it relates to pay, other benefits of employment, seniority, pension rights and other similar matters and the period of continuous employment until the determination or settlement of the complaint. The amount of pay, which must be specified in the order, shall be the amount the employee would reasonably be expected to earn and shall be paid on the normal pay days during the period of the order. Any payment made by the employer during the contract of employment, or by way of a lump sum in lieu of wages, shall be taken into account in determining the amount payable under the order.[8]

PAID TIME OFF WORK

An employer is required to permit an employee who is an official of an independent trade union recognised by the employer for bargaining purposes to take paid time off work for certain specific purposes.[9] The first of these purposes is to carry out those duties of his as such an official which are concerned with industrial relations between his employer and an associated employer, and their employees. The word "official" would appear not to apply to a per-

---

[6] E.P.C.A. 1978, s.76A.
[7] Or where the order for reinstatement or re-engagement is not complied with—s.79(2).
[8] E.P.C.A. 1978, ss.77 and 78.
[9] E.P.C.A. 1978, s.27. Recognition requires proof of intent by the employer to recognise which may be derived from a number of factors. Recognition is for purposes of collective bargaining and not, for example, as safety representatives—*Cleveland County Council* v. *Springett* [1985] I.R.L.R. 131. See pp. 292–295, *supra*.

son merely elected or appointed the delegate to a conference outside the workplace. If, however, a workers' representative were to wish to go to such a conference, being an official his right to paid leave would depend on the rest of the statutory definition.

The Act does not, as it might have done, use the words "connected with industrial relations." It may be thought that the words "concerned with" require a closer affinity. Although the heads of industrial relations are numerous, it seems reasonable to suggest that the matter in issue should fall directly within one such head rather than be a by-product of something in the list. The ACAS Code originally stated that an official's duties are those duties pertaining to his or her role in the jointly agreed procedures or customary arrangements for collective bargaining and grievance handling. It then listed six specific sub-headings including: collective bargaining with appropriate levels of management; meetings with other lay officials or full-time officers on matters concerned with industrial relations between his employer and the employees; appearing on behalf of constituents before an outside official body dealing with industrial relations matters concerning the employer, and interviews with and on behalf of constituents on grievance and disciplinary matters concerning them and their employer. It seems to be generally accepted that to this list should be added the duties of a safety representative under the Health and Safety at Work, etc., Act 1974. Even with this addition, the list would appear to be closely linked with the basic concepts of industrial relations. In *British Bakeries (Northern) Ltd.* v. *Adlington*[10] it was held that the right extended to attending a meeting to campaign against amendment of the Baking Industry (Hours of Work) Act on the ground that it was a matter of fact for an industrial tribunal whether preparatory work was sufficiently proximate to the discharge of industrial relations activities.

Matters connected with industrial relations

The question of what falls within the scope of matters connected with industrial relations duties was considered in *Beal* v. *The Beecham Group Ltd.*[11] in relation to the not unusual situation in which officials normally negotiate on a plant basis but wish to co-ordinate a policy covering a group of companies. In this instance the group was divided into two sub-groups containing five and six divisions respectively. The sub-groups were divided for industrial relations purposes into common interest groups, and it was at that level that collective bargaining was carried on. The extent of the unions' negotiating rights varied considerably between these common interest groups. Officials sought paid time off to attend a meeting of the National Advisory Committee for the Beecham Group "to enable representatives . . . to discuss matters of an industrial relations nature and to plan a co-ordinated strategy."

The E.A.T. held that it would be unduly restrictive to interpret "concerned with industrial relations between" employers and their employees to exclude

---

[10] *The Times*, February 17, 1989 (C.A.).
[11] [1981] I.R.L.R. 127 (E.A.T); [1982] I.R.L.R. 192 (C.A.). See also *Allen* v. *Thomas Scott and Son (Bakers) Ltd.* [1983] I.R.L.R. 11.

this function. The duties of a trade union official are not limited to bargaining and the precise terms of a recognition agreement. Although the employer was not required to deal with the N.A.C. the meeting in question was concerned with industrial relations. The meeting did not involve a mere exchange of information and, even if it had done so, it might still have been concerned with industrial relations. The actual decision in *Sood* v. *G.E.C. Elliott Process Automation Ltd.*[12] that an exchange of information was not within the permission does not mean that such a function can never be more than purely educative. The facts of each case would have to be looked at to see whether the processes of industrial relations were involved. Moreover, a co-ordinated approach is a legitimate objective and is not, therefore, too remote to constitute a duty.

The Court of Appeal confirmed this. O'Connor L.J. said:

"[The provisions of the ACAS Code of Practice, para. 13] which expressly are not comprehensive show that the code envisages that what is a union meeting may well be concerned with industrial relations. The code uses collective bargaining in a restricted sense as it separates matters of grievance and discipline, but it shows that what may be called preparatory work and explanatory work by officials may well be in fulfilment of duties concerned with industrial relations.

Finally, Mr. Field submitted that as the NAC had no negotiating function with the employers—indeed no function at all with the employers—attending its meetings could not be for the purpose of enabling the official to carry out his duties concerned with industrial relations. Once it is recognised that preparatory work falls within the discharge of duties concerned with industrial relations, then one looks to see if the preparatory work had some direct relevance to an industrial relations matter, and if so, it qualifies under s.27(1)(a). As I have said, attending the NAC to exchange information would not have that direct relevance but to determine policies nationally may well be directly relevant, depending upon what the policies are. The agenda and minutes of the meeting show that some at least of the policies were concerned with industrial relations matters that were to go into the 1979 wage claim.

It follows that in my judgment when the respondents attended the NAC meeting it was for the purpose of enabling them to carry out their duties concerned with industrial relations.

It must be remembered that time off under s.27(1) is subject to, and in accordance with, subsection (2). This is the safeguard for employers against any attempt by a union to dress up what is an activity to make it look like a duty concerned with industrial relations. So too is it under subsection (2) that the question has to be decided whether it was reasonable for the respondents to seek time off with pay for the NAC meeting in addition to their accepted CIG meeting."

So far as this interpretation accepts the inclusion of activities away from the place of employment it was confirmed by the Court of Appeal in *British Bakers (Northern) Ltd.* v. *Adlington*[13] but it is proposed to reverse this by legislation in the near future.

---

[12] [1980] I.C.R. 1.
[13] *Supra.*

Training

The second main purpose for which paid time off may be claimed is to undergo training in aspects of industrial relations relevant to the carrying out of the duties of the official concerned with industrial relations and approved by the Trades Union Congress or the independent trade union of which the employee is an official. This does not have the effect which might at first sight seem to be intended. There is nothing to stop an employer giving time off for his own courses. In *White* v. *Pressed Steel Fisher Ltd.*[14] the E.A.T. held that it did not follow that an employer's course was not adequate because it had not been approved by a trade union. Furthermore, the existence of an adequate course offered by the employer might provide a reasonable ground for refusing time off to attend a course approved by a trade union.

On the question of permissible training, the Code suggests two main areas: (1) initial basic training as soon as possible after the official is elected or appointed; (2) further training relevant to any special responsibilities or necessary to meet special circumstances. It is necessary to consider the nature of the official's duties in deciding whether the course is one which it is reasonable to permit him to attend.[15]

Conditions

Reasonable limits may be placed on the amount of time; the purposes for which; the occasions on which; and any conditions subject to which time off may be taken.[16] It is, of course, impossible to specify all the considerations which may justify such limits. The Code of Practice sets out quite a number in reasonably general terms. These include the operational requirements of the business; safety considerations; the obligations of the industry or service; accordance with agreed procedures and consistency with wider agreements; arrangements, where necessary, for other employees to cover the work; and the convenience of the times. Some of these enter into areas of great difficulty in terms of industrial relations. Manning agreements are not uncommon in certain areas of industry. In such areas there is little doubt that the employer will seek trade union agreement to refrain from requiring a replacement for an absent official. Although such agreement may at first sight seem reasonable, there are many reasons why, for instance, a trade union should resist any attempt to establish the fact that the machinery can be run with fewer employees than a manning agreement specifies. So far as the actual purpose for which the time is required is concerned it does not follow that the right is established as soon as it can be shown that the matter is concerned with the industrial relations duties of the official. The existence of an established procedure or an agreed solution to a problem may mean that it is reasonable for

---

[14] [1980] I.R.L.R. 176.
[15] *Sood* v. *G. E. C. Elliott Ltd.* [1981] I.R.L.R. 127 (E.A.T.); [1982] I.R.L.R. 192 (C.A.); *Menzies* v. *Smith and McLaurin Ltd.* [1980] I.R.L.R. 180. Compare *Young* v. *Carr Fasteners Ltd.* [1979] I.C.R. 844; The standard is that of whether the employer acted reasonably on the knowledge he might reasonably have—*Ministry of Defence* v. *Crook and Irving* [1982] I.R.L.R. 488.
[16] s.27(2).

an employer to refuse paid time off so that an official may take part in an unofficial procedure or seek a different solution.[17]

Pay

Where an official is permitted to take time off under this section, then the employer is required to pay him the amount of remuneration he would receive for the work he would ordinarily have been doing during that time as if he had worked for the whole of that time.[18] If it is reasonable to take the time off the employer is not entitled to impose a condition that it should be without pay.[18a] If the employee's remuneration for that work varies with the amount of work done, then he must receive an amount calculated by reference to the average hourly earnings for the work. This formula uses actual pay and not the notion of a normal week's pay. It appears to follow, therefore, that if time off is permitted during what would normally be overtime working, the employee is entitled to remuneration at the premium rate for that time off. Any contractual remuneration paid to the employee in respect of the time off may be set off against the statutory entitlement.[19]

An employee who is an official of an independent trade union recognised by the employer may present a complaint to an industrial tribunal that his employer has failed to permit him to take time off as required by the section or to pay him the whole or part of any amount so required to be paid.[20] This is, in fact, the only formal method provided by the Act for resolving any dispute as to the right of an official to time off or the reasonableness of any conditions to be attached to that right. It is perhaps unfortunate for the operation of this statutory provision that the effect of this is that any doubts can only finally be resolved by a refusal to grant the time off or the pay and resort to what is usually seen in this country as an adversary procedure.

Unpaid time for union activities

An employee who is a member of an independent recognised trade union has a right[21] to unpaid time off during working hours for the purpose of taking part in any activity of the union of which he is a member or for which he is acting as a representative, excluding activities which themselves consist of industrial action, whether or not in contemplation or furtherance of a trade dispute.

This latter exclusion clearly is not intended to exclude from the right unpaid time off to organise industrial action.[22] Again, the amount of time off which an employee is to be permitted to take, the purposes for which, the occasions on which, and any conditions subject to which this unpaid time off may be so taken, must be those that are reasonable in all the circumstances, having regard to the Code of Practice issued by the Advisory Conciliation and Arbitration Service.[23]

---

[17] *Depledge* v. *Pye Telecommunications Ltd.* [1981] I.C.R. 82.
[18] s.27(3).
[18a] *Beecham Group Ltd.* v. *Beal (No. 2)* [1983] I.R.L.R. 317.
[19] s.27(6).
[20] s.27(1).
[21] s.28.
[22] s. 28(2).
[23] s. 28(3).

STATUTORY ASSISTANCE TO BARGAINING

Consistently with the hands-off approach of Governments in the United Kingdom until the 1980s, statutory assistance in the processes of collective negotiation of terms and conditions of employment has been much less evident than in most other industrialised countries. Nevertheless there has, from time to time, arisen a situation in which it was apparent either, in the case of the establishment of Wages Councils, that the strength of the parties was so dissimilar that support was necessary or, in the case of the establishment of the Commission for Industrial Relations (which became the Advisory Conciliation and Arbitration Service), that some monitorial supervision or, latterly, simply advice and assistance would make for improved relations.

Wages councils

Trade Boards, later renamed Wages Councils, were first set up under the Trade Boards Act of 1909. Their initial purpose was to provide a minimum wage in sections of industry which trade unions found it hard to penetrate and where "sweated labour" had become a disgrace. Following the report of the Whitley Committee in 1917 they were extended to other sections of industry, where trade union organisation was poor, with the primary purpose of establishing a habit of collective bargaining so that purely voluntary bargaining could replace them. The Agricultural Wages Board operated under separate legislation but to a similar pattern. The report of the Royal Commission on Trade Unions[24] gave widespread publicity to fundamental criticism of the operation of Wages Councils, not least by trade unions which considered that they inspired apathy among the workforce towards forming their own organisation for bargaining.

Initially, trade unions were pleased with the added status that a Wages Council gave them and with the apparent resultant draw towards membership, but since the 1920s there has been a constant feeling that the existence of a council positively discourages union organisation. In evidence to the Royal Commission[25] the Transport and General Workers' Union commented that the existence of a Wages Council tended to produce the impression that a system of wage fixing existed which obviated the need for union membership, and that the incentive to the trade union movement itself to set up voluntary machinery was weakened. In the catering and hotel industry, which is a major sector for the operation of Wages Councils, only 4 per cent. of employees are in trade unions. In industry generally the figures of trade union membership in Wages Council sectors are between 75 and 25 per cent. of that for employment as a whole, revealing, if nothing else, that progress towards the original objective has been either slow or non-existent.[26]

Two responses are obvious. Either Wages Councils should be abolished or they should be made more effective. Both solutions were applied. In 1978, for instance, the Road Haulage Wages Council was abolished and nine councils in retail distribution were amalgamated to form two. The C.I.R. also recom-

---

[24] Cmnd. 3623 (1968).

[25] Cmnd. 3623, para. 229.

[26] F. J. Bayliss, *British Wage Councils* (Blackwell 1962) at pp. 140–141 thought these figures had to do with the character of the trade. That is true, but the Wages Council failed to change that character.

mended that 10 councils in clothing should be reduced to three, thereby removing 170,000 workers from their supervision.

In some cases abolition was obviously long overdue. When, in October 1973, the C.I.R. recommended the abolition of the Boot and Floor Polish Wages Council it had not met since 1967 and had no influence on pay of the 1,500 workers in the industry. On the other hand, when in the same month the abolition of three metalware councils was recommended , it was admitted that there would remain vulnerable minorities of employees for whom some protection might be needed. It was said, however, that such protection would not be afforded by continuing the Wages Councils. Rather, it was hoped that it would be forthcoming from a more general consideration of the problem of low-paid sections of industry. In the case of the Paper Box Wages Council[27] abolition was recommended despite the contention of the employers that no voluntary machinery existed to take its place. In both these latter cases there is obviously present an element of incentive to produce the necessary voluntary machinery.

Simultaneously, the Wages Councils Act 1979 extended the jurisdiction of remaining councils from the fixing of wage rates and holidays with pay to all terms and conditions of employment.[28] The Employment Protection Act 1975 conferred on the Secretary of State power, on his own initiative or on the application of the employers' or workers' organisations represented in the council to convert a Wages Council (but not the Agricultural Wages Board) into a "statutory joint industrial council" having the powers of a Wages Council and also having power to request the Advisory Conciliation and Arbitration Service to attempt to settle a dispute which the council had failed to resolve. The ACAS had power to appoint an arbitrator in such a case if it was unable to bring about a settlement by other means.[29] A statutory joint industrial council would not contain independent members.

The Secretary of State was also given power to establish a central co-ordinating committee to operate in relation to any two or more statutory joint industrial councils. He already had such power in relation to Wages Councils. If the Secretary of State was of the opinion that, if a statutory joint industrial council was abolished, adequate machinery would be established for the effective regulation of wages, terms and conditions of employment, and that such machinery was likely to be maintained he might, by order, abolish the council. The Secretary of State might vary the field of operation of a Wages Council and this included power to exclude from that field any employer who was a member of an organisation, party to an agreement regulating remuneration or other terms and conditions of employment. By this means areas of more advanced unionisation could be hived off without the need to abolish the whole council.

The Wages Act 1986, however, signalled a reversal of this extension of powers. Young people under 21 are now excluded from the operation of Wages Councils. It is said that this will enable employers to offer such workers wages which reflect their level of training and experience so as to enable them to "get a foothold on the ladder of employment and so improve

---

[27] C.I.R. Report No. 83 (1974).
[28] s.14.
[29] *Ibid.* ss.10 and 11.

their long-term prospects."[30] The idea that wages below the minimum set by a Wages Council could be beneficial would have struck the Whitley Committee as odd, especially had they envisaged that such levels would remain well below average for industry as a whole. The general power to fix terms and conditions was abolished and Wages Councils returned to the limited function of fixing a single, basic minimum hourly rate applicable to all time workers covered by the council and rates of deduction for living accommodation.[31] Piece rates are left to be worked out in accordance with this standard.[32] One hopes the author of an article in the Employment Gazette[33] does not intend his suggestion that the reason for this was that employers had found it difficult to understand the more detailed wages orders to be taken seriously. No one, knowing the history of Wages Councils and the minimal standard they have been able to maintain would consider a reduction of their powers anything but a deliberate attempt to weaken them.

In case the point had been missed, however, the 1986 Act destroys the power to create new councils and the process of abolition is simplified. It is, for instance, no longer necessary for the Secretary of State even to consult ACAS before a council is abolished or its scope varied although proposals for abolition or variation must be approved by both Houses of Parliament. The Secretary of State may abolish a Wages Council either on his own initiative or upon the application of a Joint Industrial Council, a conciliation board or some similar *joint* body substantially representative of organisations of workers and employers, on the ground that they jointly provide machinery which is, and is likely to remain, adequate for the effective regulation of remuneration and conditions of employment. To these powers the Industrial Relations Act 1971 added a unilateral right to apply for a winding-up by any organisation of workers which represents a substantial portion of the workers with respect to whom the council operates. The Act also substituted as the general ground for a winding-up that the existence of a Wages Council is no longer necessary for the purpose of maintaining a reasonable standard of remuneration for the workers with respect to whom it operates. Both these extensions were preserved by the Trade Union and Labour Relations Act 1974.[34]

Wages Councils fix wages by making a Wages Order, which becomes a term of the contract of employment of each worker covered by it. Before making the order the council must publish notice of the rate it proposes and allow 28 days[35] for the submission of any representations which, if they are in writing, must be considered.

Amended proposals must be given further publicity if it appears to the council that as a result of the modifications those affected should have an opportunity for further consideration. The order is operative from a date specified in it, not earlier than the date of the Wages Council's agreement to the proposals.[35a]

---

[30] (1986) 94 *Employment Gazette*, p. 371.
[31] Wages Act 1986, s.14.
[32] *Ibid.* s.15.
[33] *Supra*, n. 30.
[34] Sched. III, para. 9(3). See now, Wages Councils Act 1979, s.5.
[35] Wages Act 1986, Sched. III, para. 1.
[35a] s. 14(5)–(7)

A wages regulation order may be enforced as a term of his contract by any affected worker or, on his behalf, by a wages inspector. The worker may recover by this means up to six years' back pay. Alternatively, he may be awarded up to two years' back pay in summary criminal proceedings against the employer for infringement of the order. In practice there are virtually no civil or criminal proceedings for offences of this nature but the evidence suggests that the inspectorate is active and that the absence of court actions indicates that this method of ensuring observance is satisfactory.

Conciliation and arbitration

The conciliation powers of the Department of Employment originated in the Conciliation Act 1896, which provided that where a difference existed or was apprehended between employers and workmen or between different classes of workmen the [Secretary of State] might:

(i) take such steps as may seem expedient [to him] for the purpose of enabling the parties to the difference to meet together, by themselves or their representatives, under the presidency of a chairman mutually agreed upon or nominated by the [Secretary of State] or by some other person or body, with a view to the amicable settlement of the difference;

(ii) on the application of employers or workmen interested, and after taking into consideration the existence and adequacy of means available for conciliation in the district or trade and the circumstances of the case, appoint a person to act as a conciliator or as a board of conciliation.[36]

Though the Department could not refer a dispute to the Arbitration Board until satisfied that the agreed procedure in the industry had failed to obtain a settlement, it was in its discretion at what stage in a dispute it might introduce conciliation. In order to encourage voluntary procedure for conciliation, however, it was the practice of the Department not to intervene until the agreed procedure had been exhausted or, if there was no agreed procedure, until the parties had attempted to settle the dispute. The services of a conciliator appointed by the Department were regarded as available merely to assist the parties to find a mutually acceptable basis for settlement. To this end the conciliator had to avoid identification with either side.

Despite a general impression that these industrial relations functions of the Department had suffered badly from doubts as to its impartiality raised by a succession of Government pay policies, this does not appear to have been true of conciliation.

The Advisory Conciliation and Arbitration Service has power[37] where a trade dispute exists or is apprehended to offer its assistance, by way of conciliation or other means, to bring about a settlement. It is provided that the Service shall have regard to the desirability of encouraging use of agreed procedure for settlement of disputes, but the former principle of requiring exhaustion of such private procedures has been removed.

---

[36] Conciliation Act 1896, c. 30, s.2.
[37] E.P.A. 1975, s.2. ACAS also has an extensive individual conciliation function in respect of claims made to industrial tribunals for unfair dismissal. *Supra*, p. 319.

Where a trade dispute exists or is apprehended, ACAS at the request of one or more parties *and with the consent of all parties to the dispute*, may refer all or any of the matters in dispute to arbitration by one or more persons appointed by the Service, or to the Central Arbitration Committee. In this instance the Service must consider the likelihood of the dispute being settled by conciliation. Where there exist appropriate agreed procedures for negotiation or settlement of disputes ACAS should not refer a matter to arbitration unless those procedures have been used and failed to produce a settlement or unless the Service is of the opinion that there is a special reason which justifies arbitration as an alternative to those procedures.

The Central Arbitration Committee is the direct successor of the Industrial Court first established in 1919. It once dealt with claims of breach of the Fair Wages Resolution by failure of government contractors (and some others) to observe rates of wages and terms and conditions of employment not less beneficial than those established in a section of trade or industry and locality. To this was added a more extensive, but similar, jurisdiction under Schedule 11 of the E.P.A. 1975. The Resolution has been revoked and the Schedule repealed and most of the other jurisdiction of the C.A.C. has also gone.[38] It retains power to deal with complaints of failure to supply information for bargaining purposes[39] and the power to arbitrate generally on questions referred from ACAS.

ACAS maintains lists of available arbitrators who may act singly or jointly, usually as a group of three, one of whom acts as chairman. For some reason parties seem to prefer single arbitrators. A single arbitrator may be provided with assessors, although arrangements are often not that precise and he may have to work out whether the decision is ultimately his or whether the parties (and his two colleagues) assume he can be outvoted. Usually parties approaching ACAS will be given lists of arbitrators together with some background information and will endeavour to agree a chairman, then appointing one member each if tripartite arbitration is desired. This power of choice is, probably, the attraction this system has over reference of the dispute for arbitration by the C.A.C. which will arrange its own constitution for the occasion. The C.A.C., a little reluctantly but with an eye to the fact that when its jurisdiction was more extensive it was quite likely to be subjected to judicial review, adopted the practice of setting out the main considerations it had taken into account in arriving at its decision. The more normal practice among other arbitrators is not to give reasons. This practice is usually explained as preventing further dispute arising between the parties as to errors they detect in the reasoning or the assumptions of fact apparent therefrom.

In truth, industrial arbitration has no very high reputation in the United Kingdom, partly because of its relative rarity suggesting a lack of consistent experience among the arbitrators. Inevitably, because they are likely to be regarded as least directly involved in the issues, the majority of arbitrators are academics. The very advantage of lack of involvement, however, tends to suggest a lack of background knowledge. On the whole, it seems true to say

---

[38] Its power to consider overtly discriminatory provisions in collective agreements under the E.P.A. 1970, s.3 disappeared in February 1987 under the S.D.A. 1986.
[39] *Supra*, pp. 296–300.

that most employers and trade unions in Britain would not voluntarily refer to arbitration an issue which they considered significant. A lot of arbitration, therefore, relates to individual discipline and the tag end of a number of matters which have been in dispute. The principal advantage of going to arbitration is, for many parties, the avoidance of the need to accept, on a subsequent occasion, that they agreed to the outcome produced by the arbitrator. In some situations, indeed, it is possible to see that the parties know what the outcome will be in the hands of any reasonable person; but one, or both, does not wish to admit that.

One of the principal complaints against arbitrators has long been that they tend to split the difference between claim and offer, or otherwise produce some compromise or fudge. If it is objected that very often the parties resolve their own disputes far less satisfactorily the answer would probably be that more was expected of the arbitrator. In order to overcome this objection there has, in recent years, been developed what is called "pendulum" arbitration when it is expressly stated in the arbitrator's terms of reference that he must choose between the claim and the offer and is not free to adopt an intermediate position. Apart from ensuring that the arbitrator does not produce a result undesirable from the point of view of both parties this device ensures that neither party adopts an extreme and indefensible position at the end of joint negotiations. To do so would be to increase the risk that the arbitrator would be forced to favour the position of the other party.

Contrary to general supposition employers are less opposed to arbitration clauses than are trade unions. Probably, both see the presence of such a clause as affording an inducement to settle. Resort to industrial action will not be a breach of procedure if arbitration is only available with the agreement of both parties but there is, naturally, a certain weakening of position if an available alternative is rejected out of hand. The objections of both mostly derive from their own failure to develop this method of dispute settlement. The fact that arbitrators may be inexperienced and are even more likely to know little of the background can easily be avoided by the use of tripartite machinery and resort to a regular arbitrator. Because arbitration cases are usually of minor importance the preparation and presentation of the case is often startlingly inept and casual—especially when one remembers the care which employers in particular devoted to preparation of cases at the C.A.C. in the late 1970s. Arbitration as a method of dispute settlement in the United Kingdom remains a device the potential of which has never been realised.

CHAPTER IX

LEGAL CONTROL OF INDUSTRIAL ACTION

The acceptable limits of control

Frequently industrial action is extremely damaging not only to workers and employers but to the national economy. A major dogma of the Thatcher government is that the poor economic performance of the United Kingdom, relative to the rest of Europe, in the years from 1950 to 1980 was, to a significant degree, attributable to misuse of the power of trade unions. A sizeable proportion of this blame would derive from their ability to secure inflationary wage claims whilst, by restrictive practices, reducing productivity. But a significant element would derive from the effect of industrial disruption. Particularly, it is often said that the economy of the United Kingdom was damaged by large numbers of local, short-lived, strikes attributable to the power of the shop-floor union organisation. As a result, even statistics which revealed a higher incidence of industrial activity in other countries might be deceptive if that rate was produced by a few major (and long foreseen) stoppages, against which damage control methods were both more possible and more effective. On the other hand, at least so far as strikes are concerned, it can be argued that the worker, whose labour it is, should be free to withdraw it and, if combination is no longer itself reprehensible, to do so in combination.

More significantly, however, for about one hundred years, since 1875, it has been accepted by United Kingdom governments that the power of capital (which is, after all, a form of combination) may properly be opposed by combined power of labour. The two in conflict will produce an equilibrium in which neither is unacceptably oppressed.

In this atmosphere the function of the law is to define the boundaries of permissible action and so hold the ring in what is accepted as an inevitable conflict of interest. Between 1875, subject to major reassertion in 1906, and 1980, this definition was not seen by government as a regulator to be applied liberally or severely as the balance of power would seem to demand. The courts, however, interpreting the fairly elemental statutory principles, responded more obviously to the state of this balance at each stage of economic development. A policy of political non-intervention said to have been accepted somewhere vaguely between 1906 and 1918, was once thought to be characteristic of United Kingdom law. Now it is seen as no more than an epoch, some would say an interval, between periods of judicial repression of industrial action, explicable by the weakness of collective labour power between the two World Wars. However this may be, it seems likely that it was the absence of any prolonged threat from industrial action which perpetuated the 1906 formula for balance for so long.

It follows that few would contend for total prohibition of industrial action even if prohibition was thought likely to be effective. More, no doubt, would argue for total freedom on the ground that the worker's economic dependence on wages will act as a far more effective brake on the incidence of industrial action than legal restriction.

INDUSTRIAL ACTION AS A CRIME

For various, rather obvious, reasons the early days of the industrial revolution produced an all time low in legal recognition of the freedom of organised labour. The legislature, at least until 1833, was dominated by property owners, many of whom were developing extensive interests in the new industries. The supreme importance of the economic power which trade conferred is never likely to be far from the minds of a British government but, next to the problems of the Napoleonic wars, was then pre-eminent. These same wars were a constant reminder of the threat of, and resultant instability arising from, working class revolution. The very suggestion of wage regulation was anathema to this state of mind. The legislative grant of power to magistrates to fix wages, dating from 1349, would have been abolished from 1813, had it been exercised to any significant extent in the previous century. That abolition when it came probably owed more to a formal indication of the predominance of market freedom than to a desire to rid the statute book of out-dated and ineffective provisions. Criminal law had long provided the principal sanction by which workers were protected against their assumed predilections for idleness and combination to force up the value of their labour. As Wedderburn[1] puts it: "Prosecutions for leaving or 'neglecting' work were a major mechanism for combating unions and militant workers. . . . As late as 1872 there were 10,400 convictions under the provisions of the Master and Servant Acts which made breach of the contract of employment a criminal offence." It was natural, therefore, to seek to deal with combinations of workers for similar purposes by similar means. There was ample legislative precedent for the Combination Acts 1799 and 1800 which imposed criminal sanctions on combinations, even if only in the temporary form of a meeting, and agreements arising from them for increasing wages or changing hours. The judges, coming from a class thus frightened of combination, not surprisingly applied the established common law weapon of criminal conspiracy to any situation where two or three workers gathered together to seek a means of raising their wages.

The fears of the old and new rich and their protectors, distributed thickly through the establishment, were evidently well justified for, incredibly, between 1800 and 1824 combinations of workers flourished. True, this flourishing was an overall trend, whilst individual organisations appeared and disappeared with a speed that would have convinced the casual observer of any one of them that it was no more than a transitory upsurge of dissatisfaction. In some ways the Combination Acts, which were undoubtedly extensively deployed, served the interests of their supporters badly since they forced worker combinations to operate clandestinely and, sometimes, in disguise as friendly societies with the apparently predominant object of providing financial

---

[1] *The Worker and the Law*, (3rd ed.), p. 141.

benefits to their members in sickness, old-age or death. They received considerable support from middle class philosophers of reform. As early as 1824, as some, including the Prime Minister, would have it, without the government actually being aware of what was going on, and in a carefully packed unreformed Parliament, this unlikely conspiracy secured the repeal of the Combination Acts. Some of the middle classes who had supported this move because they thought it would actually remove the incentive to worker combination were, no doubt, startled by a year of, often violent, industrial action provoked by price rises. Much of the former severity of the law was restored by the Combination Act 1825 which, though it formally legalised combinations of workers solely to agree their own hours and wages, imposed a series of criminal offences aimed at industrial action, though appearing in the guise of restriction on unacceptable methods. The courts, therefore, readily found molestation, intimidation and obstruction virtually inherent in industrial action. Two important lessons had plainly been learnt:

(a) The real power of labour is derived from the ability of groups of workers to support each other rather than merely look after themselves; and

(b) it is largely impossible to prevent the formation of such groups but their power can be diminished by making illegal the weapon by which they achieve their purpose.

Organisers of the quality of those who had successfully led the movement for less oppressive laws until 1824 were not found in the next quarter of a century but the "New Model" unions emerging after 1850 were a different matter. Governments of both political persuasions were recognising, probably because the extension of the franchise made them conscious that they were dependent on the support of a steadily widening public, the need to take into account the wishes of workers. The improved organisation for giving voice to these wishes and the increasing desire to listen produced the Royal Commission of 1867 but, perhaps more significantly, a government which, in 1871 implemented the *minority* report of that Commission. The Trade Union Act 1871 recognised, and provided a basic organisational structure for, combinations of workers. The Criminal Law Amendment Act repealed the Combination Act 1825, though it left many forms of criminality in existence. The judiciary were a little slow to get the message and a Conservative Government (not to be equated with the Whig governments of the 1980s), again acknowledging the working class vote, passed the Conspiracy and Protection of Property Act 1875 which repealed the Master and Servant Acts and destroyed criminal conspiracy as a weapon against acts in contemplation or furtherance of a trade dispute; unless the act would have been criminal without the element of combination. It took another hundred years[2] finally to abolish the concept of criminality derived from the fact of combination alone, but the criminal law was not to have any further significant use as a weapon against combined industrial action. Indeed, it became virtually axiomatic that criminal sanctions were not an appropriate, or effective, method of dealing with peaceful industrial action.

A few remnants of criminal liability, arising from the infliction of economic

---

[2] See the Criminal Law Act, 1977.

harm as distinct from illegal means, survived. The Conspiracy and Protection of Property Act 1875 preserved the idea of an intentional breach of the contract of employment as a criminal offence in its application to protection of essential services (gas, water and, later, electricity). This was repealed by the Industrial Relations Act 1971, partly because it seems never to have been invoked and partly because there is a reluctance in the United Kingdom to single out groups of employees (even public employees) for particular restriction. Equally unused has been the still surviving criminal offence of wilful and malicious breach of a contract of service or hiring (a rare assimilation of employment and self-employment), knowing or having reasonable cause to believe that the probable consequence will be to endanger human life, cause serious bodily injury or expose valuable property (when is property not valuable?) to destruction or serious injury. Even the change from a pattern of short, relatively localised, strikes in private industry, in which light the Royal Commission Report of 1968 saw little risk in leaving this section in force, to a greater significance for widespread major confrontations in both public and private sectors, has produced no resort to this provision. We cannot say that criminal sanctions against industrial action are a thing of the past, although they have been for well over a century. That depends on whether there is public acceptance of the essential criminality of such action. The Royal Commission, in an appendix, gave lasting publicity to a comedy, which might otherwise have been forgotten, in which wartime criminal sanctions were invoked against the mere act of striking, with such morale-shattering results to the instruments of law enforcement that prosecutions were not enforced against those who did not pay their fines—inspiring those who did to ask for their money back. As we saw at the beginning of this chapter it is possible to present a logical argument that industrial action which irresponsibly creates vast damage to the national economy ought to be regarded as criminal. One member of the Royal Commission did so. Apart from the obvious reluctance of the courts to sit in judgment on what is irresponsible (presumably in the sense of lacking justification), organised labour is still recognised as entitled to oppose its view of the economic interests of industrial workers to the welfare of the national economy, not yet recognised as the be-all-and-end-all of everyone's existence. The mere act of collective withdrawal of labour is difficult to present as criminal to those who accept that no individual can be compelled to work.

INDUSTRIAL ACTION AS A BREACH OF CONTRACT

A strike is defined for some legal purposes as a concerted, deliberate, and total withdrawal of labour designed to bring pressure to bear upon an employer.[3] It is arguable that other elements should be added to this definition but it is true of any legal definition that some particular interest group, such as social workers or doctors of medicine, would wish to add qualifications. The law is not concerned to ask who primarily caused the dispute, or

---

[3] See E.P.C.A. 1978, Sched. 13, para. 24. In *Express and Star Ltd.* v. *Bunday* [1987] I.R.L.R. 422 the Court of Appeal said that this definition could not be applied throughout the Act and that the best appreciation of whether a situation involves a strike or a lock out would come from the tribunal.

to subdivide strikes into different categories. In *Barretts and Baird (Whole-salers) Ltd.* v. *I.P.C.S.*[4] the strike was of fixed duration and had been called without notice. It is, of course, general knowledge that strikes may be indefinite and may be preceded by lengthy notice—which may, indeed, be part of the bargaining strategy. There was a time when one would have come across the term "proper notice." This would have implied that the strikers, or a trade union acting on their behalf, had given at least the same notice to strike as the individual employees would have been required to give to terminate their employment. It was commonly assumed before 1964 that such notice would prevent a strike from being in breach of contract.[5] This assumption was challenged by Lord Devlin in *Rookes* v. *Barnard*.[6] Lord Denning endorsed his view in *J.T. Stratford and Son Ltd.* v. *Lindley*,[7] but retreated from that proposition in *Morgan* v. *Fry*,[8] preferring an ill-defined type of suspension of obligations. The Royal Commission on Trade Unions[9] rejected the proposition that a strike preceded by "proper" notice would not be in breach of the contracts of employment of the participants. As Phillips J. pointed out in *Simmons* v. *Hoover Ltd.*[10] Lord Denning was the only member of the Court of Appeal to take that view and he failed to deal with any of the problems arising from the concept of suspension in a strike situation.[11] Phillips J. considered therefore that *Morgan* v. *Fry* provided no authority binding on him to contradict his own view that a withdrawal of labour, with or without notice, unless intended to terminate the contract of employment, would constitute a breach of the employee's obligation to be available for work. That proposition has never since been questioned.[12] And as Henry J. said in *Barretts* v. *Baird*, no striker gives notice to terminate his employment. If nothing else such action would contradict the understanding of both employer and employee that the employment relationship is intended to continue throughout the strike. It follows that, effectively, all strikes are now regarded as undertaken in breach of the contract of employment. In fact this does not explain the situation as fully as Phillips J. inferred. It is, for instance, normal for an employer not to pay wages during a strike (though he may agree as part of a settlement to pay a portion of the money lost). Strictly speaking, if he elects not to rescind the contract it could be argued that he is obliged to pay the wages due. As we have seen[13] that contention may now be effectively answered by the recent

---

[4] [1987] I.R.L.R. 3.
[5] The Contracts of Employment Act, 1963 was actually founded on this proposition intending to deny continuity of employment to those who struck without proper notice.
[6] [1964] A.C. 1129.
[7] [1965] A.C. 307.
[8] [1968] 2 Q.B. 710.
[9] Para. 937.
[10] [1977] I.C.R. 61.
[11] See Royal Commission on Trade Unions, para. 943.
[12] But in *Boxfoldia Ltd.* v. *N.G.A.(1982)* [1988] I.R.L.R. 383 Saville J. in the Queen's Bench Division held out the possibility of notice to strike being construed as termination of the contract.
[13] See pp. 76–78 *supra*. The explanation is that participation in a strike affords the employer no chance of acceptance of partial performance. When partial performance occasioned by other forms of industrial action is rejected there is, equally, no obligation to pay wages—*Miles* v. *Wakefield M.D.C.* [1987] I.C.R. 368.

decisions suggesting a right to withhold wages in proportion to non-performance of the obligation to be available for work, but that is a new development which does not explain legally the long established practice of non-payment during a strike.

The fact that strikers lose wages has long induced most trade unions to pay strike, or dispute, benefit to their members although it is now rare for this to be a substantial sum. This means that a lengthy, widespread, strike can be very expensive to the unions organising it and, knowing of this, the employer may calculate that his bargaining position becomes stronger the longer the stoppage continues. Because of this it is not uncommon to organise selective strikes in which relatively small groups of key workers are called out or, at no notice to the employers, workers in a selected locality, or unit, strike briefly and are followed by another group elsewhere. It is unlikely that a group of workers, merely waiting for the call, would be regarded as in anticipatory breach but it has been established[14] that an employer cannot, by injunction, be prevented from threatening to dismiss them unless they undertake not to obey such a call.

Except in those industries whose employees may have alternative sources of work, or rebates on income tax reduce the actual monetary loss, a strike of any duration is likely, therefore, to be a last resort. It is only fair to say that this is not necessarily true of very short stoppages. Withdrawal of labour for half an hour each morning may be very disruptive of production but it is unlikely, at least initially, that the employer will regard it as worth deducting wages.[15] The cost of a strike to an employee has been a major reason why this and other disruptive techniques are used. The "work to rule" is the best known. Many jobs involve specified procedures. Even a simple rule that postal workers must ensure that the seals on mail bags are intact implies some procedural activity. It may be argued that the passing glance by which this duty is normally carried out is actually a failure to observe the rule which really requires the seal to be prodded with a penknife to ensure that it is attached. The Fatstock Inspectors in *Barretts and Baird* v. *I.P.C.S.*[16] could certainly have applied a number of such restrictions. No doubt, on that occasion they preferred a more open demonstration. So the "work to rule" may often equally well be called a "go-slow," and the go-slow more euphamistically described as "working without enthusiasm." All such devices may avoid loss of wages, in practice, simply because the employer does not wish to sacrifice what productivity remains by resorting to dismissal, or a lockout. Again, the recent decisions indicating that he might withhold a portion of wages for partial performance are more likely to affect this practice. It may still be difficult for him to value what has been withheld, but it is unlikely that the workers would resort to the court to challenge his assessment.

We shall see that it is of great significance to the availability of injunctions prohibiting industrial action, to determine whether that action was in breach

---

[14] *Chappell* v. *Times Newspapers Ltd.* [1975] 2 All E.R. 233.
[15] Before *Miles* v. *Wakefield MCD*, *supra*, it would have been questionable whether withdrawal for a portion of the day followed by agreed resumption of work would have entitled the employer to deduct a portion of the days wages.
[16] *Supra.*

of the contract of employment. As *Barretts and Baird* acknowledges, most applicable tort liability requires the use of unlawful means. Davies and Freedland suggest that this is not so in the case of primary action where they say interference with contract is direct. It is suggested, however, that if the complaint is of interference with commercial contracts by means of industrial action that interference will be indirect. Unlawful means are provided by the organisers inducement of breach of the contract of employment. There was a time when the work to rule was thought to be properly regarded as a strict observance, rather than a breach, of contract. The Court of Appeal virtually destroyed this argument in *Secretary of State for Employment* v. *ASLEF (No. 2)*.[17] There is no need to consider the dubious proposition advanced primarily by Lord Denning M.R., in that case that an employee taking part in a work to rule would commit a breach of the implied obligation not wilfully to disrupt his employer's undertaking. This would make breach or observance of contract depend on motive. On that basis even a refusal to work voluntary overtime would constitute a breach of contract if made with such intention.[18] The Court of Appeal pointed out that a work to rule is only within the contract if the restricted work correctly interprets the contractual obligations. With convincing logic it said that the parties, when adopting the rule, must have intended that it would lead to normal working. Interpretation of a rule, as requiring a practice that would bring chaos to the normal operation of the railways, was considerably less likely to be correct than one which permitted the railways to run to schedule. This is not quite as obvious as it sounds. A guard dismissed for failure to take sufficient care to ensure that carriage doors were shut before a train left the station may reflect that the normal practice is less than is formally required. On the other hand, those wishing to apply coercive pressure by means of a work to rule are unlikely to balance the restriction correctly between slightly slapdash normal practice and over-assiduous application. Injunctions are usually interim on the basis of likely observance or breach and it seems unlikely that the courts would fail to see in a work to rule potential breach.

Similar judicial attention has not been paid to deciding how much enthusiasm the employee should display. Donaldson J. once suggested in argument[19] that, contractually speaking, an employee was bound to work just as hard as his employer required. This seems unlikely to be correct, but even if the enthusiasm falls below a reasonable level it may be difficult for the employer to collect enough tangible evidence to persuade a court of a likely breach of a specific term. Resort to this device to avoid a breach of contract was mooted in the 1970s but never really caught on. Possibly the feeling grew that, if pushed, the courts would find an argument for regarding it as in breach of contract. More probably, trade unions regarded it as recognition of legalism and nothing is more likely to put a trade unionist off a course of action than the feeling that he is pandering to some legal nicety.

---

[17] [1972] I.C.R. 19.

[18] But the implied contractual obligation to maintain trust and confidence, in its application to the conduct of the employee suggested in *W.M. Car Services* v. *Woods*, comes very close to producing a similar effect.

[19] *Seaboard Airlines Ltd.* v. *Transport and General Workers Union* [1973] I.C.R. 458.

We have already seen[20] that though legislation refers to "industrial action"[21] neither it nor the courts offer any satisfactory general definition. The newest judicial attempts suggest the two main ingredients of concerted coercion. This may be criticised as a typical lawyers' generalisation, deliberately ignoring other important elements. Nor, in itself, does it solve the problem of deciding when the process of preparation of the ultimate action becomes, in itself, industrial action.[22] But this failure is not our problem. The difficulty of defining industrial action only arises if liability is made to depend on the existence of such action. In English law liability, as we have just seen, depends on interference with contract and it suffices, therefore, as we have done, to consider the available forms of industrial action. If motive were introduced as a factor leading to breach it might occasionally be necessary to consider such problems as that of the unwilling participant[23] or the willing non-participant.[24] Unless that suggestion develops (either from *Secretary of State* v. *ASLEF* or *W.M. Car Services* v. *Woods*) the law controlling industrial action never needs to ask the question whether industrial action is actually taking place. The key to liability is whether those involved are in breach of their contracts of employment. What we have just said suggests that that will normally be so even in the case of the imposition of bans on non-contractual extras such as voluntary overtime. To reach such a conclusion, however, it may be necessary to conduct legalistic exercises which seem to have no relevance to a policy desire to forbid concerted coercion.[25]

This chapter is mostly concerned with collective liability for the effect of concerted individual breaches of contract. Before continuing, however, it ought to be pointed out that the individual who actually takes the industrial action runs the risk of more than the frustration of his efforts by an injunction. The employee's personal breach of contract is unlikely to lead to an action by the employer for damages and, it cannot lead to an injunction. The first is because it is not worth the time and trouble for an employer to collect small sums of damages which the courts will attribute to the individual breach of contract. The second results from the provision of section 16 of T.U.L.R.A. 1974 which forbids the grant of an injunction having the effect of compelling an employee to work. We shall discover, however,[26] that an employer is effectively at liberty to dismiss those participating in industrial action (not, notice, those committing breaches of contract) provided only that he dismisses all those still participating at the date of dismissal. This freedom extends even to those who are performing all their contractual obligations but have withdrawn from voluntary extra duties, since it is founded on the definition of industrial action based on concerted coercion rather than breach of contract.

---

[20] *Supra*, p. 324.
[21] *e.g.* E.P.C.A., s.62.
[22] *Naylor* v. *Orton and Smith Ltd.* [1983] I.R.L.R. 233; Compare: *Rasool* v. *Hepworth Pipe Co. Ltd.* [1980] I.R.L.R. 137.
[23] *Coates and Venables* v. *Modern Methods Ltd.* [1982] I.R.L.R. 318.
[24] *Hindle Gears Ltd.* v. *McGinty* [1984] I.R.L.R. 477.
[25] Consider, for instance, the question whether a union meeting in working time is "industrial action"—*Naylor* v. *Orton and Smith Ltd.* [1983] I.R.L.R. 233, and then ask whether it constitutes a breach of the contract of employment.
[26] See pp. 371–373, *infra*, and E.P.C.A., s.62.

Industrial Action as a Tort

Legal control of industrial action in the United Kingdom is imposed primarily, if not in practice exclusively, by means of an injunction (usually an interim injunction) to restrain a tort or a threatened tort. The situation in *Barratts and Baird* was a straightforward one in which a union organised its members to break their contracts of employment in order to disrupt their employer's undertaking. The unusual factor was that it was their employer's customers who were complaining. In fact, of course, damage to customers, clients, suppliers or other contractors is inevitable. They will not normally take action against the union themselves, preferring to leave it to those who have the power to resolve the dispute to decide which action to pursue. The incentive to the affected employer of preventing loss of customers to rivals is usually at least as great as any incentive upon the customer to ensure continued supplies or services. That consideration did not apply in this case. The customer who was bearing almost all the real loss was left alone to seek a remedy. Whether the customer, or the employer against whom the action is taken, sues, the picture is the same. An organiser, usually an official of a trade union, "induces" employees to take industrial action which almost inevitably interferes with commercial contracts of the employer. That interference is, of course, also an interference with the other party's rights in that same contract. Some unlawfulness, other than breach of the contract of employment, may exist in the means used to achieve this result. In *Barretts and Baird* it was alleged unsuccessfully that the plaintiffs, as customers, could complain of unlawfulness in the breach by the employer of his statutory duty to provide them with a service. This is an unusual feature. Normally, since it is the employer, whose contracts of employment are interfered with, who complains of interference with his commercial contracts, any illegality he may be induced to commit is irrelevant to the means used to interfere with him. Surprisingly, although this element of unlawful means is required in most of the tort liability invoked in practice, the explanation for the existence of this element differs.

(a) Conspiracy

Little is heard these days of the tort of conspiracy. It is, as Lord Diplock said in *Lonhro Ltd.* v. *Shell Petroleum (No. 2)*,[27] an anomalous head of liability depending solely on judicial disapproval of action in combination. If that action would be illegal when done by individuals why not leave it at that and proceed against the individual conspirators? If the action would not be illegal why should the fact that it is done in combination make it illegal.[28] The answer, as Lord Diplock says, lies in the supposition that a combination may be more oppressive than a single person. Given that a single person can be a powerful corporation this was no more true when the proposition was first devised than it is now. On the other hand, as criminal sanctions appeared more and more inappropriate the courts turned to civil liability which, even if

---

[27] [1982] A.C. 173.
[28] In *Allen* v. *Flood* [1848] A.C. 1, it was held that however malicious the motive of an individual in causing injury, he was not liable unless he had used unlawful means.

it might ultimately be enforceable, as in contempt of an injunction, lacked that implicit unacceptablity. The House of Lords relied on this fact when developing civil conspiracy, to take the place of the criminal law, at the beginning of the twentieth century. In *Allen* v. *Flood*[29] the defendant had threatened to impose a withdrawal of labour, not seen at the time as involving any illegality, unless certain other employees the defendant desired to punish were dismissed without breach of their contracts by their employer. This lawful course of action was held not to be rendered unlawful by the clear intention of the defendant to injure the dismissed employees. In *Quinn* v. *Leathem*[30] the facts were essentially similar. Leathem was requested by certain union officials to dismiss non-unionists employed by him. He refused and a customer of his was induced, by threat of strike action, to cease dealing with him until he complied. Again it was assumed that no breaches of contract were involved, although this assumption would probably not be made at the present time. Nevertheless, the House of Lords held that the union officials were liable for civil conspiracy. The distinction between the two decisions is usually regarded as dependent on the element of conspiracy producing, as Lord Dunedin said in *Sorrell* v. *Smith*,[31] liability where economic harm was intentionally inflicted by a combination of individuals employing means which would not have produced liability had they been used by a individual with the same intention. The decision is doubly strange because a combination of shipowners to cut their rates so as to force out of business a shipowner, not a member of their federation, who had himself threatened their price maintenance arrangements, was held justified by their own self-interest.[32] Years later, and in an atmosphere different in almost every respect, both these principles were confirmed and applied to industrial action. In *Crofter Handwoven Harris Tweed Co. Ltd.* v. *Veitch*[33] a union had approached employers who made tweed cloth on the Island of Lewis to negotiate a wage rise on behalf of its members. The employers were subject to market pressure from yarn spun on the mainland and sent to Lewis for weaving so that it could be sold, though at lower prices, as tweed. The request must have seemed a somewhat unexpected answer to a prayer since the union could, and did, stop the import of the mainland yarn, simply by instructing others of its wide ranging membership, who were dockers at the port of Stornoway, not to handle the yarn. In return the union secured a closed shop. The House of Lords defined the elements of the tort of conspiracy primarily to cause economic loss without other unlawful means and made it clear that primary self interest would provide a defence of justification. The other branch of civil conspiracy arising from a combination to use unlawful means was not thought of as capable of justification.

In 1906 it was unlikely that such a judicial recognition of the legitimate interests of trade unions would occur and so effectively eliminate from the pursuit of trade disputes the weapon of conspiracy. Statute, therefore, provided that no action for civil conspiracy should arise from conduct in contemplation or furtherance of a trade dispute. As it turned out, a degree of such

---

[29] [1898] A.C. 1.
[30] [1901] A.C. 495.
[31] [1925] A.C.700.
[32] *Mogul Steamship Co. Ltd.* v. *McGregor, Cow and Co. Ltd.* [1892] A.C. 25.
[33] [1942] A.C. 435.

recognition, applying specifically to the closed shop, and which made the decision in *Crofter* almost certain, occurred during the era of non-intervention between the two world wars.[34] As intervention again developed after the second world war the limits this placed on liability for conspiracy to injure would have made it difficult to develop it as a weapon even without statutory protection. Some commentators point to the decision in *Huntley* v. *Thornton*[35] as an indication of the continued availability of conspiracy as a weapon against industrial action. The plaintiff had refused to take part in industrial action, which might well have been called improperly according to the rules of the union. He was expelled by his branch, but the National Executive of the union declined to confirm the expulsion and instructed the branch to reinstate him. Branch officials, however, continued to behave as if the plaintiff was not a union member and secured his dismissal from employment in union shops. They were held liable for the tort of conspiracy on the ground of a primary intention to injure Huntley rather than to act in their own, or their members', interests. The same malicious motive prevented them from claiming to be acting in contemplation or furtherance of a trade dispute so as to invoke statutory immunity. It is, of course, easy to see that they could hardly be said to be acting in the interests of the union which had ordered them to act differently. On the other hand, they may well have supposed that they were acting in the interests of the local members and it seems clear that self interest must be a matter of subjective intention. The answer to that question must depend on the evidence and the Chancery Division concluded that they were pursuing a personal vendetta. So far as the report goes that conclusion appears to depend solely on their single minded pursuance of the plaintiff, in defiance of their union. If that is all the support for the court's conclusion, it must be pointed out that it no more indicates a personal vendetta than a mistaken view of their interests. On the face of it, therefore, the decision does seem to confirm the possibility of liability for groups of trade union officials pressing objectives not in accordance with union policy.

Conspiracy is now seen much more clearly as a matter of chance rather than a badge of combined strength against which the law should react. As Lord Diplock said in *Lonrho Ltd.* v. *Shell Petroleum Co. Ltd.*[36] acts done by two street-corner grocers in concert are no more oppressive and dangerous than those of a string of supermarkets owned by a single corporation. Although he accepted that liability for conspiracy to injure was too well established to be discarded, there can be little doubt that the fact that such liability seems to the courts anomolous will cause them to lean in favour of limitation. In the *Lonrho* case, self interest, which began life as the measure of distinction between the elements of tortious liability and the absence thereof is seen rather as a defence available to any combination and seemed to have been extended to both limbs of the tort. Liability would exist if unlawful means are actually used but it appeared to be the view of the House of Lords, that no liability would arise merely from the existence of a combination intending to use such means. This appearance was denied in *Metall und Rohstoff AG* v.

---

[34] See *Reynolds* v. *Shipping Federation* [1924] 1 Ch. 28.
[35] [1957] 1 W.L.R. 321.
[36] [1981] 3 W.L.R. 33.

Donaldson Lufkin and Jenrette Inc.[36a] It is probably too much to expect courts to accept self interest as justifying the contemplation in combination of the use of unlawful means.

This use of justification is a little confusing for there is authority to suggest a wholly different concept of a defence of justification which, in varying degrees, extends to other economic torts. In *Scala Ballroom (Wolverhampton) Ltd.* v. *Ratcliffe*[37] the Musicians' Union was held not liable for conspiracy to injure the plaintiff's business by forbidding its members to perform in the plaintiff's dance-halls until the latter ceased to ban blacks from attending. The Court of Appeal chose to find the element of justification in the conclusion that the union considered a colour bar contrary to the interests of its members. No doubt it was concerned not to have to define some concept of public policy as a justification. It seems that justification as a defence, if it develops at all, will rest upon public policy whilst self-interest as an element of the tort is an entirely different, and infinitely wider concept.

(b) Intimidation

The prospect of conspiracy apparently steadily withdrawing from industrial conflict is untypical. Such withdrawal must be explained as arising from judicial dissatisfaction with the concept of a liability wholly derived from the existence of a combination which may or may not be powerful and which is neither the only, nor the most marked, form of "collective" power. Other forms of economic tort have, since the second world war, advanced into tactical positions surrounding industrial action.

The first to do so was the tort of Intimidation. It was applied in *Rookes* v. *Barnard*[38] because it had not been emasuclated, as had conspiracy, nor immunised, as had the tort of inducement to breach of contract. So far as the pleadings in that case go, it seems to have evolved out of an attempt to develop liability for conspiracy by the use of threats. With startling understatement, Lord Wedderburn says[39] that it had played little role in the law between 1793 and 1964. It seems to have been the text-book writer Salmond who, in 1909, had developed the elements of a recognised head of tort from a few cases which had recognised civil liability for threats of violence.[40] From this he had suggested liability for injury caused by threats of unlawful action. It may be strange to all save lawyers well used to the proposition, that criminal and civil liability are entirely different concepts likely to rest on different philosophy, that whereas the statutory crime of intimidation had actually been restricted to threats of violence after 1875, the tort of intimidation was to be extended beyond in in 1965. Salmond isolated two forms of intimidation, that against the plaintiff himself causing him injury[41] and intimidation of third parties

---

[36a] *The Times*, April 14, 1988, a chambers judgment reported with leave.
[37] [1958] 1 W.L.R. 1057.
[38] [1964] A.C. 1129.
[39] (3rd ed.) at p. 617.
[40] See *Garrett* v. *Taylor* (1620) Cro.Jac. 567; *Tarleton* v. *M'Gawley* (1793) 1 Peake 270.
[41] For which there was no authority save the opinion of Hawkins J. advising the H.L. in *Allen* v. *Flood* [1898] A.C. 1 at 17.

intending to compel them to act in a manner causing loss to the plaintiff. Both forms plainly require threats of unlawful action.[42] In *Rookes* v. *Barnard* it was argued that Salmond had invented a separate tort from the element of threat contained in early conspiracy cases but the Court of Appeal and the House of Lords confirmed that such a separate head of liability did exist. The Court of Appeal, however,[43] was anxious not to outflank the contractual doctrine of privity by permitting to a plaintiff an action in tort for the effects of a threat of breach of contract to which he was not a party. Consequently it suggested that authority only justified liability for threats of "some gross illegality" (*per,* Pearson L.J.) and fell short of imposing liability for threats of breach of contract.[44] The House of Lords rejected this limitation.

The plaintiff Rookes was employed by BOAC as a draughtsman. He left his trade union because he disagreed with its policies. In the view of the relevant branch of the union this was an unacceptable breach of a one-hundred-per-cent. trade union membership situation which had been established at his workplace. Branch officials and the full-time district officer of the union conveyed to the employers a branch resolution in favour of strike action if Rookes was not dismissed within three days. At this time it was unclear whether the court would regard a withdrawal of labour as a breach of continuing contractual obligations to be available for work (as is now in practice always the case) or as a termination of the contract of employment, lawful if proper notice was given (as is now only theoretically possible, should the strikers actually clearly give such notice). Various members of the Court of Appeal and the House of Lords supported the view that in a normal strike situation the withdrawal of labour is not intended to terminate the contract so that withdrawal breaches the continuing contract, but counsel for the defendants had conceded the alternative contention of the plaintiff that a collective agreement not to take industrial action before exhaustion of negotiating procedures had been incorporated in the individual contracts of employment (which would now be regarded as doubtful). Since no attempt had been made to negotiate the branch officials who were employed by BOAC were, therefore, threatening a breach of their contracts. The full time union official was not. He was, at worst, threatening to induce others to break their contracts and statutory immunity prevented that from being regarded as an unlawful action. He was, however, with very little reasoned argument in the judgment, deemed to be part of a conspiracy to threaten a breach of the employees' contracts.

The House of Lords held that the tort of intimidation was constituted by a threat of breach of contract. It is surprising to think that BOAC might have released the defendants from liability to Rookes by waiving the breach. Much later in *Barretts and Baird* v. *I.P.C.S.*[45] a judge of the Queen's Bench Division was to indicate grave doubts as to the propriety of regarding a strike, resorted to after a ballot required by statute, as properly to be regarded as

---

[42] *Hodges* v. *Webb* [1920] 2 Ch. 70; and see *Morgan* v. *Fry* [1968] 2 Q.B. 710.
[43] [1963] 1 Q.B. 623.
[44] See also, Wedderburn, *"The Right to Threaten Strikes"* (1961) M.L.R. 572; (1962) 25 M.L.R. 513.
[45] [1987] I.R.L.R. 3. See now, also, *Boxfoldia Ltd.* v. *N.G.A.* [1988] I.R.L.R. 383.

unlawful breach of contract. By then however, there was little alternative but
to conclude that the law had decided that such an action fitted more comfortably into the category of unlawful, rather than lawful, action. In *Morgan* v.
Fry[46] Russell L.J. had shown a somewhat similar concern about the effect of a
largely coincidental illegality when he concluded that the decision in *Rookes*
v. *Barnard* that breach of a no strike provision in the contract of employment
furnished sufficient unlawful means for the tort of intimidation, was not a precedent for saying that the absence of a few day's notice which could properly
have terminated the contract would suffice. As he pointed out it is not the
date when the action starts but its indefinite duration which produces the
pressure.

(c) Inducement to breach of contract, interference with contract and with trade

   Though greatly neglected by jurists, the development of the tort of inducement to breach of contract is a fascinating example of the expansionist ten-
dencies of the common law.
   In *Lumley* v. *Gye*[47] one of the piecemeal moulds of early civil liability was
broken (as many in the area of negligence liability were later to be) when the
court declined to confine liability to the factual situation of enticement of a
servant to leave his service and accepted that the inducement of a breach of
contract to work was actionable. This apparently obvious extension of principle was, however, a fundamental step from protection of property (the master's right of property in his servant's labour) to protection of contract in
general. It is doubtful whether modern practice would regard the opera singer
in that case as an employee. Nor is it true that the tort was confined to inducement to breach of contracts to work until extended by *Thomson* v. *Deakin*[48]
to commercial contracts.[49]
   For the first one hundred years, the tort of inducement to breach of contract applied both to contracts of employment and to commercial contracts
but did not look beyond what would now be called direct liability—that is to
say a situation where the defendant, by his own actions, brings pressure on
the contract breaker. So it was that, in the case of organisers of industrial
action, liability was seen as confined to inducement to breach of contracts of
employment. If we look at a typical industrial action situation diagrammati-
cally (opposite) this will be apparent.
   The trade union official is directly inducing employees to break their contracts of employment. This was so held in *South Wales Miners Federation* v.
Glamorgan Coal Co. Ltd.[50] in which the House of Lords confirmed the generality of the tort. Those officials were not directly influencing the employer.
Although the employees, taking the action, may, in theory, have been
directly inducing breaches of the commercial contracts between him and his

---

[46] [1968] 2 Q.B. 710.
[47] (1853) 2 E. and B. 216.
[48] [1952] Ch. 646.
[49] See, *e.g.* *GWK* v. *Dunlop* (1926) 42 T.L.R. 376; *BMTA* v. *Salvadori* [1949] Ch. 556.
[50] [1905] A.C. 239.

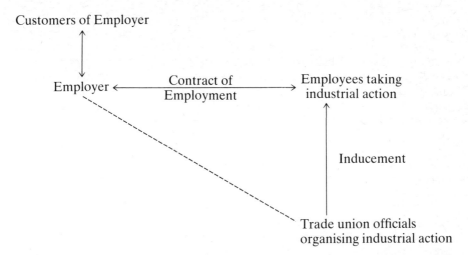

customers, no one would have thought of proceeding against them. It seems that it must have been the difficulty of conceiving of indirect liability, represented by the diagonal line, as arising from intention to injure a party who could not himself sue if he gave in to the pressure and allowed the commercial contracts to be affected which concealed from the courts the fact that it was well recognised that commercial contracts were no less entitled to protection than contracts of employment. So effective was the concealment that the statutory protection afforded in 1906 to those acting in contemplation or furtherance of a trade dispute[51] only extended to liability for inducement of a contract of employment.

If we remember that before 1964 industrial action would not have been regarded as almost inevitably involving a breach of the contract of employment, the need for statutory protection in 1906 was not quite so pressing as is sometimes inferred.[52] Union power in collective bargaining would not then have been seen as destroyed by the decision in the *Glamorgan Coal Co.* case. Short notice of a strike would usually have sufficed to raise the assumption that the contract of employment had been properly terminated. This assumption, when examined in an atmosphere of judicial intervention, was found to be insubstantial but it is interesting that in 1906 the legislature saw fit to protect even forms of industrial action involving no notice. Now, when it is established that virtually all industrial action save withdrawal of voluntary overtime involves a breach of the contract of employment, the organisation of such action without statutory protection almost inevitably raises tort liability for direct breach of (or interference with) the contract of employment.

The significance of industrial action lies, of course, in the intention of its participants to interfere with the commercial undertaking in which they are employed. Since it is generally accepted that those on strike are not entitled to wages, strike action would scarcely.be a weapon if it was not intended to disrupt commercial contracts. The predominance of that intention could readily have been more apparent than it was in *D.C. Thomson and Co. Ltd.*

---

[51] Trade Disputes Act 1906, s.3.
[52] *e.g.* R. Kidner, "*Lessons in Trade Union Reform*" (1982) 2 L.S. 34 at 51.

v. *Deakin.*[53] The Transport and General Workers Union had no quarrel with Bowaters Ltd. and no wish to injure that employer by seeking to induce a breach of its contracts of employment. Bowaters had no wish to make anything of this inducement so that, by not giving orders to their employees to which the union would have objected, Bowaters prevented an inducement of breach of the contract of employment from occurring. The plaintiffs, who operated a policy of not employing trade unionists, were the object of the attack; the sole purpose of which was to impose a boycott by cutting off supplies of paper, usually supplied by Bowaters, in breach of a commercial contract. The Court of Appeal affirmed the proposition in *Allen* v. *Flood*[54] that a malicious motive alone cannot produce civil liability and accepted the established liability for knowing violation of a legal right by direct interference with a contractual relationship. By "direct" the Court of Appeal clearly indicated that it meant pressure by the defendant directly upon the breaker of the contract, the subject of the action. (The Court also acknowledged another form of direct inducement in which the defendant without necessarily influencing either party does an act which, in their hands, would have been a breach of contract.) Here, however, there was no direct invasion of the plaintiff's rights under the commercial contract. The breach of contracts of employment which the union might have induced did not involve any breach of Bowaters' contract with Thomsons.

> "Nevertheless," said Jenkins L.J.,[55] "I think that in principle an actionable interference with contractual relations may be committed by a third party who, with knowledge of a contract between two other persons and with the intention of causing its breach, or of preventing its performance, persuades, induces or procures the servants of one of those parties, on whose services he relies for the performance of his contract, to break their contracts of employment. . . . "

The elements of the tort of inducement of breach of contract at this time, therefore, were either:

(a) Procurement of the contract breaker by the defendant. This did not depend on the element of malicious motive for its authority, but in the illegality of intentional intervention to destroy a contractual relationship. As Lord Evershed M.R. put it, " . . . the result is, for practical purposes, as though in substance he, the intervener, is breaking the contract."[56]

(b) Action by the intervener, wrongful in itself, preventing the performance of the contract;

(c) Achievement of the same result, incidently, by procuring a third party, by an unlawful act, to bring pressure to bear directly on the contract breaker.

So long, in all cases, as the elements of knowledge of the contract and intention to cause its breach are present.

The defendant in all three instances is, therefore, directly associated with

---

[53] [1952] Ch. 646.
[54] [1898] A.C. 1.
[55] At p. 696.
[56] At p. 677.

the procurement of an unlawful act. In the first the unlawful act is the breach of contract itself. In the third, and now so far as industrial action is concerned, the most usual case it is the unlawful action of the intervener. The union official directly induces a breach of the contracts of employment of those he organises to take industrial action. It may be that their breach of their own contract makes them liable also. The defendant has, therefore, directly procured or done an unlawful act in all three cases. The intention and the cause of the damage in all three is the intended breach of contract to which the plaintiff was a party, even though in the third case that breach is one stage removed from the unlawful pressure. Union officials do not stand apart from the contract breaker and they can usually be said to have acted both directly and indirectly. The unlawful means need not themselves be actionable at the suit of the plaintiff. In the case of direct inducement they will be because they exist in breach of the very contract on which the plaintiff relies. In the case of direct inducement it has been said that the person upon whom the pressure is brought cannot complain of injury arising because he did not resist it[57] but this prohibition cannot apply in either situations (b) or (c) above where the contract breaker can do nothing about the illegality of the defendant's actions and could hardly be excluded for failing to resist the effect of that illegal action. In a case of indirect inducement, therefore, we must conclude that either party to the contract intentionally interfered with has a cause of action.

A rather different problem arises if we have to consider whether, in indirect inducement, the inducer himself must be acting illegally. It seems to have been assumed in industrial action cases that the illegality of the organiser's action arises from the fact that he has directly induced a breach of the employee's contract of employment, and he himself, thereby, is separately liable to action in tort. This seems to have derived from an interpretation of *Thomson* v. *Deakin* as requiring the use of unlawful means to induce the breach. This is, however, not how Evershed M.R. saw it. He plainly refers to the unlawful act of the *intermediary*; namely breach of the contracts of employment as a result of the industrial action.

Since *Thomson* v. *Deakin*, however, the unlawful means arising from industrial action seems normally to have been taken to be in the tort of the inducer rather than the breach of contract of employment by the intermediary. At the present stage of our discussion the distinction may not seem to matter. The inducer could scarcely escape liability by asserting that the illegality is his own, rather than that of the intermediary. If, therefore, the tort is broadened from inducement to breach of contract to extend to lesser interference, the fact that employees may not have broken their contracts, and so may be acting legally, will not remove the liability in tort of the inducer in otherwise interfering with those contracts. That unlawfulness will suffice to form the necessary element for liability for indirect interference with commercial contracts. What we have not yet considered is the reverse of this situation in which tortious liability for interference with contract is removed by statute but contractual liability for breach is unaffected. In that situation the inducer is not guilty of unlawful means unless the final act of the intermediary can be so considered. This possibility was finally considered at first instance in

---

[57] Upjohn L.J. in *Boulting* v. *ACTT* [1963] 2 Q.B. 606 at 634–40.

Barretts and Baird (Wholesalers) Ltd. v. *I.P.C.S.*[58] Henry J. clearly favoured the view (which it is submitted is in line with the reasoning in *Thomson* v. *Deakin*) that illegal means employed either by the inducer or his intended intermediary will suffice.

In this case also, inducement to breach of statutory duty was accepted as furnishing the element of unlawful means although such inducement was held not to have occurred in the circumstances since there was no statutory obligation to carry out duties of inspection on the particular days disrupted by industrial action.

As a result of the decision of the House of Lords in *Hadmor Productions* v. *Hamilton*[59] it seems clear that the required unlawful means must be actionable. Lord Denning M.R., who questioned the need for illegal means at all,[60] took the view that a practice referable to the Restrictive Trade Practice Court under the Restrictive Trade Practices Act, 1956, would be regarded by the Court of Appeal as unlawful before such reference. Perhaps he shared the view of Russell L.J. that, if referred, it would inevitably be held contrary to the public interest.[61] In *Associated Newspapers Group Ltd.* v. *Wade*[62] Lord Denning also suggested that behaviour contrary to the public interest, such as interference with the freedom of the Press, would constitute unlawful means. The question will one day have to be faced of whether a statutory offence provides unlawful means. In *Merkur Island Shipping Corporation* v. *Laughton*[63] the Court of Appeal held that breaches of contracts of employment amounted to unlawful means even though the contracts were not with either party to the commercial contracts interfered with. The House of Lords supported this.[64]

The decision in *Merkur Island* maintains the *Thomson* v. *Deakin* insistence on proof that the organisers *intended* to attack the commercial contract in question and that interference with that contract was a necessary consequence of the unlawful means. Only the second of those restrictive elements which the Court of Appeal obviously deliberately built in to indirect inducement to keep it within bounds has survived intact. The requirement that the organisers of the action should have knowledge of the contracts attacked has ceased to be a significant element. In *J.T. Stratford and Son Ltd.* v. *Lindley*[65] union officials had placed an embargo on barges delivered to the appellant company for repair in order to bring pressure to bear on another company controlled by the same person, so that the latter would agree to negotiate with their union in addition to negotiation with the Transport and General Workers Union. The House of Lords unanimously concluded that there would be contracts of hiring which could not be fulfilled by the return of the barges at the end of the period of hiring. Lord Pearce said[66]:

> "It is no answer to a claim based on wrongfully inducing a breach of contract to assert that the respondents did not know with exactitude all the terms of the con-

---

[58] [1987] I.R.L.R. 3.
[59] [1982] I.C.R. 114.
[60] A position from which he later withdrew—*Torquay Hotel Ltd.* v. *Cousins* [1969] 2 Ch. 106.
[61] *Daily Mirror Newspapers Ltd.* v. *Gardner* [1968] 2 Q.B. 768.
[62] [1979] I.C.R. 664.
[63] [1983] I.C.R. 178.
[64] [1983] I.C.R. 490.
[65] [1965] A.C. 269.
[66] At p. 332.

tract. The relevant question is whether they had sufficient knowledge of the terms to know that they were inducing a breach of contract . . . it seems unlikely that they would be ignorant of the simple commonplace obligation of the hirers under the courses of dealing whereby they had a duty to return the barges to the appellants. . . . "

Like most such applications these proceedings were interlocutory and it was easy enough to add that evidence at the trial would illuminate this point. It is arguable, however, that the prima facie inference can only be justified by the conclusion that the respondents must take the risk of resultant breach once they know that contracts exist the purpose of which would not be fulfilled as a result of their action. The contracts in question in *Stratford* v. *Lindley* were based on customary understanding and it is actually highly unlikely that failure to return the barges because of industrial action would result in any enforcement of liability against the hirers. Why then should action not be taken to have produced no breach in these circumstances rather than a breach which was not pursued? Certainly it was this attitude of assumption of risk which was adopted by the Court of Appeal in *Emerald Construction Co.* v. *Lowthian.*[67] Officials of a building union, concerned at the spread of "labour only contracts" under which a main contractor hired gangs of self-employed workers, required the main contractor for the construction of a power station to terminate such contracts under threat of industrial action, which ultimately was taken. The main contractors did terminate the contracts without notice. The respondents argued that though they knew of the contracts they had no knowledge of the terms on which they might be terminated. It was clear that they did not care whether the contracts were terminated lawfully or by breach and there is some reason to suppose that the time limit they set would have permitted lawful termination. Lord Denning M.R., in rejecting this argument, made two significant points, one in relation to knowledge and the other to intention:

(a) One who turns a blind eye to the contracts of which he knows will be treated as having the knowledge which he had the means of acquiring; and,

(b) recklessness of the consequences produces the same liability as intention.

There might still, on occasion, be a residual question of both knowledge and intention. In *Torquay Hotel Co. Ltd.* v. *Cousins*[68] Lord Denning M.R. said "the person must know of the contract or, at any rate, turn a blind eye to it."[69] In *Stratford* an attack on a commercial relationship was presumed to be made with knowledge that it was carried out by means of contract. In *Emerald* the blindness related to the details of a known contract. It is possible to envisage industrial action aimed at a relationship which need not be a contractual one and in which the respondents had no knowledge that contracts existed. Apart from that, however, extension of liability from inducement to breach to intentional interference with significant aspects of the contract has further weakened any element of knowledge. Once there is knowledge of, or

---

[67] [1966] 1 W.L.R. 69.
[68] [1969] 2 Ch. 106.
[69] At p. 138.

indifference to, the existence of a contract it will be practically impossible to show an absence of both knowledge of and indifference to the fact that it will be interfered with. There has never been any suggestion that the actual interference which occurs must be envisaged and, in *Metropolitan Borough of Solihull* v. *NUT*,[70] even honest belief that the obligations were not contractual did not excuse, either on the basis of lack of knowledge or of intention.

Extension of liability to interference with contract also occurred in the 1960s. In *Torquay Hotel Co. Ltd.* v. *Cousins*[71] the commercial contract in question contained a provision excluding liability for breach if occasioned by industrial action. Strictly speaking, therefore, the organisers of the industrial action produced an agreed suspension of obligations rather than a breach. It is probably too much to expect the Court of Appeal to accept that the liability of a potential tortfeasor can be removed by the action of third parties *inter se* and the opportunity was provided for Lord Denning to suggest that the time had come to extend liability to deliberate and direct interference short of breach. Although he uses the word direct he goes on to indicate similar liability for indirect interference provided that it was occasioned by unlawful means. Lord Reid had suggested a possibility of such an extension in *Stratford* v. *Lindley* but Lord Donovan had firmly rejected liability arising from such "indefinable interference." Lord Denning had built up to his proposition by remarking in *Emerald* v. *Lowthian* that some people would take that view, and he expressly referred to "interference by unlawful means" in *Daily Mirror* v. *Gardner*. The other members of the Court of Appeal in *Torquay* v. *Cousins* did not support him but his view gained ground.[72] Finally, the House of Lords confirmed the existence of such liability in *Merkur Island Shipping Corporation* v. *Laughton*.[73] The House of Lords sought to meet Lord Donovan's objection to the indefinable nature of the interference by defining it as "prevention of due performance of a primary obligation." This would certainly deal with the effect of exclusion clauses as in *Torquay* v. *Cousins* and it would exclude interference to prevent the formation of a contract.[74] Apart from that, however, it adds little to certainty.

It is, however, likely that Lord Denning was wrong in *Torquay* v. *Cousins* to define a direct form of the tort of interference with contract, since this would contradict the decision in *Allen* v. *Flood*. Unless, that is, we are to engage on another front the proposition that acts can be unlawful even if not actionable. If the respondents have neither used unlawful means nor intentionally produced a result actionable in itself (*i.e.* a breach of contract) it seems incorrect, by saying that parties have a right not to have their contractual relations interfered with, thereby, and thereby alone, to confer a right of action upon them.

Several of the cases which have established the tort of interference with contract by unlawful means have loosely referred to interference with trade.[75]

---

[70] [1985] I.R.L.R. 211.

[71] [1969] 2 Ch. 106.

[72] See, *e.g. Acrow (Automotion) Ltd.* v. *Rex Chain Belt Incorporated* [1971] 1 W.L.R. 1676; *Esso Petroleum Co. Ltd.* v. *Kingswood Motors Ltd.* [1974] Q.B. 142.

[73] [1983] I.C.R. 490.

[74] See *Midland Cold Storage Ltd.* v. *Steer* [1972] I.C.R. 435.

[75] *e.g.* Lord Denning M.R. in *Torquay Hotels Ltd.* v. *Cousins* [1969] 2 Ch. 106 at 139; and, with the support of Watkins L.J., in *Hadmor Productions Ltd.* v. *Hamilton* [1981] 3 W.L.R. 139.

The House of Lords, however, used the same term without adverse comment in *Hadmor*[76] but, as we have seen, defined the tort as interference with the primary obligations of an existing contract. It seems, therefore, that the reference in *Brekkes Ltd.* v. *Cattel*[77] to interference with an established course of dealing likely to lead to such contracts, should be regarded as no more than an early, and now incorrect, definition of interference with contract. It has become commonplace, however, to refer to the tort we have been discussing as interference with trade or business[78] without thereby implying any extension beyond interference with the primary obligations of existing contracts, which Lord Donovan in *Rookes* v. *Barnard* had intended as an example of unacceptable imprecision but which the House of Lords in *Hadmor* v. *Hamilton* adopted as a definition of its scope. Davies and Freedland,[79] however, say of the decision in *Meade* v. *Haringey LBC*[80] that if the organisers of the industrial action, by which school caretakers withdrew their service, had used unlawful means which had brought about closure of the schools affected they would have been liable for interference with the local authority's business. This involves an assumption of liability without proof of any interference with primary obligations of contract. The local authority had no contractual obligation to keep the schools open nor any contract with parents to educate their children. Contracts ancillary to the running of the schools might have been affected but to include them would be stretching "intention" a long way, as well as assuming evidence which does not seem to have been given. It is suggested that there is no authority for extension of the tort of interference with business (if that is what it is now to be called) beyond interference with contract.

(d) Other relevant torts

There seems no logical obstacle to the proposition that breach of statutory duty, at least if the duty is owed to individuals and the breach constitutes a tort, should constitute unlawful means so as to produce that element of liability in the torts we have so far discussed. As tortious liability arising from breach of statutory duties shows there is no need for specific provision of a civil remedy and the express provision of criminal sanctions will not precude the grant of a right of action in tort. On the other hand, the courts will not thus extend statutory penalties into private rights where the obligations are not obviously intended to benefit individuals.[81] It must remain open to question whether breach of such a duty is capable of founding liability for interference with contract. In *Barretts and Baird (Wholesalers) Ltd.* v. *I.P.C.S.*,[82] however, the suggestion by Lord Denning M.R. in *Meade* v. *Haringey LBC*[83] of the existence of civil liability for inducement to breach of statutory duty was accepted as capable of supplying the unlawful element. Presumably such

---

[76] [1982] I.C.R. 114.
[77] [1972] Ch. 105.
[78] See, *e.g. Barretts and Baird (Wholesalers) Ltd.* v. *I.P.C.S.* [1987] I.R.L.R. 3; Davies and Freedland at pp. 745 and 756.
[79] At p. 756.
[80] [1989] I.C.R. 494.
[81] See, *e.g. Lonrho Ltd.* v. *Shell Petroleum (No. 2)* [1982] A.C. 173.
[82] [1987] I.R.L.R. 3.
[83] [1979] I.C.R. 494.

a tort could only exist in the case of statutory duties which would give rise to individual rights of action. Such was presumably the case in respect of the duty of a local education authority to provide schooling but it seems somewhat more doubtful in relation to the duty to inspect abattoirs to ensure compliance with EC standards. If there is such a tort it seems uncertain whether it requires the use of unlawful means or whether there are direct and indirect forms of it. If the latter, it seems as if both *Meade* and *Barretts* would be examples of indirect inducement.

Wedderburn[84] raises the possibility of more numerous forms of tortious inducement specifically in relation to equitable duties. Elias, Napier and Wallington[85] called attention to the earlier case of *Prudential Assurance Co. Ltd.* v. *Lorenz*[86] in which an interlocutory injunction had been granted to prevent insurance agents withdrawing from their employers the submission of weekly accounts in breach of an equitable (as well as contractual) duty to account.

Quite apart from this suggestion, equity has long been prepared to set aside an obligation incurred under duress and to order restitution. In *Universe Tankships Inc. of Monrovia* v. *ITF*[87] the House of Lords held that an action for economic duress arose from pressure imposed by an industrial boycott. Superficially, the action, apart from the availability of a wider range of remedies, resembles intimidation and the House of Lords, in this case, did not furnish any detailed discussion to enable us to be sure how the differences there outlined might develop. In *Morgan* v. *Fry*[88] Russell L.J. considered that the unlawful means in intimidation should themselves produce the coercive effect, but he was primarily concerned to distinguish the coercive effect of the lawful situation from the enhancement of it by the unlawful element. No one seems ever to have suggested that a plaintiff who actually has complied with the intimidatory pressure cannot complain if the intimidating acts are not of a nature that would normally override free-will. It was said in *Universe Tankships* that duress must be such as to overbear the will of the plaintiff. In *Hennessy* v. *Craigmyle and Co. Ltd. and ACAS*[89] the Court of Appeal held that duress is only a ground for avoidance if it leaves no real alternative but for the plaintiff to acquiesce.

Of more significance is consideration of the nature of the means required. Lord Scarman in *Universe Tankships* said that duress can exist even if the means are lawful. Liability depends on the illegitimate nature of the demand, not the nature of the pressure. This, of course, is in conformity with its equitable origin and Lord Diplock stressed that economic duress is, strictly speaking, not a tort but gives rise to an action for restitution rather than damages. Confusingly, Lord Scarman himself has said that duress is a tort. Whatever the uncertainties this development has considerable potential in the control of individual disputes, which almost always contain elements of coercion. One of the likely problems is that the coercion exercised by an employer is

---

[84] 3rd ed., at p. 649.
[85] At pp. 2424–3.
[86] (1971) II K.I.R. 78.
[87] [1982] I.C.R. 262.
[88] [1968] 2 Q.B. 710.
[89] [1986] I.R.L.R. 300.

inherent in the system of capital employment of labour, whilst coercion by the employee usually appears as a definable action.

STATUTORY IMMUNITY

The heads of liability affected

The device of rendering normal trade union activity permissible, by granting statutory immunity from forms of civil liability which appear unduly restrictive, was first adopted in the Trade Union Act of 1871 which freed trade unions from liability for acting in restraint of trade. This approach, whereby unions were given freedom to pursue their normal objectives rather than having specific rights conferred upon them by legislation, may well be a reflection of the feeling at that time, and for almost a century after, that British trade unions were self-made and should not seek to depend on legislative grant.[90] The policy of matching judicial developments in civil liability with legislative protection had produced a structure of law which can best be described as crazy. Nevertheless, such a "hands-off" approach had much to commend it whilst successive governments could be relied on to accept that the ring should be left clear of intervention so that the opposed forces of capital and labour could be left to match their strength. That acceptance is no more and, with hindsight, it may seem a pity that the previous century had not been used to establish legal rights for organised labour which, if accepted over a period, would have resisted attack more effectively than immunities were able to resist withdrawal.[91]

However this may be, when the possibility of judicial extension of civil liability at the beginning of the twentieth century threatened the freedom to resort to industrial action, the Liberal government responded in the Trade Disputes Act 1906, by granting total immunity from tort to trade unions as such, and immunity to individuals acting in contemplation or furtherance of a trade dispute from those specific heads of tort—namely conspiracy, inducement to breach of contract, and (in case it existed) interference with trade—which were in the forefront of the threat.

In 1906, immunity was confined[92] to inducement to breach of the contract of employment or interference with trade, business or employment, or the right of a person to dispose of his capital or labour as he wills. As has been explained, it was not until the decision in *Thomson* v. *Deakin*[93] that it was contemplated that liability for industrial action would extend to indirect inducement to break commercial contracts. It was not until *Rookes* v. *Barnard*[94] that serious doubts began to be felt about the effect of the immunity thus granted to the most likely unlawful means used in such indirect inducement to break commercial contracts. A majority of the Royal Commission on Trade Unions, reporting in 1968,[95] recommended that immunity should be extended to inducement to breach of commercial contracts. It is perhaps for-

---

[90] See Wedderburn, *Industrial Relations and the Courts* (1980) 9 I.L.J. 65.
[91] On the relative merits of positive rights see Davies and Freedland, pp. 786–789.
[92] Trade Disputes Act 1906, s.3.
[93] [1952] Ch. 646.
[94] [1964] A.C. 1129.
[95] Cmnd. 3623.

tunate that this change did not take place immediately or it might have omitted the further extension of tort liability to interference with contract. Eventually, in 1976,[96] immunity was extended to inducement to breach or interference with any contract. Section 13 of the Trade Union and Labour Relations Act 1974, as so amended, provides that:

> "An act done by a person in contemplation or furtherance of a trade dispute shall not be actionable in tort on the ground only:
> (a) that it induces another person to breach a contract or interferes or induces any other person to interfere with its performance."

At that point immunity was, again, co-extensive with the tort of interference with contract. Wedderburn[97] powerfully argues that this effect was no greater than had been intended by the legislature in 1906. Tort liability had extended and the statutory immunity had extended to the same point.

The second part of section 3 of the 1906 Act was, "for the avoidance of doubt" re-enacted in T.U.L.R.A. 1974[98] notwithstanding that the tort of interference with trade, thought to be threatened in 1906, had never materialised. It was repealed in 1982,[99] apparently for that reason. This cautious provision had its moment in *Rookes* v. *Barnard*[1] when it was contended that it did not refer to a specific head of tort (because no such head of liability had ever existed) but to the consequences of any action. It would be difficult to explain the words "on the ground only that," plainly lending immunity to one head of tort in the first part of the single sentence which comprises section 3 of the 1906 Act whilst, in the second part rendering immune all tort liability unless it produced damage other than interference with trade. Historically, the reason for the second limb was quite plain and the House of Lords, in rejecting this argument, said so. The repeal of this provision may be regretted if the tort called interference with business breaks the bounds of interference with contract but for the moment the second limb can be said never to have had any effect.

The tort of conspiracy was active in 1906 and a legislature intent on immunity naturally provided[2] that an act done in combination or agreement in contemplation or furtherance of a trade dispute should not be actionable unless it would have been actionable if done without such combination or agreement; thereby extending to civil liability the immunity earlier provided for criminal liability. Re-enactment of this provision in 1974[3] is in these words:

> "An agreement or combination by two or more persons to do or procure the doing of any act in contemplation of furtherance of a trade dispute shall not be actionable in tort if the act is one which, if done without any such agreement or combination, would not be actionable in tort."

Since the chances of an action being based on conspiracy are currently

---

[96] T.U.L.R.A., 1976.
[97] 3rd ed., at p. 596.
[98] s.3(2).
[99] E.A. 1982, Sched. 4.
[1] *Supra*.
[2] Trade Disputes Act 1906, s.1.
[3] T.U.L.R.A., s.13(4).

remote there is little point in discussing the possible effect of the insertion of the second reference to tort. Presumably a conspiracy to break a contract would not fall within the protective effect of the section. But this would be a surprising conclusion, allowing conspiracy to act as the unlawful element in interference with commercial contracts arising from industrial action in breach of contract induced by union officials who rarely resort to such incitement without consultation with those taking the action. In *Rookes* v. *Barnard* the full-time union official, Silverthorne, had no contract of employment to break and was immune from the consequences of inducing a breach of contract by the employees. Nevertheless he was considered part of a conspiracy to *threaten* to break contracts of employment (and so he would, surely, have been part of a conspiracy to break those contracts had this actually occurred) despite the fact that only the agreement or combination made him liable. It is submitted that this conclusion must be unjustified (though the authority of the House of Lords will make it difficult to dispose of) and that a union official would not be liable for conspiracy to use unlawful means if none of his individual acts were actionable had the words "in tort" not been added. It is the double negative which causes the problem.

The draftsmen of section 3(3) of the Trade Union and Labour Relations Act 1974 excelled themselves in dealing, in a remarkably short space, with several problems of "unlawful means" which would usually provide the key to primary liability for economic torts. They seem to have made only one slip in referring to avoidance of doubt in one of their two secondary immunities which, without doubt, had not previously existed. The subsection first provided that activities granted immunity by subsection (1) should not be capable of furnishing unlawful means. As we have already said the better opinion has always been that there is not some intermediary category between actionable wrongs and legal activities which encompasses things the courts would like to consider wrongful but which they are prevented by statute from so regarding. The House of Lords confirmed this view in *Hadmor Productions Ltd.* v. *Hamilton*[4] but, before that, some judges, in *Stratford* v. *Lindley* and *Rookes* v. *Barnard*, had dropped hints that they might think otherwise. The second part of section (3), however, provided that actual breach of contract in contemplation or furtherance of a trade dispute would not constitute such unlawful means. In *Barratts and Baird (Wholesalers) Ltd.* v. *I.P.C.S.*[5] Henry J. apparently saw some considerable reason for this, at least so far as it relates to the breach of contract usually inherent in otherwise lawful industrial action. It does seem somewhat surprising that a collective withdrawal of labour—which it is normally assumed workers are free to engage in and which the legislature has recently apparently approved provided it is preceded by a ballot of likely participants—should nevertheless be "unlawful." Henry J., however, reluctantly concluded that a breach of contract was better described as unlawful than as lawful so that, with the repeal of subsection 3,[6] a breach of contract, as distinct from an interference therewith, was again available as the unlawful means of an actionable inducement to breach of statutory duty. By implication he accepted that the first part of subsection (3) had been purely declar-

---

[4] [1983] 1 A.C. 191.
[5] [1987] I.R.L.R. 3.
[6] By the E.A. of 1982, Sched. 4.

atory so that it remained correct to say that statutorily immune actions would not constitute unlawfulness.

Finally, part (b) of section 3(1) of T.U.L.R.A. 1974 deals with immunity from liability for intimidation arising from a threat of breach of, or interference with, any contract, and from threats to induce others to break or interfere with a contract.

Immunity of trade unions

The immunities summarised above now apply to actions against individuals and actions against trade unions as such. In 1906 total immunity had been afforded to trade unions from actions in tort without the restriction that the act in question should be in contemplation or furtherance of a trade dispute. This really was a statutory privilege. It arose from the fact that before 1901 it would have been considered necessary to sue a trade union as an unincorporated association by way of a representative action against its members. In practice, it would scarcely have been possible to satisfy the condition for representative action that the same group of members had been responsible for the authorisation of the act as are represented in the action arising from it. Effectively, therefore, trade union funds were immune from action in tort. In 1901 the House of Lords had held that a registered trade union was sufficiently recognised by legislation to be sued in its own name. The 1906 Act, therefore, restored an immunity which arose from a purely procedural difficulty and had no justification as a means of relieving from liability for carrying out its industrial relations function. The immunity was reduced in 1974 to permit actions in tort for negligence, nuisance and breach of duty, and those arising from the possession of property, but it was entirely repealed in 1982.[7] That repealing provision sets out in detail the circumstances in which a trade union will be deemed to have authorised industrial action. If these conditions are satisfied the trade union is subject to action in its own name[8] in the same way, and subject to the same immunities, as an individual, save that the amount of damages per cause of action is limited and the political and provident funds of the union are not available to satisfy the judgment. This makes little difference in practice since such actions normally give rise to interlocutory injunctions. The list of specified authorising bodies or persons contains the principal executive committee, or an official regularly attending its meetings; any person empowered by the union rules to authorise or endorse acts of the kind; an employed official of the union or any committee to which such employed official regularly reports (unless prevented by the rules from such authorisation or endorsement or unless the act of the employed official or committee has been repudiated by the principal executive committee or an official regularly attending its meetings, as soon as is reasonably practicable and by written notice to the person (sic) who purported to authorise or endorse the act). Shop stewards, unless authorised by the rules or regulations, or attending the principal executive committee, will not, therefore, by endorsing industrial action, impose liability on the union.[9]

---

[7] E.A. 1982, s.15.

[8] T.U.L.R.A. 1974, s.2.

[9] See the difference of opinion between the Court of Appeal and the House of Lords in *Heaton's Transport (St. Helens) Ltd.* v. *T.G.W.U.* [1972] I.C.R. 308.

This repeal effects arguably the most significant reduction of immunity in the legislation of the 1980s. The injunction is the principal sanction against industrial action. Neither the threat of injunctions nor damages greatly inhibit individuals seeking to organise industrial action and the grant of an injunction against them, which can only be against named defendants, does no more than remove a few potential organisers from the field. An injunction obtained against a trade union may not only order it to take active steps to prevent all its officials from organising such action but, if not obeyed, may lead to fine and indefinite sequestration of the funds of the union and, of course, subsequent fines if it persists in its contempt.

Despite the apparent championship of section 13 immunities by the House of Lords in the late 1970s this is, in fact, the point at which the attitude of the legislature in 1906 was abandoned. No more obvious declaration, that in future a different policy would be adopted towards the freedom of organised labour to balance the power of capital by industrial action, can be found than this passage from the judgment of Lord Diplock in *Duport Steels Ltd.* v. *Sirs*[10] in which the House of Lords actually rejected any suggestion that secondary action was not covered by immunity offered to action in contemplation or furtherance of a trade dispute. Nevertheless, Lord Diplock said[11]:

"That conclusion as to the meaning of words that have been used by successive Parliaments since the Trade Disputes Act 1906, to describe acts for which the doer is entitled to immunity from the law of tort over an area that has been much extended by the Acts of 1974 and 1976, is . . . one which is intrinsically repugnant to anyone who has spent his life in the practice of the law or the administration of justice. Sharing these instincts it was a conclusion that I myself reached with considerable reluctance, for given the existence of a trade dispute it involves granting to trade unions a power, which has no other limits than their own self-restraint, to inflict by means which are contrary to the general law, untold harm to industrial enterprises, to members of the public and to the nation itself, so long as those in whom the control of the trade union is vested honestly believe that to do so may assist it, albeit in a minor way, in achieving its objectives in the dispute."

"Contemplation or furtherance of a trade dispute"

It will have been observed that all the provisions conferring immunity do so in respect of acts in contemplation or furtherance of a trade dispute. A trade dispute is now defined[12] as:

" . . . a dispute between workers and their employer which relates wholly or mainly to one or more of the following, that is to say:
(a) terms and conditions of employment, or the physical conditions in which any workers are required to work";

Working practices, as well as contractual terms are included in this[13]:

"(b) engagement or non-engagement, or termination or suspension of employment or the duties of employment, of one or more workers";

---

[10] [1980] 1 W.L.R. 142.
[11] At p. 156.
[12] T.U.L.R.A., 1974, s.29; as amended by the E.A. 1982, s.18.
[13] Denning M.R. in *Hearn* v. *BBC* [1977] I.C.R. 685.

But this category, which was once capable of permitting fear of redundancy to be put forward as a reason for opposition to a merger or privatisation of a public undertaking, is less effective in that respect since the amendment which requires that the dispute must relate wholly or mainly to that consequence[14]:

> "(c) allocation of work or the duties of employment as between workers or groups of workers;"[15]
> (d) matters of discipline;
> (e) membership or non-membership of a trade union on the part of a worker;
> (f) facilities for officials of trade unions; and
> (g) machinery for negotiation or consultation, and other procedures, relating to any of the foregoing matters, including recognition . . . of the right to represent workers."

The list, though detailed, was plainly drawn up with the intention of comprehensively covering all matters likely to arise from the subject matter of industrial relations. It settles some long-standing arguments such as that as to whether a recognition claim could be connected with the terms and conditions of labour of the workers concerned.

Before the 1982 amendments the dispute was only required to be "connected with" one or more of these matters and the House of Lords, in *NWL Ltd.* v. *Woods*,[16] seemed to conclude that any genuine element of such a matter, as distinct from a sham or a pretext, brought the dispute within the immunity.[17] It seems that this view was more lenient than that in some earlier decisions which had inclined to require the dispute to be *about* a trade matter.[18] It would have been difficult to detect a sham if it had been included in the original statement of dispute and courts had even shown a willingness to imply a trade connection. By 1982, and, of course, in the light of the forthcoming legislative restriction, the House of Lords was regretting its generosity.[19]

The Employment Act 1982 replaced the words "connected with" by "relates wholly or mainly to." The question in future is to be resolved by deciding whether it is the "trade" or the "political" elements of a dispute which are subsidiary. The chances are that attempts to create two or more separate disputes will not find favour with the courts.[20] It is clear from the decision in *Mercury Communications Ltd.* v. *Scott-Garner*,[21] in which the Court of Appeal held that the amendment directed attention to what the dispute was "about," that it did not mean that word in the old sense, possibly incorporating more than one principal motive. The Court of Appeal clearly inferred that if the dispute was about more than one matter a single principal purpose had to be identified. It will be apparent that a lot depends on how far

---

[14] *Mercury Communications Ltd.* v. *Scott-Garner* [1984] Ch. 27.
[15] *Infra*, p. 350.
[16] [1979] I.R.L.R. 478.
[17] *BBC* v. *Hearn* [1977] I.C.R. 685 even a nominal addition of a requirement that in future contracts of employment should make provision for a "non-trade" matter had seemed possible.
[18] *e.g. J.T. Stratford & Son Ltd.* v. *Lindley* [1965] A.C. 307.
[19] *Universe Tankships Inc. of Monrovia* v. *ITF* [1982] I.C.R. 262.
[20] See: *Star Sea Transport Corporation of Monrovia* v. *Slater* [1978] I.R.L.R. 507.
[21] [1984] Ch. 27.

courts are prepared to go along the chain of causation. The simple answer is "not far." In *Stratford* v. *Lindley* where, despite statutory use of the word "connected," the courts had tended to treat the question as what the dispute was about, the courts had concentrated on the object furthered and not the underlying reason why that was a matter of dispute. The same view was taken by Sir John Donaldson M.R. in *Mercury*. He, like the other members of the Court of Appeal, rejected the contention that refusal to connect Post Office telephone systems to those of a private company could be said to relate mainly to a fear of ultimate redundancy springing from privatisation of tele-communications. May L.J., because his approach led him nowhere near fear of job losses which, he said, was the only "trade" matter in the whole range of possible causes, said the question must be treated like one of causation. It would be wrong to treat the reason for the industrial action in question rather than, for instance, why that reason was a matter of dispute, as the sole deter-mining factor. In his view, the trade union had clearly induced the industrial action and that action was a direct response to the order to connect the sys-tems, but it would be wrong not to consider the motive which produced the dispute about that action. He concluded, however, that that motive was, on a commonsense view, the unions opposition to privatisation, rather than the fear of redundancy arising therefrom but on a more distant horizon. It is sug-gested that though the outcome of each approach was the same in *Mercury*, in general the approach of May L.J. is likely to be more restrictive. There are many examples of industrial action which can be directly related to a trade matter without asking why that connection should cause a dispute. Where that connection is obvious, as in the case of industrial action to secure a pay rise, the courts are unlikely to enquire further although the truth is often that pay claims spring from an underlying uncertainty about jobs (which would, of course, also constitute a trade matter). It is where motives are obviously mixed that the courts are likely to abandon the direct connection and look for deeper motives. Where, for example, the International Transport Workers Federation takes action against ships flying flags of convenience, the dispute is regarded by the courts as primarily related to the "political" objection to such a policy.[22] If the chain were pursued it could readily be seen that the Feder-ation's objection to flags of convenience was motivated almost entirely by the fact that that device facilitated poor terms and conditions of employment and rates of pay. The Donaldson approach would see only the fact that the action was brought about by a flag of convenience. The May approach ought to be capable of looking beyond the policy of opposing flags of convenience. In practice, however, just as it failed to look beyond opposition to privatisation in *Mercury*, so as to ask whether that opposition sprang from political dogma or fear of the consequences upon trade matters, so it is likely to stop short of asking why flags of convenience are opposed. In short, the May approach is only causation in the sense of causation limited by a remoteness which is in the discretion of the courts. Some light is shed on secondary motives by the decision of the Northern Ireland Court of Appeal in *Norbrook Laboratories Ltd.* v. *King*[23] in which personal animosity—considered likely to develop in many disputes—was held capable of displacing a trade motive only if it

---

[22] *e.g. Star Sea Transport Corporation of Monrovia* v. *Slater* [1978] I.R.L.R. 507.
[23] [1984] I.R.L.R. 200.

became the sole motivation. In this case a genuine trade motive had originally existed whereas in *Huntley* v. *Thornton*[24] it had not. There being no primary purpose to displace the court was to discard, as subsidiary or as not a motivating factor at all, the possibility of a genuine desire to maintain a closed shop. Certainly this discretion, whether a common sense approach or not, will effectively destroy any attempt to link a dispute to a trade matter either on the simple basis of *BBC* v. *Hearn*[25] or the more sophisticated suggestion of entirely concealing the underlying motive by the form in which the dispute is presented.

The 1982 amendment to the definition of a trade dispute incorporated two separate but interrelated changes. Disputes between workers and workers were excluded, as they had been in 1971. In itself this appears as part of the "neutral" employer approach which had given rise to the partial exclusion from immunity of secondary action.[26] In the 1960s demarcation disputes had been a prominent issue. The majority of the Donovan Commission had decided against withdrawal of immunity because of the difficulty of defining an employer having no responsibility for the dispute. Demarcation disputes, which are by far the main source of disputes between worker and worker, had become much less of an issue by 1982, but the opportunity was taken to place upon the courts the task of defining employer involvement.[27]

Much more significant, it is submitted, is the requirement that a dispute, in order to enjoy protection, must be between an employer and *his* workers. This is fortified by the fact that "worker" is defined as one employed by that employer (or one who was employed but who was dismissed in connection with the dispute, or whose dismissal was one of the circumstances in connection with the dispute). Wherever the term worker appears in the definition of a trade dispute, therefore, it has this limited meaning. A demarcation dispute concerns allocation of work and so falls within the third head of definition. Such a dispute will exist between a non-neutral employer and his workers but, if it involves allocation of work between them and employees of another employer, it will not fall within the third head. That speaks of "allocation . . . between workers" and can only refer to allocation between workers for a single employer.[28] It is a somewhat surprising result that industrial action should be protected if an employer proposes to alter the allocation of work among his own employees but not if he proposes to transfer work to employees of another company which he may control.

In origin the second of these amendments probably had little to do with demarcation disputes. The classic example of a dispute with an employer who had no dispute with his own employees arose when the Society of Lithographic Artists and Engravers successfully compelled upwards of 5,000 employees of small artwork companies to join that union. Virtually none of them had previously been union members and few apparently wished to be. S.L.A.D.E. had taken little interest in them until photographic methods enabled their artwork to be directly prepared for printing, thus bypassing the

---

[24] [1957] 1 W.L.R. 321.
[25] [1977] I.C.R. 685.
[26] E.A. 1980, s.17, *infra* p. 352.
[27] See *Cory Lighterage Co. Ltd.* v. *T.G.W.U.* [1973] I.C.R. 334.
[28] *Dimbleby and Sons Ltd.* v. *NUJ* [1984] I.R.L.R. 69 (C.A.); [1984] I.R.L.R. 161 (H.L.).

traditional engraving skills upon which trade the union had been founded. S.L.A.D.E. members were, however, in a position to refuse to handle this material when it was submitted to printing companies in which they were represented. The dispute as to whether these employees should be forced by their employers to join the union was, of course, within the pre-1982 definition and so no legal action could be taken to prevent the otherwise unanswerable pressures. The 1982 limitation is bound to go much further than this. Its principal casualty is, currently, the International Transport Workers Federation. Crews of ships flying flags of convenience are often glad to have work on any terms and so they are unlikely to wish to raise a dispute about terms and conditions with their employer, least of all to benefit seamen in countries where the beneficial ownership of the ship lies and who would be likely to be taken on if labour costs were the same.

It remains to be seen whether a dispute between an employer and his employees can only be raised initially by the objection of one of those employees. In *Beetham* v. *Trinidad Cement Ltd.*[29] the Privy Council held that a trade union could be regarded as authorised by its members to raise a claim for recognition and so could be said to be acting for its members. If this is followed, a trade union would be entitled to claim protection for a dispute it initiated on behalf of its members employed by the employer. There seems no reason why the same should not apply if the union was asked to do so by employees not members of the union as in the I.T.F. flags of convenience situation. The union would have to be careful first to approach the employer so as to ensure the existence of a dispute before taking industrial action.[30]

Finally, the action in question must be "in contemplation or furtherance" of a trade dispute. This phrase provided the battle ground for those, and primarily certain members of the Court of Appeal, who in the late 1970s sought by judicial decision to limit the scope of the statutory immunity. It had long been a niggling source of doubt. In *Conway* v. *Wade*[31] Lord Shaw had said that "contemplation" did not refer to "something as yet wholly within the mind [of the intervener] and of a subjective character." Lord Scarman in *NWL Ltd.* v. *Woods*[32] affirmed this point. On the other hand, in *Beetham* v. *Trinidad Cement Ltd.*[33] it was said that the parties did not have to be locked in combat. Steps taken at this doubtful stage will rarely form the basis for legal preventive action[34] so that little more light is likely to be shed on the precise point of contemplation at which the line should be drawn. Lord Denning M.R., in particular, concentrated on the word "furtherance," apparently assuming that "contemplation" referred to the period before positive action was taken. In a series of decisions in the Court of Appeal he suggested that an action might be too remote to be in furtherance of the dispute in which it purported to relate and that furtherance implied objective judgment so that a mere belief that the dispute was being advanced by the action would not suffice. His third point, which was that an overriding motive might lead to the conclusion that actions, even if related to trade matters, were not in further-

[29] [1960] A.C. 132.
[30] *J.T. Stratford and Son Ltd.* v. *Lindley* [1965] A.C. 307.
[31] [1909] A.C. 506.
[32] [1979] I.C.R. 67.
[33] [1960] A.C. 132.
[34] But see *Bents Brewery Co. Ltd.* v. *Hogan* [1945] 2 All E.R. 570.

ance of a trade dispute, has effectively become the basis for the 1982 statutory restriction to actions wholly or mainly related to trade matters. The House of Lords rejected all these limitations in *NWL Ltd.* v. *Woods*[35] and *Express Newspapers Ltd.* v. *McShane.*[36] The legislature, however, not only adopted the limitation to a principal motive but, as we shall see, also accepted the concept of remoteness in its application to secondary action, which the House of Lords had, distinctly reluctantly, rejected in *Duport Steels Ltd.* v. *Sirs.*[37] As a result it is more feasible to argue now than it was in 1980 that "furtherance" is intended by the legislature to involve such limitations as Lord Denning suggested.

The defintion of trade dispute contains some general extensions. As amended in 1982[38] a trade dispute exists even though it relates to matters occurring outside the United Kingdom, so long as the persons whose actions are said to be in contemplation or furtherance of such a dispute are likely to be affected in one or more of the aspects set out in the list of trade matters. "Likely to be affected" does not suggest a strong element of involvement but the provision which was originally designed to make it clear that disputes outside *Great Britain* could be supported from within now casts doubt on the freedom to conduct purely sympathetic action.

Section 29(5) of the 1974 Act has survived intact so as to provide that an act, threat or demand which would have led to a trade dispute shall still be treated as in contemplation or furtherance of a trade dispute, notwithstanding that the other against whom it is made submits or accedes so that no dispute arises. This refers to a pre-combat situation but, as we have seen, actions in such a situation will normally be in contemplation or furtherance of a trade dispute. It seems extremely unlikely that the purely subjective state of mind which precedes a dispute could produce an act, threat or demand which was complied with. In any event it must be born in mind that the subsection does not say that there is a trade dispute in such a situation but merely that actions taken before compliance are protected.

Exclusions from immunity

(a) *Secondary action*

Apart from restrictive amendments to the definitions of the extent of immunity, the 1980s have been marked, at regular intervals, by legislative exclusion of certain types of industrial action from that protection.

The first, relating to secondary action, was made by the Employment Act 1980[39] which provision the courts have often said is so complex as to defy comprehension. The section defines what is meant by secondary action as: inducement to breach or interference with a contract of employment or a threat that a contract of employment will be broken or its performance interfered with (whether the contract is that of the threatener or another), where the employer under the contract of employment is not a party to the trade dispute. Industrial action is thereby defined in terms of an attack on an unin-

---

[35] [1979] I.C.R. 867.
[36] [1980] I.C.R. 42.
[37] [1980] 1 W.L.R. 142.
[38] s.18.
[39] s.17.

volved employer by way of interference with his contracts of employment or a threat of such interference. One might have expected the actual breaches of contract caused by industrial action to be included but this provision is only concerned to lift the immunity which would otherwise be available and that does not include actual breach of contract. To secondary action thus defined it is provided that the normal statutory immunity shall not apply. The complications then set in. Section 17(3)–(5) defines three situations which would clearly fall within this basic definition to which, nonetheless, immunity is still to extend.

The first is, with reservations, the simplest example of secondary action in which the purpose of the action is directly to prevent or disrupt the supply, during the dispute, of goods or services between an employer party to the dispute and the employer against whom the secondary action is directed. The reservations are:

(a) that the secondary action was likely to achieve that purpose (*i.e.* the purpose of disrupting the supply—not of furthering the dispute); and

(b) the supply intended to be disrupted must be in pursuance of contracts subsisting at the time of the action. In practice it will be relatively uncommon for secondary action to have, as its purpose, only the disruption of existing contracts. It is far more likely to be a general attack on trade intended to include prevention of the formation of new contracts. The commercial contracts must also be between the employer in dispute and the employer attacked. If they lie between the employer attacked and an intermediary not acting as agent for the employer in dispute the immunity will not be restored by this provision.

In *Merkur Island Shipping Corporation* v. *Laughton*[40] the I.T.F., objecting to terms and conditions of employment offered to the crew of a ship sailing under a flag of convenience, blacked the ship while it was in a British port. The blacking was implemented by tugmen who refused to handle the ship in breach of their contracts of employment. I.T.F. officials had, therefore, taken secondary action by interfering with contracts of employment of an employer not involved in that dispute. Their purpose was the disruption of commercial contracts namely, the contract for dock services between the charterers of the ship and the tug owners. But neither of them was party to the dispute. The employer in dispute was the shipowner. Indirectly, of course, the I.T.F. might be said to have been interfering with the contract of charter to which the employer was a party but the subsection refers only to direct intention. In *Shipping Company Uniform Inc.* v. *ITWF*[41] it was accepted that it might seem surprising that liability for industrial action depended on who was legally responsible to provide certain services, which it might not be easy to tell. In this case the charterers had introduced another safeguard by appointing an "agent" who might contract for port services either on their behalf or as a principal. The court rejected the suggestion that a direction from the owner that the agents were not to contract on his behalf was a sham. The involvement of subsidiary companies (of which trade unions are unlikely to know)[42]

---

[40] [1983] 2 A.C. 570.
[41] [1985] I.R.L.R. 71.
[42] *Dimbleby and Son Ltd.* v. *NUJ* [1984] I.R.L.R. 161.

introduces a further element of uncertainty in ascertaining whether the commercial contracts directly attacked are made with the employer in dispute. In *Dimbleby's* case the dispute lay with T.B.F. Ltd. The plaintiff had entered into contracts with T.B.F. (Printers) Ltd., a separate, though associated, company. It seems likely, therefore, that if all employees are transferred to a separate company which acts only as employer and does not enter into commercial contracts the effect of the subsection in restoring immunity for secondary action can be effectively eliminated.

The complexity of subsection (3) is nothing compared to that of subsection (4), which is designed to restore immunity to secondary action against those who afford substitute services to replace contracts disrupted by a trade dispute. This subsection refers to secondary action the purpose of which is directly to prevent or disrupt the supply of goods or services during the dispute in pursuance of subsisting contracts between any person and an associated employer of the employer in dispute, where the goods or services are in substitution for goods or services which, but for the dispute, would have fallen to be supplied to, or by, the employer party to the dispute. The secondary action must be taken against an employer party to such a substitute contract and be likely to achieve the disruptive purpose. The two subsections together, therefore, produce the following picture:

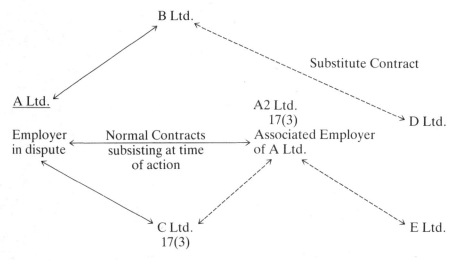

Whilst the normal contracts subsist, secondary action against B, C and A2 is permitted. Whilst the substitute contracts persist, secondary action against C, E and A2 is permitted by section 17(4), but D may not be attacked with impunity, nor may B, if its normal contract with A has ceased.

"Associated employer"[43] refers to a situation in which one is a company of which the other (directly or indirectly) has control or both are companies of which a third person (or a group of persons) (directly or indirectly) has control. As we have seen[44] the weight of authority now favours limiting the concept of control to holding a majority of the company's shares. This is a rather

[43] T.U.L.R.A., s.30(5).
[44] *Supra* p. 223.

mechanical way of fixing the bounds of permissible response to the measures taken to offset the effect of industrial action. It is also, somewhat impracticably, involved. As *Dimbleby and Sons* v. *NUJ*[45] reveals, a trade union may well finds itself attacking an associate of the employer with which it is in dispute, but not with a view to interfering with substitute contracts. Associate status, moreover, is a variable concept. Some associate companies are nothing more than an administrative variant of a single organisation. Others possibly as a result of diversification policies by the parent, have all the appearance of a separate enterprise. Wedderburn[46] rightly describes the remaining immunity as "a hit-and-miss affair at best."

Finally, provision is made for immunity for certain secondary action by means of picketing. Confusingly the word "secondary" is used in a different sense in relation to picketing as referring to pickets at other than their own places of employment. This shorthand form should be avoided and here "secondary" will only be used in the sense defined in section 17 as an attack on an employer not party to the dispute. As we shall see,[47] picketing at one's own place of employment is declared to be lawful.[48] Immunity is offered[49] to a worker picketing at his own place of work and employed by a party to the dispute. Such a worker may be involved in secondary action because his aim is to disrupt the contracts of an employer not involved in that dispute, although it seems unlikely in practice that such contracts will not fall within section 17(3) as being made with the employer picketed.[50] Subsection (5) also protects the union official accompanying his members picketing at their own place of work and in this case the protection extends to all such picketing, even if the employer picketed is not a party to the dispute. It seems possible, therefore, that at their own place of work pickets whose employer was not involved in the dispute would have no immunity because neither subsections (3), (4) or (5) applied to them; but their trade union official attending at the same picket would be immune.

(b) *Inducement to union only labour*

The Employment Act 1982[51] declares void any contractual term for the supply of goods or services which requires that at least some part of the work is done only by persons who are, or who are not, members of trade unions generally, or members of a particular union. It also[52] renders void any contractual term for the supply of goods or services requiring recognition of or negotiation or consultation with, or with any official of, one or more trade unions. Should industrial action be taken to induce incorporation of such a term it will not enjoy immunity under T.U.L.R.A., s.13.[53] The same loss of

---

[45] *Supra.*
[46] 3rd ed., at p. 603.
[47] *Infra,* p. 364.
[48] E.A. 1980, s.16, substituting a revised s.15 into T.U.L.R.A., 1974.
[49] E.A. 1980, s.17(5).
[50] In the N.U.S. Ferry dispute at Dover in 1988 "place of work" might have been said to be the whole harbour complex. Pickets at the entrance employed by one ferry company might be said to be at their place of work although they were also taking secondary action against another company.
[51] s.12.
[52] s.13.
[53] E.A. 1982, s.14(1).

immunity occurs in respect of action designed to induce contravention of the statutory prohibitions on excluding a person from a list of those invited to tender, or to include the name of a person on such a list, failing to permit a person to tender or otherwise determining not to enter into a contract with a particular person or terminating a contract for the supply of goods or services on the ground that the work will be done by union members or non-union members or that the contractor does not recognise, or negotiate, or consult with one or more trade unions. In all such cases that act of inducement itself will not constitute a tort[54] but otherwise tortious acts of inducement lose their immunity.

Immunity is also removed from interference with contracts of employment (including inducement to breach) or threats thereof which interferes, *or can reasonably be expected to interfere, with* the supply of goods or services (whether under contract or not) where the reason, or one of the reasons, for doing the act is that the work has been, or is likely to be, done by persons who are, or who are not, members of trade unions or of particular trade unions or that the supplier does not recognise negotiate or consult with one or more trade unions, unless in the case of each of these reasons the workers are employed by, or the supplier is, the actual employer whose contracts of employment are attacked.

There is no doubt that many contractors, usually large and unionised companies, did require their sub-contractors to recognise unions or employ union labour on the contracts. There were other reasons for this than union pressure in many cases.

(c) *Action not supported by ballot*

Statutory immunity is withdrawn from inducement to breach of, or interference with a contract of employment by means of industrial action not supported by a ballot.[55] Immunity is similarly withdrawn where such an attack on the contract of employment in turn induces breach of, or interference with, a commercial contract.

The Conservative government, first elected in 1979, had consistently maintained that industrial action was not resolved upon by democratic means and should be subjected to a ballot of all those members of a trade union who, at the time of the ballot, it is reasonable for the union to believe will be induced to take part in the industrial action. If anyone not entitled to vote is subsequently called upon to take part in the industrial action the ballot will be invalidated.[56] No one else must be entitled to vote. The ballot must be conducted by means of marking a ballot paper, so far as reasonably practicable in secret, without interference or, so far as possible, cost to the voter. The answer "yes" or "no" must be required to the question whether the voter is prepared to take part in a strike or is prepared to take part in some industrial action other than a strike. The statement, "If you take part in a strike or other industrial action, you may be in breach of your contract of employment," must appear on every ballot paper. If both strikes and other industrial action are envisaged two separate questions must be asked. The ballot must either

---

[54] ss.12(7) and 13(4).
[55] Trade Union Act 1984, s.10(1).
[56] Trade Union Act 1984, s.11(1) as amended by Employment Act 1988.

be by post or, during or immediately before or after work, at the workplace. Normally a separate ballot must be held for each workplace involved but this is not so if all union members or all members employed by one or more employers are balloted. Nor is it so if those balloted share a "common distinguishing factor" other than one consequent on the place of work alone. No act before a majority of those voting have answered "yes" to the question whether they are prepared to take part in the industrial action enjoys immunity and the first authorisation or endorsement of action and the act itself must occur within four weeks of that date.[57] Once the action has been authorised by ballot and commenced within this period, however, it may be suspended and later resumed without a further ballot, although difficult decisions may have to be made about what is a resumption of previous industrial action and what is a new industrial action in pursuit of fresh objectives.[58]

The Secretary of State is empowered, and intends, to issue a code of practice on desirable balloting and election practices.[59] Long before this legislation the rules of many trade unions required a ballot before industrial action was taken. Other unions, particularly those which allowed local shop-stewards more freedom to initiate industrial action, were strongly opposed to the introduction of a statutory ballot requirement, especially one backed by so effective a sanction as the illegitimacy of action without such a ballot. No doubt the requirement of a ballot has, in many instances, forced the abandonment of planned industrial action where local officials were unsure of the support of their members. Some well-publicised instances exist of ballots producing a majority against the proposed action. Where, however, a ballot produces a majority in favour of action it is obvious that the fact considerably strengthens the authority of the union and, thus, its bargaining position. In a situation where they are likely to receive majority support, therefore, union officials are more likely than not to welcome the opportunity to hold a ballot. It is also likely to be true in many cases that full time union officials are not entirely opposed to the effect it will have on controlling the power of shop-stewards. It could be that a future government would reduce the severity of the sanction but total repeal of the ballot requirement seems unlikely. Union recognition of the usefulness of a ballot in certain circumstances is emphasised by the efforts of the national Union of Seamen in April 1988 to hold a ballot in favour of industrial action by the crews of cross-channel ferries, despite the fact that such action would, for other reasons, not have enjoyed immunity from legal action. In this instance an injunction was applied for by the employers to prevent the holding of a ballot, on the ground that it would tend to the authorisation of unlawful action. Although the union called off the action, an award of such an injunction would have been strange, in view of the fact that the whole purpose of the ballot is to authorise what would otherwise be unlawful.

A member of a trade union is given the right by the Employment Act 1988[60] to apply to the High Court (or the Court of Session in Scotland) where he claims that the union has, without the support of a ballot, authorised or

---

[57] s.10(3).
[58] *Monsanto plc* v. *T.G.W.U.* [1986] I.R.L.R. 406.
[59] E.A. 1988, s.18.
[60] s.1.

endorsed any industrial action participated in by employees and in which members of the union, including himself, are likely to be, or have been, induced by the union to take part or continue. Such right exists regardless of whether the industrial action is legal and regardless of whether the inducement would be effective. If the court is satisfied on all these points including the fact that the applicant is likely to be, or has been, induced to participate, it may make such order as it considers appropriate for requiring the union to take steps to ensure both that the inducement ceases and that no member of the union engages in the action after the order by virtue of having been induced to do so before the order. Authorisation by the union depends on the same rules as are contained in section 15 of the Employment Act 1982.[61]

PICKETING

Picketing, which is, for some unexplained reason, an activity best known in the English speaking world, is regarded in the United States of America as protected by the free speech provisions of the Constitution. As this indicates, it is, and should be regarded as, primarily a means of communication, persuasive though that communication may be.

In this country, however, it is not protected by any such fundamental right. The activities involved in picketing, in the absence of any special statutory immunity, fall, therefore, to be judged according to the ordinary law. A person or a group of people, whether they be pickets or not, is free to stand on a street corner or outside a building and communicate information or seek to persuade others to adopt a course of action. There is no inalienable freedom to do so and there is no right in the sense of corresponding duty on others to listen. All the ordinary laws of obstruction and assault apply and such activities may be considered by the police to give rise to a reasonable anticipation of a breach of the peace.[61a]

Specific criminal liability

Whilst abolishing liability for criminal conspiracy[62] in 1876 the legislature retained the criminal sanction against certain forms of wrongful action. It was provided by section 7 of the Conspiracy and Protection of Property Act 1875, that:

> "Every person who, with a view to compel any other person to abstain from doing or to do any act which such other person has a legal right to do or abstain from doing, wrongfully and without legal authority,
> (1) uses violence to or intimidates such other person or his wife or children, or injures his property;
> (2) persistently follows such other person about from place to place;
> (3) hides any tools, clothes or other property owned or used by such other person, or deprives him of, or hinders him in the use thereof;
> (4) watches or besets the house or other place where such other person resides or works or carries on business, or happens to be, or the approach to such house or place; or

---

[61] See p. 346, *supra*.
[61a] *Hubbard* v. *Pitt* [1976] Q.B. 142.
[62] This part of the section was repealed by s.2(2) of the Trade Disputes Act 1906.

(5) follows such other person with two or more other persons in an disorderly
    manner in or through any street or road,

shall on conviction thereof by a court of summary jurisdiction, or on indictment as
hereinafter mentioned be liable to pay a penalty not exceeding £20, or to be
imprisoned for a term not exceeding 3 months. . . . "

In *J. Lyons & Sons* v. *Wilkins*[63] the Court of Appeal held that pickets who
sought to persuade people not to enter into the plaintiff's employment were
doing more than this provision permitted and were "watching and besetting"
within the criminal provisions of the rest of the section.[64] In the second hearing before the Court of Appeal, Lindley M.R., who was not noted for sympathy towards trade union objectives, said:

"The truth is that to watch or beset a man's house with a view to compel him to do
or not to do what is lawful for him not to do or to do is wrongful and without lawful authority unless some reasonable justification for it is consistent with the evidence. Such conduct seriously interferes with the ordinary comfort of human
existence and ordinary enjoyment of the house beset, and such conduct would
support an action on the case for a nuisance at common law."

It will be observed that the Master of the Rolls here makes two points:

(i) that "watching and besetting" outside the protection mentioned is
    itself wrongful;
(ii) that in the circumstances what happened was common law nuisance.

It is, of course, the first of these which is of greatest significance. Chitty L.J.
supported it by pointing out that in the section the description "wrongful"
was applied to all the subsections and, since it applied equally to violence,
intimidation and injury to property and to watching and besetting, it must follow that this last was regarded as equally unlawful with the first three. In
Ward, Lock and Co. v. *Operative Printers' Assistants' Society*,[65] however, a
different view was taken. The words "wrongfully and without legal authority"
were regarded as intended to make it clear that the crimes specified in section
7 would only be committed where the conduct was otherwise unlawful so as to
give rise to a civil remedy. Fletcher Moulton L.J. said of the section:

"It legalises nothing, and it renders nothing wrongful that was not so before. Its
object is solely to visit certain selected classes of acts which were previously
wrongful, *i.e.* were at least civil torts, with penal consequences capable of being
summarily inflicted."

In contra-distinction to the tort of 'intimidation," criminal intimidation
appears to be confined to threats of personal violence[66] but actual fear need
not be proved.[67] It is sufficient if the act in question would have been enough
to produce fear in men of normal courage. The exhibition or threat of force or
violence without their use, will suffice.[68] "Persistent following," as an

[63] [1896] 1 Ch. 811; [1899] 1 Ch. 255.
[64] *Infra.*
[65] (1906) 22 T.L.R. 327; followed in *Fowler* v. *Kibble* [1922] 1 Ch. 487. But see now *The Mersey
Dock and Harbour Co.* v. *Verrinder* [1982] I.R.L.R. 152 *infra.*
[66] *Gibson* v. *Lawson* [1891] 2 Q.B. 545.
[67] *Agnew* v. *Munro* (1891) 28 S.L.R. 335.
[68] *R.* v. *Jones and Others* [1974] I.C.R. 310.

offence, raises some problems. In *Smith* v. *Thomasson*[69] it was said that the offence does not require proof of actual or threatened violence nor, in view of the offence in the fifth head, does it require disorderliness. Yet this would suggest that persistent following is rendered wrongful *de novo*, since there is no civil liability merely for following a person about from place to place. It is suggested that this decision is incorrect and that, as in the case of the fifth head (where the element of disorderly conduct was described in *R.* v. *McKenzie*[70–71] as "the gist and pith of the offence") disorderly conduct, or some other illegal element, is also necessary to provide the unlawful element in the offence. The distinction between the second and fifth head, therefore, is simply that liability under the second head, in respect of following by a single person, will only arise if that following is persistent.

In the same way, the hiding of tools, clothes or other property will not be criminal under this section unless accompanied by measures which are otherwise wrongful. Very commonly, of course, such means would be constituted by the trespass upon the property hidden; but in *Fowler* v. *Kibble*[72] a colliery lampsman had been persuaded, by lawful means, to refuse to issue lamps to certain non-union miners before they went down the mine. The lampsman might be said to have been induced to break his contract of employment by this act, but because of the effect of what was then section 3 of the Trade Disputes Act 1906, such inducement would not have been actionable. There was, therefore, no unlawfulness in the activity concerned and it was held that no offence had been committed under section 7.

"Watching and besetting" is simply a description of certain forms of picketing. It seems to follow that once the prerequisite that the watching and besetting is otherwise wrongful is established the criminal offence under the section is made out, provided that its object is that specified in the section.[73]

Apart from these special statutory provisions, picketing is particularly likely to give rise to general types of criminal conduct. In *R.* v. *Jones*[74] the indictment against six pickets contained 42 counts. The first three charged them all with conspiracy, unlawful assembly and affray. The remaining 39 charged offences under section 7, as well as damaging, attempting to damage or threatening to destroy property, threatening behaviour and assault. Pickets may also be guilty of criminal offences of unlawful assembly and even, in some situations, of affray.[75]

Police powers

In *Piddington* v. *Bates*[76] eight employees were, at the time, at work in the premises of the Free Press Ltd. during the major printing stoppage of 1959. The company employed non-union labour and was owned by an organisation generally regarded as anti-union. A party of 18 pickets arrived in two

[69] (1891) 62 L.T. 68.
[70–71] [1892] 2 Q.B. 519.
[72] [1922] 1 Ch. 487.
[73] See *Farmer* v. *Wilson* (1900) 69 L.J.Q.B. 496.
[74] [1974] I.C.R. 310.
[75] *R.* v. *Jones, supra.*
[76] [1961] 1 W.L.R. 162.

vehicles. Two pickets were stationed at the front gate and four at the rear gate. A constable arrived and informed the pickets at the rear gate that two pickets were sufficient there. Two of them departed. The constable made his way to the front gate and, on his way, passed the appellant, who was clearly going back to the gate. The constable told the appellant several times that two pickets would be enough there, but the appellant asserted that he knew his rights and could stand at the rear gate if he chose. He attempted to push past the constable and was arrested and charged with obstructing a policeman in the exercise of his duty. It was alleged that the duty involved was the prevention of a breach of the peace which the constable reasonably anticipated. The court held that, in the circumstances, it could not say that the constable had no reasonable grounds for such anticipation. Lord Parker C.J.[77] indicated the existence of a considerable protection against abuse of the powers of the police which may not, in practice, exist:

"The law is reasonably plain. First, the mere statement by a constable that he did anticipate that there might be a breach of the peace is clearly not enough. There must exist proved facts from which a constable could reasonably have anticipated such a breach.

"Secondly, it is not enough that his contemplation is that there is a remote possibility of a breach of the peace. Accordingly in every case it becomes a question whether, on the particular facts, there were reasonable grounds on which the constable charged with this duty reasonably anticipated that a breach of the peace might occur."

It is fairly obvious, however, that a court will not be over-anxious to discard the assessment of a policeman on the spot.

An attempt was made in *Kavanagh* v. *Hiscock*[78] to restrict this police power by asserting a right to picket. The divisional court, following the decision in *Hunt* v. *Broome*[79] confirmed that immunities did not amount to rights. May J. said[80]:

"Both before the learned stipendiary magistrate and in this court the appellant contended that section 134 of the Industrial Relations Act 1971[81] gave him a right, in the sense of a positive entitlement, to picket peacefully, that is to seek peacefully to persuade the driver of the coach to cease carrying the electricians who were not on strike. In my judgment this is not the effect of section 134(1) nor what, by its plain terms, it enacts. Section 134 merely provides, as did its statutory predecessors, that the activity specified in subsection (1), which may loosely be described as peaceful picketing, shall not, of itself, and these words require to be stressed, constitute a criminal offence or a civil wrong."

Picketing which, by reason of the application of excessive means, does not fall within the statutory protection, is usually referred to as "non-peaceful"

---

[77] At p. 169.
[78] [1974] 2 All E.R. 177.
[79] [1974] I.C.R. 24.
[80] At p. 185.
[81] Which at that time contained the statutory protection for picketing.

picketing. This must not be taken necessarily to refer to the existence of violence.[82]

Since the legislative indications of added restrictions upon picketing, it appears that the police have, as a matter of combined policy, extended the use of their powers. In *Moss* v. *McLachlan*,[83] during the lengthy miners' strike in 1985, certain miners were stopped by the police whilst travelling some miles away from a number of collieries. They were informed that the police had reason to believe they intended to demonstrate at these pits and that this was likely to cause a breach of the peace. They attempted to push through the police cordon and were arrested and convicted of wilful obstruction of a police officer in the execution of his duty. A Divisional Court held that there was ample evidence to support the conclusion that the police honestly and reasonably feared an imminent breach of the peace. The Divisional Court, on this occasion, said that the breach was not too remote in view of the proximity of the pits, but it is difficult to see why that should be relevant and instances were reported of police turning back miners from the Kent coalfield at the Dartford Tunnel, apparently on their way to the Nottingham coalfields. Where an arrest occurs in such circumstances it is, of course, likely that those charged will be released on bail. In *R.* v. *Mansfield Justices, ex p. Sharkey*[84] Lord Lane permitted the imposition of such conditions on bail as the court considered necessary to prevent the accused committing another offence while on bail. Although the schedule to the Act makes it clear that such a condition must be necessary it was, in his view, sufficient if the court perceived a real, rather than a fanciful, risk of such an offence. He held that in the present case the magistrates were justified in concluding that further picketing, threatening the peace, would be indulged in by the accused and were entitled, therefore, to impose a condition that those bailed should not attend at pickets in furtherance of their dispute.

The code of practice

A Code of Practice for the conduct of picketing, has been issued which is increasingly relied on by lower courts to set permissible standards beyond which the picketing ceases to be lawful. It is doubtful whether the Code is correct to say "the law gives the police discretion to take whatever measures may reasonably be considered necessary to ensure that picketing remains peaceful and orderly."[85] A disorderly picket protected by the statutory immunity does not seem to commit any offence (nor even incur civil liability) merely by reason of that fact, and it is submitted that not all disorderly conduct can reasonably be foreseen as likely to provoke a breach of the peace. In the same way it is not the fear of disorder among the pickets that entitles the police to limit their numbers.[86] These provisions seem designed to suggest to magistrates that it is an offence for a picket to refuse to obey the request of a policeman to move.

Is a "disorderly" picket one not supervised according to paragraph 32?

---

[82] See, *e.g. Ryan* v. *Cooke and Quinn* [1938] I.R. 512—placards bearing gross misrepresentations.
[83] [1985] I.R.L.R. 76.
[84] [1984] I.R.L.R. 496.
[85] Para. 26.
[86] Para. 28.

"An experienced person, preferably a trade union official who represents those picketing, should always be in charge of the picket line. He should have a letter of authority from his union which he can show to police officers or to people who want to cross the picket line. Even when he is not on the picket line himself he should be available to give the pickets advice if a problem arises."

More significantly, the Code contains the following guidelines[87]:

"Large numbers on a picket line are also likely to give rise to fear and resentment amongst those seeking to cross that picket line even where no criminal offence is committed. They exacerbate disputes and sour relations not only between management and employees but between the pickets and their fellow employees. Accordingly pickets and their organisers should ensure that in general the number of pickets does not exceed six at any entrance to a workplace; frequently a smaller number will be appropriate."[88]

It is important to realise that the powers of the police and the provisions of the criminal law are indeed very extensive.[89] The difference between tolerable levels of control and oppression of freedoms that are part of the freedom of speech is, in the area of picketing, very much dependent on the way the police exercise their powers. The distinction between instructions and guidelines is no doubt real but the Code comes perilously close to governmental instruction to the police to regard six pickets at any one point as the normal permitted maximum.

Liability of pickets in tort

The most likely objectives of a picket line are either,

(a) to persuade workers not to enter the premises where they are employed and thus to interfere with their contracts of employment; or
(b) to persuade suppliers to those premises or purchasers from them, usually through the vehicle drivers they have instructed to deliver and pick up goods, not to do business with the occupier and thus to interfere with commercial contracts.

Until 1980, however, the developing tort of interference with contract played little part in the control of industrial picketing because pickets were almost certain to be acting in contemplation or furtherance of a trade dispute and thus to enjoy immunity. When legal control of industrial action turned from primary reliance on the criminal[90] to the civil law, however, it preferred torts relating to property, even over conspiracy which obviously would have been available. In most forms of industrial action the employer can either permit those involved on his premises or exclude them, as he chooses. Unless they defy his exclusion, therefore, he is unlikely to have any cause of action in nuisance or trespass. Picketing, however, characteristically takes place on

---

[87] Para. 31.
[88] In *Thomas* v. *National Union of Mineworkers (South Wales Area)* [1985] I.R.L.R. 136 Scott J. considered this a sensible limit and relied heavily on the presence of numbers in excess to establish illegality.
[89] See, *e.g.* para. 24.
[90] Nevertheless pickets were convicted of conspiracy along with other s.7 charges in *R.* v. *Jones* [1974] I.C.R. 310.

public property; that is to say, on the road outside the gates of the place of employment. The occupier cannot directly forbid the pickets to be there. He can claim that they interfere with his freedom to use his property as he wishes, for that is their purpose. Inevitably, therefore, it occured to the courts at an early stage of the development of civil liability to consider whether a picket constituted a nuisance actionable by a private owner because the interference with the use of his property caused him damage over and above the nuisance caused to the general public. This sounds so much more obvious if we call picketing "watching and besetting" that it is hardly surprising that Lindley M.R., moved directly from that description to the conclusion that a picket seriously interfered with the "ordinary enjoyment of the house beset."[91] A great deal that occurs on public property, and especially on the highway, interferes with the enjoyment of adjacent private property. The law must strike a balance.[92] But the primary element of coercion of the will of the occupier would obviously leave most nineteenth century judges, and not least Lindley, in no doubt whose freedom was most deserving of protection. It seems to have had a good deal of influence on Scott J. in 1985.[93] It says a lot for a later Court of Appeal, in 1906,[94] that it should have been prepared to conclude that attendance outside private premises to seek to persuade people not to do business there was not inevitably an actionable nuisance. Even with that hopeful sign, however, the freedom to picket would have been left to the discretion of judges with less generous views. The legislature in 1906, accordingly declared that:

> "It shall be lawful for one or more persons, acting on their own behalf or on behalf of a trade union . . . in contemplation or furtherance of a trade dispute, to attend at or near a house or place where a person resides or works or carries on business or happens to be, if they so attend merely for the purposes of peacefully obtaining or communicating information, or of peacefully persuading any person to work or abstain from working."[95]

This provision was never thought of by the courts as doing more than declaring that peaceful persuasion by those on public property was not unlawful as such. Without it, it might be argued that picketing was a trespass to the highway or an unreasonable interference with the use of private property constituting a nuisance. There can be no doubt that the intention of the legislature was to go no further than that. It conferred no right to picket. The declaration of legality was confined to those who attended at, and not in, a place and it went no further than to neutralise peaceful persuasion, by which it meant not necessarily non-violent conduct but persuasion which, in itself, was within the law. All the statutory provision amounted to was a declaration that it shall be lawful to attend for the specified purpose, provided those attending behaved lawfully.

That the legislature was justified in taking the trouble to free lawful persuasion on the highway from inherent liability arising from nuisance or trespass

---

[91] *J. Lyons & Sons* v. *Wilkins* [1896] 1 Ch. 255.
[92] *Thomas* v. *NUM (South Wales Area)* [1985] I.R.L.R. 136.
[93] *Thomas* v. *NUM, supra.*
[94] *Ward Lock and Co.* v. *Operative Printers' Assistants' Society* (1906) 22 T.L.R. 327.
[95] The Trade Disputes Act 1906 (c. 47), s.2.

to the highway, was demonstrated years later when attendance, not in contemplation or furtherance of a trade dispute, to persuade potential customers
not to do business with an estate agent was held by a majority of the Court of
Appeal to justify an injunction to prevent trespass to the highway. The "pickets" in that case had remained on the pavement which they had, in no sense,
blocked; nor had they resorted to threats or any other illegal conduct than the
simple act of standing about rather than "passing and repassing" with the
occasional act incidental thereto.[96]

This freedom to picket was, and is, severely circumscribed. It is a freedom
to persuade and communicate; nothing more. If the purpose of the pickets
includes interference with the freedom of others in any respect their activity is
outside the scope of the statutory declaration of lawfulness. So, in *Tynan* v.
Balmer[97] the lower court had found as a fact that 40 pickets walked in a circle
so as to block a service road to a factory. The Divisional Court held that that
went beyond persuasion. The lower court had made a second point that even
if the purpose of the pickets was confined within the statutory limits it was
only necessarily lawful to take steps without which communication and persuasion could not reasonably take place. It is, for instance, excessive to attend
with more people than is necessary for mere persuasion and communication
and, since the excess persons trespass on the highway, such picketing seems to
become, however technically, unlawful. On the other hand, communication
with a vehicle driver cannot reasonably take place without stopping his
vehicle but the statutory provision says nothing about stopping people to
communicate with them. Again, therefore, obstruction of a vehicle is outside
the statutory definition of legality.[98–99]

It is difficult to understand the surprise which seems to have been felt at the
obviously correct decision of the House of Lords in *Hunt* v. *Broome*.[1] The
defendant, a strike picket, stood in front of a lorry holding a placard which
urged the driver not to work at a nearby site where there was a dispute. Perhaps the expressions of surprise arise from the feeling, shared by the magistrate, that this was a reasonable method of communication. Perhaps it was the
most inoffensive method that could be devised. But it involved obstruction of
the driver's freedom of passage and so was more than attendance to persuade.
Lord Reid said:

> "I see no ground for implying any right to require the person whom it is sought to
> persuade to submit to any kind of constraint or restriction of his personal free-
> dom. One is familiar with persons at the side of the road signalling to a driver
> requesting him to stop. It is then for the driver to decide whether he will stop or
> not. That, in my view, a picket is entitled to do. If the driver stops, the picket can
> talk to him but only for so long as the driver is willing to listen.
> That must be so, because if a picket had a statutory right to stop or to detain the
> driver, that must necessarily imply that the Act has imposed on those passing

---

[96] *Hubbard* v. *Pitt* [1976] Q.B. 142.
[97] [1967] 1 Q.B. 91.
[98–99] See *Bird* v. *O'Neal* [1960] A.C. 907.
[1] [1974] I.C.R. 84. Even Widgery C.J. in *Kavanagh* v. *Hiscock* [1974] I.C.R. 282 at 290 infers
that there is something novel in the decision.

along the road a statutory duty to stop or to remain for longer than they choose to stay. So far as my recollection goes it would be unique for Parliament to impose such a duty otherwise than by express words, and even if one envisages the possibility of such a duty being imposed by implication the need for it would have to be crystal clear."[2]

However unremarkable this view may have been to the lawyer, the decision brought sharply to the attention of trade unions the fact that, in practice, it will be very difficult to keep effective picketing within the scope of the narrow statutory provision. The Secretary of State for Employment, somewhat unwisely, declared that steps would be taken to ensure the lawfulness of reasonable picketing. The reader may enjoy the diversion of drafting a definition of what would thereby be permitted which does not use the word "reasonable" or include some similarly imprecise boundary of permission. Through the Home Secretary, the police made it quite clear that they would not be responsible for controlling picketing if its legality could only be determined after the event by a court. In favour of doing nothing was the fact that in practice, at the time there was a wide freedom to picket. Police forces generally were not in the habit of restricting reasonable picketing. *Piddington* v. *Bates*[3] was the outcome of an excess of zeal by a constable who had not been told what the policy was. It remained unlikely that anyone would seek to obtain an injunction against the organisers of a picket for technical nuisance or trespass. Despite impressions to the contrary, trade unions do not indulge in finding ways round court orders backed by solid law, but in such a situation they would probably have taken the simple step of replacing the organisers subject to the injunction with others who had not been included.

In 1982, however, two changes in the law relating to industrial action completely altered the practical vulnerability of pickets. Firstly, the removal of trade union immunity meant that injunctions could be obtained against the union so that it was no longer necessary to try to identify the organisers of pickets, knowing that they could readily be replaced. An injunction against a trade union can go so far as to instruct it to take positive steps to see that the picketing is terminated, thus making the trade union the guarantor of its officials and members. Secondly, immunity under section 13 of the 1974 Act hitherto available against liability for the tort of interference with contract, is withdrawn from picketing, even if it is in contemplation or furtherance of a trade dispute, wherever the picketing does not fall within the narrow limits of statutory lawfulness. It is not too much to say that picketing which obstructs free passage, however, non-violently, or which involves more than the minimum number necessary to communicate and persuade, is virtually bound to constitute an actionable interference with contract.

The scope of attendance declared lawful by what is now section 15 of the Trade Union and Labour Relations Act 1974 has been significantly reduced by an amendment introduced in 1980.[4] The declaration of the lawfulness of attendance (and thus, since 1980, of the availability of immunity under section 13) depends now on the presence of all the following elements:

---

[2] See also *The Mersey Dock and Harbour Co.* v. *Verrinder* [1982] I.R.L.R. 152.
[3] [1961] 1 W.L.R. 162.
[4] E.A. 1980, s.16(1).

(a) the attendance must be in contemplation or furtherance of a trade dispute; and

(b) must be for the purpose only of peacefully obtaining or communicating information or peacefully persuading any person to work or abstain from working;
(excessive purposes of others will not affect the legality of an individual's attendance, although his knowledge of them might call in question the extent of his own purposes); and

(c) *the person concerned must be attending at or near his own place of work, or to be an official of a trade union attending at or near the place of work of a member of that union whom he is accompanying and whom he represents.*

This final limitation was inserted specifically to withdraw legality from the "flying picket"; typically a group who might, or might not, be involved elsewhere in the same industry as the employer in dispute and whose purpose was to reinforce picket lines. The extension of permission to union representatives was made in recognition of the fact that the presence of union officials is considerably more likely to restrain than extend illegality. The legislative provision does not deal well with the question of what may be regarded as a place of work or, it is submitted, adequately with the position of former employees. It ignores completely the problem created by a single entrance to private property, upon which are a number of separate workplaces, so that a picket at that entrance is not only at or near his place of work.[4a] Commonsense will presumably prevail in that the nuisance to other employees occasioned by the picket, ascertaining that those seeking access to or egress from them are not within the object of the picketing will, in practice, be overlooked.[5] Where an employee has no one place of work, or attendance at his place of work is impracticable, he may attend at the place from which he works or from which his work is administered. It seems likely that this will prevent effective picketing in many instances where the employee has no obvious base, since picketing a head office is unlikely to be effective. Where a worker's employment has been terminated in connection with a trade dispute, he may picket his former place of work. No provision is made for the possibility that his employer may subsequently have transferred operations from that site.[6]

The problems that face organisers of pickets become clear from the study of the facts and the decision in *Thomas* v. *National Union of Mineworkers (South Wales Area).*[7] As Scott J. said, the striking of a balance between the freedom to persuade and the freedom to trade, or go to work, poses no problem for picketing which is "peacefully and responsibly conducted." There is no law which makes picketing *per se* a common law nuisance. Whether it is conducted at the picket's place of work or not, it need not be unlawful. But in the nature of things, feelings are likely to run high whenever a picket line is challenged. In this instance six pickets (demonstrating the influence of the

---

[4a] *Rayware Ltd.* v. *T.G.W.U.*, *The Times*, 15 November, 1988.

[5] But is a picket desirous of attacking both his own employer and another sharing the same entrance to be protected?

[6] So former employees of *The Times* were entitled to picket the old premises at Printing House Square in Grays Inn Road but not the new headquarters in Wapping.

[7] [1985] I.R.L.R. 136.

Code) were deputed to stand at the gate, presumably to conduct the actual communication. They were, however, backed up by a large attendance of their colleagues and "abuse was hurled at the vehicle" bringing in those who wished to continue to work. The very fact that workers had to be brought in in this way and that a considerable police presence was thought necessary was, in the judge's view, clear evidence of circumstances "highly intimidating to any ordinary person." In the nineteenth century "subjection to black looks" had been considered sufficient to constitute unlawful intimidation.[8] To insist, as most later cases do, on "intimidation" indicates a different view of the balance but does nothing to explain how far pickets may go. A lot of the answer lies in the impression the courts form. Many reasonable people would simply rather not experience the unpleasantness of passing through a passive, but unfriendly, picket line. The more courageous might turn away when they actually saw it. Those who do pass through are likely to sense hostility. Presumably, all this leaves the balance in favour of the freedom to picket. What if the hostility expresses itself in a muttered curse or two? The answer, yet again, is that in practice a civil action is unlikely to be brought without enough evidence to enable the courts to declare that the pickets have gone further than persuasion. Criminal actions are more likely to be founded on anticipation of a breach of the peace than on crimes which need proof of intimidation, unless, again, that proof is obviously forthcoming. Finally, in the matter of civil liability, the judgment of Scott J. in *Thomas* v. *NUM* contains suggestions of the existence of a new head of tort, which he suggested "might be described as a species of private nuisance, namely unreasonable interference with the victim's rights to use the highway . . . Unreasonable harassment of them in their exercise of that right would . . . be tortious." In *News Group Newspapers Ltd.* v. *SOGAT'82*[9] it was said that interference with the rights of others should be actionable only if it fell within an existing head of tort and gave rise to individual damage. It certainly seems unlikely that the courts will feel the pressure to invent a new head of civil liability to deal with picketing and for the moment, it is suggested, this aspect of the decision should be treated as no more than an interesting example of the fertility of the common law in the field of industrial action.

PENALTIES FOR INDUSTRIAL ACTION

Despite the apparent care with which legislation had limited the liability of trade union funds for damages arising out of each separate action in tort arising from non-immune industrial action,[10] actions for damages against unions are likely to be rare and those against individual organisers non-existent.[11] The main objective of the employer is likely to be to stop the industrial action occurring, or continuing. The injunction is particularly attractive because it can be obtained, on an interlocutory application, quickly and *ex parte*—that is

---

[8] *R.* v. *Druitt* (1867) 10 Cox. 592.
[9] [1986] I.R.L.R. 337.
[10] E.A. 1982, s.16.
[11] Though there might be a greater desire to recover money actually paid out as a result of industrial pressure—*Universe Tankships Inc. of Monrovia* v. *ITF* [1982] I.C.R. 262.

to say, on affidavit evidence without cross examination.[12] It is, moreover, necessary only to show that the evidence reveals "a serious question to be tried" and that the balance of convenience favours the grant, rather than the refusal, of an injunction.[13] Some attempt was made to restrict the availability of this injunction[14] by a provision which required that if the defendant was likely to claim that he had acted in contemplation or furtherance of a trade dispute, the court must be satisfied that all reasonable steps had been taken to allow him to be heard. But that is to permit no more than the submission of an affidavit in reply. It is also required that, in England and Wales, in such a case, regard should be had to the likelihood that the party against whom the injunction is sought will be able to show that he will be able to establish a defence under either section 13 or 15 of the 1974 Act. This latter was an attempt to offset the effect of the fact that the visible economic damage to the employer caused by industrial action, when set against the less tangible damage caused by loss of the momentum of the dispute if an injunction was granted, would usually make the balance of convenience appear to come down in favour of the grant of the injunction.[15] If an interlocutory injunction to prevent industrial action is granted or refused it will:

" . . . in effect, dispose of the action finally in favour of whichever party was successful in the application, because there would be nothing left on which it was in the unsuccessful party's interest to proceed to trial. By the time the trial came on the industrial dispute, if there were one, . . . would be likely to have been settled and it would not be in the employer's interest to exacerbate relations with his workmen. . . . Nor, if an interlocutory injunction has been granted against them, would it be worthwhile for the individual defendants to take steps to obtain a final judgment in their favour. . . . "

In the light of this consideration, Lord Diplock was of the opinion that in applications arising from industrial action the court should consider all aspects of the likelihood of the claim succeeding. In *Dimbleby and Sons Ltd.* v. *NUJ*[16] he was less sure that the interlocutory decision would not proceed to trial. In view of the union's liability introduced in 1982 so that, after that date, the injunction could be obtained against the union, followed by substantial fines for contempt if the injunction were not obeyed, this greater caution is justified. The fact that there might be a later opportunity to discuss possible defences to the action appears to infer that there is less need to consider more than the possibility of statutory immunity at the interlocutory stage. In *Mercury Communications Ltd.* v. *Scott Garner*[17] Sir John Donaldson M.R. presented this as a consideration of whether the applicant had shown a real prospect of succeeding. If this is the correct question relating to industrial action it seems to restore some of the pre-*Ethicon* restriction. In practice, as Wedderburn says, in the same way that there is little likelihood that the application will proceed to trial[18] an allegation that the union is in contempt of the

[12] Although cross examination is theoretically possible R.S.C. Ord. 38, r. 3.
[13] *American Cyanamid Co.* v. *Ethicon Ltd.* [1975] A.C. 396.
[14] T.U.L.R.A. 1974, s.17.
[15] See Lord Diplock in *NWL Ltd.* v. *Woods* [1979] 1 W.L.R. 1294 at p. 1306.
[16] [1984] I.R.L.R. 160.
[17] [1984] I.C.R. 74.
[18] (3rd ed.), at p. 686.

injunction will afford little chance of reconsideration of its justification. Wedderburn also points out[19] that practice affords little real opportunity for the defendant to consider the claims and reply.

In recent years it has become more usual to include positive instructions—mandatory elements—rather than merely a prohibition in interim labour injunctions, and the Trade Union Act 1988 reflects this.[20] It is not uncommon to order a trade union to take positive steps to ensure that industrial action is ended, thus preventing the union successfully contending that it has done its best to comply with an injunction but it has been unable to prevent individuals from continuing to organise action. The circumstances in which a union will be held responsible for organising industrial action in respect of a claim for failure to ballot its members are the same as those applicable to tort liability and are set out in section 15 of the Employment Act 1982.[21]

The availability, since 1982, of the union itself as a defendant bound by injunction, has revealed the significance of the sanction for failure to comply with an injunction. Individuals might be fined but if they did not pay, could, in practice, only be imprisoned. The latter was proved to be a distinctly double-edged weapon, tending to create martyrs. A fine levied on an organisation with sufficient assets to pay it can, however, be enforced by sequestration of those assets.[22] There is no limit to the amount of a fine for contempt and, indeed, its purpose is to express the degree of public affront felt at the disobedience. The amount will, therefore, be connected with the means of the contemnor and a subsequent fine for continuation of the contempt after the first fine is certain to be noticeably larger. Sequestration of assets and a fine may be imposed together and on the first application. A trade union, therefore, is faced with the option of obeying the injunction or incurring increasingly heavy fines. Contempt, however, is a personal offence to which vicarious liability does not contribute.[23] Disobedience to an injunction is civil contempt but it seems to become a criminal contempt when it involves deliberate defiance of the court, as in the case of intentional disobedience to an injunction. As Lightman points out[24] sequestration as a remedy for civil contempt is coercive and an assertion of the courts authority whereas the remedy of a fine for a criminal contempt is largely punitive.

An order for sequestration which may be issued by the court of its own motion, binds the property of the contemnor from the date of a writ issued to four sequestrators (of whom two actually act). It may vest possession of all the contemor's assets. In the case of a trade union, care may have to be taken to ensure that the funds belong to the union rather than, for instance, one of its branches.[25] The sequestrators have a duty to find the assets, obtain them and then deal with them as directed by the court. Not only the parties to the injunction, but all members of the public, have a duty to assist these processes, primarily, of course, by disclosing information as to the whereabouts

---

[19] pp. 687–8.
[20] s.1. See also *Express Newspapers plc* v. *Mitchell* [1982] I.R.L.R. 465.
[21] See pp. 346, *supra*.
[22] R.S.C. Ord. 45, r. 5. See, Lightman, *The Legal Constraints of Receivership and Sequestration*, (1987) 40 C.L.P. 25.
[23] *Express and Star Ltd.* v. *NGA* [1986] I.R.L.R. 222.
[24] (1987) 40 C.L.P. 25 at p. 28.
[25] *News Group Newspapers Ltd.* v. *SOGAT* [1986] I.R.L.R. 227.

of the assets.[26] On the other hand, it seems that there is no duty on third parties to co-operate with a receiver and that only positive interference is a contempt. Both sequestrators and receivers have a right to resort in private for directions to the judge who appointed them.

Lightman[27] concludes that it is open to a trade union, before the issue of an injunction, to place its assets abroad or otherwise out of reach. Presumably, after the issue of the injunction such action would be a contempt. Once sequestrators, or receivers, have been appointed, the union may continue to function (unless ordered not to) but it will have to do so without interfering with their right to possession of its assets. This means, in effect, that it will have to secure their consent to expenditure of its funds.

Sequestration orders may cover so much of the contemnor's property as the court chooses and so may be made against such property as is necessary to pay the fine. In the NUM cases to which reference has been made, however, all the unions assets were included in the orders. The orders will only be discharged when the court is satisfied that this contempt has been purged. In *Richard Read (Transport) Ltd.* v. *NUM*[28] Scott J. granted a discharge without any apology having been received from the contemnor on the ground that the union had recognised the authority of the Court. The receivership referred to in the case of the NUM was not discharged on the application of the receiver but was discharged when the union official and three of its officers tendered a formal apology without assurances that they would comply with orders of the court in future.

EMPLOYER AGAINST EMPLOYEE

As we have seen[29] the employer is free to proceed against his employees who participate in industrial action where, as will usually be the case, they have committed a breach of contract. In practice he will rarely seek damages or an injunction on this ground. The breach is, however, likely to be repudiatory, so he is entitled at common law to dismiss them without notice.

As we have also seen,[30] an employer may withhold part of the wages of those employed who restrict performance in breach of their contractual obligation. In the case of a total withdrawal of labour the contractual obligation is usually regarded as continuing. The strikers are, therefore, in breach of their continuing obligation to be available for work. There is no reason why the employer should indicate a waiver of this breach and so, of course, he may withhold all pay for that period. This right applies, presumably, however short the period of withdrawal but in the case of short periods of withdrawal, say, for an hour in the course of a day, the employer may find it expedient to accept a resumption of work. In such a situation it could be argued either that he has accepted partial performance or that no performance has occurred during a defined pay period so that the whole pay for that period can be withheld. The conclusion may well depend on how the pay period is expressed. In the case of other more obvious examples of partial performance where, for

---

[26] *Messenger Newspapers Group Ltd.* v. *NGA* [1984] I.R.L.R. 397.
[27] *Op cit.* at p. 40.
[28] [1985] I.R.L.R. 67.
[29] *Supra*, pp. 324–329.
[30] *Supra*, pp. 76–78.

instance, the employees refuse to perform certain tasks and the employer, rather than dispensing with their services altogether, accepts performance of other tasks, it now seems that the employer can withhold a portion of the remuneration, reasonable in relation to the services withheld.

In 1971 dismissal of those engaged in strikes or other irregular industrial action was declared fair unless one or more employees was selected for dismissal from among a larger number of strikers and the reason for the selection was an inadmissible reason. This provision underwent a number of changes over the years, not all of them as a result of relevant considerations. The concept of irregular industrial action involving a breach of contract was abandoned in 1974 and in the haste to repeal the 1971 Act it seems that the word "irregular" was deleted from this provision without very clear realisation that this would render fair dismissal regardless of the absence of any breach of contract.[30a] There is no reason why such a breach should be considered a relevant factor in determining the law in relation to industrial action. Nevertheless it does point out sharply the practical consequences of different types of industrial action to which, however, a common legal consequence is assigned. The explanation by the N.I.R.C. of the provision was that it was a means whereby the employer could avoid the ruin of his business.[31]

The provision that dismissal on account of industrial action should be fair was changed to a provision that an industrial tribunal should not have jurisdiction to decide upon the fairness of a dismissal. In 1975 even the reason disappeared and the provision which became section 62 of the Employment Protection (Consolidation) Act 1978 merely referred to dismissal where the employee took part in industrial action or the employer was conducting a lock-out. The reference to prohibited reasons for discrimination among those concerned was dropped in favour of a general prohibition on selective dismissal regardless of the reason.

Section 62 was further amended by the Employment Act 1982[32] and the current provision is as follows:

(1) The provisions of this section shall have effect in relation to an employee (the "complainant") who claims that he has been unfairly dismissed by his employer where at the date of dismissal:
   (a) the employer was conducting or instituting a lock-out, or
   (b) the complainant was taking part in a strike or other industrial action.

(2) In such a case an industrial tribunal shall not determine whether the dismissal was fair or unfair unless it is shown:
   (a) that one or more relevant employees of the same employer have not been dismissed, or
   (b) that any such employee has, before the expiry of the period of three months beginning with that employee's date of dismissal, been offered re-engagement and that the complainant has not been offered re-engagement.

(3) Where it is shown that the condition referred to in paragraph (b) of subsection (2) is fulfilled, the provision of sections 57 to 60 shall have

---

[30a] See, *Bolton Roadways Ltd.* v. *Edwards* [1987] I.R.L.R. 392.
[31] *Heath* v. *J.F. Longman Ltd.* [1973] 2 All E.R. 1228.
[32] s.9.

effect as if in those sections for any reference to the reason or principal reason for which the complainant was dismissed there were substituted a reference to the reason or principal reason for which he has not been offered re-engagement.

(4) In this section:
  (a) "date of dismissal" means:
    (i) where the employee's contract of employment was terminated by notice, the date on which the employer's notice was given, and
    (ii) in any other case, the effective date of termination;
  (b) "relevant employees" means:
    (i) in relation to a lock-out, employees who were directly interested in the dispute in contemplation or furtherance of which the lock-out occurred, and
    (ii) in relation to a strike or other industrial action, those employees at the establishment who were taking part in the action at the complainant's date of dismissal;
    "establishment," in sub-paragraph (ii), meaning that establishment of the employer at or from which the complainant works and
  (c) any reference to an offer of re-engagement is a reference to an offer (made either by the original employer or by a successor of that employer or an associated employer) to re-engage an employee, either in the job which he held immediately before the date of dismissal or in a different job which would be reasonably suitable in his case.

Interpretation of the provisions

It should be noted that it is not always clear whether the employees are taking part in industrial action. The question is one of fact, not the reasonable belief of the employer.[32a] In *Rasool* v. *Hepworth Pipe Co. Ltd. (No. 2)*[33] participation in a union meeting was held to be a union activity but not to constitute industrial action, even though the employer had expressly warned his employees that no permission had been given for them to attend the union meeting. On the other hand, as we have seen, the fact that the action is not in breach of an employee's obligations does not mean that it does not constitute industrial action.[34] It is not even clear when industrial action may be said to have ended. In *Bloomfield* v. *Springfield Hosiery Finishing Co. Ltd.*[35] the N.I.R.C., with considerable perception of the industrial relations realities of the matter, regarded strikes as part of the process of industrial relations and concluded that, for the purposes of continuity of employment, a strike could be said still to be in progress even though the employer had dismissed the strikers because of their action. On the other hand, in *Clarke Chapman— John Thompson Ltd.* v. *Walters*[36] it was said that a strike was at an end when

---

[32a] *Bolton Roadways Ltd.* v. *Edwards, supra.*
[33] [1980] I.R.L.R. 137.
[34] *Power Packing Casemakers* v. *Faust* [1981] I.C.R. 484.
[35] [1972] I.C.R. 91.
[36] [1972] 1 W.L.R. 378.

the employees are ready to return to work, even though they have not yet been taken back.[37]

The provisions added to the section by the Employment Act 1982 were designed to overcome the effect of the decision in *Stock* v. *Jones (Frank) (Tipton) Ltd.*[38] that an employer could only claim protection from any decision as to unfair dismissal if he had dismissed all those who had ever taken part in the strike in question regardless of whether some of them had returned to their jobs by the time of the dismissal. It had also appeared that an unconscious re-employment of one of the strikers some time after the dismissal would offend the provision in the 1978 Act concerning subsequent re-engagement.

In fact, however, the amendments afford the employer more scope than is necessary to overcome this problem. The prohibition on selection is stated to cover the "relevant employees." These are defined as those employees who were taking part in the action at the date of the complainant's dismissal. The effect of this is to allow the employer to select a point of time when he may dismiss all those still on strike. Inevitably, in some cases, this will tend to mean that a hard core who remain on strike may be dismissed without remedy. The employer is also entitled to dismiss strikers at one establishment but not at another.

It should be noted that if the employer does dismiss strikers he can still claim the protection of the section even though he does not re-engage all of them in their previous jobs. It is provided that re-engagement means the offer of any job reasonably suitable in the particular employee's case. So in *Williams* v. *National Theatre Board Ltd.*[39] it was held that an offer of re-engagement to one striker on condition that he should be regarded as under a second warning did not entitle him to claim an unfair dismissal. The E.A.T. did not hold this condition suitable. It held that suitability only extended to consideration of the nature of the job. If this decision is correct it entitles the employer selectively to impose discriminatory conditions upon re-engagement regardless of their unreasonableness, provided only that they do not affect the job content. Finally, after three months, the employer is now to be released from any obligation not selectively to re-engage.

UNION MEMBERS AGAINST UNION

A union member not in sympathy with the industrial action which has been undertaken in breach of the rules of the union may seek an injunction against his union to prevent it acting in breach of its rules. Such action could lie on the ground of prevention of breach of contract. In that case it might prove difficult to obtain an injunction, either because the individual had suffered little damage, since he was free to disobey the instruction and go to work, or because damages would be an adequate remedy. It is more common to seek to restrain the actions of a union in breach of its rules on the ground that an action not authorised by the rules of the union is *ultra vires* the union.[40]

---

[37] A threat of action, however, does not constitute the start of industrial action—*Midland Plastics Ltd.* v. *Till* [1983] I.R.L.R. 9.
[38] [1978] I.C.R. 347 (H.L.).
[39] [1981] I.C.R. 248.
[40] *Taylor* v. *NUM (Derbyshire Area)* [1985] I.R.L.R. 99. See p. 396 *infra*.

In *Taylor* v. *NUM* (*Yorkshire area*)[40a] by an order dated October 10, 1984, Nicholls J. fined the President of the Union £1,000 and the Union £200,000 for disregarding injunctions. The fines had not been paid by October 25, when the same judge gave leave to the plaintiffs to issue a writ of sequestration against the property of the Union. On November 8, certain members of the Union commenced action for the removal of the trustees and the appointment of a receiver. This removal was confirmed by the application of the principles in *Ethicon* and on the ground that the trustees had sought to move the Union's property abroad, out of reach of the sequestrators. It was reinforced by the conclusion that the trustees' conduct, if not checked, might lead to further fines. Other decisions[40b] have held that the trade union, not its members, is the beneficiary of the trust and it is difficult to see, therefore, how this individual intervention in a private trust was justified.

If there was such a doubt, however, the right of the individual union member to seek removal of the trustees has been confirmed by the Employment Act 1988.[41] Where trustees have caused or permitted any unlawful application of union property, or complied, or propose to comply, with any unlawful direction given, or purportedly given, under the rules of the union, any union member at the time of the misapplication may apply to the High Court. The Court may make any order it considers appropriate, including a requirement that the trustees take any specified steps to recover the property, the appointment of a receiver (or judicial factor in Scotland), and the removal of any one or more of the trustees. If the misapplication is contrary to an order of the Court the trustees must be removed unless they satisfy the Court that there is good reason for them to remain. The generality of its powers would, presumably, permit the Court to appoint new trustees. This reverses the effect of the decision of Vinelott J. in *Taylor* v. *NUM*[42] that the union, by its normal governmental procedure, could excuse its trustees from liability for compliance with the union's own instructions.

The Employment Act 1988[43] gives a union member a right to apply to the court for an order to restrain his union from inducing him and other members to take any kind of industrial action in the absence of a properly conducted secret ballot in which the majority of those voting indicate their wish to take industrial action, whether by strike or otherwise. This right, therefore, is independent of the union rules and of any question of illegality involved in the action. If the court is satisfied that the union authorised, or endorsed,[44] any industrial action without the support of a ballot and members, including the applicant, are likely to be, or have been, induced to take part, or continue to take part, it may order the union to ensure that there is no further inducement (or that the likelihood of it does not materialise). It may also order the union to ensure that no member does anything after the order as a result of unlawful inducement before the order. The union, therefore, can be ordered to make clear to members that authorisation or endorsement is at an end. Failure to comply with the order is punishable as a contempt.

[40a] For the order from which this contempt arose, see, [1984] I.R.L.R. 445.
[40b] *Hughes* v. *T.G.W.U.* [1985] I.R.L.R. 382.
[41] s.9.
[42] *Supra*, n.40.
[43] s.1.
[44] See E.A. 1982, s.15.

THE STATE AND THE EMPLOYEE

It has been observed that, until recently, it was the policy of the legislature to refrain from intervention in the control of industrial action, leaving it to the parties, relatively free from legal inequalities, to match their strength. Early this century, in accordance with this policy, social security was withheld from those who lost work and pay as a direct consequence of industrial action, whether by workers or employers. It was thought inappropriate for the State to be seen to be supporting financially those on strike, thus enabling them to continue the stoppage. It would have been politically impossible to appear to distinguish between the merits of a strike and of a lock-out by paying benefit in the latter case. Wedderburn,[45] points out that this can scarcely be called neutrality since the absence of benefit will tend to induce a return to work, just as its presence would have tended to prolong the stoppage. Nevertheless the "policy" has been widely regarded as justified.

(a) *Unemployment benefit*

An unemployed person is not disqualified from receiving unemployment benefit because he declines as unsuitable, "employment in a situation vacant in consequence of a stoppage of work due to a trade dispute."[46] On the other hand, there is no similar exemption from disqualification of an employee who leaves work for good cause during a dispute. Most such employees, and all who participate in industrial action or are laid off as a result of strikes, lock-outs or other industrial action, are likely to fall within the general disqualification from benefit[47]:

> "(1) A person who has lost employment as an employed earner by reason of a stoppage of work which was due to a trade dispute at his place of employment shall be disqualified for receiving unemployment benefit so long as the stoppage continues, except in a case where, during the stoppage, he has become bona fide employed elsewhere in the occupation which he usually follows or has become regularly engaged in some other occupation; but this subsection does not apply in the case of a person who proves—
>> (*a*) that he is not participating in or directly interested in the trade dispute which caused the stoppage of work."

The dispute must have occurred at the claimant's place of employment.[48] If at that place there are separate departments doing work which would normally be undertaken at separate establishments,[49] a man in one such department, who loses work because of a dispute in another, may avoid the disqualification.[50]

---

[45] 3rd ed. at pp. 675–6.

[46] This long-standing provision is now contained in the S.S.A. 1975, s.20(4).

[47] Now contained in the S.S.A. 1975, s.19(1) as amended by the E.P.A. 1975, s.111.

[48] Defined in s.22(6)(*a*). It may be wide enough, for instance, to include the car body and assembly plants at Cowley as one place of employment. See also R(U) 8/71.

[49] As to what would normally be done elsewhere, see R(U) 1/70—car trim not "normally" manufactured at separate establishments.

[50] See, *e.g.* R(U) 24/57; R(U) 5/61; compare R(U) 3/62; R(U) 23/64; but see R(U) 1/70—Fords of Dagenham—factory. A majority of the Royal Commission rejected the contention that the removal of disqualification should be extended to exclude the effects of disputes in any other department, whether a normally integrated part of the establishment or not—see Cmnd. 3623, para. 972.

A question that often arises is whether the continuing unemployment is due to the dispute or whether that dispute has ended. A convenient starting point for discussion is a classic, but much misunderstood, decision of the Commissioner.[51] An employee was dismissed because of a shortage of materials. Other employees complained of this and gave notice to terminate their contracts. They were, however, dismissed with wages in lieu of notice on the ground that they were troublemakers. The Commissioner said:

"A stoppage of work [for this purpose] must be in the nature of a strike or lock-out, that is to say, it must be a move in a contest between an employer and his employees, the object of which is that employment shall be resumed on certain conditions. If a stoppage is not designed for this purpose but was a result of a decision to cease to be employed or to give employment (as the case may be), it would not in our opinion be due to a trade dispute within the meaning of the subsection, notwithstanding that this decision was because of the existence of a trade dispute. . . . The mere fact that notice to terminate employment is given is not usually significant. Such notice is commonly required by the contract of employment and the fact that it is given is not inconsistent with an intention to resume employment on fresh terms."

For some time it was assumed that this decision meant that a stoppage due to a trade dispute would continue to be so, after settlement of the dispute, pending, for example, the resumption of full production[52] but that a stoppage made permanent by the permanent closing of the plant, or the intended permanent dismissal of the employees to whom the claim related, would cease to be the result of a trade dispute. In a later decision, however,[53] it was said that the original decision in 1952:

" . . . decides only that a stoppage of work which is due to dismissal is not, for the dismissed employee, due to a trade dispute . . . it affords no authority for holding that, if a stoppage of work is due to a trade dispute, a determination by either party to sever relations permanently with the other brings the stoppage to an end."

A trade dispute stoppage may come to an end without the settlement of the dispute if sufficient workers return to provide the employer with enough workers to prevent work being hindered.[54] Those who remain out of work will not be disentitled to benefit unless it can be shown that a fresh dispute exists. Such a fresh dispute might arise, for example from an argument about the payment of wages during the original stoppage.[55] In one case,[56] certain printers who had taken part in a national stoppage were prepared to resume work on a specified day. By then the employer had finally dismissed them and he refused to take them back save as non-unionists. It was held that there was a fresh dispute concerning the terms of re-employment. From this it is clear that the existence of a dispute does not depend on the taking of hostile action. Claim-

---

[51] R(U) 17/52. It is interesting to compare the attitude of the Commissioners with that of the courts in relation to dismissal during industrial action. *Supra*, p. 373.
[52] R(U) 19/51.
[53] R(U) 1/65.
[54] R(U) 25/57; R(U) 11/63. Compare, *Heath* v. *Longman Ltd.* [1973] I.R.L.R. 214.
[55] R(U) 3/69; (1970) 7 K.I.R. 517.
[56] R(U) 12/60.

ants who had lost their work because they refused to terminate a meeting about working conditions which extended beyond the meal break were held to have been engaged in a trade dispute concerning the rejection of the claims for better conditions.[57]

A worker indefinitely suspended within 12 days of a stoppage is rebuttably presumed to have lost work by reason of the dispute leading to that stoppage.[58]

With the repeal of the Trade Disputes Act 1906, and the provision by the Trade Union and Labour Relations Act 1974 of a new definition of "trade dispute," the definition of a trade dispute for the purposes of this provision becomes somewhat isolated from the rest of the law of industrial disputes. It is defined in the Social Security Act 1975 as: "Any dispute between employers and employees, or between employees and employees, which is connected with the employment or non-employment or the terms of employment or the conditions of employment of any persons, whether employees in the employment of the employer with whom the dispute arises, or not."[59] This is very similar to the old general definition but differs from the new definition of an industrial dispute in that it is less detailed. The definition has already given rise to some surprising decisions; for example, that a claimant who was prevented from working by pickets was disqualified from benefit because of the existence of a trade dispute between him and the pickets.

A claimant may seek to show that he is not participating or directly interested in the trade dispute.[60] Of this provision the Royal Commission said[61]: "There is general agreement that a person participating in a trade dispute at his place of employment and becoming unemployed in consequence ought not to be supported by the insurance fund during such unemployment." On its face, this appears to be a reasonable attitude, but it must be pointed out that even the narrow term "participation" can be given a surprisingly wide meaning. It has been said[62] that a person participates in a dispute if he knowingly does something or refrains from doing something which contributes to the continuance of the dispute. This is somewhat inelegantly phrased but its width is borne out by the cases. In one case,[63] a colliery "repairer" lost employment due to a stoppage of "brushers." Repairers, who could be required to work as brushers, were offered such work in this instance, but refused to take it. It was held that they were participating in the dispute. Some form of active support is necessary, however, and mere failure to attend a union meeting to vote against a stoppage does not involve participation.[64] In the same way if one attempts to go to work but is prevented against one's will by the activities of pickets, it cannot be said that there is participation in *their*

---

[57] R(U) 21/59.
[58] See R(U) 20/27—where the presumption was considered to have been rebutted.
[59] Social Security Act 1975, s.19(2)(*b*).
[60] The practice is then for a test case to be taken and for the Department of Social Security to accept the result as normally applicable to all similar claimants—see, *e.g.* R(U) 3/69.
[61] Report, Cmnd. 3623, para. 982.
[62] Calvert, *Social Security Law* (2nd ed.), p. 165.
[63] R(U) 41/56.
[64] R(U) 3/69—had the decision been otherwise it would have been necessary to show that *all* the members of the claimant's grade or class attended the meeting, but see, *Coates and Venables* v. *Modern Methods and Materials Ltd.* [1982] I.R.L.R. 318 (C.A.).

dispute on that ground alone.[65] But an employee may withdraw from the action and thereby cease participation.[66]

"Direct interest," like "participation," would give little cause for objection if it was narrowly construed. There were a number of decisions in which what was said to be direct interest looks somewhat indirect. It has been said that a direct interest must be a "substantial and material" one,[67] but again it has been stated that the provision is concerned with the nature of the interest and not with the magnitude of it.[68] In the latter decision the only matter in dispute which would affect the claimant was a proposal to do away with the afternoon tea-break. He was held to be directly interested in the dispute as a whole. In some cases the claimant has had no option but to be in a position where he can be said to be interested. In one such,[69] the dispute concerned the level of heating in a workshop. The platers stopped work, and a plater's helper was held to be directly interested in the dispute since he was bound to be affected by the physical conditions in the workshop. But the mere question of whether the employee should return to work does not involve a direct interest.[70]

This wide approach to "direct interest" has been confirmed by the House of Lords in *Presho* v. *DHSS*[71] to avoid, as Lord Brandon put it, narrow legalism allowing deliberate and calculated evasion of the statutory purpose. In that case it was held that "direct interest" included not only interest in the dispute but also in its outcome. There is a direct interest where, automatically, the employer will apply the outcome both to the participants' and the claimant's group of employees. It is, however, necessary for this common application to be automatic, that is to say, not just something that happens but something established by collective agreement, custom or practice applicable to the workplace in question.

As we have seen, there is no temporal limit on the period of disqualification save the length of the stoppage of work. Strikers and those locked-out may, therefore, be without income for considerable periods. They themselves may not receive supplementary benefits but, subject to qualifications, their families may. Strikers are deemed to receive a certain weekly benefit from their trade union. When introduced in 1980 this was £12, but this is increased on average by about £1 per year. This deduction from benefit entitlement is made even if it is clear that the union pays no strike benefit and even if the person concerned is not a union member.

Urgent need payments, which were available to single employees, were abolished in 1980. If supplementary benefits are paid to the employee's family they may be continued for 15 days after the end of the dispute. Amounts paid in this period are, however, recoverable from wages, normally at source.[72] Family income supplement payable when the gross income from both spouses

---

[65] R(U) 5/66. Compare, *McCormick* v. *Horsepower Ltd.* [1981] I.C.R. 535 (C.A.)—refusal to cross a picket line did not involve participation in industrial action in the absence of a common purpose.

[66] CU 39/1985. Though he might remain disqualified by direct interest and see R(U) 2/85.

[67] R(U) 18/58.

[68] R(U) 3/62.

[69] R(U) 4/65, see also *Punton* v. *Ministry of Pensions and National Insurance* [1963] 1 W.L.R. 186.

[70] R(U) 3/69.

[71] [1984] I.C.R. 463.

[72] See also S.S.A. 1986, s.23(8).

falls below a certain minimum has been held to depend on normal earnings when at work and so is also likely to be denied to the family of a striker who, but for the stoppage, would earn more than the minimum.[73] Tax rebates will be taken into account in assessing income for the purposes of such benefits but the Finance Act 1981 permits them to be withheld where unemployment benefit is being paid or the employee is involved in a trade dispute.

---

[73] *Lowe* v. *Rigby* [1985] 2 All E.R. 903 (C.A.).

CHAPTER X

INTERNAL TRADE UNION AFFAIRS

The definition of a trade union

The Trade Union Act 1871 which first created a definition of trade unions was primarily concerned to offer some formal structure to a wide variety of industrial organisations not previously recognised by the law. Consequently, the legislature at that time had no need to distinguish between the membership of such organisations but was concerned rather to define them according to their purpose of regulating industrial relations and the conditions of the trade.[1] The resulting definition, therefore, included employers' associations and organisations of workers. So long as its principal purpose remained to define an organisation to which a particular, but not particularly restrictive, structure should apply, this caused no problems.

Only in 1971 when the legislature desired to impose substantial restrictions on workers' organisations was it necessary to construct a legal definition which distinguished them from organisations which, though possessing the same basic purpose of regulating industrial relations, adopted methods of doing so radically different from those of workers' organisations. In practice, of course, it was this line of distinction which had long been recognised as the most significant and the popular concept of a trade union which clearly separated it as a workers' organisation from the lesser known and less powerful employers' organisation. Employers are not only inclined to further their individual interests but, being more powerful as such than the individual worker are able to do so more effectively. It follows that they have less need and less reason to confer power on their own groupings, and the distinguishing features of such employers' associations and trade unions support the popular conception that the one has no practical similarity to the other.[2]

The report of the Royal Commission on Trade Unions and Employers' Associations 1965–68[3] not surprisingly in view of the distinction recognised in its own title, recommended that the term "trade union" should be confined to organisations of employed persons. This recommendation was given effect by the Industrial Relations Act 1971. The current definition contained in the Trade Union and Labour Relations Act 1974[4] maintains the distinction

---

[1] Trade Union Act 1871, s.23 subsequently amended by Trade Union (Amendment) Act 1876, s.16 and Trade Union Act 1913, ss.1 and 2.

[2] But employers' associations also desire to maintain common standards and some of them have been seriously weakened by repeal of legislation, such as Sched. 11 of the E.P.C.A., designed to provide enforcement of such standards.

[3] Cmnd. 3623, para. 766.

[4] s.28(1).

between organisations of workers and organisations of employers. A trade union:

> "consists wholly or mainly of workers of one or more descriptions and is an organisation [whether permanent or temporary] whose principal purposes include the regulation of relations between workers of that description or those descriptions and employers or employers associations."

Constituent or affiliated organisations or federations of such organisations which fulfil this requirement and their representatives may also be regarded as trade unions provided that they possess a sufficient degree of organisation.[5]

"Worker" is wider than "employee," extending to those who perform personally work or services for another person who is not a professional client.[6] So the Law Society was held not to be an "organisation of workers" under the provisions of the Industrial Relations Act 1971.[7] In *Broadbent* v. *Crisp*[8] the definition of worker was confined to those whose contracts actually obliged them to perform the work personally. This would appear to be the correct interpretation of the words used in the definition but it confines the term to those who accept an obligation which would not apply to many self-employed persons. Indeed, one of the characteristics of employment accepted in *Ready Mixed Concrete (South East) Ltd.* v. *Minister of Pensions*[9] was inability to assign performance to another.

One of the organisation's principal purposes must be the regulation of relations between workers and employers or associations of employers. Though it is submitted that this places it beyond doubt that the definition is not intended to be exclusive of any other purpose and so disposes of any lingering suspicion that *Osborne* v. *A.S.R.S.*[10] is still the law it does have the effect of excluding organisations whose only primary purpose is to act as a pressure group.[11] An organisation merely to take industrial action in support of negotiations by others would not be a trade union.

Independent trade unions

Independence is defined[12] as denoting a trade union not under the domination or control of an employer or of a group of employers or of one or more employers' associations and:

> "not liable to interference by an employer or any such group or association (arising out of the provision of financial or material support or by any other means whatsoever) tending towards such control."

In the Annual Report of the Certification Officer for 1978[13] it is pointed out that the crucial question is what is meant by "liable to interference." The cer-

---

[5] *Midland Cold Storage* v. *Steer* [1972] I.C.R. 230.
[6] s.30(1) and (2).
[7] *Carter* v. *The Law Society* [1973] I.C.R. 113.
[8] [1974] I.C.R. 248.
[9] [1968] 2 Q.B. 497.
[10] [1910] A.C. 87.
[11] *Midland Cold Storage* v. *Steer* [1972] I.C.R. 230.
[12] T.U.L.R.A. 1974, s.30.
[13] Para. 2.7.

tification officer there states that his office took the view that it meant "vulnerable to" or "exposed to the risk of" interference and that in considering this it was proper to consider the organisation's history, membership base, organisation and structure, finance, collective bargaining record and use of employer-provided facilities. This approach was endorsed by the Court of Appeal in *Squibb U.K. Staff Association* v. *Certification Officer*[14] which rejected the test of likelihood of interference adopted by the E.A.T. in favour of the vulnerability test in the sense of subjection to a real possibility of interference. As Shaw L.J. said[15]:

> "If the facts present a possibility of interference tending towards control, and if it is a possibility which cannot be dismissed as trivial or fanciful or illusory, then it can properly be asserted that the union is at risk of and therefore liable to such interference. The risk need be no more than one which is recognisable and capable in the ordinary course of human affairs of becoming an actuality."

The fact that it is unlikely that the employer will exploit the vulnerability is not relevant.

This sub-grouping of unions is clearly intended to exclude employer-dominated organisations from the benefit of statutory assistance to the functions of trade unions. Certain statutory requirements to consult are confined to independent recognised unions.[16]

The status of a trade union

The Royal Commission on Trade Unions which reported in 1968[17] recommended that trade unions be given full legal entity. There is no doubt in popular understanding that a trade union has functions and powers which give it a quality different from that of most voluntary associations. The courts, on the other hand, were hesitant to recognise that difference as productive of different legal status if it seemed that this would confer legal advantages.

In the leading case of *Taff Vale Railway Co.* v. *Amalgamated Society of Railway Servants*[18] only Lord Brampton said that a trade union was a legal entity, although a majority of the House of Lords permitted it to be sued in its own name. In *Kelly* v. *NatSOPA*[19] the Court of Appeal regarded the union as no more in law than a collection of individuals so that an individual member was debarred from obtaining damages for wrongful expulsion because he was either claiming against himself or had participated in authorising the wrong. On the other hand, in *National Union of General and Municipal Workers* v. *Gillian*[20] a registered union was allowed to sue for defamation of itself. The matter was not resolved by the House of Lords in *Bonsor* v. *Musicians Union*.[21] The issue was again one of the award of damages for wrongful expulsion. Although the House of Lords overthrew the decision in *Kelly*'s case two

---

[14] [1979] I.C.R. 235.
[15] At p. 247.
[16] E.P.A. 1975, s.99(1).
[17] Cmnd. 3623, paras. 769–785.
[18] [1901] A.C. 426.
[19] (1915) 84 L.J.K.B. 2236.
[20] [1946] K.B. 81.
[21] [1956] A.C. 104.

of the members of that House did so on the basis of the false logic of that
decision and not on the falsehood of the basic premise that a union is not an
entity. The judgment of Lord Morton (with whom Lord Porter substantially
agreed) comes down most strongly in favour of separate entity[22]:

> "My Lords, in my opinion the action in *Kelly's* case was an action by a member
> against his union as an entity recognised by the law and distinct from the individ-
> ual members thereof, for breach of a contract between the plaintiff and his union.
> If this is so, the foundation for the refusal to award damages is gone. I base the
> view which I have just expressed on a line of authorities, of which the first is the
> well-known case of *Taff Vale Ry. Co.* v. *Amalgamated Society of Railway Servants*
> (1900). In that case, it was held by this House that a trade union registered under
> the Trade Union Acts 1871 and 1876, could be sued in tort for the wrongful con-
> duct of its servants in the course of a strike. I find it unnecessary to set out the
> relevant provisions of these Acts, since they are sufficiently summarised for the
> present purpose in passages which I am about to quote from the judgment of Far-
> well J., in the *Taff Vale* case. That learned judge said:
>> 'The defendant society had taken out a summons to strike out their name
>> as defendants, on the ground that they are neither a corporation nor an indi-
>> vidual, and cannot be sued in a quasi-corporate or any other capacity . . .
>> Now it is undoubtedly true that a trade union is neither a corporation, nor an
>> individual, nor a partnership between a number of individuals; but this does
>> not by any means conclude the case.'
> After referring to section 16 of the Trade Union Act 1876, and to an argument
> advanced on behalf of the defendant, the learned judge continued (*ibid.*):
>> 'The questions that I have to consider are what, according to the true con-
>> struction of the Trade Union Acts, has the legislature enabled the trade
>> unions to do, and what, if any, liability does a trade union incur for wrongs
>> done to others in the exercise of its authorized powers? The Acts commence
>> by legalising the usual trade union contracts, and proceed to establish a
>> registry of trade unions, give to each trade union an exclusive right to the
>> name in which it is registered, authorize it through the medium of trustees to
>> own a limited amount of real estate, and unlimited personal estate 'for the
>> use and benefit of such trade union and the members thereof'; provide that it
>> shall have officers and treasurers, and render them liable to account; require
>> that annual returns be made to the registry of the assets and liabilities and
>> receipts and expenditure of the society; provide that it shall have rules and a
>> registered office, imposing a penalty on the trade union for non-compliance;
>> and permit it to amalgamate with other trade unions, and to be wound up.
>> The funds of the society are appropriated to the purposes of the society, and
>> their misappropriation can be restrained by injunction: *Wolfe* v. *Matthews*;
>> and on a winding up, such funds are distributed amongst the members in
>> accordance with the rules of the society: *Strick* v. *Swansea Tin-Plate Co.*
>> Further, the Act of 1871 contains a schedule of matters which must be pro-
>> vided for by the rules.'
> The Court of Appeal set aside the orders made by Farwell, J., but this House
> was unanimous in restoring them. . . . My Lords, in my view, the *Taff Vale* case
> goes far to decide the question now before your Lordships' House. It may be that
> Lords MacNaghten and Lindley thought that an action against the union was an
> action against all the individual members—indeed, that view was expressed again
> by Lord MacNaghten in *Russell's* case and by Lord Lindley in *Yorkshire Miners'*
> *Assocn.* v. *Howden* but I am satisfied that it has never been more than a minority

---

[22] At p. 121.

view, inconsistent with the relevant authorities from the *Taff Vale* case onwards, with the solitary exception of *Kelly*'s case."

Lord Macdermott (supported by Lord Somervell) equally emphatically rejected this conclusion.[23]

Lord Keith of Avonholme, who might have produced the majority, appears to conclude that whilst it would not be wrong to call a union a legal entity it was not an entity distinct at any point of time from its individual members. These two concepts are contradictory and there is no reliable indication in his judgment of what was meant by them.

It is apparent that the system of registration introduced by the 1871 Act is central to the issue of legal entity. That difference of opinion lies in whether the legislature intended, by introducing that system, to confer entity as previously it had conferred such status on incorporated companies which were also required to register. It is clear that some care was taken by the system of incorporation to separate a company from its members. The requirement of registration may well be seen as ancillary to incorporation rather than as possessing a special significance of its own. Alternatively the system of registration may be viewed less as an instrument by which legal status is conferred but as a means of recognition that such separate identity has been achieved in practice. Whichever view is taken of registration the common element is that the State must confer or recognise a separate identity before it can be accepted as producing legally recognised consequences.

In the absence of any judicial consensus, legislation has taken to providing directly a more or less ambiguous answer. For a time the Industrial Relations Act 1971 suspended the argument by providing that trade unions registered under that Act should enjoy full legal entity whilst unregistered unions should not enjoy such status but should be capable of suing and being sued in their own name.[24] Trade unionists saw this as a device intended to convey an air of inferiority to the large well-established unions which declined to register whilst ensuring that the funds of all unions should be available to satisfy claims for damages for "unfair industrial practices."

The Trade Union and Labour Relations Act 1974 repealed this and provided[25]:

> A trade union which is not a special register body shall not be, or be treated as if it were, a body corporate but:
> (a) it shall be capable of making contracts
> (c) . . . it shall be capable of suing and being sued in its own name . . . in proceedings relating to . . . any . . . cause of action whatsoever.
> (e) any judgment, order or award made in proceedings of any description brought against the trade union . . . shall be enforceable . . . against any property held in trust for the trade union to

---

[23] At p. 137.
[24] s.75. For the case law on this provision, see *Midland Cold Storage Ltd.* v. *Turner* [1972] I.C.R. 230; *Midland Cold Storage Ltd.* v. *Steer* [1972] I.C.R. 435; *Heaton's Transport Ltd.* v. *T.G.W.U.* [1972] I.C.R. 308 at 338 and 339.
[25] s.2.

the extent and in the like manner as if the union were a body corporate.

Even without so positive a statement as that contained at the beginning of this section the relegation of registration to a certification of independence not of itself conferring the sort of incidents that accompanied legal status would probably have sufficed to destroy the foundation of argument for entity. In *Electric, Electronic, Telecommunications and Plumbing Union* v. *Times Newspapers Ltd.*[26] O'Connor J. had no doubt that the effect of the statute was to deny any possibility of legal entity to a trade union:

> "When one looks at the statute, s.1(1) is in terse and quite unequivocal terms: 'The Industrial Relations Act 1971 is hereby repealed.' Thereafter, as transitional provisions, a whole series of matters dealing with different topics in that statute were preserved in Sched. 4 to the 1974 Act. That is the end of s.1. Section 2, the side note to which reads, 'Status of trade unions,' provides:
>
> > '(1) A trade union which is not a special register body shall not be, or be treated as if it were, a body corporate . . . '
>
> In my judgment, those are absolutely clear words. One must remember the position in law at that time. At that time, trade unions if they were registered were not necessarily corporate bodies; they were made corporate bodies. If they were on the provisional register they had the attributes of corporate bodies and could properly be called quasi-corporate associations, and the whole background of the position of trade unions until 1971 was that they were quasi-corporate bodies. It was a matter which was as much in their interest as any possible disability. Nevertheless here we find Parliament telling us what a trade union may not be: it 'shall not be, or be treated as if it were, a body corporate.'
>
> Now it is possible that the words 'or be treated as if it were,' got into the statute because of the dislike of the decision in the *Taff Vale* case. I do not know and it is not for me to speculate. It is my task to construe the words and if I find them to be absolutely clear then, even though the result produced may be one which strikes me as being absurd, I must give effect to them. . . . It does not follow that the result which I am driven to in the present case is necessarily an absurdity, but as I have said, it seems to me that those words are absolutely clear and they are saying that a trade union is not to be a body corporate, and it is not to be treated as if it were a body corporate. That is, it is removing from the status of a trade union that which had been accorded to it from 1901 until 1971, when the matter was changed; and there it is."

In *Taylor* v. *NUM (Derbyshire Area)*[27] Vinelott J. stated that the purpose of this section was merely to repeal the provision of the Industrial Relations Act 1971, which had created registered trade unions legal entities. This enabled him to treat a trade union as once again in the shady fairyland envisaged by Lord Keith in *Bonsor*.[28] In that land the courts are able to assign or withhold aspects of legal entity. So they apply the doctrine of *ultra vires*, which should not attach to a collection of natural persons, and conclude that property is held on trust for the union (which on other occasions does not exist) rather than for its members.[28a] Perhaps we might take advantage of this to treat the contract of membership as made with the union and not with each other individual member.

---

[26] [1980] Q.B. 585 at 598.
[27] [1985] I.R.L.R.99.
[28] *Supra.*
[28a] *Hughes* v. *T.G.W.U.* [1985] I.R.L.R. 382.

The legality of trade unions and their agreements

It was widely assumed, until the passage of the Trade Union Act 1871, that the rules of a trade union were in restraint of trade so as to make the contracts of the union unenforceable and its funds incapable of legal protection.[29] It is not very likely, even without statutory provision to the contrary, that a court at the present time would take such a view. Not only has the law relating to restraint of trade changed[30] in a way that would have restricted the generality of the disqualification applied to trade unions, but the attitude of the courts as to what may be considered a reasonable restraint has also changed. The power to order a member to go on strike would not now necessarily be regarded as an unreasonable restraint upon that member's freedom to offer his labour. More significantly, courts which before 1871 were anxious to deny legal protection to a trade union, have, more recently, been anxious to assert their jurisdiction over it.

So sharp was the reversal of the judicial approach that it threatened to undermine the assumption of common law illegality upon which the 1871 Act was based, and thus to throw the legislative system into chaos.[31] The conception of a basic illegality was only re-established with difficulty in *Russell* v. *Amalgamated Society of Carpenters and Joiners*,[32] after doubt had been thrown upon in in three earlier judgments.[33] The view taken in *Russell's* case, although it may be correct, seems difficult to explain in face of such decisions as that in *Reynolds* v. *Shipping Federation Ltd.*[34] in which a combination to enforce a closed-shop agreement with the compliance of the employers was held to be lawful. It may be said, with the Court of Appeal,[35] that though a closed shop is justifiable in the area in which a union operates it is, nonetheless, to be regarded as unlawful at common law, but it is obvious that to maintain that a trade union is an essentially unlawful organisation is to maintain a fiction in order to accommodate the presumptions upon which statute law was based.

So far as the validity of union rules is concerned the matter is again dealt with in the Trade Union and Labour Relations Act 1974.[36]

> "The purposes of any trade union . . . shall not, by reason only that they are in restraint of trade, be unlawful, so as:
>> (a) to make any member of the organisation or body liable to criminal proceedings for conspiracy or otherwise; or

---

[29] See, *e.g. Hornby* v. *Close* (1867) L.R. 2 Q.B. 153.

[30] Its nature was substantially affected by the decision in *Nordenfelt* v. *Maxim Nordenfelt* [1894] A.C. 535.

[31] Kahn-Freund. *The Illegality of a Trade Union* (1943) 7 M.L.R. 202—one of the classics of academic English labour law.

[32] [1910] 1 K.B. 506 (C.A.); [1912] A.C. 421 (H.L.).

[33] *Swaine* v. *Wilson* (1889) 24 Q.B.D. 252; *Gozney* v. *Bristol Trade and Provident Society* [1909] 1 K.B. 901; *Osborne* v. *Amalgamated Society of Railway Servants* [1911] 1 Ch. 540—although it must be noted that the rules of none of the associations involved in these cases were so obviously restrictive as would now be the case with an ordinary trade union. The associations involved in the first two decisions were not even typical trade unions.

[34] [1924] 1 Ch. 28.

[35] *Faramus* v. *Film Artistes Association* [1963] 2 Q.B. 527 (C.A.); [1964] A.C. 925 (H.L.).

[36] s.2(5).

(b) to make any agreement or trust void or voidable[37];
nor shall any rule of a trade union . . . be unlawful or unenforceable by reason
only that it is in restraint of trade."[38]

In *Faramus* v. *F.A.A.*[39] the Master of the Rolls had attempted to limit the
earlier section to the protection of major purposes and to argue that agreements in pursuit of an "ancillary" purpose might still be unenforceable. This
view did not commend itself to the House of Lords, but Lord Denning M.R.
returned to the attack from another direction in *Edwards* v. *Society of Graphical and Allied Trades*,[40] saying that a rule allegedly entitling a union to
expel a member for any, or no, reason could not be said to be *proper* to the
purposes of the union.[41] The provisions of the 1871 and 1971 Acts were
capable of this interpretation since they did not contain the final provision
inserted in the 1974 Act.

The effect was that the validity of the individual rules, agreements or trusts,
would be capable of challenge in the ordinary courts. The subjective nature of
such jurisdiction is revealed only too clearly by the assumption of Lord Denning M.R. that the proper function of a trade union was to protect the right of
each individual member to earn his living and take advantage of all that goes
with it. Since it is obviously the purpose of any organisation to protect its
members as a group rather than as individuals, to the point where the individual interest may have to suffer, and since this is the whole reason that people
combine, one's confidence in judicial ability to acknowledge a proper purpose
when one is observed is undermined. The effect of the extra provision added
to the 1974 legislation was to remove this method of attacking the validity of
union rules. On its face it would also seem to mean that it would not be possible to argue, by analogy with the decision in *Nagle* v. *Feilden*,[42] that an
attempt arbitrarily to exclude an applicant for membership was void because
it was in unreasonable restraint of trade and, being neither an agreement nor
trust, was still unenforceable. A new method of restricting the enforceability
of trade union rules has been introduced by the Employment Act 1988.[43]

Amalgamation

The number of trade unions in the United Kingdom is declining, almost
entirely as a result of merger of two or more unions. This decline has markedly increased during the 1980s largely as a result of general decline in union
membership which has made smaller organisations economically unstable—
particularly in the matter of providing adequate pension schemes for
employed officials. There is a case to be made for merger even of large and
viable unions within a particular industry so as to simplify the bargaining
structure and avoid duplication of services. It was, no doubt, the latter end

---

[37] Compare with the earlier provisions—Trade Union Act 1871, s.3—"The purposes of any trade
union shall not, by reason merely that they are in restraint of trade, be unlawful so as to render
void or voidable any agreement or trust."
[38] This final provision appeared for the first time in the 1974 Act.
[39] *Supra*, n. 35.
[40] [1971] Ch. 354.
[41] See in support of this the judgment of Sachs L.J.
[42] [1966] 2 Q.B. 633.
[43] s.3, p. 419, *infra*.

that was in view when the Labour Government proposed[44] to make grants available to assist union merger. It is certainly true that there are dangers in unplanned merger by which a group of workers goes to the highest bidder.

The statutory procedure for amalgamation was not substantially affected by the Industrial Relations Act 1971, although it may be said that that Act temporarily reversed the process and gave rise to numerous splinter unions. The original statute, the Trade Union Amendment Act 1876, which had required the assent of at least two-thirds of the members of each union involved before a merger could take place was modified by the Trade Union (Amalgamation) Act 1917. This required that at least 50 per cent. of those entitled to vote should do so and that the votes of those in favour should exceed by at least 20 per cent. the votes of those against. Initially this easing of the requirement had a marked effect and a considerable number of smaller unions were absorbed. But, as today, it was very difficult in a large union to produce a 50 per cent. poll. The Trade Union (Amalgamations, etc.), Act 1964[45] has further reduced the requirement to a simple majority of those voting and eliminated that of a 50 per cent. poll.[46]

Transfer of engagements, by which the unions retained nominal identities but one transferred all its obligations and assets to the others, was easier to achieve[47] in that only the support of two-thirds of the members or delegates present at a general meeting of the transferor union, summoned for the purpose, was necessary. But the consent of not less than two-thirds of the members of the transferee union had then to be obtained unless this requirement was dispensed with by the registrar.

Procedure

The present Act requires that the members of the unions concerned draft an agreed Instrument of Amalgamation or Transfer of Engagements and submit it to the trade union Certification Officer for approval. Certain matters must be contained in the Instrument, and the Certification Officer had issued a pamphlet to guide unions in preparing the Instrument.[48] The issue of merger in the terms of the Instrument must then be put to the members of each amalgamating union. If transfer of engagements rather than amalgamation is desired, only the members of the transferor union are required to vote. The ballot on acceptance of the proposals must be without interference or constraint, and every member must be entitled to vote. A secret ballot is not actually required, the Act merely requires that a ballot paper be marked. The requirement that every member should have the right to vote extends, for instance, to apprentices and superannuated members even if the union

---

[44] White Paper, *In Place of Strife* 1969, Cmnd. 3888, paras. 71 and 72, and Industrial Relations Bill 1970.

[45] The Act does not generally apply to unions registered only in Northern Ireland.

[46] This Act also applies to unincorporated employers' associations. T.U.L.R.A. 1974, Sched. 3, para. 10(3).

[47] Societies (Miscellaneous Provisions) Act 1940, s.6.

[48] There is strictly speaking no need to provide for transfer of some union property. This will automatically vest in the trustees of the amalgamated or transferee union unless such transfer is excluded by the instrument. Stock in public funds of the U.K. is not automatically transferred.

rules normally exclude them from voting in union affairs.[49] All reasonable steps must be taken by each voting union to secure that, not less than seven days before voting on the resolution begins, every member of the union is supplied with a notice in writing approved, for each union, by the Certification Officer.[50] The notice is designed to inform members of the proposals, and must contain either the complete Instrument or an account of it sufficient to enable those receiving it "to form a reasonable judgment on the main effects" of the proposal. In the second case the notice must state where copies of the Instrument may be inspected. A decision on the sufficiency of the notice is in the discretion of the Certification Officer. These provisions may not be altered by the rules of the union.

The manner of conducting the ballot is a matter for the governing body of the union. The decision, however, will be made by a simple majority unless the union rules expressly and in terms provide that this statutory requirement shall not apply and a different majority be required. It follows that all rules, contrary to this, made before the Act, are replaced by the statutory provision. This effect was necessary because a number of union rule books had incorporated the requirements of the earlier Act. This was being discarded as too restrictive and it would have been anomalous to have left in force equally restrictive rules based on it.

When the proposals have been approved by the required majority an application for registration of the Instrument must be made to the Certification Officer, accompanied by two copies of the Instrument, the proposed rules of the amalgamated or transferee union,[51] and by a statutory declaration signed by the general secretary of each union involved of compliance with the ballot requirements and verification of voting figures.

Objection

For six weeks from the date when the application for registration is submitted any member of a union involved in the voting has a right to complain to the Certification Officer on the following grounds:

(i) that every member of the union was not entitled to vote;
(ii) that there was interference with or constraint in the voting, or that a fair opportunity to vote was otherwise lacking;
(iii) that the ballot did not involve the marking of a ballot paper;
(iv) that the arrangements for voting were otherwise contrary to the union rules or the procedure laid down by its governing body;
(v) that the requisite majority was not obtained.

If it is found that the complaint is justified he may, in his discretion, declare it to be so but take no further action, or make an order specifying the steps to be taken before he will consider the application for registration. He must give reasons for his decision, orally or in writing, and he may order

---

[49] See report of an action arising from the amalgamation of the National Graphical Association and the Amalgamated Society of Lithographic Printers, *The Times*, January 15, 1969.

[50] The functions of the Registrar of Friendly Societies, briefly transferred to the Registrar of Trade Unions by the 1971 Act have now been transferred to the Certification Officer—E.P.A. 1975, s.7 and Sched. 16, Part IV, para. 10.

[51] In the case of a transfer of engagements the instrument itself must state whether the rules of the transferee union are to be altered and, if so, the effect of the alterations.

either the complainant or the union to pay costs. He may vary his order. An appeal on a point of law lies from any decision of the Certification Officer to the E.A.T.[52]

When the six-week complaint period has expired or, if there is a complaint, when it has been finally determined, the Certification Officer may register the merger.

The Act makes no provisions as to the political funds of amalgamating unions which transfer their engagements. This matter will normally be dealt with by the Instrument. In the case of unions which amalgamate, if one has no political fund, the statutory procedure for establishing one will have to be pursued by the new union formed by the amalgamation. Normally, if a union with no political fund transfers its engagements to a union which has a political fund the view will be taken that the members of the transferor union are in the position of new members of the transferee union and have one month to contract out. A problem may arise if a group of unions, for reasons of status, do not wish to merge with the largest of their number, but wish to amalgamate on equal terms, and some of them have, whilst others have not, a political fund. The normal way to avoid this problem, as indeed it is to avoid a number of others, would be to form a new nominal union, with or without a political fund according to the ultimate intention, and then for all the substantial unions to merge with the new nominal union.

The two methods of merger outlined above are the only methods available and a union may not provide some other method by its rules.

An interesting problem arises in connection with situations where amalgamation does not work and unions wish to separate. When it was reported[53] that this was the position in respect of NatSOPA and N.U.P.B.P.W. which amalgamated to form Division 1 and Division A of the Society of Graphical and Allied Trades, Division 1 issued a writ "accepting" repudiation of the contract of amalgamation brought about by the decision of Division A to stop payment into the amalgamated funds.

The political fund

The British Trade Union Movement has long been aware of the value of taking an active part in political activity in order to impress its views on governments and has for much of the present century been significantly successful in this sphere. In 1900 the Trades Union Congress took positive steps to form and support the forerunner of the present Labour Party, directly to represent the views of labour, although, paradoxically, it has often been said until the present time that the union movement has found it easier to achieve adoption of its views by a Conservative government.

Political activity of any kind requires financial support. Until 1911 it was so financed from the general funds of the unions, irrespective of the opposition of minorities within the unions. This practice was confirmed in *Steele* v. *South Wales Miners' Federation*,[54] in which Darling J. rejected the argument that the financing of political activity was *ultra vires* the union. The House of Lords however, accepted that argument three years later in *Amalgamated*

---

[52] E.P.A. 1975, Sched. 16, Part IV, para. 10.
[53] See *The Times*, October 12, 1970.
[54] [1907] 1 K.B. 361.

Society of Railway Servants v. *Osborne*.[55] The union went further than the use of its general funds by providing that one shilling and a penny per year was to be compulsorily contributed by each member to a fund for giving financial support to the Labour Representation Committee in order to secure representation of railwaymen in the House of Commons, and to support such representatives if elected. The House of Lords held that the statutory definition of a trade union, as it then existed, was exhaustive and that it did not extend to the carrying on of political activity. Such a view would, of course, exclude a great deal more of a trade union's normal functions than merely political activities. It is fair to remark that, though ameliorating legislation only controlled political matters, the reasoning behind the judgment must now be considered to be unsound. There is no doubt that a trade union may now pursue educational objects and other purposes ancillary to its principal statutory objects and this is made plain by section 3(1) of the 1913 Act.[56]

The Trade Union Act 1913 was passed to reverse the effect of the *Osborne* case so as to permit unions to use funds for political purposes, but the opportunity was taken to restrict and control this power. Any trade union may adopt "political fund" rules if their inclusion is approved, by a majority vote of those voting, in a ballot for the purpose conducted by the union by a procedure approved by the Certification Officer. In giving his approval the Certification Officer must be satisfied that the ballot complies with certain procedural requirements inserted by the Trade Union Act 1984.[57] The registrar[58] in practice had insisted on a second ballot after the proposal had been approved so as to approve the actual rules. Voters should receive a copy of the proposed political fund rules before this second ballot. If approved the union may then amend its rule book to include political fund rules and, if registered, must register such an amendment in the same way as any other alteration of its rules. In this case, however, the Certification Officer must approve the rules according to the requirements of the Act of 1913 before them become effective.[59]

The Trade Union Act 1984[60] requires validation of an existing political fund by ballot at intervals not longer than 10 years. By deeming funds approved more than nine years before to have been approved nine years before most trade unions were placed in a position where their political funds had to be revalidated in 1985 or 1986.

A union with political fund rules is not necessarily obliged to make a political levy, although it could frame the rules so as to impose an obligation.[61] If no general obligation is imposed, then the union could collect the levy from such members as it chose. It had also been the view of the registrar that the

---

[55] [1910] A.C. 87.

[56] The permissive effect of s.1 of the Trade Union Act 1913 is, therefore, no longer necessary and was repealed by the Industrial Relations Act 1971.

[57] s.13, amending s.4 of the 1913 Act.

[58] See *supra*, n. 47.

[59] At the end of 1980, 69 trade unions and two employers' associations were maintaining political funds under the statutory provisions. No applications for the establishment of new political funds had been made in that year. The total income of trade union political funds in 1980 was £5m. Some unions, in terms, commit themselves to the support of the Labour Party.

[60] c. 49, s.12.

[61] *Edwards and the National Federation of Insurance Workers*. Decision of registrar, January 21, 1949.

rules themselves could provide that certain classes of membership were not subject to the levy.[62] Organisations other than trade unions make political donations. These require to be disclosed in the case of a limited company but are otherwise regulated only by the need to fall within the stated objects of the company so as not to be *ultra vires*.[63]

Application of political funds

The objects covered are the expenditure of money:

(a) on any contribution to the funds of, or on payment of any expenses incurred directly or indirectly by a political party;
(b) on the provision of any service or property for use by or on behalf of any political party;
(c) in connection with the registration of electors, the candidature of any person, the selection of any candidate or the holding of any ballot by the union in connection with any election to a political office;
(d) on the maintenance of any holder of a political office[64];
(e) on the holding of any conference or meeting by or on behalf of a political party or of any other meeting the main purpose of which is the transaction of business in connection with a political party;
(f) on the production, publication or distribution of any literature, document, film, sound recording or advertisement, the main purpose of which is to persuade people to vote for a political party or candidate or to persuade them not to vote for a political party or candidate.

This list, replacing that of 1913, was introduced by the Trade Union Act 1984.[65] The principal feature of the amendments is their repeated reference to a political party. The original provisions had nowhere referred to a party and had only used the word "political" in the final provision relating to meetings and the distribution of literature. The new list includes not merely representatives in an elected assembly but the holders of any position in a political party. Although ordinary administrative expenses of the union were not included in the restriction the expenses of union involvement in the organisation, national or local, of a political party is so included.

It will be noted that the last two sub-divisions refer to the "main purpose" of either the meeting or the distribution of information. It is uncertain what this would mean in a situation, for example, where a trade union was opposed to the policy of a political party on an issue such as privatisation of a state-owned industry. If it pursued that opposition in the manner described in (f), above, at the time of a general election it would be likely to be considered primarily to be seeking to persuade people to vote against that party. In *Paul and Fraser* v. *NALGO*[66] Browne-Wilkinson V.-C. held that, though such persuasion could be considered the main purpose at election time, persuasion to a particular point of view unconnected with the exercise of a vote at an elec-

---

[62] So, for instance, when the Medical Practitioners' Union merged with A.S.T.M.S. it was provided that members of the medical practitioners' section should not be required to pay a political levy.
[63] Companies Act 1985, s.235.
[64] "Political office" extends to membership of the Assembly of European Communities.
[65] s.17(1).
[66] [1987] I.R.L.R. 413.

tion would not fall within the restriction. This would be so even if the persuasion took the form of express disapproval of Government policy.

Contracting out

When a union has adopted a political fund existing members must be informed of their right not to contribute.[67] The model rules contain a provision requiring that new members shall be supplied with a copy of the political fund rules and also a provision pointing out the right not to contribute. All members covered by the rules will, prima facie, contribute, in the case of existing members, one month after the publication of notice of the right not to contribute,[68] and, in the case of new members, one month after they have actually been supplied with a copy of the political fund rules. A member who does not give notice to contract out within that month is liable to pay until the first day of January next after he has given notice of his wish to contract out. Such notices may not be validly given before an applicant has been accepted for membership.[69] In *Reeves* v. *T.G.W.U.* ([1980] I.C.R. 728) the E.A.T., allowing an appeal from the Certification Officer, held that if contributions were deducted from contracted-out members and refunded, the refund might be in arrears if it was not possible to make it in advance. Under the Trade Union Act 1984[70] a contracted-out member may certify this fact to his employer who thereafter may not deduct the political contribution under any check-off of system for union dues applicable to that member.

Section 3(1)(*b*) of the 1913 Act states that:

" . . . a member who is exempt from the obligation to contribute to the political fund of the union shall not be excluded from any benefits of the union, or placed in any respect either directly or indirectly under any disability or at any disadvantage as compared with other members of the union (except in relation to the control or management of the political fund) by reason of his being so exempt."

This section was considered in *Birch's* case.[71] Birch was a contracting-out member of the National Union of Railwaymen who was elected a branch chairman. The general secretary ruled that a contracting-out member could not hold this office. The registrar held that the office of branch chairman was not "involving . . . control or management" of the political fund and that as such under the union's political fund rules (as distinct from the Model Rules) the union was bound to exclude Birch. If this was contrary to the requirements of the 1913 Act the political fund rules themselves were at fault, and the registrar declined jurisdiction to consider that argument. In the High Court it was held that the approval of the registrar did not preclude the court examining the validity of the rules adopted, and that in this case it was only proper to exclude Birch from such aspects of his office as affected the control or management of the political fund. Had the office been one, such as that of general secretary, substantially involving such control or management, it

---

[67] Trade Union Act 1913, s.5(1).
[68] See *Birns and the A.E.U.*, September 25, 1947, Reports of Selected Disputes 1938–49.
[69] *Wilson and the A.E.U.*, December 4, 1948, Reports of Selected Disputes 1938–49.
[70] s.18.
[71] *Birch and the N.U.R.*, November 8, 1948, Reports of Selected Disputes 1938–49; *Birch* v. *N.U.R.* [1959] Ch. 602.

seems that a non-contributor could properly be excluded from the entire office.[72]

It should be noted that the Act only gives a union member a right to complain of discrimination. It appears that an applicant who was refused admission because he indicated that he would not contribute would have no *locus standi* to complain under this Act.

TRADE UNIONS AND THEIR MEMBERS

The contractual approach

Until 1988 the courts controlled the internal affairs of trade unions, as they did those of most voluntary organisations solely through the law of contract. The rules of the organisation, in the case of a trade union usually contained in written form in a "rule book," are looked upon as the terms of that contract. The relation of a member to the organisation undoubtedly commences in contract but it may be that it is misleading to regard the whole subsequent course of that relationship as a matter of agreement. The rules of a trade union resemble local laws rather than terms of a contract. The group depends on the submission of its members to limitation of their freedom by rules in much the same way as the State or any other group governed by what are habitually called laws. The difference such an approach would make is surprising. Regulation by contract requires consent. Hence the principles governing the implication of terms are usually based on supposed consent. Regulation by law appears only to require an understanding of the purpose of the group to which the laws apply and a failure to reject its laws. Submission to group membership involves a restriction of individual freedom just as does the entry into a contract but it does not require continuous consent to that restriction.[73] As we saw when dealing with the employment relationship the courts have recently expressly acknowledged the different emphasis.

This acknowledgment, in the law of employment, of the co-existence of agreement and rules of law, however, in practice is only used to permit supplementation of the contract of employment. The parties, or, to be realistic, the employer as the draftsman of the contract, (as "the union" is the draftsman of the contract it offers to potential members) retain the right to override the intrusion of rules of law. Statutory intervention in the contract of membership of a trade union, however, overrides the agreement between the union and the member. We shall, shortly, examine the extent of this external control of the relationship.

The reader will now be well acquainted with the control which the courts can exercise over the content of a contract by the interconnected functions of interpretation and implication. They have had considerably less opportunity to interpret the contract of membership of a trade union at least in the last 20 years, than that of employment. When they do so, however, these attempts to produce "reasonable" results seem to lead to conclusions more at variance with the intended nature of the relationship. If for no other reason than this it

---

[72] Grunfeld, *Modern Trade Union Law*, pp. 305–306.
[73] See A. M. Honore: *Groups Laws, and Obedience*: Oxford Essays in Jurisprudence, Second Series (ed. A. W. B. Simpson).

is as well that they confine this intervention to interpretation and largely reject the invitation to imply terms. In *Radford* v. *National Society of Operative Printers, etc.*[74] Plowman J. refused to imply a term that a union member would act justly and faithfully in his dealings with the union and his fellow members and would comply with all reasonable arrangements made between the union and employers and would accept all reasonable and proper directions from the union as to his dealings with employers. In fairness, the proposition of so extensive an implied obligation could scarcely have been thought likely to do other than frighten courts away from such a process. In this instance the learned judge said that the specific enumeration in the union's disciplinary rule of the obligations of members left neither scope nor necessity for the implication of further obligations, failure in which might result in expulsion.

The courts have said, often enough, that union rules should not be interpreted too strictly, bearing in mind that they are not drafted by lawyers.[75] *Heatons'* case is a rare example of this caution actually being exercised. In *Porter* v. *NUT*[76]; Lord Dilhorne immediately qualified the caution with the words: "But custom and practice, while it may moderate the operation of a rule cannot in my opinion entitle a union to act in conflict with it"; he proceeded to a strict construction. Even if judges avoid the invitation of Lord Denning M.R. to invalidate "unreasonable" rules[77] a lawyer's view of reasonable interpretation may be unrecognisably different from that of a trade union or, it may be added, any governing body of a voluntary organisation. Judges have often recognised this and deliberately avoided interference with domestic tribunals. This self-denial has, for many years, not extended to trade unions where the conflict between the judicial view of individual rights and a trade union's view of the surrender of some individuality to the good of the group conflict in a high proportion of judicial encounters.[78]

The Ultra Vires doctrine

The effect of confining the contract to its express terms and of restrictive interpretation is enhanced by the application of the *ultra vires* rule. A natural individual may do whatever the law permits such a person to do. If statute confers extra powers on a natural person they cannot validly be exceeded, for the person has no powers in that respect save those conferred. An artificial person, such as a corporation, has no natural powers. It can only act within the powers conferred upon it by statute, charter or some similar grant, or the power it has been permitted to assume, as in the case of a limited company, by the objects clause of its articles of association. People and artificial persons may restrict their freedom of movement within these powers, for instance by a contract which will be broken if they take some other contrary action. But

---

[74] [1972] I.C.R. 484 (Ch.D.).
[75] *Porter* v. *National Union of Journalists* [1980] I.R.L.R. 404; *Heatons Transport (St. Helens) Ltd.* v. *TGWU* [1972] I.R.L.R. 25.
[76] *Supra.*
[77] *e.g.* in *Faramus* v. *Film Artistes Association* [1964] A.C. 925; *Edwards* v. *S.O.G.A.T.* [1971] Ch. 354.
[78] See, *e.g. Esterman* v. *N.A.L.G.O.* [1974] I.C.R. 625; *Loosley* v. *N.U.T.* [1988] I.R.L.R. 157. (C.A.). If the concentration of trade unions on group interest at the expense of the individual is doubted the reader only has to look at the application of the Bridlington Agreement.

they have power to break the contract. Such a breach is not void and of no effect as is an action *ultra vires*.

Trade Unions find themselves in a unique position in relation to the *ultra vires* doctrine. If they are not a legal entity they ought, save for those purposes in which statute allows their actions to have effect as if they were incorporated, to be treated as collections of natural persons. It should follow that it is *intra vires* for a trade union to take any action which its members, as individuals, might take even though such action might constitute a breach of the contract of membership or some other legal inhibition the members have accepted. This is, however, not the view of the courts. At least since *Yorkshire Miners' Association* v. *Howden*[79] the doctrine of *ultra vires* has been applied to trade unions. Later, in one of the gems of judicial confusion Romer J. said,[80] "The principle . . . does not depend on the existence of a corporation. The reasoning of it surely applies to any legal entity which . . . is composed of individuals."

The doctrine is, however, not applied to a trade union as it would be applied to other artificial entities on the basis of an objects clause, although most trade union rule books contain one.[80a] The courts, it seems, conclude that a trade union derives its power to act by grant from its members; that is to say, by restriction within all the terms of the contract of membership. A trade union, accordingly, is not only confined within broad, generally stated, objectives, but also within the more minute procedural detail of its rule book. In *Taylor* v. *NUM (Derbyshire Area)*[81] the National Union of Mineworkers possessed a rule requiring national strikes to be authorised by national ballot. Most of its regions had similar rules relating to strikes within the region. The objects clause of the union permitted it to take industrial action but the action it took was held to be *ultra vires* where it had not been authorised by a prior ballot. Nevertheless, the objects clause may be invoked where it operates to restrict, rather than extend, the powers conferred by the rules. In *Goring* v. *British Actors' Equity Association*[82] a referendum approved, by a majority, a proposal of the annual general meeting that any member working in South Africa should be subject to expulsion. The objects of the union were stated to be non-party-political and non-sectarian. Such an objective was, therefore, *ultra vires* even though an ingenious mind could find a way in which it advanced the interest of the members.

Legislative restriction

The Employment Act 1980[83] sought to provide some statutory control of the admission process. It provides:

> Every person who is, or is seeking to be, in employment [by an employer] with respect to which it is the practice, in accordance with a union membership agreement, for the employee to belong to a speci-

---

[79] [1905] A.C. 256 (H.L.).

[80] *Cotter* v. *National Union of Seamen* [1929] 2 Ch. 58.

[80a] The objects clause itself has been construed strictly so as to render certain activities *ultra vires—Goring* v. *British Actors' Equity Association* [1987] I.R.L.R. 122.

[81] [1985] I.R.L.R. 99.

[82] [1987] I.R.L.R. 122.

[83] s.4.

fied trade union or one of a number of specified trade unions [shall have the right]
  (a) not to have an application for membership of a specified trade union unreasonably refused;
  (b) not to be unreasonably expelled from a specified trade union.

Refusal includes an implied refusal after a period within which admission might reasonably have been expected. Expulsion includes any cessation of membership upon an event specified by the rules and so includes termination for financial default—although presumably it may be reasonable in such circumstances for the decision not to involve a hearing. Rejection or expulsion is conclusively deemed to be unreasonable if it is for one of the "unjustifiable" reasons listed in section 3 of the Employment Act 1988.[84]

The remedy for interference with either right is in addition to any common law remedy and is available by application to an industrial tribunal within six months of the date of refusal or expulsion or such further period as the tribunal considers reasonable in a case where it is satisfied that it was not reasonably practicable for the complaint to be presented before that time. The tribunal may make a declaration that the complaint is well founded. An appeal on either law or fact lies to the E.A.T. The matter is to be determined in accordance with equity and the substantial merits of the case. A union is not to be regarded as having acted reasonably merely because it observed its rules, or unreasonably merely because it did not.

After securing a declaration that his claim was well founded the applicant may make a claim for compensation at any time after four weeks and before six months from the date of the declaration. If at the time of the application the applicant had been admitted or readmitted to the union the compensation application lies to an industrial tribunal. If he has not been so admitted or readmitted the application to compensate lies to the E.A.T. In the case of an industrial tribunal the amount is subject to a limit of 30 weeks' pay plus the limit for compensatory awards in unfair dismissal for the loss consequent upon the refusal of admission or expulsion. The E.A.T. has a wider power to award such sum as it considers just and equitable subject to the limit applicable to industrial tribunal awards plus 52 weeks' pay.

Both awards are subject to the duty of the applicant to mitigate his loss.

Discrimination

The Race Relations Act 1976,[85] and the Sex Discrimination Act 1975[86] apply the prohibitions on illegal discrimination respectively contained in those Acts to "any organisation whose members carry on a particular profession or trade for the purposes of which the organisation exists." It is unlawful for such an organisation to discriminate against a person in the terms on which it is prepared to admit him; by refusing or deliberately omitting to accept his application for membership; or, if a member, in the way it affords him access to any benefits, facilities or services or by refusing or deliberately omitting to afford him access to them; by depriving him of membership or varying the terms on which he is a member; or by subjecting a member to any

---

[84] s.4(6), p. 420, *infra*.
[85] s.11.
[86] s.12.

other detriment. The only exception applies in the case of discrimination on the grounds of sex arising from provisions made in relation to the death or retirement from work of the member.

Judicial restriction

Every judicial attempt to find a peg on which to hang a common law action by a rejected applicant for membership of a trade union has failed. In *Davis* v. *Carew-Pole*[87] Pilcher J. suggested the possibility of a preliminary contract arising from the application and obliging the organisation to observe its rules. In *Woodford* v. *Smith*[88] Megarry J. attempted to fix receipt by the organisation of application forms as the point at which the organisation might be deemed to have made, or alternatively be estopped from denying, the existence of an offer properly to consider the application.

A more sustained and far-reaching attempt has been made, largely by Lord Denning M.R., to establish recognition of an individual's right to work in the sense of a right not to have access to the labour market restricted. He seems first to have suggested the existence of such a right as against a trade union in *Lee* v. *Showmen's Guild of Great Britain*.[89] He followed this in a totally different context in *Boulting* v. *A.C.T.A.T.*[90] and extended it to professional associations in *Nagle* v. *Feilden*[91] and *Enderby Town Football Club* v. *Football Association*.[92] In *Faramus* v. *Film Artistes Association*,[93] however, Diplock L.J. rejected the suggestion that a standard of reasonableness could be imposed on union rules.

The principal support for a cause of action alleging that exclusion from membership might constitute an unreasonable restraint of the right to work is the preliminary judgment of the Court of Appeal on the admissibility of a cause of action in *Nagle* v. *Feilden*.[94] Mrs. Nagle trained racehorses. She was, however, refused a licence to do so by the Jockey Club in pursuance of what was then its policy of never giving such a licence to a woman. In order for her horses to be allowed to run on courses controlled by the Jockey Club the licence to train was given to her "head lad." Mrs. Nagle objected to this situation and sought an injunction to compel the Jockey Club to issue her with a licence. Her initial contention depended on the argument that a contract arose when she applied for a licence. This plea was struck out. She appealed against that decision and the Court of Appeal in considering that interim matter was concerned simply to decide whether she had an arguable case. Lord Denning M.R. (with whom Salmon and Danckwerts L.JJ. agreed) said[95]:

---

[87] [1956] 1 W.L.R. 833.
[88] [1970] 1 All E.R. 1091.
[89] [1952] 2 Q.B. 329.
[90] [1963] 2 Q.B. 606.
[91] [1966] 2 Q.B. 633.
[92] [1971] Ch. 591.
[93] [1963] 2 Q.B. 527 affirmed [1964] A.C. 925 (H.L.).
[94] [1966] 2 Q.B. 633.
[95] Lord Denning's derivation of public policy from the doctrine of unreasonable restraint of trade possibly derives from a remark by Lord Evershed in *Faramus* v. *Film Artistes Association* [1964] A.C. 925 that only a contract in unreasonable restraint of trade, not saved by the then existing Trade Union Act 1871, s.3 could be struck down.

"I quite agree that if we were here considering a social club, it would be necessary for the plaintiff to show a contract. If a man applies to join a social club and is blackballed, he has no cause of action: because the members have made no contract with him. They can do as they like. They can admit or refuse him, as they please; but we are not considering a social club. We are considering an association which exercises a virtual monopoly in an important field of human activity. By refusing or withdrawing a licence, the stewards can put a man out of business. This is a great power. If it is abused, can the courts give redress? That is the question. It was urged before us that the members of a trading or professional association were like a social club. They had, it was said, an unrestricted power to admit, or refuse to admit, any person whom they choose: and that this was established by a case in 1825 concerning the Inns of Court. In R. v. Lincoln's Inn Benchers, Bayley J. said:

> 'They make their own rules as to the admission of members; and even if they act capriciously upon the subject, this court can give no remedy in such a case; because in fact there has been no violation of a right.'

I venture to question this statement, notwithstanding the eminence of the judge from whom it fell. The common law of England has for centuries recognised that a man has a right to work in his trade or profession without being unjustly excluded from it. He is not to be shut out from it at the whim of those having the governance of it. If they make a rule which enables them to reject his application arbitrarily or capriciously, not reasonably, that rule is bad. It is against public policy. The courts will not give effect to it. Such was held in the seventeenth century in the celebrated *Ipswich Tailors' Case*, where a rule was made that no person should exercise the trade of a tailor in Ipswich unless he was admitted by them to be a sufficient workman. Lord Coke C.J. held that the rule was bad, because it was 'against the liberty and freedom of the subject.' If, however, the rule is reasonable, the courts will not interfere. In the eighteenth century, the company of surgeons required as a qualification for an apprentice an understanding of the Latin tongue. The governors rejected an apprentice because on examination they found him to be totally ignorant of Latin. Lord Mansfield C.J. declined to interfere with their decision (see *R. v. Surgeons' Co. (Master)*.)"[96]

This development was overtaken by the provision in the Industrial Relations Act 1971[97] of a statutory right to complain of arbitrary exclusion regardless of the membership agreements of the union. Subsequently, development of the concept of unreasonable restraint of trade put forward in *Nagle* v. *Feilden* was precluded by a specific statutory prohibition upon applying the doctrine to trade union rules.[98] In any event is is fair to suggest that outright exclusion on arbitrary or unreasonable grounds is likely to be rare among British trade unions. Possibly because British unions are not, like their United States counterparts, operated as personal power bases the type of situation apparent in *Huntley* v. *Thornton*,[99] where the branch committee did pursue a personal vendetta, is a rare exception.

The courts are much more likely to be asked to deal with a situation where the unions have bent their rules to meet an unexpected situation—rather as they would expect rules to be bent in negotiation of a dispute. Such a situation occurred in *Martin* v. *Scottish Transport and General Workers Union*.[1] The

---

[96] At p. 644.
[97] s.65(2). Repealed by the Trade Union and Labour Relations (Amendment) Act 1976, s.1.
[98] T.U.L.R.A. 1974, s.2(5).
[99] [1957] 1 W.L.R. 321.
[1] [1952] 1 All E.R. 691 (H.L.).

plaintiff had been directed to work in the docks at Edinburgh at the beginning of the Second World War. The appropriate union branch was reluctant to admit such directed labour to membership of the trade union but a compromise was eventually agreed by which such workers were classified as temporary members. Eight or nine years later when work at the docks declined the union agreed to such temporary members being laid off before ordinary members, many of whom had joined after the plaintiff. The plaintiff argued that since the rule book made no provision for temporary membership he should be considered to have been admitted a full member. The House of Lords, however, concluded that the attempt to admit him to a class of membership which did not exist was *ultra vires* and void. The strict contractual approach revealed by the following extract from the judgment of Lord Normand is typical of the judicial approach to all trade union membership cases but, it is submitted, is out of line with the normal practice of trade unions in considering such situations[2]:

> " . . . [Any] rule governing the terms on which membership is granted must apply to all admissions until it is altered by the method prescribed by the rules themselves, and I, therefore, reject the argument put forward for the respondents that *esto* the rules in August, 1940, provided only for the admission of members without any limit on the duration of their membership, some modification of the rule so as to provide for temporary membership could be brought about by an implied ratification of admissions purporting to have been made on a temporary basis. Now, r. 15 contains this:
>> 'Every person upon being admitted a member of the union shall be deemed to agree to abide by the rules of the union in every respect, and be liable to forfeit membership at any time if in the opinion of the general executive council such person has failed to abide by the rules.'
> There is no rule providing for the admission of members on a temporary basis or for forfeiture for any reason except that prescribed by r. 15. Rule 20 provides:
>> 'No new rule shall be made, nor shall any rule herein contained or hereafter be made (*sic*), or amended, or rescinded except in accordance with a resolution duly passed at the annual meeting of the general executive council.'
> In spite of imperfections of drafting, the sense of this rule was clear. It is common ground that r. 15 was in force in August, 1940, and that it was not thereafter altered by any resolution passed at the annual meeting of the general executive council. Therefore, the officials of the branch or of the union had no authority in August, 1940, or later, to admit the appellant to membership subject to a limitation of time, and when they purported to do so they acted in excess of their powers and their act had and has no validity. I agree with the view expressed by Lord Carmont that there was an attempt to create a class of member outside the provisions of the rules and that it necessarily fails. The conclusion that the appellant never was a member may be inconvenient to both parties, because it may be difficult to work out the equitable adjustment of rights, but that is not a consideration which can affect the decision of the present appeal. I would dismiss the appeal with costs."

It is not, of course, intended to suggest that trade unions should be free to manipulate rules in order to resolve a particular problem where that manipulation will affect established rights of individual members. The courts regard

---

[2] At p. 695.

their principal purpose as the protection of individual rights. The trade unions regard their principal purpose as the pursuit of group interest. Instances where the two objectives are opposed are bound to occur. What is suggested is that the strict contractual approach adopted by the courts may, as in *Martin's* case, seem as unsatisfactory to the individual as it is alien to the union's way of thinking. In *Faramus* v. *Film Artistes Association*[3] the courts noted the union's purpose of protecting the group by excluding those whose presence would endanger it but the House of Lords took no account of this purpose in strictly construing a rule providing that anyone convicted of a criminal offence should be ineligible for membership. The effect was to permit the union, admittedly in the interest of those who remained, to reduce its membership to suit a contracting industry, using the unnecessarily wide criterion of criminal conviction.

The courts have found it possible to apply the principle of estoppel to discount procedural errors in the admission process.[4] This chance discovery that estoppel is not precluded where the result it is sought to establish is *intra vires* gives a clue to the possibility of using the expectations of the parties as the source of their rights rather than strict, and often clearly unintended, interpretation of rules. A recent decision not connected with trade unions' affairs indicates how this approach might develop. In *McInnes* v. *Onslow Fane*[5] the plaintiff applied to the British Boxing Board of Control for a licence as a boxing manager. His application was rejected on more than one occasion and, finally, without hearing or reasons. He sought a declaration that this refusal was unlawful as being unfair and contrary to natural justice. Although concluding that the applicant had no right to demand a hearing or reasons the judgment of Megarry V.-C. proceeded on the basis of what he might reasonably expect:

> "It seems plain that there is a substantial distinction between the forfeiture cases and the application cases. In the forfeiture cases, there is a threat to take something away for some reason; and in such cases, the right to an unbiased tribunal, the right to notice of the charges and the right to be heard in answer to the charges (which, in *Ridge* v. *Baldwin*, Lord Hodson said were three features of natural justice which stood out) are plainly apt. In the application cases, on the other hand, nothing is being taken away, and in all normal circumstances there are no charges, and so no requirement of an opportunity of being heard in answer to the charges. Instead, there is the far wider and less defined question of the general suitability of the applicant for membership or a licence. The distinction is well-recognised, for in general it is clear that the courts will require natural justice to be observed for expulsion from a social club, but not in an application for admission to it. The intermediate category, that of the expectation cases, may at least in some respects be regarded as being more akin to the forfeiture cases than the application cases; for although in form there is no forfeiture but merely an attempt at acquisition that fails, the legitimate expectation of a renewal of the licence or confirmation of the membership is one which raises the question of what it is that has happened to

---

[3] [1964] A.C. 925.
[4] See *Clarke* v. *National Union of Furniture Trade Operatives*, *The Times*, October 18, 1957, *per* Upjohn J. The authority of this poorly reported decision is not increased by the fact that, on the evidence, the applicant had probably been properly admitted.
[5] [1978] 3 All E.R. 211.

make the applicant unsuitable for the membership or licence for which he was previously thought suitable."[6]

On this basis it was conceded that fairness might be expected, even in cases of application for admission alone, and the judgment picks up the point[7]:

"Let the distinctions between this case and the authorities that I have mentioned be accepted. There still remains the question whether in this case the board's procedure is fair. Counsel for the plaintiff said with force that an obligation to be fair is not satisfied merely by being honest; or, to put it the other way round, that a person may be perfectly honest in reaching a decision, and yet be unfair. What should have been done, he said, was that if the board reached a provisional decision to reject the plaintiff's application, the board should then have adjourned further consideration of the application, and notified the plaintiff both of the gist of their reasons for the provisional rejection and of his right to attend for an oral hearing at which he could try to meet the objections. Alternatively, there should be an initial oral hearing at which those with objections could put them to the plaintiff, and then, if he lacked the materials with which to meet them, he should be given the opportunity of being heard again at an adjourned meeting. In each case, the procedure envisages that there might have to be two meetings before any final decision was reached. . . .

Looking at the case as a whole, in my judgment there is no obligation on the board to give the plaintiff even the gist of the reasons why they refused his application, or proposed to do so. This is not a case in which there has been any suggestion of the board considering any alleged dishonesty or morally culpable conduct of the plaintiff. A man free from any moral blemish may nevertheless be wholly unsuitable for a particular type of work. The refusal of the plaintiff's application by no means necessarily puts any slur on his character, nor does it deprive him of any statutory right. There is no mere narrow issue as to his character, but the wide and general issue whether it is right to grant this licence to this applicant. In such circumstances, in the absence of anything to suggest that the board have been affected by dishonesty or bias or caprice, or that there is any other impropriety, I think that the board are fully entitled to give no reasons for their decision, and to decide the application without any preliminary indication to the plaintiff for those reasons. The board are the best judges of the desirability of granting the licence, and in the absence of any impropriety the court ought not to interfere."

This decision is obviously designed for an association which does not appear to the courts to justify a degree of control similar to that often imposed on trade unions. Nevertheless the restrictions it reveals on control of the admission process, short of statutory control, are likely to be applied similarly.

The Bridlington Agreement and membership

This set of rules was adopted by the Trades Union Congress at Bridlington in 1939 and is designed to govern the approach of unions to recruitment of members especially where more than one union is capable of representing a particular grade of worker. They serve to reduce the proliferation of unions operating in the same area which is characteristic of the growth of British

[6] At p. 218.
[7] At p. 221.

industrial relations but which is widely recognised as detrimental to the development of orderly and stable bargaining. The Bridlington Agreement was extended in 1969 to allow the TUC to intervene in disputes between employers and workers and also to extend the powers of the TUC in inter-union disputes, not only about membership but also concerning recognition, demarcation and conditions of employment. We have already examined the effect of this agreement on union representation at the workplace and its terms are set out there.[8]

It appears[9] that in adjudicating on any dispute the Disputes Committee is primarily concerned to inquire whether the procedure laid down in the Agreement has been followed, whether the recruiting union was already the dominant employee organisation in the bargaining unit and whether it has established negotiating rights. There is no doubt that the jurisdiction favours the established unions and, therefore, appears to favour the larger unions which it protects from breakaway movements.

In some ways the Bridlington Agreement operates to suppress individual freedom of choice to a degree similar to that of closed-shop agreements. In *Spring* v. *National Amalgamated Stevedores and Dockers Society*[10] the effect of the order of the Disputes Committee which the court set aside would have been to compel a large number of union members to return to a union they wished to leave and in which they had little confidence. Most unions affiliated to the TUC countered the effect of this decision by amendment to their rules allowing them to terminate the membership of any person recruited in breach of the Bridlington Agreement. The National Graphical Association, for example, has the following power:

> "Notwithstanding anything in these rules, the National Council may by giving six weeks' notice in writing terminate the membership of any member if necessary in order to comply with a decision of the Disputes Committee of the Trades Union Congress."[11]

The judicial approach continues, however, to be at variance with that of the unions in the same two significant respects which characterise most of the membership issues. The Bridlington Agreement epitomises the union's view of the overriding importance of the group whilst the courts continue to think in terms of individual interest. Likewise, the agreement is one of the most open avowals of the unions' attitude to settling disputes without the analysis of legal issues which characterise judgments of the courts.

This conflict surfaced again in the decision of the Chancery Division in *Rothwell* v. *Association of Professional, Executive, Clerical and Computer Staff*.[12] The Association of Scientific, Technical and Managerial Staff (ASTMS) began recruiting employees of the General Accident Assurance Company. Shortly afterwards it was challenged by the newly formed "Staff Association General Accident" which subsequently merged with the Association of Professional, Executive, Clerical and Computer Staffs (APEX). Both

---

[8] *Supra*, p. 295.
[9] See Peter J. Kalis "The Adjudication of Inter Union Membership Disputes" (1977) 6 I.L.J. 19.
[10] [1956] 1 W.L.R. 585.
[11] R. 17(*b*).
[12] [1976] I.C.R. 211.

ASTMS and APEX were affiliated to the TUC. ASTMS claimed that it had recruited over 20 per cent. of the staff of General Accident and that the merger accordingly constituted a breach of principle 5 of the Bridlington Agreement. The Disputes Committee upheld this claim and ordered APEX to terminate the membership of the 3,000 or so members it had acquired by the merger. APEX had a rule similar to that of the NGA quoted above which would have enabled it to comply with this order. Not entirely surprisingly, Foster J. applied to the question of the validity of the Agreement reasoning similar to that of the approach of the courts to other membership issues. He declined to resort to arguments based on public policy to invalidate the union's own rule permitting termination of membership but concluded that not only could that rule not be invoked in bad faith, or contrary to natural justice, but also that it could not provide authority to implement an award of the Disputes Committee which was itself *ultra vires*. He applied a strictly literal interpretation of principle 5 of the Bridlington Agreement and arrived at the conclusion that no valid award could be made under that principle if the complaining union did not possess membership of 50 per cent. of the employees concerned. He also concluded that it could not be *intra vires* the Disputes Committee to require a union to take action which it had no power to take. In this case APEX had already accepted a transfer of engagements from the Staff Association and could not lawfully go back on that. Similar reasoning, of course, would apply to the action required of the recruiting union in *Spring's* case. In other words the jurisdiction of the TUC Disputes Committee is dependent on the active participation of the unions concerned.

The judgment of the E.A.T. (subsequently overruled by the Court of Appeal) in the later decision in *Cheall* v. *APEX*[13] is, however, sharply at variance with the normal judicial approach to any aspect of trade union membership and government, taking a non-interventionist approach to the operation of the Agreement. The facts disclose a fairly simple "Bridlington" situation of a union responding to an instruction of the TUC Disputes Committee to discontinue a membership which had been granted in breach of the Agreement. The union had a rule allowing it to terminate membership, by six weeks' written notice, if necessary in order to comply with a decision of the Disputes Committee. In the instant case it applied that power without giving the affected member a right to a hearing. Bingham J. seemed to experience some difficulty in explaining why there was no obligation upon the Disputes Committee to afford a hearing but less difficulty in deciding that there was equally no obligation, in the circumstances, on the union. In his view the direct relations of the TUC were with its member unions. Its first object was to promote their interests. Its conduct would affect the individual who could, therefore, be said to have an interest in it. This interest, however, gave him no right against it. It might, as simply, have been said that the individual union member has no relationship with the TUC upon which any claim can be based. The actions of the TUC are, to him, no more than an external event. The action, so far as he is concerned, can only be that of his union. Turning to this issue, the learned judge also concluded that the union had no obligation to provide a hearing because there was no other decision which it could, in reality, arrive at than to terminate membership. Significantly, he then strongly supported the view

---

[13] [1982] I.R.L.R. 91.

that trade unions should be permitted to regulate such relations and that a strong case of public policy would have to be made out to interfere with the method of so doing selected by them:

> "I turn lastly to the expert evidence. Whether the Bridlington Principles and the model rule are on balance beneficial or detrimental to British industry and industrial relations is a very large question, the resolution of which would involve much factual research and comparative study. It would be naive to suppose that a reliable view could be formed on the basis of a couple of hours' evidence, from sources however eminent. In order that a court should find the model rule to be contrary to public policy, in the absence of other indications or authority and on the strength of factual evidence, an overwhelming case would have to be made out. It suffices to say that no such case has in my view been made out here. The practical arguments in favour of the model rule are, at the least serious and substantial. Taking all these matters together I find it quite impossible to conclude that the model rule is void as being contrary to public policy."

It is suggested that it may be unwise to rely on first impressions when reading the highly coloured judgment of Lord Denning M.R. in the Court of Appeal which, by a majority, overruled the decision of Bingham J. Lord Denning obviously rejected both that decision and the philosophy behind it, but the same cannot be said of the other majority judgment of Slade L.J.[14]

The Master of the Rolls seized a last opportunity to reiterate many of the propositions about trade union membership which he had enunciated but which had lain dormant for long enough for hope to have begun to form that they would not re-emerge. In the forefront of these was the right for the individual freely to choose a particular union and to insist on joining it. He now founded this on Article 11(1) of the European Convention of Human Rights and pointed out that he had declared his broad interpretation a basic principle of English law.[15] As Donaldson L.J., dissenting, pointed out, the European Court of Human Rights in *Young* v. *The United Kingdom*[16] had not committed itself on the extent of the right. The difficulty of doing so is demonstrated by the fact that Lord Denning had to rely on *Nagle* v. *Feilden*[17] which came nowhere near to granting such a broad right as he now sought to assert. Accepting his own view of the pervasiveness of the right to join a trade union Lord Denning sought to dispose of the difficulty that such a principle was not part of the contract. Neither of the other members of the court of Appeal chose to comment on his reiteration of the far-fetched comparison between rules and by-laws let alone on the incorrect inference that, if equivalent to by-laws, such rules would be freely liable to be declared void as unreasonable or uncertain.

It is submitted that these elements of Lord Denning's judgment owe more to rhetoric than legal analysis and that the true significance of the decision is better determined by examination of the issues discussed by Slade L.J. on the one side and Donaldson L.J. on the other. Both accepted that the rules of a union constituted a contract. Donaldson L.J. dissenting, however, more

---

[14] [1982] I.R.L.R. 362.
[15] *U.K.A.P.E.* v. *A.C.A.S.* [1979] I.R.L.R. 68.
[16] [1981] I.R.L.R. 408.
[17] [1966] 2 Q.B. 633.

clearly brought out the untypical nature of that contract which, as he said, is a contract of adhesion. That being so, in his view, its interpretation depended more on the intention of the union and its pre-existing members than on that of a new member adhering to an existing agreement. From this viewpoint he was able to conclude that any implication concerning the right of the union to obey a decision of the TUC Disputes Committee must depend to a considerable extent on whether its existing members could be said to have intended that it should be forced to run the risk of disaffiliation from the TUC. Slade L.J. accepted this view but differed in the result on the ground that not all the members of the union were likely to take the same view. That, of course, is true and it is, indeed, another good reason for not embarking on the task of implication in respect of trade union rules. It led Slade L.J. to adopt a different interpretation although, as he admitted, only a minority of the membership might have intended the rule to read as he preferred.

Donaldson L.J. substantially supported the view of Bingham J. that the appellant was a third party to the dispute between APEX and TGWU which the TUC Disputes Committee had to resolve. As he said the fact that he would be affected by the outcome of that dispute could not be regarded by the courts as entitling him to participate in its resolution. He also supported Bingham J. in holding that though, when it came to his own expulsion from APEX, the appellant had a right to be treated fairly, no question of unfairness could arise in a situation in which the union took the only course feasibly open to it. The appellant must have known all along that, if it came to the crunch, the union would exclude him. Slade L.J. did not really consider these two arguments, preferring to concentrate the weight of his judgment on the somewhat arid issue of whether the union could rely on its own *wrong* in admitting the appellant in breach of the Bridlington agreement to justify its subsequent exclusion of him. Like Lord Denning M.R., who merely mentioned the point in passing, he concluded that it could not. Donaldson L.J. preferred to rely on the fact that to bring about this result it would be necessary to qualify the plain words of the union rule. Quite apart from the difficulty in reality of arriving at different results depending on whether the admission was an innocent or a guilty breach of "Bridlington" he concluded that the circumstances would suggest that anyone joining a union would accept that they would be liable to exclusion if their admission turned out to be in breach of that agreement, however that breach arose.

It is submitted that the important consideration is the extent to which the judgments of Slade and Donaldson L.JJ. support or reject the *collective reality* approach of Bingham J. Donaldson L.J. clearly supports it, but Slade L.J. does not reject it. Slade L.J. considers it necessary to support his desired qualification by looking for what he considers the real likelihood of a collective acceptance. Interestingly, Donaldson L.J. is forced to the conclusion that no implication is possible because there would be no collective consensus whilst Slade L.J. supports an implication by what he would be forced to admit might be minority intention. Slade L.J. is, therefore, assuming a presumption in favour of procedural safeguards whilst Donaldson L.J. assumes something like a presumption in favour of the accepted operation of trade union institutions. In the absence of any reasoned conclusion on this issue by Lord Denning M.R. the new approach contained in the judgment of Bingham J. can at the most be said to be in dispute.

It must be noted that the Employment Act 1988[18] designates as discipline encouragement or advice to another union not to accept an individual as a member. If the reason for that encouragement or advice is one of the matters listed as providing no justification for discipline[19] the affected member may proceed against the union of which he was, or is, a member which provided that encouragement or advice. That union may be required to pay compensation for the detriment thereby caused.

Resignation and repudiation

The common law raises a presumption of a freedom to resign membership[20] but, as may be expected of the contractual approach, allows this to be rebutted by contrary provision in the rules. Statute has intervened, it is submitted, unnecessarily, by implying into every contract of membership of a trade union a term conferring on the member a right to resign on giving reasonable notice and complying with any reasonable conditions.[21]

In fact the common law rule simply accepts the inevitable, leaving the association to seek to enforce membership obligations extra-legally if it can. In reality the most common system of resignation in trade unions is that whereby the individual ceases to pay his dues or ask for benefits. Unions have learned to deal with this by providing a quick procedure for removing such persons from the list of members. The courts have responded by avoiding the raising of any questions as to the invalidity of such a procedure. This compromise was threatened by the provision in the Code of Practice on the Closed Shop that it is reasonable to expect fair procedure in all termination situations regardless of any disciplinary content.[22] Few commentators have sought to explain in terms of legal theory the current workable, if tacit, understanding. It was at one time suggested that payment of dues might be regarded as a condition precedent to the retention of membership. Alternatively it could be argued that non-payment of dues constituted a repudiatory breach which the union accepted when it deleted the individual's name from the list of members. The courts are shy of either explanation, possibly fearing to allow into this aspect of the law doctrines which might permit alternative explanations of disciplinary termination of membership.

A more realistic and less doctrinal explanation was propounded by Megarry J. in *Re The Sick and Funeral Society of St. John's Sunday School, Golcar*.[23] The members of a long-established association decided that its object of providing sums of money for members in sickness and for the cost of members' funerals served no useful purpose in the modern welfare state. They decided, therefore, to wind up the association and distribute its assets among existing members. Certain persons who had once been members but had ceased to pay subscriptions attempted to pay these subscriptions for the

---

[18] s.3(5)(*f*).

[19] See p. 420, *infra*.

[20] *Finche* v. *Oake* [1896] 1 Ch. 409.

[21] T.U.L.R.A. 1974, s.7 as amended; replacing a more restrictive provision in the Industrial Relations Act 1971.

[22] See also *Edwards* v. *SOGAT* [1971] Ch. 354. Presumably, the threat disappears with the enforceability of the closed shop.

[23] [1973] Ch. 51.

period of default so as to establish their continuing membership and right to share in the distribution. Megarry J. said:

> "It seems to me that the answer, or an answer, lies in the decision of the Court of Appeal in *Finch* v. *Oake*, which I mentioned in the course of argument. This established that a member of a society has the unilateral right, not dependent on acceptance by the society, to resign his membership at any time, even though the rules contain no provision as to resignation. In that case, the member wrote a letter saying that he desired to withdraw his name as a member of the society, and that was held to be sufficient. There can be no magic in the word 'resign,' nor in whether the resignation is written or oral. The essence of the matter seems to me to be whether the member has sufficiently manifested his decision to be a member no more. I cannot see why such a manifestation should not be by conduct instead of by words; the only question is whether the member's decision has been adequately conveyed to the society by words or deeds. In short, in addition to resignation by words, I think there may be resignation by conduct; and I do not see why in a proper case a sufficiency of inertia should not constitute resignation by conduct. The points seem to lack authority, and so I must resolve it on principle."

Discipline

The practice

Although the advent of a code of practice suggesting standards of reasonableness in admission procedures may have its influence on the attitude of industrial tribunals to legislative intervention to control union admission procedures introduced by the Employment Act 1980 the unions have not felt much pressure to adapt their admission rules to meet judicial requirements. It is otherwise with union discipline. As we shall see, the courts have consistently applied a strict contractual approach to their jurisdiction over complaints arising from such discipline. This approach has not been adapted to suit the parties' attitudes, as has the judicial view of the contract of employment, by flexible rules of implication of terms. The unions are, therefore, confronted with such clearly established principles as that no discipline is permitted unless authorised by the rules, that the courts will construe the provisions of the rule book according to judicial concepts of reasonableness which make little concession to the objectives of the union and that the courts will impose standards of fair procedure which, with the unexpected exception of bias, are not adapted to the amateur and informal attitudes of union branch procedure.

The most obvious sign of the union response to judicial restrictiveness is the "blanket" offence. This typically provides for discipline (usually by way of expulsion) for conduct which, in the opinion of the branch or the National Executive, is contrary to the interests of the union. This concept may be worded in different ways and because of the strictness of the courts' approach to the words used these differences may allow them to produce some surprisingly narrow constructions.[24] The intention of the unions is to cover as wide an area as possible and they would justify this approach by pointing out that it would be impossible by specification of precisely defined offences to cover all situations where it might reasonably be considered in the interest of the organisation to impose discipline. Few union rule books are without such pre-

---

[24] See *Esterman* v. *NALGO* [1974] I.C.R. 625.

cise offences but it is fair to say that little effort appears to have been made to ensure that they cover all the more obviously likely offences. In other words, there can be little doubt that the narrow judicial construction of what is contrary to the union's interest must surprise most of the membership. The sort of specific and blanket offences a careful union might think to include is apparent from the following extract[25] which is typical in all save the fact that it forms a single rule. More commonly this list of offences would be scattered throughout the rule book:

1. Without prejudice to any other grounds of expulsion herein contained any member of the Union who, in the opinion of his branch or the Executive Council, shall have injured or attempted to injure the Union, or worked or acted contrary to the interests of the Union or its members, or have attempted to break up or dissolve the Union otherwise than as allowed by these rules, or otherwise brought the Union into discredit or refused to comply with the order or decision of any Committee, Council, or conference having jurisdiction over such member under these rules or requested or taken work from any employer at any place where or when a trade dispute exists between such employer and the Union or any branch thereof, or obtained or attempted to obtain any of the benefits of the Union by means of misrepresentation, or have knowingly participated in or been a party to any fraud perpetrated upon the Union, or any misappropriation or misapplication of its funds or the funds of any branch thereof, or whose conduct shall have been otherwise inconsistent with the duties of a member of this Union or who being an officer shall have refused to perform the duties imposed upon him by these rules or any of them, may be expelled by his branch, with the approval of the Executive Council, or he may be expelled or otherwise dealt with by the Executive Council. If expelled from the Union, he shall thereupon, subject to his right of appeal as in these rules provided, cease to be a member thereof. Every expelled member shall cease to have any claim on the funds and benefits of the Union (except as provided for in Rule 27 Clause 2) and shall forfeit all right to participate in the privileges thereof. It shall be necessary to give notice to any member of the intention to proceed against him under this rule and of the grounds or matters which the branch are proposing to consider, and every expelled member shall afterwards receive notice of his expulsion and the grounds thereof, and shall thereupon have the right to appeal as in these rules provided.

2. In addition and without prejudice to the foregoing if any member be satisfactorily proved to have stolen the funds or property of the Union; to have, with intent to deceive, tampered, falsified, or otherwise wilfully misused any books or other documents belonging to the Union to have, contrary to these rules, obtained possession of, or refused to give up when in his possession any books, keys, papers, or other documents or effects, belonging to the Union or any part thereof, to have refused to sign or execute any cheque, transfer, deed, or other document to which his signature or execution was required by these rules; to have refused to obey these rules, or to comply with any other by them authorised he may be fined such sum (not exceeding £5) or suspended from benefit for so long as the committee or branch meeting who have tried him may think proper.

3. Any member causing a quarrel, swearing, or using abusive language in any of the Union's meetings shall be fined [12p]. Any member not obeying the president when called to order three times shall be liable to a fine not exceeding [50p]; and should he continue disorderly, he shall be expelled from the meeting, by force if necessary. Any member refusing to pay the fine, or any member conniving at or endeavouring

---

[25] A.U.E.W.

to vindicate the conduct of a member having so offended, shall be fined [12p]. Penalties prescribed in this clause shall be imposed by the president of the meeting.

4. Any member being charged with disorderly conduct while on Unemployment or Sick Benefit shall be summoned before the branch or branch committee, and, if the charge be proved, be liable to such fine, not exceeding [£1]; as the nature of the case demands. Any member finding fault with a member's conduct while on Unemployment or Sick Benefit, and not reporting him to the president or secretary of the branch to which he belongs shall be fined [25p].

5. All fines imposed by these Rules shall be applied by the branch secretary. If the branch secretary fails to apply any fine when due, he shall be liable to a fine of [5p] which shall be applied by the branch referee. All fines shall be paid within 14 weeks from the imposition of such fine, if not then paid shall be treated as arrears of contributions.

6. The General Trustees shall, under the direction of the Executive Council, prosecute, or, if more convenient, direct any branch or district officer or officers to prosecute any member or other person suspected by them of any offence, legally punishable with reference to the affairs of the union, and they may themselves institute, or, if more convenient, may direct any branch or district officer or officers to institute civil proceedings against any member or other persons refusing to give up possession of any of the Union's property or any branch property; or doing or neglecting to do any act so as to render himself or themselves liable to legal proceedings in reference to the Union's affairs, or the affairs of any branch thereof.

7. No member shall call on or write to the secretary of any branch or District Committee at the works where he is employed, under a penalty of [12p] for each offence.

8. Any member receiving money to pay for another member, or for a person proposed or desiring to be proposed to become a member, and neglecting to do so on the first meeting night, shall be fined [12p] for such neglect. He shall also be responsible for the money paid to him, and the fines incurred, if any. All such cases shall be brought before the branch or branch committee for their decision. No member so entrusting his contribution money shall have any claim upon the Union if thrown out of benefit through the person entrusted with the said contribution money failing to pay the same, but under such circumstances no member shall be expelled.

9. Should any member refuse to pay money entrusted to him as above, together with the fine as before-mentioned, he shall be deprived of all benefit till the same be paid into the Union.

10. Any member entrusted with money from the funds, and misapplying or failing to account for the same, shall be deprived of all benefit until he has refunded the amount, and shall pay a fine of 20 per cent. on the sum so misapplied or not accounted for, such moneys to be paid to the General Office, or if so decided by the Executive Council to the money steward on a regular meeting night.

11. Any member engaged under Government auspices, by appointment or otherwise, or any member employed on the staff of any private firm, or other Trade Union, who uses the powers thus vested in him for purposes contrary to the Union's interest shall be liable to a fine of £3 or expulsion.[26]

In contrast to the relative similarity of substantive rules there is little in detail common to the rules governing disciplinary procedure. In outline such procedures do appear similar simply because the hierarchy of union tribunals

---

[26] As we have seen, in relatively recent years many unions have added to the list of causes for removal of members a provision allowing them to terminate membership in order to comply with a ruling of the T.U.C. Disputes Committee that recruitment of such a person was in contravention of the Bridlington Agreement.

follows similar patterns. Most disciplinary proceedings will be initiated before branch committees although the National Executive will very commonly be empowered to initiate such action directly. It has become much more usual to provide that expulsion should be subject to confirmation by some higher body. Not all unions allow appeals but, again, it is the usual practice to make some such provision. When it comes to the detail, however, rules seem to have grown out of what it occurred to early draftsmen to include, supplemented in a more or less haphazard fashion by later lessons from the courts. In consequence one may readily find provisions for notice of appeal much more carefully worked out than provisions for the initial branch hearing. Presumably, the unions were unwilling to impose upon the branch procedures which appeared to be unduly complex. Even the later realisation that it was at that level that errors occurred which would result in disallowance of the discipline, either on internal appeal or before the courts, will only very slowly lead to the introduction of more complex procedures.

Though surprisingly law-abiding in the conduct of their internal affairs trade unions are not over-anxious to impose upon themselves unwanted restrictions merely at the behest of the courts. There are, however, some startling examples of judicial influence. The rule book of the Musicians Union before the decision in *Bonsor* v. *Musicians Union*[27] contained what was then a very characteristic hotchpotch of offences and partial procedures. Immediately after that judgment the union thoroughly revised the disciplinary sections of the book to produce what might still be regarded by lawyers as a model. In the same way isolated pieces of guidance obviously influenced by contact with the courts often appear. The following is a good example:

> "Any member summoned to appear on a charge must be notified in writing of the detailed charge made against him. This principle must be applied by the appropriate bodies to every rule where any charge whatsoever is preferred."

One of the problems that the draftsman faces is that the standard practice of rule books is to define procedure committee by committee. Not only does this mean that disciplinary procedures will be scattered but it has a tendency to mean that the committee will be led to apply its normal business procedure to disciplinary matters. Even if later experience has led the union to include a special rule for disciplinary procedure it is likely to be found only to insert one or two extra details into this normal business procedure, producing thereby innumerable pitfalls. An excellent example of such a practice, together with a number of other common shortcomings, appears in the following extract:

> 19.—Any member violating any working rules, registration, or by-laws, disseminating false statements or any rumour which tends to depreciate the organisation, its officers, or any section appertaining to the Union, or circulating any business of the Union to unauthorised persons without authority, or who is guilty of other forms of misconduct, shall be fined a sum not exceeding £10, or otherwise dealt with by the branch or authorised committee of the Unions as may be deemed fit.

> 20.—(a) Complaints against the conduct of members may be dealt with by the branch, branch committee (where so determined by the branch), divisional committee, regional committee or the General Executive Council. A member whose

---

[27] [1956] A.C. 104.

conduct is the subject of inquiry shall be given notice of the complaint in writing with an intimation of his right to be present at the hearing.

(b) If a branch, branch committee or divisional committee, as the case may be, imposes a fine for misconduct, or for any of the offences specified in clause 19, the member shall have a right of appeal to the regional committee, whose decision shall be final. Notwithstanding the foregoing provision a regional committee shall have power to impose fines for misconduct provided that in the event of a fine being imposed by a regional committee, a member shall have a right of appeal to the General Executive Council, whose decision shall be final.

(c) Notice of appeal under the preceding clause (b) must be in writing and sent to the regional secretary or the general secretary, as the case may be, within fourteen days from the date of receipt of notification of the fine, and the appeal shall be heard at the first meeting of the regional committee or the General Executive Council, as the case may be, held following the receipt of such notice.

(d) Where a question of expulsion arises for misconduct, or for any of the offences specified in clause 19, the investigation shall be conducted by the regional committee who shall make recommendations to the General Executive Council. A member whose conduct is the subject of complaint, shall be given notice of the investigation in writing and afforded an opportunity of appearing before the regional committee. The General Executive Council may act upon the recommendation of the regional committee or make further investigation or take such steps as, in the opinion of the General Executive Council, seem just.

21.—Without prejudice to any other ground of expulsion contained in these rules, any member, or members, of the Union who, in the opinion of the General Executive Council shall have injured or attempted to injure the Union, or worked or acted contrary to the interest of the Union or its members, or whose conduct shall have been otherwise inconsistent with the duties of a member of this Union may be fined a sum not exceeding £10 and if holding office removed therefrom, or may be expelled by the General Executive Council from the Union and shall thereupon, subject to the right of appeal as in these rules provided, cease to be a member thereof.[28]

Judicial control[29]

The rule in Foss v. Harbottle

The courts from time to time express a reluctance to interfere in the domestic affairs of an association but there is little sign of such reluctance in the case of interference in the internal affairs of a trade union. The so-called rule in *Foss* v. *Harbottle*[30] springs from this reluctance. The courts state that they will not intervene where the fact of which complaint is made is *intra vires* the association so that a procedural error could subsequently be corrected. The rule was held to apply to trade unions as legal entities.[31] In *Hodgson* v. *N.A.L.G.O.*[32] Goulding J. held that it would not apply to an unregistered union which was not a legal entity. In the light of section 2 of the Trade Union

---

[28] It may be pointed out that it is not at all uncommon to find the sharp contrast between a trivial fine and expulsion as the only alternatives open to a disciplinary body. The effect may be to force the union to expel for only moderately serious offences.

[29] Complaints concerning discipline normally seek either a declaration or, more commonly, an injunction.

[30] (1843) 2 Hare 461.

[31] *Cotter* v. *National Union of Seamen* [1929] 2 Ch. 58.

[32] [1972] 1 W.L.R. 130; [1972] 2 All E.R. 15.

and Labour Relations Act 1974[33] it seems, therefore, that trade unions should not now be entitled to the benefit of the rule in *Foss* v. *Harbottle*. It is not available where the act in question is an invasion of individual rights where the individuals do not sue for a wrong done to the association but in their own right to protect from invasion their own individual rights as members.[34] In any event, as we have seen, the doctrine of *ultra vires* is applied so extensively as to cause any infringement of the rule book to go to the *vires*.

Contractual basis of jurisdiction

The strictly contractual approach is apparent in the judgment of Goff J. (as he then was) in *Silvester* v. *National Union of Printing, Bookbinding and Paper Workers*.[35] The plaintiff had been censured by the branch committee for "acting to the detriment of the interests of the union" and ordered to undertake certain work he had previously refused. While his appeal to the final appeal bodies of the union was pending he was three times charged with failing to carry out the instruction. On the third occasion the secretary of the appeals committee, without authority, withdrew the appeal:

> "Whether the plaintiff could have obtained a mandatory order compelling the union to hear the case in its final appeal court or damages for the breach of the rules in not having permitted him to appeal to that body, I am satisfied that those could not be his only remedies. In my judgment, he must be entitled to say that he only submitted to be liable to be disciplined on the terms that he should have certain prescribed rights of appeal, and that upon the union refusing him those rights the sentence, albeit only of censure, and the decision that he was bound to obey the chapel committee's instructions in that matter could not stand. . . .
>
> It follows, in my judgment, that the second and third charges must be bad, despite the provisions of rules 3(12) and 24(4). If the final appeal court had heard the appeal on the first charge and dismissed it, then, of course, the second and third would have been good, but the wrongful refusal of the appeal, in my view, made the decision on the first *ultra vires* . . .
>
> I come last to what has been described as the broken thread argument, which is that the defendant union had no power to withdraw the plaintiff's appeal to the final appeal court on the first charge and that, even if it had, it could not be exercised by the secretary. This, it is said, vitiated the decision and sentence on the first charge and also the second and third. I am satisfied that the secretary had no power to withdraw the appeal. The defendants have craved in aid the principle which applies in this court, that a party who is in contempt by disobeying an order cannot appeal from it without first purging his contempt: I very much doubt whether this principle applies to the decisions of domestic tribunals where the jurisdiction and the rights of appeal depend upon contract; but even if it does, still, in my judgment, the proper authority to stay the appeal was the final appeal court, not the appeals committee or the national executive council. If, however, it was, then it was a power which the secretary was expressly enjoined not to exercise. It must, in my view, be a decision made in an appeal without the exception 'in cases of appeals of any nature' in rule 3(17), and I cannot accept the argument that this was a mere executive or administrative act on his part. Then, what is the

---

[33] *Supra*, p. 385.
[34] *Edwards* v. *Halliwell* [1950] 2 All E.R. 1064.
[35] (1966) 1 K.I.R. 679.

result of that? In my judgment, it must, at least, invalidate the whole of the proceedings on the first charge."[36]

Express provision for discipline

It follows from the application of contractual principles that the union has no power to discipline nor terminate the contract of membership save to the extent that such powers are conferred by the contract. In *Spring* v. *National Amalgamated Stevedores and Dockers Society*[37] the defendant union had recruited members who had previously been members of the Transport and General Workers Union. The latter union protested to the T.U.C. Disputes Committee that this practice was contrary to the Bridlington Agreement.[38] The Disputes Committee ordered the N.A.S.D. to exclude the new recruits and that union purported to do so despite their refusal to leave voluntarily. Some of the individuals affected brought an action in the Lancaster Chancery Court seeking to prohibit the N.A.S.D. from excluding them. Sir Leonard Stone V.-C. refused, on the basis of the test in *Shirlaw* v. *Southern Foundries (1926) Ltd.*[39]—the "Oh, of course" test—to imply into the individual contract of membership a provision allowing the union to act in compliance with the Bridlington Agreement.

As we have seen in considering the structure of the contract of employment this, and the business efficacy, tests are applied by the courts so as to allow them to achieve a result which, in their opinion, is "reasonable." It may be as well therefore that the tests are rarely applied in trade union law largely because the courts do not wish to expand the powers of the unions by implication. Nevertheless it is worth pointing out that the way in which the learned Vice-Chancellor applied the test was, probably deliberately, naive. He supposed, probably correctly, that if the plaintiff had been asked whether he intended to include a reference to the Bridlington Agreement in his contract of membership he would have asked "What's that?" The significant question, of course, is what his reply would have been when that explanation was forthcoming. The court is on firmer ground when it rejects implication of a power to expel members in compliance with the Bridlington Agreement on the ground that the Agreement is intended only as a morally binding code regulating the relations of trade unions *inter se* and that it contains no reference to a power of expulsion.[40]

Substantive offences

Interpretation. The courts have consistently stated that since the jurisdiction is governed by contract they may construe the rule books which form the principal source of terms of that contract. They have also said that, in this

---

[36] Although most other common law jurisdictions are reluctant to imply terms and adopt the same rule concerning the need for the rules to cover the offence, some are more willing to excuse minor defects, *e.g. Reilly* v. *Hogan* 32 N.Y.S. 2d 864 (1942); *Margolis* v. *Burke* 53 N.Y.S. 2d 157 (1945); *Stephen* v. *Stewart* [1944] 1 D.L.R. 305.

[37] [1956] 1 W.L.R. 585.

[38] *Supra*, pp. 403–408.

[39] [1939] 2 All E.R. 113.

[40] See the judgment of Bingham J. in *Cheall* v. *A.P.E.X.*, discussed, *supra*, p. 405.

situation, the rules must be construed strictly.[41] In *Lee* v. *Showmen's Guild of Great Britain*[42] the rule which was being considered permitted the Guild to fine members who were guilty of "unfair competition." The plaintiff had disregarded an instruction from the Guild to yield a site he had been allotted at the annual Bradford Fair to another member. The Court of Appeal held that this conduct was not capable of being described as unfair competition. Denning L.J. said[43]:

> "But the question still remains: To what extent will the courts intervene? They will, I think, always be prepared to examine the decision to see that the tribunal have observed the law. This includes the correct interpretation of the rules. Let me give an illustration. If a domestic tribunal is given power by the rules to expel a member for misconduct, such as here for 'unfair competition,' does that mean that the tribunal is the sole judge of what constitutes unfair competition? Suppose they put an entirely wrong construction on the words 'unfair competition' and find a member guilty of it when no reasonable person could so find, has not the man a remedy? I think he has, for the simple reason that he has only agreed to the committee exercising jurisdiction according to the true interpretation of the rules, and not according to a wrong interpretation. Take this very case. If the man is found guilty of unfair competition, the committee can impose a fine on him of a sum up to £250. Then, if he has not the money to pay, or, at any rate, does not pay, within one month, the man automatically ceases to be a member of the Guild: see r. 14. To be deprived of membership in this way is a very severe penalty on a man. It means that he will be excluded from all the fair grounds of the country which are controlled by the Guild or its members: see r. 11(*g*)(ii) and r. 15(*a*). This is a serious encroachment on his right to earn a livelihood, and it is, I think, not to be permitted unless justified by the contract into which he has entered. . . .
>
> In most cases that come before such a domestic tribunal the task of the committee can be divided into two parts—(i) they must construe the rules; (ii) they must apply the rules to the facts. The first is a question of law which they must answer correctly if they are to keep within their jurisdiction. The second is a question of fact which is essentially a matter for them. The whole point of giving jurisdiction to a committee is so that they can determine the facts and decide what is to be done about them. The two parts of the task are, however, often inextricably mixed together. The construction of the rules is so bound up with the application of the rules to the facts that no one can tell one from the other. When that happens, the question whether the committee has acted within its jurisdiction depends, in my opinion, on whether the facts adduced before them were reasonably capable of being held to be a breach of the rules. If they were, then the proper inference is that the committee correctly construed the rules and have acted within their jurisdiction. If, however, the facts were not reasonably capable of being held to be a breach and yet the committee held them to be a breach, then the only inference is that the committee have misconstrued the rules and exceeded their jurisdiction. The proposition is sometimes stated in the form that the court can interfere if there was no evidence to support the finding of the committee, but that only means that the facts were not reasonably capable of supporting the finding.

---

[41] *Blackall* v. *National Union of Foundry Workers* (1923) 39 J.L.R. 431. In *Marley Tile Co. Ltd.* v. *Shaw* [1980] I.C.R. 72, Goff L.J. said, however, "the rules of a trade union are not to be construed like a statute. They grow by addition and amendment." He was, of course, not dealing with the rights of an individual member.

[42] [1952] 2 Q.B. 329. See also *Manders* v. *Showmen's Guild*, *The Times*, November 4, 1966; *Silvester* v. *N.U.P.B.P.W.* (1966) 1 K.I.R. 679.

[43] At p. 343.

My conclusion, therefore, is that the court has power in this case to intervene in the decision of the committee of the Showmen's Guild if no facts were adduced before them which could reasonably be considered to be 'unfair competition' within r. 15(c) which says that

'No member of the Guild shall indulge in unfair competition with regard to the renting, taking or letting of ground or position.' "

A similar approach was adopted by Templeman J. in *Esterman* v. *National and Local Government Officers Association*.[44] The plaintiff was threatened with expulsion as being "unfit" to be a member of the union. She had disobeyed an instruction from the union by using her spare time to assist the returning officer in local government elections. The learned judge concluded that there were many good reasons why an individual might decide not to obey such an instruction or might go so far as to consider she had a public duty to disobey. The concept of unfitness, therefore, could not extend to cover her conduct.

Similar reasoning would apply to any discipline based upon an instruction *ultra vires* the union's rules. So, if the union had power to order a strike where there was an "industrial dispute" the courts would be free to interpret the meaning of that term and might well be led to adopt a definition derived from statute.[45] It is submitted that not only does this approach make no allowance for the problem-solving approach of unions to the application of their rules but it runs the risk that the understanding of the parties as to the meaning of the words will be overlooked. It is interesting to note that both these dangers were avoided by Melford-Stevenson J. in *Santer* v. *NGA*.[46] He used the very looseness of drafting of the rules to justify a much wider view of their meaning than the courts commonly allow.

Public policy. In addition to their power of interpretation the courts have, in more recent decisions, established power to invalidate a discipline rule on grounds of public policy in exactly the same way as they have challenged admission rules. In the case of discipline, of course, this approach produces the significant difference that the successful plaintiff remains a member of the union whereas the invalidity of admission rules needs to be supported by a further development of public policy if it is to provide the desired remedy. In *Edwards* v. *Society of Graphical and Allied Trades*[47] the plaintiff was informed that his membership had automatically terminated because he was in arrears with his dues. This default had only occurred because a union official had failed to take the necessary steps to see that the dues were checked off from his wages. The union argued *inter alia* that under its rules it had power to terminate membership in its unfettered discretion. Sachs L.J. said[48]:

"The courts have always protected a man against any unreasonable restraint on his right to work even if he has bargained that right away, and it matters not whether the bargain is with an employer or with a society. A rule that in these days of closed shops entitles a trade union to withdraw the card of a capable

---

[44] [1974] I.C.R. 625.
[45] See *Sherard* v. *A.U.E.W.* [1973] I.C.R. 421.
[46] [1973] I.C.R. 60.
[47] [1971] Ch. 354.
[48] At p. 382.

craftsman of good character who for years has been a member, even if styled 'temporary' member, for any capricious reason such as (to mix conventional and practical examples) having incurred the personal enmity, for non-union reasons, of a single fellow member, the colour of his hair, the colour of his skin, the accent of his speech, or the holding of a job desired by someone not yet a member, is plainly in restraint of trade. At common law it is equally clearly unreasonable so far as the public interest is concerned.

This proposition may now, however, be doubtful in the light of the admission by Lord Denning M.R. in *British Actors Equity Association* v. *Goring*[49] that he had gone too far[50] in suggesting that union rules could be invalidated if they were unreasonable.

The normal approach of the courts leads many trade unionists to wonder whether there is any limit to the power of the courts to disallow union rules. The answer, it is submitted, must be that in the great majority of cases the issue is clear and the courts would, if the matter were brought to them, allow the union to proceed. In *Kelly* v. *National Society of Operative Printers' Assistants*[51] there can be little doubt that had the evidence established that the practice adopted by the plaintiff of undertaking two separate full-time employments did constitute him a danger to his fellow printers he might properly have been expelled for conduct detrimental to the interests of the society. The problem is that the statement in *Roebuck* v. *National Union of Mineworkers*[52] that "what is or is not to the detriment of the interests of the union is a matter which is essentially within the knowledge of the members and officers of the union" is not characteristic of the actual practice of the courts. In *Esterman's* case the union would be somewhat surprised to discover that it could not reasonably consider one who refused an instruction to withdraw her labour as a person unfit for membership. The union might have argued that the court had regard to the reactions of an individual in the abstract and that if these reactions were regarded as those of a union member involved in a pay dispute the reasonableness of imposing restrictions on freedom of action becomes much more obvious. There is obviously a marked difference of opinion not only as to whether conduct unrelated to the objects of the union can bring it into discredit[53] but also as to the criterion for determining what is unrelated.

Most unions have at some time thought it worthwhile to include in their rules the provision that the existence of an offence shall be "in the opinion of" the appropriate committee. This qualification seems to have no effect on the application of the law. In *Lee's* case Somervell L.J. pointed out that in club and professional cases where a code of ethics was being considered the opinion of the body imposing that code would be dominant. This, however, seems to be a semantic distinction. The ethics of union membership are no less real for being unwritten and not attached to a profession. The only real distinction, it is suggested, is that between private clubs and organisations controlling trade. In the former, as a matter of policy, the courts may be pre-

---

[49] [1977] I.C.R. 393.
[50] In *Bonsor* v. *Musicians' Union* [1954] Ch. 479.
[51] (1915) 31 T.L.R. 632.
[52] [1977] I.C.R. 573.
[53] See *Wolstenholme* v. *Amalgamated Musicians' Union* [1920] 2 Ch. 388.

pared not to interfere with the members' selection of whom they associate with. Romer L.J. was, therefore, on firmer ground when he emphasised the seriousness of expulsion from a trade union and said[54]:

> "I should require the use of clear language before I was satisfied that members of any body such as the defendant guild had agreed to leave exclusively to a domestic tribunal powers which it had neither the knowledge nor experience to use and which, if misused (however honestly), might have such serious consequences for the members."

Conversely, in what would now be the unusual case of a blanket offence not expressed to be a matter for opinion the courts would not interfere if in their view a reasonable tribunal, acting bona fide, could reach that decision.[55] This leaves little if any scope for the suggestion[56] that a union might reasonably reach such a conclusion even if fuller explanation might have removed the discredit.

On the other hand there has recently been some indication that the courts themselves feel they may have been too dismissive of the ability of a union properly to conduct its own affairs. In *Roebuck* v. *NUM*[57] it was said that the courts should not lightly come to the conclusion that no reasonable tribunal could have reached the decision the union has arrived at. If the remarks of Denning M.R. in *British Actors Equity Association* v. *Goring*[58] that the courts should do everything then can to construe union rules as reasonable lend support to the approach adopted in *Esterman* v. *NALGO*[59] at least they also suggest the removal of invalidity as a proper purpose of such a construction. If the words of the judgment in *Cheall* v. *APEX*[60] are extended to disciplinary expulsion they would go a long way to permit the union to express a valid opinion as to what was in its own interest.

Statutory restriction of substantive offences

Statutory restriction on the power to discipline union members was imposed by the Employment Act 1988[61] where discipline relates to failure to take industrial action or to an adherence to obligations imposed by the contract of employment in preference to those imposed by union rules. This is termed "unjustifiable discipline" and complaint lies by the affected member to an industrial tribunal within three months; or longer if it was not reasonably practicable to make the complaint in that time, or the delay is wholly or partly due to reasonable attempts to appeal, or have the decision reconsidered or reviewed. The industrial tribunal, if it finds the complaint well

---

[54] [1952] 2 Q.B. 329 at p. 349.
[55] See, *e.g. Esterman* v. *N.A.L.G.O.* [1974] I.C.R. 625.
[56] See *Evans* v. *National Union of Printing, Bookbinding and Paper Workers* [1938] 4 All E.R. 51.
[57] [1977] I.R.L.R. 573.
[58] [1977] I.L.R. 393.
[59] *Supra.*
[60] [1982] I.R.L.R. 91.
[61] s.3.

founded, may make a declaration to that effect. If the determination constituting infringement of the right not to be unjustifiably disciplined is not
revoked, or the union has failed to take all the necessary steps to secure the
reversal of anything done for the purpose of giving effect to that decision
within four weeks of the tribunal declaration, the member may apply to the
Employment Appeal Tribunal not later than six months after that declaration. Even if these actions have been taken the member may make a further
application to an industrial tribunal within the same time. Either the E.A.T.
or the industrial tribunal may, on the second application, award compensation and order the repayment of any money the member has been required to
pay to the union or any branch of it. Compensation is such amount as the tribunal considers just and equitable, subject to the member's duty of mitigation. It must not exceed the sum of the maximum permissible compensatory
award for unfair dismissal together with 30 times the weekly maximum used
for calculating the basic award.[62]

This right of complaint is displaced if there would be a right to complain of
unreasonable expulsion in the closed-shop situation[63] but in that case expulsion for any of the listed reasons is conclusively deemed to be unreasonable.

In more detail, the reasons for discipline to which this section applies are:

(i) that the applicant has failed to participate in or support, or indicated
opposition to, or lack of support for, any industrial action, whether or
not by members of that union;

(ii) that the applicant has failed to contravene, for the purposes of any
industrial action, any requirement imposed on the applicant by a contract of employment or any other agreement with a person for whom
he works or normally works;

(iii) that the applicant has made any assertion that the union, its officials or
trustees have contravened, or are proposing to contravene, any obligation even thought to be imposed by the union rules, any other agreement, by legislation or other rule of law, unless the assertion is false
and the applicant believed it was false or acted in bad faith;

(iv) that the applicant encouraged or assisted any person to perform an
obligation of that person's contract of employment or other agreement
with a person for whom he works or to vindicate any assertion mentioned in (iii), unless the assertion was false and the applicant believed
it to be false or acted in bad faith;

(v) that the applicant's conduct involves the Commissioner for the Rights
of Trade Union Members or the Certification Officer being consulted
or asked to provide assistance on any matter or involves any person
being consulted or asked to provide assistance on anything which
might form the subject-matter of an assertion under (iii);

(vi) that the applicant has contravened any requirement flowing from a
determination which was itself a contravention of the rights of the
applicant or any other person under those provisions;

---

[62] These provisions are much the same as those provided by the E.A. 1980, s.4. See p. 397,
supra.
[63] E.A. 1980, s.4.

(vii) that the conduct of the applicant consists in proposing to engage in, or doing anything preparatory to engaging in, any such conduct.

Discipline includes expulsion, fine, refusal to accept as subscriptions to the union any sum tendered for that purpose, deprival of benefits or access to benefits, services or facilities which would otherwise be available to the applicant as a member of the union, advice or encouragement to another union not to accept the applicant into membership, or subjection of the applicant to any detriment.

The reader must make up his own mind about these provisions. It seems extraordinary to the present writer that they passed into law with so little public comment. Trade unions are not unlawful organisations, nor is their activity in collective negotiation in any way unlawful. Part of this activity consists in threatening, and taking, industrial action in support of their claims, and that action may well be perfectly lawful. The very purpose of the combination of individuals is that such action should be, or appear likely to be, effective because it will be concerted action. The unions have always sought to ensure that members of the union respond to that combined purpose, in the last resort by threat of expulsion if the individual declines to accept that purpose. It can be argued that if the individual does not want to accept that combined purpose, yet is forced to belong to the union by the existence of a closed-shop agreement, he is treated unfairly. Such a person, it can be argued, should be free of one or other compulsion. Either he should be free to secure work without union membership or, if he is forced to become a union member in order to secure work, he should be free to decide how much support he gives the union. But the 1988 Act seriously curtails the power of the union to enforce union membership by placing it at risk of having to pay heavy compensation if it induces dismissal of an employee because of non-membership, whether or not there is in existence a closed-shop agreement. The 1988 Act might have left power to enforce the closed shop intact but protected a member in a closed-shop situation from expulsion in the ways just mentioned. It has chosen, however, to provide that a member who has freely joined the union or, alternatively, decided to stay in the union when he was free to leave, cannot be removed from membership though he chooses to act in disregard of his collective obligations as a union member. Some might regard this as over-kill. The point may be made by asking whether expulsion of a member for such lack of support, even if the closed-shop agreement could be enforced by dismissal, would have been considered unreasonable by courts applying section 4 of the Employment Act 1980 had this not conclusively been presumed to be so by the 1988 Act.[64]

Procedural defects

Fairness. Although the normal principle of contract that custom may not override an express term was applied to the contract of union membership in *Bonsor* v. *Musicians' Union*[65]; it is common for customary practices to supplement disciplinary procedure. Nevertheless the courts will construe procedural rules as painstakingly as they do substantive rules. Their approach is typified

---

[64] s.4(6).
[65] [1956] A.C. 105.

in the judgment of Melford Stevenson J. in *Santer* v. *National Graphical Association*[66]:

> "Rule 38 lays down the procedure which has to be followed in the event of any contravention of the rules of the union. It says that:
>
> > '(1) All allegations of contravention of these rules by a member shall be investigated by the committee of the branch to which for the time being the member belongs. The member concerned shall have the right at any such investigation to answer the charge, either in writing or in person, and call witnesses. The chapel officers concerned in the charge shall be present. The branch committee shall either dismiss the charge or, if they consider the charge proved, communicate their decision and the penalty recommended to the member and to the executive council. In so communicating their decision and recommendation, the branch committee shall make clear to the member that, provided he notifies the branch secretary within seven days of his desire so to do, he has the right to answer the charge before the executive council, in writing or in person, and to call witnesses. The executive council shall then investigate the charge and recommendation and, when the member has notified his desire to answer the charge and in fact attends with or without witnesses when called upon so to do, or sends to the executive council a written answer after hearing the member and his witnesses, if any, or considering any written answer, either dismiss the charge or impose the penalty recommended by the branch or any other penalty permitted by these rules as it sees fit. No penalty shall be imposed except by the executive council whose decision shall be final.'
>
> Applying my mind as best I can to those two rules and in particular rule 38, it is quite plain that rule 38 contemplates the formulation of a charge against a member when it appears that an offence against union rules has been committed. I can find no other explanation of the phrase in rule 38(1) 'answer the charge,' and I think that it follows that a charge having been formulated—the rule does not say 'in writing' but it is, at least, desirable it should be—that the member has an opportunity to consider and prepare any defence he thinks he may have to the charge, and I cannot interpret the word 'investigated' in the second line of rule 38a(1) except by saying that it must contemplate an investigation by the committee in the presence of a member who has had an opportunity to prepare any answer he may wish to make to the charge formulated against him, and I am equally satisfied that in the present case the steps to which I have referred were not taken. I have no doubt that the committee did decide to recommend expulsion, but I am quite satisfied on the balance of probabilities on the evidence of the plaintiff as against the evidence of Mr. Nash and Mr. Donkin that not only did they not properly communicate their decision to the plaintiff, but that the committee did not make clear to him that provided he notified the branch secretary within seven days of his desire to do so, he had the right to answer the charge before the executive council in writing or in person, and to call witnesses. It follows that what, in my view, is a vital part of rule 38 was not observed. He was not told of his right to appeal and there was not the equivalent notice of appeal in seven days such as the rules contemplate, and there is no evidence before me to suggest (indeed, the indications are all to the contrary) that the executive council to whom the recommendation of the committee was communicated ever investigated the matter at all."

Natural justice

Whatever procedural rules or practices the union may apply they must

---

[66] [1973] I.C.R. 60 at p. 60; see also *Hiles* v. *Amalgamated Society of Woodworkers* [1968] Ch. 440.

observe what has traditionally been called "the rule of natural justice." More recently the courts have taken to describing this procedural requirement simply as "fairness."[67] Essentially what is required is that anybody making a decision which will directly affect an individual's rights and freedoms must give that person a fair and impartial hearing. A great deal of detail may be added to this outline which will vary with the circumstances to meet the basic concept of fairness.

The basis for the imposition of this requirement has considerably developed over the years. Originally it was attached to the concept of property rights because it originated in equitable jurisdictions which had established the principle that equitable remedies were not available to protect purely personal interests.[68] Protection of property rights become the theoretical basis of the entire jurisdiction over membership rights.[69] Following *Cooper* v. *Wandsworth Board of Works*[70] it was regarded as established that natural justice would apply to all judicial and quasi-judicial procedures. The House of Lords in *Ridge* v. *Baldwin*[71] accepted the then well-established criticism that such could not be the test for the requirement of natural justice since all it provided was that when there was a hearing that hearing should be fair. That decision preferred to base the requirement on the existence of power to impose a penalty or deprive of a right. In its particular application to trade union discipline this principle was expressed in *Stevenson* v. *United Road Transport Union*[72] to apply "where one party has a discretionary power to terminate the tenure or enjoyment by another of an employment or an office or a post or a privilege [and] that power [is] conditional upon the party invested with the power being first satisfied upon a particular point which involves investigating some matter upon which the other party ought in fairness to be heard or to be allowed to give his explanation or put his case." In other cases the basis for the requirement had been stated even more widely,[73] but subjected to discretionary limitations inherent in so broad a concept as "fairness" and to a distinction between adjudication and administration.[74] The first-instance decision in *Cheall* v. *APEX*[75] breaks entirely new ground so far as trade union affairs are concerned in suggesting that natural justice is not required when its presence is unlikely to affect the result.

It is clear, therefore, that this requirement is a rule of law.[76] Only common law courts obsessed with founding the jurisdiction on contract could have involved themselves in argument as to whether the requirement could be

[67] See, *e.g. Breen* v. *Amalgamated Engineering Union* [1971] 2 Q.B. 175; *McInnes* v. *Onslow Fane* [1978] 3 All E.R. 211.
[68] *Gee* v. *Pritchard* (1818) 2 Swans 402.
[69] *Rigby* v. *Connel* (1880) L.R. 14 Ch.D. 492 although Jessel M.R. referred to it as a very technical ground.
[70] (1863) 14 C.B.(N.S.) 180.
[71] [1964] A.C. 40.
[72] [1977] I.C.R. 893.
[73] See, *e.g. R.* v. *Gaming Board for Great Britain, ex p. Benaim* [1970] 2 Q.B. 417; *Pearlberg* v. *Varty* [1972] 2 All E.R. 6; *Re Liverpool Taxi Owners' Association* [1972] 2 All E.R. 589.
[74] *e.g. Glynne* v. *Keele University* [1971] 1 W.L.R. 487; *Breen* v. *Amalgamated Engineering Union* [1971] 2 Q.B. 175.
[75] [1982] I.R.L.R. 91.
[76] See *Breen* v. *Amalgamated Engineering Union, supra, per* Denning M.R.

excluded by express provision in the contract of membership.[77] It is submitted that the rules are not implied into the contract but are extraneous to it and so cannot be excluded by it. Whether or not this is the correct explanation it is now clear that the courts deny any power to exclude "natural justice" by contract. Lord Denning M.R. has consistently so asserted and did so as early as 1949 in the case of *Russell* v. *Duke of Norfolk*.[78] In *Radford* v. *NatSOPA*[79] Plowman J. stated categorically that a rule providing for automatic forfeiture of membership as a disciplinary measure without the necessity of charge and hearing would be *ultra vires* and void.[80] Doubts expressed in earlier cases[81] and repeated as late as *Lawlor* v. *Union of Post Office Workers*[82] can now, it is submitted, be regarded as resolved.

This does, however, pose a problem. In *Edwards* v. *SOGAT*[83] the Court of Appeal applied this principle of the non-exclusion of natural justice to a case in which non-payment of dues was in issue. If the court will not normally consider the idea of repudiatory breach which has only to be accepted[84] they are bound to face difficulty in explaining the nature of termination for non-payment as anything but a form of discipline attracting natural justice. On the other hand, as we have seen, it is common to treat non-payment as a form of resignation, and the need to offer a hearing in each case would impose a severe burden.[85] It seems clear in practice that unions do not commonly afford a hearing in such situations. The explanation the courts might reasonably apply if they chose would be that if natural justice has become fairness there is nothing unfair in acting without a hearing on the undisputed fact of non-payment in applying the only available specific penalty of termination. This would be to go along the line developed by Industrial Tribunals when dealing with the procedural aspects of unfair dismissal but now rejected by the House of Lords[85a] whose judgment clearly implies that absence of proper procedure cannot be reasonable. The language of some judgments suggests little acceptance of this course. So Lord Denning M.R. in *Edwards* v. *SOGAT* said[86]:

> "Just think. A man may fall into arrears without any real fault of his own. It may be due to an oversight on his part, or because he is away sick, or on holiday. It may be due, as here, to the union's own fault in not forwarding the 'check-off' slip. . . . No union can stipulate for automatic exclusion of a man without giving him an opportunity of being heard. . . . "

---

[77] See *Roebuck* v. *National Union of Mineworkers* [1977] I.C.R. 573.

[78] [1949] 1 All E.R. 109. See also *Lee* v. *Showmen's Guild of Great Britain* [1952] 2 Q.B. 329 at 341; *Abbott* v. *Sullivan* [1952] 1 K.B. 189 at 198; *Bonsor* v. *Musicians' Union* [1954] Ch. 479 at 485–486.

[79] [1972] I.C.R. 484. See also *Hiles* v. *Amalgamated Society of Woodworkers* [1968] Ch. 440.

[80] But see *Cheall* v. *A.P.E.X.* [1982] I.R.L.R. 91 where Bingham J. at first instance would only disallow a rule compelling absence of procedure.

[81] *e.g. McLean* v. *The Workers Union* (1929) 1 Ch. 602 at 623–624.

[82] [1965] Ch. 712.

[83] [1971] Ch. 354.

[84] *Supra*, p. 408.

[85] But see the Code of Practice which suggests that any exclusion without procedure should be regarded as unreasonable.

[85a] *Polkey* v. *A. E. Dayton Ltd.* [1988] I.C.R. 242.

[86] At p. 377.

Nevertheless, exactly this argument was used to check but not abolish the power of tribunals to dispense with natural justice in dismissal situations in *Williams* v. *Compair Maxam Ltd.*[87]

Notice

It is quite clear that the common law requires notice of charges.[88]

Briefly, the Industrial Relations Act 1971 imposed a requirement of written notice of a charge, allowing sufficient time for the preparation of a defence.[89] With the repeal of this provision, however, the law reverts to the far less precise requirements of the common law. It is possible to argue that in certain circumstances it would only be possible to achieve fairness by a written charge but there is no reported case where writing has been required.[90] The common law, however, did require notice in time to prepare a defence although in *Stevenson* v. *United Road Transport Union*[91] it was said that there might be cases so uncomplicated that natural justice would not require particular notice of the charge.

Differing views were expressed by the members of the Court of Appeal in *Abbott* v. *Sullivan*[92] as to the necessary content of the notice. Only Morris L.J., however, was prepared to go so far as to state that a failure to communicate the essential facts to the accused, who certainly knew them already, would invalidate the procedure. Denning L.J. held that the notice was inadequate in the circumstances but Evershed M.R. was inclined to regard it as sufficient.[93] In *Payne* v. *ETU*[94] personal knowledge was allowed to supplement the notice, as it was in *Russell* v. *Duke of Norfolk*.[95] In *Wolstenholme* v. *Amalgamated Musicians' Union*[96] Eve J. accepted a charge, in the terms of the rules, of "conduct detrimental to the interests of the union" as sufficient.

It must follow that a charge cannot be changed without fresh, and adequate notice and the Privy Council so held in *Annamunthodo* v. *Oilfield Workers' Trade Union*.[97] In *Russell* v. *Duke of Norfolk*,[98] however, Tucker L.J., it is submitted incorrectly, excused the absence of notice of the specific charge because no specific charge had emerged before the hearing. He may, however, have been influenced by the fact that the appellant had shown himself aware of the nature of the charge.

An entirely separate aspect of notice, often apparently overlooked, is the requirement that notice must be given to all members of the tribunal. In *Young* v. *Ladies' Imperial Club*[99] the court was uncompromising in its

---

[87] [1982] I.R.L.R. 83.
[88] *Annamunthodo* v. *Oilfield Workers' Trade Union* [1961] A.C. 945.
[89] s.65(8)(*a*).
[90] But see Morris L.J. in *Abbott* v. *Sullivan* [1952] 1 K.B. 189 at 211.
[91] [1977] I.C.R. 893.
[92] [1952] 1 K.B. 189.
[93] See also *Davis* v. *Carew-Pole* [1956] 1 W.L.R. 833; *Ridge* v. *Baldwin* [1962] 2 W.L.R. 716 at 734.
[94] *The Times*, April 14, 1960.
[95] [1949] 1 All E.R. 109. Strangely enough the much earlier case of *Innes* v. *Wylie* (1844) 1 Car. and K. 257 at 262–263 provided a detailed and strict requirement as to the content of notice.
[96] [1920] 2 Ch. 388.
[97] [1961] A.C. 945.
[98] *Supra.*
[99] [1920] 2 K.B. 523.

requirement that notice specifying the business must be sent to members if it would be physically possible for the person to attend and that failure to notify one member would invalidate an otherwise unanimous decision. It has been said that the same result will follow if notice is dispatched but not received.[1]

Hearing

The hearing is the opportunity for the accused either to deny the charges or invoke mitigating circumstances. It seems difficult to say with certainty in any situation that no mitigating circumstance could be advanced.[2] In unfair dismissal we have seen that it is not uncommon in practice for the accused not to be present throughout the hearing and that it seems to be assumed that this absence may be excused if his "representatives" are permitted to attend, notwithstanding that they may have more than his individual interests to consider.[3]

The prima facie right to be heard before the imposition of discipline is well-established in all common law jurisdictions but it is equally clear that strict judicial procedures are not required. The detailed requirements of the hearing may well vary from case to case. Wherever there is likely to be a significant dispute as to the evidence, however, it is submitted that the accused has the right, either personally or through his representatives, to confront his accusers.[4] On the other hand it would go too far to say that there must be a right to cross-examine.[5] Indeed, in *Breen* v. *AEU*[6] it was considered that in some circumstances a purely written "hearing" would suffice.

Bias

The primary requirement of a fair hearing is that it should be before an impartial tribunal. Since all courts accept the fact that preconceptions are inevitable and look rather for evidence of a closed mind it is submitted that the test most often cited in the books[7] of whether a member could reasonably be suspected of bias goes too far. Whilst it is clear that courts look for the appearance, rather than the proved existence, of bias it is submitted that it is the appearance of a "real likelihood" rather than a suspicion which is significant. In *R.* v. *Barnsley Licensing Justices*[8] Devlin L.J. said:

> "We have not to inquire what impression might be left on the minds of the present applicants or on the minds of the public generally. We have to satisfy ourselves that there was a real likelihood of bias—not merely satisfy ourselves that that was the sort of impression that might reasonably get abroad. The term 'real likelihood of bias' . . . is used to show that it is not necessary that actual bias should be proved . . . 'Real likelihood' depends on the impression which the court gets

---

[1] *Leary* v. *National Union of Vehicle Builders* [1971] Ch. 34.

[2] *Parker* v. *Clifford Dunn Ltd.* [1979] I.C.R. 463. Compare *Conway* v. *Matthew Wright and Nephew Ltd.* [1977] I.R.L.R. 89, where it could be said to be clear that the employee did not intend to plead mitigation, with *Carr* v. *Alexander Russell Ltd.* [1976] I.T.R. 39.

[3] *Gray Dunn and Co. Ltd.* v. *Edwards* [1980] I.R.L.R. 23.

[4] e.g. *Willard* v. *N.U.P.B.P.W.*, *The Times*, May 29, 1938; *Payne* v. *E.T.U.*, *The Times*, April 14, 1960.

[5] See de Smith, "Administrative Hearings in English Law," 68 Harv.L.R. at 58 (1955).

[6] [1971] 2 Q.B. 175. Compare *Payne* v. *E.T.U.*, *The Times*, April 14, 1960.

[7] Derived from *Allinson* v. *General Council of Medical Education and Registration* [1894] 1 Q.B. 750 at 758–759.

[8] [1960] 2 Q.B. 167 at p. 187, following *R.* v. *Tempest* (1902) 86 L.T. 585.

from the circumstances in which the justices were sitting . . . Bias is or may be an unconscious thing and a man may honestly say that he is not actually biased and did not allow his interest to affect his mind, although, nevertheless, he may have allowed it unconsciously to do so."

Nevertheless some conduct will inevitably incline a court to regard bias as likely. In *Roebuck* v. *NUM*[9] Templeman J. said:

"In the present case, the fact that there was an overlap between the membership of the executive committee and the area council seems to me to be irrelevant. In this kind of domestic tribunal that must happen and is acceptable. But it is to be observed that the test is the likelihood of bias; in *Hannan* v. *Bradford Corporation*, Cross L.J said,[10]

'If a reasonable person who has no knowledge of the matter beyond knowledge of the relationship which subsists between some members of the tribunal and one of the parties would think that there might well be bias, then there is in his opinion a real likelihood of bias. Of course, someone else with inside knowledge of the characters of the members in question, might say: "Although things don't look very well, in fact there is no real likelihood of bias." That, however, would be beside the point, because the question is not whether the tribunal will in fact be biased, but whether a reasonable man with no inside knowledge might well think that it might be biased.'

That seems to me an answer to the plea of Mr. Turner-Samuels that the trial ought to take place so that one can find out exactly what happened at the relevant meetings; what the members of the various tribunals thought; what the plaintiffs, Mr. Roebuck and Mr. O'Brien thought and said; and whether in fact, despite the appearance, justice, or rough justice, was done.

As I have said already, a man before a tribunal of this kind must put up with the fact that as members of the union, and as officers, the members of the tribunal itself are rightly and properly concerned to uphold the union and its officers. But Mr. Scargill was in a different position from which the likelihood of bias was plain and evident. It is not sufficient to satisfy either the court or the (and I use Mr. Turner-Samuels' adjective) robust members of the trade union, that justice, or rough justice, was meted out to Mr. Roebuck and Mr. O'Brien. The fact is that even a guilty man is entitled to a proper tribunal and a tribunal is not properly constituted if the chairman has been personally involved and is likely to be biased, consciously or unconsciously. It is no answer to say, or prove, that Mr. Scargill in fact had no influence on the result."

In *Breen* v. *A.E.U.*[11] Lord Denning M.R. seems to have thought that vitiating bias could arise from the fact of believing incorrect evidence even if that belief is simply communicated to the tribunal by a non-voting official:

Mr. Townsend certainly was influenced by the bad reason. He wrote it down in the letter. He repeated it later, saying to the plaintiff: 'You had the money Brother.' I expect the judge thought that Mr. Townsend's state of mind did not matter because he had no vote. But I think it mattered a lot. He was the district secretary, a paid official, there permanently. The others were elected annually. They came and went. He stayed on. He knew all about the episode in 1958. It was his job to know it. It is true that he had no vote, but he had a voice and he had a

---

[9] [1978] I.C.R. 676 at p. 682.
[10] See Paul Jackson (1971) 34 M.L.R. 445.
[11] [1971] 2 Q.B. 175.

pen. The judge finds that there was little discussion at the meeting, but I would venture to ask: were there not private discussions beforehand? We know that does happen in the most sophisticated committees. Things are often decided beforehand so as to save discussion and dissension at the meeting itself."[12]

Edmund-Davies L.J. in the majority on this question, makes it clear that this suggestion arises from the courts' belief that the person so influenced did not have an honest belief that the evidence was accurate. It is then clear that the bias in that case derived from the "well-established hostility" towards the accused. Even this proposition poses problems. In *White* v. *Kuzych*[13] the Privy Council warned of the inevitability of a certain amount of ill-feeling. What the court is really looking for is either a closed mind or significant influence from factors not relevant to the charge in hand:

"Whatever the correct details may be, their Lordships are bound to conclude that there was, before and after the trial, strong and widespread resentment felt against the respondent by many in the union and that Clark, among others, formed and expressed adverse views about him. If the so-called 'trial' and the general meeting which followed had to be conducted by persons previously free from all bias and prejudice, this condition was certainly not fulfilled. It would, indeed, be an error to demand from those who took part the strict impartiality of mind with which a judge should approach and decide an issue between two litigants—that 'icy impartiality of a Rhadamanthus' which Bowen L.J., in *Jackson* v. *Barry Rly. Co.* thought could not be expected of the engineer-arbitrator—or to regard as disqualified from acting any members who had held and expressed the view that the 'closed shop' principle was essential to the policy and purpose of the union. What those who considered the charges against the respondent and decided whether he was guilty ought to bring to their task was a will to reach an honest conclusion after hearing what was urged on either side and a resolve not to make up their minds beforehand on his personal guilt, however firmly they held their conviction as to union policy and however strongly they had shared in previous adverse criticism of the respondent's conduct."[14]

So it is that peculiar personal interests will almost always lead to a conclusion of disqualifying bias. This applies particularly to direct financial interest, however small.[15] The mere possibility of deriving an indirect economic advantage from a decision one way or another will not suffice[16] otherwise no trade union tribunal would ever be qualified to consider allegations of financial default. Personal interest is less common but a good example occurred in *Roebuck* v. *National Union of Mineworkers (Yorkshire Area) (No. 2).*[17] The union area president, acting on behalf of the union, had successfully sued a newspaper for libel. Two union members had given evidence for the newspaper and, at the instigation of the area president, were charged with conduct detrimental to the interests of the union. The area executive which had resolved to prefer the charges also found them proved and its decision was confirmed by the area council which had initially referred the matter to the

---

[12] At p. 192.
[13] [1951] A.C. 585.
[14] *Per* Viscount Simon at p. 595.
[15] *Dimes* v. *Grand Junction Canal Co.* (1852) H.L.C. 759.
[16] See *R.* v. *Barnsley Licensing Justices* [1960] 2 Q.B. 167.
[17] [1978] I.C.R. 676.

executive. The area president was chairman of both bodies and participated in the proceedings, questioning the accused and taking part in the subsequent discussion, though he did not actually vote on the issue.

Templeman J. said[18]:

> "Mr. Roebuck and Mr. O'Brien were entitled to be tried by a tribunal whose chairman did not appear to have a special reason for bias, conscious or unconscious, against them. True it is that all the members of the executive committee and the area council, in common with all members of a domestic tribunal where the interests of their own organisation are at stake, have a general inclination to defend the union and its officers against attack from any source; this fact, every trade unionist and every member of a domestic organisation knows and accepts."

The presence of a tribunal member disqualified by bias or bad faith will not invalidate the proceedings if he takes no part in them.[19]

Bad faith

Although bad faith is invariably referred to as a disqualifying element on its own there does not seem to be any reported case in which the invalidity of discipline rested on this factor without support from any other.[20] Rather, bad faith is usually a conclusion drawn from and, in turn, supporting other disqualifying defects. In the club case of *Dawkins* v. *Antrobus*[21] Brett L.J. assimilated bad faith to malice and it will be obvious that such an element is likely to appear as bias.

Appeal procedures

A large proportion of trade union rule books make provision for internal appeal. Where such provision is made the procedures must be complied with.[22] In *Silvester* v. *National Union of Printing, Bookbinding and Paper Workers*[23] the plaintiff had been censured for acting to the detriment of the union in refusing to do routine overtime which he was not contractually bound to undertake but which his chapel wished him to work. Goff J. held that since it was not the clear policy of the union to encourage overtime working it could not be said to be detrimental to the union that a member should refuse to undertake such work. The plaintiff had appealed to the appeals committee of the national executive committee of the union against the instruction to do overtime. This appeal was unsuccessful and he then appealed to the final appeal court of the union. Meanwhile the plaintiff continued to disobey the instruction to do overtime and because of this failure the secretary of the appeals committee, without authority, withdrew the appeal. Goff J. held that the wrongful refusal of the right of appeal, even on one of a number of charges, placed the appellate tribunals in an impossible position from which they probably could not, but certainly did not, extricate themselves.

---

[18] At p. 681.
[19] *Lane* v. *Norman* (1891) 61 L.J.Ch. 149; *Leary* v. *National Union of Vehicle Builders* [1971] Ch. 34.
[20] See Lord Cooper in *Martin* v. *Scottish T.G.W.U.* 1951 S.C. 129 at 141.
[21] (1881) 17 Ch.D. 615.
[22] *Braithwaite* v. *Electrical Electronics and Telecommunications Union* [1969] 2 All E.R. 859; *Santer* v. *National Graphical Association* [1973] I.C.R. 60.
[23] (1966) 1 K.I.R. 679.

The unions might be forgiven for supposing that though they were bound strictly to follow their rules as to appeal procedures, the aggrieved member is not. It is logical enough to conclude that the act of appealing is not an affirmation of the union's actions. As was pointed out by the Privy Council in *Annamunthodo* v. *Oilfield Workers Trade Union*,[24] on the contrary, it is a disaffirmation. Nor, moreover, is the opportunity afforded by the appeal of a fair hearing or removal of the prejudice already suffered by the individual. It is less easy for the unions to understand, however, why, if the appeal body actually does grant a full rehearing the original basis of complaint can remain unaffected. In *Leary* v. *National Union of Vehicle Builders*[25] Megarry J. said[26]:

> "Now in the present case the hearing by the appeals council seems to me to have been in substance a complete rehearing, with the witnesses called and heard, and complete liberty of action for the plaintiff to present his case in full. Indeed, the members of the quite differently constituted branch committee might well have been put in some practical difficulty if they had been required to devote two days to disposing of the case. Nevertheless, it was not to the appeals council that the rules confided the issue of expulsion or no. It may be that the matter was properly brought before the appeals council by the combined effect of r. 2(13), r. 6(1) and the decision of the executive committee; but any such jurisdiction is merely appellate. If a man has never had a fair trial by the appropriate trial body, is it open to an appellate body to discard its appellate functions and itself give the man a fair trial that he has never had?
>
> I very much doubt the existence of any such doctrine. Central bodies and local bodies often differ much in their views and approach; and the evidence before me certainly does not suggest that this is a union free from any such differences. Suppose the case of a member whose activities have pleased some of his fellow members in the locality but have displeased headquarters and other branches. Suppose further that in his absence, and without hearing his explanations, a local committee is persuaded to expel him. Is it any answer to his complaint that he has not received the benefit of natural justice to say 'Never mind, one of the central bodies will treat your appeal as if it were an initial trial.'? Can he not say 'I want to be tried properly and fairly by the only body with power under the rules to try me in the first place, namely, the local committee'? I appreciate that the appeals council is composed of members elected from each of the union's 12 divisions, and is not an emanation of the NEC or other central body; but I do not think that this affects the point.
>
> That is not all. If one accepts the contention that a defect of natural justice in the trial body can be cured by the presence of natural justice in the appellate body, this has the result of depriving the member of his right of appeal from the expelling body. If the rules and the law combine to give the member the right to a fair trial and the right of appeal, why should he be told that he ought to be satisfied with an unjust trial and a fair appeal? Even if the appeal is treated as a hearing de novo, the member is being stripped of his right to appeal to another body from the effective decision to expel him. I cannot think that natural justice is satisfied by a process whereby an unfair trial, although not resulting in a valid expulsion, will nevertheless have the effect of depriving the member of his right of appeal when a valid decision to expel him is subsequently made. Such a deprivation would be a powerful result to be achieved by what in law is a mere nullity;

---

[24] [1961] A.C. 945.
[25] [1970] 2 All E.R. 713.
[26] At p. 720.

and it is no mere triviality that might be justified on the ground that natural justice does not mean perfect justice. As a general rule, at all events, I hold that a failure of natural justice in the trial body cannot be cured by a sufficiency of natural justice in an appellate body."

Exclusion of jurisdiction

Consistently with the desire to maintain their ultimate power of control the courts maintain that contract may not exclude the right of resort to the courts.[27] It is, in other areas, generally assumed that this does not prevent contractual postponement of the right to take a justiciable issue to the courts pending the exhaustion of some other remedial procedure. Many trade union rule books contain such provisions and some go further so as expressly to challenge the position in *Scott* v. *Avery*. It was at one time apparently assumed that a void provision for total exclusion of the right to resort to the courts would be construed as a valid postponement. In *Leigh* v. *National Union of Railwaymen*[28] Goff J. destroyed this latter assumption and significantly reduced the effectiveness of postponement. He, further, advanced these three rules:

(i) A court is not absolutely precluded by an express requirement in the rules that internal remedies should be exhausted before resort to the courts because its jurisdiction cannot be ousted. In such a situation, however, the plaintiff will have to demonstrate that the circumstances justify disregarding the contractual position.

(ii) Where there is no such express requirement the courts may, more readily, intervene before exhaustion but may require the plaintiff first to exhaust internal remedies.[29]

(iii) A rule purporting to oust the jurisdiction of the courts is void and cannot be read as a valid requirement of exhaustion of remedies before resort to the courts.[30]

In addition to this power to invalidate, or ignore, any provision in union rules requiring members to resort to internal remedies statute now permits any court to ignore such provision wherever the matter is required or allowed under those rules to be submitted for determination or conciliation in accordance with the rules. This applies whenever any member or past member of a trade union has made application for the matter to be submitted for determination or conciliation and allowed six months to elapse between the date when the union received that application and the commencement of the court proceedings. If the application to the union is invalid this invalidity is to be ignored unless the union informs the applicant, within 28 days of receipt, of all the circumstances in which the application contravenes the requirements of the rules. If the court is satisfied that any delay in the determination or con-

---

[27] *Scott* v. *Avery* (1856) 25 L.J.Ex. 308.

[28] [1970] Ch. 326.

[29] These principles were extracted from the judgments in *White* v. *Kuzych* [1951] A.C. 585 and *Lawlor* v. *Union of Post Office Workers* [1965] Ch. 712. The second was relied on in *Radford* v. *NatSOPA* [1972] I.C.R. 484 on the ground that the courts were the most appropriate tribunal to decide matters affecting the construction of union rules and the sufficiency of evidence.

[30] See also Denning M.R. in *Enderby Town F.C.* v. *The Football Association* [1971] 1 All E.R. 215.

ciliation was attributable to the unreasonable conduct of the person who commenced the proceedings it may extend the period of six months during which postponement of resort to the courts is effective by such period as it deems appropriate.[31]

TRADE UNION GOVERNMENT

When Davies and Freedland[32] originally suggested that the legislature and the courts should seek to "maximise representativeness" of the machinery of union government there was a good deal of evidence that national and local leadership were not characterised by being in touch with the membership and that that situation was of long standing. In many cases national leadership, if it was subject to periodic election at all, had fallen into a cosy state of assuming it would be re-elected because its names were better known to the members than those of potential replacements. The shocked disbelief felt by the general secretary of the Wallpaper Workers' Union when he was ousted in the 1970s would have been shared by most of his contemporaries had any such unlikely misfortune befallen them. It might be thought that the same could not be true of branch committees, but they were equally secure in the assumption that few of the membership wanted the job. In fairness, a good many branch officials would happily have resigned had any replacement been available. More damaging for the public image of trade unions was the picture of representation operating on the ancient Greek principle of a show of hands at a mass meeting, or by majority vote at a branch meeting, returning the vote of the entire branch membership, or by some complex system of indirect election. It is true that Boards of Directors are not noticeably more democratic but it is fair to assume that all most shareholders want is profits. Those whose organisation can deprive them of a living present a better case for the right to an individual voice and this cannot be denied just because that case is presented to some who see the encouragement of individualism as a means of undermining the effect of collective criteria.

In the later 1970s the Labour Government made what it called a "social contract" with trade unions under which a programme of employment protection and trade union freedom was offered in return for union adherence to pay limits. This considerably enhanced the apparent power of national leadership. Once Press and public concentrated attention on them it could readily be seen that most of them made their own decisions. Day-to-day consultation with membership is not possible, but widespread disregard of any attempt to ascertain the wishes of that membership became apparent. The breakdown of the social contract brought union leadership into open conflict with government serving to increase the significance of irresponsibility.

Legislative provision

It is scarcely surprising that the Conservative Government which was formed in 1979 saw that one way to keep this power in check was to ensure that it was required to be responsive to the membership. As it dealt with con-

---

[31] E.A. 1988, s.2(2).
[32] 1st ed., p. 561.

trol of industrial action so it pursued this policy little by little. The Employment Act 1980[33] made public funds available to cover the expenses of a postal ballot which can cost a large union half a million pounds. This gentle persuasion was replaced by express obligation in 1984.[34] Secret ballots were required for election to membership of the principal governing body (usually the National Executive Committee), to authorise industrial action[35] and to establish, and periodically confirm, political funds.

Every voting member of the principal executive committee of a trade union, other than one having no individual members or which consists wholly or mainly of affiliated unions, must be elected by secret ballot at not more than five-yearly intervals.[36] This obligation was extended to non-voting members in 1988[37] when it was seen that great influence could be exerted by senior national officers without the vote. The 1988 requirement cannot be avoided by permitting attendance without membership,[38] but it goes further than that so as to deem the president and general secretary, or their equivalents, to be members of the principal executive[39] so long as they are to hold office for more than 13 months, or have held the same office during the previous 12 months. An employee of the union will be affected by these extensions unless he has been an employee for a total of at least 10 years, will reach retirement age in two years and is entitled by the rules of the union to hold the office until retirement age[40] and so long as he does not continue in the office after retirement age.

A member not re-elected may continue in office for a reasonable period not exceeding six months as required to give effect to the election result.[41] The actions of the principal executive committee are not made invalid by the participation of a member or other person who does not satisfy these requirements.[42]

Entitlement to vote at contested elections must be accorded to all, save overseas, members of the trade union other than those not in employment, or in arrears of contribution or subscription or who are apprentices, trainees, student or new members. It is also permissible, under the rules of the union, to exclude from the ballot all members of a class determined by reference to any trade, occupation or geographical area or which is treated by virtue of the union rules as a separate section, or which is a class determined by any combination of these factors.

So far as is reasonably practicable voting shall be by secret postal ballot without cost to the member. Votes must be fairly and accurately counted and the result be determined by the number of votes directly cast for each candidate, or by the single transferable vote system. No member of the union may be unreasonably excluded from standing as a candidate and no candidate may

---

[33] s.1.
[34] Trade Union Act 1984, ss.1, 10 and 12.
[35] See pp. 356–358, *supra*.
[36] Trade Union Act 1984, s.1(1).
[37] E.A. 1988, s.12(1).
[38] s.12 inserting s.(6A)(b) into the 1984 Act.
[39] 1984 Act, s.1(6B).
[40] 1988 Act, s.12(5).
[41] 1984 Act, s.1(3).
[42] 1984 Act, s.1(6).

be required, directly or indirectly, to be a member of a political party (although it is presumably open to the union to ban members of a particular party so long as this does not amount to unreasonable exclusion). Despite this it is expressly provided that it is not unreasonable to exclude the candidacy of all members of a particular class so long as that class is not determined by reference to those the union chooses to exclude.[43] Candidates must be given the opportunity to prepare an election address of not less than 100 words for distribution by the union to those entitled to vote, without expense to the candidate. Apart from the minimum length the union may decide what matters the address shall contain so long as the same restrictions apply to each candidate.[44]

The union must appoint an independent scrutineer to supervise the production and distribution of the voting papers and to whom those papers are to be returned. He must report, as soon as reasonably practicable after the close of the ballot, the number of ballot papers distributed, the number returned, the number of valid and invalid votes and his satisfaction, or otherwise, with statutory requirements and arrangements for handling, and maintaining security of, the votes. A copy of this report must be sent to every member of the union within three months of its receipt unless the contents of the report are otherwise notified to the members in the way which it is the practice of the union to adopt when matters of general interest need to be brought to the attention of its members.[45] Every trade union must maintain an up to date register of the names and addresses of its members.[46]

These ballot provisions also apply to ballots in respect of the political fund.[47]

Any member of the union who, if the application relates to an election, was a member at the time of the election, claiming failure to comply with any of these provisions for ballots may apply to the Certification Officer or the court for a declaration of failure. If the application relates to an election it must be made within a year of the date when the result of the election was announced. The declaration must specify the provisions which have not been complied with and, if made by the court, must contain an enforcement order, unless the court considers this inappropriate. The enforcement order imposes on the union a duty to secure the holding of a specified election and to take specified steps to remedy the failure and to abstain from any acts specified with a view to securing that the same, or a similar, failure does not arise on the part of the union. The order, if it requires a fresh election, may specify how that election is to be conducted.[48]

The union's rules on government

Judicial control of union government is based on the contract of memberships derived from the union rule book. When dealing with the necessarily detailed procedural provisions the courts, inevitably, adopt a strictness of construction unlikely to have been envisaged by the draftsmen.

---

[43] 1985 Act, s.2.
[44] 1988 Act, s.13.
[45] 1988 Act, s.15.
[46] 1984 Act, s.4.
[47] See p. 392, *supra*.
[48] 1984 Act, s.5.

In *Drake* v. *Morgan*[49] the national executive committee of a union was empowered to expend union funds to assist members in such legal matters as it deemed necessary to protect the interests of the union and in the payment of legal charges, costs and damages. That committee passed a resolution that the union would indemnify members in respect of fines imposed for picketing offences. Forbes J. resolved the matter in the following way[50]:

"The first argument of Mr. Melville Williams is that the resolution comes within the first sentence of rule 10(p), because (if I may abridge his argument) the N.E.C. is the sovereign authority and rule 10(1) gives them power to determine what is or what is not a purpose of the union. It is quite clear from the rules that the N.E.C. is intended to be the sovereign authority between annual delegate meetings and it is so described in rule 21(c): 'Nothing in this rule shall derogate from the N.E.C.'s sovereign authority between A.D.M.'s.' But as I read the first part of rule 10(1) the N.E.C. is only empowered to act on behalf of the union in accordance with the rules themselves. The committee is thus circumscribed by those rules. Indeed, in my view, the first sentence of rule 10(p) makes a deliberate distinction between the expenditure of money for union purposes, which must be purposes specified in the rules, and the expenditure for those purposes set out in (i) and (ii) over which the N.E.C. are to have an absolute discretion. I cannot find that the payment of fines for members is a purpose specified in the rules, so that the first sentence of rule 10(p) does not, in my view, cover these resolutions.

Mr. Melville Williams somewhat tentatively advanced a proposition that the second sentence in rule 10(1) would cover these resolutions on the basis that by passing them the N.E.C. was effectively determining a question on which the rules were silent; but I think he virtually withdrew this point when it was pointed out that there was no evidence that the N.E.C. had ever purported to exercise an interpretative role, nor bent their intelligence to any question as to whether the rules were or were not silent on this point.

Both counsel accept that rule 10(p)(ii) cannot cover these resolutions: it refers in terms and only to legal charges, costs and damages and cannot, therefore, cover the payment of fines. But Mr. Melville Williams says that rule 10(p)(i) does cover the situation. The payment of a fine for a member must, he says, be assistance in a legal matter or proceeding and as long as the N.E.C., in its absolute discretion, deems it necessary to pay such a fine to protect the interests of the union, such a decision falls squarely within this sub-rule.

Mr. Still will not accept this. First he says you must read (i) and (ii) together and thus read (i) as a general provision which is particularised in (ii). I do not think this rule can be so read. It is clear that (i) and (ii) are intended to be two separate matters on which money can be expended by the N.E.C. in its absolute discretion. They are both concerned with legal matters and proceedings: (ii) specifically deals with legal charges, costs and damages; (i) is much wider and must be assumed to be dealing with matters other than those detailed in (ii). I can see no reason for excluding the payment of fines from the ambit of rule 10(p)(i) subject to one matter to which I shall have to return.

Mr. Still's other point is that it cannot be in the interests of the union that its members should be encouraged to break the law by having their fines paid, or that justices imposing penalties should increase them in the knowledge that the union was paying, or even impose penalties other than financial in order to hit the offender rather than the union. There is much force in this argument, but the rules, it seems to me, do not provide for intervention by the courts on this ground.

---

[49] [1978] I.C.R. 56.
[50] At p. 59.

A judge cannot substitute his judgment for that of the N.E.C. because the rules provide that it is the N.E.C. who shall have absolute discretion and be the sole judge of what is necessary to protect the interests of the union. It may be that if the N.E.C. decided to do that which no reasonable committee could possibly think was in the interests of the union the courts might interfere, but that is very far from being this case."

Similarly, in *British Actors Equity Association* v. *Goring*[51] the House of Lords had to consider the interaction of a rule providing for alteration of the rules by a two-thirds majority and a rule providing for the submission of any question to a referendum the majority vote in which would be binding. Lord Dilhorne stated that the purpose of the court was to construe the rules, like any other written document, so as to give the words a reasonable interpretation according with what the court thought must have been intended. Not one word of his judgment, however, indicates the consideration of evidence, other than that of the words themselves, as to this intention. Such an examination, common enough when construing the contract of employment, would have revealed a great deal of the understanding of the union and its membership as to how its structure and purpose might be served by one method or another.

Union office and elections

One of the principal unresolved aspects of the judicial approach to the administration of trade unions is whether, because it involves and reflects on the interests of individuals, that administration should be governed by the same extra-contractual procedural safeguards as are attached to discipline. It is obvious that many such decisions affecting individuals must be taken and that the government of the union would become impossible if all were to be subjected to natural justice. It is, therefore, perhaps surprising that the court hesitated in reaching the conclusion in *Brown* v. *Amalgamated Union of Engineering Workers*[52] that it was for the executive council to resolve the question of the length of the period of office of the plaintiff following his restoration to that office. Walton J. said[53]:

"I find this a by no means easy point to resolve, but I start from this, that the rules are silent as to the date from which any successful candidate's term of office runs. That being so, the only way in which such commencement can be determined must, I think, be by the executive council in exercise of their powers under rule 15(18). In the present case on December 6, 1973, the general secretary of the union wrote to the plaintiff saying:
    'The executive council has now given further consideration to this matter and have decided that you should commence your three year period of office on January 7, 1974.'
This appears to me to be perfectly valid administrative decision of the executive council which it was fully entitled to take. Accordingly, I think it means what it says, namely, that the three year term of office envisaged for the holder of the office of divisional organiser started, so far as the plaintiff is concerned, on Janu-

---

[51] [1978] I.C.R. 791.
[52] [1976] I.C.R. 147.
[53] At p. 168.

ary 7, 1974, and will therefore run until January 6, 1977. Having regard to the extremely democratic structure of the union, this was an administrative decision which might have been challenged within a period of eight weeks in the manner indicated in rule 20(2). That period having elapsed, it is now beyond challenge. I should note that Mr. Pain sought to put his case on this precise point on the question of estoppel. He said that the letter contained a representation made on behalf of the union on the faith of which his client acted to his detriment by giving up his previous employment and taking service with the union as a divisional organiser. I see the force of that, but I do not think this would have availed the plaintiff if the executive council had had no power under the rules to do what it in fact did. I do not think it possible for a body to give itself power which it does not in fact have, via the doctrine of estoppel."

Cusack J. had had no hesitation in arriving at a similar conclusion in *Breen* v. *Amalgamated Engineering Union*[54] concerning the administrative nature of the process of approving the plaintiff's candidature for office, but the Court of Appeal overruled him and held that the decision entitled the plaintiff to be heard. Even if they do not go that far the courts will usually construe the union rules with care to ensure that the administrative action is not *ultra vires*.[55] As we have seen this may even extend to questioning the right of the union to make policy decisions. So, in *Esterman* v. *National and Local Government Officers Association*[56] it was said that:

"A member could take the view that action against the returning officers had never been submitted to a ballot and that whether or not a ballot was strictly necessary the national executive council, following the spirit as well as the letter of the instructions with regard to strikes, ought not to order, but rather—if they wished—to recommend, action against the returning officer. A member may have thought that such an order did not reasonably command obedience and that there was a possibility that it gave the appearance of coercing those who thought that action against the returning officers was not in the best interests of NALGO. He might take the view that, in all the extraordinary background of this case, he could not conscientiously accept an order given by the national executive council without a ballot or a fresh ballot against the wishes of the Minister and the secretary of the Trades Union Congress and in the existing national conditions, particularly since 100 per cent. obedience to the order of the national executive council would seem to imply that 100 per cent. of the members were firmly in support of the action which was being taken. A member might take the view that the national executive council order was an abuse of their powers, because, without any mandate by way of a ballot, it had the appearance, some might think, of seeking to wreck the local elections for the purpose of bringing pressure to bear on the Minister. A member might think that if the public thought that, then the reputation of NALGO might be irreparably damaged. In brief in my judgment, a member was entitled to take the view that this was an order which he might be under a positive duty to disobey. Of course, the suspicions or fears of a member that the national executive council had no power to issue the order aimed against the returning officers, or that the national executive council, even if they had the power, were misusing it and exercising it in a way objectionable to numbers of members and injurious to the reputation of NALGO, all those fears could be ill-

[54] [1971] 2 Q.B. 175.
[55] *Sherard* v. *Amalgamated Union of Engineering Workers* [1973] I.C.R. 421; *MacLelland* v. *National Union of Journalists* [1975] I.C.R. 116.
[56] [1974] I.C.R. 625.

founded. But, in my judgment, a member, faced with an órder, was entitled to
doubt. On the face of the order and the constitution and the rules and against all
the background, there was a very large question mark hanging over the validity of
the order and whether it was a proper order to issue even if there was power to do
so.

Those doubts were due entirely to the insistence, as I have said no doubt bona
fide and thought to be in the best interests of NALGO, but nevertheless the insistence, of the national executive council on taking a step which not only had never
been put to a ballot but really was an extraordinary step to take, peremptorily
ordering every member of NALGO to withdraw assistance from the local election, when what they were after dealt with London weighting allowance and they
had no quarrel with the returning officers."[57]

In relation to elections, when they are not overridden by statute union rules
will also be construed on the basis of the contractual approach.[58]

In *Leigh* v. *NUR*[58a] the plaintiff had been nominated for office as president
of his union. The general secretary refused to accept the nomination on the
ground that, as a member of the Communist Party, the plaintiff would be
unable to attend TUC or Labour Party conferences. Goff J. said[59]:

"The plaintiff submits that r. 4(1) of the union's rules specifies the whole of the
qualifications which a candidate for the office of president must have at the time
of his nomination, and he supports this by reference to the fact that in other rules
where provision is made for different offices the necessary qualifications are similarly expressly laid down. Prima facie, this appears to me to be correct, but the
defendants argue that the matter is not so simple because something must be
implied. First they submit that some general discretion arises under r. 4(2) from
the reference there to approval of nominations. The second defendant puts it in
his affidavit in this way:
    'Rule 4(2), imposes upon me in conformity with the general objects the
    administrative duty to approve the nomination and also to consider the issue
    of eligibility of any candidate for the Presidency of the Union.'
The plaintiff says that I should not make any such implication and should confine
the general secretary to the purely administrative and mechanical duty of chec-
king that the nomination is correct on the face of it and that the candidate has the
qualifications prescribed by r. 4(1). I accept that submission. There is not even a
provision that nominations shall be approved. It is one stage removed in that cir-
culars are not to be sent out until the nominations are approved. Moreover, once
one goes beyond the narrow ground on which the plaintiff stands, I see nowhere
to stop short of a discretion to review generally the suitability of the candidate,
which may depend on all kinds of personal considerations. Further, this is not, as
one often finds in rules of this kind, a power or discretion given to the executive
committee or even a sub-committee. I do not think it would be right to make any
such wide implication and I decline to do so.

Then the defendants argue that, the duty imposed by r. 4(4) on the candidate,
if elected, to attend the Trades Union Council and Labour Party conference
implies that he must at the time of nomination be an individual member of the
Labour Party because by its constitution unless he be such he will be ineligible to
attend. Further, or alternatively, they ask me to imply that he must not be a mem-

---

[57] *Per* Templeman J. at p. 633.
[58] *Leigh* v. *National Union of Railwaymen* [1970] Ch. 326; *Breen* v. *Amalgamated Engineering
Union* [1971] 2 Q.B. 175; *Watson* v. *Smith* [1941] 2 All E.R. 725.
[58a] *Supra.*
[59] At p. 331.

ber of any one of the large number of bodies proscribed by the Labour Party. Ought I to make any such implication? In my judgment the answer is 'No,' because it is not necessary to give to the contract contained in the rules business efficacy although it may make it more efficient. The election does not take place for two or three months after the latest date for nominations, the successful candidate does not take office until 1st January next following, that is some six months later, and there is an interval after that before the first conference which he is required to attend. He therefore has a considerable time in which to obtain the required qualification for attendance, and he has some time before the election itself so that the electors can judge of the genuineness of his intention to join the Labour Party and the likelihood of success in that endeavour. Implication of additional requirements of eligibility over and above those expressed should not be made unless one is really driven to it, and in my judgment one is not. In my view the inability of the candidate at the moment of nomination if elected to perform his duties under r. 4(4), is a matter for the electors, not of his right to stand."

In *Brown* v. *Amalgamated Union of Engineering Workers*[60] Walton J. held that the union rules gave no power to avoid the result of an election, once that result had been declared, unless the whole election was a nullity.

Given this approach the courts are in no position to decline the application of any restrictive rule the union may possess unless they regard the rule as contrary to the statutory requirements we have noted,[61] ineffective or unreasonable.[62] Nevertheless they have been prepared to avoid this restriction by holding that the application of electoral rules amounts to the imposition of a penalty which may be *ultra vires* either because it is imposed by a body without disciplinary powers or because the grounds for exercise of those powers do not exist. In *Losinska* v. *Civil and Public Services Association*[63] the Court of Appeal affirmed the grant of an injunction restraining the union from publishing resolutions of the national executive committee deploring the conduct of a candidate for the Presidency. In *Breen* v. *AEU*[64] the Court of Appeal supplemented the union rules as to qualification to stand for election with the requirements of natural justice.

There is little sign in this of any reflection of the judicial attitude to specific enforcement of the contract of service. It is true that the element of personal service is missing from elected office but it seems more than arguable that where the authoritative organs of the union clearly express lack of confidence in an individual he may claim damages for any breach of contract resulting but may not seek to perform his office. Exceptionally, this was the view of Megarry J. in *Leary* v. *National Union of Vehicle Builders*.[65] The plaintiff had been full-time area organiser of the union for 14 years. At a meeting of his branch of which he had not been given notice and which he did not attend it was decided to exclude him from the union on the ground that he was more than six months in arrears with dues. Eventually, after hearing the plaintiff,

---

[60] [1976] I.C.R. 147.
[61] *Supra*, pp. 432–434.
[62] *Carling* v. *N.U.G.M.W.* [1973] I.C.R. 267. The statutory powers under which this case was decided—Industrial Relations Act 1971, s.65(4)—no longer exist.
[63] [1976] I.C.R. 473.
[64] [1971] 2 Q.B. 175.
[65] [1970] 2 All E.R. 713.

the national executive committee endorsed this decision. The learned judge held that the failure of natural justice before the branch could not be cured by appeal and the exclusion of the plaintiff was, therefore, invalid. He quoted from the judgment of Buckley L.J. in the unreported case of *Shanks* v. *Plumbing Trades Union* to the effect that there was a difference between specific performance of the contract of employment and reinstatement of an office holder removed by somebody other than those who elected him.

In *Stevenson* v. *United Road Transport Union*[66] the Court of Appeal side-stepped the issue by applying the argument, usually thought to be the basis of the decision in *Vine* v. *National Dock Labour Board*,[67] that there is no objection to a declaration that a purported removal from office is *ultra vires*.

Services and benefits

It seems likely that entitlement to the services and benefits offered by the union is the matter foremost in the mind of most union members when considering the propriety of the action of the union. Of these the right to fair representation would no doubt rank high. Yet of all his rights this is likely to be least protected by the law. English law recognises no obligation to bargain in good faith. The structure of most union rule books as interpreted by the courts leads to the inference that whilst negotiation is usually a declared object of the union it does not produce a contractual obligation as between it and its members. Again, it is possible to compare this approach adversely with that adopted to the contract of employment where such a central objective of the relationship would almost certainly produce the implication of a contractual obligation.

The importance to an individual's employment position of collective bargaining is obvious but the facts in *Blackman* v. *The Post Office*[68] lend it added emphasis. Difficulties had arisen in recruiting a sufficient number of post and telegraph officers. The union agreed not to object to recruiting on an unestablished basis from outside the Post Office. The agreement with the union provided that candidates whose service had been satisfactory would be expected to seek establishment in an open written examination. Subsequently it was agreed that candidates in the plaintiff's position would be allowed three opportunities to pass a special aptitude test. The plaintiff sat the test three times and only just failed the third attempt. The employer had no other cause of complaint against him but the union refused to agree to modify its agreement to permit him and others in a similar position to remain in employment and he was eventually dismissed. The union may impose very considerable sanctions upon a member by refusing him the benefit of its services as it did in *Oddy* v. *Transport Salaried Staffs Association*.[69] In that case the service in question was representation in individual negotiations with the employer. Sir High Griffiths in the N.I.R.C., however, decided that no right to such representation could be construed from the declaration that it was an object of the union to protect the interests of its members.

---

[66] [1977] I.C.R. 893.
[67] [1956] 1 Q.B. 658.
[68] [1974] I.C.R. 151.
[69] [1973] I.C.R. 524.

Fair representation

So far, neither legislature nor courts have shown any tendency to develop obligations fairly to represent members.

The only obligations towards its members arising outside the union rules are those concerning discrimination declared to be illegal by statute. In *FTATU* v. *Modgill*,[70] however, the fact that the union was doing no more for sixteen African Asians than it was for the rest of its members at the place of work in question provided a complete answer to a claim of discrimination.

The extent to which the individual may be dependent on the efficiency of his union in affording him services is illustrated in other ways. In *Gray Dunn and Co. Ltd.* v. *Edwards*[71] Lord McDonald was ready to accept the proposition that an employee's right to be heard before dismissal would be satisfied by the presence at some stages only of his union representatives. There is no doubt that this makes good sense in the light of normal industrial practice. The union, however, is representing the group as much as the individual and without inferring any bad faith on its part it is almost certainly true that wider policy considerations may at times modify the case it puts forward. In *Chappell* v. *Times Newspapers Ltd.*[72] the Court of Appeal confirmed that the willingness of union members to respond to calls from their union could be effective to destroy the trust and confidence of their employer in their readiness to fulfil their obligations as employees. The dependence of the member may actually be increased by statute. In *Times Newspapers Ltd.* v. *O'Regan*[73] the E.A.T. retreated from the more lenient attitude adopted by the N.I.R.C. in *Owen* v. *Crown House Engineering Ltd.*[74] and refused to allow delay to permit negotiations to be completed to be presented to excuse the filing out of time of a complaint of unfair dismissal.

Negligence

So far the courts have acknowledged only one source of protection for the non-contractual rights of a member. The law of negligence may provide, intermittently, remedies for failure by union officials adequately to represent or provide services for union members. So far, however, even this opportunity has not been developed. In *Buckley* v. *National Union of General and Municipal Workers*[75] the discussion was limited to the application of the law of negligence to the carrying out of contractual obligations and the court was anxious not to require too high a degree of skill. In *Cross* v. *British Iron, Steel and Kindred Trades Association*[76] Salmon L.J. considered only a contractual duty of care and concluded that the obligation the union had accepted was satisfied by delegation to those reasonably thought competent.

It is suggested that the courts, which have often stated an awareness of the power of trade unions spreading far beyond the rule book, should realise that in order to provide a system of protection of a member's rights in respect of the organisation of the union they must look beyond the narrow confines of

---

[70] [1980] I.R.L.R. 142.
[71] [1980] I.R.L.R. 23. See also *Ellis* v. *Brighton Co-operative Society* [1976] I.R.L.R. 419.
[72] [1975] I.C.R. 145.
[73] [1977] I.R.L.R. 101.
[74] [1973] I.C.R. 511.
[75] [1967] 3 All E.R. 767.
[76] [1968] 1 All E.R. 250.

the rule book. It is essential to consider the field of action of the union, and particularly the stated purposes of the union as a source of implied obligation to the member. The almost insuperable difficulty in the way of judicial development of this line of thought, however, is that that obligation is to the member as one of a group. Discipline cases reveal no evidence of judicial comprehension of such a status but the Court of Appeal, in *Twanuszezak* v. G.M.B.A.T.U.[77] clearly rejected any suggestion of an individual duty of care applicable to collective bargaining. This, of course, is the explanation for the difference. Lawyers, thinking instinctively of the individualisation of rights, apply that approach when an individual is disciplined under a set of rules conveniently individualised as the terms of a contract. Those rules, at best, only look peripherally on the bargaining process which even lawyers can readily see must consider the wellbeing of the group. It is not surprising that when faced with so obvious a collective function Lloyd L.J. should say that when the collective interests of the union conflict with the interests of an individual member it only makes sense that the collective interests of the members as a whole should prevail. It is, of course, inconceivable that an individual in the bargaining unit should have a cause of action for individual injury occasioned by the union's pursuit of the collective good. Yet the view expressed by Lloyd L.J. is contrary to the individualistic attitude characterising almost every other aspect canvassed in this chapter, whether viewed in the light of judicial or legislative approaches. If trade unions are to be regulated on the assumption that they are something different from voluntary associations it is time legislature and courts defined the nature of that difference so as to pursue a tolerably consistent policy. Until they do they can hardly complain if the conflict continues.

---

[77] [1988] I.R.L.R. 219.

INDEX